Software Testing

Software Testing

A Craftsman's Approach

Fifth Edition

Paul C. Jorgensen and Byron DeVries

CRC Press
Taylor & Francis Group
Boca Raton London New York

CRC Press is an imprint of the
Taylor & Francis Group, an **informa** business

AN AUERBACH BOOK

Fifth edition published [2021]
by CRC Press
6000 Broken Sound Parkway NW, Suite 300, Boca Raton, FL 33487-2742

and by CRC Press
2 Park Square, Milton Park, Abingdon, Oxon, OX14 4RN

[First edition published by CRC Press 1995]
[Fourth edition published by CRC Press 2014]

CRC Press is an imprint of Taylor & Francis Group, LLC

ISBN: 978-0-367-35849-5 (hbk)
ISBN: 978-0-367-76762-4 (pbk)
ISBN: 978-1-003-16844-7 (ebk)

Typeset in Garamond
by SPi Global, India

To Carol, Kirsten, and Katia; Angela, Bryce, and Wesley

Contents

Preface..**xix**
Authors...**xxi**

PART I   A Mathematical Context

1   A Perspective on Testing **3**
    1.1   Basic Definitions 3
    1.2   Test Cases 4
    1.3   Insights from a Venn Diagram.. 5
    1.4   Identifying Test Cases 7
           1.4.1   Specification-based Testing 7
           1.4.2   Code-based Testing... 8
           1.4.3   The Specification-based versus Code-based Debate 9
    1.5   Fault Taxonomies 10
    1.6   Levels of Testing.. 12
    Exercises 13
    References.. 14

2   Examples.. **15**
    2.1   Structural Elements of Pseudo-code and Java.................... 15
    2.2   The Triangle Problem 19
           2.2.1   Problem Statement 19
           2.2.2   Discussion... 20
           2.2.3   Java Implementation... 20
    2.3   The NextDate Function.. 21
           2.3.1   Problem Statement 21
           2.3.2   Discussion... 21
            2.3.3   Java Implementation... 22
    2.4   The Foodies-Wish-List Online Shopping Application 24
           2.4.1   Problem Statement 25
           2.4.2   Discussion... 25
    2.5   The Garage Door Controller.. 29
    2.6   Examples in Exercises... 30
           2.6.1   The Quadrilateral Program 30

2.6.2 The NextWeek Function 31
2.6.3 The Windshield Wiper Controller 31
Exercises 31
References.. 32

3 Discrete Math for Testers 33
3.1 Set Theory 33
3.1.1 Set Membership 34
3.1.2 Set Definition 34
3.1.3 The Empty Set.. 35
3.1.4 Venn Diagrams.. 35
3.1.5 Set Operations 36
3.1.6 Set Relations 37
3.1.7 Set Partitions 38
3.1.8 Set Identities 39
3.2 Functions... 39
3.2.1 Domain and Range 40
3.2.2 Function Types 40
3.2.3 Function Composition 41
3.3 Relations.. 42
3.3.1 Relations among Sets... 42
3.3.2 Relations on a Single Set 44
3.4 Propositional Logic 45
3.4.1 Logical Operators 46
3.4.2 Logical Expressions 47
3.4.3 Logical Equivalence 47
3.4.4 Probability Theory 48
Exercises 50
Reference 51

4 Graph Theory for Testers 53
4.1 Graphs.. 53
4.1.1 Degree of a Node 54
4.1.2 Incidence Matrices... 54
4.1.3 Adjacency Matrices 55
4.1.4 Paths... 56
4.1.5 Connectedness... 57
4.1.6 Condensation Graphs 57
4.1.7 Cyclomatic Number 58
4.2 Directed Graphs... 58
4.2.1 Indegrees and Outdegrees 59
4.2.2 Types of Nodes.. 60
4.2.3 Adjacency Matrix of a Directed Graph 60
4.2.4 Paths and Semipaths 61
4.2.5 Reachability Matrix 62
4.2.6 n-Connectedness.. 63
4.2.7 Strong Components 63

4.3 Graphs for Testing...64
    4.3.1 Program Graphs 64
    4.3.2 Finite State Machines...66
    4.3.3 Petri Nets...67
    4.3.4 Event-Driven Petri Nets 70
    4.3.5 Statecharts..73
Exercises 75
Reference 75

PART II Unit Testing

5 Boundary Value Testing **79**
5.1 Normal Boundary Value Testing..80
    5.1.1 Generalizing Boundary Value Analysis 81
    5.1.2 Limitations of Boundary Value Analysis 82
5.2 Robust Boundary Value Testing..82
5.3 Worst Case Boundary Value Testing 83
5.4 Special Value Testing..85
5.5 Examples 85
    5.5.1 Test Cases for the Triangle Problem 85
    5.5.2 Test Cases for the NextDate Function...................................85
5.6 Random Testing..92
5.7 Guidelines for Boundary Value Testing...93
Exercises 95

6 Equivalence Class Testing **97**
6.1 Equivalence Classes 97
6.2 Traditional Equivalence Class Testing 98
6.3 Improved Equivalence Class Testing 99
    6.3.1 Weak Normal Equivalence Class Testing 100
    6.3.2 Strong Normal Equivalence Class Testing..........................100
    6.3.3 Weak Robust Equivalence Class Testing 101
    6.3.4 Strong Robust Equivalence Class Testing 102
6.4 Equivalence Class Test Cases for the Triangle Problem.......................103
6.5 Equivalence Class Test Cases for the NextDate Function 104
6.6 Equivalence Class Test Cases for the completeOrder Method.............108
6.7 "Edge Testing" 110
6.8 Reflections on Invalid Classes 111
6.9 Guidelines and Observations..111
Exercises 112
References...113

7 Decision Table-Based Testing **115**
7.1 Decision Tables 115
7.2 Decision Table Techniques 116
7.3 Test Cases for the Triangle Problem..120

7.4 Test Cases for the NextDate Function 121
    7.4.1 First Try 121
    7.4.2 Second Try 122
    7.4.3 Third Try 124
7.5 Cause and Effect Graphing 127
7.6 Guidelines and Observations 128
Exercises 128
References 129

8 Code-Based Testing **131**
8.1 Program Graphs 131
8.2 DD-Paths 132
8.3 Code Coverage Metrics 135
    8.3.1 Program Graph-Based Coverage Metrics 135
    8.3.2 E. F. Miller's Coverage Metrics 136
        8.3.2.1 Statement Testing 137
        8.3.2.2 DD-Path Testing 137
        8.3.2.3 Simple Loop Coverage 138
        8.3.2.4 Predicate Outcome Testing 138
        8.3.2.5 Dependent Pairs of DD-Paths 138
        8.3.2.6 Complex Loop Coverage 138
        8.3.2.7 Multiple Condition Coverage 139
        8.3.2.8 "Statistically Significant" Coverage 140
        8.3.2.9 All Possible Paths Coverage 140
    8.3.3 A Closer Look at Compound Conditions 140
        8.3.3.1 Boolean Expression (per Chilenski) 140
        8.3.3.2 Condition (per Chilenski) 141
        8.3.3.3 Coupled Conditions (per Chilenski) 141
        8.3.3.4 Masking Conditions (per Chilenski) 141
        8.3.3.5 Modified Condition Decision Coverage 142
    8.3.4 Examples 143
        8.3.4.1 Condition with Two Simple Conditions 143
        8.3.4.2 Example: Compound Condition from NextDate 143
        8.3.4.3 Test Coverage Analyzers 150
        8.3.4.4 Java Code for Tests in Table 8.8 151
        8.3.4.5 Junit Test Results 155
        8.3.4.6 Capabilities of Selected Code Coverage Tools 156
8.4 Basis Path Testing 156
    8.4.1 McCabe's Basis Path Method 157
    8.4.2 Observations on McCabe's Basis Path Method 160
    8.4.3 Essential Complexity 160
8.5 Guidelines and Observations 163
Exercises 163
References 164

9   Testing Object-Oriented Software **165**
  9.1   Unit Testing Frameworks 165
      9.1.1   Common Unit Testing Frameworks 166
      9.1.2   JUnit Examples 166
  9.2   Mock Objects and Automated Object Mocking 169
  9.3   Dataflow Testing 171
      9.3.1   Define/Use Testing Definition 171
      9.3.2   Define/Use Testing Metrics 173
      9.3.3   Define/Use Testing Example 174
  9.4   Object-Oriented Complexity Metrics 181
      9.4.1   WMC—Weighted Methods per Class 181
      9.4.2   DIT—Depth of Inheritance Tree 182
      9.4.3   NOC—Number of Child Classes 182
      9.4.4   CBO—Coupling Between Classes 182
      9.4.5   RFC—Response for Class 182
      9.4.6   LCOM—Lack of Cohesion on Methods 182
  9.5   Issues in Testing Object-Oriented Software 183
      9.5.1   Implications of Composition and Encapsulation 183
      9.5.2   Implications of Inheritance 183
      9.5.3   Implications of Polymorphism 185
  9.6   Slice-Based Testing 190
      9.6.1   Example 192
      9.6.2   Style and Technique 197
      9.6.3   Slice Splicing 197
      9.6.4   Program Slicing Tools 198
  Exercises 198
  References 199

10   Retrospective on Unit Testing **201**
  10.1   The Test Method Pendulum 202
  10.2   Traversing the Pendulum 204
      10.2.1   Program Graph-Based Testing 204
      10.2.2   Basis Path Testing 204
      10.2.3   Dataflow Testing 206
      10.2.4   Slice-Based Testing 209
      10.2.5   Boundary Value Testing 210
      10.2.6   Equivalence Class Testing 210
      10.2.7   Decision Table Testing 211
  10.3   Insurance Premium Case Study 213
  10.4   Specification-Based Testing 214
      10.4.1   Code-Based Testing 218
          10.4.1.1   Path-based Testing 219
          10.4.1.2   Dataflow Testing 221
          10.4.1.3   Slice Testing 221
  10.5   Guidelines 221
  Exercises 223
  References 223

PART III Beyond Unit Testing

11 Life Cycle-Based Testing... **227**
   11.1 Traditional Waterfall Testing... 227
       11.1.1 Waterfall Testing 229
       11.1.2 Pros and Cons of the Waterfall Model 229
   11.2 Testing in Iterative Lifecycles.. 230
       11.2.1 Waterfall Spin-Offs... 230
       11.2.2 Specification-Based Life Cycle Models........................ 232
   11.3 Agile Testing.. 234
       11.3.1 About User Stories.. 234
           11.3.1.1 Behavior-Driven Development........................ 235
           11.3.1.2 Use Cases 241
       11.3.2 Extreme Programming... 242
       11.3.3 Scrum 242
       11.3.4 Test-Driven Development... 243
       11.3.5 Agile Model-Driven Development................................ 245
       11.3.6 Model-Driven Agile Development................................ 245
   11.4 Remaining Questions... 246
       11.4.1 Specification or Code Based? 246
       11.4.2 Configuration Management?... 246
       11.4.3 Granularity?.. 248
   11.5 Pros, cons, and Open Questions of TDD 248
   11.6 Retrospective on MDD vs. TDD.. 249
   References.. 251

12 Integration Testing.. **253**
   12.1 Decomposition-Based Integration 253
       12.1.1 Top-down Integration... 256
       12.1.2 Bottom-up Integration.. 258
       12.1.3 Sandwich Integration 258
       12.1.4 Pros and Cons... 259
   12.2 Call Graph-Based Integration 260
       12.2.1 Pairwise Integration 261
       12.2.2 Neighborhood Integration.. 262
       12.2.3 Pros and Cons... 264
   12.3 Path-Based Integration.. 265
       12.3.1 New and Extended Concepts 265
       12.3.2 MM-Path Complexity 268
       12.3.3 Pros and Cons... 268
   12.4 Example: Procedural integrationNextDate 269
       12.4.1 Decomposition-Based Integration................................ 269
       12.4.2 Call Graph-Based Integration....................................... 270
       12.4.3 Integration Based on MM-Paths................................... 272
       12.4.4 Observations and Recommendations............................ 275
   12.5 Example: O-O integrationNextDate.. 275
   12.6 Model-Based Integration Testing.. 280
       12.6.1 Message Communication.. 281

12.6.2 Pairwise Integration 282
12.6.3 FSM/M Path Integration 286
12.6.4 Scenario 1: Normal Account Creation 286
Exercises 287
References... 289

13 System Testing **291**
13.1 Threads.. 291
13.1.1 Thread Possibilities... 292
13.1.2 Thread Definitions.. 293
13.2 Identifying Threads in Single-Processor Applications 294
13.2.1 User Stories/Use Cases 294
13.2.2 How Many Use Cases?.. 295
13.2.2.1 Incidence with Input Events and Messages 297
13.2.2.2 Incidence with Output Actions and Messages 300
13.2.2.3 Incidence with Classes.. 300
13.2.3 Threads in Finite State Machines 301
13.2.3.1 Paths in a Finite State Machine................................ 301
13.2.3.2 How Many Paths?... 303
13.2.4 Atomic System Functions 305
13.3 Identifying Threads in Systems of Systems 305
13.3.1 Dialogues 305
13.3.2 Communicating FSMs 307
13.3.3 Dialogues as Sequences of ASFs 309
13.4 System Level Test Cases 309
13.4.1 An Industrial Test Execution System..................................... 310
13.4.2 Use Cases to Test Cases 311
13.4.3 Finite State Machine Paths to Test Cases 312
13.4.4 Dialogue Scenarios to Test Cases 313
13.4.5 Communicating Finite State Machines to Test Cases............... 313
13.5 Coverage Metrics for System Testing... 314
13.5.1 Use Case-Based Test Coverage 315
13.5.2 Model-Based Test Coverage... 318
13.6 Long Versus Short Test Cases... 320
13.6.1 Supplemental Approaches to System Testing 324
13.6.2 Operational Profiles.. 324
13.6.2.1 Risk-Based Testing.. 327
13.7 Non-functional System Testing 332
13.7.1 Stress Testing Strategies 332
13.7.1.1 Compression... 333
13.7.1.2 Replication... 333
13.7.2 Mathematical Approaches 334
13.7.2.1 Queueing Theory 334
13.7.2.2 Reliability Models... 334
13.7.2.3 Monte Carlo Testing 335
Exercises 335
References... 336

14 Model-Based Testing **337**
14.1 Testing Based on Models 337
14.2 Appropriate Models 338
    14.2.1 Peterson's Lattice 338
    14.2.2 Expressive Capabilities of Mainline Models 340
    14.2.3 Modeling Issues 340
    14.2.4 Making Appropriate Choices 342
14.3 Commercial Tool Support for Model-Based Testing 342
    14.3.1 TestOptimal 342
    14.3.2 Conformiq 343
    14.3.3 Verified Systems International GmbH 346
Exercises 349
References 351

15 Software Complexity **353**
15.1 Unit Level Complexity 354
    15.1.1 Cyclomatic Complexity 354
        15.1.1.1 "Cattle Pens" and Cyclomatic Complexity 355
        15.1.1.2 Node Outdegrees and Cyclomatic Complexity 356
        15.1.1.3 Decisional Complexity 357
    15.1.2 Computational Complexity 358
        15.1.2.1 Halstead's Metrics 358
        15.1.2.2 Example: Day of Week with Zeller's Congruence 359
15.2 Integration Level Complexity 361
    15.2.1 Integration Level Cyclomatic Complexity 362
    15.2.2 Message Traffic Complexity 363
15.3 Software Complexity Example 364
15.4 Object-Oriented Complexity 366
    15.4.1 WMC—Weighted Methods per Class 366
    15.4.2 DIT—Depth of Inheritance Tree 367
    15.4.3 NOC—Number of Child Classes 367
    15.4.4 CBO—Coupling between Classes 367
    15.4.5 RFC—Response for Class 367
    15.4.6 LCOM—Lack of Cohesion on Methods 367
15.5 System Level Complexity 367
    15.5.1 Cyclomatic Complexity of Source Code 368
    15.5.2 Complexity of Specification Models 368
    15.5.3 Use Case Complexity 368
    15.5.4 UML Complexity 369
Exercise 369
References 372

16 Testing Systems of Systems **373**
16.1 Characteristics of Systems of Systems 374
16.2 Sample Systems of Systems 375
    16.2.1 The Garage Door Controller (Directed) 375

16.2.2 Air Traffic Management System (Acknowledged) 376
16.2.3 The Foodie Wish List System 377
16.3 Software Engineering for Systems of Systems 378
16.3.1 Requirements Elicitation.. 378
16.3.2 Specification with a Dialect of UML.. 378
16.3.2.1 Air Traffic Management System Classes 379
16.3.2.2 Air Traffic Management System Use Cases and
Sequence Diagrams.. 379
16.3.3 Testing.. 382
16.4 Communication Primitives for Systems of Systems 382
16.4.1 ESML Prompts as Petri Nets 383
16.4.1.1 Petri Net Conflict 383
16.4.1.2 Petri Net Interlock 383
16.4.1.3 Enable, Disable, and Activate...................................... 384
16.4.1.4 Trigger 385
16.4.1.5 Suspend and Resume 385
16.4.2 New Prompts as Swim Lane Petri Nets.. 386
16.4.2.1 Request 386
16.4.2.2 Accept 386
16.4.2.3 Reject 386
16.4.2.4 Postpone 388
16.4.2.5 Swim Lane Description of the November 1993
Incident... 389
16.5 Effect of Systems of Systems Levels on Prompts 389
16.5.1 Directed and Acknowledged Systems of Systems 390
16.5.2 Collaborative and Virtual Systems of Systems 390
Exercises 390
References.. 390

17 Feature Interaction Testing **391**
17.1 Feature Interaction Problem Defined.. 391
17.2 Types of Feature Interactions 393
17.2.1 Input Conflict... 394
17.2.2 Output Conflict.. 397
17.2.3 Resource Conflict... 398
17.3 A Taxonomy of Interactions 399
17.3.1 Static Interactions in a Single Processor...................................... 399
17.3.2 Static Interactions in Multiple Processors.................................... 401
17.3.3 Dynamic Interactions in a Single Processor 402
17.3.4 Dynamic Interactions in Multiple Processors 405
17.4 Interaction, Composition, and Determinism 406
Exercises 407
References.. 407

18 Case Study: Testing Event-Driven Systems **409**
18.1 The Garage Door Controller Problem Statement................................. 410
18.2 Modeling with Behavior Driven Development (BDD)........................... 410

18.3 Modeling with Extended Finite State Machines....................................... 412
    18.3.1 Deriving a Finite State Machine from BDD Scenarios 412
    18.3.2 Top-down Development of a Finite State Machine 414
18.4 Modeling with Swim Lane Event-Driven Petri Nets........................... 418
    18.4.1 Normal Garage Door Closing.. 419
    18.4.2 Garage Door Closing with an Intermediate Stop 420
    18.4.3 Garage Door Closing with a Laser Beam Crossing 421
    18.4.4 The Door Opening Interactions... 421
18.5 Deriving Test Cases from Swim Lane Event-Driven
    Petri Nets 423
18.6 Failure Mode Event Analysis (FMEA) 425
Exercises 430
References.. 430

19 A Closer Look at All Pairs Testing... 431
19.1 The All Pairs Technique 431
    19.1.1 Program Inputs 433
    19.1.2 Independent Variables... 433
    19.1.3 Input Order... 435
    19.1.4 Failures Due only to Pairs of Inputs 439
19.2 A Closer Look at the NIST Study... 440
19.3 Appropriate Applications for All-Pairs Testing................................. 440
19.4 Recommendations for All Pairs Testing... 441
Exercises 442
References.. 442

20 Software Technical Reviews 443
20.1 Economics of Software Reviews.. 443
20.2 Types of Reviews 445
    20.2.1 Walkthroughs.. 445
    20.2.2 Technical Inspections 445
    20.2.3 Audits 446
    20.2.4 Comparison of Review Types... 446
20.3 Roles in a Review.. 446
    20.3.1 Producer... 447
    20.3.2 Review Leader... 447
    20.3.3 Recorder... 447
    20.3.4 Reviewer 448
    20.3.5 Role Duplication 448
20.4 Contents of an Inspection Packet.. 448
    20.4.1 Work Product Requirements 448
    20.4.2 Frozen Work Product... 448
    20.4.3 Standards and Checklists.. 449
    20.4.4 Review Issues Spreadsheet... 449
    20.4.5 Review Reporting Forms 450
    20.4.6 Fault Severity Levels 451
    20.4.7 Review Report Outline 451

20.5 An Industrial-Strength Inspection Process 452
    20.5.1 Commitment Planning.. 453
    20.5.2 Reviewer Introduction.. 453
    20.5.3 Preparation 453
    20.5.4 Review Meeting 454
    20.5.5 Report Preparation 454
    20.5.6 Disposition.. 455
20.6 Effective Review Culture.. 455
    20.6.1 Etiquette.. 455
    20.6.2 Management Participation in Review Meetings........................ 456
    20.6.3 A Tale of Two Reviews 456
        20.6.3.1 A Pointy-Haired Supervisor Review 456
        20.6.3.2 An Ideal Review 457
20.7 Inspection Case Study.. 457
References.. 459

21 **Epilogue: Software Testing Excellence** **461**
21.1 Craftsmanship 461
21.2 Best Practices of Software Testing.. 462
21.3 Our Top 10 Best Practices for Software Testing Excellence 463
    21.3.1 Carefully Performed Technical Inspections 463
    21.3.2 Careful Definition and Identification of Levels of Testing 463
    21.3.3 Model-Based Testing at All Levels.. 464
    21.3.4 System Testing Extensions 464
    21.3.5 Incidence Matrices to Guide Regression Testing..................... 464
    21.3.6 Use of xUnit and Object Mocking at the Unit Level................. 464
    21.3.7 Intelligent Combination of Specification-Based
        and Code-Based Unit Level Testing 465
    21.3.8 Use of Appropriate Tools at All Testing Levels........................ 465
    21.3.9 Exploratory Testing During Maintenance 465
    21.3.10 Test-Driven Development.. 465
21.4 Mapping Best Practices to Diverse Projects 465
    21.4.1 A Mission Critical Project 465
    21.4.2 A Time Critical Project... 465
    21.4.3 Corrective Maintenance of Legacy code 466
21.5 An Extreme Example 466
References.. 468

Appendix A: Complete Technical Inspection Packet **469**

Appendix B: Foodies Wish List Example **481**

Index **503**

Preface

The fifth edition of *Software Testing—A Craftsman's Approach* appears 25 years after the first edition and now there is a co-author, Dr. Byron DeVries. Together, Paul and Byron have 32 years of industrial experience and a few more years of university teaching and research in Software Engineering. Paul's testing experience is on telephone switching systems software; Byron's is on avionics systems.

The book has evolved over four editions and 25 years of classroom and industrial use. We continue the pattern of presenting theory, using it to describe testing techniques, and illustrating all of this with carefully selected examples. We retained some of the classical examples and replaced others with a comprehensive web-based example, the Foodies Wish List, that is used throughout where appropriate. This lends a unifying "leitmotif" to our book.

Here are some the highlights of the Fifth Edition…

- This book now has a website, softwaretestcraft.org (also .com) that contains all Java code, powerpoint presentations, and various notes.
- Parts 2, 3, and 4 are essentially object-oriented. All pseudo-code examples are now converted to Java. Unit testing examples use JUnit.
- We included specific information on commercial and open-source tools for code-based testing. Also, we added three examples of commercial Model-Based Testing products to the Model-Based Testing chapter.
- Testing object-oriented software is consolidated in a single chapter.
- There is a new chapter on the feature interaction problem.
- There is a new emphasis (and example) for modeling and testing event-driven systems.
- We retained the chapter on technical inspections and the corresponding appendix.

Some things have remained constant across all five editions. In the Preface to the First Edition, Paul wrote:

> *We huddled around the door to the conference room, each taking a turn looking through the small window. Inside, a recently hired software designer had spread out source listings on the conference table and carefully passed a crystal hanging from a long chain over the source code. Every so often, the designer marked a circle in red on the listing. Later, one of my colleagues asked the designer what he had been doing in the conference room. The nonchalant reply: "Finding the bugs in my program." This is a true story, it happened in the mid-1980s when people had high hopes for hidden powers in crystals.*

For the past 25 years, the goal of this book is to provide you with a better set of crystals. As the title suggests, we believe that software (and system) testing is a craft, and we have some mastery of that craft. We bring our combined industrial and academic backgrounds to the theory, techniques, and examples. We hope that all of this will crystalize into your software testing craft.

Paul C. Jorgensen
Rockford, Michigan

Byron DeVries
Grand Rapids, Michigan
December, 2020

Authors

Paul Jorgensen, Ph.D., spent his 20-year first career in all phases of software development for the research and development laboratory of a telephone switching systems company. He began his university career in 1986 teaching graduate courses in software engineering at Arizona State University, and since 1988, at Grand Valley State University where he is a full professor. Paul retired from the university in the summer of 2017 and is now a Professor Emeritus. He jokes that he has seven-day weekends, every week. This schedule permits a lot of family contact and also allows time for his consulting business, Software Paradigms. He has served on major CODASYL, ACM, IEEE, and ISTQB committees, and in 2012, his university recognized his lifetime accomplishments with its "Distinguished Contribution to a Discipline Award."

In addition to this software testing book, he is also the author of *Modeling Software Behavior: A Craftsman's Approach* and *The Craft of Model-Based Testing*. He is a co-author of *Mathematics for Data Processing* (McGraw-Hill, 1970) and *Structured Methods--Merging Models, Techniques, and CASE* (McGraw-Hill, 1993).

Living and working in Italy for three years made him a confirmed "Italophile." He, his wife Carol, and daughters Kirsten and Katia have visited friends there several times. Paul and Carol have volunteered at the Porcupine School on the Pine Ridge Reservation in South Dakota for 19 years. His preferred email addresses are jorgensp@gvsu.edu; paul@softwaretestcraft.org

Byron DeVries, Ph.D., has taught undergraduate and graduate software engineering courses at Grand Valley State University since he joined the faculty in 2017 as an assistant professor. Prior to teaching, he spent over a dozen years in a variety of avionics software development roles, often focused on verification. He actively publishes in and serves on program committees for a variety of IEEE and ACM conferences. In 2021, he was recognized by his university with the "Distinguished Early Career Scholar Award."

In the summers, you can most often find him either close to, or on, the water around West Michigan with his wife, Angela. Though an avid sailor, he begrudgingly spends more time on power boats for the sake of his two young boys: Bryce and Wesley. You can reach him at his email addresses: devrieby@gvsu.edu and byron@softwaretestcraft.org.

A MATHEMATICAL CONTEXT

Chapter 1

A Perspective on Testing

Why do we test? The two main reasons are: to make a judgment about quality or acceptability and to discover problems. We test because we know that we are fallible—this is especially true in the domain of software and software-controlled systems. The goal of this chapter is to create a framework within which we can examine software testing.

1.1 Basic Definitions

Much of testing literature is mired in confusing (and sometimes inconsistent) terminology, probably because testing technology has evolved over decades and via scores of writers. The International Software Testing Qualification Board (ISTQB) has an extensive glossary of testing terms (see the website http://www.istqb.org/downloads/glossary.html). The terminology here (and throughout this book) is compatible with the ISTQB definitions, and they, in turn, are compatible with the standards developed by the Institute of Electronics and Electrical Engineers (IEEE) Computer Society. To get started, here is a useful progression of terms.

Error—people make errors. A good synonym is mistake. When people make mistakes while coding, we call these mistakes bugs. Errors tend to propagate; a requirements error may be magnified during design and amplified still more during coding.

Fault—a fault is the result of an error. It is more precise to say that a fault is the representation of an error, where representation is the mode of expression, such as narrative text, UML diagrams, hierarchy charts, source code, and so on. Defect (see ISTQB Glossary) is a good synonym for fault, as is bug. Faults can be elusive. An error of omission results in a fault is that something is missing that should be present in the representation. This suggests a useful refinement, we might speak of faults of commission and faults of omission. A fault of commission occurs when we enter something into a representation that is incorrect. Faults of omission occur when we fail to enter correct information. Of these two types, faults of omission are more difficult to detect and resolve.

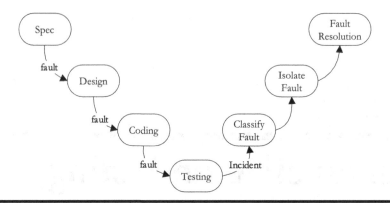

Figure 1.1   A testing life cycle.

Failure—a failure occurs when the code corresponding to a fault executes. Two subtleties arise here: one is that failures only occur in an executable representation, which is usually taken to be source code, or more precisely, loaded object code; the second subtlety is that this definition relates failures only to faults of commission. How can we deal with failures that correspond to faults of omission? We can push this still further: What about faults that never happen to execute, or perhaps do not execute for a long time? Technical reviews (see Chapter 20) prevent many failures by finding faults; in fact, well-done reviews can find faults of omission.

Incident—when a failure occurs, it may or may not be readily apparent to the user (or customer or tester). An incident is the symptom associated with a failure that alerts the user to the occurrence of a failure.

Test—testing is obviously concerned with errors, faults, failures, and incidents. A test is the act of exercising software with test cases. A test has two distinct goals: to find failures or to demonstrate correct execution.

Test Case—test case has an identity and is associated with a program behavior. A test case also has a set of inputs and expected outputs.

Figure 1.1 portrays a life cycle model for testing. Notice that, in the development phases, three opportunities arise for errors to be made, resulting in faults that may propagate through the remainder of the development process. The Fault Resolution step is another opportunity for errors (and new faults). When a fix causes formerly correct software to misbehave, the fix is deficient. We will revisit this when we discuss regression testing.

From this sequence of terms, we see that test cases occupy a central position in testing. The process of testing can be subdivided into separate steps: test planning, test case development, running test cases, and evaluating test results. The focus of this book is how to identify useful sets of test cases.

1.2 Test Cases

The essence of software testing is to determine a set of test cases for the item to be tested. A test case is (or should be) a recognized work product. A complete test case will contain a test case identifier, a brief statement of purpose (*e.g.,* a business rule), a description of pre-conditions, the actual test case inputs, the expected outputs, a description of expected post-conditions, and an execution history. The execution history is primarily for test management use—it may contain the date when the test was run, the person who ran it, the version on which it was run, and the Pass/Fail result.

The output portion of a test case is frequently overlooked, which is unfortunate because this is often the hard part. Suppose, for example, you were testing software that determined an optimal route for an aircraft, given certain FAA air corridor constraints and the weather data for a flight day. How would you know what the optimal route really is? Various responses can address this problem. The academic response is to postulate the existence of an oracle that "knows all the answers." One industrial response to this problem is known as Reference Testing, where the system is tested in the presence of expert users. These experts make judgments as to whether outputs of an executed set of test case inputs are acceptable.

Test case execution entails establishing the necessary preconditions, providing the test case inputs, observing the outputs, comparing these with the expected outputs, and then ensuring that the expected post-conditions exist to determine whether the test passed. From all of this, it becomes clear that test cases are valuable—at least as valuable as source code. Test cases need to be developed, reviewed, used, managed, and saved.

1.3 Insights from a Venn Diagram

Testing is fundamentally concerned with behavior, and behavior is orthogonal to the code-based view common to software (and system) developers. A quick distinction is that the code-based view focuses on what it *is* and the behavioral view considers what it *does*. One of the continuing sources of difficulty for testers is that the base documents are usually written by and for developers; the emphasis is therefore on code-based, instead of behavioral, information. In this section, we develop a simple Venn diagram that clarifies several nagging questions about testing.

Consider a universe of program behaviors. (Notice that we are forcing attention on the essence of testing.) Given a program and its specification, consider the set S of specified behaviors, and the set P of programmed behaviors. Figure 1.2 shows the relationship between the specified and programmed behaviors. Of all the possible program behaviors, the specified ones are in the circle labeled S; and all those behaviors

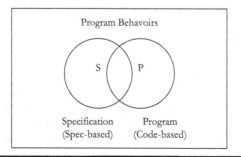

Figure 1.2　Specified and implemented program behaviors.

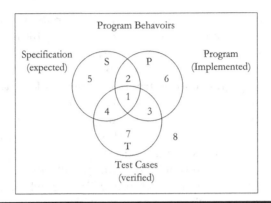

Figure 1.3   Specified, implemented, and tested behaviors.

actually programmed are in P. With this diagram, we can see more clearly the problems that confront a tester. What if certain specified behaviors have not been programmed? In our earlier terminology, these are faults of omission. Similarly, what if certain programmed (implemented) behaviors have not been specified? These correspond to faults of commission and to errors that occurred after the specification was complete. The intersection of S and P (the football-shaped region) is the "correct" portion, that is, behaviors that are both specified and implemented. A very good view of testing is that it is the determination of the extent of program behavior that is both specified and implemented. (As an aside, note that "correctness" only has meaning with respect to a specification and an implementation. It is a relative term, not an absolute.)

The new circle in Figure 1.3 is for test cases. Notice the slight discrepancy with our universe of discourse and the set of program behaviors. Because a test case results in a program behavior, the mathematicians might forgive us. Now, consider the relationships among the sets S, P, and T. There may be specified behaviors that are not tested (regions 2 and 5), specified behaviors that are tested (regions 1 and 4), and test cases that correspond to unspecified behaviors (regions 3 and 7).

Similarly, there may be programmed behaviors that are not tested (regions 2 and 6), programmed behaviors that are tested (regions 1 and 3), and test cases that correspond to behaviors that were not implemented (regions 4 and 7).

Each of these regions is important. If specified behaviors exist for which no test cases are available, the testing is necessarily incomplete. If certain test cases correspond to unspecified behaviors, some possibilities arise: either such a test case is unwarranted, the specification is deficient, or the tester wishes to determine that specified non-behavior does not occur. (In my experience, good testers often postulate test cases of this latter type. This is a fine reason to have good testers participate in specification and design reviews.)

We are already at a point where we can see some possibilities for testing as a craft: what can a tester do to make the region where these sets all intersect (region 1) as large as possible? Another approach is to ask how the test cases in the set T are identified. The short answer is that test cases are identified by a testing method. This framework gives us a way to compare the effectiveness of diverse testing methods, as we shall see in Chapter 10.

1.4 Identifying Test Cases

Two fundamental approaches are used to identify test cases; for decades, these have been called functional and structural testing. Why functional? In a sense, a program is a function that maps elements of its input space to elements of its output space. The "structural" part is less clear—to be generous, it might refer to the structure of the code being tested. Specification-based and code-based are more descriptive names, and they will be used here. Both approaches have several distinct test case identification methods, they are generally just called testing methods. They are methodical in the sense that two testers following the same "method" will devise very similar (equivalent?) test cases.

1.4.1 Specification-based Testing

The reason that specification-based testing was originally called "functional testing" is that any program can be considered to be a function that maps values from its input domain to values in its output range. (Function, domain, and range are defined in Chapter 3.) This notion is commonly used in engineering, when systems are considered to be black boxes. This led to another synonymous term—black box testing, in which the content (implementation) of the black box is not known, and the function of the black box is understood completely in terms of its inputs and outputs (see Figure 1.4). Many times, we operate very effectively with black box knowledge; in fact, this is central to object orientation. As an example, most people successfully operate automobiles with only black box knowledge.

With the specification-based approach to test case identification, the only information used is the specification of the software. Therefore, the test cases have two distinct advantages: (1) they are independent of how the software is implemented, so if the implementation changes, the test cases are still useful; and (2) test case development can occur in parallel with the implementation, thereby reducing overall project development interval. On the negative side, specification-based test cases frequently suffer from two problems: significant redundancies may exist among test cases, compounded by the possibility of gaps of untested software.

Figure 1.5 shows the results of test cases identified by two specification-based methods. Method A identifies a larger set of test cases than does Method B. Notice that, for both methods, the set of test cases is completely contained within the set of specified behavior. Because specification-based methods are based on the specified behavior, it is hard to imagine these methods identifying behaviors that are not specified. In Chapter 10, we will see direct comparisons of test cases generated by various specification-based methods for the examples defined in Chapter 2.

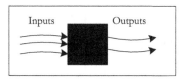

Figure 1.4   An engineer's black box.

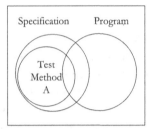 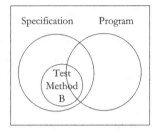

Figure 1.5   Comparing specification-based test case identification methods.

In Chapters 5, 6, and 7, we will examine the mainline approaches to specification-based testing, including boundary value analysis, robustness testing, worst-case analysis, special value testing, input (domain) equivalence classes, and decision table-based testing. The common thread running through these techniques is that all are based on definitional information of the item tested. Some of the mathematical background presented in Chapter 3 applies primarily to the specification-based approaches.

1.4.2 Code-based Testing

Code-based testing is the other fundamental approach to test case identification. To contrast it with black box testing, it is sometimes called white box (or even clear box) testing. The clear box metaphor is probably more appropriate, because the essential difference is that the implementation (of the black box) is known and used to identify test cases. The ability to "see inside" the black box allows the tester to identify test cases based on how the function is actually implemented.

Code-based testing has been the subject of some fairly strong theory. To really understand code-based testing, familiarity with the concepts of linear graph theory (Chapter 4) is essential. With these concepts, the tester can rigorously describe exactly what is tested. Because of its strong theoretical basis, code-based testing lends itself to the definition and use of test coverage metrics. Test coverage metrics provide a way to explicitly state the extent to which a software item has been tested, and this in turn makes testing management more meaningful.

Figure 1.6 shows the results of test cases identified by two code-based methods. As before, Method A identifies a larger set of test cases than does Method B. Is a larger set of test cases necessarily better? This is an excellent question, and code-based testing provides important ways to develop an answer. Notice that, for both methods, the set of test cases is completely contained within the set of programmed

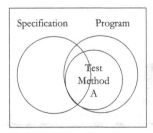 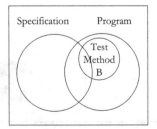

Figure 1.6   Comparing code-based test case identification methods.

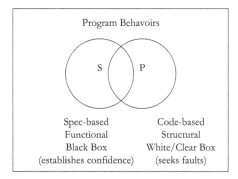

Figure 1.7   Sources of test cases.

behavior. Because code-based methods are based on the program, it is hard to imagine these methods identifying behaviors that are not programmed. It is easy to imagine, however, that a set of code-based test cases is relatively small with respect to the full set of programmed behaviors. In Chapter 10, we will see direct comparisons of test cases generated by various code-based methods.

1.4.3 The Specification-based versus Code-based Debate

Given the two fundamentally different approaches to test case identification, it is natural to question which is better. If you read much of the literature, you will find strong adherents to either choice.

The Venn diagrams presented earlier yield a strong resolution to this debate. Recall that the goal of both approaches is to identify test cases. Specification-based testing uses only the specification to identify test cases, while code-based testing uses the program source code (implementation) as the basis of test case identification. Later chapters will establish that neither approach by itself is sufficient. Consider program behaviors: if all specified behaviors have not been implemented, code-based test cases will never be able to recognize this. Conversely, if the program implements behaviors that have not been specified, this will never be revealed by Specification-based test cases. (A Trojan Horse is a good example of such unspecified behavior.) The quick answer is that both approaches are needed; the testing craftsperson's answer is that a judicious combination will provide the confidence of specification-based testing and the measurement of code-based testing. Earlier, we asserted that specification-based testing often suffers from twin problems of redundancies and gaps. When specification-based test cases are executed in combination with code-based test coverage metrics, both of these problems can be recognized and resolved.

The Venn diagram view of testing provides one final insight. What is the relationship between the set T of test cases and the sets S and P of specified and implemented behaviors? Clearly, the test cases in T are determined by the test case identification method used. A very good question to ask is how appropriate (or effective) is this method? To close a loop from an earlier discussion, recall the causal trail from error to fault, failure, and incident. If we know what kind of errors we are prone to make, and if we know what kinds of faults are likely to reside in the software to be tested, we can use this to employ more appropriate test case identification methods. This is the point at which testing really becomes a craft.

1.5 Fault Taxonomies

Our definitions of error and fault hinge on the distinction between process and product: process refers to how we do something, and product is the end result of a process. The point at which testing and Software Quality Assurance (SQA) meet is that SQA typically tries to improve the product by improving the process. In that sense, testing is clearly more product oriented. SQA is more concerned with reducing errors endemic in the development process, while testing is more concerned with discovering faults in a product. Both disciplines benefit from a clearer definition of types of faults. Faults can be classified in several ways: the development phase in which the corresponding error occurred, the consequences of corresponding failures, difficulty to resolve, risk of no resolution, and so on. My favorite is based on anomaly (fault) occurrence: one time only, intermittent, recurring, or repeatable.

For a comprehensive treatment of types of faults, see the IEEE Standard Classification for Software Anomalies (IEEE, 1993). (A software anomaly is defined in that document as "a departure from the expected," which is pretty close to our definition.) The IEEE standard defines a detailed anomaly resolution process built around four phases (another life cycle): recognition, investigation, action, and disposition. Some of the more useful anomalies are given in Tables 1.1 through 1.5; most of these are from the IEEE standard, but we have added some of our favorites.

Since the primary purpose of a software review is to find faults, review checklists (see Chapter 20) are another good source of fault classifications. Karl Wiegers has an excellent set of checklists on his website: [http://www.processimpact.com/pr_goodies.shtml].

Table 1.1   Input/Output Faults

Type	Instances
Input	Correct input not accepted
	Incorrect input accepted
	Description wrong or missing
	Parameters wrong or missing
Output	Wrong format
	Wrong result
	Correct result at wrong time (too early, too late)
	Incomplete or missing result
	Spurious result
	Spelling/grammar
	Cosmetic

Table 1.2   Logic Faults

Missing case(s)
Duplicate case(s)
Extreme condition neglected
Misinterpretation
Missing condition
Extraneous condition(s)
Test of wrong variable
Incorrect loop iteration
Wrong operator (e.g., < instead of ≤)

Table 1.3   Computation Faults

Incorrect algorithm
Missing computation
Incorrect operand
Incorrect operation
Parenthesis error
Insufficient precision (round-off, truncation)
Wrong built-in function

Table 1.4   Interface Faults

Incorrect interrupt handling
I/O timing
Call to wrong procedure
Call to nonexistent procedure
Parameter mismatch (type, number)
Incompatible types
Superfluous inclusion

Table 1.5   Data Faults

Incorrect initialization
Incorrect storage/access
Wrong flag/index value
Incorrect packing/unpacking
Wrong variable used
Wrong data reference
Scaling or units error
Incorrect data dimension
Incorrect subscript
Incorrect type
Incorrect data scope
Sensor data out of limits
Off by one
Inconsistent data

1.6 Levels of Testing

Thus far, we have said nothing about one of the key concepts of testing—levels of abstraction. Levels of testing echo the levels of abstraction found in the Waterfall Model of the software development life cycle. Although this model has its drawbacks, it is useful for identifying distinct levels of testing and for clarifying the objectives that pertain to each level. A diagrammatic variation of the Waterfall Model, known as the V-Model in ISTQB parlance, is given in Figure 1.8; this variation emphasizes the correspondence between testing and design levels. Notice that, especially in terms of Specification-based testing, the three levels of definition (specification, preliminary design, and detailed design) correspond directly to three levels of testing—system, integration, and unit testing.

A practical relationship exists between levels of testing versus Specification-based and code-based testing. Most practitioners agree that code-based testing is most appropriate at the unit level, while Specification-based testing is most appropriate at the system level. This is generally true, but it is also a likely consequence of the base information produced during the requirements specification, preliminary design, and detailed design phases. The constructs defined for code-based testing make the most sense at the unit level, and similar constructs are only now becoming

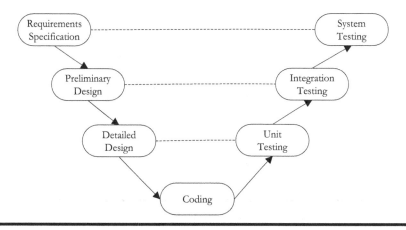

Figure 1.8   Levels of abstraction and testing in the Waterfall Model.

available for the integration and system levels of testing. We develop such structures in Chapters 9, 12, and 13 to support code-based testing at the integration and system levels for both traditional and object-oriented software.

Exercises

1.1 Make a Venn Diagram that reflects a part of the following statement: "… we have left undone that which we ought to have done, and we have done that which we ought not to have done …"

1.2 Make a Venn Diagram that reflects the essence of Reinhold Niebuhr's "Serenity Prayer":

> God, grant me the serenity to accept the things I cannot change,
> Courage to change the things I can,
> And wisdom to know the difference.

1.3 Describe each of the eight regions in Figure 1.3. Can you recall examples of these in software you have written?

1.4 One of the folk tales of software lore describes a disgruntled employee who writes a payroll program which contains logic that checks for the employee's identification number before producing paychecks. If the employee is ever terminated, the program creates havoc. Discuss this situation in terms of the error, fault, and failure pattern and decide which form of testing would be appropriate.

1.5 Figure 1.9 shows the V-Model (aka the Waterfall Model) phases in which mistakes might be made, thereby becoming faults. Try to map the faults in Tables 1.1 through 1.5 into the "fault insertion" phases in Figure 1.9.

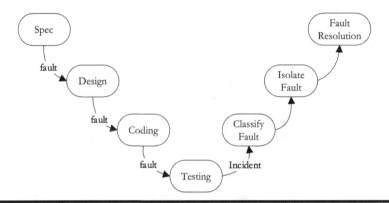

Figure 1.9 Possibilities for Fault Insertion in the V-Model.

References

IEEE Computer Society, *IEEE Standard Glossary of Software Engineering Terminology*, 4th Edition. 1983, ANSI/IEEE Std 729–1983.

IEEE Computer Society, *IEEE Standard Classification for Software Anomalies*, 1993, IEEE Std 1044–1993.

Chapter 2

Examples

Three examples will be used in Chapters 5 through 10 to illustrate the various unit testing methods: the triangle problem (a venerable example in testing circles); a logically complex function, NextDate; and an online shopping example that typifies MIS applications, Foodies-Wish-List. Taken together, these examples raise most of the issues that testers will encounter at the unit level. The discussion of higher levels of testing in Chapters 11 through 17 uses a garage door controller example which also illustrates some of the issues of "systems of systems." Finally, Section 2.6 describes three examples that will be used in the exercise portions of selected chapters.

For the purposes of code-based testing, Java implementations of the three unit-level examples are given in this chapter. System-level descriptions of the garage door controller are given in Chapters 11 through 17. These applications are modeled with finite state machines, variations of Event-Driven Petri Nets, selected statecharts, and with the Universal Modeling Language (UML).

2.1 Structural Elements of Pseudo-code and Java

Previous editions of this book used pseudo-code as an "implementation" of code examples. Most of the pseudo-code has been rewritten as Java code. The pseudo-code was deliberately similar to Visual Basic for Applications (VBA). Tables 2.1 and 2.2 show most language constructs in "VBA" form and in Java.

Table 2.1

Comments	"VBA"	' <text>
	Java	//<text>
Data Structure / Class Declaration	"VBA"	Type <type name><list of field descriptions>
	Java	public class <class name> {<list of data declarations>

(Continued)

Table 2.1 (Continued)

Data Declaration	"VBA"	Dim \<variable list\> As \<type\>
	Java	\<type\> \<variable list\>;
Input/Output	"VBA"	Input (\<variable list\>) Output (\<variable list\>)
	Java	NA
Variable Naming	"VBA" and Java	A sequence of alphanumeric (and selected special) characters with no length limit. Descriptive names are preferred. By convention, variable names begin with a lower case letter. If the variable name consists of two or more words, the first letter of each successive word is capitalized, *e.g.,,* accountBalance.

Binary Arithmetic Operators Same for both "VBA" and Java		
Addition	both	+
Subtration	both	-
Multiplication	both	*
Division	both	/
Remainder	both	%

Unary Arithmetic Operators, Java only		
Positive value	Java	+
Negative value	Java	-
Increment by 1	Java	++
Decrement by 1	Java	--
Logical complement	Java	! (reverses value of a boolean variable)

Relational Operators		
Equals	"VBA"	=
	Java	==
Not Equals	"VBA"	<>
	Java	!=
Greater than	both	>
Greater than or equal	both	>=
Less than	both	<
Less than or equal	both	<=

(*Continued*)

Table 2.1 (Continued)

Conditional Operators		
Conjunction	"VBA"	AND
	Java	&&
Disjunction	"VBA"	OR
	Java	||
Negation	"VBA"	NOT
	Java	!
Expressions		In both "VBA" and java, an expression can be a single variable, a single procedure, (or method invocation) or a compound built out of these with operators.
Assignment Statement	both	<variable> = <expression>

Table 2.2

Control Flow Statements (usually more than one line)		
Conditional Statement	"VBA"	Java
If-then	If <condition> Then <block of statements> EndIf	if <condition> { <block of statements> ; }
If-then-else	If <condition> Then <block of statements> Else <block of statements> EndIf	if <condition> { <block of statements> ; } else { <block of statements> ; }
If-ElseIF	If <condition> Then <block of statements> ElseIF <block of statements> ElseIF <block of statements> ... EndIf	if <condition> { <block of statements> ; } else if <condition> { <block of statements> ; } else if <condition> { <block of statements> ; }

(*Continued*)

Table 2.2 (Continued)

Mutual Exclusive Alternatives	Case <variable> of
	
	Case 1 variable = value
	
	Case 2 variable = value
	
	Case 3 variable = value
	
	End Case
		switch <variable> {
		
		case 1: <block of statements>
		
		break;
		
		case 2: <block of statements>
		
		break;
		
		}

Pre-test loop	While <condition>
	
	<block of statements>
	
	EndWhile
		while <condition> {
		
		<block of statements>
		
		}

For (also a pre-test loop)	For Index = first, last, increment
	
	<block of statements>
	
	EndFor
		for(<type> index = first, index <= last, index++) {
		
		<block of statements>
		
		}

Post-test loop	Do <block of statements> Until <condition>	do { <block of statements> } while <condition> ;
Other (Java only) Sequence-changing Statements		
Branching Statement	Java (description)	
break	Terminates a switch or repetition	
continue	Terminates innermost repetition, Then continues the loop	
return <value>	Returns <value> and exits from a method	
return	Exits from a void method	
Procedure/Method Definition		
	"VBA"	Java
	Procedure <procedure name> (Input: <list of variables>;Output: <list of variables>) <body>	<modifier> <return type> methodName (<parameter list>) {modifiers: public, private, protected; return type is the type of value returned (items in the parameter list are preceded by their type
	End <procedure name>	}

(Continued)

Table 2.2 (Continued)

Functions	Function functionName(<parameter list>)	NA
	a Function is treated as a variable, *e.g., x = squareRoot(49*	
Inter-unit Communication	Call procedureName(<parameter list>	A message can be treated as a variable
Class/Object Definition		
	<name> (<attribute list>; <method list>, <body>) End <name>	public class <class name> {<list of data declarations>}
Object Instantiation		
	Instantiate <class name>.<object name> (list of attribute values)	<class name> <object name> = new <class name>(<parameter list>);

2.2 The Triangle Problem

The triangle problem is the most widely used example in software testing literature. Some of the more notable entries in four decades of testing literature are Gruenberger (1973); Brown (1975); Myers (1979); Pressman (1982) and subsequent editions; Clarke (1983); Clarke (1984); Chellappa (1987); and Hetzel (1988). There are others, but this list makes the point.

2.2.1 Problem Statement

Simple version: The triangle program accepts three integers, a, b, and c, as input. These are taken to be sides of a triangle. The output of the program is the type of triangle determined by the three sides: Equilateral, Isosceles, Scalene, or Not A Triangle. Sometimes this problem is extended to include right triangles as a fifth type; we will use this extension in some of the exercises.

   Improved version: The triangle program accepts three integers, a, b, and c, as input. These are taken to be sides of a triangle. The integers a, b, and c must satisfy the following conditions:

$c1.$	$1 \leq a \leq 200$	$c4.$	$a < b + c$
$c2.$	$1 \leq b \leq 200$	$c5.$	$b < a + c$
$c3.$	$1 \leq c \leq 200$	$c6.$	$c < a + b$

The output of the program is the type of triangle determined by the three sides: Equilateral, Isosceles, Scalene, or NotATriangle. If an input value fails any of conditions c1, c2, or c3, the program notes this with an output message, for example,

"Value of b is not in the range of permitted values." If values of a, b, and c satisfy conditions c1, c2, and c3, one of four mutually exclusive outputs is given:

1. If all three sides are equal, the program output is Equilateral.
2. If exactly one pair of sides is equal, the program output is Isosceles.
3. If no pair of sides is equal, the program output is Scalene.
4. If any of conditions c4, c5, and c6 is not met, the program output is NotATriangle.

2.2.2 Discussion

Perhaps one of the reasons for the longevity of this example is that it contains clear but complex logic. It also typifies some of the incomplete definitions that impair communication among customers, developers, and testers. The first specification presumes the developers know some details about triangles, particularly the Triangle Inequality: the sum of any pair of sides must be strictly greater than the third side. The upper limit of 200 is both arbitrary and convenient; it will be used when we develop boundary value test cases in Chapter 5.

We use this example because:

■ it is well-known in the software testing literature.
■ it is easy to determine expected outputs, and
■ it is an easy example for infeasible program paths.

The Java code is given next. Note, for this and other examples, Java source code will be written in Monaco 8.5 font.

2.2.3 Java Implementation

```java
public class Triangle {
        public static final int OUT_OF_RANGE = -2;
        public static final int INVALID = -1;
        public static final int SCALENE = 0;
        public static final int ISOSELES = 1;
        public static final int EQUILATERAL = 2;

        public static int triangle(int a, int b, int c) {
                boolean c1, c2, c3, isATriangle;

                // Step 1: Validate Input
                c1 = (1 <= a) && (a <= 200);
                c2 = (1 <= b) && (b <= 200);
                c3 = (1 <= c) && (c <= 200);

                int triangleType = INVALID;
                if (!c1 || !c2 || !c3)
                        triangleType = OUT_OF_RANGE;
                else {
                        // Step 2: Is A Triangle?
                        if ((a < b + c) && (b < a + c) && (c < a + b))
                                isATriangle = true;
                        else
                                isATriangle = false;
```

```
                    // Step 3: Determine Triangle Type
                    if (isATriangle) {
                            if ((a == b) && (b == c))
                                    triangleType = EQUILATERAL;
                            else if ((a != b) && (a != c) && (b != c))
                                    triangleType = SCALENE;
                            else
                                    triangleType = ISOSELES;
                    } else
                            triangleType = INVALID;
            }

            return triangleType;
        }
}
```

2.3 The NextDate Function

The complexity in the triangle program is due to relationships between inputs and correct outputs. We will use the NextDate function to illustrate a different kind of complexity—logical relationships among the input variables.

2.3.1 Problem Statement

NextDate is a function of three variables: month, date, and year. It returns the date of the day after the input date. The month, date, and year variables have integer values subject to these conditions (the year range ending in 2042 is arbitrary, and is from the First Edition):

c1. $1 \leq$ month ≤ 12
c2. $1 \leq$ day ≤ 31
c3. $1842 \leq$ year ≤ 2042

As we did with the triangle program, we could make our problem statement more specific. This entails defining responses for invalid values of the input values for the day, month, and year. We could also define responses for invalid combinations of inputs, such as June 31 of any year. If any of conditions c1, c2, or c3 fails, NextDate produces an output indicating the corresponding variable has an out-of-range value—for example, "Value of month not in the range 1...12." Because numerous invalid day–month–year combinations exist, NextDate collapses these into one message: "Invalid Input Date."

2.3.2 Discussion

Two sources of complexity exist in the NextDate function: the complexity of the input domain discussed previously, and the rule that determines when a year is a leap year. A year is 365.2422 days long; therefore, leap years are used for the "extra day" problem. If we declared a leap year every fourth year, a slight error would occur. The Gregorian calendar (after Pope Gregory) resolves this by adjusting leap years on century years. Thus, a year is a leap year if it is divisible by 4, unless it is a century year. Century years are leap years only if they are multiples of 400 (Inglis, 1961); so 1996,

2016, and 2000 are leap years, while the year 1900 is not a leap year. The NextDate function also illustrates a sidelight of software testing. Many times, we find examples of Zipf's Law, which states that 80% of the activity occurs in 20% of the space. Notice how much of the source code is devoted to leap year considerations. In the second implementation, notice how much code is devoted to input value validation.

2.3.3 *Java Implementation*

```java
public class NextDate {

    public static SimpleDate nextDate(SimpleDate date) {

        int tomorrowDay, tomorrowMonth, tomorrowYear;

        tomorrowMonth = date.month;
        tomorrowDay = date.day;
        tomorrowYear = date.year;
        switch (date.month) {

        // 31 day months (except Dec.)
        case 1:
        case 3:
        case 5:
        case 7:
        case 8:
        case 10:
                if (date.day < 31)
                        tomorrowDay = date.day + 1;
                else {
                        tomorrowDay = 1;
                        tomorrowMonth = date.month + 1;
                }
                break;

        // 30 day months
        case 4:
        case 6:
        case 9:
        case 11:
                if (date.day < 30)
                        tomorrowDay = date.day + 1;
                else {
                        tomorrowDay = 1;
                        tomorrowMonth = date.month + 1;
                }
                break;
        // December
        case 12:
                if (date.day < 31)
                        tomorrowDay = date.day + 1;
                else {
                        tomorrowDay = 1;
                        tomorrowMonth = 1;
                        if (date.year == 2042)
                                System.out.println("Date beyond 2042 ");
                        else
```

```
                                    tomorrowYear = date.year + 1;
                    }
                    break;
            // February
            case 2:
                    if (date.day < 28)
                            tomorrowDay = date.day + 1;
                    else {
                            if (date.day == 28) {
                                    if (date.isLeap())
                                            tomorrowDay = 29;
                                    else {
                                            tomorrowDay = 1;
                                            tomorrowMonth = 3;
                                    }
                            } else if(date.day == 29) {
                                    tomorrowDay = 1;
                                    tomorrowMonth = 3;
                            }              .
                    }
                    break;
            }
            return new SimpleDate(tomorrowMonth, tomorrowDay,
tomorrowYear);
    }
}
public class SimpleDate {
        int month;
        int day;
        int year;
        public SimpleDate(int month, int day, int year) {
                if(!rangesOK(month, day, year))
                        throw new IllegalArgumentException("Invalid Date");
                this.month = month;
                this.day = day;
                this.year = year;
        }
        public int getMonth() {
                return month;
        }
        public void setMonth(int month) {
                this.month = month;
        }
        public int getDay() {
                return day;
        }
        public void setDay(int day) {
                this.day = day;
        }
        public int getYear() {
                return year;
        }
}
```

```java
    public void setYear(int year) {
        this.year = year;
    }
    boolean rangesOK(int month, int day, int year) {
        boolean dateOK = true;

        dateOK &= (year > 1841) && (year < 2043); // Year OK?
        dateOK &= (month > 0) && (month < 13); // Month OK?
        dateOK &= (day > 0) && (
                    ((month == 1 || month == 3 || month == 5
|| month == 7 || month == 8 || month == 10 || month == 12) && day < 32) ||
                    ((month == 4 || month == 6 || month == 9
|| month == 11) && day < 31) ||
                        ((month == 2 && isLeap(year)) && day < 30) ||
                        ((month == 2 && !isLeap(year)) && day < 29));
        return dateOK;
    }

    private boolean isLeap(int year) {
        boolean isLeapYear = true;
        if(year % 4 != 0)
            isLeapYear = false;
        else if(year % 100 != 0)
            isLeapYear = true;
        else if(year % 400 != 0)
            isLeapYear = false;

        return isLeapYear;
    }
    public boolean isLeap() {
        return isLeap(year);
    }

    @Override
    public boolean equals(Object obj) {
        boolean areEqual = false;
        if(obj instanceof SimpleDate) {
            SimpleDate simpleDate = (SimpleDate) obj;

            areEqual = simpleDate.getDay() == getDay() &&
                        simpleDate.getMonth() == getMonth() &&
                        simpleDate.getYear() == getYear();
        }
        return areEqual;
    }
}
```

2.4 The Foodies-Wish-List Online Shopping Application

Foodies-Wish-List is an online shopping service for extremely rare (and expensive!) gourmet foods. It can be used either on a one-time basis as a guest, or repeatedly by members. There is no initial cost for either category, but to be a Foodies-Wish-List member, one must register with customary information, such as:

■ member name
■ address

- shipping address
- telephone number
- email address
- preferred payment method
  - member credit card
  - PayPal

The registration process ends with an account number being assigned to the new Foodies-Wish-List member.

Registered Foodies-Wish-List members receive discounts based on the price of an individual order as follows:

- orders less than $200 receive no discount
- orders between $200 and $800 (inclusive) receive a 10% discount
- orders over $800 receive a 15% discount

There is no discount for any guest order.

Foodies-Wish-List members receive free shipping on any order over $200. For orders less than $200, there is a standard shipping price of $5.00. All guest orders are charged a $10 shipping fee.

Foodie Items

1. Vanilla beans; $112/pound
2. hop shoots; $128/pound
3. Jamon Iberico de Belotta; $220/pound
4. Kopi Luwak coffee; $200/pound
5. Kobe beef; $200/pound
6. Moose House cheese; $400 – $500/pound
7. Italian white truffles: $2000/pound
8. Saffron; $4540/pound, $10/gram
9. Almas caviar; $11,364/pound

2.4.1 Problem Statement

The full Foodies Wish List problem will be used as an integration testing and data-flow testing example. Here we only describe two parts of the problem—building an order and computing the final price.

2.4.2 Discussion

The public void method completeOrder is used to illustrate how Behavior-Driven Development (BDD) and decision tables can be combined to improve the bottom-up process inherent in agile software development.

The usual format for a BDD scenario uses key words Given, When, and Then. Here we move from this format directly into a partial decision table, and then expand the table using the mechanisms of a decision table.

Given: the running price total of an Order
And: the Order was placed by a Member,
When: the Member selects "Finish"

Then: compute discount
And: apply any taxes
And: apply shipping charges
And: open Payment Screen

The Given, When portions are modeled as conditions, and the Then portion is the action portion of the decision table.

c1. Member Order
c2. Order price < $20
c3. Member selects "Finish"
a1. no discount.
a2. 10% discount.
a3. 15% discount.
a4. apply any taxes.
a5. apply shipping charges.
a6. open Payment Screen.

This scenario yields the first rule of a decision table:

c1. Member Order	T
c2. Order price < $20	T
c3. Member selects "Finish"	T
a1. no discount	x
a2. 10% discount	—
a3. 15% discount	—
a4. apply any taxes	x
a5. apply shipping charges	x
a6. open Payment Screen.	x

Since this is a Limited Entry Decision Table (LEDT), we can mechanically expand it to the following (incomplete) decision table: (DT1).

c1. Member Order	T	T	T	T	F	F	F	F
c2. Order price < $200	T	T	F	F	T	T	F	F
c3. Member selects "Finish"	T	F	T	F	T	F	T	F
a1. no discount	x	—	—	—	—	—	—	—
a2. 10% discount	—	—	—	—	—	—	—	—
a3. 15% discount	—	—	—	—	—	—	—	—
a4. apply any taxes	x	—	—	—	—	—	—	—
a5. apply shipping charges	x	—	—	—	—	—	—	—
a6. open Payment Screen.	x	—	—	—	—	—	—	—

The mechanical expansion raises a few questions; these might be answered by additional BDD scenarios, or by discussion with the Customer. (Note that one of the values of a good model is that it stimulates discovery. One historical example: the Periodic Table of Elements predicted the existence of several chemical elements before they were shown to exist.) We can/should ask:

1. What does it mean for c1. Member order to be false?
2. What is so special about c2. Order price < $200?
3. What happens when c3. Member selects "Finish" is false?

Some possible answers are as follows:

1. More than one category of people submitting an order. For now, we will assume just one category, Non-member.
2. Actions a1, a2, and a3 suggest there are three ranges of order prices. For now, we could call them small, medium, or large.
3. Since this is an online shopping example, we might assume that when c3. Member selects "Finish" is false, the customer selects a "Order" screen. This, in turn, will create a new action, a7. Order. A simpler solution is to just not perform action a6.

c1. Member Order	T	T	T	T	F	F	F	F
c2. Order price < $200	T	T	F	F	T	T	F	F
c3. Member selects "Finish"	T	F	T	F	T	F	T	F
a1. no discount	x	—	—	—	—	—	—	—
a2. 10% discount	—	—	—	—	—	—	—	—
a3. 15% discount	—	—	—	—	—	—	—	—
a4. apply any taxes	x	—	—	—	—	—	—	—
a5. apply shipping charges	x	—	—	—	—	—	—	—
a6. open Payment Screen.	x	—	—	—	—	—	—	—
a7. open Order screen	—	x	—	x	—	x	—	x

With these assumptions, the Member half of our decision table is

c1. Order by	Member					
c2. Order price is	< $200		$200 to $800		> $800	
c3. Member selects "Finish"	T	F	T	F	T	F
a1. no discount	x	—	—	—	—	—

(Continued)

a2. 10% discount	—	—	x	—	—	—
a3. 15% discount	—	—	—	—	x	—
a4. apply any taxes	x	—	x	—	x	—
a5. apply shipping charges	x	—	x	—	x	—
a6. open Payment Screen.	x	—	x	—	x	—
a7. open Continue Shopping screen	—	x	—	x	—	x

and the non-Member half is (note change to "Guest"):

c1. Order by	Guest					
c2. Order price is	< $200		$200 to $800		> $800	
c3. Member selects "Finish"	T	F	T	F	T	F
a1. no discount	x	—	—	—	—	—
a2. 10% discount	—	—	—	—	—	—
a3. 15% discount	—	—	—	—	—	—
a4. apply any taxes	x	—	x	—	x	—
a5. apply shipping charges	x	—	x	—	x	—
a6. open Payment Screen.	x	—	x	—	x	—
a7. open Continue Shopping screen	—	x	—	x	—	x

At this point, the modeler must either seek new BDD scenarios or speak with the Customer. For now, assume the modeler learns that

1. guests receive no discount, regardless of order size, and
2. shipping charges are applied to any order of price < $200.

This reduces the Guest portion to:

c1. Order by	Guest	
c2. Order price is	—	
c3. Member selects "Finish"	T	F
a1. no discount	x	x

(Continued)

a2. 10% discount	—	—
a3. 15% discount	—	—
a4. apply any taxes	x	—
a5. apply shipping charges	x	x
a6. open Payment Screen.	x	—
a7. open Continue Shopping screen	—	x

And the final decision table is

c1. Order by	Member						Guest	
c2. Order price is	< $200		$200 to $800		> $800		—	
c3. Member selects "Finish"	T	F	T	F	T	F	T	F
a1. no discount	x	x	—	—	—	—	x	x
a2. 10% discount	—	—	x	—	—	—	—	—
a3. 15% discount	—	—	—	—	x	—	—	—
a4. apply any taxes	x	x	x	—	x	—	x	—
a5. apply shipping charges	x	—	—	—	—	—	x	—
a6. open Payment Screen.	x	—	x	—	x	—	x	—
a7. open Order screen	—	x	—	x	—	x	—	x

2.5 The Garage Door Controller

A system to open a garage door is comprised of several components: a drive motor, a drive chain, the garage door wheel tracks, end-of-track sensors, and a wireless control keypad. The garage door is controlled by the wireless keypad. In addition, there are two safety features, a laser beam near the floor, and an obstacle sensor. These latter two devices operate only when the garage door is closing. If the light beam is interrupted (possibly by a pet), the door immediately stops, and then reverses direction until the door is fully open. If the door encounters an obstacle while it is closing (say a child's tricycle left in the path of the door), the door stops and reverses direction until it is fully open. There is a third way to stop a door in motion, either when it is closing or opening—a signal from the wireless keypad. The response to this signal is different—the door stops in place. A subsequent signal starts the door in the same direction as when it was stopped. Finally, the end-of-track sensors detect when the door has moved to one of the extreme positions, either fully open or fully closed, and stop the drive motor.

2.6 Examples in Exercises

We identify three examples that we will use in the Exercise portions of selected chapters. Each example is similar to an ongoing example, yet different enough to be thought provoking.

2.6.1 The Quadrilateral Program

The Quadrilateral Program is deliberately similar to the Triangle Program. It accepts four integers, a, b, c, and d, as input. These are taken to be sides of a four-sided figure and they must satisfy the following conditions:

c1. $1 \leq a \leq 200$ (top)
c2. $1 \leq b \leq 200$ (left side)
c3. $1 \leq c \leq 200$ (bottom)
c4. $1 \leq d \leq 200$ (right side)

The output of the program is the type of quadrilateral determined by the four sides (see Figure 2.1): Square, Rectangle, Trapezoid, or General. (Since the problem statement only has information about lengths of the four sides, a square cannot be distinguished from a rhombus, similarly, a parallelogram cannot be distinguished from a rectangle.)

1. A *square* has two pairs of parallel sides (a||c, b||d), and all sides are equal (a = b = c = d).
2. A *kite* has two pairs of equal sides, but no parallel sides (a = d, b = c).
3. A *rhombus* has two pairs of parallel sides (a||c, b||d), and all sides are equal (a = b = c = d).
4. A *trapezoid* has one pair of parallel sides (a||c) and one pair of equal sides (b = d).
5. A *parallelogram* has two pairs of parallel sides (a||c, b||d), and two pairs of equal sides (a = c, b = d).
6. A *rectangle* has two pairs of parallel sides (a||c, b||d) and two pairs of equal sides (a = c, b = d).
7. A *(general) quadrilateral* has four sides, none equal and none parallel (aka a trapezium).

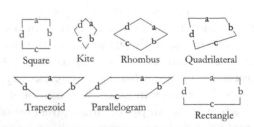

Figure 2.1   The Seven Quadrilaterals.

2.6.2 The NextWeek Function

The complexity in the quadrilateral program is primarily computational. The complexity of the NextWeek function, as with its clone, NextDate, is due to logical relationships among the input variables. NextWeek is a function of three variables: month, date, and year. It returns the date of the day one week after the input date. The month, date, and year variables have integer values subject to these conditions:

c1. $1 \leq$ month ≤ 12
c2. $1 \leq$ day ≤ 31
c3. $1842 \leq$ year ≤ 2042

2.6.3 The Windshield Wiper Controller

An automobile windshield wiper is controlled by a lever with a dial. The lever has four positions: OFF, INT (for intermittent), LOW, and HIGH; and the dial has three positions, numbered simply 1, 2, and 3. The dial positions indicate three intermittent speeds, and the dial position is relevant only when the lever is at the INT position. The decision table below shows the windshield wiper speeds (in wipes per minute) for the lever and dial positions.

c1. Lever	OFF	INT	INT	INT	LOW	HIGH
c2. Dial	n/a	1	2	3	n/a	n/a
a1. Wiper	0	4	6	12	30	60

Exercises

1. Recall the discussion from Chapter 1 about the relationship between the specification and the implementation of a program. If you study the implementation of NextDate carefully, you will see a problem. Look at the Switch clause for 30-day months (4, 6, 9, 11). There is no special action for day = 31. Discuss whether this implementation is correct. Repeat this discussion for the treatment of values of day 29 in the Switch clause for February.

2. In Chapter 1, we mentioned that part of a test case is the expected output. What would you use as the expected output for a NextDate test case of June 31, 1942? Why?

3. One common addition to the triangle problem is to check for right triangles. Three sides constitute a right triangle if the Pythagorean relationship is satisfied: $c^2 = a^2 + b^2$. This change makes it convenient to require that the sides be presented in increasing order, i.e., a <= b <= c. Extend public static int triangle3 to include the right triangle feature.

4. What would the public static int triangle3 do for the sides -3, -3, 5 if it did not contain the input validation code?

```
// Step 1: Validate Input
c1 = (1 <= a) && (a <= 200);
```

```
c2 = (1 <= b) && (b <= 200);
c3 = (1 <= c) && (c <= 200);
```

Discuss this in terms of the considerations we made in Chapter 1.

5. Consider a function YesterDate as the inverse of NextDate. Given a mon th, day, year, YesterDate returns the date of the day before. Develop a program for YesterDate. This is a "symmetric" program to NextDate. For testing purposes, we could implement

NextDate(YesterDate(mm. dd. yyyy)

and get the original date as a result.

6. Develop a program for NextWeek.

References

Brown, J.R. and Lipov, M., *Testing for software reliability, Proceedings of the International Symposium on Reliable Software*, Los Angeles, April 1975, pp. 518–527.

Chellappa, Mallika, Nontraversible Paths in a Program, *IEEE Transactions on Software Engineering*, Vol. SE-13, No. 6, June 1987, pp. 751–756.

Clarke, Lori A. and Richardson, Debra J., The application of error sensitive strategies to debugging, *ACM SIGSOFT Software Engineering Notes*, Vol. 8, No. 4, August 1983.

Clarke, Lori A. and Richardson, Debra J., A reply to Foster's comment on "The Application of Error Sensitive Strategies to Debugging", *ACM SIGSOFT Software Engineering Notes*, Vol. 9, No. 1, January 1984.

Gruenberger, F., Program testing, the historical perspective, in *Program Test Methods*, William C. Hetzel, Ed., Prentice-Hall, New York, 1973, pp. 11–14.

Hetzel, Bill, *The Complete Guide to Software Testing*, 2nd ed., QED Information Sciences, Inc., Wellesley, MA, 1988.

Inglis, Stuart J., *Planets, Stars, and Galaxies*, 4th Ed., John Wiley & Sons, New York, 1961.

Myers, Glenford J., *The Art of Software Testing*, Wiley Interscience, New York, 1979.

Pressman, Roger S., *Software Engineering: A Practitioner's Approach*, McGraw-Hill, New York, 1982.

Chapter 3

Discrete Math for Testers

More than any other life cycle activity, testing lends itself to mathematical description and analysis. In this chapter and in the next, testers will find the mathematics they need. Following the craftsperson metaphor, the mathematical topics presented here are tools; a testing craftsperson should know how to use them well. With these tools, a tester gains rigor, precision, and efficiency—all of which improve testing. The "for testers" part of the chapter title is important: this chapter is written for testers who either have a sketchy math background or who have forgotten some of the basics. Serious mathematicians (or maybe just those who take themselves seriously) will likely be annoyed by the informal discussion here. Readers who are already comfortable with the topics in this chapter should skip to the next chapter and start right in on graph theory.

In general, discrete mathematics is more applicable to specification-based testing, while graph theory pertains more to structural testing. "Discrete" raises a question: What might be indiscrete about mathematics? The mathematical antonym is continuous, as in calculus, which software developers (and testers) seldom use. Discrete math includes set theory, functions, relations, propositional logic, and probability theory, each of which is discussed here.

3.1 Set Theory

How embarrassing to admit, after all the lofty expiation of rigor and precision, that no explicit definition of a set exists. This is really a nuisance because set theory is central to these two chapters on math. At this point, mathematicians make an important distinction: naive versus axiomatic set theory. In naive set theory, a set is recognized as a primitive term, much like point and line are primitive concepts in geometry. Here are some synonyms for "set": collection, group, and bunch—you get the idea. The important thing about a set is that it lets us refer to several things as a group, or a whole. For example, we might wish to refer to the set of months that have exactly 30 days (we need this set when we test the NextDate function from Chapter 2). In set theory notation, we write:

M1 = {April, June, September, November}

and we read this notation as "M1 is the set whose elements are the months April, June, September, November."

3.1.1 Set Membership

The items in a set are called elements or members of the set, and this relationship is denoted by the symbol ∈. Thus, we could write April ∈ M1. When something is not a member of a set, we use the symbol ∉, so we might write December ∉ M1.

3.1.2 Set Definition

A set is defined in three ways: by simply listing its elements, by giving a decision rule, or by constructing a set from other sets. The listing option works well for sets with only a few elements as well as for sets in which the elements obey an obvious pattern. We used this method in defining M1 above. We might define the set of allowable years in the NextDate program as follows:

$$Y = \{1842, 1843, 1844, \ldots, 2041, 2042\}$$

When we define a set by listing its elements, the order of the elements is irrelevant. We will see why when we discuss set equality. The decision rule approach is more complicated, and this complexity carries both advantages and penalties. We could define the years for NextDate as:

$$Y = \{year: 1842 \leq year \leq 2042\}$$

which reads "Y is the set of all years such that (the colon is "such that") the years are between 1842 and 2042 inclusive." When a decision rule is used to define a set, the rule must be unambiguous. Given any possible value of year, we can therefore determine whether that year is in our set Y.

The advantage of defining sets with decision rules is that the unambiguity requirement forces clarity. Experienced testers have encountered "untestable requirements." Many times, the reason that such requirements cannot be tested boils down to an ambiguous decision rule. In our triangle program, for example, suppose we defined a set:

$$N = \{t: t \text{ is a nearly equilateral triangle}\}$$

We might say that the triangle with sides (300, 300, 299) is an element of N, but how would we treat the triangles with sides (50, 50, 51) or (5, 5, 6)?

A second advantage of defining sets with decision rules is that we might be interested in sets where the elements are difficult to list. In the NextDate problem, for example, we might be interested in the set:

$$S = \{years : year \text{ is a leap year}\}$$

We cannot easily write down the elements of this set; but given a particular value for year, we can easily apply the decision rule.

The main disadvantage of decision rules is that they can become logically complex, particularly when they are expressed with the predicate calculus quantifiers ∃ ("there exists") and ∀ ("for all"). If everyone understands this notation, the precision is helpful. Too often customers are overwhelmed by statements with these quantifiers. A second problem with decision rules has to do with self-reference. This is interesting, but it really has very little application for testers. The problem arises when a decision rule refers to itself, which is a circularity. As an example, the Barber of Seville "is the man who shaves everyone who does not shave himself." A more entertaining example is the business card which, on one side says "The statement on the other side is true." and the other side says "The statement on the other side is false.".

3.1.3 The Empty Set

The empty set, denoted by the symbol ∅, occupies a special place in set theory. The empty set contains no elements. At this point, mathematicians will digress to prove a lot of facts about empty sets:

1. The empty set is unique; that is, there cannot be two empty sets (we will take their word for it).
2. ∅, {∅}, {{∅}}, are all different sets (we will not need this).

It is useful to note that, when a set is defined by a decision rule that is always false, the set is empty. For instance, ∅ = {year: 2042 ≤ year ≤ 1842}.

3.1.4 Venn Diagrams

There are two traditional techniques to diagram relationships among sets: Venn diagrams, and Euler diagrams. Both help visualize concepts that have already been expressed textually. The chair of my college Mathematics Department maintained that, in her words, "Mathematics is not a function of its diagrams." Maybe not, but diagrams are certainly expressive, and they promote easy communication and understanding. Today, sets are commonly pictured by Venn diagrams—as in Chapter 1, when we discussed sets of specified and programmed behaviors. In a Venn diagram, a set is depicted as a circle; points in the interior of the circle correspond to elements of the set. Then, we might draw our set M1 of 30-day months as in Figure 3.1.

Venn diagrams were originally devised by John Venn, a British logician, in 1881. Most Venn diagrams show two or three overlapping circles. (It is impossible to show a Venn diagram of five sets showing all the possible intersections.) Shading is used in two opposite ways—most often, shaded regions are subsets of interest, but occasionally, shading is used to indicate an empty region. It is therefore important to include a legend explicitly stating the meaning of shading. Also, Venn diagrams should be placed within a rectangle that represents the universe of discourse. Figures 1.3 and 1.4 in Chapter 1 are examples of two- and three-set Venn diagrams. When the circles overlap, there is no presumption of relationships among the sets; at the same time, the overlapping regions

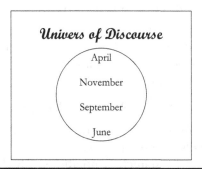

Figure 3.1   Venn diagram of the set of 30-day months.

describe all the potential intersections. It is topologically impossible to draw a Venn diagram of five sets. Finally, there is no way to diagram the empty set.

Venn diagrams communicate various set relationships in an intuitive way, but some picky questions arise. What about finite versus infinite sets? Both can be drawn as Venn diagrams; in the case of finite sets, we cannot assume that every interior point corresponds to a set element. We do not need to worry about this, but it is helpful to know the limitations. Sometimes, we will find it helpful to label specific elements.

Another sticking point has to do with the empty set. How do we show that a set, or maybe a portion of a set, is empty? The common answer is to shade empty regions, but this is often contradicted by other uses in which shading is used to highlight regions of interest. The best practice is to provide a legend that clarifies the intended meaning of shaded areas.

It is often helpful to think of all the sets in a discussion as being subsets of some larger set, known as the universe of discourse. We did this in Chapter 1 when we chose the set of all program behaviors as our universe of discourse. The universe of discourse can usually be guessed from given sets. In Figure 3.1, most people would take the universe of discourse to be the set of all months in a year. Testers should be aware that assumed universes of discourse are often sources of confusion. As such, they constitute a subtle point of miscommunication between customers and developers.

3.1.5 Set Operations

Much of the expressive power of set theory comes from basic operations on sets: union, intersection, and complement. Other handy operations are used: relative complement, symmetric difference, and Cartesian product. Each of these is defined next. In each of these definitions, we begin with two sets, A and B, contained in some universe of discourse U. The definitions use logical connectives from the propositional calculus: and ($\wedge$), or ($\vee$), exclusive–or ($\oplus$), and not ($\sim$).

Definition

Given sets A and B,

Their *union* is the set $A \cup B = \{x: x \in A \vee x \in B\}$.
Their *intersection* is the set $A \cap B = \{x: x \in A \wedge x \in B\}$.
The *complement* of A is the set $A' = \{x: x \notin A\}$.
The *relative complement of B with respect to A* is the set.
   $A - B = \{x: x \in A \wedge x \notin B\}$
The *symmetric difference of A and B* is the set $A \oplus B = \{x: x \in A \oplus x \in B\}$.

Venn diagrams for these sets are shown in Figure 3.2.

The intuitive expressive power of Venn diagrams is very useful for describing relationships among test cases and among items to be tested. Looking at the Venn diagrams in Figure 3.2, we might guess that:

$$A \oplus B = (A \cup B) - (A \cap B)$$

This is the case, and we could prove it with propositional logic.

Venn diagrams are used elsewhere in software development: together with directed graphs, they are the basis of the statechart notations, which are among the most rigorous specification techniques supported by Computer-Aided Software Engineering

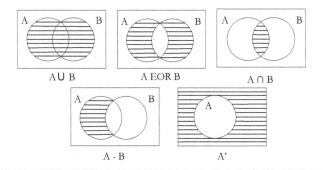

Figure 3.2   Venn diagrams of basic sets.

(CASE) technology. Statecharts are also the control notation chosen for the UML, the Unified Modeling Language from the IBM Corp. and the Object Management Group.

The Cartesian product (also known as the cross product) of two sets is more complex; it depends on the notion of ordered pairs, which are two element sets in which the order of the elements is important. The usual notation for unordered and ordered pairs is:

> unordered pair: (a, b)
> ordered pair: <a, b>

The difference is that, for a ≠ b, (a, b) = (b, a), but <a, b > ≠ < b, a>. This distinction is important to the material in Chapter 4; as we shall see, the fundamental difference between ordinary and directed graphs is exactly the difference between unordered and ordered pairs.

Definition

The Cartesian product of two sets A and B is the set.

$$A \times B = \{<x, y>: x \in A \land y \in B\}.$$

Venn diagrams do not show Cartesian products, so we will look at a short example. The Cartesian product of the sets A = {1, 2, 3} and B = {w, x, y, z} is the set:

$$A \times B = \begin{Bmatrix} <1, w>, <1, x>, <1, y>, <1, z>, <2, w>, <2, x>, \\ <2, y>, <2, z>, <3, w>, <3, x>, <3, y>, <3, z> \end{Bmatrix}$$

The Cartesian product has an intuitive connection with arithmetic. The cardinality of a set A is the number of elements in A and is denoted by $|A|$. (Some authors prefer Card(A).) For sets A and B, $|A \times B| = |A| \times |B|$. When we study specification-based testing in Chapter 5, we will use the Cartesian product to describe test cases for programs with several input variables. The multiplicative property of the Cartesian product means that this form of testing generates a large number of test cases.

3.1.6 Set Relations

We use set operations to construct interesting new sets from existing sets. When we do, we often would like to know something about the way the new and the old sets are related. Given two sets, A and B, we define three fundamental set relationships:

Definition

> *A is a subset of B*, written $A \subseteq B$, if and only if (iff) $a \in A \Rightarrow a \in B$.
> *A is a proper subset of B*, written $A \subset B$, iff $A \subseteq B \land B - A \neq \varnothing$.
> *A and B are equal sets*, written $A = B$, iff $A \subseteq B \land B \subseteq A$.

Mathematicians use "iff" for "if and only if." In plain English, set A is a subset of set B if every element of A is also an element of B. In order to be a proper subset of B, A must be a subset of B and there must be some element in B that is not an element of A. Finally, the sets A and B are equal if each is a subset of the other.

3.1.7 Set Partitions

A partition of a set is a very special situation that is extremely important for testers. Partitions have several analogs in everyday life: we might put up partitions to separate an office area into individual offices; we also encounter political partitions when a state is divided up into legislative districts. In both of these, notice that the sense of "partition" is to divide up a whole into pieces such that everything is in some piece and nothing is left out. More formally:

Definition

Given a set A, and a set of subsets A1, A2, …, An of A, the subsets are a *partition* of A iff

$$A1 \cup A2 \cup \ldots \cup An = A, \text{ and } i \neq j \Rightarrow Ai \cap Aj = \varnothing.$$

Because a partition is a set of subsets, we frequently refer to individual subsets as elements of the partition.

The two parts of this definition are important for testers. The first part guarantees that every element of A is in some partition subset, while the second part guarantees that no element of A is in two of the partition subsets.

This corresponds well with the legislative districts example: everyone is represented by some legislator, and nobody is represented by two legislators. A jigsaw puzzle is another good example of a partition.

Partitions are helpful to testers because the two definitional properties yield important assurances: completeness (everything is somewhere) and non-redundancy. When we study specification-based testing, we shall see that its inherent weakness is the vulnerability to both gaps and redundancies: some things may remain untested,

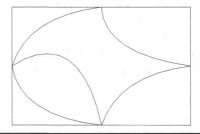

Figure 3.3 A partition of the universe of discourse.

while others are tested repeatedly. One of the difficulties of specification-based testing centers on finding an appropriate partition. In the Triangle Program, for example, the universe of discourse is the set of all triplets of positive integers. (Note that this is actually a Cartesian product of the set of positive integers with itself three times.) We might partition this universe three ways:

1. Into triangles and non-triangles
2. Into equilateral, isosceles, scalene, and non-triangles
3. Into equilateral, isosceles, scalene, right, and non-triangles

At first, these partitions seem okay, but there is a problem with the last partition. The sets of scalene and right triangles are not disjoint (the triangle with sides 3,4,5 is a right triangle that is scalene.)

3.1.8 Set Identities

Set operations and relations, when taken together, yield an important class of set identities that can be used to algebraically simplify complex set expressions. Math students usually are asked to derive all these; we will just list them and (occasionally) use them.

Name	Expression
Identity Laws	$A \cup \emptyset = A$ $A \cap \cup = A$
Domination Laws	$A \cup U = U$ $A \cap \emptyset = \emptyset$
Idempotent Laws	$A \cup A = A$ $A \cap A = A$
Complementation Laws	$(A')' = A$
Commutative Laws	$A \cup B = B \cup A$ $A \cap B = B \cap A$
Associative Laws	$A \cup (B \cup C) = (A \cup B) \cup C$ $A \cap (B \cap C) = (A \cap B) \cap C$
Distributive Laws	$A \cup B \cap C) = (A \cup B) \cap (A \cup C)$ $A \cap (B \cup C) = (A \cap B) \cup (A \cap C)$
DeMorgan's Laws	$(A \cup B)' = A' \cap B'$ $(A \cap B)' = A' \cup B'$

3.2 Functions

Functions are a central notion to software development and testing. The whole functional decomposition paradigm, for example, implicitly uses the mathematical notion of a function. Informally, a function associates elements of sets. In the NextDate program, for example, the function of a given date is the date of the following day, and in the triangle problem, the function of three input integers is the kind of triangle formed by sides with those lengths.

Any program can be thought of as a function that associates its outputs with its inputs. In the mathematical formulation of a function, the inputs are the domain and the outputs are the range of the function.

Definition

Given sets A and B, a *function* f is a subset of A × B such that, for a_i, $a_j \in$ A, b_i, $b_j \in$ B, and $f(a_i) = b_i$, $f(a_j) = b_j$, $b_i \neq b_j \Rightarrow a_i \neq a_j$.

Formal definitions like this one are notoriously terse, so let us take a closer look. The inputs to the function f are elements of the set A, and the outputs of f are elements of B. What the definition says is that the function f is "well behaved" in the sense that an element in A is never associated with more than one element of B. (If this could happen, how would we ever test such a function? This would be an example of non-determinism.)

3.2.1 Domain and Range

In the definition just given, the set A is the domain of the function f, and the set B is the range. Because input and output have a "natural" order, it is an easy step to say that a function f is really a set of ordered pairs in which the first element is from the domain and the second element is from the range. Here are two common notations for function:

$$f: A \rightarrow B$$

$$f \subseteq A \times B$$

We have not put any restrictions on the sets A and B in this definition. We could have A = B, and either A or B could be a Cartesian product of other sets.

3.2.2 Function Types

Functions are further described by particulars of the mapping. In the definition below, we start with a function f: A → B, and we define the set:

$$f(A) = \{b_i \in B: b_i = f(a_i) \text{ for some } a_i \in A\}$$

This set is sometimes called the image of A under f.

Definition

f is a *function from A onto B* iff f(A) = B.
f is a *function from A into B* iff f(A) $\subset$ B (note the proper subset here!)
f is a *one-to-one function from A to B* iff, for all a_i, $a_j \in$ A, $a_i \neq a_j \Rightarrow f(a_i) \neq f(a_j)$.
f is a *many-to-one function from A to B* iff, there exists a_i, $a_j \in$ A, $a_i \neq a_j$ such that $f(a_i) = f(a_j)$.

Back to plain English, if f is a function from A onto B, we know that every element of B is associated with some element of A. If f is a function from A into B, we know that there is at least one element of B that is not associated with an element of A. One-to-one functions guarantee a form of uniqueness: distinct domain elements are never mapped to the same range element. (Notice this is the inverse of the "well-behaved" attribute described earlier.) If a function is not one-to-one, it is many-to-one; that is, more than one domain element can be mapped to the same range element. In these terms, the "well-behaved" requirement prohibits functions from being one-to-many. Testers familiar with relational databases will recognize that all these possibilities (one-to-one, one-to-many, many-to-one, and many-to-many) are allowed for relations.

Referring again to our testing examples, suppose we take A, B, and C to be sets of dates for the NextDate program, where:

$$A = \{date : 1 January 1842 \leq date \leq 31 December 2042\}$$

$$B = \{date : 2 January 1842 \leq date \leq 1 January 2043\}$$

$$C = A \cup B$$

Now, NextDate: $A \rightarrow B$ is a one-to-one, onto function, and NextDate: $A \rightarrow C$ is a one-to-one, into function.

It makes no sense for NextDate to be many-to-one, but it is easy to see how the triangle problem can be many-to-one. When a function is one-to-one and onto, such as NextDate:$A \rightarrow B$ previously, each element of the domain corresponds to exactly one element of the range; conversely, each element of the range corresponds to exactly one element of the domain. When this happens, it is always possible to find an inverse function (see the YesterDate excercise in Chapter 2) that is one-to-one from the range back to the domain.

All this is important for testing. The into versus onto distinction has implications for domain- and range-based specification-based testing, and one-to-one functions may require much more testing than many-to-one functions.

3.2.3 Function Composition

Suppose we have sets and functions such that the range of one is the domain of the next:

$$f: A \rightarrow B$$

$$g: B \rightarrow C$$

$$h: C \rightarrow D$$

When this occurs, we can compose the functions. To do this, let us refer to specific elements of the domain and range sets $a \in A$, $b \in B$, $c \in C$, $d \in D$, and suppose that $f(a) = b$, $g(b) = c$, and $h(c) = d$. Now the composition of functions h, g, and f is:

$$
\begin{aligned}
h \circ g \circ f(a) &= h(g(f(a))) \\
&= h(g(b)) \\
&= h(c) \\
&= d
\end{aligned}
$$

Function composition is a very common practice in software development; it is inherent in the process of defining procedures and subroutines.

Composed chains of functions can be problematic for testers, particularly when the range of one function is a proper subset of the domain of the "next" function in the chain. A special case of composition can be used, which helps testers in a curious way. Recall we discussed how one-to-one onto functions always have an inverse function. It turns out that this inverse function is unique and is guaranteed to exist (again, the math folks would prove this). If f is a one-to-one function from A onto B, we denote its unique inverse by f^{-1}. It turns out that for $a \in A$ and $b \in B$, $f^{-1} \cdot f(a) = a$ and $f \cdot f^{-1}(b) = b$. The NextDate and YesterDate programs are such inverses. The way this helps testers is that, for a given function, its inverse acts as a "cross-check," and this can often expedite the identification of specification-based test cases.

3.3 Relations

Functions are a special case of a relation: both are subsets of some Cartesian product, but in the case of functions, we have the "well-behaved" requirement that says that a domain element cannot be associated with more than one range element. This is borne out in everyday usage: when we say something "is a function" of something else, our intent is that there is a deterministic relationship present. Not all relationships are strictly functional. Consider the mapping between a set of patients and a set of physicians. One patient may be treated by several physicians, and one physician may treat several patients—a many-to-many mapping.

3.3.1 Relations among Sets

Definition

Given two sets A and B, a *relation* R is a subset of the Cartesian product A × B.

Two notations are popular; when we wish to speak about the entire relation, we usually just write $R \subseteq A \times B$; for specific elements $a_i \in A$, $b_i \in B$, we write $a_i \, R \, b_i$. Most math texts omit treatment of relations; we are interested in them because they are essential to both data modeling and object-oriented analysis.

Next, we need to explain an overloaded term—cardinality. Recall that, as it applies to sets, cardinality refers to the number of elements in a set. Because a relation is also a set, we might expect that the cardinality of a relation refers to how many ordered pairs are in the set $R \subseteq A \times B$. Unfortunately, this is not the case.

Definition

Given two sets A and B, a relation $R \subseteq A \times B$, the *cardinality of relation R* is:

One-to-one iff R is a one-to-one function from A to B.

Many-to-one iff R is a many-to-one function from A to B.

One-to-many iff at least one element $a \in A$ is in two ordered pairs in R, that is $<a, b_i > \in R$ and $< a, b_j > \in R$.

Many-to-many iff at least one element $a \in A$ is in two ordered pairs in R, that is $<a, b_i > \in R$ and $< a, b_j > \in R$ and at least one element $b \in B$ is in two ordered pairs in R, that is $<a_i, b > \in R$ and $< a_j, b > \in R$.

The distinction between functions into and onto their range has an analog in relations—the notion of participation.

Definition

Given two sets A and B, a relation R ⊆ A × B, the *participation of relation R* is:

Total iff every element of A is in some ordered pair in R
Partial iff some element of A is not in some ordered pair in R
Onto iff every element of B is in some ordered pair in R
Into iff some element of B is not in some ordered pair in R

In plain English, a relation is total if it applies to every element of A, and partial if it does not apply to every element. Another term for this distinction is mandatory versus optional participation. Similarly, a relation is onto if it applies to every element of B, and into if it does not. The parallelism between total/partial and onto/into is curious and deserves special mention here. From the standpoint of relational database theory, no reason exists for this; in fact, a compelling reason exists to avoid this distinction. Data modeling is essentially declarative, while process modeling is essentially imperative. The parallel sets of terms force a direction on relations, when in fact no need exists for the directionality. Part of this is a likely holdover from the fact that Cartesian products consist of ordered pairs, which clearly have a first and second element.

The cardinality and participation concepts are nicely merged in the UML (min, max) notation for relations. For a relation R(min,max) on sets A and B (see Figure 3.4), we have the following:

In A(min, max), if min = 0 participation in relation R is partial; if min = 1 participation in relation R is total. In B(min, max), if min = 0 the mapping is into; if min = 1 the mapping is onto. Here are some examples:

In Figure 3.5,

R1 is a partial one-to-one mapping of A into B,
R2 is a total one-to-one mapping of A onto B,
R3 is a partial one-to-many mapping of A into B, and
R4 is a total one-to-many mapping of A onto B.

So far, we have only considered relations between two sets. Extending relations to three or more sets is more complicated than simply the Cartesian product. Suppose, for example, we had three sets, A, B, and C, and a relation R ⊆ A × B × C. Do we intend the relation to be strictly among three elements, or is it between one element and an ordered pair (there would be three possibilities here)? This line of thinking also

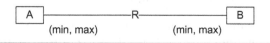

Figure 3.4 Relation R on sets A and B.

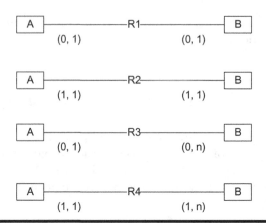

Figure 3.5   Examples of (min,max) related to Cardinality and Participation.

needs to be applied to the definitions of cardinality and participation. It is straight-forward for participation, but cardinality is essentially a binary property. (Suppose, for example the relation is one-to-one from A to B and is many-to-one from A to C.) We discussed a three-way relation in Chapter 1, when we examined the relationships among specified, implemented, and tested program behaviors. We would like to have some form of totality between test cases and specification–implementation pairs; we will revisit this when we study functional and structural testing.

Testers need to be concerned with the definitions of relations because they bear directly on software properties to be tested. The onto/into distinction, for example, bears directly on what we will call output-based functional testing. The mandatory–optional distinction is the essence of exception handling, which also has implications for testers.

3.3.2 Relations on a Single Set

Two important mathematical relations are used, both of which are defined on a single set: ordering relations and equivalence relations. Both are defined with respect to specific properties of relations.

Let A be a set, and let $R \subseteq A \times A$ be a relation defined on A, with <a, a>, <a, b>, <b, a>, <b, c>, <a, c > ∈ R. Relations have four special attributes:

Definition

A relation $R \subseteq A \times A$ is:

   Reflexive iff for all a ∈ A, <a, a > ∈ R.
   Symmetric iff < a, b > ∈ R ⇒ <b, a > ∈ R.
   Antisymmetric < a, b>, <b, a > ∈ R ⇒ a = b.
   Transitive iff < a, b>, <b, c > ∈ R ⇒ <a, c > ∈ R.

Family relationships are nice examples of these properties. You might want to think about the following relationships and decide for yourself which attributes apply: brother of, sibling of, and ancestor of. Now we can define the two important relations.

Definition

A relation $R \subseteq A \times A$ is an *ordering relation* if R is reflexive, antisymmetric, and transitive.

Ordering relations have a sense of direction; some common ordering relations are Older than, $\geq$, $\Rightarrow$, and Ancestor of. (The reflexive part usually requires some fudging—we really should say Not Younger Than and Not a Descendant of.) Ordering relations are a common occurrence in software: data access techniques, hashing codes, tree structures, and arrays are all situations in which ordering relations are used.

The power set of a given set is the set of all subsets of the given set. The power set of the set A is denoted P(A). The subset relation $\subseteq$ is an ordering relation on P(A), because it is reflexive (any set is trivially a subset of itself), it is antisymmetric (the definition of set equality), and it is transitive.

Definition

A relation $R \subseteq A \times A$ is an *equivalence relation* if R is reflexive, symmetric, and transitive.

Mathematics is full of equivalence relations: equality and congruence are two quick examples. A very important connection exists between equivalence relations and partitions of a set. Suppose we have some partition $A_1, A_2, ..., A_n$ of a set B, and we say that two elements, b_1 and b_2 of B, are related (i.e., $b_1 \, R \, b_2$) if b_1 and b_2 are in the same partition element. This relation is reflexive (any element is in its own partition), it is symmetric (if b_1 and b_2 are in a partition element, then b_2 and b_1 are), and it is transitive (if b_1 and b_2 are in the same set, and if b_2 and b_3 are in the same set, then b_1 and b_3 are in the same set). The relation defined from the partition is called the equivalence relation induced by the partition.

The converse process works in the same way. If we start with an equivalence relation defined on a set, we can define subsets according to elements that are related to each other. This turns out to be a partition, and it is called the partition induced by the equivalence relation. The sets in this partition are known as equivalence classes. The end result is that partitions and equivalence relations are interchangeable, and this becomes a powerful concept for testers. Recall that the two properties of a partition are notions of completeness and non-redundancy. When translated into testing situations, these notions allow testers to make powerful, absolute statements about the extent to which a software item has been tested. In addition, great efficiency follows from testing just one element of an equivalence class and assuming that the remaining elements will behave similarly.

3.4 Propositional Logic

We have already been using propositional logic notation; if you were perplexed by this usage definition before, you are not alone. Set theory and propositional logic have a chicken-and-egg relationship—it is hard to decide which should be discussed first. Just as sets are taken as primitive terms and are therefore not defined, we take propositions to be primitive terms. A proposition is a sentence that is either true or false, and we call these the truth values of the proposition. Furthermore, propositions are unambiguous: given a proposition, it is always possible to tell whether it is true or false. The sentence "Mathematics is difficult" would not qualify as a proposition because of the ambiguity. There are also temporal and spatial aspects of propositions. For example, "It is raining" may be true at some times at false at others. In addition, it may be true for one person and false for another at the same time but different locations. We usually denote propositions with lower-case letters p, q, and r. Propositional logic has operations, expressions, and identities that are very similar (in fact, they are isomorphic) to set theory.

3.4.1 Logical Operators

Logical operators (also known as logical connectives or operations) are defined in terms of their effect on the truth values of the propositions to which they are applied. This is easy, only two values are used: T (for true) and F (for false). Arithmetic operators could also be defined this way (in fact, that is how they are taught to children), but the tables become too large. The three basic logical operators are and ($\wedge$) or ($\vee$), and not ($\sim$); these are sometimes called conjunction, disjunction, and negation. Negation is the only unary (one operand) logical operator; the others are all binary. These, and other logical operators, are defined by "truth tables" such as this one that defines and ($\wedge$) or ($\vee$), and not ($\sim$).

p	q	$p \wedge q$	$p \vee q$	$\sim p$
T	T	T	T	F
T	F	F	T	F
F	T	F	T	T
F	F	F	F	T

Conjunction and disjunction are familiar in everyday life: a conjunction is true only when all components are true, and a disjunction is true if at least one component is true. Negations also behave as we expect. Two other common connectives are used: exclusive–or ($\oplus$) and IF–THEN ($\rightarrow$). They are defined as follows:

p	q	$p \oplus q$	$p \rightarrow q$
T	T	F	T
T	F	T	F
F	T	T	T
F	F	F	T

An exclusive–or is true only when one of the propositions is true, while a disjunction (inclusive–or) is true also when both propositions are true. The IF–THEN connective usually causes the most difficulty. The easy view is that this is just a definition; but because the other connectives all transfer nicely to natural language, we have similar expectations for IF–THEN. The quick answer is that the IF–THEN connective is closely related to the process of deduction: in a valid deductive syllogism, we can say "if premises, then conclusion" and the IF–THEN statement will be a tautology.

3.4.2 Logical Expressions

We use logical operators to build logical expressions in exactly the same way that we use arithmetic operators to build algebraic expressions. We can specify the order in which operators are applied with the usual conventions on parentheses, or we can employ a precedence order (negation first, then conjunction followed by disjunction). Given a logical expression, we can always find its truth table by "building up" to it following the order determined by the parentheses. For example, the expression $\sim((p \rightarrow q) \land (q \rightarrow p))$ has the following truth table (note the equivalence to Exclusive OR):

p	q	$p \rightarrow q$	$q \rightarrow p$	$(p \rightarrow q) \land (q \rightarrow p)$	$\sim((p \rightarrow q) \land (q \rightarrow p))$
T	T	T	T	T	F
T	F	F	T	F	T
F	T	T	F	F	T
F	F	T	T	T	F

3.4.3 Logical Equivalence

The notions of arithmetic equality and identical sets have analogs in propositional logic. Notice that the expressions $\sim((p \rightarrow q) \land (q \rightarrow p))$ and $p \oplus q$ have identical truth tables. This means that, no matter what truth values are given to the base propositions p and q, these expressions will always have the same truth value. This property can be defined in several ways; we use the simplest.

Definition

Two *propositions p and q are logically equivalent* (denoted $p \Leftrightarrow q$) iff their truth tables are identical.

By the way, the curious "iff" abbreviation we have been using for "if and only if" is sometimes called the bi-conditional, so the proposition p iff q is really $(p \rightarrow q) \land (q \rightarrow p)$, which is denoted $p \Leftrightarrow q$.

Definition

A proposition that is always true is a *tautology*; a proposition that is always false is a *contradiction*.

In order to be a tautology or a contradiction, a proposition must contain at least one connective and two or more primitive propositions. We sometimes denote a tautology as a proposition T, and a contradiction as a proposition F. We can now state several laws that are direct analogs of the ones we had for sets.

Law	Expression
Identity	$p \wedge T \Leftrightarrow p$
	$p \vee F \Leftrightarrow p$
Domination	$p \vee T \Leftrightarrow T$
	$p \wedge F \Leftrightarrow F$
Idempotent	$p \wedge p \Leftrightarrow p$
	$p \vee p \Leftrightarrow p$
Complementation	$\sim(\sim p) \Leftrightarrow p$
Commutative	$p \wedge q \Leftrightarrow q \wedge p$
	$p \vee q \Leftrightarrow q \vee p$
Associative	$p \wedge (q \wedge r) \Leftrightarrow (p \wedge q) \wedge r$
	$p \vee (q \vee r) \Leftrightarrow (p \vee q) \vee r$
Distributive	$p \wedge (q \vee r) \Leftrightarrow (p \wedge q) \vee (p \wedge r)$
	$p \vee (q \wedge r) \Leftrightarrow (p \vee q) \wedge (p \vee r)$
DeMorgan's Laws	$\sim(p \wedge q) \Leftrightarrow \sim p \vee \sim q$
	$\sim(p \vee q) \Leftrightarrow \sim p \wedge \sim q$

3.4.4 Probability Theory

We will have two occasions to use probability theory in our study of software testing: one deals with the probability that a particular path of statements executes, and the other generalizes this to a popular industrial concept called an operational profile (see Chapter 13). Because of this limited use, we will only cover the rudiments here.

As with both set theory and propositional logic, we start out with a primitive concept—the probability of an event. Here is the definition provided by a classic textbook (Rosen, 1991):

> The probability of an event E, which is a subset of a finite sample space S of equally likely outcomes, is $p(E) = |E|/|S|$, where $|E|$ denotes the cardinality (number of elements) of the set E.

This definition hinges on the idea of an experiment that results in an outcome, the sample space is the set of all possible outcomes, and an event is a subset of outcomes. This definition is circular: What are "equally likely" outcomes? We assume these have equal probabilities, but then probability is defined in terms of itself.

The French mathematician Laplace had a reasonable working definition of probability two centuries ago. To paraphrase it, the probability that something occurs is the number of favorable ways it can occur divided by the total number of ways (favorable and unfavorable). Laplace's definition works well when we are concerned with drawing colored marbles out of a bag (probability folks are unusually concerned with their marbles; maybe there's a lesson here), but it does not extend well to situations in which it is hard to enumerate the various possibilities.

We will use our (refurbished) capabilities in set theory and propositional logic to arrive at a more cohesive formulation. As testers, we will be concerned with things that happen; we will call these events and say that the set of all events is our universe of discourse. Next, we will devise propositions about events, such that the propositions refer to elements in the universe of discourse. Now, for some universe U and some proposition p about elements of U, we make a definition:

Definition

The *truth set* T of a proposition p, written T(p), is the set of all elements in the universe U for which p is true.

Propositions are either true or false, therefore, a proposition p divides the universe of discourse into two sets, T(p) and (T(p))', where T(p) U (T(p))' = U. Notice that (T(p))' is the same as T(~p). Truth sets facilitate a clear mapping among set theory, propositional logic, and probability theory.

Definition

The *probability that a proposition p is true*, denoted Pr(p), is $|T(p)|/|U|$.

With this definition, Laplace's "number of favorable ways" becomes the cardinality of the truth set T(p), and the total number of ways becomes the cardinality of the universe of discourse. This forces one more connection: because the truth set of a tautology is the universe of discourse, and the truth set of a contradiction is the empty set, the probabilities of $\varnothing$ and U are, respectively, 0 and 1.

The NextDate problem is a good source of examples. Consider the month variable and the proposition:

$$p(m): \text{ m is a 30-day month}$$

The universe of discourse is the set U = {Jan., Feb., …, Dec.}, and the truth set of p(m) is the set

$$T(p(m)) = \{\text{Apr., June, Sept., Nov.}\}$$

Now, the probability that a given month is a 30-day month is:

$$Pr(p(m)) = |T(p(m))|/|U| = 4/12.$$

A subtlety exists in the role of the universe of discourse; this is part of the craft of using probability theory in testing—choosing the right universe. Suppose we want to know the probability that a month is February. The quick answer: 1/12. Now, suppose we want the probability of a month with exactly 29 days. Less easy—we need a universe that includes both leap years and common years. We could use congruence arithmetic and choose a universe that consists of months in a period of four consecutive years—say 1991, 1992, 1993, and 1994. This universe would contain 48 "months," and in this universe, the probability of a 29-day month is 1/48. Another possibility would be to use the 200 year range of the NextDate program, in which the year 1900 is not a leap year. This would slightly reduce the probability of a 29-day month. One conclusion: getting the right universe is important. A bigger conclusion: it is even more important to avoid "shifting universes."

Here are some facts about probabilities that we will use without proof. They refer to a given universe, propositions p and q, with truth sets T(p) and T(q):

$$Pr(\sim p) = 1 - Pr(p)$$

$$Pr(p \wedge q) = Pr(p) \times Pr(q)$$

$$Pr(p \vee q) = Pr(p) + Pr(q) - Pr(p \wedge q)$$

These facts, together with the tables of set theory and propositional identities, provide a strong algebraic capability to manipulate probability expressions.

Exercises

Operation	Propositional Logic	Set Theory
Disjunction	Or	Union
Conjunction	And	Intersection
Negation	Not	Complement
Implication	If, Then	Subset
	Exclusive or	Symmetric difference

1. A very deep connection (an isomorphism) exists between set operations and the logical connectives in the propositional logic (see the table above). For sets A and B....
   a. Express A ⊕ B in words.
   b. Express (A ∪ B) – (A ∩ B) in words.
   c. Convince yourself that A ⊕ B and (A ∪ B) – (A ∩ B) are the same set.
   d. Is it true that A ⊕ B = (A – B) ∪ (B – A)?
2. In many parts of the U.S., real estate taxes are levied by different taxing bodies, for example, a school district, a fire protection district, a township, and so on. Discuss whether these taxing bodies form a partition of a state. Do the 50 states form a partition of the United States of America? (What about the District of Columbia?)

3. Is brotherOf an equivalence relation on the set of all people?? How about sib-lingOf?, sameBirthdayAs?

4. In the text after Figure 3.5, four relations are given as examples. In A(min, max), min can have the values 0 and 1, and max can have the values 1 and n (where n means "many"). Similarly, in B(min, max), min can have the values 0 and 1, and max can have the values 1 and n. List all the combinations of (min, max) values to identify the full set of possible relation types between two sets A and B. Try to express a few of them as examples.

Here is one example, a relation between patients (A) and physicians (B): Some facts:

1. a patient may be treated by more than one physician
2. a physician may treat more than one patient
3. some patients are not treated by any physician
4. some physicians might not treat any patients

Taken together, these facts define a many-to-many relation between patients and physicians, that is Partial (point 3) and Into (point 4). We could write this as A(0,n) and B(0,n).

Reference

Rosen, Kenneth H., *Discrete Mathematics and Its Applications*, McGraw-Hill, New York, 1991.

Chapter 4

Graph Theory for Testers

Graph theory is a branch of topology that is sometimes referred to as "rubber sheet geometry." Curious, because the rubber sheet parts of topology have little to do with graph theory; furthermore, the graphs in graph theory do not involve axes, scales, points, and curves as you might expect. Whatever the origin of the term, graph theory is probably the most useful part of mathematics for computer science—far more useful than calculus—yet it is not commonly taught. Our excursion into graph theory will follow a "pure math" spirit: in which definitions are as devoid of specific interpretations as possible. Postponing interpretations results in maximum latitude in interpretations later, much like well-defined abstract data types promote reuse.

Two basic kinds of graphs are used: undirected and directed. Because the latter are a special case of the former, we begin with undirected graphs. This will allow us to inherit many concepts when we get to directed graphs.

4.1 Graphs

A graph (also known as a linear graph) is an abstract mathematical structure defined from two sets—a set of nodes and a set of edges that form connections between nodes. A computer network is a fine example of a graph. More formally.

Definition

A *graph* $G = (V, E)$ is composed of a finite (and nonempty) set V of nodes and a set E of unordered pairs of nodes (edges between nodes).

The usual notation is for a graph with m nodes and p edges is $V = \{n_1, n_2, ..., n_m\}$ and $E = \{e_1, e_2, ..., e_p\}$, where each edge $e_k = \{n_i, n_j\}$ for some nodes $n_i, n_j \in V$. Nodes are sometimes called vertices; edges are sometimes called arcs; and we sometimes call nodes the endpoints of an arc. The common visual form of a graph shows nodes as circles and edges as lines connecting pairs of nodes, as in Figure 4.1. We will use this figure as a continuing example, so take a minute to become familiar with it.

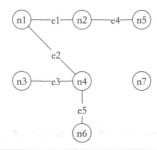

Figure 4.1   A graph with seven nodes and five edges.

In the graph in Figure 4.1, the node and edge sets are

$$V = \{n_1, n_2, n_3, n_4, n_5, n_6, n_7\}$$

$$E = \{e_1, e_2, e_3, e_4, e_5\}$$

$$= \{(n_1, n_2), (n_1, n_4), (n_3, n_4), (n_2, n_5), (n_4, n_6)\}$$

To define a particular graph, we must first define a set of nodes and then define a set of edges between pairs of nodes. We can think of nodes as program statements or as program units, and we have various kinds of edges, representing, for instance, flow of control, define/use relationships, or message connection.

4.1.1 Degree of a Node

Definition

The *degree of a node* in a graph is the number of edges that have that node as an endpoint. We write deg(n) for the degree of node n.

We might say that the degree of a node indicates its "popularity" in a graph. In fact, social scientists use graphs to describe social interactions, in which nodes are people, edges often refer to things like "friendship," "communicates with," and so on. If we make a graph in which classes are nodes and edges are messages, the degree of a node (object) indicates the extent of integration testing that is appropriate for the class.

The degrees of the nodes in Figure 4.1 are:

$$\deg(n_1) = 2, \deg(n_2) = 2, \deg(n_3) = 1, \deg(n_4) = 3, \deg(n_5) = 1, \deg(n_6) = 1, \text{and} \deg(n_7) = 0.$$

4.1.2 Incidence Matrices

Graphs need not be represented pictorially—they can be fully represented in an incidence matrix. This concept becomes very useful for testers, so we will formalize it here. When graphs are given a specific interpretation, the incidence matrix always provides useful information for the new interpretation.

Definition

The *incidence matrix of a graph* G = (V, E) with m nodes and n edges is an m × n matrix, where the element in row i, column j is a 1 if and only if node i is an endpoint of edge j; otherwise, the element is 0.

The incidence matrix of the graph in Figure 4.1 is

	e1	e2	e3	e4	e5
n1	1	1	0	0	0
n2	1	0	0	1	0
n3	0	0	1	0	0
n4	0	1	1	0	1
n5	0	0	0	1	0
n6	0	0	0	0	1
n7	0	0	0	0	0

We can make some observations about a graph by examining its incidence matrix. First, notice that the sum of the entries in any column is 2. That is because every edge has exactly two endpoints. If a column sum in an incidence matrix is ever something other than 2, there is a mistake somewhere. Thus, forming column sums is a form of integrity checking similar in spirit to that of parity checks. Next, we see that the row sum is the degree of the node. When the degree of a node is zero, as it is for node n_7, we say the node is isolated. (This might correspond to unreachable code, or to objects that are included but never used.)

4.1.3 Adjacency Matrices

The adjacency matrix of a graph is a useful supplement to the incidence matrix. Because adjacency matrices deal with connections, they are the basis of many later graph theory concepts. Given a graph, we can always find its adjacency matrix, and, given an adjacency matrix, we can always create a member of a set of topologically equivalent graphs (the placement of nodes may be different, but the connectivity will be the same. This might seem like a trivial point, but consider the two graphs in Figure 4.2. They are visually different, but topologically equivalent (because they have the same adjacency matrix).

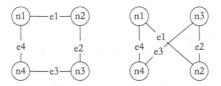

Figure 4.2   Two equivalent graphs.

Definition

The *adjacency matrix of a graph* G = (V, E) with m nodes is an m × m matrix, where the element in row i, column j is a 1 if and only if an edge exists between node i and node j; otherwise, the element is 0.

The adjacency matrix is symmetric (element i,j always equals element j,i), and a row sum is the degree of the node (as it was in the incidence matrix). The adjacency matrix of the graph in Figure 4.1 is:

	n1	*n2*	*n3*	*n4*	*n5*	*n6*	*n7*
n1	0	1	0	1	0	0	0
n2	1	0	0	0	1	0	0
n3	0	0	0	1	0	0	0
n4	1	0	1	0	0	1	0
n5	0	1	0	0	0	0	0
n6	0	0	0	1	0	0	0
n7	0	0	0	0	0	0	0

4.1.4 Paths

As a preview of how we will use graph theory, the code-based approaches to testing (see Part II) all center on types of paths in a program. Here, we define (interpretation-free) paths in a graph.

Definition

A *path* is a sequence of edges such that, for any adjacent pair of edges e_i, e_j in the sequence, the edges share a common (node) endpoint.

Paths can be described either as sequences of edges or as sequences of nodes; the node sequence choice is more common. Some paths in the graph in Figure 4.1:

Path	Node Sequence	Edge Sequence
Between n1 and n5	n1, n2, n5	e1, e4
Between n6 and n5	n6, n4, n1, n2, n5	e5, e2, e1, e4
Between n3 and n2	n3, n4, n1, n2	e3, e2, e1

Paths can be generated directly from the adjacency matrix of a graph using a binary form of matrix multiplication and addition. In our continuing example, edge e_1 is between nodes n_1 and n_2, and edge e_4 is between nodes n_2 and n_5. In the product of the adjacency matrix with itself, the element in position (1, 2) forms a product with the element in position (2, 5), yielding an element in position (1, 5), which corresponds to the two-edge path between n_1 and n_5. If we multiplied the product matrix by the original adjacency matrix again, we would get all three edge paths, and so on.

At this point, the pure math folks go into a long digression to determine the length of the longest path in a graph; we will not bother. Instead, we focus our interest on the fact that paths connect "distant" nodes in a graph.

The graph in Figure 4.1 predisposes a problem. It is not completely general, because it does not show all the situations that might occur in a graph. In particular, no paths exist in which a node occurs twice in the path. If it did, the path would be a loop (or circuit). We could create a circuit by adding an edge between nodes n_3 and n_6.

4.1.5 Connectedness

Paths let us speak about nodes that are connected; this leads to a powerful simplification device that is very important for testers.

Definition

Two *nodes are connected* if and only if they are in the same path.

"Connectedness" is an equivalence relation (see Chapter 3) on the node set of a graph. To see this, we can check the three defining properties of equivalence relations:

1. Connectedness is reflexive, because every node is, by default, in a path of length 0 with itself. (Sometimes, for emphasis, an edge is shown that begins and ends on the same node.)
2. Connectedness is symmetric, because if nodes n_i and n_j are in a path, then nodes n_j and n_i are in the same path.
3. Connectedness is transitive (see the discussion of adjacency matrix multiplication for paths of length 2).

Equivalence relations induce a partition (see Chapter 3 if you need a reminder); therefore, we are guaranteed that connectedness defines a partition on the node set of a graph. This permits the definition of components of a graph:

Definition

A *component of a graph* is a maximal set of connected nodes.

Nodes in the equivalence classes are components of the graph. The classes are maximal due to the transitivity part of the equivalence relation. The graph in Figure 4.1 has two components: $\{n_1, n_2, n_3, n_4, n_5, n_6\}$ and $\{n_7\}$.

4.1.6 Condensation Graphs

We are finally in a position to formalize an important simplification mechanism for testers.

Definition

Given a graph G = (V, E), its *condensation graph* is formed by replacing each component by a condensing node.

Developing the condensation graph of a given graph is an unambiguous (i.e., algorithmic) process. We use the adjacency matrix to identify path connectivity and then use the equivalence relation to identify components. The absolute nature of this process is important: the condensation graph of a given graph is unique. This implies that the resulting simplification represents an important aspect of the original graph.

The components in our continuing example are $S_1 = \{n_1, n_2, n_3, n_4, n_5, n_6\}$ and $S_2 = \{n_7\}$.

No edges can be present in a condensation graph of an ordinary (undirected) graph. Two reasons are:

1. Edges have individual nodes as endpoints, not sets of nodes. (Here, we can finally use the distinction between n_7 and $\{n_7\}$.)
2. Even if we fudge the definition of edge to ignore this distinction, a possible edge would mean that nodes from two different components were connected, thus in a path, thus in the same (maximal!) component.

The implication for testing is that components are independent in an important way, thus they can be tested separately. For large graphs, the corresponding condensation graphs are a way to reduce the problem(s) of size without losing and important connectivity among condensation nodes.

4.1.7 Cyclomatic Number

The cyclomatic complexity property of graphs has deep implications for testing.

Definition

The *cyclomatic number of a graph* G is given by $V(G) = e - n + p$, where

e is the number of edges in G
n is the number of nodes in G
p is the number of components in G

$V(G)$ is the number of distinct regions in a strongly connected directed graph. In Chapter 8, we will examine a formulation of code-based testing that considers all the paths in a program graph to be a vector space. There are $V(G)$ elements in the set of basis vectors for this space. The cyclomatic number of our example graph is $V(G) = 5 - 7 + 2 = 0$. This is not a very good example for cyclomatic complexity. When we use cyclomatic complexity in Chapter 8, and expand on it in Chapter 14, we will (usually) have strongly connected graphs, which will have a larger cyclomatic complexity than this small example.

4.2 Directed Graphs

Directed graphs are a slight refinement to ordinary graphs: edges acquire a sense of direction. Symbolically, the unordered pairs (n_i, n_j) become ordered pairs $<n_i, n_j>$, and we speak of a directed edge going from node n_i to n_j, instead of being between the nodes.

Definition

A *directed graph (or digraph)* $D = (V, E)$ consists of a finite set $V = \{n_1, n_2, ..., n_m\}$ of nodes, and a set $E = \{e_1, e_2, ..., e_p\}$ of edges, where each edge $e_k = <n_i, n_j>$ is an ordered pair of nodes $n_i, n_j \in V$.

In the directed edge $e_k = <n_i, n_j>$, n_i is the initial (or start) node, and n_j is the terminal (or finish) node. Edges in directed graphs fit naturally with many software concepts: sequential behavior, imperative programming languages, time-ordered events, define/reference pairings, messages, function and procedure calls, and so on. Given this, you might ask why we spent (wasted?) so much time on ordinary graphs. The difference between ordinary and directed graphs is very analogous to the difference between declarative and imperative programming languages. In imperative languages (e.g., COBOL, FORTRAN, Pascal, C, Java, Ada®), the sequential order of source language statements determines the execution time order of compiled code. This is not true for declarative languages (such as Prolog). The most common declarative situation for most software developers is Entity/Relationship modeling. In an E/R model, we choose entities as nodes and identify relationships as edges. (If a relationship involves three or more entities, we need the notion of a "hyper-edge" that has three or more endpoints.) The resulting graph of an E/R model is more properly interpreted as an ordinary graph. Good E/R modeling practice suppresses the sequential thinking that directed graphs promote.

When testing a program written in a declarative language, the only concepts available to the tester are those that follow from ordinary graphs. Fortunately, most software is developed in imperative languages so testers usually have the full power of directed graphs at their disposal.

The next series of definitions roughly parallels the ones for ordinary graphs. We modify our now familiar continuing example to the one shown in Figure 4.3.

We have the same node set $V = \{n_1, n_2, n_3, n_4, n_5, n_6, n_7\}$, and the edge set appears to be the same: $E = \{e_1, e_2, e_3, e_4, e_5\}$. The difference is that the edges are now ordered pairs of nodes in V:

$$E = \{<n_1, n_2>, <n_1, n_4>, <n_3, n_4>, <n_2, n_5>, <n_4, n_6>, <n_6, n_3>\}$$

4.2.1 Indegrees and Outdegrees

The degree of a node in an ordinary graph is refined to reflect direction, as follows:

Definition

The *indegree of a node* in a directed graph is the number of distinct edges that have the node as a terminal node. We write indeg(n) for the indegree of node n.

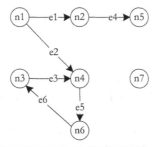

Figure 4.3 A directed graph.

The *outdegree of a node* in a directed graph is the number of distinct edges that have the node as a start point. We write outdeg(n) for the outdegree of node n.

The nodes in the digraph in Figure 4.3 have the following indegrees and outdegrees:

indeg(n1) = 0 outdeg(n1) = 2
indeg(n2) = 1 outdeg(n2) = 1
indeg(n3) = 0 outdeg(n3) = 1
indeg(n4) = 2 outdeg(n4) = 1
indeg(n5) = 1 outdeg(n5) = 0
indeg(n6) = 1 outdeg(n6) = 0
indeg(n7) = 0 outdeg(n7) = 0

Ordinary and directed graphs meet through definitions that relate obvious correspondences, such as: deg(n) = indeg(n) + outdeg(n).

4.2.2 Types of Nodes

The added descriptive power of directed graphs lets us define different kinds of nodes:

Definition

A node with indegree = 0 is a *source node.*
A node with outdegree = 0 is a *sink node.*
A node with indegree ≠ 0 and outdegree ≠ 0 is a *transfer node.*

Source and sink nodes constitute the external boundary of a graph. If we made a directed graph of a context diagram (from a set of dataflow diagrams produced by structured analysis), the external entities would be source and sink nodes.

In our continuing example, n_1, n_3, and n_7 are source nodes; n_5, n_6, and n_7 are sink nodes; and n_2 and n_4 are transfer (also known as interior) nodes. A node that is both a source and a sink node is an isolated node, *e.g.*, n_7.

4.2.3 Adjacency Matrix of a Directed Graph

As we might expect, the addition of direction to edges changes the definition of the adjacency matrix of a directed graph. (It also changes the incidence matrix, but this matrix is seldom used in conjunction with digraphs.)

Definition

The *adjacency matrix of a directed graph* D = (V, E) with m nodes is an m × m matrix: A = (a(i, j)) where a(i, j) is a 1 if and only if there is an edge from node i to node j; otherwise, the element is 0.

The adjacency matrix of a directed graph is not necessarily symmetric. A row sum is the outdegree of the node; a column sum is the indegree of a node. The adjacency matrix of our continuing example is:

	n_1	n_2	n_3	n_4	n_5	n_6	n_7
n_1	0	1	0	1	0	0	0
n_2	0	0	0	0	1	0	0
n_3	0	0	0	1	0	0	0
n_4	0	0	0	0	0	1	0
n_5	0	0	0	0	0	0	0
n_6	0	0	0	0	0	0	0
n_7	0	0	0	0	0	0	0

One common use of directed graphs is to record family relationships, in which siblings, cousins, and so on are connected by an ancestor; and parents, grandparents, and so on are connected by a descendant. Entries in powers of the adjacency matrix now show existence of directed paths. As we saw with ordinary graphs, given a directed graph, we can always find its adjacency matrix, and, given an adjacency matrix, we can always create a member of a set of topologically equivalent directed graphs (the placement of nodes may be different, but the connectivity will be the same. This might seem like a trivial point but consider the two graphs in Figure 4.4. Both are cycles (to be defined later), but this is more readily apparent in the left graph. (My undergraduate math professor always maintained that mathematics is NOT a function of its drawings, but if our goal is communication, the difference is clear.)

4.2.4 Paths and Semipaths

Direction permits a more precise meaning to paths that connect nodes in a directed graph. As a handy analogy, think of edges as one-way and two-way streets.

Definition

A *(directed) path* is a sequence of edges such that, for any adjacent pair of edges e_i, e_j, in the sequence, the terminal node of the first edge is the initial node of the second edge.

A *cycle* is a directed path that begins and ends at the same node.

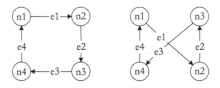

Figure 4.4   Two equivalent graphs.

A *chain* is a sequence of nodes such that each interior node has indegree = 1 and outdegree = 1. The initial node may have indegree = 0 or indegree >1. The terminal node may have outdegree = 0 or outdegree >1, (we will use this concept in Chapter 8).

A *(directed) semipath* is a sequence of edges such that, for at least one adjacent pair of edges e_i, e_j in the sequence, the initial node of the first edge is the initial node of the second edge or the terminal node of the first edge is the terminal node of the second edge.

Our continuing example contains the following paths and semipaths (not all are listed):

A path from n_1 to n_6
A semipath between n_1 and n_3
A semipath between n_2 and n_4
A semipath between n_5 and n_6

4.2.5 Reachability Matrix

When we model an application with a digraph, we often ask questions that deal with paths that let us reach (or "get to") certain nodes. This is an extremely useful capability and is made possible by the reachability matrix of a digraph.

Definition

The *reachability matrix of a directed graph* D = (V, E) with m nodes is an m × m matrix R = (r(i, j)), where r(i, j) is a 1 if and only if there is a path from node i to node j, otherwise the element is 0.

The reachability matrix of a directed graph D can be calculated from the adjacency matrix A as follows:

$$R = I + A + A^2 + A^3 + \ldots + A^k$$

where k is the length of the longest path in D, and I is the identity matrix. The reachability matrix for our continuing example is:

	n1	*n2*	*n3*	*n4*	*n5*	*n6*	*n7*
n1	1	1	0	1	1	1	0
n2	0	1	0	0	1	0	0
n3	0	0	1	1	0	1	0
n4	0	0	0	1	0	1	0
n5	0	0	0	0	1	0	0
n6	0	0	0	0	0	1	0
n7	0	0	0	0	0	0	1

The reachability matrix tells us that nodes n_2, n_4, n_5, and n_6 can be reached from n_1, node n_5 can be reached from n_2, and so on.

4.2.6 *n-Connectedness*

Connectedness of ordinary graphs extends to a rich, highly explanatory concept for digraphs.

Definition

Two nodes n_i and n_j in a directed graph are:

0-connected iff no path exists between n_i and n_j
1-connected iff a semi-path but no path exists between n_i and n_j
2-connected iff a path exists between n_i and n_j
3-connected iff a path exists from n_i to n_j and a path exists from n_j to n_i

No other degrees of connectedness exist.

We need to modify our continuing example to show 3-connectedness. The change is the addition of a new edge e_6 from n_6 to n_3, so the graph contains a cycle.

With this change, we have the following instances of n-connectivity in Figure 4.5 (not all are listed):

n_1 and n_7 are 0-connected
n_2 and n_6 are 1-connected,
n_1 and n_6 are 2-connected
n_3 and n_6 are 3-connected

4.2.7 *Strong Components*

The analogy continues. We get two equivalence relations from n-connectedness: 1-connectedness yields what we might call "weak connection," and this in turn yields weak components. (These turn out to be the same as we had for ordinary graphs, which is what should happen, because 1-connectedness effectively ignores direction.) The second equivalence relation, based on 3-connectedness, is more interesting. As

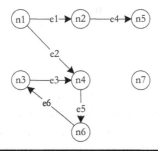

Figure 4.5   A directed graph with a cycle.

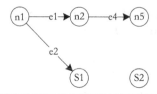

Figure 4.6   Condensation graph of the digraph in Figure 4.5.

before, the equivalence relation induces a partition on the node set of a digraph, but the condensation graph is quite different. Nodes that previously were 0-, 1-, or 2-connected remain so. The 3-connected nodes become the strong components.

Definition

A *strong component of a directed graph* is a maximal set of three-connected nodes.

   In our amended example, the strong components are the sets $\{n_3, n_4, n_6\}$ and $\{n_7\}$. The condensation graph for our amended example is shown in Figure 4.6.

   Strong components let us simplify testing source code by removing loops and isolated nodes. Although this is not as dramatic as the simplification we had in ordinary graphs, it does solve a major testing problem. Notice that the condensation graph of a digraph will never contain a loop. (If it did, the loop would have been condensed by the maximal aspect of the partition.) These graphs have a special name: directed acyclic graphs, sometimes written as DAG.

   Many papers on structured testing make quite a point of showing how relatively simple programs can have millions of distinct execution paths. The intent of these discussions is to convince us that exhaustive testing is exactly that—exhaustive. The large number of execution paths comes from nested loops. Condensation graphs eliminate loops (or at least condense them down to a single node); therefore, we can use this as a strategy to simplify situations that otherwise are computationally untenable.

4.3 Graphs for Testing

We conclude this chapter with four special graphs that are widely used for testing. The first of these, the program graph, is used primarily at the unit testing level. The other three, finite state machines, statecharts, and Petri nets, are best used to describe system-level behavior, although they can be used at lower levels of testing.

4.3.1 Program Graphs

At the beginning of this chapter, we made a point of avoiding interpretations on the graph theory definitions to preserve flexibility in later applications. Here, we give the most common use of graph theory in software testing—the program graph. To better connect with existing testing literature, the traditional definition is given, followed by an improved definition.

Definition

Given a program written in an imperative programming language, its *program graph* is a directed graph in which:

1. (Traditional Definition)
   Nodes are program statements, and edges represent flow of control (there is an edge from node i to node j iff the statement corresponding to node j can be executed immediately after the statement corresponding to node i).
2. (Improved Definition)
   Nodes are either entire statements or fragments of a statement, and edges represent flow of control (there is an edge from node i to node j iff the statement or statement fragment corresponding to node j can be executed immediately after the statement or statement fragment corresponding to node i).

It is cumbersome to always say "statement or statement fragment," so we adopt the convention that a statement fragment can be an entire statement. The directed graph formulation of a program enables a very precise description of testing aspects of the program. For one thing, a very satisfying connection exists between this formulation and the precepts of structured programming. The basic structured programming constructs (sequence, selection, and repetition) all have the directed graphs as shown in Figure 4.7.

When these constructs are used in a structured program, the corresponding graphs are either nested or concatenated. The single entrance and single exit criteria result in unique source and sink nodes in the program graph. In fact, the old (non-structured) "spaghetti code" resulted in very complex program graphs. GOTO statements, for example, introduce edges; and when these are used to branch into or out of loops, the resulting program graphs become even more complex. One of

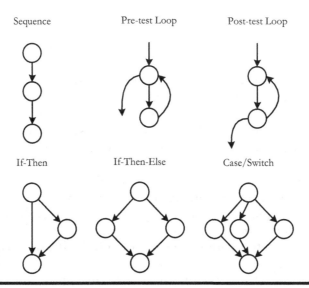

Figure 4.7 Digraphs of the structured programming constructs.

the pioneering analysts of this is Thomas McCabe, who popularized the cyclomatic number of a graph as an indicator of program complexity (McCabe, 1976). When a program executes, the statements that execute comprise a path in the program graph. Loops and decisions greatly increase the number of possible paths and therefore similarly increase the need for testing.

One of the problems with program graphs is how to treat nonexecutable statements such as comments and data declaration statements. The simplest answer is to ignore them. A second problem has to do with the difference between topologically possible and semantically feasible paths. We will discuss this in more detail in Chapter 8.

4.3.2 Finite State Machines

Finite state machines have become a widely adopted notation for requirements specification. All the real-time extensions of structured analysis use some form of finite state machine, and nearly all forms of object-oriented analyses require them.

Definition

A *finite state machine* is a directed graph FSM = (S, T) in which states in S are nodes and transitions in T are edges.

Source and sink states become initial and terminal nodes, sequences of transitions are modeled as paths, and so on. Most finite state machine notations add information to the edges (transitions) to indicate the cause of the transition and actions that occur as a result of the transition.

Figure 4.8 is a finite state machine for the Garage Door Controller described in Chapter 2. (We will revisit this finite state machine in Chapters 13 and 17.) The labels on the transitions follow a convention that the "numerator" is the event that causes the transition, and the "denominator" is the action that is associated with the transition. The events are mandatory—transitions do not just happen, but the actions are optional. Finite state machines are simple ways to represent situations in which a variety of events may occur, and their occurrences have different consequences.

Finite state machines can be executed, but a few conventions are needed first. One is the notion of the active state. We speak of a system being "in" a certain state; when the system is modeled as a finite state machine, the active state refers to the state "we are in." Another convention is that finite state machines may have an initial state, which is the state that is active when a finite state machine is first entered. (Initial and final states are recognized, respectively, by the absence of incoming and outgoing transitions.) Exactly one state can be active at any time. We also think of transitions as instantaneous occurrences, and the events that cause transitions also occur one at a time. To execute a finite state machine, we start with an initial state and provide a sequence of events that causes state transitions. As each event occurs, the transition changes the active state and a new event occurs. In this way, a sequence of events selects a path of states (or equivalently, of a sequence of transitions) through the machine.

Notice that, in the definition of finite state machines, the states are never actually defined. This is deliberate, because then they can be interpreted in

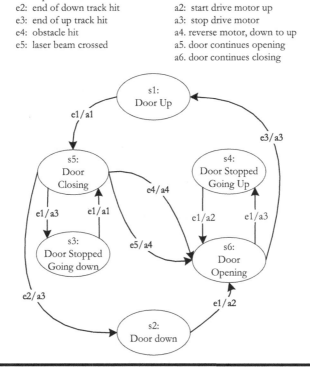

Input events
e1: depress controller button
e2: end of down track hit
e3: end of up track hit
e4: obstacle hit
e5: laser beam crossed

Output events (actions)
a1: start drive motor down
a2: start drive motor up
a3: stop drive motor
a4. reverse motor, down to up
a5. door continues opening
a6. door continues closing

Figure 4.8   Finite state machine for the Garage Door Controller.

application-dependent ways, as in Figure 4.8. One general way to think about "state" is that a state is an interval of time in which some proposition is true. In the Garage Door FSM, state s1 has the proposition "The door is open." When event e1 occurs (depress controller button), action a1 (start drive motor down) occurs and the state s1 proposition is no longer true. Instead, the proposition for state s5 (Door is closing) is true. In a well-formed finite state machine, the state propositions are mutually exclusive, and at any "point in time" exactly one state proposition is true. (This guarantees that an FSM can only be "in" one state at a time.) The second convention is that no two events can occur simultaneously. In the Garage Door FSM, one example is that only one of the two events that could occur in state s6 (e1 or e3) can actually occur, thus only one of states s1 and s4 could be entered. This preserves the convention that only one state can be "active" at any point in time.

4.3.3 Petri Nets

Petri nets were the topic of Carl Adam Petri's Ph.D. dissertation in 1963; today, they are the accepted model for protocols and other applications involving concurrency and distributed processing. Petri nets are a special form of directed graph: a bipartite directed graph. (A bipartite graph has two sets of nodes, V_1 and V_2, and a set of edges E, with the restriction that every edge has its initial node in one of the sets V_1, V_2, and its terminal node in the other set.) In a Petri net, one of the sets is referred to as "places," and the other is referred to as "transitions." These sets are usually denoted as P and T, respectively. Places are inputs to and outputs of transitions; the input and output relationships are functions, and they are usually denoted as In and Out, as in the following definition.

Definition

A *Petri net* is a bipartite directed graph (P, T, In, Out), in which P and T are disjoint sets of nodes, and In and Out are sets of edges, where In $\subseteq$ P $\times$ T, and Out $\subseteq$ T $\times$ P.

For the sample Petri net in Figure 4.9, the sets P, T, In, and Out are:

$$P = \{p_1, p_2, p_3, p_4, p_5\}$$
$$T = \{t_1, t_2, t_3\}$$
$$In = \{<p_1, t_1>, <p_5, t_1>, <p_5, t_3>, <p_2, t_3>, <p_3, t_2>\}$$
$$Out = \{<t_1, p_3>, <t_2, p_4>, <t_3, p_4>\}$$

Petri nets are executable in more interesting ways than finite state machines. The next few definitions lead us to Petri net execution.

Definition

A *marked Petri net* is a 5-tuple (P, T, In, Out, M) in which (P, T, In, Out) is a Petri net and M is a set of mappings of places to positive integers.

The set M is called the marking set of the Petri net. Elements of M are n-tuples, where n is the number of places in the set P. For the Petri net in Figure 4.10, the set M contains elements of the form $<n_1, n_2, n_3, n_4, n_5>$, where the n's are the integers associated with the respective places. The number associated with a place refers to the number of tokens that are said to be "in" the place. Tokens are abstractions that can be interpreted in modeling situations. For example, tokens might refer to the number of times a place has been used, or the number of things in a place, or whether the place is true. Figure 4.10 shows a marked Petri net.

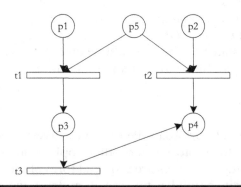

Figure 4.9   A Petri net.

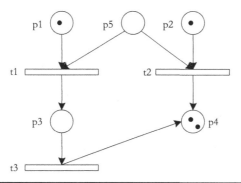

Figure 4.10   A marked Petri net.

Definition

A transition in a Petri net is *enabled* if at least one token is in each of its input places. The marking tuple for the marked Petri net in Figure 4.10 is <1, 1, 0, 2, 0>. We need the concept of tokens to make two essential definitions. No transitions in the marked Petri net in Figure 4.10 are enabled. If we put a token in place p_3, then transition t_3 would be enabled.

Definition

When an enabled Petri net *transition fires*, one token is removed from each of its input places and one token is added to each of its output places.

In Figure 4.11, transition t_2 is enabled in the left net and has been fired in the right net. The marking sequence for the net in Figure 4.11 contains two tuples—the first shows the net when t_2 is enabled, and the second shows the net marking after t_2 has fired:

$$M = \{< 1,1,0,2,1 >, < 1,0,0,3,0 >\}.$$

Tokens may be created or destroyed by transition firings. Under special conditions, the total number of tokens in a net never changes; such nets are called conservative. We usually do not worry about token conservation. Markings let us execute Petri nets

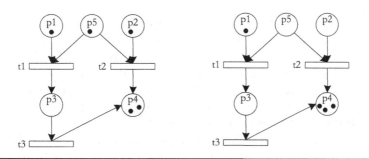

Figure 4.11   Before and after firing t_2.

in much the same way that we execute finite state machines. (It turns out that finite state machines are a special case of Petri nets.)

Look again at the net in Figure 4.11; in left net (before firing any transition), places p_1, p_2, and p_5 are all marked. With such a marking, transitions t_1 and t_3 are both enabled. We choose to fire transition t_2, the token in place p_5 is removed, and t_1 is no longer enabled. Similarly, if we choose to fire t_1, we disable t_2. This pattern is known as Petri net conflict. More specifically, we say that transitions t_1 and t_2 are in conflict with respect to place p_5. Petri net conflict exhibits an interesting form of interaction between two transitions; we will revisit this (and other) interactions in Chapters 13 and 16.

4.3.4 Event-Driven Petri Nets

Basic Petri nets need two slight enhancements to become Event-Driven Petri Nets (EDPNs). The first enables them to more closely express event-driven systems, and the second deals with Petri net markings that express event quiescence, an important notion in object-oriented applications. Taken together, these extensions result in an effective, operational view of software requirements; they were originally known as known as OSD nets (for Operational Software Development) (Jorgensen, 1989).

Definition

An *Event-Driven Petri Net* (abbreviated as EDPN) is a tripartite-directed graph (P, D, S, In, Out) composed of three sets of nodes, P, D, and S, and two mappings, In and Out, where:

P is a set of port events
D is a set of data places
S is a set of transitions

In is a set of ordered pairs from (P $\cup$ D) × S.
Out is a set of ordered pairs from S × (P $\cup$ D).

EDPNs express four of the five basic system constructs defined in Chapter 13; only devices are missing. The set S of transitions corresponds to ordinary Petri net transitions, which are interpreted as actions.

Two kinds of places, port events and data places, are inputs to or outputs of transitions in S as defined by the input and output functions In and Out. A thread is a sequence of transitions in S, so we can always construct the inputs and outputs of a thread from the inputs and outputs of the transitions in the thread. EDPNs are graphically represented in much the same way as ordinary Petri nets; the only difference is the use of triangles for port event places. The EDPN in Figure 4.12 has four transitions, s_7, s_8, s_9, and s_{10}; two port input events, p_3 and p_4; and three data places, d_5, d_6, and d_7. It does not have port output events.

This EDPN corresponds to a finite state machine developed for the dial portion of the windshield wiper controller. The components of this net are described in Table 4.1.

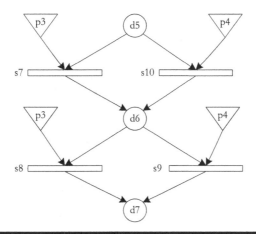

Figure 4.12   An Event-Driven Petri Net.

Table 4.1   EDPN Elements in Figure 4.12

Element	Type	Description
p3	port input event	rotate dial clockwise
p4	port input event	rotate dial counterclockwise
d5	data place	dial at position 1
d6	data place	dial at position 2
d7	data place	dial at position 3
s7	transition	state transition: d5 to d6
s8	transition	state transition: d6 to d7
s9	transition	state transition: d7 to d6
s10	transition	state transition: d6 to d5

Markings for an EDPN are more complicated because we want to be able to deal with event quiescence.

Definition

A *marking M of an EDPN* (P, D, S, In, Out) is a sequence M = <m1, m2, ... > of p-tuples, where p = k + n, and k and n are the number of elements in the sets P and D, and individual entries in a p-tuple indicate the number of tokens in the event or data place.

By convention, we will put the data places first, followed by the input event places and then the output event places. An EDPN may have any number of markings; each corresponds to an execution of the net. Table 4.2 shows a sample marking of the EDPN in Figure 4.12.

Table 4.2   A Marking of the EDPN in Figure 4.12

tuple	(p3, p4, d5, d6, d7)	Description
m1	(0, 0, 1, 0, 0)	Start in state d5
m2	(1, 0, 1, 0, 0)	p3 occurs
m3	(0, 0, 0, 1, 0)	in state d6
m4	(1, 0, 0, 1, 0)	p3 occurs
m5	(0, 0, 0, 0, 1)	in state d7
m6	(0, 1, 0, 0, 1)	p4 occurs
m7	(0, 0, 0, 1, 0)	in state d6

Table 4.3   Enabled and Fired Transitions in Table 4.2

tuple	$(p_3, p_4, d_5, d_6, d_7)$	Description
m_1	(0, 0, 1, 0, 0)	nothing enabled
m_2	(1, 0, 1, 0, 0)	s_7 enabled; s_7 fired
m_3	(0, 0, 0, 1, 0)	nothing enabled
m_4	(1, 0, 0, 1, 0)	s_8 enabled; s_8 fired
m_5	(0, 0, 0, 0, 1)	nothing enabled
m_6	(0, 1, 0, 0, 1)	s_9 enabled; s_9 fired
m_7	(0, 0, 0, 1, 0)	nothing enabled

The rules for transition enabling and firing in an EDPN are exact analogs of those for traditional Petri nets; a transition is enabled if there is at least one token in each input place; and when an enabled transition fires, one token is removed from each of its input places, and one token is placed in each of its output places. Table 4.3 follows the marking sequence given in Table 4.2, showing which transitions are enabled and fired.

The important difference between EDPNs and traditional Petri nets is that event quiescence can be broken by creating a token in a port input event place. In traditional Petri nets, when no transition is enabled, we say that the net is deadlocked. In EDPNs, when no transition is enabled, the net is at a point of event quiescence. (Of course, if no event occurs, this is the same as deadlock.) Event quiescence occurs four times in the thread in Table 4.3; at m_1, m_3, m_5, and m_7.

The individual members in a marking can be thought of as snapshots of the executing EDPN at discrete points in time; these members are alternatively referred to as time steps, p-tuples, or marking vectors. This lets us think of time as an ordering that allows us to recognize "before" and "after." If we attach instantaneous time as an attribute of port events, data places, and transitions, we obtain a much clearer picture of thread behavior. One awkward part to this is how to treat tokens in a port output event place. Port output places always have outdegree = 0; in an ordinary Petri net, tokens cannot be removed from a place with a zero outdegree. If the tokens in a port output event place persist, this suggests that the event occurs indefinitely. Here again, the time attributes resolve the confusion; this time we need a duration of the marked output event. (Another possibility is to remove tokens from a marked output event place after one-time step; this works reasonably well.)

4.3.5 Statecharts

David Harel had two goals when he developed the statechart notation: he wanted to devise a visual notation that combined the ability of Venn diagrams to express hierarchy and the ability of directed graphs to express connectedness (Harel, 1988). Taken together, these capabilities provide an elegant answer to the "state explosion" problem of ordinary finite state machines. The result is a highly sophisticated and very precise notation that is supported by commercially available CASE tools, notably the StateMate system. Statecharts are now the control model of choice for the unified modeling language (UML) from IBM. (See http://www-306.ibm.com/software/rational/uml/ for more details.)

Harel uses the methodology neutral term "blob" to describe the basic building block of a statechart. Blobs can contain other blobs in the same way that Venn diagrams show set containment. Blobs can also be connected to other blobs with edges in the same way that nodes in a directed graph are connected. In Figure 4.13, blob A contains two blobs (B and C), and they are connected by edges. Blob A is also connected to blob D by an edge.

As Harel intends, we can interpret blobs as states, and edges as transitions. The full statechart system supports an elaborate language that defines how and when transitions occur (their training course runs for a full week, so this section is a highly simplified introduction). Statecharts are executable in a much more elaborate way than ordinary finite state machines. Executing a statechart requires a notion similar to that of Petri net markings. The "initial state" of a statechart is indicated by an edge that has no source state.

When states are nested within other states, the same indication is used to show the lower level initial state. In Figure 4.14, state A is the initial state; and when it is entered, state B is also entered at the lower level. When a state is entered, we can think of it as active in a way analogous to a marked place in a Petri net. (The statechart tool used colors to show which states are active, and this is equivalent to marking places in a Petri net.) A subtlety exists in Figure 4.15, the transition from

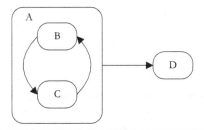

Figure 4.13 Blobs in a Statechart.

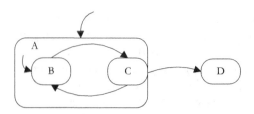

Figure 4.14 Initial states in a Statechart.

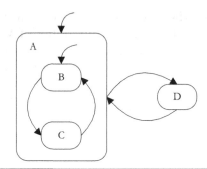

Figure 4.15 Default entry into substates.

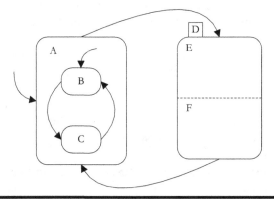

Figure 4.16 Concurrent states.

state A to state D seems ambiguous at first because it has no apparent recognition of states B and C. The convention is that edges must start and end on the outline (Harel uses the term "contour") of a state. If a state contains substates, as state A does, the edge "refers" to all substates. Thus, the edge from A to D means that the transition can occur either from state B or from state C. If we had an edge from state D to state A, as in Figure 4.14, the fact that state B is indicated as the initial state means that the transition is really from state D to state B. This convention greatly reduces the tendency of finite state machines to look like "spaghetti code."

The last aspect of statecharts we will discuss is the notion of concurrent statecharts. The dotted line in state D (see Figure 4.16) is used to show that state D really refers to two concurrent states, E and F. (Harel's convention is to move the state label of D to a rectangular tag on the perimeter of the state.) Although not shown here, we can think of E and F as separate devices that execute concurrently. Because the edge from state A terminates on the perimeter of state D, when that transition occurs, both devices E and F are active (or marked, in the Petri net sense).

Exercises

1. Propose a definition for the length of a path in a graph.
2. What loop(s) is/are created if an edge is added between nodes n_5 and n_6 in the graph in Figure 4.1?
3. Convince yourself that 3-connectedness is an equivalence relation on the nodes of a digraph.
4. Compute the cyclomatic complexity for each of the structured programming constructs in Figure 4.7.
5. The digraphs in Figure 4.17 were obtained by adding nodes and edges to the digraph in Figure 4.5. Compute the cyclomatic complexity of each new digraph and explain how the changes affected the complexity.
6. Suppose we make a graph in which nodes are people and edges correspond to some form of social interaction, such as "talks to" or "socializes with." Find graph theory concepts that correspond to social concepts such as popularity, cliques, and hermits. What implications might this have for someone who wants to analyze Facebook friends?
7. Discuss the popular "six degrees of separation" in terms of graph theory. (in 2008, after examining 30 Billion electronic conversations, Microsoft researchers computed the degree of separation between any two people on the planet as 6.6, which would have to be rounded to 7.)
   How might an epidemiologist use directed graphs to do contact tracing a viral epidemic?

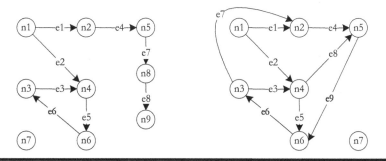

Figure 4.17 Effect of adding edges on cyclomatic complexity.

Reference

Harel, David, On visual formalisms, *Communications of the ACM*, Vol. 31, No. 5, pp. 514–530, May, 1988.

UNIT TESTING

The term "unit" needs explanation. There are several interpretations about exactly what constitutes a unit. In a procedural programming language, a unit can be

- a single procedure,
- a function,
- a body of code that implements a single function,
- source code that fits on one page,
- a body of code that represents work done in 4 to 40 hours (as in a Work Breakdown Structure),
- the smallest body of code that can be compiled and executed by itself.

In an object-oriented programming language, there is general agreement that a class is a unit. However, methods of a class might be described by any of the above "definitions" of a unit for procedural code.

The bottom line is that "unit" is probably best defined by organizations implementing code. My personal definition of a unit is a body of software that is designed, coded, and tested by either one person, or possibly a programmer pair. Chapters 5 through 10 cover unit level testing.

Chapter 5

Boundary Value Testing

In Chapter 3, we saw that a function maps values from one set (its domain) to values in another set (its range) and that the domain and range can be cross products of other sets. Any program can be considered to be a function in the sense that program inputs form its domain and program outputs form its range. In this and the next two chapters, we examine how to use knowledge of the functional nature of a program to identify test cases for the program. Input domain testing (also called "Boundary Value Testing") is the best-known specification-based testing technique. Historically, this form of testing has focused on the input domain; but it is often a good supplement to apply many of these techniques to develop range-based test cases.

There are two independent considerations that apply to input domain testing. The first asks if we are concerned with invalid values of variables. Normal Boundary Value Testing is concerned only with valid values of the input variables. Robust Boundary Value Testing considers invalid and valid variable values. The second consideration is whether we make the "single fault" assumption common to reliability theory. This assumes that faults are due to incorrect values of a single variable. If this is not warranted, meaning that we are concerned with interaction among two or more variables, we need to take the cross-product of the individual variables. Taken together, the two considerations yield four variations of boundary value testing:

- Normal Boundary Value Testing, sometimes abbreviated here as NBVT
- Robust Boundary Value Testing, RBVT
- Worst Case Boundary Value Testing, WCBVT and
- Robust Worst Case Boundary Value Testing, RWCBVT.

For the sake of comprehensible drawings, the discussion in this chapter refers to a function, F, of two variables x_1 and x_2. When the function F is implemented as a program, the input variables x_1 and x_2 will have some (possibly unstated) boundaries:

$$a \leq x_1 \leq b$$

$$c \leq x_2 \leq d$$

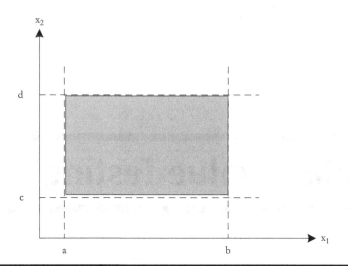

Figure 5.1   Input domain of a function of two variables.

Unfortunately, the intervals [a, b] and [c, d] are referred to as the ranges of x_1 and x_2, so right away we have an overloaded term. The intended meaning will always be clear from its context. Strongly typed languages (such as Ada® and Pascal) permit explicit definition of such variable ranges. In fact, part of the historical reason for strong typing was to prevent programmers from making the kinds of errors that result in faults that are easily revealed by boundary value testing. For programs written in languages are not strongly typed, boundary value testing is more appropriate. The input space (domain) of our function F is shown in Figure 5.1. Any point within the shaded rectangle and including the boundaries is a legitimate input to the function F.

5.1 Normal Boundary Value Testing

All four forms of boundary value testing focus on the boundary of the input space to identify test cases. The rationale behind boundary value testing is that errors tend to occur near the extreme values of an input variable. Loop conditions, for example, may test for < when they should test for ≤, and counters often are "off by one." (In some programming languages counting begins at zero, in others at one.) The basic idea of boundary value analysis is to use input variable values at their minimum, just above the minimum, a nominal value, just below their maximum, and at their maximum. As far back as the early 1990s, there was a commercially available testing tool (originally named T) that generated such test cases for a properly specified program. This tool has been successfully integrated with two popular front-end CASE tools (Teamwork from Cadre Systems, and Software through Pictures from Aonix (part of Atego). For more information, see http://www.aonix.com/pdf/2140-AON.pdf). The T tool refers to these values as min, min+, nom, max-, and max. The robust forms add two values, min- and max+.

The next part of boundary value analysis is based on a critical assumption; it is known as the "single fault" assumption in reliability theory. This says that failures are only rarely the result of the simultaneous occurrence of two (or more) faults. The normal and robust cases are obtained by holding the values of all but one variable at their nominal values, and letting that one variable assume its full set of test values.

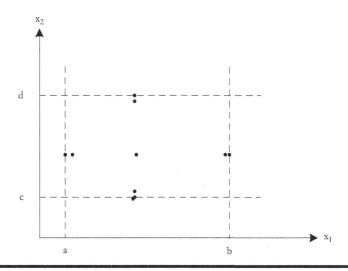

Figure 5.2 Boundary value analysis test cases for a function of two variables.

The normal boundary value analysis test cases for our function F of two variables (illustrated in Figure 5.2) are:

$\{<x_{1nom}, x_{2min}>, <x_{1nom}, x_{2min+}>, <x_{1nom}, x_{2nom}>, <x_{1nom}, x_{2max-}>, <x_{1nom}, x_{2max}>, <x_{1min}, x_{2nom}>,$
$<x_{1min+}, x_{2nom}>, <x_{1max-}, x_{2nom}>, <x_{1max}, x_{2nom}>\}$

The All Pairs testing approach (described in Chapter 18) contradicts the single fault assumption, with the observation that, in software-controlled medical systems, almost all faults are the result of interaction between a pair of variables. This is the rationale for the Worst Case variations of boundary value testing.

5.1.1 Generalizing Boundary Value Analysis

The basic boundary value analysis technique can be generalized in two ways: by the number of variables and by the kinds of ranges. Generalizing the number of variables is easy: if we have a function of n variables, we hold all but one at their nominal values and let the remaining variable assume the min, min+, nom, max-, and max values, repeating this for each variable. Thus, for a function of n variables, boundary value analysis yields 4n + 1 unique test cases.

Generalizing ranges depends on the nature (or more precisely, the type) of the variables themselves. In the NextDate function, for example, we have variables for the month, the day, and the year. One implementation approach would be to encode these, so that January would correspond to 1, February to 2, and so on. In a language that supports user-defined types (like Pascal or Ada), we could define the variable month as an enumerated type {Jan., Feb., ..., Dec.}. Either way, the values for min, min+, nom, max-, and max are clear from the context. When a variable has discrete, bounded values, as the variables in the commission problem have, the min, min+, nom, max-, and max are also easily determined. When no explicit bounds are present, as in the triangle problem, we usually must create "artificial" bounds. The lower bound of side lengths is clearly 1 (a negative side length is silly); but what might we do for an upper bound? By default, the largest representable integer (called MAXINT in some languages) is one possibility; or we might impose an arbitrary upper limit such as 200 or 2000. For other data types, as long as a variable supports an ordering relation (see Chapter 3 for a definition), we can usually infer the min, min+, nominal, max-, and max values. Test values for lower case alphabet characters, for example, would be {a, b, m, y, and z}.

Boundary value analysis does not make much sense for Boolean variables; the extreme values are TRUE and FALSE, but no clear choice is available for the remaining three. We will see in Chapter 7 that Boolean variables lend themselves to decision table-based testing. Logical variables also present a problem for boundary value analysis. In login examples, a customer's PIN is a logical variable, as are cell phone directory numbers. We could go through the motions of boundary value analysis testing for such variables, but the exercise is not very satisfying to the tester's intuition.

5.1.2 Limitations of Boundary Value Analysis

Boundary value analysis works well when the program to be tested is a function of several independent variables that represent bounded physical quantities. Mathematically, the variables need to be described by a true ordering relation, in which, for every pair <a, b> of values of a variable, it is possible to say that a <= b. (See Chapter 3 for a detailed definition of ordering relations.) Sets of car colors, for example, or football teams, do not support an ordering relation, thus no form of boundary value testing is appropriate for such variables. The key words here are *independent* and *physical quantities*. A quick look at the boundary value analysis test cases for NextDate (in Section 5.5) shows them to be inadequate. Very little stress occurs on February and on leap years. The real problem here is that interesting dependencies exist among the month, day, and year variables. Boundary value analysis presumes the variables to be truly independent. Even so, boundary value analysis happens to catch end-of-month and end-of-year faults. Boundary value analysis test cases are derived from the extrema of bounded, independent variables that refer to physical quantities, with no consideration of the nature of the function, nor of the semantic meaning of the variables. We see boundary value analysis test cases to be rudimentary because they are obtained with very little insight and imagination. As with so many things, you get what you pay for.

The physical quantity criterion is equally important. When a variable refers to a physical quantity, such as temperature, pressure, air speed, angle of attack, load, and so forth, physical boundaries can be extremely important. (In an interesting example of this, Sky Harbor International Airport in Phoenix had to close on June 26, 1992, because the air temperature was 122°F. Aircraft pilots were unable to make certain instrument settings before take-off: the instruments could only accept a maximum air temperature of 120°F.) In another case, a medical analysis system uses stepper motors to position a carousel of samples to be analyzed. It turns out that the mechanics of moving the carousel back to the starting cell often causes the robot arm to miss the first cell.

5.2 Robust Boundary Value Testing

Robust boundary value testing is a simple extension of normal boundary value testing: in addition to the five normal boundary value analysis values of a variable, we see what happens when the extrema are exceeded with a value slightly greater than

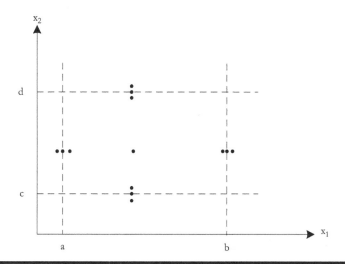

Figure 5.3   Robustness test cases for a function of two variables.

the maximum (max+) and a value slightly less than the minimum (min-). Robust boundary value test cases for our continuing example are shown in Figure 5.3.

Most of the discussion of boundary value analysis applies directly to robustness testing, especially the generalizations and limitations. The most interesting part of robustness testing is not with the inputs, but with the expected outputs. What happens when a physical quantity exceeds its maximum? If it is the angle of attack of an airplane wing, the aircraft might stall. If it is the load capacity of a public elevator, we hope nothing special would happen. If it is a date, like May 32, we would expect an error message. The main value of robustness testing is that it forces attention on exception handling. With strongly typed languages, robustness testing may be very awkward. In strongly typed languages, if a variable is defined to be within a certain range, values outside that range result in run-time errors that abort normal execution. This raises an interesting question of implementation philosophy: is it better to perform explicit range checking and use exception handling to deal with "robust values," or is it better to stay with strong typing? The exception handling choice mandates robustness testing.

There are situations where robustness testing cannot occur, for example, water temperature might have the boundaries 0° C<= waterTemperature <= 100° C. For temperatures below 0° C, water is actually ice, and above 100° C, it is steam. If the application that uses waterTemperature is dealing with liquid properties such as viscosity or ability to dissolve salts, robustness testing cannot produce anything useful.

5.3 Worst Case Boundary Value Testing

Both Normal and Robust boundary value testing, as we said earlier, make the single fault assumption of reliability theory. Due to their similarity, we treat both Normal Worst Case Boundary Testing and Robust Worst Case Boundary Testing in this subsection. Rejecting single-fault assumption means that we are interested in what happens when more than one variable has an extreme value. In electronic circuit analysis, this is called "worst-case analysis"; we use that idea here to generate worst-case test cases. For

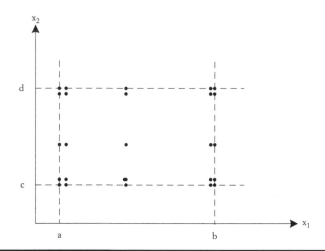

Figure 5.4   Worst-case test cases for a function of two variables.

each variable, we start with the five-element set that contains the min, min+, nom, max-, and max values. We then take the Cartesian product (see Chapter 3) of these sets to generate test cases. The result of the two-variable version of this is shown in Figure 5.4.

Worst-case boundary value testing is clearly more thorough in the sense that boundary value analysis test cases are a proper subset of worst-case test cases. It also represents much more effort: worst-case testing for a function of n variables generates on the order of 5n test cases, as opposed to 4n + 1 test cases for boundary value analysis.

Worst-case testing follows the generalization pattern we saw for boundary value analysis. It also has the same limitations, particularly those related to independence. Probably the best application for worst-case testing is where physical variables have numerous interactions, and where failure of the function is extremely costly. In extreme situations, we could go to robust worst-case testing. This involves the Cartesian product of the seven-element sets we used in robustness testing resulting in nearly 7n test cases. Figure 5.5 shows the robust worst-case test cases for our two-variable function.

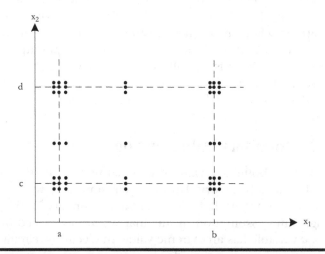

Figure 5.5   Robust worst-case test cases for a function of two variables.

5.4 Special Value Testing

Special value testing is probably the most widely practiced form of functional testing. It also is the most intuitive and the least uniform. Special value testing occurs when a tester uses domain knowledge, experience with similar programs, and information about "soft spots" to devise test cases. We might also call this *ad hoc* testing. No guidelines are used other than "best engineering judgment." As a result, special value testing is very dependent on the abilities of the tester.

Despite all the apparent negatives, special value testing can be very useful. In the next section, you will find test cases generated by the methods we just discussed for our two continuing examples. If you look carefully at these, especially for the NextDate function, you find that none is very satisfactory. Special value test cases for NextDate will include several test cases involving February 28, February 29, and leap years. Even though special value testing is highly subjective, it often results in a set of test cases that is more effective in revealing faults than the test sets generated by boundary value methods—testimony to the craft of software testing.

5.5 Examples

Our two continuing examples are both functions of three variables. Printing all the test cases from all the methods for each problem is very space consuming, so we just have selected examples (values "near the corners") for Worst Case Boundary Value and Robust Worst Case Boundary Value testing.

5.5.1 Test Cases for the Triangle Problem

In the problem statement, no conditions are specified on the triangle sides, other than being integers. Obviously, the lower bounds of the ranges are all 1. We arbitrarily take 200 as an upper bound. For each side, the test values are {1, 2, 100, 199, 200}. Robust boundary value test cases will add {0, 201}. Table 5.1 contains boundary value test cases using these ranges. Notice that test cases 3, 8, and 13 are identical (bold face in the table); two should be deleted. Also, notice that there is no test case for scalene triangles.

The cross-product of test values will have 125 test cases (some of which will be repeated)—too many to list here. (The full set is easily generated as a spreadsheet.) Table 5.2 only lists the first 25 Worst Case boundary Value test cases for the Triangle Problem. You can picture them as a plane slice through the cube (actually it is a rectangular parallelepiped) in which a = 1 and the other two variables take on their full set of cross-product values. As we saw for Normal Boundary Value test cases, there is no test case for scalene triangles.

5.5.2 Test Cases for the NextDate Function

All 125 worst case test cases for NextDate are listed in Table 5.3. Take some time to examine it for gaps of untested functionality and for redundant testing. For example, would anyone actually want to test January 1 in five different years? The end of February is not tested sufficiently—there are no test cases for February 28, nor for February 29.

Table 5.1   Normal Boundary Value Test Case

Case	a	b	c	Expected Output
1	100	100	1	Isosceles
2	100	100	2	Isosceles
3	**100**	**100**	**100**	**Equilateral**
4	100	100	199	Isosceles
5	100	100	200	Not a Triangle
6	100	1	100	Isosceles
7	100	2	100	Isosceles
8	**100**	**100**	**100**	**Equilateral**
9	100	199	100	Isosceles
10	100	200	100	Not a Triangle
11	1	100	100	Isosceles
12	2	100	100	Isosceles
13	**100**	**100**	**100**	**Equilateral**
14	199	100	100	Isosceles
15	200	100	100	Not a Triangle

Table 5.2   (Selected) Worst-Case Boundary Value Test Cases

Case	A	B	C	Expected Output
1	1	1	1	Equilateral
2	1	1	2	Not a Triangle
3	1	1	100	Not a Triangle
4	1	1	199	Not a Triangle
5	1	1	200	Not a Triangle
6	1	2	1	Not a Triangle
7	1	2	2	Isosceles
8	1	2	100	Not a Triangle
9	1	2	199	Not a Triangle
10	1	2	200	Not a Triangle
11	1	100	1	Not a Triangle

(Continued)

Table 5.2 (*Continued*)

Case	A	B	C	Expected Output
12	1	100	2	Not a Triangle
13	1	100	100	Isosceles
14	1	100	199	Not a Triangle
15	1	100	200	Not a Triangle
16	1	199	1	Not a Triangle
17	1	199	2	Not a Triangle
18	1	199	100	Not a Triangle
19	1	199	199	Isosceles
20	1	199	200	Not a Triangle
21	1	200	1	Not a Triangle
22	1	200	2	Not a Triangle
23	1	200	100	Not a Triangle
24	1	200	199	Not a Triangle
25	1	200	200	Isosceles

Table 5.3   Worst-Case Test Cases

Case	Month	Day	Year	Expected Output
1	1	1	1842	1, 2, 1842
2	1	1	1843	1, 2, 1843
3	1	1	1942	1, 2, 1942
4	1	1	2041	1, 2, 2041
5	1	1	2042	1, 2, 2042
6	1	2	1842	1, 3, 1842
7	1	2	1843	1, 3, 1843
8	1	2	1942	1, 3, 1942
9	1	2	2041	1, 3, 2041
10	1	2	2042	1, 3, 2042
11	1	15	1842	1, 16, 1842
12	1	15	1843	1, 16, 1843

(Continued)

Table 5.3 (*Continued*)

Case	Month	Day	Year	Expected Output
13	1	15	1942	1, 16, 1942
14	1	15	2041	1, 16, 2041
15	1	15	2042	1, 16, 2042
16	1	30	1842	1, 31, 1842
17	1	30	1843	1, 31, 1843
18	1	30	1942	1, 31, 1942
19	1	30	2041	1, 31, 2041
20	1	30	2042	1, 31, 2042
21	1	31	1842	2, 1, 1842
22	1	31	1843	2, 1, 1843
23	1	31	1942	2, 1, 1942
24	1	31	2041	2, 1, 2041
25	1	31	2042	2, 1, 2042
26	2	1	1842	2, 2, 1842
27	2	1	1843	2, 2, 1843
28	2	1	1942	2, 2, 1942
29	2	1	2041	2, 2, 2041
30	2	1	2042	2, 2, 2042
31	2	2	1842	2, 3, 1842
32	2	2	1843	2, 3, 1843
33	2	2	1942	2, 3, 1942
34	2	2	2041	2, 3, 2041
35	2	2	2042	2, 3, 2042
36	2	15	1842	2, 16, 1842
37	2	15	1843	2, 16, 1843
38	2	15	1942	2, 16, 1942
39	2	15	2041	2, 16, 2041
40	2	15	2042	2, 16, 2042
41	2	30	1842	Invalid date

(*Continued*)

Table 5.3 (*Continued*)

Case	Month	Day	Year	Expected Output
42	2	30	1843	Invalid date
43	2	30	1942	Invalid date
44	2	30	2041	Invalid date
45	2	30	2042	Invalid date
46	2	31	1842	Invalid date
47	2	31	1843	Invalid date
48	2	31	1942	Invalid date
49	2	31	2041	Invalid date
50	2	31	2042	Invalid date
51	6	1	1842	6, 2, 1842
52	6	1	1843	6, 2, 1843
53	6	1	1942	6, 2, 1942
54	6	1	2041	6, 2, 2041
55	6	1	2042	6, 2, 2042
56	6	2	1842	6, 3, 1842
57	6	2	1843	6, 3, 1843
58	6	2	1942	6, 3, 1942
59	6	2	2041	6, 3, 2041
60	6	2	2042	6, 3, 2042
61	6	15	1842	6, 16, 1842
62	6	15	1843	6, 16, 1843
63	6	15	1942	6, 16, 1942
64	6	15	2041	6, 16, 2041
65	6	15	2042	6, 16, 2042
66	6	30	1842	7, 1, 1842
67	6	30	1843	7, 1, 1843
68	6	30	1942	7, 1, 1942
69	6	30	2041	7, 1, 2041
70	6	30	2042	7, 1, 2042

(*Continued*)

Table 5.3 (*Continued*)

Case	Month	Day	Year	Expected Output
71	6	31	1842	Invalid date
72	6	31	1843	Invalid date
73	6	31	1942	Invalid date
74	6	31	2041	Invalid date
75	6	31	2042	Invalid date
76	11	1	1842	11, 2, 1842
77	11	1	1843	11, 2, 1843
78	11	1	1942	11, 2, 1942
79	11	1	2041	11, 2, 2041
80	11	1	2042	11, 2, 2042
81	11	2	1842	11, 3, 1842
82	11	2	1843	11, 3, 1843
83	11	2	1942	11, 3, 1942
84	11	2	2041	11, 3, 2041
85	11	2	2042	11, 3, 2042
86	11	15	1842	11, 16, 1842
87	11	15	1843	11, 16, 1843
88	11	15	1942	11, 16, 1942
89	11	15	2041	11, 16, 2041
90	11	15	2042	11, 16, 2042
91	11	30	1842	12, 1, 1842
92	11	30	1843	12, 1, 1843
93	11	30	1942	12, 1, 1942
94	11	30	2041	12, 1, 2041
95	11	30	2042	12, 1, 2042
96	11	31	1842	Invalid date
97	11	31	1843	Invalid date
98	11	31	1942	Invalid date

(*Continued*)

Table 5.3 (*Continued*)

Case	Month	Day	Year	Expected Output
99	11	31	2041	Invalid date
100	11	31	2042	Invalid date
101	12	1	1842	12, 2, 1842
102	12	1	1843	12, 2, 1843
103	12	1	1942	12, 2, 1942
104	12	1	2041	12, 2, 2041
105	12	1	2042	12, 2, 2042
106	12	2	1842	12, 3, 1842
107	12	2	1843	12, 3, 1843
108	12	2	1942	12, 3, 1942
109	12	2	2041	12, 3, 2041
110	12	2	2042	12, 3, 2042
111	12	15	1842	12, 16, 1842
112	12	15	1843	12, 16, 1843
113	12	15	1942	12, 16, 1942
114	12	15	2041	12, 16, 2041
115	12	15	2042	12, 16, 2042
116	12	30	1842	12, 31, 1842
117	12	30	1843	12, 31, 1843
118	12	30	1942	12, 31, 1942
119	12	30	2041	12, 31, 2041
120	12	30	2042	12, 31, 2042
121	12	31	1842	1, 1, 1843
122	12	31	1843	1, 1, 1844
123	12	31	1942	1, 1, 1943
124	12	31	2041	1, 1, 2042
125	12	31	2042	1, 1, 2043

5.6 Random Testing

At least two decades of discussion of random testing are included in the literature. Most of this interest is among academics, and in a statistical sense, it is interesting. Our two continuing sample problems lend themselves nicely to random testing. The basic idea is that, rather than always choose the min, min+, nom, max-, and max values of a bounded variable, use a random number generator to pick test case values. This avoids any form of bias in testing. It also raises a serious question: How many random test cases are sufficient? Later, when we discuss structural test coverage metrics, we will have an elegant answer. For now, Tables 5.4 and 5.5 show the results of randomly generated test cases. They are derived from a Visual Basic application that picks values for a bounded variable a ≤ x ≤ b as follows:

$$x = \text{Int}\big((b - a + 1) * \text{Rnd} + a\big)$$

where the function Int returns the integer part of a floating point number, and the function Rnd generates random numbers in the interval [0, 1]. The program keeps generating random test cases until at least one of each output occurs. In each table, the program went through seven "cycles" that ended with the "hard-to-generate" test case. In Tables 5.4 and 5.5, the last line shows what percentage of the random test cases was generated for each column. In the table for NextDate, the percentages are very close to the computed probability given in the last line of Table 5.5. Even in the smallest sets of random test cases, 1289 for the Triangle Program, and 913 for NextDate, there is extensive redundancy before the "difficult" test cases are reached randomly. Since every form of random testing only generates the input portion of a test case, the expected outputs must be generated somehow. This is easy for NextDate, but in general, this will be in enormous task. Our conclusion? Random testing is of academic interest only.

Table 5.4 Random Test Cases for the Triangle Program

Test Cases	Non-triangles	Scalene	Isosceles	Equilateral
1289	663	593	32	1
15436	7696	7372	367	1
17091	8556	8164	367	1
2603	1284	1252	66	1
6475	3197	3122	155	1
5978	2998	2850	129	1
9008	4447	4353	207	1
Percentage	49.83%	47.87%	2.29%	0.01%

Table 5.5   Random Test Cases for the NextDate Program

Test Cases	Days 1–30 of 31-day months	Day 31 of 31-day months	Days 1–29 of 30-day months	Day 30 of 30-day months
913	542	17	274	10
1101	621	9	358	8
4201	2448	64	1242	46
1097	600	21	350	9
5853	3342	100	1804	82
3959	2195	73	1252	42
1436	786	22	456	13
percentage	56.76%	1.65%	30.91%	1.13%
Probability	56.45%	1.88%	31.18%	1.88%
Days 1–27 of Feb.	Feb. 28 of a leap year	Feb. 28 of a non-leap year	Feb. 29 of a leap year	Impossible days
45	1	1	1	22
83	1	1	1	19
312	1	8	3	77
92	1	4	1	19
417	1	11	2	94
310	1	6	5	75
126	1	5	1	26
7.46%	0.04%	0.19%	0.08%	1.79%
7.26%	0.07%	0.20%	0.07%	1.01%

5.7 Guidelines for Boundary Value Testing

With the exception of special value testing, the test methods based on the input domain of a function (program) are the most rudimentary of all specification-based testing methods. They share the common assumption that the input variables are truly independent; and when this assumption is not warranted, the methods generate unsatisfactory test cases (such as June 31, 1942 for NextDate). Each of these methods can be applied to the output range of a program.

Another useful form of output-based test cases is for systems that generate error messages. The tester should devise test cases to check that error messages are generated when they are appropriate and are not falsely generated. Boundary value analysis can also be used for internal variables, such as loop control variables, indices, and pointers. Strictly speaking, these are not input variables; but errors in the use of these variables are quite common. Robustness testing is a good choice for testing internal variables.

There is a discussion in Chapter 10 about "the testing pendulum"—it refers to the problem of syntactic versus semantic approaches to developing test cases. Here is a short example given both ways. Consider a function F of three variables, a, b, and c. The boundaries are: 0 <= a <10,000; 0 <= b <10,000, and 0 <= c <18.8. The function F is: F = (a − b)/c; Table 5.6 shows the normal boundary value test cases. Absent semantic knowledge, the test cases in Table 5.6 are what a boundary value testing tool would generate (a tool would not generate the expected output values). Even just the syntactic version is problematic—it does not avoid the division by zero possibility in test case 11. (Note: the redundant test cases are in **bold** font.)

When we add the semantic information that F calculates the miles per gallon of an automobile, where a and b are end and start trip odometer values, and c is the gas tank capacity, we see more severe problems:

1. We must always have a >= b. this will avoid the negative values of F (test cases 1, 2, 9, and 10).

Table 5.6   Normal Boundary Value Test Cases for F = (a − b)/c

Test Case	a	b	c	F
1	0	5000	9.4	−531.9
2	1	5000	9.4	−531.8
3	**5000**	**5000**	**9.4**	**0.0**
4	9998	5000	9.4	531.7
5	9999	5000	9.4	531.8
6	5000	0	9.4	531.9
7	5000	1	9.4	531.8
8	**5000**	**5000**	**9.4**	**0.0**
9	5000	9998	9.4	−531.7
10	5000	9999	9.4	−531.8
11	5000	5000	0	#DIV/0!
12	5000	5000	1	0.0
13	**5000**	**5000**	**9.4**	**0.0**
14	5000	5000	18.7	0.0
15	5000	5000	18.8	0.0

Table 5.7 Semantic Boundary Value Test Cases for F = (a − b)/c

Test Case	End Odometer	Start Odometer	Tank Capacity	Miles Per Gallon
4	9998	5000	9.4	531.7
5	9999	5000	9.4	531.8
6	5000	0	9.4	531.9
7	5000	1	9.4	531.8
8	5000	5000	9.4	0.0

2. Test cases 3, 8, and 12 - 15 all refer to trips of length 0, so they could be collapsed into one test case, probably test case 8.
3. Division by zero is an obvious problem, thereby eliminating test case 11. Applying the semantic knowledge will – result in the better set of case cases in Table 5.8.
4. Table 5.7 is still problematic—we never see the effect of boundary values on the tank capacity.

Exercises

1. Make a Venn diagram showing the relationships among test cases from boundary value analysis, robustness testing, worst-case testing, and robust worst-case testing.
2. Apply Special Value Testing to the miles per gallon example in Tables 5.8 and 5.9. Provide reasons for your chosen test cases.
3. What would we learn from Robust Normal Boundary Value test cases for the Quadrilateral Program? The values are:
   c1. $0 \leq a \leq 201$ (top)
   c2. $0 \leq b \leq 201$ (left side)
   c3. $0 \leq c \leq 201$ (bottom)
   c4. $0 \leq d \leq 201$ (right side)
4. Discuss the extent to which any form of boundary value testing would be helpful/appropriate for the Quadrilateral Program.
5. Repeat questions 3 and 4 for the NextWeek function. Use these range values:
   c1. $0 \leq month \leq 13$
   c2. $0 \leq day \leq 32$
   c3. $1841 \leq year \leq 2043$

Chapter 6

Equivalence Class Testing

The use of equivalence classes as the basis for functional testing has two motivations: we would like to have a sense of complete testing; and, at the same time, we would hope to avoid redundancy. Neither of these hopes is realized by boundary value testing—looking at the tables of test cases, it is easy to see massive redundancy, and looking more closely, serious gaps exist. Equivalence class testing echoes the two deciding factors of boundary value testing, robustness, and the single/multiple fault assumption. This chapter presents the traditional view of equivalence class testing, followed by a coherent treatment of four distinct forms based on the two assumptions. The single versus multiple fault assumption yields the weak/strong distinction and the focus on invalid data yields second distinction: normal versus robust. Taken together, these two assumptions result in Weak Normal, Strong Normal, Weak Robust, and Strong Robust Equivalence Class testing.

Two problems occur with robust forms. The first is that, very often, the specification does not define what the expected output for an invalid input should be. (We could argue that this is a deficiency of the specification, but that does not get us anywhere.) Thus, testers spend a lot of time defining expected outputs for these cases. The second problem is that strongly typed languages eliminate the need for the consideration of invalid inputs. Traditional equivalence testing is a product of the time when languages such as FORTRAN and COBOL were dominant; thus, this type of error was common. In fact, it was the high incidence of such errors that led to the implementation of strongly typed languages.

6.1 Equivalence Classes

In Chapter 3, we noted that the important aspect of equivalence classes is that they form a partition of a set, where partition refers to a collection of mutually disjoint subsets, the union of which is the entire set. This has two important implications for testing—the fact that the entire set is represented provides a form of completeness, and the disjointedness ensures a form of non-redundancy. Because the subsets are determined by an equivalence relation, the elements of a subset have something in common. The idea of equivalence class testing is to identify test cases by using one element from each equivalence class. If the equivalence classes are chosen wisely, this greatly reduces the potential redundancy among test cases. In the Triangle Problem, for example, we would certainly have a test case for an equilateral triangle, and we might pick the triple (5, 5, 5) as inputs for a test case. If we did this, we would not expect to learn much from test cases such as (6, 6, 6) and (100, 100, 100). Our intuition tells us that these would be "treated the same" as the first test case; thus, they would be redundant. When we consider code-based testing in Chapter 8, we shall see that "treated the same" maps onto "traversing the same execution path." The four forms of equivalence class testing all address the problems of gaps and redundancies that are common to the four forms of boundary value testing. Since the assumptions align, the four forms of boundary value testing also align with the four forms of equivalence class testing. There will be one point of overlap—this occurs when equivalence classes are defined by bounded variables. In such cases, a hybrid of boundary value and equivalence class testing is appropriate. The ISTQB syllabi refer to this as "edge testing." We will see this in the discussion in Section 6.3.

6.2 Traditional Equivalence Class Testing

Most of the standard testing texts (*e.g.,* Myers, 1979; Mosley, 1993) discuss equivalence classes based on valid and invalid variable values. Traditional equivalence class testing is nearly identical to weak robust equivalence class testing (see Section 6.3.3). This traditional form focuses on invalid data values, and it is/was a consequence of the dominant style of programming in the 1960s and 1970s. Input data validation was an important issue at the time, and "Garbage In, Garbage Out" was the programmer's watchword. In the early years, it was the program user's responsibility to provide valid data. There was no guarantee about results based on invalid data. The term soon became known as GIGO. The usual response to GIGO was extensive input validation sections of a program. Authors and seminar leaders frequently commented that the afferent portion in the classic afferent/central/efferent architecture of structured programming often represented 80% of the total source code. In this context, it is natural to emphasize input data validation. The early defense against GIGO was to have extensive testing to assure data validity. The gradual shift to modern programming languages, especially those that feature strong data typing, and then to graphical user interfaces (GUIs) obviated much of the need for input data validation. Indeed, good use of user interface devices such as drop-down lists and slider bars reduces the likelihood of bad input data.

Traditional equivalence class testing echoes the process of boundary value testing. Figure 6.1 shows test cases for a function F of two variables x_1 and x_2., as we had in Chapter 5. The extension to more realistic cases of n variables proceeds as follows:

1. Test F for valid values of all variables. If this is successful, then
2. Test F for invalid values of x_1 with valid values of the remaining variables. Any failure will be due to a problem with an invalid value of x_1.
3. Repeat step 2 for the remaining variables.

One clear advantage of this process is that it focuses on finding faults due to invalid data. Since the GIGO concern was on invalid data, the kinds of combinations that we

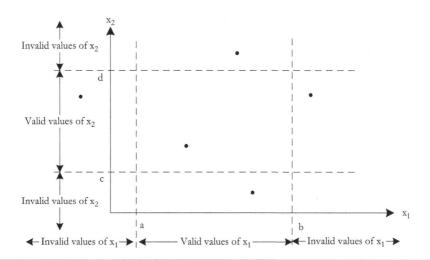

Figure 6.1   Traditional equivalence class test cases.

saw in the worst case variations of boundary value testing were ignored. Figure 6.1 shows the five test cases for this process for our continuing function F of two variables.

6.3 Improved Equivalence Class Testing

The key (and the craft!) of equivalence class testing is the choice of the equivalence relation that determines the classes. Very often, we make this choice by second-guessing the likely implementation and thinking about the functional manipulations that must somehow be present in the implementation. We will illustrate this with our continuing examples. We need to enrich the function we used in boundary value testing. Again, for the sake of comprehensible drawings, the discussion relates to a function, F, of two variables x_1 and x_2. When F is implemented as a program, the input variables x_1 and x_2 will have the following boundaries, and intervals within the boundaries:

$$a \leq x_1 \leq d, \text{ with intervals } [a, b), [b, c), [c, d]$$
$$e \leq x_2 \leq g, \text{ with intervals } [e, f), [f, g]$$

where square brackets and parentheses denote, respectively, closed and open interval endpoints. The intervals presumably correspond to some distinction in the program being tested. These ranges are equivalence classes. Invalid values of x_1 and x_2 are: $x_1 < a$, $x_1 > d$, and $x_2 < e$, $x_2 > g$. The equivalence classes of valid values are:

V1={x_1 : a <= x_1 < b}, V2={x_1 : b <= x_1 < c},V3={x_1 : c <= x_1 <= d}, V4={x_2 : e <= x_2 < f}, V5={x_2 : f <= x_2 <= g}

The equivalence classes of invalid values are:

NV1={x_1 : x_1 < a}, NV2={x_1 : d < x_1}, NV3={x_2 : x_2 < e}, NV4 ={x_2 : g < x_2 }

The equivalence classes V1, V2, V3, V4, V5, NV1, NV2, NV3, and NV4 are disjoint, and their union is the entire plane. In the following discussions, we will just use the interval notation rather than the full formal set definition.

6.3.1 Weak Normal Equivalence Class Testing

With the notation as given previously, weak normal equivalence class testing is accomplished by using one variable from each equivalence class (interval) in a test case. (Note the effect of the single fault assumption.) For the running example, we would end up with the three weak equivalence class test cases shown in Figure 6.2. This figure will be repeated for the remaining forms of equivalence class testing, but, for clarity, without the indication of valid and invalid ranges. These three test cases use one value from each equivalence class. The test case in the lower left rectangle corresponds to a value of x_1 in the class [a, b), and to a value of x_2 in the class [e, f). The test case in the upper center rectangle corresponds to a value of x_1 in the class [b, c) and to a value of x_2 in the class [f, g). The third test case could be in either rectangle on the right side of the valid values. We identified these in a systematic way, thus the apparent pattern. In fact, we will always have the same number of weak equivalence class test cases as classes in the partition with the largest number of subsets.

What can we learn from a weak normal equivalence class test case that fails, *i.e.,* one for which the expected and actual outputs are inconsistent? There could be a problem with x_1, or a problem with x_2, or maybe an interaction among the two. This ambiguity is the reason for the "weak" designation. If the expectation of failure is low, as it is for regression testing, this can be an acceptable choice. When more fault isolation is required, the stronger forms, discussed next, are indicated.

6.3.2 Strong Normal Equivalence Class Testing

Strong equivalence class testing is based on the multiple fault assumption, so we need test cases from each element of the Cartesian product of the equivalence classes, as shown in Figure 6.3. Notice the similarity between the pattern of these test cases and the construction of a truth table in propositional logic. The Cartesian product guarantees that we have a notion of "completeness" in two senses: we cover all the equivalence classes, and we have one of each possible combination of inputs. As we shall see from our continuing examples, the key to "good" equivalence class testing is the selection of the equivalence relation. Watch for the notion of inputs being "treated the same." Most of the time, equivalence class testing defines classes of the

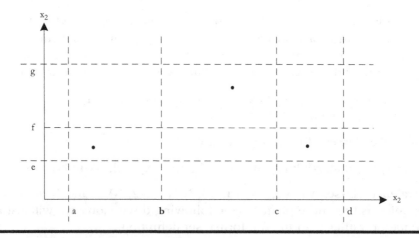

Figure 6.2 Weak normal equivalence class test cases.

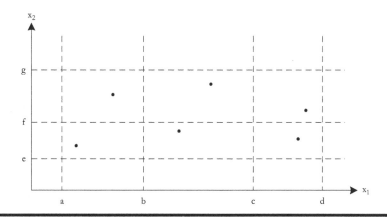

Figure 6.3   Strong normal equivalence class test cases.

input domain. There is no reason why we could not define equivalence relations on the output range of the program function being tested; in fact, this is the simplest approach for the Triangle Problem.

6.3.3 Weak Robust Equivalence Class Testing

The name for this form is admittedly counterintuitive and oxymoronic. How can something be both weak and robust? The robust part comes from consideration of invalid values, and the weak part refers to the single fault assumption. The process of weak robust equivalence class testing is a simple extension of that for weak normal equivalence class testing—pick test cases such that each equivalence class is represented. In Figure 6.4, the test cases for valid classes are as they were in Figure 6.2. The two additional test cases cover all four classes of invalid values. The process is similar to that for boundary value testing:

1. For valid inputs, use one value from each valid class (as in what we have called weak normal equivalence class testing. Note that each input in these test cases will be valid.)

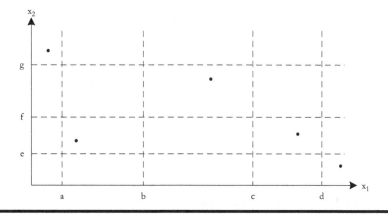

Figure 6.4   Weak robust equivalence class test cases.

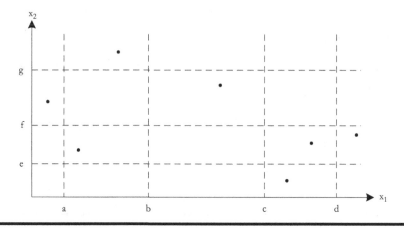

Figure 6.5   Revised weak robust equivalence class test cases.

2. For invalid inputs, a test case will have one invalid value and the remaining values will all be valid. (Thus, a "single failure" should cause the test case to fail.)

The test cases resulting from this strategy are shown in Figure 6.4. There is a potential problem with these test cases. Consider the test cases in the upper left and lower right corners. Each of the test cases represents values from two invalid equivalence classes. Failure of either of these could be due to the interaction of two variables. Figure 6.5 presents a compromise between "pure" weak normal equivalence class testing and its robust extension.

6.3.4 Strong Robust Equivalence Class Testing

At least the name for this form is neither counterintuitive nor oxymoronic, just redundant. As before, the robust part comes from consideration of invalid values, and the strong part refers to the multiple fault assumption. We obtain test cases from each element of the Cartesian product of all the equivalence classes, both valid and invalid, as shown in Figure 6.6.

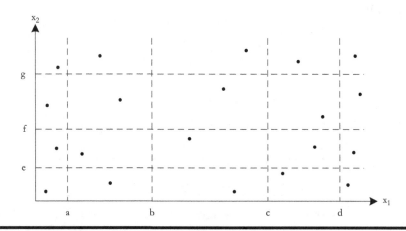

Figure 6.6   Strong robust equivalence class test cases.

6.4 Equivalence Class Test Cases for the Triangle Problem

In the problem statement, we note that four possible outputs can occur: NotATriangle, Scalene, Isosceles, and Equilateral. We can use these to identify output (range) equivalence classes as follows.

R1 = {<a, b, c>: the triangle with sides a, b, and c is equilateral}
R2 = {<a, b, c>: the triangle with sides a, b, and c is isosceles}
R3 = {<a, b, c>: the triangle with sides a, b, and c is scalene}
R4 = {<a, b, c>: sides a, b, and c do not form a triangle}

Four weak normal equivalence class test cases, chosen arbitrarily from each class are:

Test Case	a	b	c	
WN1	5	5	5	Equilateral
WN2	2	2	3	Isosceles
WN3	3	4	5	Scalene
WN4	4	1	2	Not a Triangle

Because no valid subintervals of variables a, b, and c exist, the strong normal equivalence class test cases are identical to the weak normal equivalence class test cases.

Considering the invalid values for a, b, and c yields the following additional weak robust equivalence class test cases. (The invalid values could be zero, any negative number, or any number greater than 200.)

Test Case	a	B	c	Expected Output
WR1	−1	5	5	Value of a is not in the range of permitted values
WR2	5	−1	5	Value of b is not in the range of permitted values
WR3	5	5	−1	Value of c is not in the range of permitted values
WR4	201	5	5	Value of a is not in the range of permitted values
WR5	5	201	5	Value of b is not in the range of permitted values
WR6	5	5	201	Value of c is not in the range of permitted values

Here is one "corner" of the cube in 3-space of the additional strong robust equivalence class test cases:

Test Case	a	b	c	Expected Output
SR1	−1	5	5	Value of a is not in the range of permitted values
SR2	5	−1	5	Value of b is not in the range of permitted values
SR3	5	5	−1	Value of c is not in the range of permitted values

(Continued)

Test Case	a	b	c	Expected Output
SR4	−1	−1	5	Values of a, b are not in the range of permitted values
SR5	5	−1	−1	Values of b, c are not in the range of permitted values
SR6	−1	5	−1	Values of a, c are not in the range of permitted values
SR7	−1	−1	−1	Values of a, b, c are not in the range of permitted values

Notice how thoroughly the expected outputs describe the invalid input values.

Equivalence class testing is clearly sensitive to the equivalence relation used to define classes. Here is another instance of craftsmanship. If we base equivalence classes on the input domain, we obtain a richer set of test cases. What are some of the possibilities for the three integers, a, b, and c? They can all be equal, exactly one pair can be equal (this can happen in three ways), or none can be equal.

$D1 = \{<a, b, c>: a = b = c\}$
$D2 = \{<a, b, c>: a = b, a \neq c\}$
$D3 = \{<a, b, c>: a = c, a \neq b\}$
$D4 = \{<a, b, c>: b = c, a \neq b\}$
$D5 = \{<a, b, c>: a \neq b, a \neq c, b \neq c\}$

As a separate question, we can apply the triangle property to see if they even constitute a triangle. (For example, the triplet <1, 4, 1> has exactly one pair of equal sides, but these sides do not form a triangle.)

$D6 = \{<a, b, c>: a \geq b + c\}$
$D7 = \{<a, b, c>: b \geq a + c\}$
$D8 = \{<a, b, c>: c \geq a + b\}$

If we wanted to be still more thorough, we could separate the "greater than or equal to" into the two distinct cases; thus, the set D6 would become:

$D6' = \{<a, b, c>: a = b + c\}$
$D6'' = \{<a, b, c>: a > b + c\}$

and similarly for D7 and D8.

6.5 Equivalence Class Test Cases for the NextDate Function

The NextDate function illustrates very well the craft of choosing the underlying equivalence relation. Recall that NextDate is a function of three variables: month, day, and year, and these have intervals of valid values defined as follows:

$M1 = \{month: 1 \leq month \leq 12\}$
$D1 = \{day: 1 \leq day \leq 31\}$
$Y1 = \{year: 1842 \leq year \leq 2042\}$

The invalid equivalence classes are:

M2 = {month: month < 1}
M3 = {month: month > 12}
D2 = {day: day < 1}
D3 = {day: day > 31}
Y2 = {year: year < 1842}
Y3 = {year: year > 2042}

Because the number of valid classes equals the number of independent variables, only one weak normal equivalence class test case occurs, and it is identical to the strong normal equivalence class test case:

Case ID	Month	Day	Year	Expected Output
WN1, SN1	6	15	1942	6/16/1942

Here is the full set of weak robust test cases:

Case ID	Month	Day	Year	Expected Output
WR1	6	15	1942	6/16/1942
WR2	−1	15	1942	Value of month not in the range 1..12
WR3	13	15	1942	Value of month not in the range 1..12
WR4	6	−1	1942	Value of day not in the range 1..31
WR5	6	32	1942	Value of day not in the range 1..31
WR6	6	15	1841	Value of year not in the range 1842..2042
WR7	6	15	2043	Value of year not in the range 1842..2042

As with the Triangle Problem, here is one "corner" of the cube in 3-space of the additional strong robust equivalence class test cases:

Case ID	Month	Day	Year	Expected Output
SR1	−1	15	1942	Value of month not in the range 1..12
SR2	6	−1	1942	Value of day not in the range 1..31
SR3	6	15	1841	Value of year not in the range 1842..2042
SR4	−1	−1	1942	Value of month not in the range 1..12 Value of day not in the range 1..31
SR5	6	−1	1841	Value of day not in therange 1..31 Value of year not in the range 1842..2042
SR6	−1	15	1841	Value of month not in the range 1..12 Value of year not in the range 1842..2042

(Continued)

Case ID	Month	Day	Year	Expected Output
SR7	–1	–1	1841	Value of month not in the range 1..12 Value of day not in the range 1..31 Value of year not in the range 1842..2042

If we more carefully choose the equivalence relation, the resulting equivalence classes will be more useful. Recall that earlier we said that the gist of the equivalence relation is that elements in a class are "treated the same way." One way to see the deficiency of the traditional approach is that the "treatment" is at the valid/invalid level. We next reduce the granularity by focusing on more specific treatment.

What must be done to an input date? If it is not the last day of a month, the NextDate function will simply increment the day value. At the end of a month, the next day is 1 and the month is incremented. At the end of a year, both the day and the month are reset to 1, and the year is incremented. Finally, the problem of leap year makes determining the last day of a month interesting. With all this in mind, we might postulate the following equivalence classes:

M1 = {month: month has 30 days}
M2 = {month: month has 31 days}
M3 = {month: month is February}
D1 = {day: $1 \leq$ day ≤ 28}
D2 = {day: day = 29}
D3 = {day: day = 30}
D4 = {day: day = 31}
Y1 = {year: year = 2000}
Y2 = {year: year is a non-century leap year}
Y3 = {year: year is a common year}

By choosing separate classes for 30- and 31-day months, we simplify the question of the last day of the month. By taking February as a separate class, we can give more attention to leap year questions. We also give special attention to day values: days in D1 are (nearly) always incremented, while days in D4 only have meaning for months in M2. Finally, we have three classes of years, the special case of the year 2000, leap years, and non-leap years. This is not a perfect set of equivalence classes, but its use will reveal many potential errors.

These classes yield the following weak equivalence class test cases. As before, the inputs are mechanically selected from the approximate middle of the corresponding class:

Case ID	Month	Day	Year	Expected Output
WN1	6	14	2000	6/15/2000
WN2	7	29	1996	7/30/1996
WN3	2	30	2002	Invalid Input Date
WN4	6	31	2000	Invalid Input Date

Mechanical selection of input values makes no consideration of our domain knowledge, thus the two impossible dates. This will always be a problem with "automatic" test case generation because all of our domain knowledge is not captured in the choice of equivalence classes. The strong normal equivalence class test cases for the revised classes are:

Case ID	Month	Day	Year	Expected Output
SN1	6	14	2000	6/15/2000
SN2	6	14	1996	6/15/1996
SN3	6	14	2002	6/15/2002
SN4	6	29	2000	6/30/2000
SN5	6	29	1996	6/30/1996
SN6	6	29	2002	6/30/2002
SN7	6	30	2000	7/1/2000
SN8	6	30	1996	7/1/1996
SN9	6	30	2002	7/2002
SN10	6	31	2000	Invalid Input Date
SN11	6	31	1996	Invalid Input Date
SN12	6	31	2002	Invalid Input Date
SN13	7	14	2000	7/15/2000
SN14	7	14	1996	7/15/1996
SN15	7	14	2002	7/15/2002
SN16	7	29	2000	7/30/2000
SN17	7	29	1996	7/30/1996
SN18	7	29	2002	7/30/2002
SN19	7	30	2000	7/31/2000
SN20	7	30	1996	7/31/1996
SN21	7	30	2002	7/31/2002
SN22	7	31	2000	8/1/2000
SN23	7	31	1996	8/1/1996
SN24	7	31	2002	8/1/2002
SN25	2	14	2000	2/15/2000
SN26	2	14	1996	2/15/1996
SN27	2	14	2002	2/15/2002

(Continued)

Case ID	Month	Day	Year	Expected Output
SN28	2	29	2000	3/1/2000
SN29	2	29	1996	3/1/1996
SN30	2	29	2002	Invalid Input Date
SN31	2	30	2000	Invalid Input Date
SN32	2	30	1996	Invalid Input Date
SN33	2	30	2002	Invalid Input Date
SN34	2	31	2000	Invalid Input Date
SN35	2	31	1996	Invalid Input Date
SN36	2	31	2002	Invalid Input Date

Moving from weak to strong normal testing raises some of the issues of redundancy that we saw with boundary value testing. The move from weak to strong, whether with normal or robust classes, always makes the presumption of independence; and this is reflected in the cross-product of the equivalence classes. Three month classes, four day classes, and three year classes result in 36 strong normal equivalence class test cases. Adding two invalid classes for each variable will result in 150 strong robust equivalence class test cases (too many to show here!).

We could also streamline our set of test cases by taking a closer look at the year classes. If we merge Y1 and Y2, and call the result the set of leap years, our 36 test cases would drop down to 24. This change suppresses special attention to considerations in the year 2000, and it also adds some complexity to the determination of which years are leap years. Balance this against how much might be learned from the present test cases.

6.6 Equivalence Class Test Cases for the completeOrder Method

In Chapter 2, the Behavior-Driven Development of the completeOrder method resulted in a decision table with three conditions and seven actions. Since the condition (c3) regarding the "Finish" option is not needed, we are left with the following decision table (Table 6.1).

Conditions c1 and c2 define equivalence classes on the Source of an order (Member or Guest) and the Price ranges:

S1 = {Member}, S2 = {Guest}, P1 = {<$200}, P2 = {$200 to $800}, and P3 = {>$800}

We have an identical set of equivalence classes to those in the discussion in Section 6.3. Figures 6.7 and 6.8 show the equivalence classes of the normal forms of Equivalence Class test cases.

The shaded cells in Tables 6.2 and 6.3 show the coverage of the normal forms of Equivalence Class test cases for the completeOrder method.

Table 6.1   Reduced Decision Table for the completeOrder Method

c1. Order by	Member			Guest
c2. Order price is	< $200	$200 to $800	> $800	—
a1. no discount	x	—	—	x
a2. 10% discount	—	x	—	—
a3. 15% discount	—	—	x	—
a4. apply any taxes	x	x	x	x
a5. apply shipping charges	x	—	—	x
a6. open Payment Screen	x	x	x	x

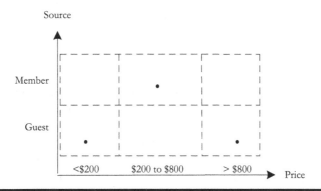

Figure 6.7   Weak Normal Equivalence Classes for completeOrder.

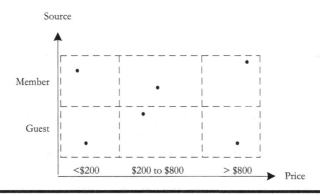

Figure 6.8   Strong Normal Equivalence Classes for completeOrder.

Table 6.2   Coverage of Weak Normal Equivalence Classes for completeOrder

c1. Order by	Member	Member	Member	Guest	Guest	Guest
c2. Order price is	< $200	$200 to $800	> $800	< $200	$200 to $800	> $800

Table 6.3   Coverage of Strong Normal Equivalence Classes for completeOrder

c1. Order by	Member	Member	Member	Guest	Guest	Guest
c2. Order price is	< $200	$200 to $800	> $800	< $200	$200 to $800	> $800

The robust forms of equivalence class testing do not apply well to the completeOrder method because the classes Member and Guest span the full set of Foodies-WishList users, and the three price ranges span all possible order prices. We could revise the < $200 class to a "normal price ($0 < orderPrice < $ 200) and negative prices, thereby creating some robustness.

6.7 "Edge Testing"

The ISTQB Advanced Level Syllabus [ISTQB 2012] describes a hybrid of boundary value analysis and equivalence class testing and gives it the name "edge testing." This need for this occurs when contiguous ranges of a particular variable constitute equivalence classes. Figure 6.2 shows three equivalence classes of valid values for x_1 and two classes for x_2. Presumably, these classes refer to variables that are "treated the same" in some application. This suggests that there may be faults near the boundaries of the classes, and edge testing will exercise these potential faults. For the example in Figure 6.2, a full set of edge testing test values are as follows:

> Normal test values for x_1: {a, a+, b-, b, b+, c-, c, c+, d-, d}
> Robust test values for x_1: {a-, a, a+, b-, b, b+, c-, c, c+, d-, d, d+}
> Normal test values for x_2: {e, e+, f-, f, f+, g-, g}
> Robust test values for x_2: {e-, e, e+, f-, f, f+, g-, g, g+}

One subtle difference is that edge test values do not include the nominal values that we had with boundary value testing. Once the sets of edge values are determined, edge testing can follow any of the four forms of equivalence class testing. The numbers of test cases obviously increase.

The set of edge testing test case values for orderPrice is:

$$\{\$0, \$1, \$199, \$200, \$201, \$799, \$800, \$801\}$$

Combining these edge test case values with the two types of users will yield 8 Weak Normal edge test cases and 16 Strong Normal edge test cases.

6.8 Reflections on Invalid Classes

When the set on which an equivalence relation holds is clearly defined, it is relatively easy to identify invalid equivalence classes. This is particularly true for the abstract example of a bounded function of two variables in Section 6.3. In the NextDate example, if we use numbers for days and months, it is similarly easy to identify invalid equivalence classes. Sets that do not conform to the definition of the set in question are good candidates for invalid equivalence classes.

More generally, the input domain (X) of some function-under-test (X->Y) may either cover the entire set of possible inputs or not. The datatype (D) used to describe X may include values outside of X, that is D is not a subset of X, thus some value d in D is not in X. Just as there may be some values in D that aren't in X for continuous functions (e.g., -1 is in D but not in X for a square root function without imaginary numbers). The opposite is true as well. Some continuous functions exist where D = X (e.g., addition has no inputs that are invalid). Robustness testing would cover invalid values inputs *iff* some d exists in D but not in X.

What about discrete sets that are defined by enumeration, rather than by a rule? Suppose we have a set C of colors:

$$C = \{red, orange, yellow, green, blue, indigo, violet\}$$

We might recognize this as the set of rainbow colors and then decide that Infra-red and Ultra-violet are members of an invalid equivalence class. But consider the set F:

$$F = \{red, white, green\}$$

Now we have little, if any, insight as to invalid equivalence classes. All Non-F? That would include Lewis Carroll's "shoes and ships - and sealing wax and cabbages and kings." There can be no general rule for this question, but we can return to the idea of craftsmanship. Even for sets defined by enumeration, there is an underlying universe of discourse and the testing craftsperson could use that insight to define useful invalid equivalence classes.

6.9 Guidelines and Observations

Now that we have gone through our two continuing examples, we conclude with some observations about, and guidelines for, equivalence class testing.

1. Obviously, the weak forms of equivalence class testing (normal or robust) are not as comprehensive as the corresponding strong forms.
2. If the implementation language is strongly typed (and invalid values cause runtime errors), it makes no sense to use the robust forms.
3. If error conditions are a high priority, the robust forms are appropriate.
4. Equivalence class testing is appropriate when input data is defined in terms of intervals and sets of discrete values. This is certainly the case when system malfunctions can occur for out-of-limit variable values.

5. Equivalence class testing is strengthened by a hybrid approach with boundary value testing, *i.e.,* edge testing. (We can "reuse" the effort made in defining the equivalence classes.)
6. Equivalence class testing is indicated when the program function is complex. In such cases, the complexity of the function can help identify useful equivalence classes, as in the NextDate function.
7. Strong equivalence class testing makes a presumption that the variables are independent, and the corresponding multiplication of test cases raises issues of redundancy. If any dependencies occur, they will often generate "error" test cases, as they did in the NextDate function. (The decision table technique in Chapter 7 resolves this problem.)
8. Several tries may be needed before the "right" equivalence relation is discovered, as we saw in the NextDate example. In other cases, there is an "obvious" or "natural" equivalence relation. When in doubt, the best bet is to try to second-guess aspects of any reasonable implementation.
9. The difference between the strong and weak forms of equivalence class testing is helpful in the distinction between progression and regression testing.

Exercises

1. Starting with the 36 strong normal equivalence class test cases for the NextDate function, revise the day classes as discussed, and then find the other nine test cases.
2. If you use a compiler for a strongly typed language, discuss how it would react to robust equivalence class test cases.
3. Compare and contrast the single/multiple fault assumption with boundary value and equivalence class testing.
4. In the completeOrder method, revise the "< $200" class to a "normal price ($0 < orderPrice < $ 200) and negative prices, and generate the corresponding Robust equivalence Class test cases. Compare and contrast this to the Edge Testing test cases of Section 6.7.
5. The spring and fall changes between standard and daylight savings time create an interesting problem for telephone bills. In the spring, this switch occurs at 2:00 a.m. on a Sunday morning (early March,) when clocks are reset to 3:00 a.m. The symmetric change takes place usually on the first Sunday in November, when the clock changes from 2:59:59 back to 2:00:00.
6. Develop equivalence classes for a long-distance telephone service function that bills calls using the following rate structure:
   ■ Call Duration < = 20 minutes charged at $0.05 per each minute or fraction of a minute
   ■ Call Duration > 20 minutes charged at $1.00 plus $0.10 per each minute or fraction of a minute in excess of 20 minutes.
   ■ Make these assumptions:
      – Chargeable time of a call begins when the called party answers and ends when the calling party disconnects.
      – Call durations of seconds are rounded up to the next larger minute.
      – No call lasts more than +30 hours.

7. Develop a set of equivalence classes for the NextWeek function. Are they significantly different from the NextDate equivalence classes?
8. Use the seven definitions of quadrilateral types (see Figure 2.1) to develop a set of equivalence classes for the Quadrilateral Program. Does it make any sense to consider the four variations of equivalence class testing? Or would it be sufficient just to test based on your equivalence classes?

References

Mosley, Daniel J., *The Handbook of MIS Application Software Testing*, Yourdon Press, Prentice Hall, Englewood Cliffs, NJ, 1993.
Myers, Glenford J., *The Art of Software Testing*, Wiley Interscience, New York, 1979.
ISTQB Advanced Level Working Party, ISTQB Advanced Level Syllabus, 2012

Chapter 7

Decision Table-Based Testing

Of all the functional testing methods, those based on decision tables are the most rigorous because of their strong logical basis. Two closely related methods are used: Cause and Effect Graphing (Elmendorf, 1973; Myers, 1979) and the decision tableau method (Mosley, 1993). These are more cumbersome to use and are fully redundant with decision tables; both are covered in Mosley (1993). For the curious, or for the sake of completeness, section 7.5 offers a short discussion of Cause and Effect Graphing.

7.1 Decision Tables

Decision tables have been used to represent and analyze complex logical relationships since the early 1960s. They are ideal for describing situations in which various combinations of actions are taken under varying sets of conditions. Some of the basic decision table terms are illustrated in Decision Table 7.1.

A decision table has four portions: the part to the left of the bold vertical line is the stub portion; to the right is the entry portion. The part above the bold horizontal

Decision Table 7.1   Sample Decision Table

	Rules							
	1	*2*	*3*	*4*	*5*	*6*	*7*	*8*
c1	T	T	T	T	F	F	F	F
c2	T	T	F	F	T	T	F	F
c3	T	F	T	F	T	F	T	F
a1	X	X			X			
a2	X					X		
a3		X			X			
a4			X	X			X	X

	Rules					
	1	*2*	*3,4*	*5*	*6*	*7,8*
c1	T	T	T	F	F	F
c2	T	T	F	T	T	F
c3	T	F	—	T	F	—
a1	X	X		X		
a2	X				X	
a3		X		X		
a4			X			X

line is the condition portion, and below is the action portion. Thus, we can refer to the condition stub, the condition entries, the action stub, and the action entries. A column in the entry portion is a rule. Rules indicate which actions, if any, are taken for the circumstances indicated in the condition portion of the rule. In the decision tables in 7.1, when conditions c1, c2, and c3 are all true, actions a1 and a2 occur. When c1 and c2 are both true and c3 is false, then actions a1 and a3 occur. The right decision table is derived from the left one as follows: notice that the action entries for rules 3 and 4 are identical. We conclude that condition c3 has no effect on the actions to be performed. The "—" entry for c3 is called a "don't care" entry. The don't care entry has two major interpretations: the condition is irrelevant, or the condition does not apply. Sometimes people will enter the "n/a" symbol for this latter interpretation.

When we have binary conditions (true/false, yes/no, 0/1), the condition portion of a decision table is a truth table (from propositional logic) that has been rotated 90°. This structure guarantees that we consider every possible combination of condition truth values. When we use decision tables for test case identification, the completeness property of a decision table guarantees a form of complete testing. Decision tables in which all the conditions are binary are called limited entry decision tables (LEDT). If conditions have several values, the resulting tables are called extended entry decision tables (MEDT). When both limited entry and mixed entry conditions are present, we have a mixed entry decision table (MEDT). These distinctions will become important when we use rule counting to identify complete decision tables. Decision tables are deliberately declarative (as opposed to imperative); no particular order is implied by the conditions, and selected actions do not occur in any particular order.

7.2 Decision Table Techniques

To identify test cases with decision tables, we interpret conditions as inputs and actions as outputs. Sometimes conditions end up referring to equivalence classes of inputs, and actions refer to major functional processing portions of the item tested. The rules are then interpreted as test cases. Because the decision table can mechanically be forced to be complete, we have some assurance that we will have a comprehensive set of test cases. Several techniques that produce decision tables are more useful to testers. One helpful style is to add an action to show when a rule is logically impossible. In the decision table in 7.2, we see examples of don't care entries and impossible rule usage. If the integers a, b, and c do not constitute a triangle, we do not even care about possible equalities, as indicated in the first rule. In rules 3, 4, and6, if two pairs of integers are equal, by transitivity, the third pair must be equal so these rules impossible. Rules 2 and 9 describe equilateral and scalene triangles, and rules 5, 7, and 8 describe three ways a triangle can be isosceles.

The Decision Table 7.3 illustrates another consideration: the choice of conditions can greatly expand the size of a decision table. Here, we have expanded the old condition (c1: a, b, c form a triangle?) to a more detailed view of the three inequalities of the triangle property. If any one of these fails, the three integers do not constitute sides of a triangle.

We could expand this still further because there are two ways an inequality could fail: one side could equal the sum of the other two, or it could be strictly greater.

When conditions refer to equivalence classes, decision tables have a characteristic appearance. Conditions in the decision table in 7.4 are from the NextDate Problem;

Decision Table 7.2 Decision Table for the Triangle Problem

	1	2	3	4	5	6	7	8	9
c1: a, b, c form a triangle?	F	T	T	T	T	T	T	T	T
c2: a = b?	—	T	T	T	T	F	F	F	F
c3: a = c?	—	T	T	F	F	T	T	F	F
c4: b = c?	—	T	F	T	F	T	F	T	F
a1: Not a triangle	X								
a2: Scalene									X
a3: Isosceles					X		X	X	
a4: Equilateral		X							
a5: Impossible			X	X		X			

Decision Table 7.3 Refined Decision Table for the Triangle Problem

c1: a<b+c?	F	T	T	T	T	T	T	T	T	T	T
c2: b<a+c?	—	F	T	T	T	T	T	T	T	T	T
c3: c<a+b?	—	—	F	T	T	T	T	T	T	T	T
c4: a = b?	—	—	—	T	T	T	T	F	F	F	F
c5: a = c?	—	—	—	T	T	F	F	T	T	F	F
c6: b = c?	—	—	—	T	F	T	F	T	F	T	F
a1: Not a triangle	X	X	X								
a2: Scalene											X
a3: Isosceles							X		X	X	
a4: Equilateral				X							
a5: Impossible					X	X		X			

they refer to the mutually exclusive possibilities for the month variable. Because a month is in exactly one equivalence class, we cannot ever have a rule in which two entries are true. In this case, the don't care entries (—) really mean "must be false."

Use of don't care entries has a subtle effect on the way in which complete decision tables are recognized. For limited entry decision table with n conditions exist, there must be 2^n independent rules. When don't care entries really indicate that the condition is irrelevant, we can develop a rule count as follows: rules in which no don't care entries occur count as one rule, and each don't care entry in a rule doubles the count of that rule. The rule counts for the decision table in Decision Table 7.3 are shown in Decision Table 7.4. Notice that the sum of the rule counts is 64 (as it should be).

If we applied this simplistic algorithm to the decision table in 7.5, we get the rule counts shown in Decision Table 7.6. We should only have eight rules, so we clearly

Decision Table 7.4   Decision Table for Decision Table 7.3 with Rule Counts

c1: a<b+c?	F	T	T	T	T	T	T	T	T	T	T
c2: b<a+c?	—	F	T	T	T	T	T	T	T	T	T
c3: c<a+b?	—	—	F	T	T	T	T	T	T	T	T
c4: a = b?	—	—	—	T	T	T	T	F	F	F	F
c5: a = c?	—	—	—	T	T	F	F	T	T	F	F
c6: b = c?	—	—	—	T	F	T	F	T	F	T	F
Rule count	32	16	8	1	1	1	1	1	1	1	1
a1: Not a triangle	X	X	X								
a2: Scalene											X
a3: Isosceles								X		X	X
a4: Equilateral				X							
a5: Impossible					X	X		X			

Decision Table 7.5   Decision Table with Mutually Exclusive Conditions

	R1	R2	R3
c1: month in M1?	T	—	—
c2: month in M2?	—	T	—
c3: month in M3?	—	—	T
a1			

Decision Table 7.6   Rule Counts for a Decision Table with Mutually Exclusive Conditions

	R1	R2	R3
c1: month in M1?	T	—	—
c2: month in M2?	—	T	—
c3: month in M3?	—	—	T
Rule count	4	4	4
a1			

have a problem. To see where the problem lies, we expand each of the three rules, replacing the "—" entries with the T and F possibilities, as shown in Decision Table 7.7.

If we applied this simplistic algorithm to the Decision Table in 7.5, we get the rule counts shown in Decision Table 7.6. We should only have eight rules, so we clearly have a problem. To see where the problem lies, we expand each of the three rules, replacing the "—" entries with the T and F possibilities, as shown in Decision Table 7.7.

Decision Table 7.7 Expanded rules in Decision Table 7.6

Conditions	Rule 1				Rule 2				Rule 3			
expanded	a	b	c	d	e	f	g	h	i	j	k	l
c1: in M1	**T**	**T**	**T**	**T**	T	T	F	F	T	T	F	F
c2: in M2	T	T	F	F	**T**	**T**	**T**	**T**	T	F	T	F
c3: in M3	T	F	T	F	T	F	T	F	**T**	**T**	**T**	**T**
Rules	1	1	1	1	1	1	1	1	1	1	1	1
a1.	X	X	X	—	X	X	X	—	X	X	X	—

Notice that we have three rules in which all entries are T: rules 1.1, 2.1, and 3.1. We also have two rules with T, T, F entries: rules 1.2 and 2.2. Similarly, rules 1.3 and 3.2 are identical; so are rules 2.3 and 3.3. If we delete the repetitions, we end up with seven rules; the missing rule is the one in which all conditions are false. The result of this process is shown in Decision Table 7.8. The impossible rules are also shown.

The ability to recognize (and develop) complete decision tables puts us in a powerful position with respect to redundancy and inconsistency. The decision table in Decision Table 7.9 is redundant—three conditions and nine rules exist. (Rule 9 is identical to rule 4.) Notice that the action entries in rule 9 are identical to those in rules 1 – 4. If the actions in a redundant rule are identical to the corresponding part

Decision Table 7.8 Mutually Exclusive Conditions with Impossible Rules

Rules	a	b	c	d	g	h	l	
c1: in M1	**T**	**T**	**T**	**T**	F	F	F	F
c2: in M2	T	T	F	F	**T**	**T**	F	F
c3: in M3	T	F	T	F	T	F	**T**	F
Rule count	1	1	1	1	1	1	1	1
a1.	X	X	X	—	X	—	—	X

Decision Table 7.9 A Redundant Decision Table

Rules	1–4	5	6	7	8	9
c1	T	F	F	F	F	T
c2	—	T	T	F	F	F
c3	—	T	F	T	F	F
a1	X	X	X	—	—	X
a2	—	X	X	X	—	—
a3	X	—	X	X	X	X

Decision Table 7.10 An Inconsistent Decision Table

Rules	1–4	5	6	7	8	9
c1	T	F	F	F	F	T
c2	–	T	T	F	F	F
c3	–	T	F	T	F	F
a1	X	X	X	–	–	–
a2	–	X	X	X	–	X
a3	X	–	X	X	X	–

of the decision table, we do not have much of a problem. If the action entries are different, as in Decision Table 7.10, we have a bigger problem.

The ability to recognize (and develop) complete decision tables puts us in a powerful position with respect to redundancy and inconsistency. The decision table in Decision Table 7.9 is redundant—three conditions and nine rules exist. (Rule 9 is identical to what would be rule 4.) Notice that the action entries in rule 9 are identical to those in rule 4. If the actions in a redundant rule are identical to the corresponding part of the decision table, we do not have much of a problem. If the action entries are different, as in Decision Table 7.10, we have a bigger problem.

If the decision table in Decision Table 7.10 were to process a transaction in which c1 is true and both c2 and c3 are false, both rules 4 and 9 apply. We can make two observations:

1. Rules 4 and 9 are inconsistent.
2. The decision table is nondeterministic.

Rules 4 and 9 are inconsistent because the action sets are different. The whole table is nondeterministic because there is no way to decide whether to apply rule 4 or rule 9. The bottom line for testers is that care should be taken when don't care entries are used in a decision table.

7.3 Test Cases for the Triangle Problem

Using the decision table for the Triangle Problem in Decision Table 7.3, we obtain 11 functional test cases: three impossible cases, three ways to fail the triangle property, one way to get an equilateral triangle, one way to get a scalene triangle, and three ways to get an isosceles triangle (see Decision Table 7.11). We still need to provide actual values for the variables in the conditions, but we cannot do this for the impossible rules. If we extended the decision table to show both ways to fail an inequality, we would pick up three more test cases (where one side is exactly the sum of the other two). Some judgment is required in this because of the exponential growth of rules. In this case, we would end up with many more don't care entries and more impossible rules.

Decision Table 7.11   Test Cases from Decision Table 7.3

Case ID	a	b	c	Expected Output
DT1	4	1	2	Not a Triangle
DT2	1	4	2	Not a Triangle
DT3	1	2	4	Not a Triangle
DT4	5	5	5	Equilateral
DT5	?	?	?	Impossible
DT6	?	?	?	Impossible
DT7	2	2	3	Isosceles
DT8	?	?	?	Impossible
DT9	2	3	2	Isosceles
DT10	3	2	2	Isosceles
DT11	3	4	5	Scalene

7.4 Test Cases for the NextDate Function

The NextDate function was chosen because it illustrates the problem of dependencies in the input domain. This makes it a perfect example for decision table-based testing, because decision tables can highlight such dependencies. Recall that, in Chapter 6, we identified equivalence classes in the input domain of the NextDate function. One of the limitations we found in Chapter 6 was that indiscriminate selection of input values from the equivalence classes resulted in impossible test cases, such as finding the next date to June 31, 1842. The problem stems from the presumption that the variables are independent. If they are, a Cartesian product of the classes makes sense. When logical dependencies exist among variables in the input domain, these dependencies are lost (suppressed is better) in a Cartesian product. The decision table format lets us emphasize such dependencies using the notion of the "impossible" action to denote impossible combinations of conditions (which are actually impossible rules). In this section, we will make three tries at a decision table formulation of the NextDate function.

7.4.1 First Try

Identifying appropriate conditions and actions presents an opportunity for craftsmanship. In Decision Table 7.12 we start with a set of equivalence classes close to the one we used in Chapter 6.

M1 = {month : month has 30 days}
M2 = {month : month has 31 days}
M3 = {month : month is February}

Decision Table 7.12   First Try Decision Table with 256 Rules (232 impossible rules)

Conditions/Rules	1	2	3	4	5	6	7	8
c1: month in M1?	T	T	T	T	T	T	T	T
c2: month in M2?	—	—	—	—	—	—	—	—
c3: month in M3?	—	—	—	—	—	—	—	—
c4: day in D1?	T	T	—	—	—	—	—	—
c5: day in D2?	—	—	T	T	—	—	—	—
c6: day in D3?	—	—	—	—	T	T	—	—
c7: day in D4?	—	—	—	—	—	—	T	T
c8: year in Y1?	T	F	T	F	T	F	T	F
a1: impossible	—	—	—	—	—	—	—	—
a2: next date	X	X	X	X	X	X	X	X

$$D1 = \{day : 1 \leq day \leq 28\}$$
$$D2 = \{day : day = 29\}$$
$$D3 = \{day : day = 30\}$$
$$D4 = \{day : day = 31\}$$
$$Y1 = \{year : year \text{ is a leap year}\}$$
$$Y2 = \{year : year \text{ is not a leap year}\}$$

The corresponding limited entry decision table will have 256 rules (we can use T, F entries for condition c8: year in Y1?). There will be 24 useful rules; the first eight are shown in Decision Table 7.12.

7.4.2 Second Try

If we focus on the leap year aspect of the NextDate function, we could use the set of equivalence classes as they were in Chapter 6. These classes have a Cartesian product that contains 36 triples, with several that are impossible.

To illustrate another decision table technique, this time we will develop an extended entry decision table, and we will take a closer look at the action stub. In making an extended entry decision table, we must ensure that the equivalence classes form a true partition of the input domain. (Recall from Chapter 3 that a partition is a set of disjoint subsets where the union is the entire set.) If there were any "overlaps" among the rule entries, we would have a redundant case in which more than one rule could be satisfied. Here, Y2 is the set of years between 1842 and 2042, evenly divisible by four excluding the year 2000.

$$M1 = \{month : month \text{ has 30 days}\}$$
$$M2 = \{month : month \text{ has 31 days}\}$$
$$M3 = \{month : month \text{ is February}\}$$

D1 = {day : 1 ≤ day ≤ 28}
D2 = {day : day = 29}
D3 = {day : day = 30}
D4 = {day : day = 31}
Y1 = {year : year = 2000}
Y2 = {year : year is a non-century leap year}
Y3 = {year : year is a common year}

In a sense, we could argue that we have a "gray box" technique, because we take a closer look at the NextDate problem statement. In order to produce the next date of a given date, only five possible actions are needed: incrementing and resetting the day (day++ and day = 1), incrementing and resetting the month (month++ and month = 1), and incrementing the year (year++). (We will not let time go backward by resetting the year.) To follow the metaphor, we still cannot see inside the implementation box—the implementation could be a table look-up. (See Decision Tables 7.13a and 7.13b)

These conditions would result in a decision table with 36 rules that correspond to the Cartesian product of the equivalence classes. Combining rules with don't care entries yields the two-part decision table in Decision Table 7.13, which has 16 rules. We still have the problem with five logically impossible rules, but this formulation helps us identify the expected outputs of a test case. If you complete the action entries in this table, you will find some cumbersome problems with December (in rule 8) and other problems with Feb. 28 in rules 8, 9, and 11. We need more precise information about the day classes.

Decision Table 7.13a Second Try Decision Table with 36 Rules (first half)

	1	2	3	4	5	6	7	8
c1: month in	M1	M1	M1	M1	M2	M2	M2	M2
c2: day in	D1	D2	D3	D4	D1	D2	D3	D4
c3: year in	—	—	—	—	—	—	—	—
Rule count	3	3	3	3	3	3	3	3
a1: impossible				X				
a2: day++	X	X			X	X	X	
a3: day = 1			X					X
a4: month++			X					?
a5: month = 1								?
a6: year++								?

Decision Table 7.13b   Second Try Decision Table with 36 Rules (second half)

	9	10	11	12	13	14	15	16
c1: month in	M3	M3	M3	M3	M3	M3	M3	M3
c2: day in	D1	D1	D1	D2	D2	D2	D3	D4
c3: year in	Y1	Y2	Y3	Y1	Y2	Y3	—	—
Rule count	1	1	1	1	1	1	3	3
a1: impossible				X		X	X	X
a2: day++	X	X	?					
a3: day = 1			?		X			
a4: month++	?		?		X			
a5: month = 1								
a6: year++								

7.4.3 Third Try

We can clear up the end-of-year considerations with a third set of equivalence classes. This time, we are very specific about days and months, and we revert to the simpler leap year or common year condition of the first try—so the year 2000 gets no special attention. (We could do a fourth try, showing year equivalence classes as in the second try, but by now you get the point.)

> M1 = {month : month has 30 days}
> M2 = {month : month has 31 days except December}
> M3 = {month : month is December}
> M4 = {month : month is February}
> D1 = {day : 1 ≤ day ≤ 27}
> D2 = {day : day = 28}
> D3 = {day : day = 29}
> D4 = {day : day = 30}
> D5 = {day : day = 31}
> Y1 = {year : year is a leap year}
> Y2 = {year : year is a common year}

The Cartesian product of these contains 40 elements. The result of combining rules with don't care entries is given in Decision Table 7.14; it has 22 rules, compared with the 36 of the second try. Recall from Chapter 1 the question of whether a large set of test cases is necessarily better than a smaller set. Here, we have a 22-rule decision table that gives a clearer picture of the NextDate function than does the 36-rule decision table. The first five rules deal with 30-day months; notice that the leap year considerations are irrelevant. The next two sets of rules (6 – 15) deal with 31-day

Decision Table 7.14a   Decision Table for the NextDate Function (Rules 1 – 10)

	1	2	3	4	5	6	7	8	9	10
c1: month in	M1	M1	M1	M1	M1	M2	M2	M2	M2	M2
c2: day in	D1	D2	D3	D4	D5	D1	D2	D3	D4	D5
c3: year in	—	—	—	—	—	—	—	—	—	—
a1: impossible					X					
a2: day++	X	X	X			X	X	X	X	
a3: day = 1				X						X
a4: month++				X						X
a5: month = 1										
a6: year++										

Decision Table 7.14b   Decision Table for the NextDate Function (Rules 11 – 22)

	11	12	13	14	15	16	17	18	19	20	21	22
c1: month in	M3	M3	M3	M3	M3	M4	M4	M4	M4	M4	M4	M4
c2: day in	D1	D2	D3	D4	D5	D1	D2	D2	D3	D3	D4	D5
c3: year in	—	—	—	—	—	—	Y1	Y2	Y1	Y2	—	—
a1: impossible										X	X	X
a2: day++	X	X	X	X		X	X					
a3: day = 1					X			X	X			
a4: month++								X	X			
a5: month = 1					X							
a6: year++					X							

months, where rules 6 – 10 deal with months other than December and rules 11 – 15 deal with December. No impossible rules are listed in this portion of the decision table, although there is some redundancy that an efficient tester might question. Eight of the ten rules simply increment the day. Would we really require eight separate test cases for this subfunction? Probably not; but note the insights we can get from the decision table. Finally, the last seven rules focus on February in common and leap years.

The decision table in Decision Table 7.14 is the basis for the source code for the NextDate function in Chapter 2. As an aside, this example shows how good testing can improve programming. All the decision table analysis could have been done during the detailed design of the NextDate function.

We can use the algebra of decision tables to further simplify these 22 test cases. If the action sets of two rules in a limited entry decision table are identical, there must be at least one condition that allows two rules to be combined with a don't care entry. This is the decision table equivalent of the "treated the same" guideline that we used to identify equivalence classes. In a sense, we are identifying equivalence classes of rules. For example, rules 1, 2, and 3 involve day classes D1, D2, and D3 for 30-day months (call this class D6). These can be combined similarly for day classes D1, D2, D3, and D4 (call this class D7) in the 31-day month rules, and D4 and D5 for February. The result is in Decision Table 7.15.

The corresponding test cases are shown in Decision Table 7.16. The progression across our three tries is exactly how decision table based testing should work.

Decision Table 7.15a   Reduced Decision Table for the NextDate Function

	1–3	4	5	6–9	10	11–14	15
c1: month in	M1	M1	M1	M2	M2	M3	M3
c2: day in	D6	D4	D5	D7	D5	D7	D5
c3: year in	—	—	—	—	—	—	—
a1: impossible			X				
a2: day++	X			X		X	
a3: day = 1		X			X		X
a4: month++		X			X		
a5: month = 1							X
a6: year++							X

Decision Table 7.15b   Reduced Decision Table for the NextDate Function

	16	17	18	19	20	21	22
c1: month in	M4	M4	M4	M4	M4	M4	M4
c2: day in	D1	D2	D2	D3	D3	D4	D5
c3: year in	—	Y1	Y2	Y1	Y2	—	—
a1: impossible					X	X	X
a2: day++	X	X					
a3: day = 1			X	X			
a4: month++			X	X			
a5: month = 1							
a6: year++							

Decision Table 7.16 Test Cases for NextDate

Test Case	Columns	Month	Day	Year	Expected Output
1	1–3	4	15	2018	4/16/2018
2	4	4	30	2018	5/1/2018
3	5	4	31	2018	Invalid Date
4	6–9	1	15	2018	1/16/2018
5	10	1	31	2018	2/1/2018
6	11–14	12	15	2018	12/16/2018
7	15	12	31	2018	1/1/2019
8	16	2	15	2018	2/16/2018
9	17	2	28	2020	2/29/2020
10	18	2	28	2018	3/1/2018
11	19	2	29	2020	3/1/2020
12	20	2	29	2018	Invalid Date
13	21	2	30	2018	Invalid Date
14	22	2	31	2018	Invalid Date

We seldom get thigs right on our first attempt. Going from the First Try (256 Rules of which 232 are impossible) to the Second Try (36 rules of which 10 are impossible), we arrive at the Third Try, with 22 rules of which 4 are impossible. By the third try, we are left with a very small set of test cases and we are confident of their completeness.

7.5 Cause and Effect Graphing

In the early years of computing, the software community borrowed many ideas from the hardware community. Sometimes this worked well, but other times, the problems of software just did not fit well with established hardware techniques. Cause and Effect Graphing is a good example of this. The base hardware concept was the practice of describing circuits composed of discrete components with AND, OR, and NOT gates. There was usually an input side of a circuit diagram, and the flow of inputs through the various components could be generally traced from left to right. With this, the effects of hardware faults such as stuck-at-one/zero could be traced to the output side. This greatly facilitated circuit testing.

Cause and effect graphs attempt to follow this pattern, by showing unit inputs on the left side of a drawing, and using AND, OR, Exclusive OR (EOR) and NOT "gates" to express the flow of data across processing stages of a unit. Figure 7.1 shows the basic Cause and Effect Graph structures. They can be augmented by less used operations: Identity, Masks, Requires, and Only One.

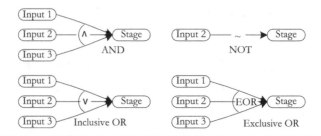

Figure 7.1 Cause and effect graphing operations.

The most that can be learned from a Cause and Effect Graph is that, if there is a problem at an output, the path(s) back to the inputs that affected the output can be retraced. There is little support for actually identifying test cases.

7.6 Guidelines and Observations

As with the other testing techniques, decision table-based testing works well for some applications (such as NextDate) and is not worth the trouble for others. Not surprisingly, the situations in which it works well are those in which a lot of decision making takes place (such as the Triangle Problem), and those in which important logical relationships exist among input variables (the NextDate function).

1. The decision table technique is indicated for applications characterized by any of the following:
   - Prominent if-then-else logic
   - Logical relationships among input variables
   - Calculations involving subsets of the input variables
   - Cause-and-effect relationships between inputs and outputs
   - High cyclomatic complexity (see Chapter 9)
2. Decision tables do not scale up very well (a limited entry table with n conditions has 2n rules.) There are several ways to deal with this — use extended entry decision tables, algebraically simplify tables, "factor" large tables into smaller ones, and look for repeating patterns of condition entries. Try factoring the extended entry table for NextDate (Decision Table 7.14).
3. As with other techniques, iteration helps. The first set of conditions and actions you identify may be unsatisfactory. Use it as a stepping-stone, and gradually improve on it until you are satisfied with a decision table.

Exercises

1. Develop a decision table for the NextWeek function. Compare the results with those for boundary value testing in the Chapter 5 exercises, and with those for equivalence class testing in the chapter 6 exercises.
2. Develop a decision table for the Quadrilateral Problem. Compare the results with those for boundary value testing in the Chapter 5 exercises, and with those for equivalence class testing in the chapter 6 exercises.

3. Develop a decision table for the Windshield Wiper Controller (see Chapter 2 exercises).

4. Discuss how well decision table testing deals with the multiple fault assumption.

5. Develop decision table test cases for the time change problem (Chapter 6, Problem 6.)

6. In 2010, the Michigan state legislature changed the retirement plan for public school teachers. Retirement pension salary of a Michigan public school teacher is a percentage of the average of their salary for last three years of teaching. Normally, the number of years of teaching service is the percentage multiplier. To encourage senior teachers to retire early, the Michigan legislature enacted the following incentive structure:

   ■ Teachers must apply for the incentive before June 11, 2010.

   ■ Teachers who are currently eligible to retire (age >= 63) shall have a multiplier of 1.6% on their salary up to, and including $90,000, and 1.5% on compensation in excess of $90,000.

   ■ Teachers who meet the 80 total years of age plus years of teaching shall have a multiplier of 1.55% on their salary up to and including $90,000 and 1.5% on compensation in excess of $90,000.

   Make a decision table to describe the retirement pension policy, be sure to consider the retirement eligibility criteria carefully. What are the compensation multipliers for a person who is currently 64 with 20 years of teaching whose salary is $95,000?

References

Elmendorf, William R., Cause–Effect Graphs in Functional Testing, *IBM System Development Division, Poughkeepsie, NY*, TR-00.2487, 1973.

Mosley, Daniel J., *The Handbook of MIS Application Software Testing*, Yourdon Press, Prentice Hall, Englewood Cliffs, NJ, 1993.

Myers, Glenford J., *The Art of Software Testing*, Wiley Interscience, New York, 1979.

Chapter 8

Code-Based Testing

The distinguishing characteristic of code-based testing methods is that, as the name implies, they are all based on the source code of the program tested, and not on the specification. Because of this absolute basis, code-based testing methods are very amenable to rigorous definitions, mathematical analysis, and useful measurement. In this chapter, we examine the two most common forms of path testing. The technology behind these has been available since the mid-1970s, and the originators of these methods now have companies that market very successful tools that implement the techniques. Both techniques start with the program graph; we repeat the improved definition from Chapter 4 here.

8.1 Program Graphs

Definition

Given a program written in an imperative programming language, its *program graph* is a directed graph in which nodes are statement fragments, and edges represent flow of control. (A complete statement is a "default" statement fragment.)

If i and j are nodes in the program graph, an edge exists from node i to node j if and only if the statement fragment corresponding to node j can be executed immediately after the statement fragment corresponding to node i.

Deriving a program graph from a given program is an easy process. It is illustrated here with four of the basic structured programming constructs (Figure 8.1), and also with our Java implementation of the triangle program from Chapter 2. Line numbers refer to statements and statement fragments. An element of judgment can be used here: sometimes it is convenient to keep a fragment as a separate node, other times it seems better to include this with another portion of a statement. For example: it is visually useful to use an end brace (}) as a node.

We also need to decide whether to associate nodes with non-executable statements such as variable and type declarations; here we do not. Figure 8.1 shows program graph possibilities for the basic constructs of structured programming.

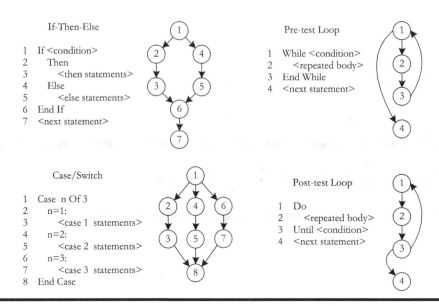

Figure 8.1 Program graphs of four structured pseudo-code programming constructs.

A program graph of the third version of the Triangle Problem (see Chapter 2) is given in Figure 8.2.

Nodes 1 through 5 are a sequence, nodes 6 through 23 contain several nested if-then-else constructs. Nodes 1 and 24 are the program source and sink nodes, corresponding to the single entry, single-exit criteria. No loops exist, so this is a directed acyclic graph. The importance of program graphs is that program executions correspond to paths from the source to the sink nodes. Because test cases force the execution of some such program path, we now have a very explicit description of the relationship between a test case and the part of the program it exercises. We also have an elegant, theoretically respectable way to deal with the potentially large number of execution paths in a program.

There are detractors of code-based testing. Figure 8.3 is a graph of a simple (but unstructured!) program; it is typical of the kind of example detractors use to show the computational difficulty of completely testing even simple programs. (This example first appeared in [Schach, 1993].) In this program, five paths lead from node B to node F in the interior of the loop. If the loop may have up to 18 repetitions, some 4.77 trillion distinct program execution paths exist. (Actually, it is 4,768,371,582,030 paths.) The detractor's argument is a good example of the logical Fallacy of Extension—take a situation, extend it to an extreme, show that the extreme supports your point, and then apply it back to the original question. The detractors miss the point of code-based testing—later in this chapter, we will see how this enormous number can be reduced, with good reasons, to a more manageable size.

8.2 DD-Paths

The best-known form of code-based testing is based on a construct known as a decision-to-decision path (DD-Path) (Miller, 1977). For "modern" programming languages, Miller's DD-Paths are similar to "blocks" with no internal decisions. In Java, a multi-line block of code is surrounded by curly braces ({}) and is indented. The name

```
1    public static int triangle3(int a, int b, int c) {
1
1      boolean c1, c2, c3, isATriangle;
1
1      // Step 1: Validate Input
2      c1 = (1 <= a) && (a <= 300);
3      c2 = (1 <= b) && (b <= 300);
4      c3 = (1 <= c) && (c <= 300);
5
5      int triangleType = INVALID;
6      if(!c1 || !c2 || !c3)
7        triangleType = OUT_OF_RANGE;
8      else {
8
8        // Step 2: Is A Triangle?
9        if((a < b + c) && (b < a + c) && (c < a + b))
10         isATriangle = true;
11       else
12         isATriangle = false;
12
12       // Step 3: Determine Triangle Type
13       if(isATriangle) {
14         if((a == b) && (b == c))
15           triangleType = EQUILATERAL;
16         else if((a != b) && (a != c) && (b != c))
17           triangleType = SCALENE;
18         else
19           triangleType = ISOSELES;
20       } else
21         triangleType = INVALID;
22     }
23
23     return triangleType;
24   }
```

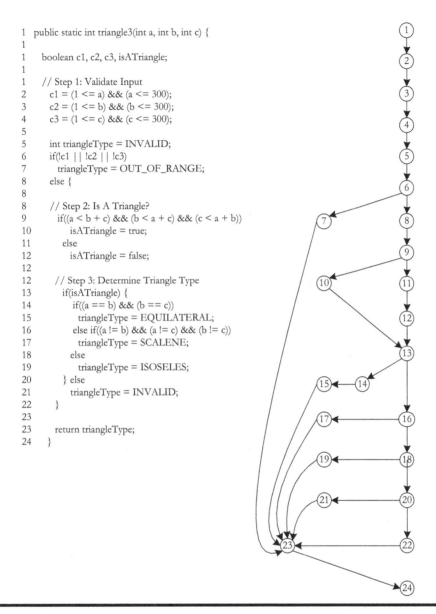

Figure 8.2   Program graph of the triangle program.

refers to a sequence of statements that, in Miller's words, begins with the "outway" of a decision statement and ends with the "inway" of the next decision statement. Miller's original definition works well for languages like COBOL and FORTRAN, because decision-making statements use statement labels to refer to target statements. With modern languages (e.g., Pascal, Ada®, C, Visual Basic, Java), the notion of statement fragments resolves the difficulty of applying Miller's original definition. Otherwise we end up with program graphs in which some statements are members of more than one DD-Path. In the ISTQB literature, and also in Great Britain, the DD-Path concept is known as a "Linear Code Sequence And Jump" and is abbreviated by the acronym LCSAJ. Same idea, longer name, hard to pronounce.

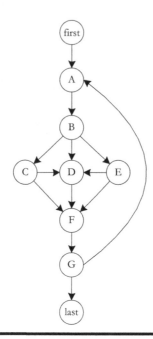

Figure 8.3   Trillions of paths.

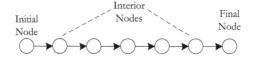

Figure 8.4   A chain of nodes in a directed graph.

Definition

A *chain* in a directed graph is a sequence of nodes in which the initial node has an. indegree > = 0, and the final node has an outdegree > = 0. Every internal node has indegree = outdegree = 1. In a degenerate case, a chain could consist of a single node.

No internal branches occur in such a sequence, so the corresponding code is like a row of dominoes lined up so that when the first falls, all the rest in the sequence fall. (See Figure 8.4.)

Definition

A *DD-Path* is a chain of statement fragments.

Definition

Given a program written in an imperative language, its *DD-Path graph* is the directed graph in which nodes are DD-Paths of its program graph, and edges represent control flow between successor DD-Paths.

In effect, a DD-Path graph is a form of condensation graph (see Chapter 4); in this condensation, 2-connected components are collapsed into individual nodes. DD-Path

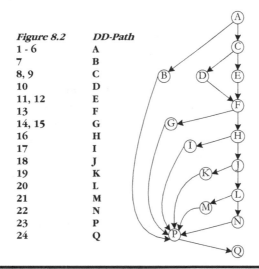

Figure 8.2	*DD-Path*
1 - 6	A
7	B
8, 9	C
10	D
11, 12	E
13	F
14, 15	G
16	H
17	I
18	J
19	K
20	L
21	M
22	N
23	P
24	Q

Figure 8.5   DD-Path graph of the triangle program in Figure 8.2.

graphs are most useful for computation intensive programs. Since the DD-Paths in Figure 8.5 are very short (only one or two actual program nodes), Figure 8.5 is not much of a condensation of Figure 8.2.

8.3 Code Coverage Metrics

The *raison d'être* of DD-Paths is that they enable very precise descriptions of the extent to which a set of test cases covers the corresponding source code. Recall (from Chapters 5, 6, and 7) that one of the fundamental limitations of specification-based testing is that it is impossible to know either the extent of redundancy or the possibility of gaps corresponding to the way a set of functional test cases exercises a program. Back in Chapter 1, we had a Venn diagram showing relationships among specified, programmed, and tested behaviors. Code coverage metrics express the extent to which a set of test cases covers (or exercises) the code of a program.

8.3.1 Program Graph-Based Coverage Metrics

Given a program graph, we can define the following set of test coverage metrics. We will use them to relate to other published sets of coverage metrics.

Definition

Given a set of test cases for a program, they constitute *node coverage* if, when executed on the program, every node in the program graph is traversed. Denote this level of coverage as G_{node}, where the G stands for program graph.

Since nodes correspond to statement fragments, this guarantees that every statement fragment is executed by some test case. If we are careful about defining statement fragment nodes, this also guarantees that statement fragments that are outcomes of a decision-making statement are executed.

Definition

Given a set of test cases for a program, they constitute *edge coverage* if, when executed on the program, every edge in the program graph is traversed. Denote this level of coverage as G_{edge}.

The difference between G_{node} and G_{edge} is that, in the latter, we are assured that all outcomes of a decision-making statement are executed. In our Triangle Problem (see Figure 8.2), nodes 9, 10, 11, 12, and 13 are a complete if-then-else statement. If we required nodes to correspond to full statements, we could execute just one of the decision alternatives and satisfy the statement coverage criterion. Because we allow statement fragments, it is natural to divide such a statement into separate nodes (the condition test, the True outcome, and the False outcome. Doing so results in predicate outcome coverage. Whether or not our convention is followed, these coverage metrics require that we find a set of test cases such that, when executed, every node of the program graph is traversed at least once.

Definition

Given a set of test cases for a program, they constitute *chain coverage* if, when executed on the program, every chain of length greater than or equal to 2 in the program graph is traversed. Denote this level of coverage as G_{chain}.

The G_{chain} coverage is the same as node coverage in the DD-Path graph that corresponds to the given program graph. Since DD-Paths are important in E. F. Miller's original formulation of test covers (defined in Section 8.3.2), we now have a clear connection between purely program graph constructs and Miller's test coverage metrics.

Definition

Given a set of test cases for a program, they constitute *path coverage* if, when executed on the program, every path from the source node to the sink node in the program graph is traversed. Denote this level of coverage as G_{path}.

This coverage is open to severe limitations when there are loops in a program (as in Figure 8.3). E. F. Miller partially anticipated this when he postulated metrics for loop coverage that covered a subset of paths from source to sink nodes. Referring to Chapter 4, observe that every loop in a program graph represents a set of strongly connected (i.,e., 3-connected) nodes. To deal with the size implications of loops, we simply exercise every loop with two test cases—one to traverse the loop, and the other to exit the loop, and then form the condensation graph of the original program graph, which must be a directed acyclic graph.

8.3.2 E. F. Miller's Coverage Metrics

Several widely accepted test/code coverage metrics are used; most of those in Table 8.1 are due to the early work of E.F. Miller who used the term "test coverage" (Miller, 1977). Having an organized view of the extent to which a program is tested makes it possible to sensibly manage the testing process. Most quality organizations now expect the C_1 metric (DD-Path coverage) as the minimum acceptable level of test coverage.

These coverage metrics form a lattice in which some are equivalent, and some are implied by others. The importance of the lattice is that there are always fault types

Table 8.1 Miller's Test Coverage Metrics

Metric	Description of Coverage
C_0	Every statement
C_1	Every DD-Path
C_{1p}	Every predicate to each outcome
C_2	C_1 coverage + loop coverage
C_d	C_1 coverage + Every dependent pair of DD-Paths
C_{MCC}	Multiple condition coverage
C_{ik}	Every program path that contains up to k repetitions of a loop (usually $k = 2$)
C_{stat}	"Statistically significant" fraction of paths
C_∞	All possible execution paths

that can be revealed at one level and can escape detection by less thorough levels of testing. E. F. Miller observes that when DD-Path coverage is attained by a set of test cases, roughly 85% of all faults are revealed (Miller, 1991). The test coverage metrics in Table 8.1 tell us what to test but not how to test it. In this section, we take a closer look at techniques that exercise source code. We must keep an important distinction in mind: Miller's test coverage metrics are based on program graphs in which nodes are full statements, whereas our formulation allows statement fragments (which can be entire statements to be nodes).

8.3.2.1 Statement Testing

Because our formulation of program graphs allows statement fragments to be individual nodes, Miller's C_0 metric is subsumed by our G_{node} metric.

Statement coverage is generally viewed as the bare minimum. If some statements have not been executed by the set of test cases, there is clearly a gap in the test coverage. Although less adequate than DD-Path coverage, the statement coverage metric (C_0) is still widely accepted: it is mandated by ANSI Standard 187B and has been used successfully throughout IBM since the mid-1970s.

8.3.2.2 DD-Path Testing

When every DD-Path is traversed (the C_1 metric), we know that each predicate outcome has been executed; that is, traversing every edge in the DD-Path graph (or program graph). Therefore, the C_1 metric is exactly our G_{chain} metric.

For if-then and if-then-else statements, this means that both the true and the false branches are covered (C_{1p} coverage). For CASE/Switch statements, each clause is covered. Beyond this, it is useful to ask how we might test a DD-Path. Longer DD-Paths generally represent complex computations, which we can rightly consider as individual functions. For such DD-Paths, it may be appropriate to apply a number of functional tests, especially those for boundary and special values.

8.3.2.3 Simple Loop Coverage

The C_2 metric requires DD-Path coverage (the C_1 metric) plus loop testing.

The simple view of loop testing is that every loop involves a decision, and we need to test both outcomes of the decision: one is to traverse the loop, and the other is to exit (or not enter) the loop. This is carefully proved in [Huang 1979]. Notice that this is equivalent to G_{edge} test coverage, where an edge exists to repeat the loop and another exists to exit the loop.

8.3.2.4 Predicate Outcome Testing

This level of testing requires that every outcome of a decision (predicate) must be exercised. Because our formulation of program graphs allows statement fragments to be individual nodes, Miller's C_{1p} metric is subsumed by our G_{edge} metric. Neither E. F. Miller's test covers, nor the graph-based covers, deal with decisions that are made on compound conditions. They are the subjects of Section 8.3.3.

8.3.2.5 Dependent Pairs of DD-Paths

Identification of dependencies must be made at the code level. This cannot be done just by considering program graphs. The C_d metric foreshadows the topic of Chapter 9—dataflow testing. The most common dependency among pairs of DD-Paths is the define/reference relationship, in which a variable is defined (receives a value) in one DD-Path and is referenced in another DD-Path. The importance of these dependencies is that they are closely related to the problem of infeasible paths. We have good examples of dependent pairs of nodes in Figure 8.2. The variable IsATriangle is set to TRUE at node 10 (DD-Path D), and FALSE at node 12 (DD-Path D). Node 14 (DD-Path D) is the branch taken when IsATriangle is TRUE in the condition at node 13 (DD-Path F). Any path containing nodes 10 and 21 (DD-Path M) is infeasible. Simple DD-Path coverage might not exercise these dependencies, thus a deeper class of faults would not be revealed.

8.3.2.6 Complex Loop Coverage

Miller's C_{ik} metric extends the loop coverage metric to include full paths from source to sink nodes that contain loops.

The condensation graphs we studied in Chapter 4 provide us with an elegant resolution to the problems of testing loops. Loop testing has been studied extensively, and with good reason — loops are a highly fault-prone portion of source code. To start, an amusing taxonomy of loops occurs (Beizer, 1984): concatenated, nested, and knotted, shown in Figure 8.6.

Concatenated loops are simply a sequence of disjoint loops, while nested loops are such that one is contained inside another. Knotted (Beizer calls them "horrible") loops cannot occur when the structured programming precepts are followed, but they can occur in languages like Java with try/catch. When it is possible to branch into (or out from) the middle of a loop, and these branches are internal to other loops, the result is Beizer's knotted loop. We can also take a modified boundary value approach, where the loop index is given its minimum, nominal, and maximum values

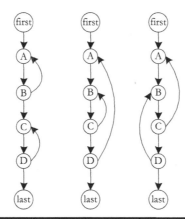

Figure 8.6   Concatenated, nested, and knotted loops.

(see Chapter 5). We can push this further to full boundary value testing and even robustness testing. If the body of a simple loop is a DD-Path that performs a complex calculation, this should also be tested, as discussed previously. Once a loop has been tested, the tester condenses it into a single node. If loops are nested, this process is repeated starting with the innermost loop and working outward. This results in the same multiplicity of test cases we found with boundary value analysis, which makes sense, because each loop index variable acts like an input variable. If loops are knotted, it will be necessary to carefully analyze them in terms of the dataflow methods discussed in Chapter 9. As a preview, consider the infinite loop that could occur if one loop tampers with the value of the other loop's index.

8.3.2.7 Multiple Condition Coverage

Miller's C_{MCC} metric addresses the question of testing decisions made by compound conditions. Look closely at the compound conditions in DD-Paths B and H. Instead of simply traversing such predicates to their true and false outcomes, we should investigate the different ways that each outcome can occur. One possibility is to make a decision table; a compound condition of three simple conditions will have eight rules (see Table 8.2), yielding eight test cases. Another possibility is to reprogram

Table 8.2   Decision Table for the Program Fragment in Figure 8.7

Conditions	rule 1	Rule 2	Rule 3	Rule 4	Rule 5	Rule 6	Rule 7	Rule 8
a	T	T	T	T	F	F	F	F
b	T	T	F	F	T	T	F	F
c	T	F	T	F	T	F	T	F
a AND (b OR c)	True	True	True	False	False	False	False	False
Actions								
y = 1	x	x	X	—	—	—	—	—
y = 2	—	—	—	x	x	x	x	x

compound predicates into nested simple if-then-else logic, which will result in more DD-Paths to cover. We see an interesting trade-off: statement complexity versus path complexity. Multiple condition coverage assures that this complexity is not swept under the DD-Path coverage rug. This metric has been refined to Modified Condition Decision Coverage, as we will see in Section 8.3.3.

8.3.2.8 "Statistically Significant" Coverage

The C_{stat} metric is awkward—what constitutes a statistically significant set of full program paths? Maybe this refers to a comfort level on the part of the customer/user.

8.3.2.9 All Possible Paths Coverage

The subscript in Miller's C_∞ metric says it all—this can be enormous for programs with loops, *a la* Figure 8.3. This can make sense for programs without loops, and also for programs for which loop testing reduces the program graph to its condensation graph, which is always acyclic.

8.3.3 A Closer Look at Compound Conditions

There is an excellent reference [Chilenski] that is 214 pages long and is available. on the web. The definitions in this subsection are derived from this reference. They will be related to the definitions in Sections 8.3.1 and 8.3.2.

8.3.3.1 Boolean Expression (per Chilenski)

A *boolean expression* evaluates to one of two possible (Boolean) outcomes traditionally known as False and True.

A Boolean expression may be a simple Boolean variable, or a compound expression containing one or more Boolean operators. Chilenski clarifies Boolean operators into four categories:

Operator Type	Boolean Operators
Unary (single operand)	NOT ($\sim$,!)
Binary (two operands)	AND($\wedge$, &), OR($\vee$, |), XOR($\oplus$)
Short circuit operators	AND (AND-THEN), OR (OR-ELSE)
Relational operators	$=, \neq, <, \leq, >, \geq$

In mathematical logic, Boolean expressions are known as *Logical Expressions*, where a logical expression can be:

1. a simple proposition that contains no logical connective, or
2. a compound proposition that contains at least one logical connective.

Synonyms: predicate, proposition, condition.

In programming languages, Chilenski's Boolean expressions appear as conditions in decision-making statements: If-Then, If-Then-Else, If-ElseIf, Case/Switch, For, While, and Until loops. This subsection is concerned with the testing needed for compound conditions. Compound conditions are shown as single nodes in a program graph, hence the complexity they introduce is obscured.

8.3.3.2 Condition (per Chilenski)

A *condition* is an operand of a Boolean operator (Boolean functions, objects, and operators).

Generally, this refers to the lowest level conditions (i.e., those operands that are not Boolean operators themselves), which are normally the leaves of an expression tree. Note that a condition is a Boolean (sub)expression.

In mathematical logic, Chilenski's conditions are known as simple, or atomic, propositions. Propositions can be simple or compound, where a compound proposition contains at least one logical connective. Propositions are also called predicates, the term that E. F. Miller uses.

8.3.3.3 Coupled Conditions (per Chilenski)

Two (or more) conditions are *coupled* if changing one also changes the other(s).

When conditions are coupled, it may not be possible to vary individual conditions, because the coupled condition(s) might also change. Chelinski notes that conditions can be strongly or weakly coupled. In a strongly coupled pair, changing one condition always changes the other. In a weakly coupled triplet, changing one condition may change one other coupled condition, but not the third one. Chelinski offers these examples:

In $(((x = 0)$ AND A) OR $((x \neq 0)$ AND B)), the conditions $(x = 0)$ and $(x \neq 0)$ are strongly coupled.

In $((x = 1)$ OR $(x = 2)$ OR $(x = 3))$, the three conditions are weakly coupled.

8.3.3.4 Masking Conditions (per Chilenski)

"The process *masking conditions* involves of setting the one operand of an operator to a value such that changing the other operand of that operator does not change the value of the operator.

Referring to Chapter 3.4.3, masking uses the Domination Laws. For an AND operator, masking of one operand can be achieved by holding the other operand False.

(X AND False = False AND X = False no matter what the value of X is.)

For an OR operator, masking of one operand can be achieved by holding the other operand True.

(X OR True = True OR X = True no matter what the value of X is.)

8.3.3.5 *Modified Condition Decision Coverage*

Modified Condition Decision Coverage (MCDC) is required for "Level A" software by testing standard DO-178B. Modified Condition Decision Coverage (MCDC) has three variations: Masking MCDC, Unique-Cause MCDC, and Unique-Cause + Masking MCDC. These are explained in exhaustive detail in [Chilenski], which concludes that Masking MCDC, while demonstrably the weakest form of the three, is recommended for compliance with DO-178B. The definitions below are quoted from [Chilenski].

Definition

Modified Condition Decision Coverage (MCDC) requires:

1. Every statement must be executed at least once,
2. Every program entry point and exit point must be invoked at least once,
3. All possible outcomes of every control statement are taken at least once,
4. Every non-constant Boolean expression has been evaluated to both True and False outcomes,
5. Every non-constant condition in a Boolean expression has been evaluated to both True and False outcomes, and
6. Every non-constant condition in a Boolean expression has been shown to independently affect the outcomes (of the expression).

The basic definition of MCDC needs some explanation. Control statements are those that make decisions, such as If statements, Case/Switch statements, and looping statements. In a program graph, control statements have an outdegree greater than 1. Constant Boolean expressions are those that always evaluate to the same end value. For example, the Boolean expression $(p \lor \sim p)$ always evaluates to True, as does the condition $(a = a)$. Similarly, $(p \land \sim p)$ and $(a \neq a)$ are constant expressions (that evaluate to False). In terms of program graphs, MCDC requirements 1 and 2 translate to node coverage, and MCDC requirements 3 and 4 translate to edge coverage. MCDC requirements 5 and 6 get to the complex part of MCDC testing. In the following, the three variations discussed by Chilenski are intended to clarify the meaning of point 6 of the general definition, namely, the exact meaning of "independence."Definition (per Chilenski)

"*Unique-Cause MCDC* [requires] a unique cause (toggle a single condition and change the expression result) for all possible (uncoupled) conditions."

Definition (per Chilenski)

"*Unique-Cause + Masking MCDC* [requires] a unique cause (toggle a single condition and change the expression result) for all possible (uncoupled) conditions. In the case of strongly coupled conditions, masking [is allowed} for that condition only, i.e., all other (uncoupled) conditions will remain fixed."

Definition (per Chilenski)

"*Masking MCDC* allows masking for all conditions, coupled and uncoupled. (toggle a single condition and change the expression result) for all possible (uncoupled) conditions. In the case of strongly coupled conditions, masking [is allowed] for that condition only (i.e., all other (uncoupled) conditions will remain fixed."

```
1.    if ((a && ( b || c)) {
2.        y = 1;
3.    else
4.        y = 2;
5.    }
```

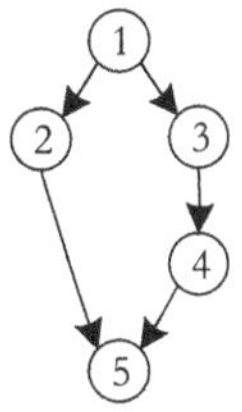

Figure 8.7   A compound condition and its program graph.

Chilenski comments: "In the case of strongly coupled conditions, no coverage set is possible as DO-178B provides no guidance on how such conditions should be covered."

8.3.4 Examples

The examples in this section are directed at the variations of testing code with compound conditions.

8.3.4.1 Condition with Two Simple Conditions

Consider the program fragment in Figure 8.7. It is deceptively simple, with a cyclomatic complexity of 2.

The decision table (see Chapter 7) for the condition (a AND (b OR c)) is in Table 8.2. Decision Coverage is attained by exercising any pair of rules such that each action is executed at least once. Test cases corresponding to Rules 3 and 4 provide Decision Coverage, as do Rules 1 and 8. Condition coverage is attained by exercising a set of rules such that each condition is evaluated to both True and False. Test cases corresponding to Rules 1 and 8 provide Decision Coverage, as do Rules 4 and 5.

To attain Modified Condition Decision Coverage, each condition must be evaluated to both True and False while holding the other conditions constant, and the change must be visible at the outcome. Rules 1 and 5 toggle condition a; rules 2 and 4 toggle condition b, and rules 3 and 4 toggle condition c.

In its expanded form, (a AND b) OR (a AND c), the Boolean variable "a" cannot be subjected to unique cause MCDC testing, because it appears in both AND expressions.

Given all the complexities here (see the Chelinski for much, much more), the best practical solution is to just make a decision table of the actual code, and look for impossible rules. Any dependencies will typically generate an impossible rule.

8.3.4.2 Example: Compound Condition from NextDate

Tolstoy's novel, *Anna Karenina*, begins with the line "Happy families are all alike; every unhappy family is unhappy in its own way." This pattern has become known as the "Anna Karenina Principle": success requires the conjunction of several factors, while the lack of any one of them leads to failure. We see this in hospital medical monitors that check factors like pulse rate, systolic and diastolic blood pressure, and so on. If all the factors are within acceptable ranges, there is no problem. When any factor slips out of range, an alarm is sounded. It is easy to imagine similar

```
1.    int day, int month, int year;
1.    boolean dayOK, monthOK, yearOK, rangesOK;
1.    java.util.Scanner inputScanner = new java.util.Scanner(System.in);

2.    rangesOK = false;

3.    do
3.      {
4.          month = inputScanner.nextInt();
4.          day = inputScanner.nextInt();
4.          year = inputScanner.nextInt();
4.          inputScanner.close();

5.          if ((day > 0) &&(day < 32))
6.              dayOK = true;
7.          else {
8.              dayOK = false;
9.          }

10.         if ((month > 0) &&(month < 13))
11.             monthOK = true;
12.         else {
13.             monthOK = false;
14.         }

15.         if ((year > 1841) &&(year < 2043))
16.             yearOK = true;
17.         else {
18.             yearOK = false;
19.         }
20.     }

21.   while (!(dayOK && monthOK && yearOK));

22.   rangesOK = true;
```

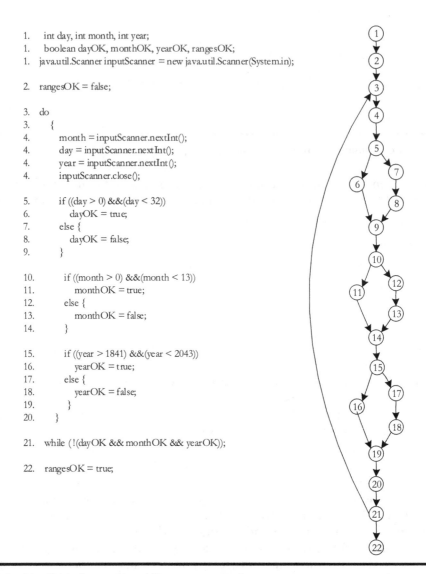

Figure 8.8   NextDate fragment and its program graph.

requirements for nuclear reactors, where factors such as reactor temperature, cooling liquid temperature, and pump power are used to monitor the nuclear reaction in order to prevent a meltdown. Indeed, this pattern is common to many control systems, and there is a corresponding need to test such situations.

Here we use a portion of our continuing NextDate problem that does range checking for valid inputs of the day, month, and year variables. A Java fragment for this and its program graph are in Figure 8.8 and one possible decision table is Table 8.3. Since the day, month, and year variables are all independent, each can be either True or False.

If we used Table 8.3 to define Multiple Condition Coverage, we could use the eight test cases in Table 8.4.

The test cases in Table 8.4 only test one way that the dayOK, monthOK, and yearOK variables can be false. We should really have the more complete decision

Table 8.3   Decision Table for the NextDate Fragment

Conditions	Rule 1	Rule 2	Rule 3	Rule 4	Rule 5	Rule 6	Rule 7	Rule 8
DayOK	T	T	T	T	F	F	F	F
monthOK	T	T	F	F	T	T	F	F
YearOK	T	F	T	F	T	F	T	F
Until condition	True	False	False	False	False	False	False	False
Actions								
Exit loop	x	—	—	—	—	—	—	—
Repeat loop	—	x	x	x	x	x	x	x

Table 8.4   Test Cases Derived from Table 8.3

	Test 1	Test 2	Test 3	Test 4	Test 5	Test 6	Test 7	Test 8
Day	3	3	3	3	32	32	32	32
Month	8	8	13	13	8	8	13	13
Year	2019	1819	2019	1819	2019	1819	2019	1819
Exit loop	x	—	—	—	—	—	—	—
Repeat loop	—	x	x	x	x	x	x	x

Table 8.5   Closer Look at Part of Table 8.3

day >0	T	T	F	F
day <32	T	F	T	F
Impossible	—	—	—	x
dayOK is	true	false	false	—

table with known boundary conditions (i.e., day >0, day <32, month >0, month <13, year >1841, and year <2043). If we include all combinations of True and False results for these six conditions, the result is a decision table of $2^6 = 64$ rules; of these, 37 are impossible, and dayOK, monthOK and yearOK are each true nine times. In Table 8.5 we take a closer look at the portion of the decision table for conditions day >0 and day <32. and the resulting impossible rules.

The rule in which both conditions are False requires the value of day to be both less than 0 and greater than 32. This nicely illustrates the masking aspect of the Modified Condition Decision Coverage (MCDC) code coverage standard. Full Multiple Condition Coverage presumes that the conditions are truly independent (as they are in Table 8.3).

Decision Coverage is attained by exercising any pair of rules such that each action is executed at least once. Test cases corresponding to rule 1 and any one of rules 2–8 provide Decision Coverage. Multiple condition coverage requires exercising a set of rules such that each condition is evaluated to both True and False. The eight test cases corresponding to all eight rules are necessary to provide Decision Coverage.

The decision table in Table 8.6 was reduced from the full decision table with 64 rules by eliminating the impossible rules. We will use the test case numbers to refer

Table 8.6   Reduced Decision Table for Range Check

Original rule numbers															
	1	2	3	5	6	7	9	10	11	17	18	19	21	22	23
day >0	T	T	T	T	T	T	T	T	T	T	T	T	T	T	T
day <32	T	T	T	T	T	T	T	T	T	F	F	F	F	F	F
month >0	T	T	T	T	T	T	F	F	F	T	T	T	T	T	T
month <13	T	T	T	F	F	F	T	T	T	T	T	T	F	F	F
year >1841	T	T	F	T	T	F	T	T	F	T	T	F	T	T	F
year <2043	T	F	T	T	F	T	T	F	T	T	F	T	T	F	T
Impossible															
dayOK is T	x	x	x	x	x	x	x	x	x						
monthOK is T	x	x	x							x	x	x			
yearOK is T	x			x			x			x			x		
Test Case	1	2	3	4	5	6	7	8	9	10	11	12	13	14	15

Original rule numbers												
	25	26	27	33	34	35	37	38	39	41	42	43
day >0	T	T	T	F	F	F	F	F	F	F	F	F
day <32	F	F	F	T	T	T	T	T	T	T	T	T
month >0	F	F	F	T	T	T	T	T	T	F	F	F
month <13	T	T	T	T	T	T	F	F	F	T	T	T
year >1841	T	T	F	T	T	F	T	T	F	T	T	F
year <2043	T	F	T	T	F	T	T	F	T	T	F	T
Impossible												
dayOK is T												
monthOK is T				x	x	x						
yearOK is T	x			x				x		x	x	
Test Case	16	17	18	19	20	21	22	23	24	25	26	27

to test cases derived from the corresponding rule to describe various levels of test coverage in the code fragment in Figure 8.8.

We can follow the nodes in Figure 8.8 to describe the path traversed by test cases derived from Table 8.6. Since this is a little tedious, we will only do this for a few test cases.

Test Case 1 traverses nodes 1, 2, 3, 4, 5, 6, 9, 10, 11, 14, 15, 16, 19, 20, 21, 22
Test case 14 traverses nodes 1, 2, 3, 4, 5, 7, 8, 9, 10, 12, 13, 14, 15, 17, 18, 19, 20, 21, 3
Test cases 15, 19, 23, 25, 26, and 28 traverse the same nodes as test case 14.

8.3.4.2.1 Program Graph-Based Coverage Metrics

Taken together, test cases 1 and any one of test cases 14, 15, 19, 23, 25, 26, and 27 provide the following levels of code coverage:

node (statement fragment),
edge (decision outcome),
loop coverage (run one of test cases 14, 15, 19, 23, 25, 26, and 27 first, followed by test
case 1), and
path coverage.

Nodes 5, 10, 15, and 21 each refer to a compound condition and this is not visible in a program graph. This is a limitation of program graphs, and compound conditions are the point at which graph theory-based coverage criteria must be replaced by code-based criteria. Fortunately, the decision table formulation permits the recognition and analysis of the complexities due to compound conditions as expressed in the decision table rules.

8.3.4.2.2 Model-Based (Decision Table) Code Coverage Metrics

First, note that test case 1 (the "happy path") exercises each of the four compound conditions in which every simple condition is true. We first look at the compound condition at node 21 (dayOK && monthOK && yearOK). Examining the decision table (Table 8.6) yields the following "toggles":

- rule 17 (aka test case 10) together with the happy path is a toggle for day <32
- rule 33 (aka test case 20) is a toggle for day >0. Similarly,
- rule 9 (aka test case 7) is a toggle for month >0, and
- rule 5 (aka test case 4) is a toggle for month <13.
- Finally, rule 2 (aka test case 2) is a toggle for year <2043, and
- rule 3 (aka test case 3) is a toggle for year >1841.

The six test cases (2, 3, 4, 7, 10, and 20), together with the happy path test case 1, constitute complete tests for the compound conditions ((day >0) &&(day <32)), ((month >0) &&(month <13)), and ((year >1841) &&(year <2043)). These seven test cases (1, 2, 3, 4, 7, 10, and 20) provide Modified Condition Decision Coverage (MCDC). The full set of 27 test cases from Table 8.6 provides full Compound Condition Coverage (aka Multiple Condition Coverage). See next page.

Test Case Values from Table 8.6.

Test	Rule	day	month	year	dayOK	monthOK	yearOK	Loop
1	1	9	8	2019	T	T	T	Exit
2	2	9	8	2044	T	T	F	Repeat
3	3	9	8	1840	T	T	F	Repeat
4	5	9	14	2019	T	F	T	Repeat
5	6	9	14	2044	T	F	F	Repeat
6	7	9	14	1840	T	F	F	Repeat
7	9	9	0	2019	T	F	T	Repeat
8	10	9	0	2044	T	F	F	Repeat
9	11	9	0	1840	T	F	F	Repeat
10	17	33	9	2019	F	T	T	Repeat
11	18	33	9	2044	F	T	F	Repeat
12	19	33	9	1840	F	T	F	Repeat
13	21	33	14	2019	F	F	T	Repeat
14	22	33	14	2044	F	F	F	Repeat
15	23	33	14	1840	F	F	F	Repeat
16	25	33	0	2019	F	F	T	Repeat
17	26	33	0	2044	F	F	F	Repeat
18	27	33	0	1840	F	F	F	Repeat
19	33	0	9	2019	F	T	T	Repeat
20	34	0	9	2044	F	T	F	Repeat
21	35	0	9	1840	F	T	F	Repeat
22	37	0	14	2019	F	F	T	Repeat
23	38	0	14	2044	F	F	F	Repeat
24	39	0	14	1840	F	F	F	Repeat
25	41	0	0	2019	F	F	T	Repeat
26	42	0	0	2044	F	F	F	Repeat
27	43	0	0	1840	F	F	F	Repeat

```
9.      if ((a < b + c) && (b < a + c) && (c < a + b)) {
10.         IsA Triangle = true;
11.     else
12.         IsA Triangle = false;
13.     }
```

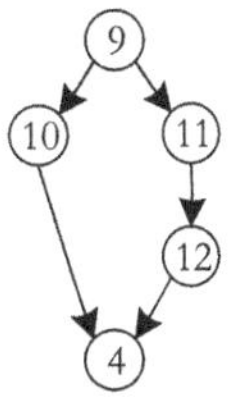

Figure 8.9   Triangle Program fragment and its program graph.

8.3.4.2.3 Compound Condition from the Triangle Program

This example is included to show important differences between it and the first two examples. The code fragment in Figure 8.9 is the part of the Triangle Program that checks to see of the values of sides a, b, and c constitute a triangle. The test incorporates the definition that each side must be strictly less than the sum of the other two sides. Notice that the program graphs in Figures 8.7 and 8.9 are identical. The NextDate fragment and the Triangle Program fragment are both functions of three variables. The second difference is that a, b, and c in the Triangle Program are dependent, whereas dayOK, monthOK, and yearOK in the NextDate fragment are truly independent variables.

The dependence among a, b, and c is the cause of the four impossible rules in the decision table for the fragment in Table 8.7; this is proved next.

Fact: It is numerically impossible to have two of the conditions false.
Proof (by contradiction): Assume any pair of conditions can both be true. Arbitrarily choosing the first two conditions that could both be true, we can write the two inequalities:

$$a > (b + c)$$

$$b > (a + c)$$

Adding them together, we have.

$$(a + b) > (b + c) + (a + c)$$

and rearranging the right side, we have.

$$(a + b) > (a + b) + 2c$$

But a, b, and c are all >0, so we have a contradiction. QED.

Decision Coverage is attained by exercising any pair of rules such that each action is executed at least once. Test cases corresponding to rules 1 and 2 provide Decision Coverage, as do rules 1 and 3, and rules 1 and 5. Rules, 4, 6, 7, and 8 cannot be used due to their numerical impossibility.

Condition coverage is attained by exercising a set of rules such that each condition is evaluated to both True and False. Test cases corresponding to rules 1 and 2 toggle the (c < a + b) condition, rules 1 and 3 toggle the (b < a + c) condition, and 1 and 5 toggle the (a < b + c) condition.

Table 8.7 Decision Table for the Triangle Program Fragment

Conditions	rule 1	rule 2	rule 3	rule 4	rule 5	rule 6	rule 7	rule 8
(a < b + c)	T	T	T	T	F	F	F	F
(b < a + c)	T	T	F	F	T	T	F	F
(c < a + b)	T	F	T	F	T	F	T	F
IsATriangle = True	x	—	—	—	—	—	—	—
IsATriangle = False	—	x	x	—	x	—	—	—
impossible	—	—	—	x		x	x	x

Modified Condition Decision Coverage is complicated by the numerical (and hence logical) impossibilities among the three conditions. The four of pairs (rules 1 and 2, rules 1 and 3, and rules 1 and 5 constitute Modified Condition Decision Coverage.

In complex situations such as these examples, falling back on decision tables is an answer that will always work. Rewriting the compound condition with nested-If logic, we will have (preserving the original statement numbers):

```
9.1   if (a < b + c) {
9.2       if (b < a + c) {
9.3           if (c <a + b) {
10.               IsATriangle = true;
11.1          else
12.1              IsATriangle =false;
11.2          }
11.3      else
12.2          IsATriangle =false;
11.4      }
11.5      else
12.3          IsATriangle =false;
11.6  }
```

This code fragment avoids the numerically impossible combinations of a, b, and c. there are four distinct paths through its program graph, and these correspond to rules 1, 2, 3, and 5 in the decision Table.

8.3.4.3 Test Coverage Analyzers

Coverage analyzers are a class of test tools that offer automated support for this approach to testing management. With a coverage analyzer, the tester runs a set of test cases on a program that has been "instrumented" by the coverage analyzer. The analyzer then uses information produced by the instrumentation code to generate a coverage report. In the common case of DD-Path coverage, for example, the instrumentation identifies and labels all DD-Paths in an original program. When the instrumented program is executed with test cases, the analyzer tabulates the DD-Paths traversed by each test case. In this way, the tester can experiment with different sets of test cases to determine the coverage of each set.

8.3.4.4 *Java Code for Tests in Table 8.8*

```java
import static org.junit.Assert.*;
import org.junit.Test;

public class SimpleDateTest {

    @Test
    public void testInvalidDates() {

        SimpleDate simpleDate = new SimpleDate(1, 1, 2000);

        assertFalse(simpleDate.rangesOK(8, 9, 2044)); // Invalid
        assertFalse(simpleDate.rangesOK(8, 9, 1840)); // Invalid
        assertFalse(simpleDate.rangesOK(14, 9, 2019)); // Invalid
        assertFalse(simpleDate.rangesOK(14, 9, 2044)); // Invalid
        assertFalse(simpleDate.rangesOK(14, 9, 1840)); // Invalid
        assertFalse(simpleDate.rangesOK(0, 9, 2019)); // Invalid
        assertFalse(simpleDate.rangesOK(0, 9, 2044)); // Invalid
        assertFalse(simpleDate.rangesOK(0, 9, 1840)); // Invalid
        assertFalse(simpleDate.rangesOK(9, 33, 2019)); // Invalid
        assertFalse(simpleDate.rangesOK(9, 33, 2044)); // Invalid
        assertFalse(simpleDate.rangesOK(9, 33, 1840)); // Invalid
        assertFalse(simpleDate.rangesOK(14, 33, 2019)); // Invalid
        assertFalse(simpleDate.rangesOK(14, 33, 2044)); // Invalid
        assertFalse(simpleDate.rangesOK(14, 33, 1840)); // Invalid
        assertFalse(simpleDate.rangesOK(0, 33, 2019)); // Invalid
        assertFalse(simpleDate.rangesOK(0, 33, 2044)); // Invalid
        assertFalse(simpleDate.rangesOK(0, 33, 1840)); // Invalid
        assertFalse(simpleDate.rangesOK(9, 0, 2019)); // Invalid
        assertFalse(simpleDate.rangesOK(9, 0, 2044)); // Invalid
        assertFalse(simpleDate.rangesOK(9, 0, 1840)); // Invalid
        assertFalse(simpleDate.rangesOK(14, 0, 2019)); // Invalid
        assertFalse(simpleDate.rangesOK(14, 0, 2044)); // Invalid
    }

    @Test
    public void testValidDates() {
        SimpleDate simpleDate = new SimpleDate(1, 1, 2000);
        assertTrue(simpleDate.rangesOK(8, 9, 2019)); // Invalid
    }

    @Test
    public void testValidDateConstructor() {
        new SimpleDate(8, 9, 2019);
    }

    @Test(expected = IllegalArgumentException.class)
    public void testInvalidDateConstructor1() {
        new SimpleDate(8, 9, 2044);
    }

    @Test(expected = IllegalArgumentException.class)
    public void testInvalidDateConstructor2() {
        new SimpleDate(8, 9, 1840);
```

```java
    }

    @Test(expected = IllegalArgumentException.class)
    public void testInvalidDateConstructor3() {
        new SimpleDate(14, 9, 2019);
    }

    @Test(expected = IllegalArgumentException.class)
    public void testInvalidDateConstructor4() {
        new SimpleDate(14, 9, 2044);
    }

    @Test(expected = IllegalArgumentException.class)
    public void testInvalidDateConstructor5() {
        new SimpleDate(14, 9, 1840);
    }

    @Test(expected = IllegalArgumentException.class)
    public void testInvalidDateConstructor6() {
        new SimpleDate(0, 9, 2019);
    }

    @Test(expected = IllegalArgumentException.class)
    public void testInvalidDateConstructor7() {
        new SimpleDate(0, 9, 2044);
    }

    @Test(expected = IllegalArgumentException.class)
    public void testInvalidDateConstructor8() {
        new SimpleDate(0, 9, 1840);
    }

    @Test(expected = IllegalArgumentException.class)
    public void testInvalidDateConstructor9() {
        new SimpleDate(9, 33, 2019);
    }

    @Test(expected = IllegalArgumentException.class)
    public void testInvalidDateConstructor10() {
        new SimpleDate(9, 33, 2044);
    }

    @Test(expected = IllegalArgumentException.class)
    public void testInvalidDateConstructor11() {
        new SimpleDate(9, 33, 1840);
    }

    @Test(expected = IllegalArgumentException.class)
    public void testInvalidDateConstructor12() {
        new SimpleDate(14, 33, 2019);
    }

    @Test(expected = IllegalArgumentException.class)
    public void testInvalidDateConstructor13() {
        new SimpleDate(14, 33, 2044);
```

```
}

@Test(expected = IllegalArgumentException.class)
public void testInvalidDateConstructor14() {
    new SimpleDate(9, 33, 1840);
}

@Test(expected = IllegalArgumentException.class)
public void testInvalidDateConstructor15() {
    new SimpleDate(14, 33, 2019);
}

@Test(expected = IllegalArgumentException.class)
public void testInvalidDateConstructor16() {
    new SimpleDate(14, 33, 2044);
}

@Test(expected = IllegalArgumentException.class)
public void testInvalidDateConstructor17() {
    new SimpleDate(14, 33, 1840);
}

@Test(expected = IllegalArgumentException.class)
public void testInvalidDateConstructor18() {
    new SimpleDate(0, 33, 2019);
}

@Test(expected = IllegalArgumentException.class)
public void testInvalidDateConstructor19() {
    new SimpleDate(0, 33, 2044);
}

@Test(expected = IllegalArgumentException.class)
public void testInvalidDateConstructor20() {
    new SimpleDate(0, 33, 1840);
}

@Test(expected = IllegalArgumentException.class)
public void testInvalidDateConstructor21() {
    new SimpleDate(9, 0, 2019);
}

@Test(expected = IllegalArgumentException.class)
public void testInvalidDateConstructor22() {
    new SimpleDate(9, 0, 2044);
}

@Test(expected = IllegalArgumentException.class)
public void testInvalidDateConstructor23() {
    new SimpleDate(9, 0, 1840);
}

@Test(expected = IllegalArgumentException.class)
public void testInvalidDateConstructor24() {
    new SimpleDate(14, 0, 2019);
```

```
        }

        @Test(expected = IllegalArgumentException.class)
        public void testInvalidDateConstructor25() {
            new SimpleDate(14, 0, 2044);
        }

        @Test
        public void testEqual() {
                assertTrue(new SimpleDate(8, 9, 2019).equals(new
SimpleDate(8,   9, 2019)));
        }

        @Test
        public void testUnequal() {
                assertFalse(new SimpleDate(8, 9, 2019).equals(new
SimpleDate(8,   10, 2019)));
        }
}


public class SimpleDate {

        int month;
        int day;
        int year;

        public SimpleDate(int month, int day, int year) {

                if(!rangesOK(month, day, year))
                        throw new IllegalArgumentException("Invalid Date");

                this.month = month;
                this.day = day;
                this.year = year;
        }

        public int getMonth() {
            return month;
        }
        public void setMonth(int month) {
            this.month = month;
        }
        public int getDay() {
            return day;
        }
        public void setDay(int day) {
            this.day = day;
        }
        public int getYear() {
            return year;
        }
        public void setYear(int year) {
            this.year = year;
        }
```

```
    boolean rangesOK(int month, int day, int year) {

        boolean dateOK = true;

        dateOK &= (year > 1841) && (year < 2043); // Year OK?
        dateOK &= (month > 0) && (month < 13); // Month OK?
        dateOK &= (day > 0) && (
            ((month == 1 || month == 3 || month == 5 || month == 7 ||
            month == 8
            || month == 10 || month == 12) && day < 32)
            || ((month == 4 || month == 6 || month == 9 || month == 11)
                && day < 31)
            || ((month == 2 && isLeap(year)) && day < 30)
            || ((month == 2 && !isLeap(year)) && day < 29));

        return dateOK;
    }
    private boolean isLeap(int year) {

            boolean isLeapYear = true;

            if(year % 4 != 0)
                isLeapYear = false;
            else if(year % 100 != 0)
                isLeapYear = true;
            else if(year % 400 != 0)
                isLeapYear = false;

            return isLeapYear;
    }

    public boolean isLeap() {

        return isLeap(year);
    }

    @Override
    public boolean equals(Object obj) {

            boolean areEqual = false;
            if(obj instanceof SimpleDate) {
                SimpleDate simpleDate = (SimpleDate) obj;
                areEqual = simpleDate.getDay() == getDay() &&
                    simpleDate.getMonth() == getMonth() &&
                    simpleDate.getYear() == getYear();
            }
            return areEqual;
    }
}
```

8.3.4.5 *Junit Test Results*

```
Test run finished after 147 ms.
        [3 containers found].
        [0 containers skipped]
```

```
[3 containers started]
[0 containers aborted]
[3 containers successful]
[0 containers failed]
[30 tests found]
[0 tests skipped]
[30 tests started]
[0 tests aborted]
[30 tests successful]
[0 tests failed]
```

8.3.4.6 *Capabilities of Selected Code Coverage Tools*

Tool name	Line/ Statement	Block	Untouched Code	Decision	Condition	MCDC	Path
Clover	x	x	x	x			
JaCoCo	x	x	x				
McCabeIQ	x	x	x	x	x	x	x
Parasoft Jtest	x	x	x	x	x	x	x
squish coco	x	x	x	x	x		
Testwell	x	x	x	x	x	x	

8.4 Basis Path Testing

The mathematical notion of a "basis" has attractive possibilities for code-based testing. Every vector space has a basis and the basis has very important properties with respect to the entire set.

Definition

For a set V to be a *vector space*, two operations (addition and scalar multiplication) must be defined for elements in the set. In addition, the following criteria must hold for all vectors x, y, and z $\in$ V, and for all scalars k, l, 0, and 1:

1. if x, y $\in$ V, the vector x + y $\in$ V.
2. x + y = y + x.
3. (x + y) + z = x + (y + z).
4. there is a vector 0 $\in$ V such that x + 0 = x.
5. for any x $\in$ V, there is a vector -x $\in$ V such that x + (−x) = 0.
6. for any x $\in$ V, the vector kx $\in$ V, where k is a scalar constant.
7. k(x + y) = kx + ky.
8. (k + l)x = kx + lx.
9. k(lx) = (kl)x.
10. 1x = x.

The basis of a vector space is a set of vectors that are independent of each other and "span" the entire vector space in the sense that any other vector in the space can be expressed in terms of the basis vectors.

Definition

Given a vector space V, a set B of vectors in V is a *basis of the vector set V* if Bis a maximal set of vectors such that

1. the elements of B are independent, and
2. Every vector $v \in V$ can be written as a linear combination of the elements in B.

A set of basis vectors somehow represents "the essence" of the full vector space: everything else in the space can be expressed in terms of the basis vectors, and if one basis element is deleted, this spanning property is lost. The hope for this theory for testing was that, if we can view a program as a vector space, then the basis for such a space would be a very interesting set of elements to test. If the basis elements are all correct, we could hope that everything that can be expressed in terms of the basis is also correct.

Consider the set P of all paths in a given program. Unfortunately, this set P is not a vector space:

- there is no meaning to an "addition operation" that adds two elements of P,
- there is also no meaning to the notion of scalar multiplication of a program path,
- there is no "identity element" O such that for any $p \in P$, $p + O = p$,
- we can imagine a $0 \in P$, possibly an empty path, or a path of length 0,
- given an element $p \in P$, there is no such "inverse element -p" such that $p + -p = 0$

Given all this, the set of paths in a program is not a vector space. In this section, we examine the early work of Thomas McCabe (McCabe 1982).

8.4.1 McCabe's Basis Path Method

McCabe's basis path method centers on a major result from graph theory, which states that the cyclomatic number (see Chapter 4) of a strongly connected graph is the number of linearly independent circuits in the graph. While program graphs are not strongly connected, the program graph of a program that conforms to the precepts of Structured Programming can be turned onto a strongly connected directed graph by adding an edge from the (unique) sink node to the unique start node. Notice that, if the single-entry, single-exit precept is violated, we greatly increase the cyclomatic number, because we need to add edges from each sink node to each source node. This bears directly on the use of Return statements in object-oriented programs. We first look at the Triangle Program in Figure 8.2 (repeated here as Figure 8.10 for convenience).

With this change, a given program graph must have its cyclomatic number of independent circuits. If we ignore the added edge from sink to source node, we have

Table 8.8 Basis Paths in Figure 8.2

Path	Node Sequence	triangleType
p1	1–6, 8, 9, 11, 12, 13, 16, 18, 20, 22, 23, 24	(infeasible path)
p2 flip 9	1–6, 8, 9, 10, 13, 16, 18, 20, 22, 23, 24	(infeasible path)
p3 flip 13	1–6, 8, 9, 11, 12, 13, 14, 15, 23, 24	EQUILATERAL
p4 flip 16	1–6, 8, 9, 11, 12, 13, 16, 17, 23, 24	SCALENE
p5 flip 18	1–6, 8, 9, 11, 12, 13, 16, 18, 19, 23, 24	ISOSCELES
p6 flip 20	1–6, 8, 9, 11, 12, 13, 16, 18, 20, 21, 23, 24	NOT A TRIANGLE
p7 flip 6	1–6, 7, 23, 24	OUT OF RANGE

independent program paths. Some confusion exists in the literature about the correct formula for cyclomatic complexity. Some sources give the formula as.

$V(G) = e - n + p$, while others use the formula $V(G) = e - n + 2p$; everyone agrees that e is the number of edges, n is the number of nodes, and p is the number of connected regions. The confusion apparently comes from the transformation of a program graph into a strongly connected directed graph. The added edge clearly affects value computed by the formula, but it should not affect the number of circuits. Counting or not counting the added edge accounts for the change to the coefficient of p, the number of connected regions. Since p is usually 1, adding the extra edge means we move from 2p to p.

McCabe next develops an algorithmic procedure (called the baseline method) to determine a set of basis paths. The method begins with the selection of a baseline path, which should correspond to some "normal case" program execution. This can be somewhat arbitrary; McCabe advises choosing a path with as many decision nodes as possible. Next the baseline path is retraced, and in turn each decision is "flipped"; that is, when a node of outdegree ≥2 is reached, a different edge must be taken. Each new path is clearly independent of the previous path. The flipping process continues until we have the cyclomatic number of paths. Table 8.8 contains the result of this process for the Java program in Figure 8.2 (repeated here for convenience).

The cyclomatic complexity of the Java program graph in Figure 8.2 is $V(G) = 29 - 24 + 2 = 7$, so the basis path agorithm results in the correct number of basis paths. It is awkward to think of an infeasible path as a basis path, but this is a consequence of the way program graphs obscure semantic information of the statements that correspond to nodes.

Next we look at a portion of the NextDate Program that verifies that day, month, and year are all in the appropirate ranges. The Javecode and program graph are in Figure 8.8 (also repeated here for convenience). This example has cyclomatic complexity $V(G) = 5$. Table 8.9 echoes the analysis done on Figure 8.2 for Figure 8.8.

The basis path algorithm works pretty well in this example. There is a little problem with the loop control decision. Normally, path p1 (the happy path) would exit

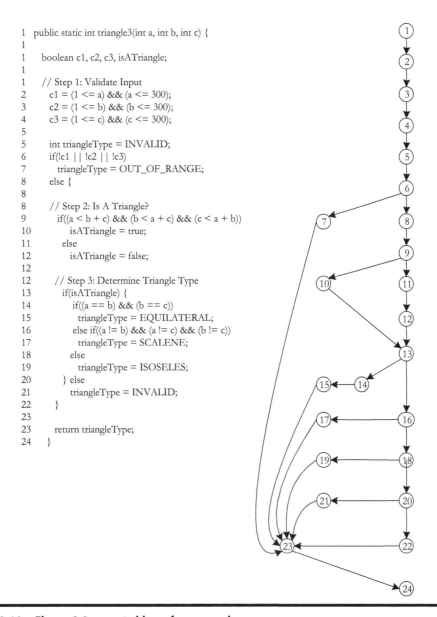

```
1   public static int triangle3(int a, int b, int c) {
1
1     boolean c1, c2, c3, isATriangle;
1
1     // Step 1: Validate Input
2       c1 = (1 <= a) && (a <= 300);
3       c2 = (1 <= b) && (b <= 300);
4       c3 = (1 <= c) && (c <= 300);
5
5       int triangleType = INVALID;
6       if(!c1 || !c2 || !c3)
7         triangleType = OUT_OF_RANGE;
8       else {
8
8       // Step 2: Is A Triangle?
9         if((a < b + c) && (b < a + c) && (c < a + b))
10          isATriangle = true;
11        else
12          isATriangle = false;
12
12        // Step 3: Determine Triangle Type
13        if(isATriangle) {
14          if((a == b) && (b == c))
15            triangleType = EQUILATERAL;
16          else if((a != b) && (a != c) && (b != c))
17            triangleType = SCALENE;
18          else
19            triangleType = ISOSELES;
20        } else
21          triangleType = INVALID;
22      }
23
23      return triangleType;
24    }
```

Figure 8.10   Figure 8.2 repeated here for convenience

Table 8.9   Basis Paths in Figure 8.8

Path	Node Sequence	Result
p1	1, 2, 3, 4, 5, 6, 9, 10, 11, 14, 15, 16, 19, 20, 21	rangesOK = True
p2 flip 5	1, 2, 3, 4, 5, 7, 8, 9, 10, 11, 14, 15, 16, 19, 20, 21, 3	dayOK = False
p3 flip 10	1, 2, 3, 4, 5, 6, 9, 10, 12, 13, 14, 15, 16, 19, 20, 21, 3	monthOK = False
p4 flip 15	1, 2, 3, 4, 5, 6, 9, 10, 11, 14, 15, 17, 18, 19, 20, 21, 3	yearOK = False
p5 flip 21	1, 2, 3, 4, 5, 6, 9, 10, 11, 14, 15, 16, 19, 20, 21, 22	Exit loop

the loop, but we know (semantically) that paths p2, p3, and p4 all must repeat the loop. Once again, the semantically clear dependence interferes with the algorithm.

8.4.2 Observations on McCabe's Basis Path Method

Even though paths in a program graph are not a vector space, the basis path algorithm correctly identifies a set of independent paths, and the set has the correct (cyclomatic number) of elements. Some confusion will always be unavoidable because a program graph does not contain semantic information in the code (see the Testing Pendulum discussion in Chapter 10). A bigger problem—there is nothing in the basis path algorithm that prevents the identification of an infeasible path as a basis path. Finally, the suggestion that a set of basis paths is a sufficient test of the ecorresponding code is an oversimplification. It happened to work well on the two decision-intensive examples in the previous section, but that is no guarantee with repsect to higher levels of code coverage.

8.4.3 Essential Complexity

Part of McCabe's work on cyclomatic complexity does more to improve programming than testing. In this section, we take a quick look at this elegant blend of graph theory, structured programming, and the implications these have for testing. This whole package centers on the notion of essential complexity (McCabe, 1982), which is only the cyclomatic complexity of yet another form of condensation graph. Recall that condensation graphs are a way of simplifying an existing graph; so far, our simplifications have been based on removing either strong components or DD-Paths. Here, we condense around the structured programming constructs, which are repeated as Figure 8.11.

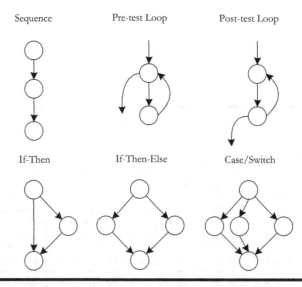

Figure 8.11 Structured programming constructs.

Identifying essential complexity begins with the program graph of interest. The basic idea is to look for the graph of one of the structured programming constructs, collapse it into a single node, and repeat until no more structured programming constructs can be found. The cyclomatic complexity of such a condensed program graph is McCabe's "essential complexity." This process is followed in Figure 8.12, which starts with the graph of the Java range check code in Figure 8.8. The if-else construct involving nodes 5, 6, 7, and 8 is condensed into node a. Similarly, the other two if-else constructs are condensed into nodes b and c. The sequence of nodes 4, a, b, c, 20 is condensed into node d. Next, the do-while loop of nodes 3, d, and 21 is condensed to e. Finally, the sequence of nodes 2, e, and 22 is condensed to node f, resulting in a condensed graph with essential cyclomatic complexity EV(G) = 1. In general, when

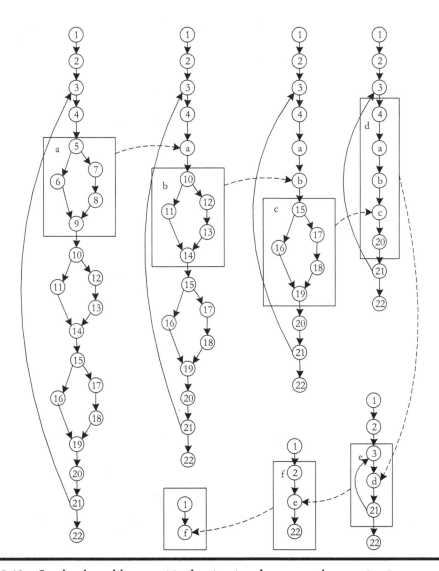

Figure 8.12   Condensing with respect to the structured programming constructs.

a program is well structured (i.e., is composed solely of the structured programming constructs), it can always be reduced to a graph with one path, *i.e.,* a program graph of cyclomatic complexity 1.

McCabe went on to find elemental "unstructures" that violate the precepts of structured programming (McCabe, 1976). These are shown in Figure 8.13. Each of these violations contains three distinct paths, as opposed to the two paths present in the corresponding structured programming constructs; one conclusion is that such violations increase cyclomatic complexity. The *pièce de resistance* of McCabe's analysis is that these violations cannot occur by themselves: if one occurs in a program, there must be at least one more, so a program cannot be only slightly unstructured. Because these increase cyclomatic complexity, the minimum number of test cases is thereby increased. In the next chapter, we will see that the violations have interesting implications for dataflow testing.

The bottom line for testers is this: programs with high cyclomatic complexity require more testing. Of the organizations that use the cyclomatic complexity metric, most set some guideline for maximum acceptable complexity; V(G) = 10 is a common choice. What happens if a unit has a higher complexity? Two possibilities: either simplify the unit or plan to do more testing. If the unit is well structured, its essential complexity is 1; so it can be simplified easily. If the unit has an essential complexity greater than 1, often the best choice is to eliminate the violations.

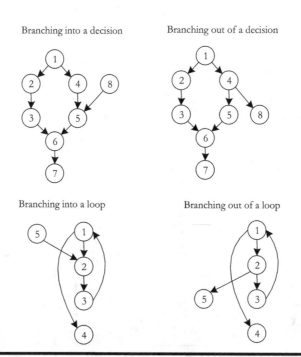

Figure 8.13 Violations of structured programming constructs.

8.5 Guidelines and Observations

In our study of specification-based testing, we observed that gaps and redundancies can both exist and, at the same time, cannot be recognized. The problem was that specification-based testing removes us too far from the code. The path testing approaches to code-based testing represent the case where the pendulum has swung too far the other way: moving from code to directed graph representations and program path formulations obscures important information that is present in the code, in particular the distinction between feasible and infeasible paths. Also, no form of code-based testing can reveal missing functionality that is specified in the requirements. In the next chapter, we look at dataflow-based testing. These techniques move closer to the code, so the pendulum will swing back from the path analysis extreme.

McCabe was partly right when he observed, "It is important to understand that these are purely criteria that measure the quality of testing, and not a procedure to identify test cases" (McCabe, 1982). He was referring to the DD-Path coverage metric and his basis path heuristic based on cyclomatic complexity metric. Basis path testing therefore gives us a lower boundary on how much testing is necessary.

Code-based testing also provides us with a set of metrics that act as crosschecks on specification-based testing. We can use these metrics to resolve the gaps and redundancies question. When we find that the same program path is traversed by several functional test cases, we suspect that this redundancy is not revealing new faults. When we fail to attain DD-Path coverage, we know that there are gaps in the functional test cases. As an example, suppose we have a program that contains extensive error handling, and we test it with boundary value test cases (min, min+, nom, max-, and max). Because these are all permissible values, DD-Paths corresponding to the error-handling code will not be traversed. If we add test cases derived from robustness testing or traditional equivalence class testing, the DD-Path coverage will improve. Beyond this rather obvious use of coverage metrics, an opportunity exists for real testing craftsmanship. Any of the coverage metrics in Section 8.3 can operate in two ways: either as a blanket-mandated standard (e.g., all units shall be tested to attain full DD-Path coverage) or as a mechanism to selectively test portions of code more rigorously than others. We might choose multiple-condition coverage for modules with complex logic, while those with extensive iteration might be tested in terms of the loop coverage techniques. This is probably the best view of structural testing: use the properties of the source code to identify appropriate coverage metrics, and then use these as a crosscheck on functional test cases. When the desired coverage is not attained, follow interesting paths to identify additional (special value) test cases.

Exercises

1. Find the cyclomatic complexity of the graph in Figure 8.3.
2. Identify a set of basis paths for the graph in Figure 8.3.
3. Discuss McCabe's concept of "flipping" for nodes with outdegree ≥3.
4. Develop multiple-condition coverage test cases for statement 21 in Figure 8.8: Until (dayOK && monthOK && yearOK).

5. In Chapter 2, you were asked to develop a program for NextWeek (Exercise 6). Apply your boundary value test cases from the exercises in Chapter 5 to your NextWeek program. What test coverage is attained?
6. Apply your equivalence class test cases from the exercises in Chapter 6 to your NextWeek program. What test coverage is attained?
7. (For mathematicians only.) For a set V to be a vector space, two operations (addition and scalar multiplication) must be defined for elements in the set. In addition, the following criteria must hold for all vectors x, y, and z $\in$ V, and for all scalars k, l, 0, and 1:
   a. if x, y $\in$ V, the vector x + y $\in$ V.
   b. x + y = y + x.
   c. (x + y) + z = x + (y + z).
   d. there is a vector 0 $\in$ V such that x + 0 = x.
   e. for any x $\in$ V, there is a vector $-x \in$ V such that x + ($-x$) = 0.
   f. for any x $\in$ V, the vector kx $\in$ V, where k is a scalar constant.
   g. k(x + y) = kx + ky.
   h. (k + l)x = kx + lx.
   i. k(lx) = (kl)x.
   j. 1x = x.
   How many of these 10 criteria hold for the "vector space" of paths in a program?

References

Beizer, Boris, *Software Testing Techniques*, Van Nostrand, New York, 1984.

Chilenski, John Joseph, "An Investigation of Three Forms of the Modified Condition Decision Coverage (MCDC) Criterion," *DOT/FAA/AR-01/18*, April 2001 [http://www.faa.gov/about/office_org/headquarters_offices/ang/offices/tc/library/, see actlibrary.tc.faa.gov]

Huang, J.C., Detection of dataflow anomaly through program instrumentation, *IEEE Transactions on Software Engineering,* SE-5, 226–236, 1979.

Miller, Edward F. Jr., Tutorial: program testing techniques, *COMPSAC '77 IEEE Computer Society*, 1977.

Miller, Edward F. Jr., Automated software testing: a technical perspective, *Amer. Programmer*, Vol. 4, No. 4, April 1991, 38–43.

McCabe, Thomas J., A complexity metric, *IEEE Transactions on Software Engineering*, Vol. SE-2, No. 4, December 1976, 308–320.

McCabe, Thomas J., Structural Testing: A Software Testing Methodology Using the Cyclomatic Complexity Metric, *National Bureau of Standards* (Now NIST), Special Publication 500–599, Washington, D.C., 1982.

McCabe, Thomas J., *Structural Testing: A Software Testing Methodology Using the Cyclomatic Complexity Metric,* McCabe and Associates, Baltimore, 1987.

Perry, William E., *A Structured Approach to Systems Testing,* QED Information Systems, Inc., Wellesley, MA, 1987.

Schach, Stephen R., *Software Engineering,* 2nd ed., Richard D. Irwin, Inc., and Aksen Associates, Inc., 1993.

Chapter 9

Testing Object-Oriented Software

Die Grenzen meiner Sprache bedeuten die Grenzen meiner Welt.

Ludvig Wittgenstein

Wittgenstein observes that the limits (boundaries) of his language are the limits of his world. In this chapter, we introduce two concepts—Define/Use paths and program slices. With this improved vocabulary, we can more accurately describe software testing issues. Define/Use paths are particularly appropriate for object-oriented software; Slices are appropriate primarily at the unit level, but they can be extended to object-oriented software.

Both theoretical and practical work on the testing of object-oriented software has flourished since the second half of the 1990s, leading to the clear dominance of the paradigm in 2013. One of the original hopes for object-oriented software was that objects could be reused without modification or additional testing. This was based on the assumption that well-conceived objects encapsulate functions and data "that belong together," and once such objects are developed and tested, they become reusable components. The new consensus is that there is little reason for this optimism—object-oriented software has potentially more severe testing problems than those for traditional software. In this chapter, we cover two methods useful in combatting the additional difficulties of testing object-oriented software: unit testing and dataflow analysis.

9.1 Unit Testing Frameworks

The origins of unit testing can be traced back to Kent Beck's work with Smalltalk and his creation of SUnit [Beck 1994]. While SUnit was designed for OO software, and a precursor (and vital component of) extreme programming and the agile manifesto, unit testing works and has been adapted for other software lifecycles and language paradigms, respectively. In fact, the ideas of unit testing were used well before the origins of SUnit in the form of small executables that would run tests on a module of software. The advent of SUnit spurred on the formalization and popularization of automatically executing unit tests. JUnit for Java, perhaps the most popularized unit testing framework, leads to the XUnit format and spurred on the creation of unit testing frameworks for a plethora of languages [https://martinfowler.com/bliki/Xunit.html]. Importantly, unit testing does not guarantee correct code, even if every line of code is tested [Gaffney 2004].

9.1.1 Common Unit Testing Frameworks

There are close to 100 languages with unit testing support [https://en.wikipedia.org/wiki/List_of_unit_testing_frameworks] in addition to roughly a dozen languages that directly support unit testing [https://en.wikipedia.org/wiki/Unit_testing]. Following the XUnit format, a selected set of widely used unit testing frameworks are as follows:

- JUnit for Java
- NUnit for C#
- CPPUnit for C++

In order to match the Java source code listings in this text, we illustrate several examples using JUnit.

9.1.2 JUnit Examples

The SimpleDate class below (Listing 9.1) is an implementation of a calendar day (e.g., month, day, year) along with appropriate getters/setters and a constructor. The implementation depends on the function rangesOK to ensure that the provided month, day, and year are valid for some calendar day. The rangesOK function depends upon the isLeap function to determine if the provided year is a leap year (e.g., includes February 29th) or is not a leap year.

LISTING 9.1 JAVA CODE FOR A SIMPLEDATE CLASS

```
1    public class SimpleDate {

2        int month;
3        int day;
4        int year;

5        public SimpleDate(int month, int day, int year) {

6            if(!rangesOK(month, day, year))
7                throw new IllegalArgumentException("Invalid Date");

8            this.month = month;
9            this.day = day;
10           this.year = year;
11       }

12       public int getMonth() {
13           return month;
14       }
```

```
15    public void setMonth(int month) {
16        this.month = month;
17    }
18    public int getDay() {
19        return day;
20    }
21    public void setDay(int day) {
22        this.day = day;
23    }
24    public int getYear() {
25        return year;
26    }
27    public void setYear(int year) {
28        this.year = year;
29    }

30    boolean rangesOK(int month, int day, int year) {

31        boolean dateOK = true;

32        dateOK &= (year > 1841) && (year < 2043); // Year OK?
33        dateOK &= (month > 0) && (month < 13); // Month OK?
34        dateOK &= (day > 0) && (
35            ((month == 1 || month == 3 || month == 5 || month == 7
            || month == 8
36                || month == 10 || month == 12) && day < 32)
37                || ((month == 4 || month == 6 || month == 9 ||
                    month == 11) && day < 31)
38                || ((month == 2 && isLeap(year)) && day < 30)
39                || ((month == 2 && !isLeap(year)) && day < 29));

40        return dateOK;
41    }

42    protected boolean isLeap(int year) {

43        boolean isLeapYear = true;

44        if(year % 4 != 0)
45            isLeapYear = false;
46        else if(year % 100 != 0)
47            isLeapYear = true;
48        else if(year % 400 != 0)
49            isLeapYear = false;

50        return isLeapYear;
51    }

52    public boolean isLeap() {

53        return isLeap(year);
54    }

55    @Override
56    public boolean equals(Object obj) {

57        boolean areEqual = false;
```

```
58          if(obj instanceof SimpleDate) {

59              SimpleDate simpleDate = (SimpleDate) obj;

60              areEqual = simpleDate.getDay() == getDay() &&
61                  simpleDate.getMonth() == getMonth() &&
62                  simpleDate.getYear() == getYear();
63          }

64          return areEqual;
65      }
66 }
```

Typically, if we wanted to unit test the rangesOK function, we would create a JUnit test case like the one in the listing below (Listing 9.2), where the test case is the function that starts on line 5 as indicated by the annotation (i.e., "@Test") on line 4. This unit test ensures that a valid February 29th date on a leap year returns true from rangesOK while an invalid February 29th date on a non-leap year returns false.

LISTING 9.2   JUNIT TEST CASE FOR LEAP YEAR AND NON-LEAP YEAR FEBRUARY 29TH

```
1   import org.junit.Test;
2   import static org.junit.Assert.*;

3   public class SimpleDateTest {

4       @Test
5       public void testWithDependency() {
6           // This test has a dependency on SimpleDate.isLeap
7           SimpleDate simpleDate = new SimpleDate(1, 1, 2000);

8           assertTrue(simpleDate.rangesOK(2, 29, 2000)); // Valid due
                to leap year
9           assertFalse(simpleDate.rangesOK(2, 29, 2001)); // Invalid
                due to leap year
10      }
11  }
```

The problem with Listing 9.2 is that each individual date tested requires an entire line of code, despite minimal changes from any of the previous lines. Via JUnitParams [https://github.com/Pragmatists/JUnitParams], it is possible to simply list out each set of test data and pass it to your test case as a function. For example, in the listing below (Listing 9.3), an annotation indicates a test on line 9 while the parameters of the test (i.e., test data) are defined via the "@Parameters" annotation on line 10 and 11. The actual JUnit test function that starts on line 12 includes parameters for the data identified in the parameters annotation. In this case, we know we are testing for the correct response for February 29th in each test so all that needs to change is the year *and* the result we expect. One last minor change is the JUnit test class needs to be run with the JUnitParams test runner, rather than the standard running. This simple change is indicated on line 6 via the "@RunWith" annotation.

LISTING 9.3 JUNIT PARAMETERIZED TEST CASE FOR LEAP YEAR AND NON-LEAP YEAR FEBRUARY 29TH

```
1   import junitparams.JUnitParamsRunner;
2   import junitparams.Parameters;
3   import org.junit.Test;
4   import org.junit.runner.RunWith;
5   import static org.junit.Assert.assertEquals;

6   @RunWith(JUnitParamsRunner.class)
7   public class SimpleDataParamTest {

8       SimpleDate simpleDate = new SimpleDate(1, 1, 2000);

9       @Test
10      @Parameters({"2000, true",
11          "2001, false" })
12      public void daysInFebruary(int year, boolean expected) throws
        Exception {

13          assertEquals(expected, simpleDate.rangesOK(2, 29, year))
14      }
15  }
```

Using JUnit, as with any other unit testing framework, it is simple to add tests to the publicly available functions within the class. Problematically, testing the rangesOK function still depends on the protected isLeap, meaning we cannot directly tell which function causes a failure when one occurs. The next section explores a solution.

9.2 Mock Objects and Automated Object Mocking

Unit testing, as we have seen throughout Part II, focuses on testing individual pieces or modules of software rather than testing the whole application. However, not all software is written as individual components that can be tested, some is written to integrate those individual components or modules together. Unit testing software requires either mock objects or adherence to testing individual modules, synthesizing those modules into additional modules, and repeating (additional integration testing information, including this bottom-up, technique is covered in Chapter 12).

Mock objects take the place of code dependencies to allow for testing a module independently of those dependencies. As previously mentioned, some dependencies come from normal integration of software and errors can be differentiated if those dependencies are tested elsewhere. However, there are also dependencies that, regardless of their test status, should not be included in testing. For example, modules that write to a database are often dependencies that should be replaced with mock objects that simulate the interactions with the dependency without performing the actions.

Mock objects can be injected manually. For example, the listing below (Listing 9.4) includes a function that could be included in the JUnit test class in Listing 9.1 that replaces the isLeap function within an inherited mock object.

Just as before, the "@Test" annotation on line 1 indicates a JUnit test in the function on line 2. However, rather than creating a SimpleDate object, we create an anonymous child and override the isLeap function by providing another version. This version has pre-set, or canned, data for our expected test cases and throws an exception to indicate any other value was used.

LISTING 9.4   MANUAL DEPENDENCY REMOVAL FROM JUNIT TEST CASE FOR LEAP YEAR AND NON-LEAP YEAR FEBRUARY 29TH

```
1   @Test
2   public void testWithoutDependencyManual() {
3     // This test has no dependency on SimpleDate.isLeap
4     SimpleDate simpleDate = new SimpleDate(1, 1, 2000) {
5       @Override
6       protected boolean isLeap(int year) {
7         if(2000 == year)
8           return true;
9         else if(2001 == year)
10          return false;
11        else
12          throw new IllegalArgumentException("No Mock for year " +
              year);
13      }
14    };
15    assertTrue(simpleDate.rangesOK(2, 29, 2000)); // Valid due to
        leap year
16    assertFalse(simpleDate.rangesOK(2, 29, 2001)); // Valid due to
        leap year
17  }
```

While the version in Listing 9.4 removes the dependency the rangesOK function has on isLeap, it adds complexity to the test. Fortunately, several frameworks exist for automatically mocking objects and functions. For example, the listing below (Listing 9.5) includes a function that could be included in the JUnit test class in Listing 9.1 (with the addition of "import static org.mockito.Mockito.*;") that replaces the isLeap function automatically for two specific inputs using the Mockito framework [https://site.mockito.org/].

LISTING 9.5   AUTOMATIC DEPENDENCY REMOVAL FROM JUNIT TEST CASE FOR LEAP YEAR AND NON-LEAP YEAR FEBRUARY 29TH

```
1   @Test
2   public void testWithoutDependencyAutomatic() {
3     // This test removes a dependency on SimpleDate.isLeap
4     SimpleDate simpleDate = mock(SimpleDate.class,
        CALLS_REAL_METHODS);
5     when(simpleDate.isLeap(2000)).thenReturn(true);
6     when(simpleDate.isLeap(2001)).thenReturn(false);
7     assertTrue(simpleDate.rangesOK(2, 29, 2000)); // Valid due to
        leap year
8     assertFalse(simpleDate.rangesOK(2, 29, 2001)); // Invalid due to
        leap year
9   }
```

Much of Listing 9.5 looks identical to the first test we created in Listing 9.2. In fact, only lines 4, 5, and 6 differ. Line 4 automatically creates a mock object where, by default, all functions allow calls to the methods in the original SimpleDate object. Lines 5 and 6 specify specific return values for the isLeap function when specific values are passed to the function. In this case we hard-code the responses for the years 2000 and 2001. Importantly, the remainder (i.e., lines 7 and 8) are unchanged from test code where the dependency has not been mocked.

9.3 Dataflow Testing

Dataflow testing is an unfortunate term because it suggests some connection with dataflow diagrams; no connection exists. Dataflow testing refers to forms of structural testing that focus on the points at which variables receive values and the points at which these values are used (or referenced). We will see that dataflow testing serves as a "reality check" on path testing; indeed, many of the dataflow testing proponents (and researchers) see this approach as a form of path testing. Most programs deliver functionality in terms of data. Variables that represent data somehow receive values, and these values are used to compute values for other variables. Since the early 1960s, programmers have analyzed source code in terms of the points (statements and statement fragments) at which variables receive values and points at which these values are used. Many times, their analyses were based on concordances that list statement numbers in which variable names occur. Concordances were popular features of second-generation language compilers (they are still popular with COBOL programmers). Early dataflow analyses often centered on a set of faults that are now known as define/reference anomalies:

A variable that is defined but never used (referenced)
A variable that is used before it is defined
A variable that is defined twice before it is used

Each of these anomalies can be recognized from the concordance of a program. Because the concordance information is compiler generated, these anomalies can be discovered by what is known as static analysis: finding faults in source code without executing it.

9.3.1 Define/Use Testing Definition

Much of the formalization of define/use testing was done in the early 1980s [Rapps, 1985]; the definitions in this section are compatible with those in [Clarke et al. 1989], which summarizes most define/use testing theory. This body of research is very compatible with the formulation we developed in Chapters 4 and 8. It presumes a program graph in which nodes are statement fragments (a fragment may be an entire statement) and programs that follow the structured programming precepts.

The following definitions refer to a program P that has a program graph G(P) and a set of program variables V. The program graph G(P) is constructed as in Chapter 4, with statement fragments as nodes and edges that represent node sequences. G(P) has a single-entry node and a single-exit node. We also disallow edges from a node to itself. Paths, subpaths, and cycles are as they were in Chapter 4. The set of all paths in P is PATHS(P).

Definition

Node n ∈ G(P) is a *defining node of the variable v ∈ V*, written as DEF(v, n), if and only if the value of the variable v is defined at the statement fragment corresponding to node n.

Input statements, assignment statements, loop control statements, and procedure calls are all examples of statements that are defining nodes. When the code corresponding to such statements executes, the contents of the memory location(s) associated with the variables are changed.

Definition

Node n ∈ G(P) is a *usage node of the variable v ∈ V*, written as USE(v, n), if and only if the value of the variable v is used at the statement fragment corresponding to node n.

Output statements, assignment statements, conditional statements, loop control statements, and procedure calls are all examples of statements that are usage nodes. When the code corresponding to such statements executes, the contents of the memory location(s) associated with the variables remain unchanged.

Definition

A usage node USE(v, n) is a *predicate use* (denoted as P-use) if and only if the statement n is a predicate statement; otherwise, USE(v, n) is a computation use, (denoted C-use).

The nodes corresponding to predicate uses always have an outdegree ≥ 2, and nodes corresponding to computation uses always have outdegree ≤ 1.

Definition

A *definition-use path with respect to a variable v* (denoted du-path) is a path in PATHS(P) such that, for some v ∈ V, there are define and usage nodes DEF(v, m) and USE(v, n) such that m and n are the initial and final nodes of the path.

Definition

A *definition-clear path with respect to a variable v* (denoted dc-path) is a definition-use path in PATHS(P) with initial and final nodes DEF (v, m) and USE (v, n) such that no other node in the path is a defining node of v.

Testers should notice how these definitions capture the essence of computing with stored data values. Du-paths and dc-paths describe the flow of data across source statements from points at which the values are defined to points at which the values are used. Du-paths that are not definition-clear are potential trouble spots. One of the main values of du-paths is they identify points for variable "watches" and breakpoints when code is developed in an Integrated Development Environment.

9.3.2 Define/Use Testing Metrics

The whole point of analyzing a program with definition/use paths is to define a set of test coverage metrics known as the Rapps-Weyuker Dataflow metrics [Rapps and Weyuker, 1985]. The first three of these are equivalent to three of E.F. Miller's metrics in Chapter 8: All-Paths, All-Edges, and All-Nodes. The others presume that define and usage nodes have been identified for all program variables, and that du-paths have been identified with respect to each variable. In the following definitions, T is a set of paths in the program graph G(P) of a program P, with the set V of variables. It is not enough to take the cross product of the set of DEF nodes with the set of USE nodes for a variable to define du-paths. This mechanical approach can result in infeasible paths. In the next definitions, we assume that the define/use paths are all feasible.

Definition

The set T satisfies the *All-Defs criterion* for the program P if and only if for every variable v ∈ V, T contains definition-clear paths from every defining node of v to a use of v.

Definition

The set T satisfies the *All-Uses criterion* for the program P if and only if for every variable v ∈ V, T contains definition-clear paths from every defining node of v to every use of v, and to the successor node of each USE(v, n).

Definition

The set T satisfies the *All-P-Uses/Some C-Uses criterion* for the program P if and only if for every variable v ∈ V, T contains definition-clear paths from every defining node of v to every predicate use of v; and if a definition of v has no P-uses, a definition-clear path leads to at least one computation use.

Definition

The set T satisfies the *All-C-Uses/Some P-Uses criterion* for the program P if and only if for every variable v ∈ V, T contains definition clear paths from every defining node of v to every computation use of v; and if a definition of v has no C-uses, a definition-clear path leads to at least one predicate use.

Definition

The set T satisfies the *All-DU-paths criterion* for the program P if and only if for every variable v ∈ V, T contains definition clear paths from every defining node of v to every use of v and to the successor node of each USE(v, n), and that these paths are either single loop traversals or they are cycle free.

These test coverage metrics have several set-theory-based relationships, which are referred to as "subsumption" in Rapps (1985). These relationships are shown in Figure 9.1. We now have a more refined view of structural testing possibilities between the extremes of the (typically unattainable) All-Paths metric and the generally accepted minimum, All-Edges. What good is all this? Define/use testing provides a rigorous, systematic way to examine points at which faults may occur.

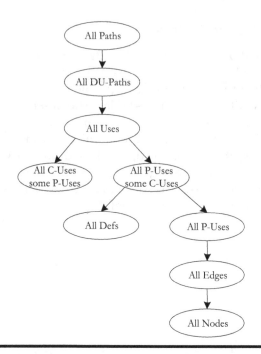

Figure 9.1   Rapps-Weyuker hierarchy of dataflow coverage metrics.

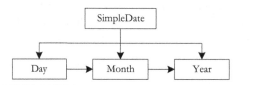

Figure 9.2   UML class diagram for SimpleDate.

9.3.3 Define/Use Testing Example

All of the define/use definitions so far make no mention of where the variable is defined and where it is used. In procedural code, this is usually assumed to be within a unit, but it can involve procedure calls to improperly coupled units. We might make this distinction by referring to these definitions as "context free," that is, the places where variables are defined and used are independent. The object-oriented paradigm changes this—we must now consider the define and use locations with respect to class aggregation, inheritance, dynamic binding, and polymorphism. The bottom line is that dataflow testing for object-oriented code moves from the unit level to the integration level, and we will revisit this discussion in Chapter 12.

However, given a concrete integration of the objects in the form of an application, or even a test, provides concrete paths and flows of data. In the listing below

(Listing 9.5), several date-related classes are presented, as well as a JUnit test class. These classes are:

- DateTest: A JUnit test class with a single test function (i.e., testSimple),
- Date: A class representing date with a month, day, and year,
- Day: A class representing a single day,
- Month: A class representing a single month,
- Year: A class representing a single year.

LISTING 9.6   NEXTDATE CLASSES AND TEST

```
     import static org.junit.jupiter.api.Assertions.*;
     import org.junit.jupiter.api.Test;

1    class DateTest {
2          @Test
2          void testSimple() {

3                Date date = new Date(Month.MAY, 27, 2020); /* msg 1 */
4                assertEquals("5-27-2020", date.getDate()); /* msg 2 */
5                date = date.nextDate();                    /* msg 3 */
6                assertEquals("5-28-2020", date.getDate()); /* msg 4 */
7          }
7    }

8    public class Date {
9          private Day day;
10         private Month month;
11         private Year year;

12         public Date(int month, int day, int year) {
13               this.year = new Year(year);               /* msg 5 */
14               this.month = new Month(month, this.year); /* msg 6 */
15               this.day = new Day(day, this.month);  /* msg 7 */
16         }

17         public String getDate() {
18               return month.getMonth() + "-" + day.getDay() + "-"
                  + year.getYear();
19         }                              /* msg 8, msg 9, msg 10 */

20         public Date nextDate() {
21               Day nextDay = day.getNextDay();          /* msg 11 */
22               Month month = nextDay.getMonth();        /* msg 12 */
23               Year year = month.getYear();             /* msg 13 */
24               return new Date(month.getMonth(), nextDay.
                  getDay(), year.getYear());
                                  /* msg14, msg15, msg16 */
25         }
26   }
```

```
27 public class Day {
28        private int day;
29        private Month month;

30        public Day(int day, Month month) {
31             this.day = day;
32             this.month = month;
33        }

34        public int getDay() {
35             return day;
36        }

37        public Day getNextDay() {
38             if(day < month.numberOfDays())   /* msg 17 */
39                     return new Day(day + 1, month); /* msg1 8 */
40             else
41                     return new Day(1, month.getNextMonth());
                       /* msg 19 */
42        }

43        public Month getMonth() {
44             return month;
45        }
46 }

47 public class Month {
48        public static final int JANUARY = 1;
49        public static final int FEBRUARY = 2;
50        public static final int MARCH = 3;
51        public static final int APRIL = 4;
52        public static final int MAY = 5;
53        public static final int JUNE = 6;
54        public static final int JULY = 7;
55        public static final int AUGUST = 8;
56        public static final int SEPTEMBER = 9;
57        public static final int OCTOBER = 10;
58        public static final int NOVEMBER = 11;
59        public static final int DECEMBER = 12;

60        private int month;
61        private Year year;

62        public Month(int month, Year year) {
63             this.month = month;
64             this.year = year;
65        }

66        public int getMonth() {
67             return month;
68        }
```

```
69        public int numberOfDays() {
70            int numberOfDays = 0;
71            switch (month) {
              // 31 day months
72            case 1: case 3: case 5: case 7: case 8: case 10: case 12:
73                    numberOfDays = 31;
74                    break;
              // 30 day months
75            case 4: case 6: case 9: case 11:
76                    numberOfDays = 30;
77                    break;
              // February
78            case 2:
79                    if(year.isLeapYear())          /* msg 20 */
80                            numberOfDays = 29;
81            else
82                            numberOfDays = 28;
84            break;
85            }
86            return numberOfDays;
87        }

88        public Month getNextMonth() {
89            if(month < 12)
90                    return new Month(month + 1, year); /* msg 21 */
91            else
92                    return new Month(1, year.getNextYear());
                      /* msg 22, msg 23 */
93        }

94        public Year getYear() {
95            return year;
96        }
97  }

98  public class Year {
99        private int year;

100        public Year(int year) {
101            this.year = year;
102        }

103        public int getYear() {
104            return year;
105        }

106        public boolean isLeapYear() {
107            boolean isLeapYear = true;

108        if(year % 4 != 0)
109                    isLeapYear = false;
110            else if(year % 100 != 0)
```

```
111                     isLeapYear = true;
112             else if(year % 400 != 0)
113                     isLeapYear = false;

114             return isLeapYear;
115         }

116         public Year getNextYear() {
117             return new Year(year + 1);              /* msg 24 */
118         }
119  }
```

The define/use nodes for each of the class member variables is listed in Table 9.1. Note that local variables also have define/use nodes, but that we skip those for brevity.

The actual dataflows based on Table 9.1 depend on the use of the classes and how they are integrated. For example, the JUnit test in Listing 9.5 in class DateTest and function testSimple executes the following lines in the following modules in the order presented in Table 9.2. Each line that specifies a message that indicates a function call to an instance whichever class has the next line number listed.

Define/Use paths based on the integrated Date, Day, Month, and Year classes include:

- Date.day: 15, 30, 31, 32, 4, 17, 18
- Date.month: 14, 62, 63, 64, 15
- Date.year: 13, 100, 101, 14
- Day.day: 31, 32, 4, 17, 18, 66, 67, 18, 34
- Day.month: 32, 4, 17, 18, 66, 67, 18, 34, 35
- Month.month: 63, 64, 15, 30, 31, 32, 4, 17, 18, 66, 67
- Month.year: No uses in this integration. However, there would be if the month February was used.
- Year.year: 101, 14, 62, 63, 64, 15, 30, 31, 32, 4, 17, 18, 66, 67, 18, 34, 35, 18, 103, 104

Table 9.1   Define/Use Nodes for Variables in the NextDate Classes and Test

Variable	Defined at Node	Used at Node
Date.day	15	18, 21
Date.month	14	15, 18, 22
Date.year	13	14, 18
Day.day	31	35, 38, 39
Day.month	32	38, 39, 41, 44
Month.month	63	67, 71, 89, 90
Month.year	64	79, 92, 95
Year.year	101	104, 108, 110, 112, 117

Table 9.2   NextDate Classes and Test Line Execution

DateTest	Date	Year	Month	Day
3 (msg 1)				
	12			
	13 (msg 5)			
		100		
		101		
	14 (msg 6)			
			62	
			63	
			64	
	15 (msg 7)			
				30
				31
				32
4 (msg 2)				
	17			
	18 (msg 8)			
			66	
			67	
	18 (msg 9)			
				34
				35
	18 (msg 10)			
		103		
		104		
5 (msg 3)				
	21 (msg 11)			
				37
				38 (msg 17)
			69	

(Continued)

Table 9.2 (*Continued*)

DateTest	Date	Year	Month	Day
			70	
			71	
			72	
			73	
			74	
			86	
				39 (msg 18)
				30
				31
				32
	22 (msg 12)			
				43
				44
	23 (msg 13)			
			94	
			95	
	24 (msg 14)			
			66	
			67	
	24 (msg 15)			
				34
				35
	24 (msg 16)			
		103		
		104		
6 (msg 4)				
	17			
	18 (msg 8)			
			66	
			67	

(*Continued*)

Table 9.2 (*Continued*)

DateTest	Date	Year	Month	Day
	18 (msg 9)			
				34
				35
	18 (msg 10)			
		103		
		104		
7				

Each of these is a dc-path, indicating that the assignment (i.e., first node) is not modified by another assignment before the value is read by the last node. However, du-paths that are not dc-paths also exist. For example, Day.day has a du-path that is not clear (modifications and reads are indicated in bold): **31**, 32, 4, 17, 18, 66, 67, 18, 34, 35, 18, 103, 104, 5, 21, 37, 38, 69, 70, 71, 72, 73, 74, 86, 39, 30, **31**, 32, 22, 43, 44, 23, 94, 95, 24, 66, 67, **34**.

Both du- and dc-paths can be used to verify that each possible definition and use combination is tested or, in this case, even indicate that the Month.year is never used since it is only used if the month is February to calculate the number of days in the month. Additional path-based methods of testing at the integration level for object-oriented code will be covered in Chapter 12.

9.4 Object-Oriented Complexity Metrics

The Chidamber/Kemerer (CK) metrics are the best-known metrics for object-oriented software [Chidamber 1994]. The names for the six CK metrics are almost self-explanatory; some can be derived from a Call Graph, others use the unit level complexity discussed in Section 15.2.

- WMC—Weighted Methods per Class
- DIT—Depth of Inheritance Tree
- NOC—Number of Child Classes
- CBO—Coupling between Classes
- RFC—Response for Class
- LCOM—Lack of Cohesion on Methods

9.4.1 WMC—Weighted Methods per Class

The WMC metric counts the number of methods in a class and weights them by their cyclomatic complexity. This weighting can easily be extended to include the notion of decisional complexity in Section 9.2. In a follow-up paper [Kemerer 2005], Kemerer observes that this metric is a good predictor of implementation and testing effort.

9.4.2 DIT—Depth of Inheritance Tree

The name says it all. If we made another call graph to show inheritance, this is the length of the longest inheritance path from root to leaf node. This is directly derivable from a standard UML Class Inheritance Diagram. While comparatively large values of the DIT metric imply good reuse, this also increases testing difficulty. One strategy is to "flatten" the inheritance classes such that all inherited methods are in one class for testing purposes. Current guidelines recommend a limit of DIT = 3. The Depth of the Inheritance Tree for the Java version of NextDate is 0, not including implicit inheritance from the Java Object class, due to a lack of inheritance between the NextDate, Day, Month, and Year classes.

9.4.3 NOC—Number of Child Classes

The Number Of Child classes of a class in the inheritance diagram for the DIT metric is simply the outdegree of each node. This is very analogous to the cyclomatic complexity of the call graph. The Number of Child Classes for the Java version of NextDate is 0, not including implicit inheritance from the Java Object class.

9.4.4 CBO—Coupling Between Classes

This metric is a carry-over from the procedural coupling metrics popularized by Yourdon and Constantine, in which coupling is increased when one unit refers to variables in another unit. In procedural code, there are six levels of coupling: Content, Common, External, Control, Stamp, and Data. Presence of most of these led to the design of object-oriented programming languages. Proper encapsulation results in "good" o-o code that is data coupled. Greater coupling implies both greater testing and greater maintenance difficulty. Well-designed classes should reduce the CBO values. The Coupling Between Classes in the Java version of NextDate is restricted to data coupling.

9.4.5 RFC—Response for Class

The RFC method refers to the length of the message sequence that results from an initial message. In Chapter 12, we saw that this is also the "length" of the integration-level testing construct, the MM-Path. The longest MM-Path in the Java version of NextDate is 4.

9.4.6 LCOM—Lack of Cohesion on Methods

Coupling and Cohesion are somewhat diametrically opposed—methods should have very low coupling with other methods, and at the same time, should be cohesive in the sense that a method has a single purpose. LCOM describes the extent to which methods are focused on a single purpose—highly cohesive methods are (or should be) a consequence of good encapsulation. The methods in the Java version of NextDate all exhibit high cohesion.

9.5 Issues in Testing Object-Oriented Software

Our goal in this section is to identify the testing issues raised by object-oriented software. First, we consider some of the implications of inheritance, encapsulation, and polymorphism; therefore, we look at ways that traditional testing can be extended to address the implications of these issues.

9.5.1 Implications of Composition and Encapsulation

Composition (as opposed to decomposition) is the central design strategy in object-oriented software development. Together with the goal of reuse, composition creates the need for very strong unit testing. Because a unit (class) may be composed with previously unknown other units, the traditional notions of coupling and cohesion are applicable. Encapsulation has the potential to resolve this concern, but only if the units (classes) are highly cohesive and very loosely coupled. Indeed, highly cohesive units that are loosely coupled not only indicate a maintainable design but are also require less testing and are generally easier to test. As coupling increases, each reference to another unit must be tested, increasing the number of required tests. Similarly, as cohesion decreases, additional, but unrelated, functionality is included and requires additional tests. At the unit level, better object-oriented complexity metrics lead to reduced tests. However, there is a point where the inherent complexity necessary to create the desired functionality is pushed out of the individual units and into the composition of the units. Microservices, for example, are highly cohesive and very loosely coupled units applicable to a multitude of applications. The definition of the application is in the composition of which microservice units are used, and how they interact with each other. The main implication of composition is that, even presuming very good unit-level testing, the real burden is at the integration testing level.

9.5.2 Implications of Inheritance

Although the choice of classes as units seems natural, the role of inheritance complicates this choice. If a given class inherits attributes and/or operations from super classes, the stand-alone compilation criterion of a unit is sacrificed. Binder suggests "flattened classes" as an answer [Binder, 1996]. A flattened class is an original class expanded to include all the attributes and operations it inherits. (Notice that flattened classes are complicated by multiple inheritance, and really complicated by selective and multiple selective inheritance. We ignore these issues here.) Unit testing on a flattened class solves the inheritance problem, but it raises another. A flattened class will not be part of a final system, so some uncertainty remains. Also, the methods in a flattened class might not be sufficient to test the class. The next work-around is to add special-purpose test methods. This facilitates class-as-unit testing but raises a final problem: a class with test methods is not (or should not be) part of the delivered system. This is perfectly analogous to the question of testing original or instrumented code in traditional software. Some ambiguity is also introduced: the test methods can also be faulty. What if a test method falsely reports a fault, or worse, incorrectly reports success? Test methods are subject to the same false positive and false negative outcomes as medical experiments. This leads to an unending chain of methods testing other methods, very much like the attempt to provide external proofs of consistency of a formal system.

Figure 9.3 shows a UML inheritance diagram of a part of a banking system. Both checking and savings accounts have account numbers and balances, and these can be accessed and changed. Checking accounts have a per-check processing charge that must be deducted from the account balance. Savings accounts draw interest that must be calculated and posted on some periodic basis.

If we did not "flatten" the checkingAccount and savingsAccount classes, we would not have access to the balance attributes, and we would not be able to change the balances. This is clearly unacceptable for unit testing. Figure 9.4 shows the "flattened" checkingAccount and savingsAccount classes. These are clearly stand-alone units that are sensible to test. Solving one problem raises another: with this formulation, we would test the getBalance and setBalance operations twice, thereby losing some of the hoped-for economies of object orientation.

Figure 9.4 shows a UML inheritance diagram of a part of the banking application in Figure 9.3. (Some functionality has been added to make this a better example.) Both checking and savings accounts have account numbers and balances, and these can be accessed and changed. Checking accounts have a per-check processing charge

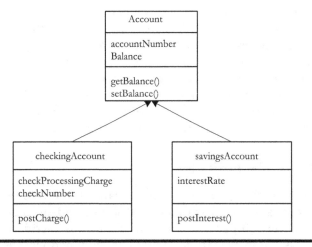

Figure 9.3   UML inheritance.

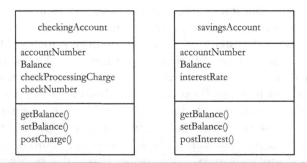

Figure 9.4   Flattened checkingAccount and savingsAccount classes.

that must be deducted from the account balance. Savings accounts draw interest that must be calculated and posted on some periodic basis.

If we did not "flatten" the checkingAccount and savingsAccount classes, we would not have access to the balance attributes, and we would not be able to access or change the balances. This is clearly unacceptable for unit testing. Figure 9.4 shows the "flattened" checkingAccount and savingsAccount classes. These are clearly stand-alone units that are sensible to test. Solving one problem raises another: with this formulation, we would test the getBalance and setBalance operations twice, thereby losing some of the hoped-for economies of object orientation.

9.5.3 Implications of Polymorphism

The essence of polymorphism is that the same method applies to different objects. Considering classes as units implies that any issues of polymorphism will be covered by the class/unit testing.

The code in Listing 9.7 has been updated to include inheritance and polymorphism to the code previously discussed in Listing 9.5. Importantly, despite changes to the structure of the code (illustrated in the UML class diagram in Figure 9.5), the previous tests (i.e., DateTest.testSimple()) remain the same in both versions.

LISTING 9.7   NEXTDATE CLASSES AND TEST WITH INHERITANCE

```
    import static org.junit.jupiter.api.Assertions.*;
    import org.junit.jupiter.api.Test;
1   public class DateTest {
2       @Test
3       void testSimple() {

4           Date date = new Date(Month.MAY, 27, 2020);
5           assertEquals("5-27-2020", date.getDate());
6           date = date.nextDate();
7           assertEquals("5-28-2020", date.getDate());
8       }

9       @Test
10      void testPolymorphismValidRange() {

11          Date date = new Date(Month.FEBRUARY, 29, 2000);
12          ValidRange arrayOfValidRanges[] = { date, date.day, date.
            month, date.year };
13          for(ValidRange validRange : arrayOfValidRanges)
14              assertTrue(validRange.validRange());
15      }

16      @Test
17      void testPolymorphismInValidRange() {

18          Date date = new Date(Month.FEBRUARY, 29, 2001);
```

```
19        ValidRange arrayOfValidRanges[] = { date, date.day, date.
          month, date.year };
20        boolean allValid = true;
21        for(ValidRange validRange : arrayOfValidRanges)
22            allValid &= validRange.validRange();

23        assertFalse(allValid);
24    }

25  }

26  abstract class ValidRange {

27      protected int minimum, maximum;

28      public ValidRange(int minimum, int maximum) {

29          this.minimum = minimum;
30          this.maximum = maximum;
31      }
32      public boolean validRange() {

33          return minimum <= getValue() && getValue() <= maximum;
34      }

35      protected abstract int getValue();
36  }

37  class Date extends ValidRange {
38      protected Day day;
39      protected Month month;
40      protected Year year;

41      public Date(int month, int day, int year) {
42          super(0, 0); // Values aren't used
43          this.year = new Year(year);
44          this.month = new Month(month, this.year);
45          this.day = new Day(day, this.month);
46      }

47      public String getDate() {
48          return month.getMonth() + "-" + day.getDay() + "-" + year.
          getYear();
49      }

50      public Date nextDate() {
51          Day nextDay = day.getNextDay();
52          Month month = nextDay.getMonth();
53          Year year = month.getYear();
54          return new Date(month.getMonth(), nextDay.getDay(), year.
          getYear());
55      }
```

```
56     @Override
57     public boolean validRange() {
58         // Inherited value overwritten
59         return year.validRange() && month.validRange() && day.
           validRange();
60     }

61     @Override
62     protected int getValue() {
63         return 0;
64     }
65 }

66  class Day extends ValidRange {
67     private int day;
68     private Month month;

69     public Day(int day, Month month) {
70         super(1, month.numberOfDays());
71         this.day = day;
72         this.month = month;
73     }

74     public int getDay() {
75         return day;
76     }

77     public Day getNextDay() {
78         if(day < month.numberOfDays())
79             return new Day(day + 1, month);
80         else
81             return new Day(1, month.getNextMonth());
82     }

83     public Month getMonth() {
84         return month;
85     }

86     @Override
87     public boolean validRange() {
88         return super.validRange() && month.validRange();
89     }

90     @Override
91     protected int getValue() {
92         return day;
93     }
94 }

95 class Month extends ValidRange {
96     public static final int JANUARY = 1;
97     public static final int FEBRUARY = 2;
98     public static final int MARCH = 3;
```

```
99     public static final int APRIL = 4;
100    public static final int MAY = 5;
101    public static final int JUNE = 6;
102    public static final int JULY = 7;
103    public static final int AUGUST = 8;
104    public static final int SEPTEMBER = 9;
105    public static final int OCTOBER = 10;
106    public static final int NOVEMBER = 11;
107    public static final int DECEMBER = 12;

108    private int month;
109    private Year year;

110    public Month(int month, Year year) {
111        super(1, 12);
112        this.month = month;
113        this.year = year;
114    }

115    public int getMonth() {
116        return month;
117    }

118    public int numberOfDays() {
119        int numberOfDays = 0;
120        switch (month) {
       // 31 day months

121        case 1: case 3: case 5: case 7: case 8: case 10: case 12:
122            numberOfDays = 31;
123            break;
       // 30 day months

124        case 4: case 6: case 9: case 11:
125            numberOfDays = 30;
126            break;
       // February

127        case 2:
128            if(year.isLeapYear())
129                    numberOfDays = 29;
130            else
131                    numberOfDays = 28;
132            break;
133        }

134        return numberOfDays;
135    }

136    public Month getNextMonth() {
137        if(month < 12)
138            return new Month(month + 1, year);
139        else
```

```
140              return new Month(1, year.getNextYear());
141    }

142    public Year getYear() {
143        return year;
144    }

145    @Override
146    public boolean validRange() {
147        return super.validRange() && year.validRange();
148    }

149    @Override
150    protected int getValue() {
151        return month;
152    }
153 }

154 class Year extends ValidRange {
155    private int year;

156    public Year(int year) {
157        super(1200, 2100);
158        this.year = year;
159    }

160    public int getYear() {
161        return year;
162    }

163    public boolean isLeapYear() {
164        boolean isLeapYear = true;

165    if(year % 4 != 0)
166            isLeapYear = false;
167        else if(year % 100 != 0)
168            isLeapYear = true;
169        else if(year % 400 != 0)
170            isLeapYear = false;

171        return isLeapYear;
172    }

173    public Year getNextYear() {
174        return new Year(year + 1);
175    }

176    @Override
177    protected int getValue() {
178        return year;
179    }
180 }
```

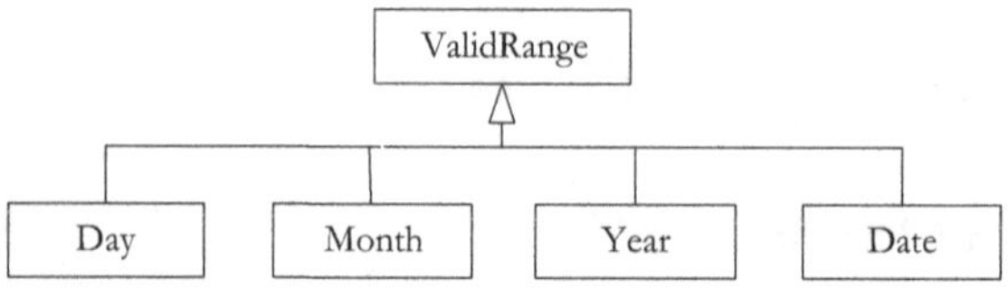

Figure 9.5 UML class diagram for revised Date classes using inheritance.

While the code listing (Listing 9.5) included no inheritance, the listing (Listing 9.7) does. While not strictly necessary, this design illustrates inheritance and polymorphism in the following ways:

- The Date class entirely overrides parent functionality (i.e., ValidRange.validRange()) in lines 56–60.
- The Day and Month classes override the parent functionality, but then use it as part of their own implementation in lines 86–89 and 145–148, respectively.
- The Year class uses the parent functionality as-is, without overriding in its own class definition.

Importantly, it is necessary to verify the behavior of each of the derived child classes to ensure correct functionality. Again, the redundancy of testing polymorphic operations sacrifices hoped-for economies.

9.6 Slice-Based Testing

Program slices have surfaced and submerged in software engineering literature since the early 1980s. They were proposed in Mark Weiser's dissertation in 1979 [Weiser79], made more generally available in [Weiser 85], used as an approach to software maintenance in [Gallagher 91], and more recently used to quantify functional cohesion in [Bieman 94]. During the early 1990s. there was a flurry of published activity on slices, including a paper [Ball 94] describing a program to visualize program slices. This latter paper describes a tool used in industry. (Note that it took about 20 years to move a seminal idea into industrial practice.)

Part of the utility and versatility of program slices is due to the natural, intuitively clear intent of the concept. Informally, a program slice is a set of program statements that contributes to, or affects the value of, a variable at some point in a program. This notion of slice corresponds to other disciplines as well. We might study history in terms of slices—U.S. history, European history, Russian history, Far East history, Roman history, and so on. The way such historical slices interact turns out to be very analogous to the way program slices interact.

We will start by growing our working definition of a program slice. We continue with the notation we used for define-use paths: a program P that has a program graph G(P) and a set of program variables V. The first try refines the definition in [Gallagher 1991) to allow nodes in P(G) to refer to statement fragments.

Definition

Given a program P and a set V of variables in P, a *slice on the variable set V at statement n*, written S(V, n), is the set of all statement fragments in P that contribute to the values of variables in V at node n.

One simplifying notion—in our discussion, the set V of variables consists of a single variable, v. Extending this to sets of more than one variable is both obvious and cumbersome. For sets V with more than one variable, we just take the union of all the slices on the individual variables of V. There are two basic questions about program slices, whether they are backward or forward slices, and whether they are static or dynamic. Backward slices refer to statement fragments that contribute to the value of v at statement n. Forward slices refer to all the program statements that are affected by the value of v and statement n. This is one place where the define-use notions are helpful. In a backward slice S(v, n), statement n is nicely understood as a Use node of the variable v, *i.e.*, Use(v, n). Forward slices are not as easily described, but they certainly depend on predicate uses and computation uses of the variable v.

The static/dynamic dichotomy is more complex. We borrow two terms from database technology to help explain the difference. In database parlance, we can refer to the intension and extensions of a database. The intension (it is unique) is the fundamental database structure, presumably expressed in a data modeling language. Populating a database creates an extension, and changes to a populated database all result in new extensions. With this in mind, a static backward slice S(v, n) consists of all the statements in a program that determine the value of variable v at statement n, independent of values used in the statements. Dynamic slices refer to execution-time execution of portions of a static slice with specific values of all variables in S(v, n). This is illustrated in Figures 9.7 and 9.8.

Listing elements of a slice S(V, n) will be cumbersome because, technically, the elements are program statement fragments. It is much simpler to list the statement fragment numbers in P(G), so we make the following trivial change.

Definition

Given a program P and a program graph G(P) in which statements and statement fragments are numbered, and a set V of variables in P, *the static, backward slice on the variable set V at statement fragment n*, written S(V, n), is the set of node numbers of all statement fragments in P that contribute to the values of variables in V at statement fragment n.

The idea of program slicing is to separate a program into components that have some useful (functional) meaning. Another refinement is whether a program slice is executable. Adding all the data declaration statements and other syntactically necessary statements clearly increases the size of a slice, but the full version can be compiled and separately executed and tested. Further, such compiled slices can be "spliced" together [Gallagher 91] as a bottom-up way to develop a program. As a test of clear diction, Gallagher suggests the term "slice splicing." In a sense, this is a precursor to agile programming. The alternative is to just consider program fragments, which we do here for space and clarity considerations. Eventually, we will develop a lattice (a directed, acyclic graph) of static slices, in which nodes are slices and edges correspond to the subset relationship.

The "contribute" part is more complex. In a sense, data declaration statements have an effect on the value of a variable. For now, we only include all executable statements. The notion of contribution is partially clarified by the predicate (P-use) and computation (C-use) usage distinction of [Rapps 85].

Recall our simplification that the slice S(V, n) is a slice on one variable; that is, the set V consists of a single variable, v. If statement fragment n is a defining node for v,

Table 9.3   Reduced Foodie Inventory for Example

Foodie Item	$/ounce
Italian white truffles	$12.50
Kobe beef	$18.75
Saffron	$28.13

then n is included in the slice. If statement fragment n is a usage node for v, then n is not included in the slice. If a statement is both a defining and a usage node, then it is included in the slice. In a static slice, P-uses and C-uses of other variables (not the v in the slice set V) are included to the extent that their execution affects the value of the variable v. As a guideline, if the value of v is the same whether a statement fragment is included or excluded, exclude the statement fragment.

9.6.1 Example

We want a computational example to show the essential features of program slices. Here we use a method of our continuing Foodies Wish List example, private static double updateShoppingCart(). The full foodies Wish List inventory is reduced to just the three items in Table 9.3. All quantities ordered are in full ounces. This method presumes an event watcher that populates the queueOfEvents variable. Figure 9.7 is a program graph of updateShoppingCart(), and Figure 9.8 is a program graph of the slice on truffleSales at line 39, denoted as S(truffleSales, 39). The source code of three simpler slices follows Figure 9.8.

Figure 9.6 shows a simple User Interface screen tor placing Foodie Wish List orders.

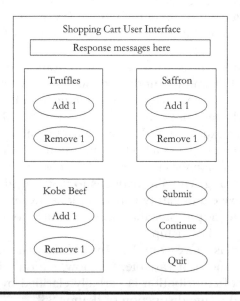

Figure 9.6   Shopping Cart User Interface.

```
1    private static double updateShoppingCart() {

2        double trufflePrice = 12.50;
3        double kobeBeefPrice = 18.75;
4        double saffronPrice = 28.13;
5        double truffleSales = 0.0;
6        double kobeBeefSales = 0.0;
7        double saffronSales = 0.0;
8        double totalSales = 0.0;

9        int totalTruffles = 0;
10       int totalKobeBeefs = 0;
11       int totalSaffrons = 0;
12       String message = "";

13       String event;
14       do {
15       while(queueOfEvents.isEmpty());
16       event = queueOfEvents.remove();

17       if(event.equalsIgnoreCase("Remove 1 Truffles")
                          && totalTruffles > 0) {
18           totalTruffles--;
19           message = "Removed 1 Truffle";
20       } else if(event.equalsIgnoreCase("Remove 1 Kobe Beef")
                          && totalKobeBeefs > 0) {
21           totalKobeBeefs--;
22           message = "Removed 1 Kobe Beef";
23       } else if(event.equalsIgnoreCase("Remove 1 Saffron")
                          && totalSaffrons > 0) {
24           totalSaffrons--;
25           message = "Removed 1 Saffron";
26       } else if(event.equalsIgnoreCase("Add 1 Truffles")) {
27           totalTruffles++;
28           message = "Added 1 Truffle";
29       } else if(event.equalsIgnoreCase("Add 1 Kobe Beef")) {
30           totalKobeBeefs++;
31           message = "Added 1 Kobe Beef";
32       } else if(event.equalsIgnoreCase("Add 1 Saffron")) {
33           totalSaffrons++;
34           message = "Added 1 Saffron";
35       }

36       truffleSales = trufflePrice * totalTruffles;
37       kobeBeefSales = kobeBeefPrice * totalKobeBeefs;
38       saffronSales = saffronPrice * totalSaffrons;
39       totalSales = truffleSales + kobeBeefSales + saffronSales;

40       setMessage(message + " total price: " + totalSales);

41       } while(!event.equalsIgnoreCase("Submit")
                          &&!event.equalsIgnoreCase("Quit"));
42       if(event.equalsIgnoreCase("Submit"))
43           return totalSales;
44       else   return 0.0;
45
46   }
```

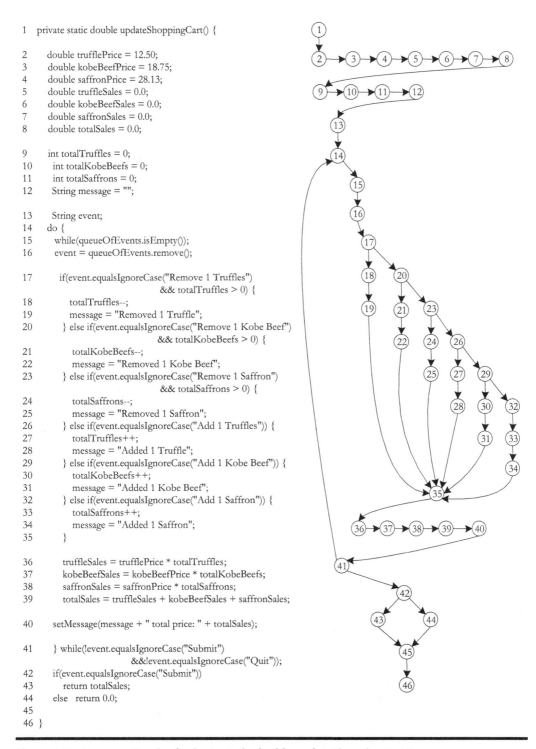

Figure 9.7   Program Graph of private static double updateShoppingCart().

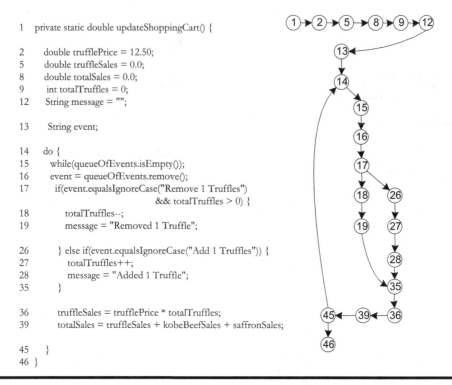

```
1   private static double updateShoppingCart() {

2       double trufflePrice = 12.50;
5       double truffleSales = 0.0;
8       double totalSales = 0.0;
9       int totalTruffles = 0;
12      String message = "";

13      String event;

14      do {
15          while(queueOfEvents.isEmpty());
16          event = queueOfEvents.remove();
17          if(event.equalsIgnoreCase("Remove 1 Truffles")
                            && totalTruffles > 0) {
18              totalTruffles--;
19              message = "Removed 1 Truffle";

26          } else if(event.equalsIgnoreCase("Add 1 Truffles")) {
27              totalTruffles++;
28              message = "Added 1 Truffle";
35          }

36          truffleSales = trufflePrice * totalTruffles;
39          totalSales = truffleSales + kobeBeefSales + saffronSales;

45      }
46  }
```

Figure 9.8   Program Graph of Slice on truffleSales at line 39 S(truffleSales, 39).

```
Slice on totalTruffles at line 36   S(totalTruffles, 36)

1   private static double updateShoppingCart() {

2       double trufflePrice = 12.50;
5       double truffleSales = 0.0;
8       double totalSales = 0.0;

9       int totalTruffles = 0;
12      String message = "";

13      String event;
14      do {
15          while(queueOfEvents.isEmpty());
16          event = queueOfEvents.remove();

17          if(event.equalsIgnoreCase("Remove 1 Truffles") && totalTruffles
            > 0) {
18              totalTruffles--;
19              message = "Removed 1 Truffle";
26          } else if(event.equalsIgnoreCase("Add 1 Truffles")) {
27              totalTruffles++;
28              message = "Added 1 Truffle";
35          }
36          truffleSales = trufflePrice * totalTruffles;
45      }
46  }
```

```
S(totalTruffles, 36) = {1,2,5,8,9,12,13,14,15,16,17,18,19,26,27,28,35,36}
```

Slice on totalTruffles at line 27 S(totalTruffles, 27)

```
1   private static double updateShoppingCart() {

2       double trufflePrice = 12.50;
5       double truffleSales = 0.0;
8       double totalSales = 0.0;

9       int totalTruffles = 0;
12        String message = "";

13        String event;
14      do {
15        while(queueOfEvents.isEmpty());
16        event = queueOfEvents.remove();

17          if(event.equalsIgnoreCase("Remove 1 Truffles") && totalTruffles
          > 0) {
18            totalTruffles--;
19            message = "Removed 1 Truffle";
26          } else if(event.equalsIgnoreCase("Add 1 Truffles")) {
27            totalTruffles++;
35          }
45      }
46  }
```

Slice on totalTruffles at line 18 S(totalTruffles, 18)

```
1   private static double updateShoppingCart() {

2       double trufflePrice = 12.50;
5       double truffleSales = 0.0;
8       double totalSales = 0.0;

9       int totalTruffles = 0;
12        String message = "";

13        String event;
14      do {
15        while(queueOfEvents.isEmpty());
16        event = queueOfEvents.remove();

17        if(event.equalsIgnoreCase("Remove 1 Truffles") && totalTruffles
          > 0) {
18            totalTruffles--;
35          }
45      }
46  }
```

These slices are all related as proper subsets. Five slices are listed here as sets of statement fragment numbers.

S(totalSales, 40)   = {1,2,3,4,5,6,7,8,9,10,11,12,13,14,15,16,17,18,19,20,21,22,23,
                          24,25,26,27,28,29,30,31,32,33,34,35,36,37,38,39,40}

S(truffleSales, 39)   = {1,2,5,8,9,12,13,14,15,16,17,18,19,26,27,28,35,36,39}

S(truffleSales, 36)   = {1,2,5,8,9,12,13,14,15,16,17,18,19,26,27,28,35,36}

S(totalTruffles, 27)   = {1,2,5,8,9,12,13,14,15,16,17,18,19,26,27,35,36}

S(totalTruffles, 18)   = {1,2,5,8,9,12,13,14,15,16,17,18,35,36}

By inspection, we see that:

S(totalTruffles, 18) ⊂ S(totalTruffles, 27) ⊂ S(totalTruffles, 36)
⊂ S(truffleSales, 39) ⊂ S(totalSales, 40)

Due to the structure of the code, we can also derive the following:

S(totalKobeBeefs,21) ⊂ S(totalKobeBeefs,30) ⊂ S(totalKobeBeefs,37)
⊂ S(kobeBeefsSales,37) ⊂ S(totalSales, 40)

S(totalSaffrons,24) ⊂ S(totalSaffrons,33)) ⊂ S(totalSaffrons,38) ⊂ S(saffronsSales,38)
⊂ S(totalSales, 40)

Figure 9.9 condenses the slice subsets into a lattice in which the ordering relation is "proper subset."

The lattice in Figure 9.9 is a roadmap for slice-based testing. Working from the leaves of a single branch in the lattice, we first assure that the contribution of total-Truffles is correct. At each step up the lattice, the slices are increasingly complete. As long as each step is tested to be correct, we know the contribution of totalTruffles to totalSales is correct. Similarly for the totalKobeBeefs and totalSaffrons lattice branches.

Notice that slice-based testing allows us to focus exactly on the program portions of interest in a well-organized way. Is all the detail necessary? For this simple example, probably not, but in larger, more complex examples, it works well.

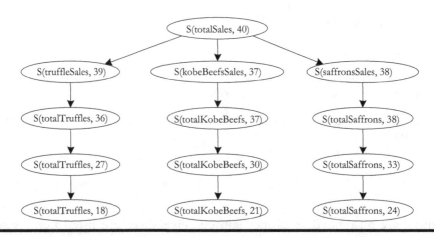

Figure 9.9   Subset Lattice of "Interesting" Slices.

9.6.2 Style and Technique

When we analyze a program in terms of interesting slices, we can focus on parts of interest while disregarding unrelated parts. We could not do this with du-paths—they are sequences that include statements and variables that may not be of interest. Before discussing some analytic techniques, we will first look at "good style." We could have built these stylistic precepts into the definitions, but then the definitions are more restrictive than necessary.

1. Never make a slice S(V, n) for which variables v of V do not appear in statement fragment n. This possibility is permitted by the definition of a slice, but it is bad practice. In our example, we defined a slice on truffleSales at node 40. Defining such slices necessitates tracking the values of all variables at all points in the program.
2. Make slices on one variable. The set V in slice S(V, n) can contain several variables, and sometimes such slices are useful. The slice S(V, 40) where

    V = { totalSales, truffleSales, kobeBeefSales, saffronSales }

    contains all the elements of the slice S_{40}: S(totalSales, 40) except statement 40.
3. Make slices for P-use nodes. When a variable is used in a predicate, the slice on that variable at the decision statement shows how the predicate variable got its value. This is very useful in decision-intensive programs such as the triangle program and NextDate.
4. Consider making slices compilable. Nothing in the definition of a slice requires that the set of statements is compilable; but if we make this choice, it means that a set of compiler directive and data declaration statements is a subset of every slice. If we added this same set of statements to all the slices we made for the updateShoppingCart() method, our lattices remain undisturbed; but each slice is separately compilable (and therefore executable).

9.6.3 Slice Splicing

Weiser [Weiser 1984] created the concept/tongue twister of "slice splicing." The updateShoppingCart() method is deliberately small, yet it suffices to illustrate the idea of slice splicing. In Figure 9.9, the updateShoppingCart() method is split into 13 slices. The three branches of the lattice correspond to the three products: truffles, Kobe beef, and saffron.

In Chapter 1, we suggested that good testing practices lead to better programming practices. Here, we have a good example. Think about developing programs in terms of compilable slices. If we did this, we could work upward from a leaf in the Lattice of slices, code a slice, and immediately test it. Notice that this is the essence of agile development! We can then code and test larger slices, knowing that the lower level slices are correct, thereby assisting in fault location. Once the three branches of the lattice have been tested, we can merge them into the full method. This is exactly the process of slice splicing.

Slice splicing also offers assistance for program comprehension needed in software maintenance. Slices allow the maintenance programmer to focus on the issues at hand and avoid the extraneous information that would be in longer du-paths.

Table 9.4   Selected Program Slicing Tools

Tool/Product	Language	Static/dynamic?
Kamkar	Pascal	Dynamic
Spyder	ANSI C	Dynamic
Unravel	ANSI C	Static
CodeSonar®	C, C++	Static
Indus/Kaveri	Java	Static
JSlice	Java	Dynamic
SeeSlice	C	Dynamic

9.6.4 *Program Slicing Tools*

Any reader who has gone carefully through the preceding section will agree that program slicing is not a viable manual approach. We hesitate assigning a slicing exercise to our university students, because the actual learning is only marginal in terms of the time spent. With good tools, however, program slicing has its place. There are a few program slicing tools, most are academic or experimental, but there are a very few commercial tools. (See [Hoffner 95] for a dated comparison.)

The more elaborate tools feature inter-procedural slicing, something clearly useful for large systems. Much of the market uses program slicing to improve the program comprehension that maintenance programmers need. One, JSlice, will be appropriate for object-oriented software. Table 9.4 summarizes a few program slicing tools.

Exercises

1. Compare and contrast DD-paths and du-paths.
2. If a mocked function includes a difference from the original could a false positive, false negative, or both be introduced? If so, provide an example. If not, provide an explanation.
3. The source code for the slice on totalTruffles at line 36, S(totalTruffles, 36), is repeated here:

```
1    private static double updateShoppingCart() {
2        double trufflePrice = 12.50;
5        double truffleSales = 0.0;
8        double totalSales = 0.0;
9        int totalTruffles = 0;
12       String message = "";
13       String event;
```

```
14    do {
15      while(queueOfEvents.isEmpty());
16      event = queueOfEvents.remove();
17      if(event.equalsIgnoreCase("Remove 1 Truffles") &&
        totalTruffles > 0) {
18        totalTruffles--;
19        message = "Removed 1 Truffle";
26      } else if(event.equalsIgnoreCase("Add 1 Truffles")) {
27        totalTruffles++;
28        message = "Added 1 Truffle";
35      }
36      truffleSales = trufflePrice * totalTruffles;
45    }
46  }
```

List the Statement fragment numbers for all Def(totalTruffles) nodes. Do the same for all Use(totalTruffles) nodes.

4. List the du-paths for the totalTruffles variable, and indicate which are definition clear. How do these du-paths align with the slices on totalTruffles?
5. List the elements in the slice S(saffronSales, 40).
6. Our discussion of slices in this chapter has actually been about "backward slices" in the sense that we are always concerned with parts of a program that contribute to the value of a variable at a certain point in the program. We could also consider "forward slices" that refer to parts of the program where the variable is used. Compare and contrast forward slices with du-paths.

References

Thomas Ball, and Stephen G. Eick, "Visualizing Program Slices", *Proceedings of the 1994 IEEE Symposium on Visual Languages*, pp. 288–295, October 1994.

Kent Beck. "Simple smalltalk testing: With patterns", *The Smalltalk Report* 4.2 (1994): 16–18.

Robert V. Binder "Testing object-oriented software: a survey." *Software Testing, Verification and Reliability* 6.3–4 (1996): 125–252.

S. R. Chidamber and C. F. Kemerer, "A metrics suite for object-oriented design", *IEEE Transactions of Software Engineering* vol. 20, No 6: pp. 476–493, (1994).

Lori A. Clarke et al., "A formal evaluation of dataflow path selection criteria", *IEEE Transactions on Software Engineering*, Vol. SE-15, No. 11, pp. 1318–1332, November 1989.

https://martinfowler.com/bliki/Xunit.html

Chris Gaffney, Christian Trefftz, and Paul Jorgensen. "Tools for coverage testing: necessary but not sufficient", *Journal of Computing Sciences in Colleges*, 20.1 (2004): 27–33.

K. B. Gallagher and J. R. Lyle, "Using program slicing in software maintenance", *IEEE Transactions on Software Engineering*, vol. SE-17, no.8, pp. 751–761, Aug. 1991.

T. Hoffner, Evaluation and comparison of Program Slicing Tools, Technical Report, Dept. of Computer and Information Science, Linkoping University, Sweden, 1995.

Paul C. Jorgensen, and Carl Erickson. "Object-oriented integration testing". *Communications of the ACM*, 37.9 (1994): 30–38.

https://github.com/Pragmatists/JUnitParams

https://site.mockito.org/

S. Rapps and E.J. Weyuker, "Selecting software test data using Dataflow information". *IEEE Transactions on Software Engineering*, Vol. SE-11, No. 4, pp. 367–375, April, 1985.

M. Weiser, Program slices: Formal psychological and practical investigations of an automatic program abstraction method. PhD thesis University of Michigan, Ann Arbor, MI.

M. D. Weiser, "Program slicing", *IEEE Transactions on Software Engineering*, vol. SE-10, no. 4, pp. 352–357, April, 1984.

https://en.wikipedia.org/wiki/List_of_unit_testing_frameworks

https://en.wikipedia.org/wiki/Unit_testing

Chapter 10

Retrospective on Unit Testing

When should unit testing stop? Here are some possible answers:

1. When you run out of time.
2. When continued testing causes no new failures.
3. When continued testing reveals no new faults.
3. When you cannot think of any new test cases.
4. When you reach a point of diminishing returns.
5. When mandated coverage has been attained.
6. When all faults have been removed.

Unfortunately, the first answer is all too common, and the seventh cannot be guaranteed. This leaves the testing craftsperson somewhere in the middle. Software reliability models provide answers that support the second and third choices; both have been used with success in industry. The fourth choice is curious: if you have followed the precepts and guidelines we have been discussing, this is probably a good answer. On the other hand, if the reason is due to a lack of motivation, this choice is as unfortunate as the first. The point of diminishing returns choice has some appeal: it suggests that serious testing has continued, and the discovery of new faults has slowed dramatically. Continued testing becomes very expensive and may reveal no new faults. If the cost (or risk) of remaining faults can be determined, the trade-off is clear. (This is a big IF.) We are left with the coverage answer, and it is a pretty good one. In this chapter, we will see how using structural testing as a cross-check on functional testing yields powerful results. First, we take a broad brush look at the unit testing methods we studied. Metaphorically, this is pictured as a pendulum that swings between extremes. Next, we follow one swing of the pendulum from the most abstract form of code-based testing through strongly semantic-based methods, and then back toward the very abstract shades of specification-based testing. We do this tour with the Triangle Program. After that, some recommendations for both forms of unit testing, followed by another case study—this time of an automobile insurance example.

10.1 The Test Method Pendulum

As with many things in life, there is a pendulum that swings between two extremes. The test method pendulum swings between two extremes of low semantic content—from strictly topological to purely functional. As testing methods move away from the extremes and toward the center, they at once become both more effective and more difficult. (See Figure 10.1.)

On the code-based side, path based testing relies on the connectivity of a program graph—the semantic meaning of the nodes is lost. A program graph is a purely topological abstraction of the code; it is nearly devoid of code meaning—only the control flow remains. This gives rise to program paths which can never be recognized as infeasible by automated means. Moving to dataflow testing, the kinds of dependencies that typically create infeasible paths can often be detected. Finally, when viewed in terms of slices, we arrive as close as we can to the semantic meaning of the code.

On the spec-based side, testing based only on boundary values of the variables is vulnerable to severe gaps and redundancies, neither of which can be known in purely spec-based testing. Equivalence class testing uses the "similar treatment" idea to identify classes, and in doing so, uses more of the semantic meaning of the specification. Finally, decision table testing uses both necessary and impossible combinations of conditions, derived from the specification, to deal with complex logical considerations.

On both sides of the testing pendulum, test case identification becomes easier as we move toward the extremes. It also becomes less effective. As testing techniques move toward higher semantic meaning, they become more difficult to automate—and more effective. Hmmm...could it be that, when he wrote "The Pit and the Pendulum," Edgar Allen Poe was actually thinking about testing as a pit, and methods as a pendulum? You decide. Meanwhile, these ideas are approximated in Figure 10.2.

These graphs need some elaboration. Starting with program graph testing, notice that the nodes contain absolutely no semantic information about the statement fragments—and the edges just describe whether one fragment can be executed after a predecessor fragment. Paths in a program graph are all topologically possible—in fact

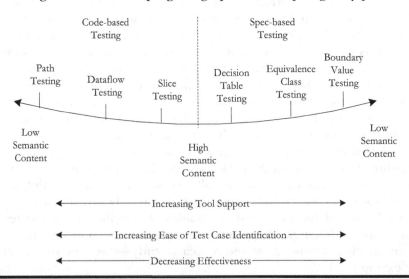

Figure 10.1   The test method pendulum.

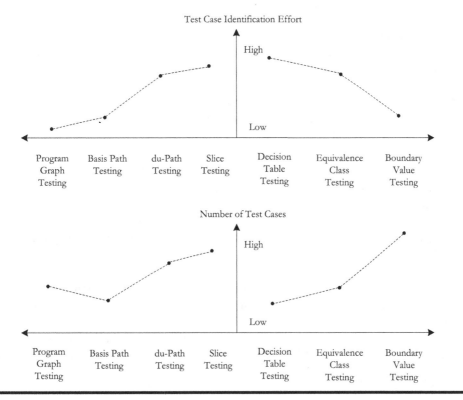

Figure 10.2 Effort and efficacy of unit test methods.

they can be generated mathematically with Warshall's Algorithm. The problem is that the set of topologically possible paths includes both feasible and infeasible paths, as we discussed in Chapter 8. Moving in the direction of McCabe's basis path testing adds a little semantic content (see Section 8.4). The recommended starting point is a mainline path that represents common unit functionality. The basis path method runs into trouble after that due to the heuristic of simply "flipping" decisions as they are encountered on the starting point path. This also leads to the possibility of infeasible paths. When testing moves to the define/use domain, we use more semantic meaning. We follow where values of variables are defined and later used. The distinction between define-use paths and definition-clear paths gives the tester even more semantic information. Finally, backward slices do two things, they eliminate unwanted detail, and thereby focus attention exactly where it is needed—all the statements affecting the value of a variable at a given point in a program. The program slicing literature contains extensive discussions of automatic slicing algorithms that are beyond the scope of this book.

On the specification-based side, the various forms of boundary value testing are shown as the most abstract. All test cases are derived from properties of the input space with absolutely no consideration about how the values are used in the unit code. When we move to equivalence class testing, the prime factor that determines a class is the "similar treatment" principle. Clearly, this moves in the direction of semantic meaning. Moving from equivalence class testing to decision table testing is usually done for two reasons: the presence of dependencies among the variables, and the possibility of impossible combinations—clearly semantic information.

The lower half of Figure 10.2 shows that, for specification-based testing, there is a true trade-off between test case creation effort and test case execution time. If the testing is automated, as in a JUnit environment, this is not a penalty. On the code-based side, as methods get more sophisticated, they concurrently generate more test cases. The bottom line to this discussion is that the combination of specification-based and code-based methods depends on the nature of the unit being tested, and this is where testers can exhibit craft rather than art.

10.2 Traversing the Pendulum

We will use a "classical" version of the Triangle Program to explore some of the lessons of the testing pendulum. We begin with a flowchart of an efficient version so popular in the early literature. We use this implementation here, mostly because it is the most frequently used in testing literature (Brown and Lipov, 1975; Pressman, 1982). The flowchart from Chapter 2 is repeated here in Figure 10.3, and it is shown as a directed graph in Figure 10.4.

We can begin to see some of the difficulties when we base testing on a program graph. There are 352 topologically possible paths in Figure 10.4 (and also in Figure 10.3), but only 11 of these are feasible; they are listed in Table 10.1. Since this is at one abstract end of the testing pendulum, we cannot expect any automated help to separate feasible from infeasible paths. Much of the infeasibility is due to the match variable. Its intent was to reduce the number of decisions. The boxes incrementing the match variable depend on tests of equality among the three pairs of sides. Of the eight paths from box 1 to box 7, the logically possible values of match are 0, 1, 2, 3, and 6. The three impossible paths correspond to exactly two pairs of sides being equal, which, by transitivity means that the sides in the third pair are equal.

Based on the flowchart, this version computes the sums of pairs (a + b, a + c, and b + c) only once and uses these later in the decisions checking the triangle inequality (decisions 8, 9, 10, 14, 17, and 19).

10.2.1 Program Graph-Based Testing

We can begin to see some of the difficulties when we base testing on a program graph (see Figure 10.4 where there are 352 topologically possible paths). Compare this to the 11 of feasible paths in Figure 10.3; they are listed in Table 10.2. Since this is at one abstract end of the testing pendulum, we cannot expect any automated help to separate feasible from infeasible paths. Some of the infeasibility is due to the match variable. Its intent was to reduce the number of decisions. The boxes incrementing the match variable depend on tests of equality among the three pairs of sides. Of the eight paths from node 1 to node 14, the logically possible values of match are 0, 1, 2, 3, and 6. Also, no pair of triangle inequalities in nodes 15 to 19 can be true, thereby eliminating four of the topologically possible paths.

10.2.2 Basis Path Testing

Moving on to basis path testing, we have another problem. Since the program graph in Figure 10.4 has a cyclomatic complexity of 14, McCabe's basis path method would ask us to find 14 test cases, but there are only 11 feasible paths. They are shown in Table 10.3.

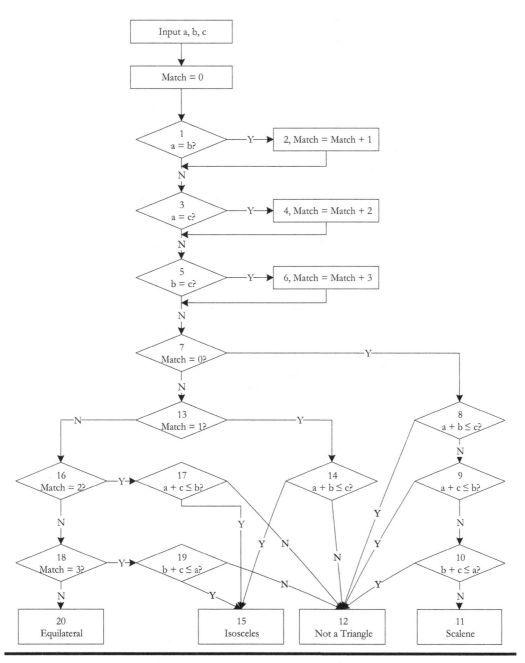

Figure 10.3   Flowchart of Efficient Triangle Program.

Table 10.4 shows one main path and its "flipped" paths, many of which are counter-intuitive. In this exercise, the main path takes the false branch for every decision except the one at node 12. This choice ignores the semantic meaning of the code associated with the nodes and therefore leads to a nearly useless set of basis paths. Other choices for a main path will have similarly useless results. The bottom line: basis path testing adds little to the information obtained from program graph based testing, and it can be worse.

Table 10.1 Feasible Paths in the Efficient Triangle Program Flowchart

Path	Node Sequence	Description
p1	1–2–3–4–5–6–7–13–16–18–20	Equilateral
p2	1–3–5–6–7–13–16–18–19–15	Isosceles (b = c)
p3	1–3–5–6–7–13–16–18–19–12	Not a Triangle (b = c)
p4	1–3–4–5–7–13–16–17–15	Isosceles (a = c)
p5	1–3–4–5–7–13–16–17–12	Not a Triangle (a = c)
p6	1–2–3–5–7–13–14–15	Isosceles (a = b)
p7	1–2–3–5–7–13–14–12	Not a Triangle (a = b)
p8	1–3–5–7–8–12	Not a Triangle (a + b ≤ c)
p9	1–3–5–7–8–9–12	Not a Triangle (b + c ≤ a)
p10	1–3–5–7–8–9–10–12	Not a Triangle (a + c ≤ b)
p11	1–3–5–7–8–9–10–11	Scalene

Table 10.2 Possible and Feasible Paths in Figure 10.4

Node Segment	Topologically Possible Paths	Feasible Paths
1 to 12	8	4
12 to 20	8	4
12 to 25	2	2
12 to 30	2	2
12 to 35	2	2
	Combinations of Segments	
1 to 20	64	4
1 to 25, 36	16	2
1 to 30, 36	16	2
1 to 35, 36	16	2
36 to 40	1	1
Total	112	11

10.2.3 Dataflow Testing

Dataflow testing will give us some valuable insights. Consider du-paths on the match variable. It has four definition nodes (5, 7, 9, and 11), three computation uses (7, 9, and 11), and four predicate uses (13, 21, 26, 31), so there are 28 possible du-paths.

```
1.    public static String triangleType(int a, int b, int c) {
1.        int match;
1.        String triangleType = "";
2.        System.out.println("Side A is " + a);
3.        System.out.println("Side B is " + b);
4.        System.out.println("Side C is " + c);
5.        match = 0;
6.        if(a == b)
7.            match = match + 1;
8.        if(a == c)
9.            match = match + 2;
10.       if(b == c)
11.           match = match + 3;
12.       if(match == 0) {
13.           if((a+b)<=c)
14.               triangleType = "NotATriangle";
15.           else if((b+c)<=a)
16.               triangleType = "NotATriangle";
17.           else if((a+c)<=b)
18.               triangleType = "NotATriangle";
19.           else
20.               triangleType = "Scalene";
21.       } else if(match == 1) {
22.           if((a+c)<=b)
23.               triangleType = "NotATriangle";
24.           else
25.               triangleType = "Isosceles";
26.       } else if(match == 2) {
27.           if((a+c)<=b)
28.               triangleType = "NotATriangle";
29.           else
30.               triangleType = "Isosceles";
31.       } else if(match == 3) {
32.           if((b+c)<=a)
33.               triangleType = "NotATriangle";
34.           else
35.               triangleType = "Isosceles";
36.       } else {
37.           triangleType = "Equilateral";
38.       }
39.       return triangleType;
40.   }
```

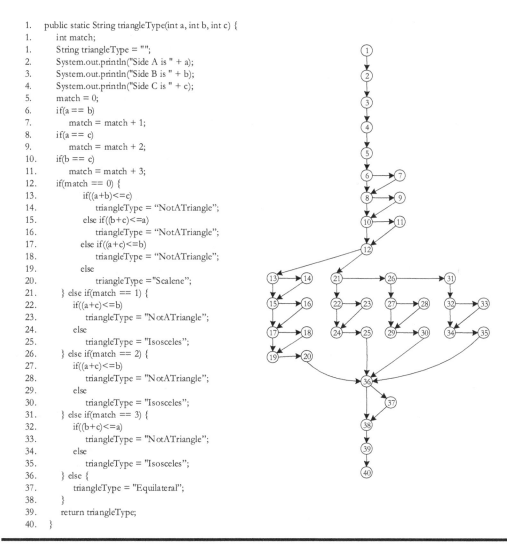

Figure 10.4   Program Graph of the Efficient Triangle Program.

The computation definition-clear paths dc(5, 7) yields the value match = 1, dc(5, 9) yields the value match = 2, and dc(5, 11) yields the value match = 3.

It is more interesting to look at du-paths involving the triangleType variable. We can assume that triangleType is initialized to "" at statement 1, and is given values at nodes 14, 16, 18, 20, 23, 25, 28, 30, 33, 35, and 37. Each of the paths from 1 to any of the later defining nodes is an important path that follows the logic of the triangle program. Six du-paths give triangleType the value "Not A Triangle": (1, 14), (1, 16), (1, 18), (1, 23), (1, 28), and (1, 33). Similarly three du-paths give triangleType the value "Isosceles": (1, 25), 1, 30), and 1, 35). There is only one du-path that gives triangleType the value "Scalene", and only one gives triangleType the value "Equilateral". Each of these du-paths echoes one of the known 11 feasible paths. (Quite an improvement over basis paths!) Looking at the du-paths for the side variables, a, b, and c is not helpful, but their role will be more important in slice-based testing.

Table 10.3   Feasible Paths in Figure 10.4

Path	Node Sequence	Match	Result
p1	1–6, 8, 10, 12, 13, 15, 17, 19, 20, 36, 38, 39, 40	0	Scalene
p2	1–6, 7, 8, 10, 12, 13, 15, 17, 19, 20, 36, 38, 39, 40	1	Isosceles a = b
p3	1–6, 8, 9, 10, 12, 26, 27, 29, 30, 36, 38, 39, 40	2	Isosceles a = c
p4	1–7, 8, 10, 11, 12, 31, 32, 34, 35, 36, 38, 39, 40	3	Isosceles b = c
p5	1–6, 8, 10, 12, 13, 14, 36, 37, 38, 39, 40	6	Equilateral
p6	1–6, 8, 10, 12, 14, 38, 39, 40	0	Not a triangle (a + b) > c
p7	1–6, 8, 10, 12, 14, 15, 16, 38, 39, 40	0	Not a triangle (b + c) > a
p8	1–6, 8, 10, 12, 14, 17, 18, 38, 39, 40	0	Not a triangle (a + c) > b
p9	1–6, 7, 8, 12, 21, 22, 23, 38, 39, 40	1	Not a triangle (a + c) > b
p10	1–6, 8, 9, 10, 12, 26, 27, 38, 39, 40	2	Not a triangle (a + c) > b
p11	1–6, 8, 10, 11, 12, 31, 32, 33, 38, 39, 40	3	Not a triangle (b + c) > a

Table 10.4   One Set of Basis Paths

Path	Flip Node	Node Sequence	Match	Result
1	main	1–6, 8, 10, 12, 13, 15, 17, 19, 20, 36, 38, 39, 40	0	Scalene
2	flip 6	1–6, 7, 8, 10, 12, 13, 15, 17, 19, 20, 36, 38, 39, 40	1	Scalene
3	flip 8	1–6, 8, 9, 10, 12, 13, 15, 17, 19, 20, 36, 38, 39, 40	2	Scalene
4	flip 10	1–6, 8, 10, 11, 12, 13, 15, 17, 19, 20, 36, 38, 39, 40	3	Scalene
5	flip 13	1–6, 7, 8, 10, 12, 13, 14, 15, 17, 19, 20, 36, 38, 39, 40	0	Scalene
6	flip 15	1–6, 7, 8, 10, 12, 13, 15, 16, 17, 19, 20, 36, 38, 39, 40	0	Scalene
7	flip 17	1–6, 7, 8, 10, 12, 13, 15, 17, 18, 19, 20, 36, 38, 39, 40	0	Scalene
8	flip 12	1–6, 8, 10, 12, 21, 22, 24, 25, 36, 38, 39, 40	0	Isosceles
9	flip 22	1–6, 8, 10, 12, 21, 22, 23, 24, 25, 36, 38, 39, 40	0	Isosceles
10	flip 21	1–6, 8, 10, 12, 21, 26, 27, 29, 36, 38, 39, 40	0	(no result)
11	flip 27	1–6, 8, 10, 12, 21, 26, 27, 28, 29, 30, 36, 38, 39, 40	0	Isosceles
12	flip 26	1–6, 8, 10, 12, 21, 26, 31, 32, 34, 35, 36, 38, 39, 40	0	Isosceles
13	flip 32	1–6, 8, 10, 12, 21, 26, 31, 32, 33, 34, 35, 36, 38, 39, 40	0	Not a triangle
14	flip 36	1–6, 7, 8, 10, 12, 13, 14, 15, 17, 19, 20, 36, 37, 38, 39, 40	0	Equilateral

10.2.4 *Slice-Based Testing*

Testing using backward static slices would be a good idea. In fact, each of the du-paths for triangleType described above lets a tester focus on where triangleType gets its value(s) at those points of the program. The advantage of slices over du-paths is that careful examination of the program logic in a slice shows how to generate test case values. Here is one example: the slice on triangleType at statement 20 (S(triangleType, 20).

```
1.     public static String triangleType(int a, int b, int c) {
1.     int match;
1.     String triangleType = "";

5.             match = 0;
6.             if(a == b)
7.                 match = match + 1;
8.             if(a == c)
9.                 match = match + 2;
10.           if(b == c)
11.               match = match + 3;
12.           if(match == 0) {
13.                   if((a+b)<=c)
14.                       triangleType = "NotATriangle";
15.                   else if((b+c)<=a)
16.                       triangleType = "NotATriangle";
17.                   else if((a+c)<=b)
18.                       triangleType = "NotATriangle";
19.                   else
20.                       triangleType ="Scalene";
```

If we look carefully at statements 5 through 20, we see that the end value of triangle-Type depends on the values of a, b, c, and match. They serve as a guideline to finding actual test case values of a, b, and c. In statements 5–11, we learn that the values of a, b, and c satisfy all three combinations of the triangle inequality. In addition, since match = 0, we know that there is no pair of equal sides. Table 10.5 shows how this logic can be applied to candidate values of the side variables.

The following source statements are the slice on triangleType at statement 14 (S(triangleType, 14).

```
1.     public static String triangleType(int a, int b, int c) {
1.     int match;
1.     String triangleType = "";

5.             match = 0;
6.             if(a == b)
7.                 match = match + 1;
8.             if(a == c)
9.                 match = match + 2;
10.           if(b == c)
11.               match = match + 3;
12.           if(match == 0) {
13.                   if((a+b)<=c)
14.                       triangleType = "NotATriangle";

39.    return triangleType
40.    }
```

Table 10.5 Test Case Values Derived from Slices

case	a	b	c	(a + b) <= c?	(b + c) < = a?	(a + c) < = b?	Equal sides?	Value of triangleType	Statement Number
1	3	4	9	yes	no	no	none	Not a Triangle	14
2	11	4	5	no	yes	no	none	Not a Triangle	16
3	3	10	5	no	no	yes	none	Not a Triangle	18
4	3	4	5	no	no	no	none	Scalene	20
5	5	5	3	yes	no	no	a = b	Not a Triangle	23
6	3	3	4	no	no	no	a = b	Isosceles	25
7	5	3	5	no	no	yes	a = c	Not a Triangle	28
8	3	4	3	no	no	no	a = c	Isosceles	30
9	3	5	5	no	yes	no	b = c	Not a Triangle	33
10	4	3	3	no	no	no	b = c	Isosceles	35
11	5	5	5	no	no	no	all	Equilateral	37

10.2.5 Boundary Value Testing

Notice that, in the pendulum swing from the very abstract program graphs to the semantically rich slice-based testing, the testing is improved. We can expect the same on the specification-based side. Here we use boundary value testing to define test cases. We will do this for both the normal and worst-case formulations. Table 10.6 shows the test cases generated using the nominal boundary value form of functional testing. The last column shows the path (from Table 10.3) taken by the test case.

The following paths are covered: p1, p2, p3, p4, p5, p6, p7; and paths p8, p9, p10, p11 are missed. Now, suppose we use a more powerful functional testing technique, worst-case boundary value testing. We saw, in Chapter 5, that this yields 125 test cases; they are summarized here in Table 10.7 so you can see the extent of the redundant path coverage.

Taken together, the 125 test cases provide full path coverage, but the redundancy is onerous.

10.2.6 Equivalence Class Testing

The next step in the pendulum progression is Equivalence Class testing. For the Triangle Problem, equivalence classes on the individual variables are pointless. Instead, we can make equivalence classes on the types of triangles, and the six ways that the variables a, b, and c can fail to be sides of a triangle. In Chapter 6 (Section 6.4), we ended up with these equivalence classes:

$$D1 = \{<a, b, c>: a = b = c\}$$
$$D2 = \{<a, b, c>: a = b, a \neq c\}$$
$$D3 = \{<a, b, c>: a = c, a \neq b\}$$
$$D4 = \{<a, b, c>: b = c, a \neq b\}$$

D5 = {<a, b, c>: a ≠ b, a ≠ c, b ≠ c}
D6 = {<a, b, c>: a > b + c}
D7 = {<a, b, c>: b > a + c}
D8 = {<a, b, c>: c > a + b}
D9 = {<a, b, c>: a = b + c}
D10 = {<a, b, c>: b = a + c}
D11 = {<a, b, c>: c = a + b}

Since these are equivalence classes, we will have just 11 test cases, and we know we will have full coverage of the 11 feasible paths in Figure 10.4.

10.2.7 Decision Table Testing

The last step is to see if decision tables will add anything to the equivalence class test cases. They do not, but they can provide some insight into the decisions in the Efficient Triangle Program flowchart. In the decision table in Table 10.8, first notice

Table 10.6   Path Coverage of Normal Boundary Values

Case	a	b	c	Expected Output	Path
1	100	100	1	Isosceles	p6
2	100	100	2	Isosceles	p6
3	100	100	100	Equilateral	p1
4	100	100	199	Isosceles	p6
5	100	100	200	Not a Triangle	p7
6	100	1	100	Isosceles	p4
7	100	2	100	Isosceles	p4
8	100	100	100	Equilateral	p1
9	100	199	100	Isosceles	p4
1	100	200	100	Not a Triangle	p5
11	1	100	100	Isosceles	p2
12	2	100	100	Isosceles	p2
13	100	100	100	Equilateral	p1
14	199	100	100	Isosceles	p2
15	200	100	100	Not a Triangle	p3

Table 10.7   Path Coverage of Nominal and Worst-case Boundary Values

	p1	p2	p3	p4	p5	p6	p7	p8	p9	p10	p11
Nominal	3	3	1	3	1	3	1	0	0	0	0
Worst-case	5	12	6	11	6	12	7	17	18	19	12

Table 10.8 Decision Table for the Efficient Triangle Program

(a) Part 1

c1. match =	0				1				2			
c2. a + b <= c?	T	F!	F!	F	T	F!	F!	F	T	F!	F!	F
c3. a + c <= b?	F!	T	F!	F	F!	T	F!	F	F!	T	F!	F
c4. b + c <= a?	F!	F!	T	F	F!	F!	T	F	F!	F!	T	F
a1. Scalene				x								
a2. Not a Triangle	x	x	x		x	x	x		x	x	x	
a3. Isosceles								x				x
a4. Equilateral												
a5. Impossible												

(b) Part 2

c1. match =	3				4	5		6			
c2. a + b <= c?	T	F!	F!	F	--	--		T	F!	F!	F
c3. a + c <= b?	F!	T	F!	F	--	--		F!	T	F!	F
c4. b + c <= a?	F!	F!	T	F	--	--		F!	F!	T	F
a1. Scalene											
a2. Not a Triangle	x	x	x					x	x	x	
a3. Isosceles				x							
a4. Equilateral											x
a5. Impossible					x	x					

that the condition on match is an extended entry. Although it is topologically possible for to have match = 4 and match = 5, these values are logically impossible. Conditions c2, c3, and c4 are exactly those used in the flowchart. We use the "F!" (must be false) notation to denote the impossibility of more than one of these conditions to be true. Also, note that there is no point in developing conditions on the individual variables a, b, and c. To conclude the traversal of the pendulum, decision table-based testing did not add much, but it did highlight why some cases are impossible (Table 10.9).

Table 10.9 Comparison of Code-Based and Spec-Based Techniques

Path	Description	Prog Graph	Basis Path	Data-flow	Slice	Boundary Value	Equiv. Class	Decision Table
p1	Equilateral	yes	yes	yes	yes	yes (3)	yes	yes
p2	Isosceles (b = c)	yes	yes	yes	yes	yes (2)	yes	yes

(Continued)

Table 10.9 (*Continued*)

Path	Description	Prog Graph	Basis Path	Data-flow	Slice	Boundary Value	Equiv. Class	Decision Table
p3	Not a Triangle (b = c)	yes	yes	yes	yes	yes (1)	yes	yes
p4	Isosceles (a = c)	yes	yes	yes	yes	yes (2)	yes	yes
p5	Not a Triangle (a = c)	yes	yes	yes	yes	yes (1)	yes	yes
p6	Isosceles (a = b)	yes	yes	yes	yes	yes (1)	yes	yes
p7	Not a Triangle (a = b)	yes	**NO**	yes	yes	yes (1)	yes	yes
p8	Not a Triangle (a + b ≤ c)	yes	**NO**	yes	yes	**NO**	yes	yes
p9	Not a Triangle (b + c ≤ a)	yes	**NO**	yes	yes	**NO**	yes	yes
p10	Not a Triangle (a + c ≤ b)	yes	**NO**	yes	yes	**NO**	yes	yes
p11	Scalene	yes	yes (6)	yes	yes	**NO**	yes	yes

10.3 Insurance Premium Case Study

Here is an example that lets us compare both specification-based and code-based testing methods and apply the guidelines. A hypothetical insurance premium program computes the semiannual car insurance premium based on two parameters: the policyholder's age and driving record:

$$\text{Premium} = \text{BaseRate} * \text{ageMultiplier} - \text{safeDrivingReduction}$$

The ageMultiplier is a function of the policyholder's age, and the safe driving reduction is given when the current points (assigned by traffic courts for moving violations) on the policyholder's driver's license are below an age-related cutoff. Policies are written for drivers in the age range of 16 to 100. Once a policyholder exceeds 12 points, the driver's license is suspended (thus, no insurance is needed). The BaseRate changes from time to time; for this example, it is $500 for a semiannual premium. The data for the Insurance Premium program are in Table 10.10.

Table 10.10 Data for the Insurance Premium Problem

Age Range	Age Multiplier	Points Cutoff	Safe Driving Reduction
16 ≤ age < 25	2.8	1	50
25 ≤ age < 35	1.8	3	50
35 ≤ age < 45	1.0	5	100
45 ≤ age < 60	0.8	7	150
60 ≤ age < 100	1.5	5	200

10.4 Specification-Based Testing

Worst-case boundary value testing, based on the input variables, age, and points, yields the following extreme values of the age and points variables (Table 10.11). The corresponding 25 test cases are shown graphically in Figure 10.5.

Nobody should be content with these test cases. There is too much of the problem statement missing. The various age cutoffs are not tested, nor are the point cutoffs. We could refine this by taking a closer look at classes based on the age ranges.

A1 = {age: $16 \leq$ age < 25}
A2 = {age: $25 \leq$ age < 35}
A3 = {age: $35 \leq$ age < 45}
A4 = {age: $45 \leq$ age < 60}
A5 = {age: $60 \leq$ age < 100}

Table 10.11   Data Boundaries for the Insurance Premium Problem

Variable	Min	Min+	Nom.	Max-	Max
Age	16	17	54	99	100
Points	0	1	6	11	12

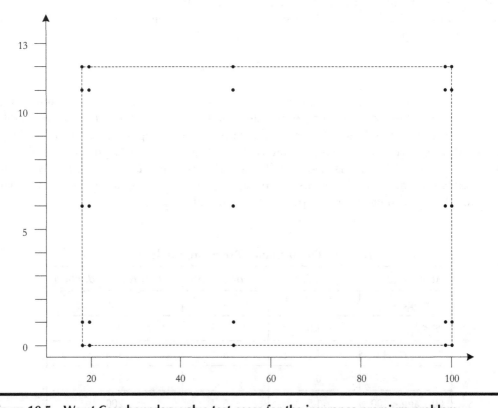

Figure 10.5   Worst Case boundary value test cases for the insurance premium problem.

Here are the age-dependent classes on license points.

P1(A1) = {points = 0, 1}, {points = 2, 3, ...,12}.
P2(A2) = {points = 0, 1, 2, 3}, {points = 4, 5, ...,12}.
P3(A3) = {points = 0, 1, 2, 3, 4, 5}, {points = 6, 7,...,12}.
P4(A4) = {points = 0, 1, 2, 3, 4, 5, 6, 7}, {points = 8, 9, 10, 11, 12}.
P5(A5) = {points = 0, 1, 2, 3, 4, 5}, {points = 6, 7,...,12}.

One added complexity is that the point ranges are dependent on the age of the policy holder and they also overlap. Both constraints are shown in Figure 10.6. The dashed lines show the age-dependent equivalence classes. A set of worst case boundary value test cases is shown only for Class A4 and its two related point classes are given in Figure 10.6. Because these ranges meet at "endpoints," we would have the worst-case test values shown in Table 10.12. Notice that the discrete values of the point variable do not lend themselves to the min + and max– convention in some cases. These are the variable values that lead to 103 test cases.

We are clearly at a point of severe redundancy; time to move on to equivalence class testing. The age sets A1–A5, and the points sets P1–P5 are natural choices for equivalence classes. The corresponding weak normal equivalence class test cases are shown in Figure 10.7. Since the point classes are not independent, we cannot do the usual cross product. Weak robust cases are of some value, because we would expect

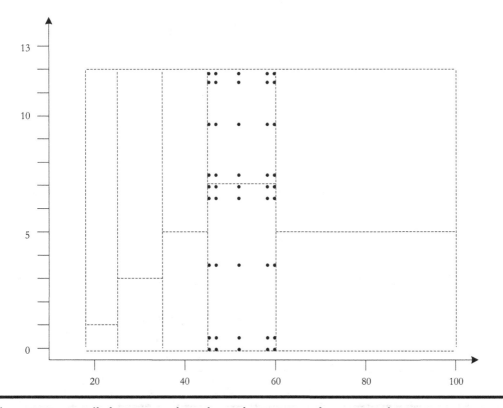

Figure 10.6 Detailed worst-case boundary value test cases for one age class.

Table 10.12   Detailed Worst-Case Values

Variable	Min	Min+	Nom.	Max-	Max
Age	16	17	20	24	
Age	25	26	30	34	
Age	35	36	40	44	
Age	45	46	53	59	
Age	60	61	75	99	100
Points(A1)	0	n/a	n/a	n/a	1
Points(A1)	2	3	7	11	12
Points(A2)	0	1	n/a	2	3
Points(A2)	4	5	8	11	12
Points(A3)	0	1	3	4	5
Points(A3)	6	7	9	11	12
Points(A4)	0	1	4	6	7
Points(A4)	8	9	10	11	12
Points(A5)	0	1	3	4	5
Points(A5)	6	7	9	11	12

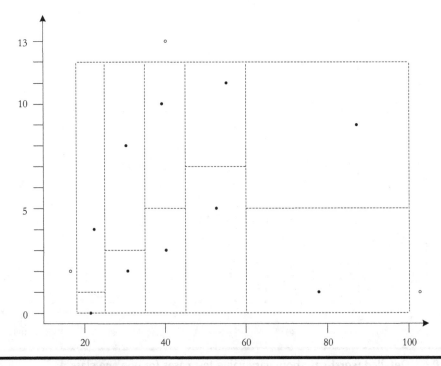

Figure 10.7   Weak and robust normal equivalence class test cases for the insurance premium program.

Table 10.13   Insurance Premium Decision Table

Variable	Min	Min+	Nom.	Max-	Max
Age	16	17	20	24	
Age	25	26	30	34	
Age	35	36	40	44	
Age	45	46	53	59	
Age	60	61	75	99	100
Points(A1)	0	n/a	n/a	n/a	1
Points(A1)	2	3	7	11	12
Points(A2)	0	1	n/a	2	3
Points(A2)	4	5	8	11	12
Points(A3)	0	1	3	4	5
Points(A3)	6	7	9	11	12
Points(A4)	0	1	4	6	7
Points(A4)	8	9	10	11	12
Points(A5)	0	1	3	4	5
Points(A5)	6	7	9	11	12

different outputs for drivers with age less than 16, and points in excess of 12. The additional weak robust test cases are shown as open circles in Figure 10.7.

The next step is to see if a decision table approach might help. Table 10.13 is a decision table based on the age equivalence classes. The decision table test cases are almost the same as those shown in Figure 10.7; the only weak robust test case missing in the decision table is that for points exceeding 12.

What are the error-prone aspects of the insurance premium program? The endpoints of the age ranges appear to be a good place to start, and this puts us back in boundary value mode. We can imagine many complaints from policy holders whose premium did not reflect a recent borderline birthday. Incidentally, this would be a good example of risk-based testing. Dealing with such complaints would be costly. Also, we should consider ages under 16 and over 100. Finally, we should probably check the values at which the safe driving reduction is lost, and maybe values of points over 12, when all insurance is lost. All of this is shown in Figure 10.7. (Notice that the responses to these were not in the problem statement, but our testing analysis provokes us to think about them.) Maybe this should be called hybrid functional testing: it uses the advantages of all three forms in a blend that is determined by the nature of the application (shades of special value testing). Hybrid appears appropriate, because such selection is usually done to improve the stock.

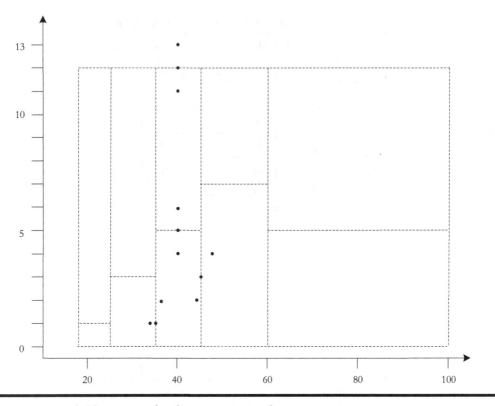

Figure 10.8   Hybrid test cases for the 35 to 45 age class.

To blend boundary value testing with weak robust equivalence class testing, note that the age class borders are helpful. Testing the max-, max, and max+ values of one age class automatically moves us into the next age class, so there is a slight economy. Figure 10.8 shows the hybrid test cases for the age range 35–45 in the insurance premium problem.

10.4.1 Code-Based Testing

Our analysis so far has been entirely specification-based. To be complete, we really need the code. It will answer questions such as whether the age variable is an integer (our assumption so far) or not. There is no question that the points variable is an integer. The pseudo code implementation is minimal in the sense that it does very little error checking. The pseudo code and its program graph are in Figure 10.9. Because the program graph is acyclic, only a finite number of paths exist—in this case, 11. The best choice is simply to have test cases that exercise each path. This automatically constitutes both statement and DD-Path coverage. The compound case predicates indicate multiple-condition coverage; this is accomplished only with the worst-case boundary test cases and the hybrid test cases. The remaining path-based coverage metrics are not applicable.

```
1.      public static PremiumResult insPremium (
1.        int driverAge, int driverPoints, double baseRate) {
2.      double premium;
3.      double ageMultiplier;
4.      int safeDriverReduction;
5.      boolean notInsurable;
6.      safeDriverReduction = 0;
7.      premium = 0;
8.      baseRate = 500;
9.      notInsurable = false;
10.       if (driverAge < 16) {
11.          notInsurable = true;
12.       } else if (driverAge < 25) {
13.          ageMultiplier = 2.8;
14.          if (driverPoints < 1)
15.            safeDriverReduction = 50;
16.       } else if (driverAge < 35) {
17.          ageMultiplier = 1.8;
18.          if (driverPoints < 3)
19.            safeDriverReduction =     50;
20.       } else if (driverAge < 45) {
21.          ageMultiplier = 1.0;
22.          if (driverPoints < 5)
23.            safeDriverReduction =     100;
24.       } else if (driverAge < 60) {
25.          ageMultiplier = 0.8;
26.          if (driverPoints < 7)
27.            safeDriverReduction = 150;
28.       } else if (driverAge < 100) {
29.          ageMultiplier = 1.5;
30.          if (driverPoints < 5)
31.            safeDriverReduction = 200;
32.       } else {
33.          notInsurable = false;
34.       }
35.     if (driverPoints > 12)
36.        notInsurable = false;
37.     premium = baseRate;
38.
39.     return new PremiumResult(premium, notInsurable);
40.   }
```

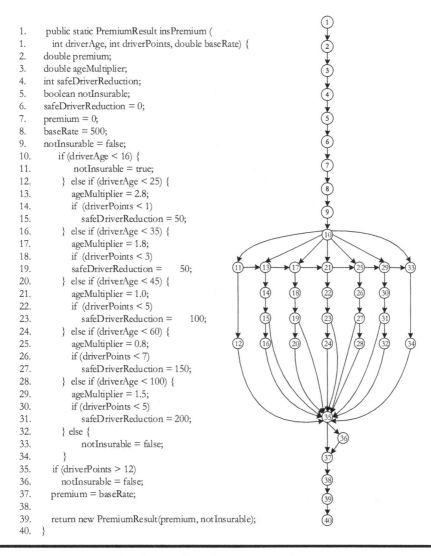

Figure 10.9   Insurance premium Java code and program graph.

10.4.1.1 Path-based Testing

The cyclomatic complexity of the program graph of the insurance premium program is V(G) = 12, and exactly 12 feasible program execution paths exist. They are listed in Table 10.14. If you follow the pseudo code for the various sets of functional test cases in Chapter 5, you will find the results shown in Table 10.15. We can see some of the insights gained from structural testing. For one thing, the problem of gaps and redundancies is obvious. Only the test cases from the hybrid approach yield complete path coverage. It is instructive to compare the results of these 25 test cases with the other two methods yielding the same number of test cases. The 25 boundary value test cases only cover six of the feasible execution paths, while the 25 weak

Table 10.14   Feasible Paths in the Insurance Premium Program

Path	Node Sequence
p1	1–9, 10, 11, 34–38
p2	1–9, 10, 12, 13, 14, 15, 34–38
p3	1–9, 10, 12, 14, 34–38
p4	1–9, 10, 12, 16, 17, 18, 19, 34–38
p5	1–9, 10, 12, 16, 17, 18, 34–38
p6	1–9, 10, 12, 16, 20, 21, 22, 23, 34–38
p7	1–9, 10, 12, 16, 20, 21, 22, 34–38
p8	1–9, 10, 12, 16, 20, 24, 25, 26, 27, 34–38
p9	1–9, 10, 12, 16, 20, 24, 25, 26, 34–38
p10	1–9, 10, 12, 16, 20, 24, 28, 29, 30, 31, 34–38
p11	1–9, 10, 12, 16, 20, 24, 28, 29, 30, 34–38
p12	1–9, 10, 12, 16, 20, 24, 28, 32, 33, 34–38

Table 10.15   Path Coverage of Functional Methods in the Insurance Program

Figure	Spec-Based Method	Test Cases	Paths covered
10.5	Normal Boundary Value	25	p2, p3, p8, p9, p10, p11
10.6	Worst Case Boundary Value	103	p2, p3, p4, p5, p6, p7, p8, p9, p10, p11
10.7	Weak Normal Equivalence Class	10	p2, p4, p6, p8, p10
10.7	Robust Normal Equivalence Class	12	p1, p2, p3, p4, p5, p6, p7, p8, p9, p10, p11, p12
10.7	Decision Table	12	p1, p2, p3, p4, p5, p6, p7, p8, p9, p10, p11, p12
10.8	Hybrid Spec-based	32	p1, p2, p3, p4, p5, p6, p7, p8, p9, p10, p11, p12

normal equivalence classes test cases cover 10 of the feasible execution paths. The next difference is in the coverage of the conditions in the case statement. Each predicate is a compound condition of the form $a <= x < b$. The only methods that yield test cases that exercise these extreme values are the worst-case boundary value (103) test cases and the hybrid (32) test cases. Incidentally, the McCabe Baseline Method will yield 11 of the 12 decision table test cases.

10.4.1.2 Dataflow Testing

Data flow testing for this problem is boring. The driverAge, points, and safeDriving Reduction variables all occur in six definition clear du-paths. The "uses" for driverAge and points are both predicate uses. Recall from Chapter 9 that the all-paths criterion implies all the lower dataflow covers.

10.4.1.3 Slice Testing

Slice testing does not provide much insight either. Four slices are of interest:

S(safeDrivingReduction, 33) = {1, 2, 3, 4, 5, 7, 8, 9, 10, 12, 13, 14, 15, 17, 18, 19, 20, 22, 23, 24, 25, 27, 28, 29, 32}
S(ageMultiplier, 33) = {1, 2, 3, 4, 5, 6, 10, 11, 15, 16, 20, 21, 25, 26, 32}
S(baseRate, 33) = {1}
S(Premium, 33) = {1, 2, 3, 4, 5, 6, 7, 8, 9, 10, 11, 12, 13, 14, 15, 16, 17, 18, 19, 20, 21, 22, 23, 24, 25, 26, 27, 28, 29, 32}

The union of these slices is the whole program. The only insight we might get from slice-based testing is that, if a failure occurred at line 33, the slices on safeDrivingReduction and ageMultiplier separate the program into two disjoint pieces, and that would simplify fault isolation.

10.5 Guidelines

One of my favorite testing stories is about an inebriated man was crawling around on the sidewalk beneath a street light. When a policeman asked him what he was doing, he replied that he was looking for his car keys. "Did you lose them here?" the policeman asked. "No, I lost them in the parking lot, but the light is better here."

This little story contains an important message for testers: testing for faults that are not likely to be present is pointless. It is far more effective to have a good idea of the kinds of faults that are most likely (or most damaging) and then to select testing methods that are likely to reveal these faults.

Many times, we do not even have a feeling for the kinds of faults that may be prevalent. What then? The best we can do is use known attributes of the program to select methods that deal with the attributes—sort of a "punishment fits the crime" view. The attributes that are most helpful in choosing specification-based testing methods are:

Whether the variables represent physical or logical quantities
Whether dependencies exist among the variables
Whether single or multiple faults are assumed
Whether exception handling is prominent

Here is the beginning of an "expert system" to help choosing a spec-based method:

1. If the variables refer to physical quantities, domain testing and equivalence class testing are indicated.
2. If the variables are independent, domain testing and equivalence class testing are indicated.
3. If the variables are dependent, decision table testing is indicated.
4. If the single-fault assumption is warranted, boundary value analysis and robustness testing are indicated.
5. If the multiple-fault assumption is warranted, worst-case testing, robust worst-case testing, and decision table testing are indicated.
6. If the program contains significant exception handling, robustness testing and decision table testing are indicated.
7. If the variables refer to logical quantities, equivalence class testing and decision table testing are indicated.

Combinations of these may occur; therefore, the guidelines are summarized as a decision table in Table 10.16.

What about code-based testing? Once again, we revert to the "punishment fits the crime" view. (But thinking of good testing as "punishment" is not appropriate.) This is where code coverage metrics are useful. As a reminder, we are focused on Unit Level testing. The first step is to examine the code for its main characteristics. Table 10.17 is a good starting point.

Table 10.16 Appropriate Choices for Functional Testing

c1	Variables (P, physical; L, logical)	P	P	P	P	P	L	L	L	L	L
c2	Independent variables?	Y	Y	Y	Y	N	Y	Y	Y	Y	N
c3	Single-fault assumption?	Y	Y	N	N	—	Y	Y	N	N	—
c4	Exception handling?	Y	N	Y	N	—	Y	N	Y	N	—
a1	Boundary value analysis		x								
a2	Robustness testing	x									
a3	Worst-case testing				x						
a4	Robust worst case			x							
a5	Weak Robust equivalence class	x		x			x		x		
a6	Weak Normal equivalence class	x	x				x	x			
a7	Strong Normal equivalence class			x	x	x			x	x	x
a8	Decision table					x					x

Table 10.17   Code Characteristics

Characteristic of code	Recommended practice(s)
Is it well structured?	Compute Cyclomatic complexity. If excessive (project dependent threshold), simplify first.
Are there violations of "structured programming?	Compute Cyclomatic complexity, then revise code. Revisit "is it well structured?"
Is it logic/decision intensive?	(Some of this will show up in the calculation of cyclomatic complexity.) Develop a program graph and apply the appropriate edge/decision coverage.
Does it contain compound conditions?	Apply either MCDC of Multiple Condition Coverage
Does it contain loops, and possibly nested loops?	Use loop coverage metrics (repeat and exit loop)
Is it computation intensive?	Use carefully selected dataflow and slice testing techniques to better understand code.
Is it hard to read/understand?	Apply "good programming practices": appropriate comments, good variable names, etc. And refactor.

Exercises

1. Repeat the gaps and redundancies analysis for the Triangle Problem using the implementation in Chapter 2 (Section 2.2.3) and its program graph in Chapter 8 Figure 8.2.
2. The Java code for the Insurance Premium Program (Figure 10.9) does not check for driver ages over 100. The Else clause (lines 32, 33) will catch this, but the output value of notInsurable is incorrect. Which functional testing techniques will reveal this fault? Which structural testing coverage, if not met, will reveal this fault?
3. In Figure 10.9, the statement at line 37 is incorrect. Which functional testing techniques will reveal this fault? Which structural testing coverage, if not met, will reveal this fault?

References

Brown, J.R. and Lipov, M., *Testing for Software Reliability, Proceedings of the International Symposium on Reliable Software*, Los Angeles, pp. 518–527, April 1975.

Pressman, Roger S., *Software Engineering: A Practitioner's Approach*, McGraw-Hill, New York, 1982.

BEYOND UNIT TESTING

In Part III, we build on the basic ideas of unit testing covered in Part II, with one major change. We are more concerned with knowing what to test and less concerned with how to test. To that end, the discussion in this part begins with the whole idea of Model-Based Testing. Chapter 11 examines testing based on models of software development life cycles, and models of software/system behavior are discussed in Chapter 19. Chapter 12 presents model-based strategies for integration testing, and these are extended to system testing in Chapter 13. Having completed this much, we are in a position to finally take a serious look at software complexity in Chapter 14. We apply much of this to a relatively recent question, testing systems of systems, in Chapter 15 and to testing Feature Interaction in Chapter 16.

Chapter 11

Life Cycle-Based Testing

In this chapter, we examine various models of the software development life cycle in terms of the implications these lifecycles have for testing. We took a general view in Chapter 1, where we identified three levels (unit, integration, and system) in terms of symmetries in the waterfall model of software development. This view has been relatively successful for decades, and these levels persist; however, the advent of alternative life cycle models mandates a deeper look at these views of testing. We begin with the traditional waterfall model, mostly because it is widely understood and is a reference framework for the more recent models. Then we look at derivatives of the waterfall model, and finally some mainline agile variations.

We also make a major shift in our thinking. We are more concerned with how to represent the item tested, because the representation may limit our ability to identify test cases.

11.1 Traditional Waterfall Testing

The traditional model of software development is the waterfall model, which is illustrated in Figure 11.1. It is sometimes drawn as a V as in Figure 11.2 to emphasize how the basic levels of testing reflect the early waterfall phases. (In ISTQB circles, this is known as "the V-Model.") In this view, information produced in one of the development phases constitutes the basis for test case identification at that level. Nothing controversial here: we certainly would hope that system test cases are clearly correlated with the requirements specification, and that unit test cases are derived from the detailed design of the unit. On the upper left side of the waterfall, the tight what/how cycles are important. They underscore the fact that the predecessor phase defines what is to be done in the successor phase. When complete, the successor phase states how it accomplishes "what" was to be done. These are also ideal points at which to conduct software reviews (see Chapter 20). Some humorists assert that these phases are the fault creation phases, and those on the right are the fault detection phases.

Two observations: a clear presumption of functional testing is used here, and an implied bottom-up testing order is used. Here, "bottom up" refers to levels of

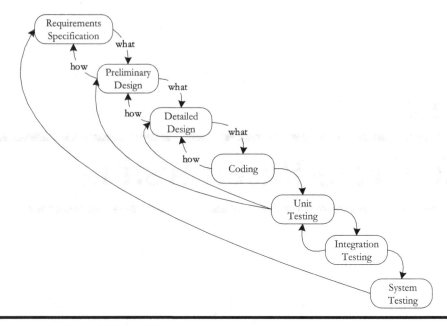

Figure 11.1 The waterfall lifecycle.

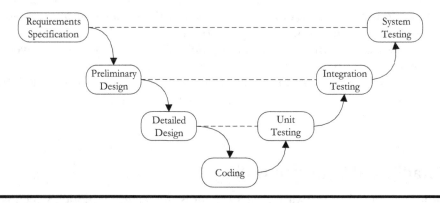

Figure 11.2 The Waterfall Lifecycle as the V Model.

abstraction—unit first, then integration, and finally, system testing. In Chapter 12, bottom up also refers to a choice of orders in which units are integrated (and tested).

Of the three main levels of testing (unit, integration, and system), unit testing is best understood. All of Part II is directed at the testing theory and techniques applicable to unit testing. System testing is understood better than integration testing, but both need clarification. The bottom-up approach sheds some insight: test the individual components, and then integrate these into subsystems until the entire system is tested. System testing should be something that the customer (or user) understands, and it often borders on customer acceptance testing. Generally, system testing is functional instead of structural; this is mostly due to the lack of higher level structural notations.

11.1.1 Waterfall Testing

The waterfall model is closely associated with top-down development and design by functional decomposition—it applies best to projects coded in a procedural language. The end result of preliminary design is a functional decomposition of the entire system into a tree-like structure of functional components. With such a decomposition, top-down integration would begin with the main program, checking the calls to the next level units, and so on until the leaves of the decomposition tree are reached. At each point, lower level units are replaced by stubs—throw-away code that replicates what the lower level units would do when called. Bottom-up integration is the opposite sequence, starting with the leaf units and working up toward the main program. In bottom-up integration, units at higher levels are replaced by drivers (another form of throw-away code) that emulate the procedure calls. The "big bang" approach simply puts all the units together at once, with no stubs or drivers. Whichever approach is taken, the goal of traditional integration testing is to integrate previously tested units with respect to the functional decomposition tree. Although this describes integration testing as a process, discussions of this type offer little information about the methods or techniques. We return to this in Chapter 12.

11.1.2 Pros and Cons of the Waterfall Model

In its history since the first publication in 1968, the Waterfall Model has been analyzed and critiqued repeatedly. The earliest compendium was by [Agresti, 1986] which stands as a good source. Agresti observes that:

- the framework fits well with hierarchical management structures,
- the phases have clearly defined end products (exit criteria), which in turn are convenient for project management, and
- the detailed design phase marks the starting point where individuals responsible for units can work in parallel., thereby shortening the overall project development interval.

More importantly, Agresti highlights major limitations of the Waterfall Model. We shall see that these limitations are answered by the derived lifecycle models. He observes that:

- there is a very long feedback cycle between requirements specification and system testing, in which the customer is absent,
- the model emphasizes analysis to the near exclusion of synthesis, which first occurs at the point of integration testing,
- massive parallel development at the unit level may not be sustainable with staffing limitations, and most importantly,
- "perfect foresight" is required, because any faults or omissions at the requirements level will penetrate through the remaining lifecycle phases.

The "omission" part was particularly troubling to the early waterfall developers. As a result, nearly all of the early papers of requirements specification demanded consistency, completeness, and clarity. Consistency is impossible to demonstrate for most requirements specification techniques (decision tables are an exception), and the need for clarity is obvious. The interesting part is completeness—all of the successor lifecycles assume incompleteness and depend on some form of iteration to gradually arrive at "completeness."

11.2 Testing in Iterative Lifecycles

Since the early 1980s, practitioners have devised alternatives in response to shortcomings of the traditional waterfall model just mentioned. The shift away from functional decomposition to an emphasis on iteration and composition is common to all these alternatives. Functional decomposition can only be well done when the system is completely understood, and it promotes analysis to the near exclusion of synthesis. The result is a very long separation between requirements specification and a completed system; and during this interval, no opportunity is available for feedback from the customer.

11.2.1 Waterfall Spin-Offs

There are three mainline derivatives of the waterfall model: incremental development, evolutionary development, and the spiral model [Boehm, 1988]. Each of these involves a series of increments or builds as shown in Figure 11.3. It is important to keep preliminary design as an integral phase, rather than to try to amortize such high-level design across a series of builds. (To do so usually results in unfortunate consequences of design choices made during the early builds that are regrettable in later builds.) This single design step cannot be done in the evolutionary and spiral models. This is also a major limitation of the bottom-up agile methods.

Within a build, the normal waterfall phases from detailed design through testing occur with one important difference: system testing is split into two steps—regression and progression testing. The main impact of the series of builds is that regression testing becomes necessary. The goal of regression testing is to ensure that things that worked correctly in the previous build still work with the newly added code.

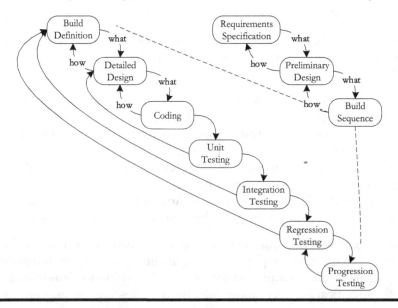

Figure 11.3   Iterative Development.

Regression testing can either precede or follow integration testing, or possibly occur in both places. Progression testing assumes that regression testing was successful and that the new functionality can be tested. Regression testing is an absolute necessity in a series of builds because of the well-known ripple effect of changes to an existing system. (The industrial average is that one change in five introduces a new fault.)

Evolutionary Development is best summarized as client-based iteration. In this spin-off, a small initial version of a product is given to users who then suggest additional features. This is particularly helpful in applications for which time-to-market is a priority. The initial version might capture a segment of the target market, and then that segment is "locked in" to future evolutionary versions. When these customers have a sense that they are "being heard," they tend to be more invested in the evolving product.

Barry Boehm's Spiral Model has some of the flavor of the evolutionary model. The biggest difference is that the increments are determined on the basis of risk rather than on client suggestions. The spiral is superimposed on an x-y coordinate plane, with the upper left quadrant referring to determining objectives, the upper right to risk analysis, the lower right refers to development (and test), and the lower left is for planning the next iteration. These four phases: determine objectives, analyze risk, develop, and test, and next iteration planning is repeated in an evolutionary way. At each evolutionary step, the spiral enlarges.

There are two views of regression testing: one is to simply repeat the tests from the previous iteration, the other is to devise a smaller set of test cases specifically focused on finding affected faults. Repeating a full set of previous integration tests is fine in an automated testing environment but is undesirable in a more manual environment. The expectation of test case failure is (or should be) lower for regression testing compared to that for progression testing. As a guideline, regression tests might fail in only 5 % of the repeated progression tests. This may increase to 20 % for progression tests. If regression tests are performed manually, there is an interesting term for special regression test cases: Soap Opera Tests. The idea is to have long, complex regression tests, akin to the complicated plot lines in television soap operas. A soap opera test case could fail in many ways, whereas a progression test case should fail for only a very few reasons. If a soap opera test case fails, clearly more focused testing is required to localize the fault. We will see this again in Chapter 20 on All-Pairs Testing.

The differences among the three spin-off models are due to how the builds are identified. In incremental development, the motivation for separate builds is usually to flatten the staff profile. With pure waterfall development, there can be a huge bulge of personnel for the phases from detailed design through unit testing. Many organizations cannot support such rapid staff fluctuations, so the system is divided into builds that can be supported by existing personnel. In evolutionary development, the presumption of a build sequence is still made, but only the first build is defined. Based on that, later builds are identified, usually in response to priorities set by the customer/user, so the system evolves to meet the changing needs of the user. This foreshadows the customer-driven tenet of the agile methods. The spiral model is a combination of rapid prototyping and evolutionary development, in which a build is defined first in terms of rapid prototyping and then is subjected to a go/no-go decision based on technology-related risk factors. From this, we see that keeping preliminary design as an integral step is difficult for the evolutionary and spiral models. To the extent that this cannot be maintained as an integral activity, integration testing is negatively affected. System testing is not affected.

Because a build is a set of deliverable end user functionality, one advantage common to all these spin-off models is that they provide earlier synthesis. This also results in earlier customer feedback, so two of the deficiencies of waterfall development are mitigated. The next section describes two approaches to deal with the "perfect foresight" problem.

11.2.2 Specification-Based Life Cycle Models

When systems are not fully understood (by either the customer or the developer), functional decomposition is perilous at best. Barry Boehm jokes when he describes the customer who says "I don't know what I want, but I'll recognize it when I see it." The rapid prototyping life cycle (Figure 11.4) deals with this by providing the "look and feel" of a system. In a sense, customers can recognize what they "see." In turn, this drastically reduces the specification-to-customer feedback loop by producing very early synthesis. Rather than build a final system, a "quick and dirty" prototype is built and then used to elicit customer feedback. Depending on the feedback, more prototyping cycles may occur. Once the developer and the customer agree that a prototype represents the desired system, the developer goes ahead and builds to a correct specification. At this point, any of the waterfall spin-offs might also be used. The agile lifecycles are the extreme of this pattern.

Rapid prototyping has no new implications for integration testing; but it has very interesting implications for system testing. Where are the requirements? Is the last prototype the specification? How are system test cases traced back to the prototype? One good answer to questions such as these is to use the prototyping cycles as information-gathering activities and then produce a requirements specification in a more traditional manner. Another possibility is to capture what the customer does

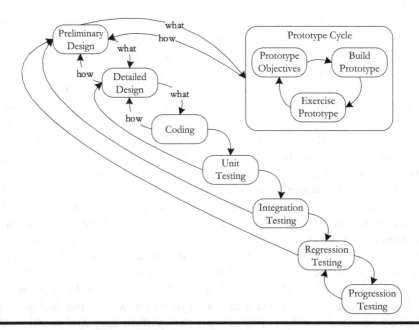

Figure 11.4   Rapid prototyping life cycle.

with the prototypes, define these as scenarios that are important to the customer, and then use these as system test cases. These could be precursors to the User Stories of the agile lifecycles. The main contribution of rapid prototyping is that it brings the operational (or behavioral) viewpoint to the requirements specification phase. Usually, requirements specification techniques emphasize the structure of a system, not its behavior. This is unfortunate, because most customers do not care about the structure, and they do care about the behavior.

Executable specifications (Figure 11.5) are an extension of the rapid prototyping concept. With this approach, the requirements are specified in an executable format (such as finite state machines, Statecharts, or Petri nets). The customer then executes the specification to observe the intended system behavior and provides feedback as in the rapid prototyping model. The executable models are, or can be, quite complex. Building an executable model requires expertise, and executing it requires an engine. Executable specification is best applied to event-driven systems, particularly when the events can arrive in different orders. David Harel, the creator of Statecharts, refers to such systems as "reactive" [Harel 1988], because they react to external events. As with Rapid Prototyping, the purpose of an executable specification is to let the customer experience scenarios of intended behavior. Another similarity is that executable models might have to be revised based on customer feedback. One side benefit is that a good engine for an executable model will support the capture of "interesting" system transactions, and it is often a nearly mechanical process to convert these into true system test cases. If this is done carefully, system testing can be traced directly back to the requirements.

Once again, this life cycle has no implications for integration testing. One big difference is that the requirements specification document is explicit, as opposed to a prototype. More importantly, it is often a mechanical process to derive system test cases from an executable specification. We will see this in Chapter 13. Although more work

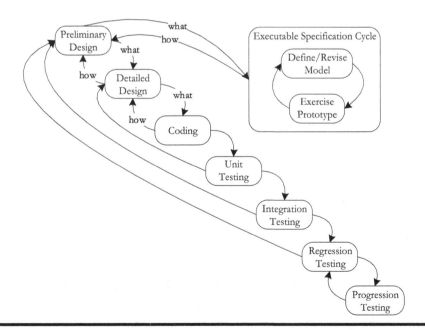

Figure 11.5   Executable specification.

is required to develop an executable specification, this is partially offset by the reduced effort to generate system test cases. Here is another important distinction: when system testing is based on an executable specification, we have an interesting form of structural testing at the system level. Finally, as we saw with rapid prototyping, the executable specification step can be combined with any of the iterative lifecycle models.

11.3 Agile Testing

The Agile Manifesto [http://agilemanifesto.org/] was written by 17 consultants, The Agile Alliance, in February, 2001. It has been translated into 42 languages and has drastically changed the software development world. The underlying characteristics of all agile lifecycles are:

- customer-driven
- bottom-up development
- flexibility with respect to changing requirements
- early delivery of fully functional components

These are sketched in Figure 11.6. Customers express their expectations in terms of "user stories," which are taken as the requirements for very short iterations of design-code-test. When does an agile project end? When the customer has no more user stories. Looking back at the iterative models, we see the progenitors of agility, especially in Barry Boehm's Spiral Model. Various websites will list as few as three to as many as 40 variations of agile software development. Here we look at three major ones and focus on how they deal with testing.

11.3.1 About User Stories

User stories are expressed by the Customer to the Developer. The most common form is a narrative in natural language. There are two other forms that lend structure to a purely narrative form—Behavior-Driven Development (BDD) scenarios and Use Cases.

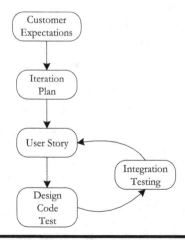

Figure 11.6   Generic Agile Lifecycle.

11.3.1.1 Behavior-Driven Development

Behavior-Driven Development (BDD) is completely consistent with agile development projects—it is an extension of Test-Driven Development (see Section 11.4.3) The BDD process centers on user stories that have a structure that translates easily into a decision table. We begin with an example from Dan North, an early proponent of BDD [Terhorst-North 2006].

> +Scenario 1: Account is in credit+.
> c1.:   Given the account is in credit
> c2:   And the card is valid
> c3:   And the dispenser contains cash
> c4:   When the customer requests cash
> a1:   Then ensure the account is debited
> a2:   And ensure cash is dispensed
> a3:   And ensure the card is returned

For transform applications such as this BDD scenario, the first four statements are conditions and the last three are actions the corresponding decision table. Decision tables work well for transform applications since the order of conditions does not matter. Here is a more formal definition of a BDD scenario:

Definition

A *well-formed BDD scenario* has the following sections and structure:

> Short ID
> IF   (<pre-condition(s)>),
> AND   (<data condition(s)>),
> AND   (<input event sequence>),
> THEN   (action sequence),
> AND   (<output event sequence>),
> AND   (<post-condition(s>).

Given a well-formed BDD scenario, the "IF" portion maps into decision table conditions, and the "THEN" portion maps into decision table actions. The full BDD scenario becomes a rule in the derived decision table. We begin a series of analyses decision table manipulations that illustrate how decision table manipulations can enhance the bottom-up nature of Behavior Driven Development (see decision tables 11.1 through 11.10).

In Decision Table 11.1, The IF portion of the BDD scenario maps to conditions c1, c2, c3, and c4; the THEN portion maps to the three action entries. The rule entries are all True.

If we mechanically expand Rule 1 using the same conditions and actions, we will have a complete Limited Entry Decision Table (LEDT), see Decision Table 11.2. The "?" action entries will gradually be removed as the final decision table is developed. Since there are 16 rules, we split the decision table into two parts. Also, we add action "a4. do nothing" in case we need it.

Decision Table 11.1   First Rule

Rule	1
c1. account is in credit	T
c2. card is valid?	T
c3. dispenser contains cash	T
c4. customer requests cash	T
a1. dispense cash	x
a2. debit customer account	x
a3. return card	x

Decision Table 11.2a   Rules 1 to 8

Rules	1	2	3	4	5	6	7	8
c1. account is in credit?	T	T	T	T	T	T	T	T
c2. card is valid?	T	T	T	T	F	F	F	F
c3. dispenser contains cash	T	T	F	F	T	T	F	F
c4. customer requests cash	T	F	T	F	T	F	T	F
a1. dispense cash	x	?	?	?	?	?	?	?
a2. debit customer account	x	?	?	?	?	?	?	?
a3. return card	x	?	?	?	?	?	?	?
a4. do nothing	—	?	?	?	?	?	?	?

Decision Table 11.2b   Rules 9 to 16

Rules	9	10	11	12	13	14	15	16
c1. account is in credit?	F	F	F	F	F	F	F	F
c2. card is valid?	T	T	T	T	F	F	F	F
c3. dispenser contains cash	T	T	F	F	T	T	F	F
c4. customer requests cash	T	F	T	F	T	F	T	F
a1. dispense cash	?	?	?	?	?	?	?	?
a2. debit customer account	?	?	?	?	?	?	?	?
a3. return card	?	?	?	?	?	?	?	?
a4. do nothing	?	?	?	?	?	?	?	?

Decision Table 11.3a   Rule 2 Action Entries Added

Rules	1	2	3	4	5	6	7	8
c1. account is in credit?	T	T	T	T	T	T	T	T
c2. card is valid?	T	T	T	T	F	F	F	F
c3. dispenser contains cash	T	T	F	F	T	T	F	F
c4. customer requests cash	T	F	T	F	T	F	T	F
a1. dispense cash	x	—	?	?	?	?	?	?
a2. debit customer account	x	—	?	?	?	?	?	?
a3. return card	x	x	?	?	?	?	?	?
a4. do nothing	—	x	?	?	?	?	?	?

This mechanical expansion may lead to additional scenarios, and in the process, additional actions. Advice: try to keep the number of conditions constant. A Limited Entry Decision Table with n binary conditions (that is what makes it a limited entry decision table) will have 2^n distinct rules.

Now, Rule 2 (in Decision Table 11.3) corresponds to a second scenario. The change to Rule 2 has no effect on Rules 9 to 16, so that half is unchanged, and is not repeated here.

> +Scenario 2: Account is in credit+.
> Given the account is in credit.
> And the card is valid.
> And the dispenser contains cash.
> If the customer does not request cash.
> Then ensure the card is returned.
> And do nothing else.

It then becomes a simple exercise to "follow" each rule to see if it corresponds to an interesting scenario. Some other scenarios might simplify the decision table. Consider the response to an invalid card: none of the other conditions will matter. As a slight digression, there is no (or should not be) any order in a decision table. We first interchange conditions 1 and 2, to get Decision Table 11.4.

Consider rules 9 through 16 in the second half of Decision Table 11.4. If the card is not valid, conditions c1, c3, and c4 are moot. The only actions are to return the invalid card and do nothing else. We show this with the "—" action entry.

Decision Table 11.4a   Conditions c1 and c2 Interchanged

Rules	1	2	3	4	5	6	7	8
c2. card is valid?	T	T	T	T	T	T	T	T
c1. account is in credit?	T	T	T	T	F	F	F	F
c3. dispenser contains cash	T	T	F	F	T	T	F	F

(Continued)

Decision Table 11.4a (Continued)

Rules	1	2	3	4	5	6	7	8
c4. customer requests cash	T	F	T	F	T	F	T	F
a1. dispense cash	x	?	?	?	?	?	?	?
a2. debit customer account	x	?	?	?	?	?	?	?
a3. return card	x	x	?	?	?	?	?	?
a4. do nothing	—	x	?	?	?	?	?	?

Decision Table 11.4b

Rules	9	10	11	12	13	14	15	16
c2. card is valid?	F	F	F	F	F	F	F	F
c1. account is in credit?	—	—	—	—	—	—	—	—
c3. dispenser contains cash	—	—	—	—	—	—	—	—
c4. customer requests cash	—	—	—	—	—	—	—	—
a1. dispense cash	—	—	—	—	—	—	—	—
a2. debit customer account	—	—	—	—	—	—	—	—
a3. return card	x	x	x	x	x	x	x	x
a4. do nothing	x	x	x	x	x	x	x	x

The "—" entries in Decision Table 11.5 mean either "don't care" or "not applicable." If the card is not valid, nothing else should happen, as shown in Rules 9 through 16 in Decision Table 11.5. (The "algebra" of decision tables results in a greatly simplified decision table. If two rules have identical action sets, there must be at least one condition that is true in one rule and false in the other. Since this difference has no effect on the actions that occur, we can combine the rules, and show that condition with a "don't care" entry "—".)

Decision Table 11.5 Rules 9 Through 16 Collapsed Into One Rule

Rules	1	2	3	4	5	6	7	8	9 - 16
c2. card is valid?	T	T	T	T	T	T	T	T	F
c1. account is in credit?	T	T	T	T	F	F	F	F	—
c3. dispenser contains cash	T	T	F	F	T	T	F	F	—
c4. customer requests cash	T	F	T	F	T	F	T	F	—
a1. dispense cash	x		?	?	?	?	?	?	—
a2. debit customer account	x		?	?	?	?	?	?	—
a3. return card	x	x	?	?	?	?	?	?	x
a4. do nothing		x	?	?	?	?	?	?	x

Decision tables force a top-down view that complements the bottom-up BDD approach. The mechanical expansion will frequently result in additional BDD scenarios that otherwise might not have occurred to the BDD developer. Also, the algebraic possibilities will usually result in much simpler tables. The example continues here, looking at the remaining rules.

Rules 3 and 4

This is an anomaly, but it might happen. If the dispenser contains no cash, the customer should be notified, but there is no action requiring that. The c4 condition entries (customer requests cash) are irrelevant since there is no cash anyway. The same comment applies to rules 7 and 8. This leads to an additional simplification, as shown in Decision Table 11.6.

At this point, the two combined rules (3 & 4 and 7 & 8) can also be combined because the action sets are identical resulting in Decision Table 11.7.

Decision Table 11.6   Action Added for Customer Notification

Rules	1	2	3 & 4	5	6	7 & 8	9 - 16
c2. card is valid?	T	T	T	T	T	T	F
c1. account is in credit?	T	T	T	F	F	F	—
c3. dispenser contains cash	T	T	F	T	T	F	—
c4. customer requests cash	T	F	—	T	F	—	—
a1. dispense cash	x	—	—	?	?	—	—
a2. debit customer account	x	—	—	?	?	—	—
a3. return card	x	x	x	?	?	x	x
a4. do nothing	—	x	—	?	?	—	x
a5: notify customer, no cash	—		x	?	?	x	—

Decision Table 11.7   Rules 3, 4, 7, and 8 Combined

Rules	1	2	3,4,7,8	5	6	9 - 16
c2. card is valid?	T	T	T	T	T	F
c1. account is in credit?	T	T	—	F	F	—
c3. dispenser contains cash	T	T	F	T	T	—
c4. customer requests cash	T	F	—	T	F	—
a1. dispense cash	x	—	—	?	?	—
a2. debit customer account	x	—	—	?	?	—
a3. return card	x	x	x	?	?	x
a4. do nothing	—	x	—	?	?	x
a5: notify customer, no cash	—		x	?	?	—

Rules 5 and 6

For now, assume there are two types of cards, credit and debit. Rules 5 and 6 refer to debit cards because the condition entry for c2 is False. Decision Table 11.8 shows that the treatment for both credit and debit cards is identical (Rules 1 and 5 have the same action sets, similarly for rules 2 and 6, resulting in Decision Table 11.9.

Look closely at condition c1: account is in credit: each condition entry is a "don't care," so we can delete that condition entirely, as in Decision Table 11.10.

We are left with four distinct rules, which correspond to four distinct BDD scenarios, each of which will become a test case.

Decision Table 11.8   Rules 5 and 6 Completed

Rules	1	2	3,4,7,8	5	6	9 - 16
c2. card is valid?	T	T	T	T	T	F
c1. account is in credit?	T	T	—	F	F	—
c3. dispenser contains cash	T	T	F	T	T	—
c4. customer requests cash	T	F	—	T	F	—
a1. dispense cash	x	—	—	x	—	—
a2. debit customer account	x	—	—	x	—	—
a3. return card	x	x	x	x	x	x
a4. do nothing	—	x	—	—	x	x
a5: notify customer, no cash	—		x	—		—

Decision Table 11.9   Rules 1 and 5 Combined, rules 2 and 6 Combined

Rules	1 & 5	2 & 6	3,4,7,8	9 - 16
c2. card is valid?	T	T	T	F
c1. account is in credit?	—	—	—	—
c3. dispenser contains cash	T	T	F	—
c4. customer requests cash	T	F	—	—
a1. dispense cash	x	—	—	—
a2. debit customer account	x	—	—	—
a3. return card	x	x	x	x
a4. do nothing	—	x	—	x
a5: notify customer, no cash	—		x	—

Decision Table 11.10   Final Decision Table

Rules	1 & 5	2 & 6	3,4,7,8	9 - 16
c2. card is valid?	T	T	T	F
c3. dispenser contains cash	T	T	F	—
c4. customer requests cash	T	F	—	—
a1. dispense cash	x	—	—	—
a2. debit customer account	x	—	—	—
a3. return card	x	x	x	x
a4. do nothing	—	x	—	x
a5: notify customer, no cash	—		x	—

11.3.1.2 Use Cases

Use Cases are central part of the Unified Modeling Language (UML). Their main advantage is that they are easily understood by both customers/users and developers. They capture the "does view" that emphasized behavior, rather than the "is view" that emphasizes structure. Customers and testers both tend to naturally think of a system in terms of the does view, so use cases are a natural choice. Decades ago, one author [Larman 2001] defined a hierarchy of use cases in which each level adds information to the predecessor level. Larman named these levels as follows:

- High level (very similar to an agile User Story)
- Essential
- Expanded Essential
- Real

The information content of these variations is shown in Venn diagram form in Figure 11.7. High-level use cases are at the level of the user stories used in agile development. A set of high level use cases gives a quick overview of the does view of a system. Essential use cases add the sequence of port input and output events. At this stage, the port boundary begins to become clear to both the customer/user and the developer. Expanded Essential use cases concentrate on pre- and post-conditions of the use cases. Real use cases replace variables in an Expanded Essential use case with actual values to be used in testing for inputs and expected outputs.

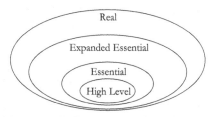

Figure 11.7   Information Content in Levels of Use Cases.

11.3.2 Extreme Programming

Extreme Programming (XP) was first applied to a project (in a documented way) in 1996 by Kent Beck [http://www.extremeprogramming.org/] while he was at the Chrysler Corporation. The clear success of the project, even though it was a revision of an earlier version, led to his book [Beck 2004]. The main aspects of XP are captured in Figure 11.8. It is clearly customer-driven, as shown by the position of user stories driving both a release plan and system testing. The release plan defines a sequence of iterations, each of which delivers a small working component. One distinction of XP is the emphasis on paired programming, in which a pair of developers work closely together, often sharing a single development computer and keyboard. One person works at the code level, while the other takes a slightly higher view. In a sense, the pair is conducting a continuous review. In Chapter 20, we will see that this is better described as a continuous code walk-through. There are many similarities to the basic iterative lifecycle shown in Figure 11.3. One important difference is that there is no overall preliminary design phase. Why? Because this is a bottom-up process. If XP were truly driven by a sequence of user stories, it is hard to imagine what can occur in the release plan phase.

11.3.3 Scrum

Scrum is probably the most frequently used of all the agile lifecycles. There is a pervading emphasis on the team members and teamwork. The name comes from the rugby maneuver in which the opposing teams are locked together and try to hook the football back to their respective sides. A rugby scrum requires organized teamwork—hence the name for the software process.

The quick view of Scrum (the development lifecycle) is that it is mostly new names for old ideas. This is particularly true about the accepted Scrum vocabulary. Three examples: roles, ceremonies, and artifacts. In common parlance, Scrum roles refer to project participants; the ceremonies are just meetings, the artifacts are work

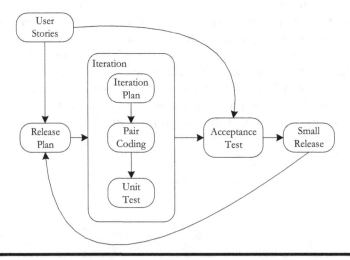

Figure 11.8   The Extreme Programming Lifecycle.

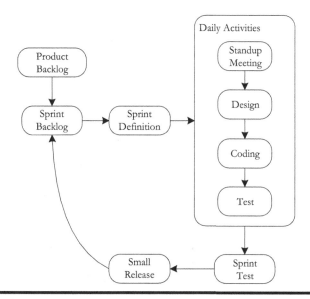

Figure 11.9 The Scrum Lifecycle.

products. Scrum projects have Scrum Masters (who act like traditional supervisors with less administrative power). Product Owners are the customers of old, and the Scrum Team is a development team. Figure 11.9 is adapted from "official" Scrum literature, the Scrum Alliance. Think about the activities in terms of the iterative lifecycle in Figure 11.3. The traditional iterations become "sprints" which last from two to four weeks. In a sprint, there is a daily stand-up meeting of the Scrum Team to focus on what happened the preceding day and what needs to be done in the new day. Then there is a short burst of design-code-test followed by an integration of the team's work at the end of the day. This is the agile part—a daily build that contributes to a sprint-level work product in a short interval. The biggest differences between Scrum and the traditional view of iterative development are the special vocabulary and the duration of the iterations.

Testing in the Scrum lifecycle occurs at two levels—the unit level at each day's end, and the integration level of the small release at the end of a sprint. Selection of the Sprint backlog from the product backlog is done by the Product Owner (the customer), which corresponds roughly to a requirements step. Sprint definition looks a lot like preliminary design because this is the point where the Scrum Team identifies the sequence and contents of individual sprints. The bottom line? Scrum has two distinct levels of testing—unit and integration/system. Why "integration/system?" The small release is a deliverable product usable by the Product Owner, so it is clearly a system level work product. But this is the point where all of the development work is integrated for the first time.

11.3.4 Test-Driven Development

Test-Driven Development (TDD) is the extreme case of agility. It is driven by a sequence of user stories, as shown in Figure 11.10. A user story can be decomposed

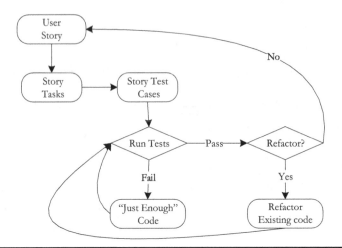

Figure 11.10   Test-Driven Development Lifecycle.

into several tasks, and this is where the big difference occurs. Before any code is written for a task, the developer decides how it will be tested. The tests become the specification. The next step is curious—the tests are run on non-existent code. Naturally, they fail, but this leads to the best feature of TDD—greatly simplified fault isolation. Once the tests have been run (and failed), the developer writes just enough code to make the tests pass, and the tests are rerun. If any test fails, the developer goes back to the code and makes a necessary change. Once all the tests pass, the next user story is implemented. Occasionally, the developer may decide to refactor the existing code. The cleaned-up code is then subjected to the full set of existing test cases, which is very close to the idea of regression testing. For TDD to be practical, it must be done in an environment that supports automated testing, typically with a member of the JUnit family of automated test environments.

Testing in TDD is interesting. Since the story level test cases drive the coding, they ARE the specification, so in a sense, TDD uses specification-based testing. But since the code is deliberately as close as possible to the test cases, we could argue that it is also code-based testing. There are two problems with TDD. The first is common to all agile flavors—the bottom-up approach prohibits a single, high-level design step. User stories that arrive late in the sequence may obviate earlier design choices. Then refactoring would have to also occur at the design level, rather than just at the code level. The agile community is very passionate about the claim that repeated refactoring results in an elegant design. Given one of the premises of agile develop-ment, namely that the customer is not sure of what is needed, or equivalently, rapidly changing requirements, refactoring at both the code and design levels seems the only way to end up with an elegant design. This is an inevitable constraint on bottom-up development.

The second problem is that all developers make mistakes—that is much of the reason we test in the first place. But consider: what makes us think that the TDD developer is perfect at devising the test cases that drive the development? Even worse: what if late user stories are inconsistent with earlier ones? A final limitation of TDD is there is no place in the lifecycle for a cross-check at the user story level.

11.3.5 Agile Model-Driven Development

Paul has a German friend Georg, who is a Ph.D. mathematician, a software developer, and a Go player. For several months, they had an email-based discussion about agile development. At one point, Georg asked if Paul plays the oriental game Go. Georg maintains that, to be a successful Go player, one needs both strategy and tactics. A deficiency in either one puts a Go player at a disadvantage. In the software development realm, he equates strategy with an overall design, and tactics as unit level development. His take on the flavors of agile development is that the strategy part is missing, and this leads us to a compromise between the agile world and the traditional views of software development. We first look at Agile Model-Driven Development (AMDD) popularized by Scott Ambler. This is followed by my mild reorganization of Ambler's work, named here as Model-Driven Agile Development (MDAD).

The agile part of AMDD is the modeling step. Ambler's advice is to model just enough for the current user story and then implement it with Test-Driven Development. The big difference between AMDD and any of the agile lifecycles is that there is a distinct design step. (The agilists usually express their distaste/disdain for modeling by calling it the "Big Design Up Front" and abbreviate it as simply the BDUF.) See Figure 11.11.

Ambler's contribution is the recognition that design does indeed have a place in agile development. As this was being written, there was a protracted discussion on LinkedIn started by the question "Is there any room for design in agile software development?" Most of the thread affirms the need for design in any agile lifecycle. Despite all this, there seems to be no room in AMDD for integration/system testing.

11.3.6 Model-Driven Agile Development

Model-Driven Agile Development (MDAD) is my proposal for a compromise between the traditional and the agile worlds. It is stimulated by Georg's view of the need for both strategy and tactics, hence the compromise. How does MDAD differ from

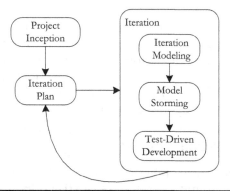

Figure 11.11 The Agile Model-Driven Development Lifecycle.

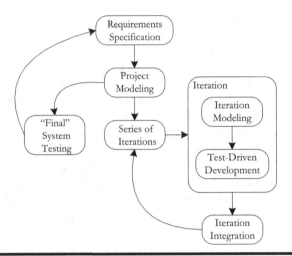

Figure 11.12 The Model-Driven Agile Development Lifecycle.

Iterative development? MDAD recommends test-driven development as the tactic and it uses Ambler's view of short iterations. The strategy part is the emphasis on an overall model, which in turn supports Model-Based Testing. In MDAD, the three levels of testing, unit, integration, and system are present.

11.4 Remaining Questions

11.4.1 Specification or Code Based?

Is Test-Driven Development code based, or specification based? In a sense, a test case is a very low level specification, so Test-Driven Development seems to be specification based. But, test cases are very closely associated with code, so it has the appearance of code-based testing. Certainly, code coverage, at least at the DD-Path level, is unavoidable. Is it a stretch to claim that the set of all test cases constitutes a requirements specification? Imagine the reaction of a Customer trying to understand a TDD program from the set of test cases. In the Agile Programming sense, however, the purpose of each test case can be considered to be a user story, and user stories are accepted by Customers. It is really a question of level of detail, and this leads to a variant of Test-Driven Development. Practitioners who object to tiny, incremental steps suggest that "larger" test cases, followed by larger chunks of code, are preferable. This has the advantage of introducing a small element of code design and probably reduces the frequency of refactoring. Then the strictly bottom-up approach of "pure" TDD is complemented by top-down thinking.

11.4.2 Configuration Management?

Superficially, Test-Driven Development appears to be a configuration management nightmare. Even a program as small as NextDate has dozens of versions in its growth from inception to completion. This is where refactoring comes in. Test-Driven

Table 11.1 User Story Granularity

Large Grain User Stories	*Fine Grain User Stories*
1. The program compiles.	1. The program compiles.
2. A date can be input and displayed.	2.1. A day can be input and displayed
	2.2.. An input month can be displayed
	2.3. An input year can be displayed
3. Invalid days can be recognized.	3.1. A day below minimum can be detected
	3.2.. A day above maximum can be detected
4. Invalid months can be recognized.	4.1.. A month below minimum can be detected
	4.2.. A month above maximum can be detected
5. Invalid years can be recognized.	5.1. A year below minimum can be detected
	5.2. A year above maximum can be detected
6. Invalid dates can be recognized.	6.1. Day = 31 in a 30 day month
	6.2. Day > = 29 in February
	6.3. Day = 29 in February in a common year
	6.4. Day = 29 in February in a leap year
7. Leap years can be recognized.	7.1. A year divisible by 4 is a leap year
	7.2. A year not divisible by 4 is a common year.
	7.3. A century year not divisible by 400 is a common year.
	7.4. A century year divisible by 400 is a leap year.
8. Valid dates can be incremented.	8.1. Increment a non-last day of a month.
	8.2. Increment the last day of a 30-day month.
	8.3. Increment the last day of a 31-day month.
	8.4. Increment December 31.
	8.5. Increment February 28 in a common year.
	8.6. Increment February 28 in a leap year.
	8.7. Increment February 29 in a leap year.

Development forces a bottom-up approach to code development. At certain points, the conscientious programmer will see that the code can be reorganized into something more elegant. There are no rules as to when refactoring should occur, but when it does, it is important to note that the original test cases are preserved. If the refactored code fails to pass all tests, there is a problem in the refactoring. Again, note the simple fault isolation. Refactoring points (once all test cases have passed) are good candidates for configuration management actions. These are points where a design object is, or can be, promoted to configuration item status. If later code causes earlier test cases to fail, this is another clear configuration management point. The configuration item should be demoted to a design object, which by definition, is subject to change.

11.4.3 Granularity?

The sequence of user stories in the example in Section 11.3.1 uses very fine-grained level of detail. As an alternative, consider the enlarged granularity of user stories in Table 11.5. With "larger" user stories, a particular user story is broken down to a series of finer tasks, and code is developed for each task. In this way, the fault isolation is preserved. To distinguish between these granularity choices, sometimes the larger version is named "story-driven development."

11.5 Pros, cons, and Open Questions of TDD

As with most innovations, Test-Driven Development has its advantages, disadvantages, claims, and unanswered questions. The advantages of TDD are very clear. Due to the extremely tight test/code cycles, something always works. In turn, this means a TDD project can be turned over to someone else, likely a programming pair, for continued development. Probably the biggest advantage of TDD is the excellent fault isolation. If a test fails, the cause must be the most recently added code. Finally, TDD is supported by an extensive variety of test frameworks, including those listed in Section 11.2.

It is nearly impossible, or at best, very cumbersome, to perform TDD in the absence of test frameworks. There really isn't much of an excuse for this, because the frameworks are readily available for most programming languages. If a tester cannot find a test framework for the project language, Test Driven Development is a poor choice. (It is probably better to just change programming languages.) At a deeper level, TDD is inevitably dependent on the ingenuity of the tester. Good test cases are necessary, but not sufficient for TDD to produce good code. Part of the reason is that the bottom-up nature of TDD provides little opportunity for elegant design. TDD advocates respond by claiming that a good design is eventually accomplished by a series of refactorings, each of which improves the code a little bit. A final disadvantage of TDD is that the bottom-up process makes it unlikely that "deeper faults," such as those only revealed by dataflow testing, will be revealed by the incrementally created test cases. These faults require a more comprehensive understanding of the code, and this disadvantage is exacerbated by the possibility of the thread interaction faults discussed in Chapter 15.

Any new technology or technique has a set of open questions, and this is certainly true for Test-Driven Development. The easiest question is that of scale-up to large applications. It would seem that there are practical limits as to how much an individual can "keep in mind" during a development. This is one of the early motivating factors for program modularity and information hiding, which are the foundations of the object-oriented paradigm. If size is a problem, complexity is even more serious. Can systems developed with TDD effectively deal with questions such as reliability and safety? Such questions usually require sophisticated models, but these are not produced in TDD. Finally, there is the question of support for long-term maintenance. The Agile Programming community and the TDD advocates maintain that there is no need for the documentation produced by the more traditional development approaches. The more extreme advocates even argue against comments in source code. Their view: the test cases *are* the specification, and well-written code, with meaningful variable and method names, is self-documenting. Time will tell.

11.6 Retrospective on MDD vs. TDD

The Northern Cheyenne people of the North American plains have teaching stories based on what they observe in nature. When they speak of the Medicine Wheel, they associate animals with each of the four directions, and the animals have qualities that are seen in nature. One interesting pair is the Eagle and the Mouse. The Eagle sees the "big picture" and therefore understands the important relationships among things. The Mouse, on the other hand, sees only the ground where it scurries, and the grasses it encounters—a very detailed view. Living by the Medicine Wheel means that each view is honored—each view is needed to have better understanding.

It is unlikely that the Northern Cheyenne ever thought much about Model-Driven Development (MDD) and Test-Driven Development (TDD), but the lessons are obvious: both are needed to have better understanding, in this case, of a program to be developed. This really is not too surprising. In the 1970s and 1980s, camps in the software community passionately debated the merits of specification-based versus code-based testing. Thoughtful people soon concluded that some blend of both approaches is necessary. To illustrate these two approaches, consider our Boolean function, isLeap, that determines whether a given year is a common or a leap year (Decision Table 11.11).

A Model-Driven approach to developing isLeap would likely begin with a decision table (Decision Table 11.11) showing the relationships among the phrases of the definition.

The advantage of using a decision table for the model is that it is complete, consistent, and not redundant. Rule 1 refers to century years that are leap years, while rule 2 refers to century years that are common years. Rule 4 describes non-century leap years, and rule 8 describes non-century common years. The other rules are

Decision Table 11.11   Leap Year Decision Table

Rules	1	2	3	4	5	6	7	8
c1. year is a multiple of 4	T	T	T	T	F	F	F	F
c2. year is a century year	T	T	F	F	T	T	F	F
c3. year is a multiple of 400	T	F	T	F	T	F	T	F
logically impossible			X		X	X	X	
a1. year is a common year		X						X
a2. year is a leap year	X			X				
test case: year =	2000	1900		2008				2011

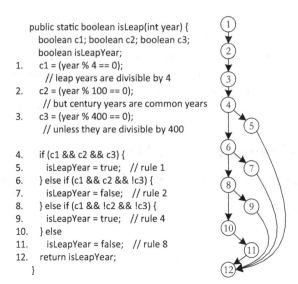

```
        public static boolean isLeap(int year) {
            boolean c1; boolean c2; boolean c3;
            boolean isLeapYear;
    1.      c1 = (year % 4 == 0);
                // leap years are divisible by 4
    2.      c2 = (year % 100 == 0);
                // but century years are common years
    3.      c3 = (year % 400 == 0);
                // unless they are divisible by 400

    4.      if (c1 && c2 && c3) {
    5.          isLeapYear = true;   // rule 1
    6.      } else if (c1 && c2 && !c3) {
    7.          isLeapYear = false;  // rule 2
    8.      } else if (c1 && !c2 && !c3) {
    9.          isLeapYear = true;   // rule 4
    10.     } else
    11.         isLeapYear = false;  // rule 8
    12.     return isLeapYear;
        }
```

Figure 11.13   MDD version of isLeap.

logically impossible. If we write isLeap from this decision table, we would get something like the following function (Figure 11.13).

Notice that there are four paths from the source node to the sink node. The path through node 5 corresponds to rule r1, the one through nodes 7 to rule r2, and so on. Coding nested If logic three levels deep is probably not what the average developer would do, at least not on the first try. (And it is even less likely that a developer would get it correct on the first try. Score one for MDD.)

The test-driven approach results in a different form of complexity. Referring to the code for User Stories 14 through 17 on Section 11.1, notice that the TDD code gradually developed a compound If statement, rather than the nested If logic in the MDD version (slightly refactored again in Figure 11.14).

As a cross check, here is the truth table for the compound condition.
(c1 AND NOT(c2)) OR (c3)

c1	c2	c3	NOT(c2)	c1 AND NOT(c2)	(c1 AND NOT(c2)) OR c3	year
T	T	T	F	F	T	2000
T	T	F	F	F	F	1900
T	F	T	T	T	T	imp
T	F	F	T	T	T	2008
F	T	T	F	F	T	imp
F	T	F	F	F	F	imp
F	F	T	T	F	T	imp
F	F	F	T	F	F	2011

```
public static boolean isLeap(int year){
      boolean c1; boolean c2; boolean c3;
1     c1 = (year %4 == 0);
2     c2 = (year %100 == 0);
3     c3 = (year % 400 == 0);
4     boolean isLeapYear = false;

5     if ((c1 && !(c2)) || (c3))
6           isLeapYear = true;

7     return isLeapYear;
8 }
```

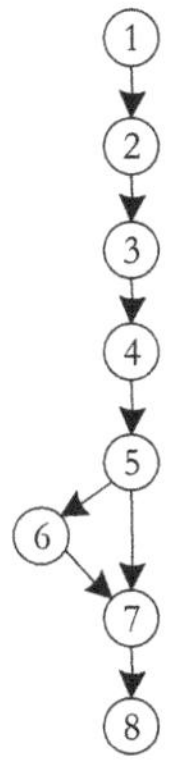

Figure 11.14   TDD version of isLeap.

Notice that the same test cases and impossibilities (the "imp" entries) occur in the rows of the truth table, and the columns of the decision table, therefore the two versions of isLeap are logically equivalent. Looking at the program graphs of the two implementations, the MDD version seems to be more complex. In fact, the cyclomatic complexity of the MDD version is 4, while that of the TDD version is only 2. From a testing standpoint, however, the compound condition in the TDD version requires multiple condition coverage. Both versions end up with the same necessary (and sufficient) four test cases.

What, if any, conclusions can we draw from this? The MDD approach yields the Eagle-eye view of the full picture. We know from the way decision tables work that the result is correct. We had to do a little more work to reach the same level of confidence with the TDD approach, but in the end, the two implementations are logically equivalent. The apparent difference in cyclomatic complexity is negated by the need for multiple condition coverage testing. The nested If complexity is moved into condition complexity—it doesn't disappear.

Any weaknesses? The MDD approach ultimately depends on the modeling skill; similarly, the TDD approach depends on testing skill. No significant difference there. What about size? The MDD version is longer: 17 statement fragments versus 9, but the TDD process requires more keystrokes. No significant difference here either.

The biggest difference would seem to be maintenance. Presumably, the modeling would be more helpful to a maintainer—the Eagle again. But the test cases from the TDD approach will help the maintainer recreate and isolate a fault—the Mouse view.

References

Agresti, W.W., *New Paradigms for Software Development*, IEEE Computer Society Press, Washington, D.C., 1986.

Beck, Kent, *Extreme Programming Explained: Embrace Change*, 2nd Edition, Addison Wesley, Boston, 2004.

Boehm, B.W., A spiral model for software development and enhancement, *IEEE Computer*, Vol. 21, No. 6, IEEE Computer Society Press, Washington, D.C., May 1988, pp. 61–72.

Harel, David, On visual formalisms, *Communications of the ACM*, Vol. 31, No. 5, pp. 514–530, May, 1988. http://www.scrumalliance.org/learn_about_scrum

Larman, C., *Applying U.M.L. and Patterns, Prentice-Hall*, Upper Saddle River, New Jersey, 2001.

Chapter 12

Integration Testing

In September 1999, the Mars Climate Orbiter mission failed after successfully traveling 416 million miles in 41 weeks. It disappeared just as it was to begin orbiting Mars. The fault should have been revealed by integration testing: Lockheed Martin Astronautics used acceleration data in English units (pounds), while the Jet Propulsion Laboratory did its calculations with metric units (newtons). NASA announced a $50,000 project to discover how this could have happened (Fordahl, 1999). They should have read this chapter. The Mars Perseverance Rover did much better in 2021.

Of the three distinct levels of software testing: unit, integration, and system, integration testing is the least well understood of these, hence in practice, it is the phase most poorly done. This chapter examines two mainline and one less well-known integration testing strategies. Traditional integration is illustrated with a continuing procedural example. Integration testing of object-oriented software is treated next, followed by a "unifying theory" for both procedural and object-oriented software. The chapter ends with a discussion of Model-Based Integration Testing.

Craftpersons are recognized by two essential characteristics: they have a deep knowledge of the tools of their trade, and they have a similar knowledge of the medium in which they work so that they understand their tools in terms of how they work with the medium. In Part II, we focused on the tools (techniques) available to the testing craftsperson at the unit level. Our goal there was to understand testing techniques in terms of their advantages and limitations with respect to particular types of software. Here, we continue our emphasis on model-based testing, with the goal of improving the testing craftsperson's judgment through a better understanding of three underlying models.

12.1 Decomposition-Based Integration

Beginning in the 1990s, and continuing 30 years later, mainline introductory software engineering texts, for example [Pressman 1992] and [Schach 1993], typically present four integration strategies based on the functional decomposition tree of the procedural software: top-down, bottom-up, sandwich, and the vividly named "big bang."

Many classic software testing texts echo this approach, [Deutsch 1982], [Hetzel 1988], [Kaner et al., 1993], [Mosley 1993], to name a few. Each of these strategies (except big bang) describes the order in which units are to be integrated. We can dispense with the big bang approach most easily: in this view of integration, all the units are compiled together and tested at once. The drawback to this is that when (not if!) a failure is observed, few clues are available to help isolate the location(s) of the fault. (Recall the distinction we made in Chapter 1 between faults and failures.)

The functional decomposition tree is the basis for this approach to integration testing because it is the main representation, usually derived from final source code, which shows the structural relationship of the system with respect to its units. All three integration orders presume that the units have been separately tested, thus, the goal of decomposition-based integration is to test the interfaces among separately tested units. A functional decomposition tree reflects the lexicological inclusion of units, in terms of the order in which they need to be compiled, to assure the correct referential scope of variables and unit names. In this chapter, our familiar NextDate unit is extended to a main program, Calendar, with procedures and functions. Figure 12.1 contains the functional decomposition tree for the calendar program. The pseudo-code is given in next.

The calendar program sketched here in acquires a date in the form mm, dd, yyyy, and provides the following functional capabilities:

- the date of the next day (our old friend, NextDate)
- the day of the week corresponding to the date (i.e., Monday, Tuesday...)
- the zodiac sign of the date
- the most recent year in which Memorial Day was celebrated on May 27
- the most recent Friday the Thirteenth

The sketch of the Calendar Program is given next, followed by a condensed "skeleton" which is the basis for the functional decomposition in Figure 12.1.

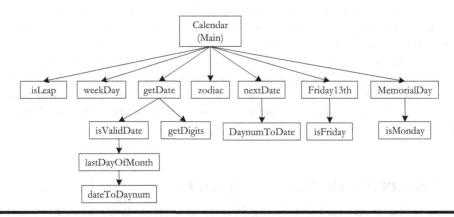

Figure 12.1 Functional decomposition of the Calendar Program.

Pseudo code for the Calendar Program

```
Main   Calendar
Data Declarations
    mm, dd, yyyy, dayNumber, dayName, zodiacSign
Function isLeap (input yyyy, returns T/F)
    (isLeap is sefl-contained)
End Function isLeap


Procedure getDate (returns mm, dd, yyyy, dayNumber)
    Function isValidDate (inputs mm, dd, yyyy; returns T/F)
        Function lastDayOfMonth (inputs mm, yyyy, returns 28, 29, 30, or 31)
            lastDayOfMonth body
                (uses isLeap)
            end lastDayOfMonth body
        End Function lastDayOfMonth

        isValidDate body
            (uses lastDayOfMonth)
        end isValidDate body
    End Function isValidDate

    Procedure getDigits(returns mm, dd, yyyy)
        (uses Function isValidDate)
    End Procedure getDigits

    Procedure memorialDay (inputs mm, dd, yyyy ; returns yyyy)
        Function isMonday (inputs mm, dd, yyyy ; returns T/F)
            (uses weekDay)
        End Function isMonday

        memorialDaybody
            isMonday
        end memorialDay
    End Procedure memorialDay
Procedure friday13th (inputs mm, dd, yyyy ; returns mm1, dd1, yyyy1)
        Function isFriday (inputs mm, dd, yyyy ; returns T/F)
            (uses weekDay)
        End Function isFriday


    friday13th body
        (uses isFriday)
    end friday13th
End Procedure friday13th

getDate body
    getDigits
    isValidDate
    dateToDayNumber
end getDate body
End Procedure getDate
Procedure nextDate (input daynum, output mm1, dd1, yyyy1)
```

```
    Procedure dayNumToDate
    dayNumToDate body
        (uses isLeap)
    end dayNumToDate body
nextDate body
    dayNumToDate
end nextDate body
End Procedure nextDate

Procedure weekDay (input mm, dd, yyyy; output dayName)
    (uses Zeller's Congruence)
End Procedure weekDay

Procedure zodiac (input dayNumber; output dayName)
    (uses dayNumbers of zodiac cusp dates)
End Procedure zodiac

Main program body
    getDate
    nextDate
    weekDay
    zodiac
    memorialDay
    friday13th
End Main program body
```

Lexicological Inclusion of Calendar Program

```
Main   Calendar
    Function isLeap
    Procedure weekDay
    Procedure getDate
        Function isValidDate
            Function lastDayOfMonth
        Procedure getDigits
    Procedure memorialDay
            Function isMonday
    Procedure friday13th
        Function isFriday
    Procedure nextDate
        Procedure dayNumToDate
    Procedure zodiac
```

12.1.1 Top-down Integration

Top-down integration begins with the main program (the root of the tree). Any lower level unit that is called by the main program appears as a "stub," where stubs are pieces of throw-away code that emulate a called unit. If we performed top-down integration testing for the Calendar program, the first step would be to develop stubs for all the units called by the main program—isLeap, weekDay, getDate, zodiac, nextDate, friday13th, and memorialDay. In a stub for any unit, the tester hard codes in a correct response to the request from the calling/invoking unit. In the stub for zodiac, for example, if the main program calls zodiac with 05, 27, 2012, zodiacStub would return "Gemini." In extreme practice, the response might be "pretend zodiac returned Gemini." The use of the pretend prefix emphasizes that it is not a real response. In practice, the effort to develop stubs is usually quite significant. There is good reason to consider stub code as part of the software project and maintain it under configuration management. In Figure 12.2, the first step in Top-Down Integration is shown. The gray-shaded units are all stubs. The goal of the first step is to check that the main program functionality is correct.

Once the main program has been tested, we replace one stub at a time, leaving the others as stubs. Figure 12.3 shows the first three steps in the gradual replacement of stubs by actual code. The stub replacement process proceeds in a breadth-first traversal of the decomposition tree until all the stubs have been replaced. (In Figures 12.2 and 12.3, the units below the first level are not shown, because they are not needed.)

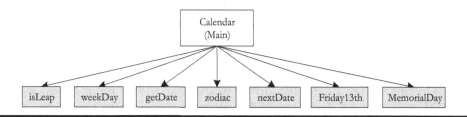

Figure 12.2 First step in Top-Down integration.

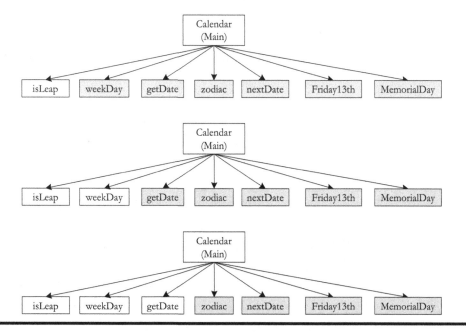

Figure 12.3 Next three steps in Top-Down integration.

The "theory" of top-down integration is that, as stubs are replaced one at a time, if there is a problem, it must be with the interface to the most recently replaced stub. (Note that the fault isolation is similar to that of Test-Driven Development). The problem is that a functional decomposition is deceptive. Because it is derived from the lexicological inclusion required by most compilers, the process generates impossible interfaces. Calendar main never directly refers to either isLeap or weekDay, so those test sessions could not occur.

12.1.2 Bottom-up Integration

Bottom-up integration is a "mirror image" to the top-down order, with the difference that stubs are replaced by driver modules that emulate units at the next level up in the tree. (In Figure 12.4, the gray units are drivers.) Bottom-up integration begins with the leaves of the decomposition tree and uses a driver version of the unit that would normally call it to provide it with test cases. (Note the similarity to test driver units at the unit level. As units are tested, the drivers are gradually replaced, until the full decomposition tree has been traversed. There is less throw-away code in bottom-up integration, but the problem of impossible interfaces persists.

Figure 12.5 shows one case where a unit (zodiac) can be tested with a driver. In this case, the Calendar driver would probably call zodiac with 36 test dates that are the day before a cusp date, the cusp date, and the day after the cusp date. The cusp date for Gemini is May 21, so the driver would call zodiac three times, with May 20, May 21, and May 22. The expected responses, respectively, would be "Taurus," "Gemini," and "Gemini." Note how similar this is to the assert mechanism in the JUnit (and related) test environments.

12.1.3 Sandwich Integration

Sandwich integration is a combination of top-down and bottom-up integration. If we think about it in terms of the decomposition tree, we are doing big bang integration

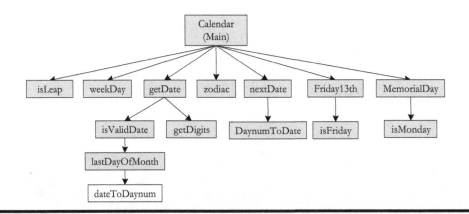

Figure 12.4 First step in bottom-up integration.

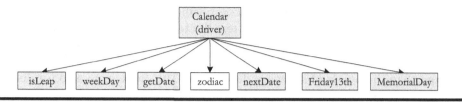

Figure 12.5 Bottom-up integration for zodiac.

on a subtree (see Figure 12.6). There will be less stub and driver development effort, but this will be offset to some extent by the added difficulty of fault isolation that is a consequence of big bang integration. (We could probably discuss the size of a sandwich, from dainty finger sandwiches to Dagwood-style sandwiches, but not now.)

A sandwich is a full path from the root to leaves of the functional decomposition tree. In Figure 12.6, the set of units is almost semantically coherent, except that isLeap is missing. This set of units could be meaningfully integrated, but test cases at the end of February would not be covered. Also note that the fault isolation capability of the top-down and bottom-up approaches is sacrificed. No stubs not drivers are needed in sandwich integration.

12.1.4 Pros and Cons

With the exception of big bang integration, the decomposition-based approaches are all intuitively clear. Build with tested components. Whenever a failure is observed, the most recently added unit is suspected. Integration testing progress is easily tracked against the decomposition tree. (If the tree is small, it is a nice touch to shade in nodes as they are successfully integrated.) The top-down and bottom-up terms

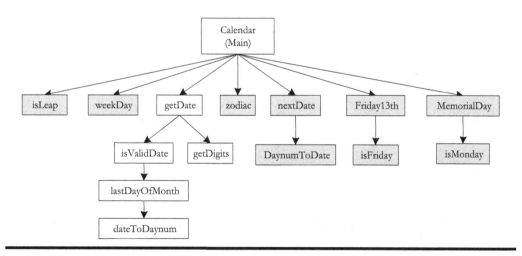

Figure 12.6 Sample sandwich integration.

suggest breadth-first traversals of the decomposition tree, but this is not mandatory. (We could use full-height sandwiches to test the tree in a depth-first manner.)

One of the most frequent objections to functional decomposition and waterfall development is that both are artificial, and both serve the needs of project management more than the needs of software developers. This holds true also for decomposition-based testing. The whole mechanism is that units are integrated with respect to structure; this presumes that correct behavior follows from individually correct units and correct interfaces. (Practitioners know better.) The development effort for stubs or drivers is another drawback to these approaches, and this is compounded by the retesting effort.

12.2 Call Graph-Based Integration

One of the drawbacks of decomposition-based integration is that the basis is the functional decomposition tree. We saw that this leads to impossible test pairs. If we use the call graph instead, we resolve this deficiency; we also move in the direction of structural testing. A Call Graph is developed by considering units to be nodes, and if unit A calls (or uses) unit B, there is an edge from node A to node B. Notice that this also applies to object-oriented software, in which nodes are o-o units, and edges are messages. The call graph for the (procedural) Calendar program is shown in Figure 12.7.

Since edges in the Call Graph refer to actual execution-time connections, the call graph avoids all the problems we saw in the decomposition-tree based versions of integration. In fact, we could repeat the discussion of Section 12.1 based on stubs and drivers in the units in Figure 12.7. This will work well, and it preserves the fault isolation feature of the decomposition-based approaches. Figure 12.8 shows the first step in call graph-based top-down integration.

The stubs in the first session could operate as follows. When the Calendar main program calls getDateStub, the stub might return May 27, 2020. The zodiacStub would return "Gemini," and so on. Once the main program logic is tested, the stubs would be replaced as we discussed in Section 12.1. The three strategies of Section 12.1 will

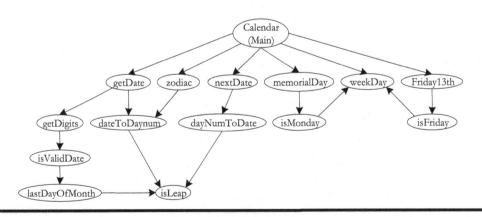

Figure 12.7   Call Graph of the Calendar Program.

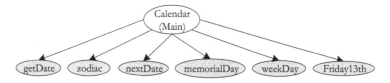

Figure 12.8   Call graph-based top-down integration of the Calendar Program.

all work well when stubs and drivers are based on the call graph rather than the functional decomposition.

We now enjoy the investment we made in the discussion of graph theory. Because the call graph is a directed graph, why not use it the way we used program graphs? This leads us to two new approaches to integration testing: we will refer to them as pairwise integration and neighborhood integration. We repeat: This discussion applies to both procedural and object-oriented code.

12.2.1 Pairwise Integration

The idea behind pairwise integration is to eliminate the stub/driver development effort. Instead of developing stubs and/or drivers, why not use the actual code? At first, this sounds like big bang integration, but we restrict a session to only a pair of units in the call graph. The end result is that we have one integration test session for each edge in the call graph. Pairwise integration results in an increased number of integration sessions when a node (unit) is used by two or more other units. In the Calendar example, there would be 15 separate sessions for top-down integration (one for each stub replacement); this increases to 19 sessions for pairwise integration (one for each edge in the call graph). This is offset by a reduction in stub/driver development. Three pairwise integration sessions are shown in Figure 12.9: getDate and getDigits, nextDate and dayNumToDate, and the third pair, weekDay and isFriday.

The main advantage of pairwise integration is the high degree of fault isolation. If a test fails, the fault must be in one of the two units. The biggest drawback is that, for

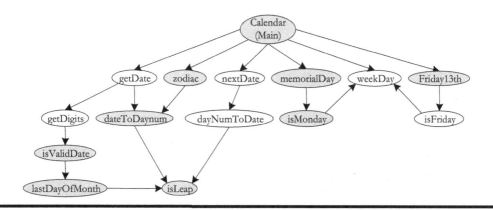

Figure 12.9   Three pairs for pairwise integration.

units involved on several pairs, a fix that works in one pair may not work in another pair. This is yet another example of the testing pendulum discussed in Chapter 10. Call graph integration is slightly better than the decomposition tree-based approach, but both can be removed from the reality of the code being tested.

12.2.2 Neighborhood Integration

We can let the mathematics carry us still further by borrowing the notion of a neighborhood from topology. The neighborhood of a node in a graph is the set of nodes that are one edge away from the given node. (Technically, this is a neighborhood of radius 1; in larger systems, it makes sense to increase the neighborhood radius.) In a directed graph, this includes all the immediate predecessor nodes and all the immediate successor nodes (notice that these correspond to the set of stubs and drivers of the node). The neighborhoods for nodes isValidDate, nextDate, and memorialDay are shown in Figure 12.10.

The 15 neighborhoods for the Calendar example (based on the call graph in Figures 12.7 and 12.10) are listed in Table 12.1. To make the table simpler, the original unit names are replaced by node numbers (in Figure 12.11), where the numbering is generally breadth-first.

The information in Table 12.1 is given below in Table 12.2 as the adjacency matrix for the call graph. The column sums show the indegrees of each node, and the row sums show the outdegrees.

We can always compute the number of neighborhoods for a given call graph. Each interior node will have one neighborhood, plus one extra in case leaf nodes are connected directly to the root node. (An interior node has a nonzero indegree and a nonzero outdegree.) We have:

$$\text{Interior nodes} = \text{nodes} - (\text{source nodes} + \text{sink nodes})$$

$$\text{Neighborhoods} = \text{interior nodes} + \text{source nodes}$$

which combine to:

$$\text{Neighborhoods} = \text{nodes} - \text{sink nodes}$$

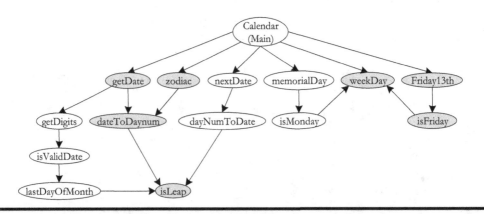

Figure 12.10   Three neighborhoods (of radius 1) for neighborhood integration.

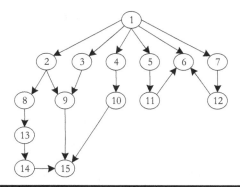

Figure 12.11   Calendar call graph with units replaced by numbers.

Table 12.1   Neighborhoods of radius 1 in the Calendar call graph

	Neighborhoods in the Calendar Program Call Graph		
Node	Unit name	Predecessors	Successors
1	Calendar (Main)	(none)	2, 3, 4, 5, 6, 7
2	getDate	1	8, 9
3	zodiac	1	9
4	nextDate	1	10
5	memorialDay	1	11
6	weekday	1, 11, 12	(none)
7	Friday13th	1	12
8	getDigits	2	13
9	dateToDayNum	3	15
10	dayNumToDate	4	15
11	isMonday	5	6
12	isFriday	7	6
13	isValidDate	8	14
14	lastDayOfMonth	13	15
15	isLeap	9, 10, 14	(none)

Neighborhood integration usually yields a reduction in the number of integration test sessions, and it reduces stub and driver development. The end result is that neighborhoods are essentially the sandwiches that we slipped past in the previous section. (It is slightly different, because the base information for neighborhoods is the call graph, not the decomposition tree.) What they share with sandwich

Table 12.2 Adjacency matrix of the Calendar Call Graph

	1	2	3	4	5	6	7	8	9	10	11	12	13	14	15	row sum
1		1	1	1	1	1	1									6
2								1	1							2
3									1							1
4										1						1
5											1					1
6																0
7												1				1
8													1			1
9															1	1
10															1	1
11							1									1
12							1									1
13														1		1
14															1	1
15																0
column sum	0	1	1	1	1	1	3	1	2	1	1	1	1	1	3	

integration is more significant—neighborhood integration testing has the fault isolation difficulties of "medium bang" integration. This is somewhat offset by reduced stub and driver effort.

12.2.3 Pros and Cons

The call graph-based integration techniques move from a purely structural basis toward a behavioral basis; the underlying assumption is an improvement. (See the Testing Pendulum in Chapter 10.) The neighborhood-based techniques also reduce the stub/driver development effort. In addition to these advantages, call graph-based integration matches well with developments characterized by builds and composition. For example, sequences of neighborhoods can be used to define builds. Alternatively, we could allow adjacent neighborhoods to merge (into villages?) and provide an orderly, composition-based growth path. All this supports the use of neighborhood-based integration for systems developed by life cycles in which composition dominates.

The biggest drawback to call graph-based integration testing is the fault isolation problem, especially for large neighborhoods. A more subtle but closely related problem occurs. What happens if (when) a fault is found in a node (unit) that appears in several neighborhoods? The adjacency matrix (Table 12.2) highlights this immediately—nodes with either a high row sum or a high column sum will be in several neighborhoods. Obviously, we resolve the fault in one neighborhood; but this means changing the unit's code in some way, which in turn means that all the previously tested neighborhoods that contain the changed node need to be retested.

Finally, a fundamental uncertainty exists in any structural form of testing: the presumption that units integrated with respect to structural information will exhibit correct behavior. We know where we are going: we want system-level threads of behavior to be correct. When integration testing based on call graph information is complete, we still have quite a leap to get to system-level threads. We resolve this by changing the basis from call graph information to special forms of paths.

12.3 Path-Based Integration

Much of the progress in the development of mathematics comes from an elegant pattern: have a clear idea of where you want to go, and then define the concepts that take you there. We do this here for path-based integration testing, but first we need to motivate the definitions.

We already know that the combination of structural and functional testing is highly desirable at the unit level; it would be nice to have a similar capability for integration (and system) testing. We also know that we want to express system testing in terms of behavioral threads. Lastly, we extend our goal for integration testing: instead of just testing interfaces among separately developed and tested units, we focus on interactions among these units. ("Co-functioning" might be a good term.) Interfaces are structural; interaction is behavioral.

When a unit executes, some path of source statements is traversed. Suppose that a call goes to another unit along such a path. At that point, control is passed from the calling unit to the called unit, where some other path of source statements is traversed. We deliberately ignored this situation in Part II, because this is a better place to address the question. Two possibilities are available: abandon the single-entry, single-exit precept and treat such calls as an exit followed by an entry or suppress the call statement because control eventually returns to the calling unit anyway. The suppression choice works well for unit testing, but it is antithetical to integration testing.

12.3.1 New and Extended Concepts

To get where we need to go, we need to refine some of the program graph concepts. As before, these refer to programs written in an imperative language. We allow statement fragments to be a complete statement, and statement fragments are nodes in the program graph.

Definition

A *source node* in a unit is a statement fragment at which unit execution begins or resumes.

The first executable statement in a unit is clearly a source node. Source nodes also occur immediately after nodes that transfer control to other units.

Definition

A *sink node* in a unit is a statement fragment at which unit execution terminates.

The final executable statement in a program is clearly a sink node; so are statements that transfer control to other units.

Definition

A *module execution path* is a sequence of statements that begins with a source node and ends with a sink node, with no intervening sink nodes.

The effect of the definitions so far is that program graphs now have multiple source and sink nodes. This would greatly increase the complexity of unit testing, but integration testing presumes that unit testing is complete.

Definition

A *message* is a programming language mechanism by which one unit transfers control to another unit and acquires a response from the other unit.

Depending on the programming language, messages can be interpreted as subroutine invocations, procedure calls, function references, and the usual messages in an object-oriented programming language. We follow the convention that the unit that receives a message (the message destination) always eventually returns control to the message source. Messages can pass data to other units. We can finally make the definitions for path-based integration testing. Our goal is to have an integration testing analog of DD-Paths.

Definition

An *MM-Path* is an interleaved sequence of module execution paths and messages.

The basic idea of an MM-Path is that we can now describe sequences of module execution paths that include transfers of control among separate units. In traditional software, "MM" is nicely understood as Module-Message; in object-oriented software, it is clearer to interpret "MM" as Method-Message. These transfers are by messages; therefore, MM-Paths always represent feasible execution paths, and these paths cross unit boundaries. The hypothetical example in Figure 12.12 shows an MM-Path (the solid edges) in which module A calls module B, which in turn calls module C. Notice that, for traditional (procedural) software, MM-Paths will always begin (and end) in the main program.

In unit A, nodes a1, a5, and a6 are source nodes (a5 and a6 are outcomes of the decision at node a5.), and nodes a4 (a decision) and a8 are sink nodes. Similarly, in unit B, nodes b1 and b3 are source nodes, and nodes b2 and b5 are sink nodes. Node b2 is a sink node because control leaves unit B at that point. It could also be a source node, because unit C returns a value used at node b2. Unit C has a single source node, c1, and a single sink node, c9. Unit A contains three module execution paths: <a1, a2, a3, a4>, <a4, a5, a7, a8>, and < a4, a6, a7, a8>. The solid edges are edges actually traversed in this hypothetical example. The dashed edges are in the program graphs of the units as stand-alone units, but they did not "execute" in the hypothetical MM-Path. We can now define an integration testing analog of the DD-Path graph that serves unit testing so effectively.

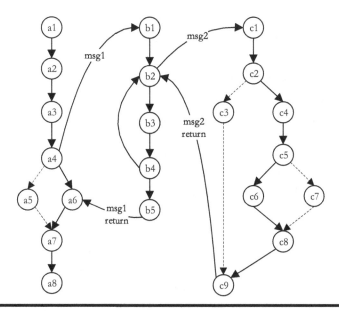

Figure 12.12   A hypothetical MM-Path across three units.

Definition

Given a set of units, their *MM-Path graph* is the directed graph in which nodes are module execution paths and edges correspond to messages and returns from one unit to another.

Notice that MM-Path graphs are defined with respect to a set of units. This directly supports composition of units and composition-based integration testing. We can even compose down to the level of individual module execution paths, but that is probably more detailed than necessary.

We should consider the relationships among module execution paths, program paths, DD-Paths, and MM-Paths. A program path is a sequence of DD-Paths, and an MM-Path is a sequence of module execution paths. Unfortunately, there is no simple relationship between DD-Paths and module execution paths. Either might be contained in the other, but more likely, they partially overlap. Because MM-Paths implement a function that transcends unit boundaries, we do have one relationship: consider the intersection of an MM-Path with a unit. The module execution paths in such an intersection are an analog of a slice with respect to the (MM-Path) function. Stated another way, the module execution paths in such an intersection are the restriction of the function to the unit in which they occur.

The MM-Path definition needs some practical guidelines. How long ("deep" might be better) is an MM-Path? The notion of message quiescence helps here. Message quiescence occurs when a unit that sends no messages is reached (like module C in Figure 12.12). In a sense, this could be taken as a "midpoint" of an MM-Path—the remaining execution consists of message returns. This is only mildly helpful. What if there are two points of message quiescence. Maybe a better answer is to take the longer of the two, or, if they are of equal depth, the latter of the two. Points of message quiescence are natural endpoints for an MM-Path.

12.3.2 MM-Path Complexity

If you compare the MM-Paths in Figures 12.13 and 12.20, it seems intuitively clear that the latter is more complex than the former. Because these are strongly connected directed graphs, we can "blindly" compute their cyclomatic complexities; recall the formula is $V(G) = e - n + 2p$, where p is the number of strongly connected regions. Since messages return to the sending unit, we will always have $p = 1$, so the formula reduces to $V(G) = e - n + 2$. Surprisingly, both graphs have $V(G) = 7$. Clearly, MM-Path complexity needs some notion of size in addition to cyclomatic complexity.

12.3.3 Pros and Cons

MM-Paths are a hybrid of functional and structural testing. They are functional in the sense that they represent actions with inputs and outputs. As such, all the functional testing techniques are potentially applicable. The net result is that the cross-check of the functional and structural approaches is consolidated into the constructs for path-based integration testing. We therefore avoid the pitfall of structural testing; and, at the same time, integration testing gains a fairly seamless junction with system testing. Path-based integration testing works equally well for software developed in the traditional waterfall process or with one of the composition-based alternative life cycle models. Finally, the MM-Path concept applies directly to object-oriented software.

The most important advantage of path-based integration testing is that it is closely coupled with actual system behavior, instead of the structural motivations of decomposition and call graph-based integration. However, the advantages of path-based integration come at a price—more effort is needed to identify the MM-Paths. This effort is probably offset by the elimination of stub and driver development.

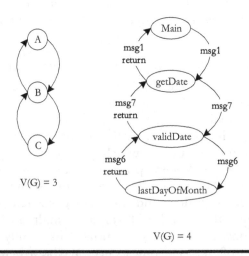

Figure 12.13   Cyclomatic complexities of two MM-Paths.

12.4 Example: Procedural integrationNextDate

Our now familiar NextDate is rewritten here as integrationNextDate, a main program with a functional decomposition into procedures and functions. The pseudo-code is very close to Visual Basic for Applications (VBA); the lines are numbered for use in the program graphs. Figures 12.14, 12.15, and 12.16 show the source code, the program graphs, and the cyclomatic complexity (see Chapter 15) of the units in the procedural version of integrationNextDate.

Figures 12.17 and 12.18 show the functional decomposition and the call graph, respectively. Figure 12.19 shows the program graphs of the units in integrationNext-Date. Figure 12.20 shows the MM-Paths for the input date May 27, 2020.

12.4.1 Decomposition-Based Integration

Pairwise integration based on the decomposition in Figure 12.17 is problematic; the isLeap and lastDayOfMonth functions are never directly called by the Main program,

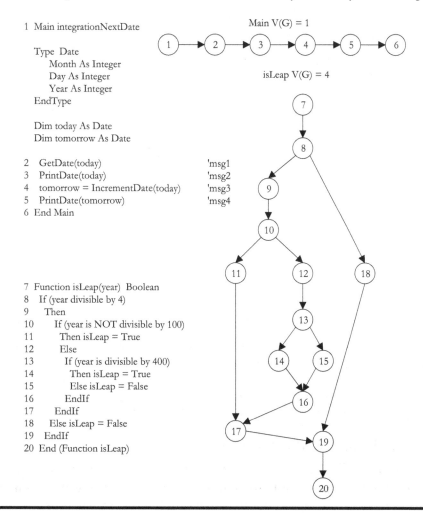

Figure 12.14 Procedural integrationNextDate Part 1.

```
21  Function lastDayOfMonth(month, year)  Integer
22    Case month Of
23      Case 1: 1, 3, 5, 7, 8, 10, 12
24        lastDayOfMonth = 31
25      Case 2: 4, 6, 9, 11
26        lastDayOfMonth = 30
27      Case 3: 2
28        If (isLeap(year))                    'msg5
29          Then lastDayOfMonth = 29
30          Else lastDayOfMonth = 28
31        EndIf
32    EndCase
33  End (Function lastDayOfMonth)
```

```
68  Function IncrementDate(aDate)  Date
69    If (aDate.Day < lastDayOfMonth(aDate.Month))  'msg8
70      Then aDate.Day = aDate.Day + 1
71      Else aDate.Day = 1
72        If (aDate.Month = 12)
73          Then aDate.Month = 1
74            aDate.Year = aDate.Year + 1
75          Else aDate.Month = aDate.Month + 1
76        EndIf
77    EndIf
78  End (IncrementDate)
```

```
79  Procedure PrintDate(aDate)
80    Output( "Day is ", aDate.Month, "/", aDate.Day, "/",
aDate.Year)
81  End (PrintDate)
```

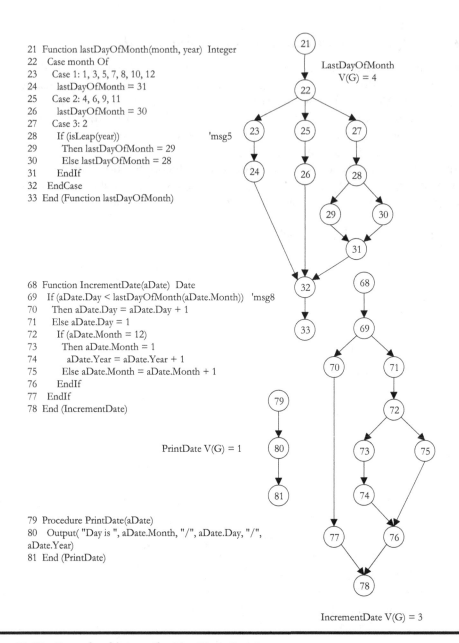

Figure 12.15   Procedural integrationNextDate Part 2.

so these integration sessions would be empty. The pairs involving integrationNext-
Date and GetDate, IncrementDate, and PrintDate are all useful (but short) sessions.

12.4.2 *Call Graph-Based Integration*

Call Graph integration based on the call graph in Figure 12.18 is an improvement
over that for the decomposition-based pairwise integration. There are no empty integration sessions because edges refer to actual unit references. There is still the problem of stubs. Sandwich integration is appropriate because this example is so small.

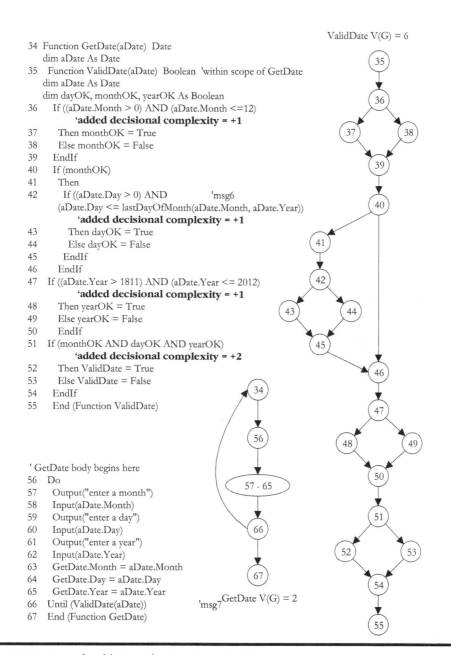

```
34 Function GetDate(aDate)  Date
   dim aDate As Date
35    Function ValidDate(aDate)  Boolean  'within scope of GetDate
      dim aDate As Date
      dim dayOK, monthOK, yearOK As Boolean
36    If ((aDate.Month > 0) AND (aDate.Month <=12)
              'added decisional complexity = +1
37      Then monthOK = True
38      Else monthOK = False
39      EndIf
40      If (monthOK)
41      Then
42        If ((aDate.Day > 0) AND           'msg6
          (aDate.Day <= lastDayOfMonth(aDate.Month, aDate.Year))
              'added decisional complexity = +1
43        Then dayOK = True
44        Else dayOK = False
45        EndIf
46      EndIf
47    If ((aDate.Year > 1811) AND (aDate.Year <= 2012)
              'added decisional complexity = +1
48      Then yearOK = True
49      Else yearOK = False
50      EndIf
51    If (monthOK AND dayOK AND yearOK)
              'added decisional complexity = +2
52      Then ValidDate = True
53      Else ValidDate = False
54      EndIf
55      End (Function ValidDate)


   ' GetDate body begins here
56   Do
57      Output("enter a month")
58      Input(aDate.Month)
59      Output("enter a day")
60      Input(aDate.Day)
61      Output("enter a year")
62      Input(aDate.Year)
63      GetDate.Month = aDate.Month
64      GetDate.Day = aDate.Day
65      GetDate.Year = aDate.Year
66   Until (ValidDate(aDate))           'msg7
67   End (Function GetDate)
```

ValidDate V(G) = 6

GetDate V(G) = 2

Figure 12.16   Procedural integrationNextDate Part 3.

In fact, it lends itself to a build sequence. Build 1 could contain Main and PrintDate. Build 2 could contain Main, GetDate, and PrintDate. IncrementDate. Finally, build 3 would add the remaining units lastDayOfMonth, isLeap, and IncrementDate in addition to the already present PrintDate, and GetDate.

Neighborhood integration based on the call graph would likely proceed with the neighborhood of lastDayOfMonth followed by the neighborhood of integrationNextDate.

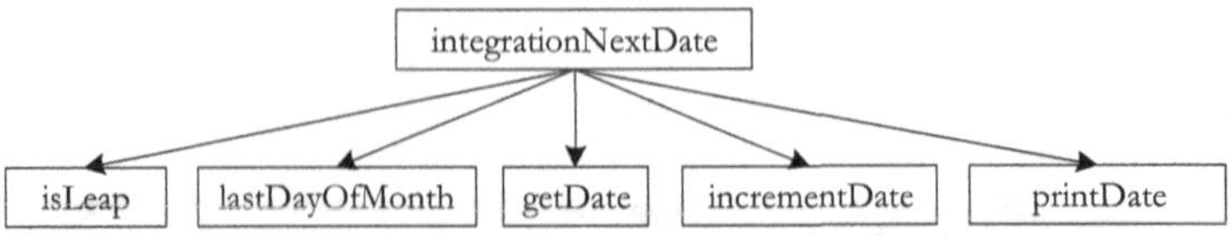

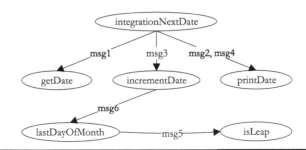

Figure 12.17 Functional decomposition of integrationNextDate.

Figure 12.18 Call graph of integrationNextDate.

12.4.3 Integration Based on MM-Paths

Because the program is data-driven, all MM-Paths begin in and return to the main program. Here are the four MM-Paths for May 27, 2020 (note the points of message quiescence). They are shown in Figure 12.20.

```
Main (1, 2, 3)
    msg1
    GetDate (35, 36, 37, 38, 39, 40, 41, 42) 'point of message quiescence
    msg1 return
Main(3, 4)
    msg2
    PrintDate(58, 59, 60) 'point of message quiescence
    msg2 return
Main(4, 5)
    msg3
    IncrementDate(43, 44)
    msg 6
    LastDayOfMonth(22, 23, 24, 25, 33, 34) 'point of message quiescence
    msg 6 return
    IncrementDate(45, 46, 56, 57)
    msg 3 return
Main(5, 6)
    msg4
    PrintDate(58, 59, 60) 'point of message quiescence
    msg4 return
Main (6, 7)
```

We are now in a strong position to describe test coverage metrics for MM-Paths of procedural code. Given a set of MM-Paths,

MMP$_0$: Every message sent
MMP$_1$: Correct response received for every message sent.
MMP$_2$: Every unit execution path is traversed

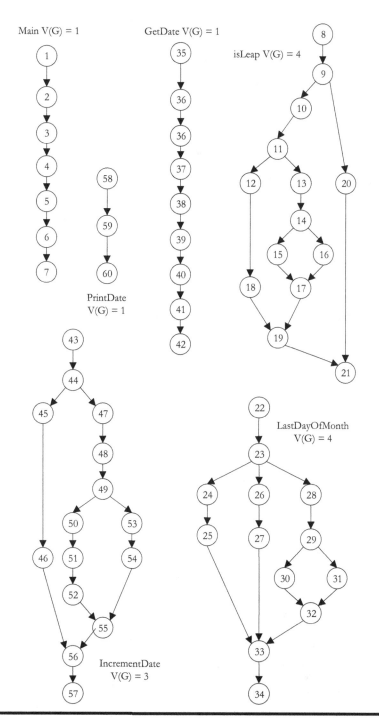

Figure 12.19   Program graphs of units in integrationNextDate.

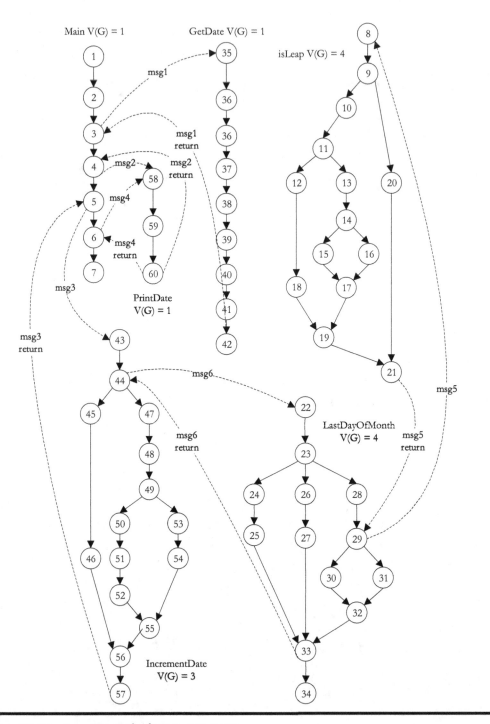

Figure 12.20   Four MM-Paths for May 27, 2020.

Table 12.3 Comparison of Integration Testing Strategies

Strategy Basis	*Ability to test Interfaces*	*Ability to test co-functionality*	*fault isolation resolution*
Functional Decomposition	acceptable but can be deceptive	limited to pairs of units	good, to faulty unit
Call Graph	acceptable	limited to pairs of units	good, to faulty unit
MM-Path	excellent	complete	excellent, to faulty unit execution path

12.4.4 *Observations and Recommendations*

Table 12.3 summarizes the observations made in the preceding discussion. The significant improvement of MM-Paths as a basis for integration testing is due to their exact representation of dynamic software behavior. MM-Paths are also the basis for present research in data flow (define/use) approaches to integration testing. Integration testing with MM-Paths requires extra effort. As a fallback position, perform integration testing based on call graphs.

12.5 Example: O-O integrationNextDate

The pseudo-code version of Section 12.4 (integrationNextDate) is rewritten here as Java code. Figures 12.17 and 12.18 show the functional decomposition and the call graph, respectively. Figure 12.19 shows the program graphs of the units in integrationNextDate. Figure 12.20 shows the MM-Path for the input date May 27, 2020.

```
import static org.junit.jupiter.api.Assertions.*;
import org.junit.jupiter.api.Test;

1   class DateTest {
2       @Test
2       void testSimple() {

3           Date date  =  new Date(Month.MAY, 27, 2020);    /* msg 1 */
4           assertEquals("5-27-2020", date.getDate());      /* msg 2 */
5           date  =  date.nextDate();                       /* msg 3 */
6           assertEquals("5-28-2020", date.getDate());      /* msg 4 */
7       }
7   }

8   public class Date {
9       private Day day;
10      private Month month;
11      private Year year;

12      public Date(int month, int day, int year) {
13          this.year  =  new Year(year);                   /* msg 5 */
```

```
14            this.month = new Month(month, this.year);      /* msg 6 */
15            this.day = new Day(day, this.month);   /* msg 7 */
16        }

17        public String getDate() {
18            return month.getMonth() +  "-" +  day.getDay()  +  "-" +
                  year.getYear();
19        }                                       /* msg 8, msg 9, msg 10 */

20        public Date nextDate() {
21            Day nextDay = day.getNextDay();                    /* msg 11 */
22            Month month = nextDay.getMonth();                  /* msg 12 */
23            Year year = month.getYear();                       /* msg 13 */
24            return new Date(month.getMonth(), nextDay.getDay(), year.
                          getYear()); /* msg14, msg15, msg16 */
25        }
26    }

27 public class Day {
28        private int day;
29        private Month month;

30        public Day(int day, Month month) {
31            this.day = day;
32            this.month = month;
33        }

34        public int getDay() {
35            return day;
36        }

37        public Day getNextDay() {
38            if(day < month.numberOfDays())                     /* msg 17 */
39                return new Day(day + 1, month);                /* msg1 8 */
40            else
41                return new Day(1, month.getNextMonth()); /* msg 19 */
42        }

43        public Month getMonth() {
44            return month;
45        }
46    }

47 public class Month {
48        public static final int JANUARY = 1;
49        public static final int FEBRUARY = 2;
50        public static final int MARCH = 3;
51        public static final int APRIL = 4;
52        public static final int MAY = 5;
53        public static final int JUNE = 6;
54        public static final int JULY = 7;
55        public static final int AUGUST = 8;
56        public static final int SEPTEMBER = 9;
57        public static final int OCTOBER = 10;
58        public static final int NOVEMBER = 11;
```

```
59      public static final int DECEMBER  =  12;

60      private int month;
61      private Year year;

62      public Month(int month, Year year) {
63          this.month  =  month;
64          this.year  =  year;
65      }

66      public int getMonth() {
67          return month;
68      }

69      public int numberOfDays() {
70          int numberOfDays  =  0;
71          switch (month) {
        // 31  day  months
72          case 1: case 3: case 5: case 7: case 8: case 10: case 12:
73              numberOfDays  =  31;
74              break;
        // 30  day  months
75          case 4: case 6: case 9: case 11:
76              numberOfDays  =  30;
77              break;
        // February
78          case 2:
79              if(year.isLeapYear())                  /* msg 20 */
80                  numberOfDays  =  29;
81              else
82                  numberOfDays  =  28;
84              break;
85          }
86          return numberOfDays;
87      }

88      public Month getNextMonth() {
89          if(month < 12)
90              return new Month(month + 1, year);    /* msg 21 */
91          else
92              return new Month(1, year.getNextYear());          /* msg
            22, msg 23 */
93      }

94      public Year getYear() {
95          return year;
96      }
97  }

98  public class Year {
99      private int year;

100     public Year(int year) {
101         this.year  =  year;
102     }
```

```
103     public int getYear() {
104         return year;
105     }

106     public boolean isLeapYear() {
107         boolean isLeapYear  =  true;

108     if(year % 4 !=   0)
109             isLeapYear  =  false;
110         else if(year % 100 !=  0)
111             isLeapYear  =  true;
112         else if(year % 400 !=  0)
113             isLeapYear  =  false;
114         return isLeapYear;
115     }

116     public Year getNextYear() {
117         return new Year(year + 1);                      /* msg 24 */
118     }
119 }
```

We can make some interesting observations between the procedural (VBA pseudo-code) and the Java implementations of the integration versions of the nextDate function (see Table 12.4). This table indicates that the total complexity stays about the same but is shifted from the procedural unit level to the object-oriented integration level. Take a minute to compare the program graphs of the procedural (Figure 12.19) and object-oriented implementations of integrationNextDate (Figure 12.21).

Since most of the object-oriented methods are simple, unit testing at the method level is (or should be) correspondingly simple. This shifts the burden in two ways: unit level testing of object-oriented code should be at the class level, and integration testing is increasingly important for object-oriented code.

Table 12.5 lists the sources, destinations, and line numbers of the 24 messages in the object-oriented implementation of integrationNextDate.

Figure 12.21 is the program graph of the five classes that implement the Java version of integrationNextDate. (Notice that the methods internal to a class are present in the overall class program graph. The cyclomatic complexity of each class is given.

Figure 12.22 shows the 24 message flows among the five classes, and Figure 12.23 shows the message flows for May 27, 2020.

Table 12.4   Comparison of Procedural and object-oriented Implementations

	Procedural	*Object-oriented*
Number of units	6	5 classes, 17 methods
Sum of unit complexities	14	40
Number of lines of code	90	119
Number of messages	7	25

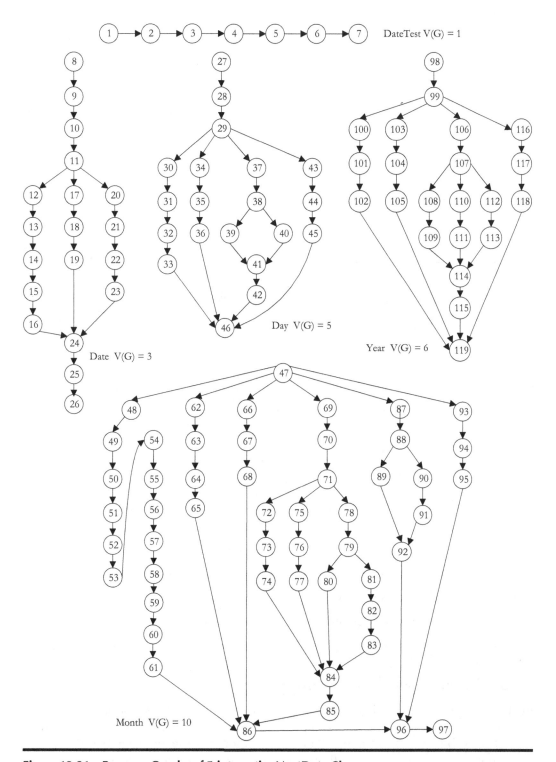

Figure 12.21   Program Graphs of 5 integrationNextDate Classes.

Table 12.5 Messages in the object-oriented implementation of integrationNextDate

Message	Source	Destination	At line
msg 1	DateTest	Date	3
msg 2	DateTest	date.getDate()	4
msg 3	DateTest	date.nextDate()	5
msg 4	DateTest	date.getDate()	6
msg 5	Date	Year	13
msg 6	Date	Month	14
msg 7	Date	Day	15
msg 8	Date.getDate	month.getMonth()	18
msg 9	Date.getDate	day.getDay()	18
msg 10	Date.getDate	year.getYear()	18
msg 11	Date.nextDate	day.getNextDay()	21
msg 12	Date.nextDate	nextDay.getMonth()	22
msg 13	Date.nextDate	month.getYear()	23
msg 14	Date.nextDate	month.getMonth()	24
msg 15	Date.nextDate	nextDay.getDay()	24
msg 16	Date.nextDate	year.getYear()	24
msg 17	Day.getNextDay	month.numberOfDays()	38
msg 18	Day.getNextDay	Day(day+1,month)	39
msg 19	Day.getNextDay	month.getNextMonth()	41
msg 20	Month.numberOfDays()	year.isLeapYear()	79
msg 21	Month.getNextMonth()	Month(month+1,year)	90
msg 22	Month.getNextMonth()	Month()	92
msg 23	Month.getNextMonth()	Month(year.getNextYear())	92
msg 24	Year.getNextYear()	Year(year+1)	117

12.6 Model-Based Integration Testing

In this section, we extend the code-based ideas of integration testing to the level of Model-Based Testing. As an example, please refer to Appendix B: The Foodies Wish List web-based application. Our starting point is the message-based interaction among models, in this case, finite state machines. For convenience, Figure B.2 is repeated here as Figure 12.24. It is a direct analog of the Call Graph we used earlier in this chapter.

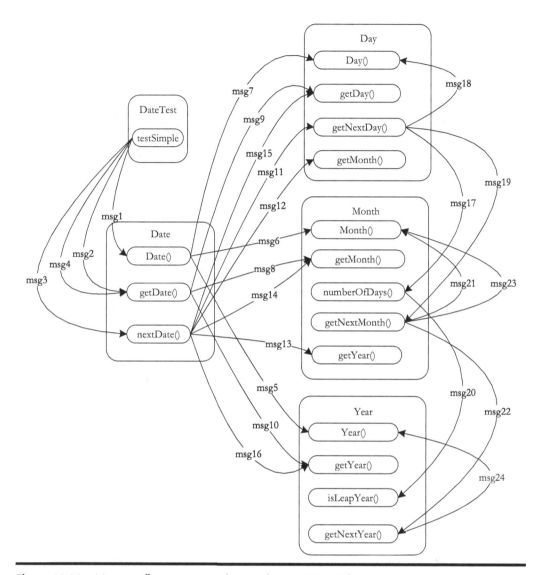

Figure 12.22 Message flows among 5 integrationNextDate Classes.

12.6.1 Message Communication

The simplest form of model-based integration testing is to verify that every message has been sent to, and received by, the correct ricipient. Figure 12.21 shows 38 messages that support the communication among the eight finite state machines. This level of testing would be most easily performed with a language-specific program such as JUnit. The ASSERT statements can be used to check the sending and receiving ends of each message. We can postulate these simple test coverage metrics:

■ Test Cover 1: every message sent to the correct recipient
■ Test Cover 2: every message received by the correct recipient

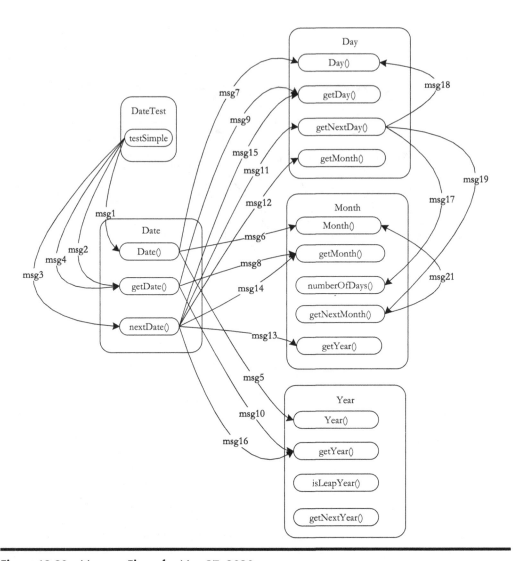

Figure 12.23   Message Flows for May 27, 2020.

12.6.2 Pairwise Integration

There are eight pairs of finite state machines (Excluding the external communication via the credit card interface) that share messages in Figure 12.24. Pairwise Integration examines each pair of message-sharing finite state machines. Here we take a closer look at the pair that includes Account Creation and Administration. They communicate using messages m7, m11, m12, m13, and m16. The message communication described in Section 12.6.1 would check that each of these five messages would have been sent and received correctly. That level of checking is a good analog of unit testing based on a program graph, in which there is no "semantic content" to the test cases. In fact, there are two responses to message m7: messages m11 and m12, depending on whether or not m7 communicated a new UserID. Pairwise Integration begins to answer "why" a response message is sent—clearly moving in

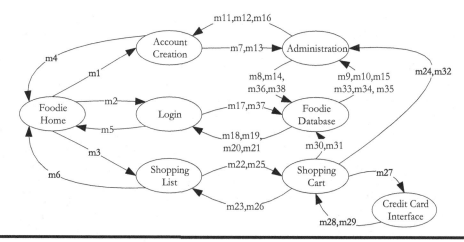

Figure 12.24   Message communication among finite state machines.

the direction of increased semantic content. We can go a step further with the observation that a new personal identification number (PIN) can be sent only after the UserID is approved by message m11.

To test this pair, we need two new objects: CreateAccountDriver, to provide user inputs to Account Creation, and FoodieDBStub to provide responses to messages sent to FoodieDB fsm by the Administration fsm. We can reduce FoodieDBStub by focusing on just the messages begun by Account Creation (See the reduced fsm in Figure 12.25). CreateAccountDriver will need to send input events e11, e12, and e13

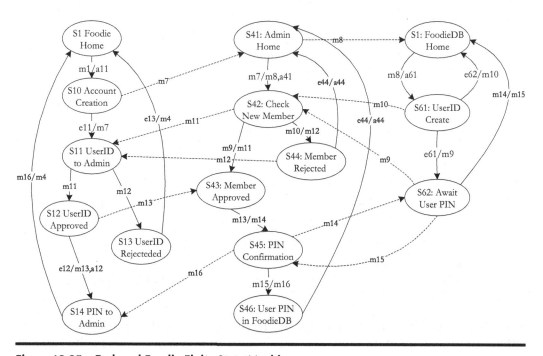

Figure 12.25   Reduced Foodie Finite State Machines.

to the AccountCreation finite state machine. FoodieDBStub will need to send messages m9, m10, and m15 to the Administration fsm. Given this set of four classes, we can test longer, semantically correct message sequences. As a caution, there is an analog of the infeasible paths we saw in program graph-based unit testing. Looking at the descriptions of the Foodie Wish List messages in Appendix B, message m12 from Admin to Account Creation rejects the proposed UserID. So any sequence containing the subsequence <m12, m13 > is logically impossible.

To identify longer pairwise integration test cases, we begin with the individual fsms, as shown in Figure 12.25. Starting at state S1 (Foodie Home), message m1 moves control to state S10 in AccountCreation. We will need AccountCreationDriver to generate message m1 (Open AccountCreation). Once opened, the AccountCreation driver can generate the input event e11 (Enter UserID), which causes the transition to state S11 and sends message m7 (Proposed UserID) to Admin. Since Admin does not know if this is an original UserID, the proposed UserID is sent to the FoodieDBStub (message m8). Since it is a stub, FoodieDBStub must have pre-programmed knowledge that the proposed UserID is either new or already in the FoodieDB. The tester will have to insure this when building FoodieDBStub. If it is a new UserID, FoodieDBStub will return message m9 (Approve New Member UserID). The Admin fsm then sends m11 (Proposed USerID Approved) back to AccountCreation. All of this is in Pairwise Test Case 1.

Pairwise Test Case 1:

Test Case Name	Original UserID Entered	
Test Case ID	pw1	
Description	User enters an original UserID	
Preconditions	The entered USerID is not in FoodieDB	
Message Sequence		
Source	Message or Input	Destination
AccountCreationDriver	m1	Account Creation
AccountCreationDriver	e11	Account Creation
Account Creation	m7	Admin
AccountCreationDriver	e12	Account Creation
Admin	m8	FoodieDBStub
FoodieDBStub	m9	Admin
Admin	m11	Account Creation

This test case is very analagous to the MM-Paths we discussed in Section 12.4.3. The difference is that the path does not send return messages as done in the original

MM-Paths. The path "ends" when control is returned to the FSM that sent the message that originated the path—in this case, CreateAccount.

Pairwise Test Case 2:

Test Case Name	Original UserID and PIN entry	
Test Case ID	pw2	
Description	User enters an original UserID and a PIN	
Preconditions	Entered USerID is not in FoodieDB, PIN is OK	
Message Sequence		
Source	Message or Input	Destination
AccountCreationDriver	e11	Account Creation
AccountCreationDriver	e12	Account Creation
Account Creation	m7	Admin
Admin	m8	FoodieDBStub
FoodieDBStub	m9	Admin
Admin	m11	Account Creation
AccountCreationDriver	e13	Account Creation
Account Creation	m13	Admin
Admin	m14	FoodieDBStub
FoodieDBStub	m15	Admin
Admin	m16	Account Creation

Pairwise Test Case 2 is actually a sequence of two FSM/M Paths—the first contains the message sequence <m7, m8, m9, m11>, and the second contains the message sequence <m13, m14, m15, m16>. This example shows that FSM/M Paths can be concatenated into full end-to-end transactions that are almost at the level of a system test case.

Pairwise Test Case 3

Test Case Name	Duplicate UserID Entered
Test Case ID	pw3
Description	User enters a duplicate UserID
Preconditions	The entered USerID is in FoodieDB

Message Sequence		
Source	Message or Input	Destination
AccountCreationDriver	e11	Account Creation
AccountCreationDriver	e12	Account Creation
Account Creation	m7	Admin
Admin	m8	FoodieDBStub
FoodieDBStub	m10	Admin
Admin	m12	Account Creation

12.6.3 FSM/M Path Integration

In this subsection, we expand the pairwise test cases from Section 12.6.2 into full FSM/M Paths. To clarify this distinction, we will refer to them as scenarios (as in Appendix B). We still need driver classes for input events in AccountCreation (events e11 and e12) and event e61 in FoodieDB. Scenarios 1 and 2 are very detailed and complete. The interactions connected with the Foodie database are more complex (three other fsms), so those scenarios will be expressed both as state sequences and as message sequences.

Definition

A *Finite State Machine Message Path (FSM/M)* is a path that originates and terminates with a Finite State Machine and connects to other FSMs using messages.

Notation

An FSM/M Path is denoted by the (interior) sequence of messages. The FSM/M Path in Pairwise Test Case 1 is the message sequence <m7, m8, m9, m11 >.

12.6.4 Scenario 1: Normal Account Creation

A Foodie User creates a UserID, sends it to Admin. Admin sends the potential UserID to the FoodieDB. The FoodieDB checks and finds no duplicate, so it approves the new UserID, and confirms this to Admin. In turn, Admin confirms this to Account Creation. The newly approved User then creates a PIN and sends it to Admin. (No check is made on validity of a PIN, since it is local to a User.) Admin sends the PIN to the FoodieDB, so that the FoodieDB can send it as the "Expected PIN" to Login.

Figure 12.26 is derived from Figure 12.25 by deleting anything not involved with Scenario 1. By examining Figure 12.26, we can derive sequence of messages and input events in scenario 1:<m1, e11, m7, m8, m9, e61, m11, e12, m13, m14, m15, e44, m16, m4>. The reason for making the state numbers global is so we can describe a scenario as a state sequence across swim lanes. The state sequence for scenario 1 is: S1, S10, S41, S60, S61, S42, S11, S12, S43, S62, S60, S45, S41, S14, S1.

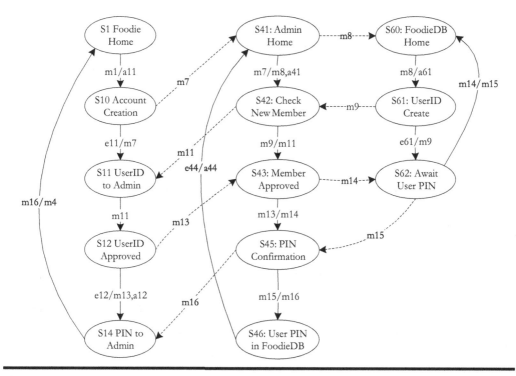

Figure 12.26 Message and state flow in Scenario 1.

For this discussion, we postulate an integration testing tool that allows a tester to "execute" paths through a set of communicating finite state machines. The verbs CAUSE and VERIFY are used as follows. A CAUSE statement can do any of the following:

■ cause an event local to a fsm (*e.g.,* e11),
■ cause message to be sent to an adjacent fsm, with parameters as needed, and
■ cause a state transition.

In an almost symmetric way, VERIFY statements can:

■ recognize the present state of the fsm in which it occurs,
■ report the name of the present state,
■ verify the value of VERIFY parameters

With just these CAUSE and VERIFY capabilities, an integration tester can define an FSM/M Path integration test procedure. Table 12.7 is derived from Figure 12.26. Steps 1 through 4 in Table 12.6 would be expressed as the test procedure in Table 12.7.

Exercises

1. Find the source and sink nodes in the DateTest class.
2. Consider some possible complexity metrics for MM-Paths:
    ■ $V(G) = e - n$
    ■ $V(G) = 0.5e - n + 2$
    ■ sum of the outdegrees of the nodes
    ■ sum of the nodes plus the sum of the edges

Table 12.6   Scenario 1 FSM/M Path Description

Step	In State	CAUSE Event/ Message	NextState	VERIFY (Result)
1	S1	m1	S10	in AccountCreation
2	S10	e11	S11	in AccountCreation
3	S10	m7: propose UserID = 'Paul'	S41	in Admin; UserID = 'Paul'
4	S41	m7	S42	in Admin; ·
5	S41	m8	S60	in FoodieDB; UserID = 'Paul'
6	S60	m8	S61	in FoodieDB;
7	S61	e61	S62	in FoodieDB;
8	S61	m9: Approve UserID = 'Paul'	S42	in Admin, UserID = 'Paul' OK
9	S42	m9	S43	in Admin
10	S42	m11	S11	in AccountCreation
11	S11	m11	S12	UserID = 'Paul' approved
12	S12	e12	S14	in AccountCreation
13	S12	m13: UserPIN defined	S43	in Admin: pass on UserPIN
14	S43	m14: UserPIN to FoodieDB	S62	UserPIN stored in FoodieDB
15	S62	m15: Confirm UserPIN	S45	in Admin
16	S45	m15	S46	in Admin
17	S45	m16: Defined PIN accepted	S14	in AccountCreation
18	S46	e44	S41	in Admin Home
19	S14	m16: Defined PIN accepted	S1	in Foodie Home

Table 12.7   Partial FSM/M Test Procedure

Step	Description
1	VERIFY (InState(S1))
2	CAUSE (SendMessage(m1))
3	VERIFY (InState(S10))
4	VERIFY (StateName = AccountCreation)
5	CAUSE (InputEvent(e11))
6	VERIFY (InState(S11))
7	CAUSE (SendMessage(m7) UserID = 'Paul")
8	VERIFY (InState(S41))
9	VERIFY (UserID = 'Paul')

Apply these to the second MM-Path in Figure 12.22 (begins with message msg2). Do they have any explanatory value?

3. Make up a few test cases, interpret them as MM-Paths, and then see what portions of the unit program graphs in Figure 12.20 are traversed by your MM-Paths. Try to devise a "coverage metric" for MM-Path-based integration testing.

4. One of the goals of integration testing is to be able to isolate faults when a test case causes a failure. Consider integration testing for a program written in a procedural programming language. Rate the relative fault isolation capabilities of the following integration strategies:

   A = Decomposition-based top-down integration.
   B = Decomposition-based bottom-up integration.
   C = Decomposition-based sandwich integration.
   D = Decomposition-based "big bang" integration.
   E = Call graph-based pairwise integration.
   F = Call graph-based neighborhood integration (radius = 2).
   G = Call graph-based neighborhood integration (radius = 1).

   Show your ratings graphically by placing the letters corresponding to a strategy on the continuum in Figure 12.27. As an example, suppose Strategies X and Y are about equal and not very effective, and Strategy Z is very effective.

Figure 12.27   continuum of Fault Isolation Capabilities.

5. Consider the process of writing an important paper (*e.g.* a formal paper or a proposal). In the (dark) days before word processors, students were encouraged to develop detailed outlines, then a draft that might be reviewed, make final changes, and TYPE a final version (ouch!). Discuss how technology has changed this process, then relate it to the life cycle models we have studied. Can you think of other situations where moving from a Waterfall-like approach to a different life cycle has improved the process?

References

Matthew Fordahl, *Elementary Mistake Doomed Mars Probe*, The Associated Press, Oct. 1, 1999; also, http://mars.jpl.nasa.gov/msp98/news/mco990930.html.

Michael S. Deutsch, *Software Verification and Validation-Realistic Project Approaches*, Prentice-Hall, Englewood Cliffs, NJ 1982.

Bill Hetzel, *The Complete Guide to SOFTWARE TESTING*, 2nd Edition, QED Information Sciences, Inc., Wellesley, MA, 1988.

Paul C. Jorgensen, *The Use of MM-Paths in Constructive Software Development*, Ph.D. dissertation, Arizona State University, Tempe, AZ, 1985.

Paul C. Jorgensen and Carl Erickson, "Object-Oriented Integration Testing", *Communications of the ACM*, Sept. 1994.

Cem Kaner, Jack Falk, & Hung Quoc Nguyen, *Testing Computer Software*, 2nd Edition, Van Nostrand Reinhold, New York, 1993.

Daniel J. Mosley, *The Handbook of MIS Application Software Testing*, Yourdon Press, Prentice-Hall, Englewood Cliffs, NJ 1993.

Roger S. Pressman, *Software Engineering: A Practitioner's Approach*, McGraw-Hill, New York, 1982.

Stephen R. Schach, *Software Engineering*, 2nd ed., Richard D. Irwin, Inc., and Aksen Associates, Inc., 1993.

Chapter 13

System Testing

Of the three levels of testing, the system level is closest to everyday experience. We test many things: a used car before we buy it, an online network service before we subscribe, and so on. A common pattern in these familiar forms is that we evaluate a product in terms of our expectations—not with respect to a specification or a standard. Consequently, the goal is not to find faults, but to demonstrate desired behavior. Because of this, we tend to approach system testing from a specification-based standpoint instead of from a code-based one. Because it is so intuitively familiar, system testing in practice tends to be less formal than it might be; and this is compounded by the reduced testing interval that usually remains before a delivery deadline.

The craftsperson metaphor continues to serve us. We need a better understanding of the medium; we will view system testing in terms of threads of system-level behavior. We begin with a new construct—an Atomic System Function (ASF)—and develop the thread concept, highlighting some of the practical problems of thread-based testing. System testing is closely coupled with requirements specification; therefore, we shall use appropriate system level models to enjoy the benefits of model-based testing. Common to all of these is the idea of "threads," so we shall see how to identify system level threads in a variety of common models. We will apply the strategy to a portion of the Foodies Wish List example (see Appendix B).

13.1 Threads

Threads are hard to define; in fact, some published definitions are either counterproductive, misleading, or wrong. We will use examples to develop a "shared vision" of a thread. Here are several views:

A scenario of normal usage
A system-level test case
A stimulus/response pair
Behavior that results from a sequence of system-level inputs
An interleaved sequence of port input and output events
A sequence of transitions in a state machine description of the system

An interleaved sequence of object messages and method executions
A sequence of machine instructions
A sequence of source instructions
A sequence of MM-paths
A sequence of atomic system funct.ions (to be defined in this chapter)

Threads have distinct levels. A unit-level thread is usefully understood as an execution-time path of source instructions or, alternatively, as a sequence of DD-Paths. An integration-level thread is an MM-Path—that is, an alternating sequence of methods/module execution paths and messages. If we continue this pattern, a system-level thread is a sequence of atomic system functions. Because atomic system functions have port events as their inputs and outputs, a sequence of atomic system functions implies an interleaved sequence of port input and output events. The end result is that threads provide a unifying view of our three levels of testing. Unit testing tests individual functions; integration testing examines interactions among units; and system testing examines interactions among atomic system functions. In this chapter, we focus on system-level threads and answer some fundamental questions, such as, "How big is a thread? Where do we find them? How do we test them?"

13.1.1 Thread Possibilities

Defining the endpoints of a system-level thread is a bit awkward. We motivate a tidy, graph theory-based definition by working backward from where we want to go with threads. Here are four candidate threads in our Foodie Wish List example:

- Entry of a digit
- Entry of a personal identification number (PIN)
- A simple Foodies Wish List shopping transaction: Login (includes UserID Entry and PIN Entry), Select a FoodeItem from the Shopping List, move the item to the Shopping Cart, and tender a credit card payment.
- A shopping session containing two or more simple transactions.

Digit entry is a good example of a minimal atomic system function. It begins with a port input event (the digit keystroke) and ends with a port output event (the screen digit echo), so it qualifies as a stimulus/response pair. This level of granularity is too fine for the purposes of system testing.

The second candidate, Personal Identification Number (PIN) Entry, is a good example of an upper limit to integration testing and, at the same time, a starting point of system testing. PIN Entry is a good example of an atomic system function. It is also a good example of a family of stimulus/response pairs (system-level behavior that is initiated by a port input event, traverses some programmed logic, and terminates in one of several possible responses (port output events)). PIN Entry entails a sequence of system-level inputs and outputs.

1. A screen requesting PIN digits
2. An interleaved sequence of digit keystrokes and system responses
3. The possibility of cancellation by the customer before the full PIN is entered
4. A system disposition: A customer has three chances to enter the correct PIN. Once a correct PIN has been entered, the Foodie customer has access to the Shopping List function. If the user fails the third PIN entry attempt, the Login fails.

Several stimulus/response pairs are evident, putting ASFs clearly in the domain of system-level testing. Other examples of ASFs include Account Creation, Shopping List item selection, Shopping Cart processing, payment processing, and Foodie database updating.

The third candidate, the simple transaction, has a sense of "end-to-end" completion. A customer could never execute PIN Entry alone (a UserID Entry is needed), but a full simple shopping transaction is commonly executed. This is a good example of a system-level thread; note that it involves the interaction of several ASFs.

The last possibility (the session) is a sequence of threads. This is also properly a part of system testing; at this level, we are interested in the interactions among threads. Unfortunately, most system testing efforts never reach the level of thread interaction.

13.1.2 Thread Definitions

We simplify our discussion by defining a new term that helps us get to our desired goal.

Definition

An *Atomic System Function* (ASF) is an action that is observable at the system level in terms of port input and output events.

In an event-driven system, ASFs are separated by points of event quiescence; these occur when a system is (nearly) idle, waiting for a port input event to trigger further processing. Event quiescence has an interesting Petri net insight. In a traditional Petri net, deadlock occurs when no transition is enabled. In an Event-Driven Petri net (as in Chapter 4), event quiescence is similar to deadlock; but an input event can bring new life to the net. The Foodie Wish List system exhibits event quiescence in several places: one is at the beginning of a Foodie Wish List session, where the system has displayed a Login screen and is waiting for a UserID and User PIN to be entered. Event quiescence is a system-level property; it is a direct analog of message quiescence at the integration level.

Definition

Given a system defined in terms of atomic system functions, the *ASF Graph* of the system is the directed graph in which nodes are ASFs and edges represent sequential flow.

Definition

A *source ASF* is an Atomic System Function that appears as a source node in the ASF graph of a system; similarly, a *sink ASF* is an Atomic System Function that appears as a sink node in the ASF graph.

In the Foodie Wish List system, the UserID Entry is a source ASF, and the payment ASF is a sink ASF. Notice that intermediary ASFs could never be tested at the system level by themselves—they need the predecessor ASFs to "get there."

Definition

A *system thread* is a path from a source ASF to a sink ASF in the ASF graph of a system.

These definitions provide a coherent set of increasingly broader views of threads, starting with very short threads (within a unit) and ending with interactions among system-level threads. We can use these views much like the ocular on a microscope, switching among them to see different levels of granularity. Having these concepts is only part of the problem; supporting them is another. We next take a tester's view of requirements specification to see how to identify threads.

13.2 Identifying Threads in Single-Processor Applications

There are three main ways to identify threads: by using user stories and use cases, finding them in models, and building them up from a set of atomic system functions. We consider each of these next, using a portion of the Foodies Wish List example.

13.2.1 User Stories/Use Cases

Use Cases are a central part of the Unified Modeling Language (UML). Their main advantage is that they are easily understood by both customers/users and developers. They capture the "does view" that emphasizes behavior, rather than the "is view" that emphasizes structure. Customers and testers both tend to naturally think of a system in terms of the does view, so use cases are a natural choice.

Decades ago, one author [Larman 2001] defined a hierarchy of use cases in which each level adds information to the predecessor level. Larman named these levels as follows:

- High level (very similar to an agile User Story)
- Essential
- Expanded Essential
- Real

The information content of these variations is shown in Venn diagram form in Figure 13.1. Tables (Use Cases) 13.2 through 13.4 show the gradual increase in Larman's use case hierarchy for the example in Table 13.1. High level use cases are at the level of the user stories used in agile development. A set of high level use cases gives a quick overview of the does view of a system. Essential use cases add the sequence of port input and output events. At this stage, the port boundary begins to become clear to both the customer/user and the developer.

Expanded essential use cases add pre- and post-conditions. We shall see that these are key to linking use cases when they are expressed as system test cases.

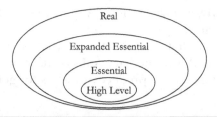

Figure 13.1 Larman's levels of Use Cases.

Table 13.1　High level Use Case for Correct PIN on First Try

Use Case Name	Correct PIN entry on first try
Use Case ID	HLUC-1
Description	A customer enters the PIN number correctly on the first attempt.

Table 13.2　Essential Use Case for Correct PIN on First Try

Use Case Name	Correct PIN entry on first try
Use Case ID	EUC-1
Description	A customer enters the PIN number correctly on the first attempt.
Event Sequence	
Input events	Output events
	1. Login Screen shows '- - - - '
2. Customer touches 1st digit	
	3. Login Screen shows '- - - * '
4. Customer touches 2nd digit	
	5. Login Screen shows '- - * * '
6. Customer touches 3rd digit	
	7. Login Screen shows '- * * * '
8. Customer touches 4th digit	
	9. Login Screen shows '* * * * '

Real use cases are at the actual system test case level. Abstract names for port events, such as "invalid PIN" are replaced by an actual invalid PIN character string. This presumes that some form of testing database has been assembled. In our Foodie Wish List system, this would likely include several user accounts with UserIDs and associated PINs.

13.2.2 How Many Use Cases?

When a project is driven by use cases, there is the inevitable question as to how many use cases are needed. Use case-driven development is inherently a bottom-up process. In the agile world, the answer is easy—the customer/user decides how many use cases are needed. But what happens in a non-agile project? Use case-driven development is still (or can be) an attractive option. In this section, we examine strategies to help decide how many bottom-up use cases are needed. Each strategy employs an incidence matrix (see Chapter 4).

Table 13.3 Expanded Essential Use Case for Correct PIN on First Try

Use Case Name	Correct PIN entry on first try
Use Case ID	EEUC-1
Description	A customer enters the PIN . number correctly on the first attempt.
Pre-Conditions	1. The expected PIN is known
	2. Login Screen is displayed
Event Sequence	
Input events	Output events
	1. Login Screen shows '- - - - '
2. Customer touches 1st digit	
	3. Login Screen shows '- - - * '
4. Customer touches 2nd digit	
	5. Login Screen shows '- - * * '
6. Customer touches 3rd digit	
	7. Login Screen shows '- * * * '
8. Customer touches 4th digit	
	9. Login Screen shows '* * * * '
10. Customer touches Enter	
	11. Login Screen shows 'Correct PIN'
Post conditions	Select Transaction screen is active

Table 13.4 Real Use Case for Correct PIN on First Try

Use Case Name	Correct PIN entry on first try
Use Case ID	RUC-1
Description	A customer enters the PIN number correctly on the first attempt.
Pre-Conditions	1. The expected PIN is '2468'
Event Sequence	
Input events	Output events
	1. Login Screen shows '- - - - '
2. Customer touches digit 2	3. Login Screen shows '- - - * '
4. Customer touches digit 4	5. Login Screen shows '- - * * '

(Continued)

Table 13.4 (Continued)

6. Customer touches digit 6	7. Login Screen shows '- * * * '
8. Customer touches digit 8	9. Login Screen shows '* * * * '
10. Customer touches Enter	11. Login Screen shows 'Correct PIN'
Post conditions	Correct PIN

13.2.2.1 Incidence with Input Events and Messages

As use cases are identified jointly between the customer/user and developers, both parties gradually identify inputs (events and messages). This very likely is an iterative process, in which use cases provoke the recognition of inputs, and they, in turn, suggest additional use cases. These are kept in an incidence matrix showing which use cases require which inputs. As the process continues, both parties reach a point where the existing set of inputs is adequate for any new use case. Once this point is reached, it is reasonable to assume that the existing set of use cases covers all the inputs.

We will use the Login constituent to illustrate the process. In the five examples used here, messages from the FoodieDB (please see Appendix B) are inputs to the Login constituent; similarly, messages to the FoodieDB are considered as outputs. The natural first use case is a valid Login with the correct PIN. The final form is Scenario 2.1; the steps are numbered to make the flow clearer:

Scenario 2.1: Valid Login, PIN correct on 1st try	
Pre-Condition: The UserID and PIN are in FoodieDB	
Account Creation	FoodieDB
1. e21: Enter valid UserID	
2. Send m17: Entered UserID to FoodieDB	3. Receive m17
5. Receive m18	4. Send m18: User ID OK; expected PIN
6. e23: Enter User PIN = expected PIN	
7. Send m37: Entered PIN	8. Receive m37
10. Receive m20	9. Send m20: User PIN OK
11. Send m5: Close Login	
Post-Condition: The UserID is logged in	

After the first step, we begin to recognize user inputs, messages, and their sources and destinations. Gradually building a spreadsheet is a convenient way to start this. The next (bottom-up) steps would probably be an exploration of the three allowed PIN entry attempts, followed by one last use case for a PIN entry failure. Since incorrect behavior is often not recognized right away, the scenario 2.5 is a failed UserID entry. As a side note, if these scenarios were used to gradually build a decision table, the identification of all five scenarios would have been facilitated. These are pre-sented in their final form as scenarios 2.2, 2.3, 2.4, and 2.5.

Scenario 2.2: Valid Login, PIN correct on 2nd try	
Pre-Condition: The UserID and PIN are in FoodieDB	
Account Creation	FoodieDB
1. e21: Enter valid UserID	
2. Send m17: Entered UserID to FoodieDB	3. Receive m17
5. Receive m18	4. Send m18: User ID OK; expected PIN
6. e24: Enter User PIN ≠ expected PIN	
7. Send m37: Entered PIN	8. Receive m37
10. Receive m21	9. Send m21: User PIN failed
11. e23: Enter User PIN = expected PIN	
12. Send m37: Entered PIN	13. Receive m37
15. Receive m20	14. Send m20: User PIN OK
16. Send m5: Close Login	
Post-Condition: The UserID is logged in	

Scenario 2.3: Valid Login, PIN correct on 3rd try	
Pre-Condition: The UserID and PIN are in FoodieDB	
Account Creation	FoodieDB
1. e21: Enter valid UserID	
2. Send m17: Entered UserID to FoodieDB	3. Receive m17
5. Receive m18	4. Send m18: User ID OK; expected PIN
6. e24: Enter User PIN ≠ expected PIN	
7. Send m37: Entered PIN	8. Receive m37
10. Receive m21	9. Send m21: User PIN failed
11. e24: Enter User PIN ≠ expected PIN	
12. Send m37: Entered PIN	13. Receive m37
15. Receive m21	14. Send m21: User PIN failed
16. e23: Enter User PIN = expected PIN	
17. Send m37: Entered PIN	18. Receive m37
20. Receive m20	19. Send m20: User PIN OK
21. Send m5: Close Login	
Post-Condition: The UserID is logged in	

Scenario 2.4: Invalid Login, PIN failed on 3rd try	
Pre-Condition: The UserID and PIN are in FoodieDB	
Account Creation	FoodieDB
1. e21: Enter valid UserID	
2. Send m17: Entered UserID to FoodieDB	3. Receive m17
5. Receive m18	4. Send m18: User ID OK; expected PIN
6. e24: Enter User PIN ≠ expected PIN	
7. Send m37: Entered PIN	8. Receive m37
10. Receive m21	9. Send m21: User PIN failed
11. e24: Enter User PIN ≠ expected PIN	
12. Send m37: Entered PIN	13. Receive m37
15. Receive m21	14. Send m21: User PIN failed
16. e24: Enter User PIN ≠ expected PIN	
17. Send m37: Entered PIN	18. Receive m37
20. Receive m21	19. Send m21: User PIN failed
21. Send m5: Close Login	
Post-Condition: The UserID is NOT logged in	

Scenario 2.5: Invalid Login, no PIN try	
Pre-Condition: The UserID and PIN are in FoodieDB	
Account Creation	FoodieDB
1. e22: Enter invalid UserID	
2. Send m17: Entered UserID to FoodieDB	3. Receive m17
5. Receive m19	4. Send m19: User ID not recognized
6. Send m5: Close Login	
Post-Condition: The UserID is not logged in	

At this point, the list of messages would appear as in Table 13.5.

The progression in Table 13.5 shows how the recognition of input events and messages expands with added use cases. The next steps in an actual development would be to explore the remaining aspects of the System of Systems. Once no new inputs are recognized, they can be reorganized, either by source or by destination. At some point, we would assign message numbers as we did for the full set of 38 messages for the Foodies Wish List in Appendix B. (If you look carefully, you will see that messages m36, m37, and m38 seem to be out of place. That is because they were identified late, after much other work had been done.) Table 13.6 shows the incidence between scenarios and input events and messages.

Table 13.5 Order in Which Messages are Recognized in Login Use Cases

Message	From	To	Content
First recognized in scenario 2.1			
	Login	FoodieDB	Entered UserID to FoodieDB
	FoodieDB	Login	User ID OK; expected PIN
	Login	FoodieDB	Entered PIN
	FoodieDB	Login	User PIN OK
First recognized in scenario 2.2			
	FoodieDB	Login	User PIN failed
First recognized in scenario 2.4			
	Login	Foodie Home	Close Login
First recognized in scenario 2.5			
	FoodieDB	Login	UserID not recognized

Table 13.6 Incidence of Input Events and Input Messages with Login Scenarios

Scenario	Port Inputs				Message Inputs				
	e21	e22	e23	e24	m2	m18	m19	m20	m21
2.1	x		x		x	x		x	
2.2	x		x	x	x	x		x	x
2.3	x		x	x	x	x		x	x
2.4	x			x	x	x			x
2.5		x			x		x		

13.2.2.2 Incidence with Output Actions and Messages

The matrix showing the incidence of use cases with port output actions and messages is developed in the same iterative way as that for input events and messages. The results are in Table 13.7 below.

It is a natural step to combine both input and output recognition into one table (Table 13.8). Table 13.8 also supports test coverage metrics.

13.2.2.3 Incidence with Classes

There is a perennial debate among object-oriented developers as to how to begin—use cases first, or classes first. One of my colleagues (a very classy person) insists on the class-first approach, while others are more comfortable with the use case first view. A good compromise is to develop an incidence matrix showing which classes are needed to support which use cases. Often, it is easier to identify classes for a use

Table 13.7 Incidence of Output Events and Output Messages with Login Scenarios

	Port Outputs		Message Outputs		
Scenario	a21	a22	m5	m17	m37
2.1	x	x	x	x	x
2.2	x	x	x	x	x
2.3	x	x	x	x	x
2.4	x	x	x	x	
2.5	x		x	x	

Table 13.8 Inputs and Outputs of the Login Scenarios

	Inputs									Outputs				
	Events				Messages					Actions		Messages		
Scenario	e 21	e 22	e 23	e 24	m2	m 18	m 19	m 20	m 21	a 21	a 22	m5	m 17	m 37
2.1	x		x		x	x		x		x	x	x	x	x
2.2	x		x	x	x	x		x	x	x	x	x	x	x
2.3	x		x	x	x	x		x	x	x	x	x	x	x
2.4	x			x	x	x			x	x	x	x	x	
2.5		x			x		x			x		x	x	

case, rather than for a full system. As with the other incidence matrices, this approach provides a good answer to when a sufficient set of classes has been identified.

13.2.3 Threads in Finite State Machines

In this section, we use the Foodies Wish List system details to illustrate how threads can be identified from models. Finite state machine models of our example system are the best place to look for system testing threads. We will start with a hierarchy of state machines; the upper level is shown in Figure 13.2; it shows the highest level view of a shopping transaction.

13.2.3.1 Paths in a Finite State Machine

It is good practice to define state machines in which transitions are caused by actual port input events, and the actions on transitions are port output events. If we have such a finite state machine, generating system test cases for these threads is a mechanical process—simply follow a path of transitions and note the port inputs and outputs as they occur along the path. Table 13.9 traces one such path through the PIN try finite state machine in Figure 13.4. This path corresponds to a thread in which a PIN is correctly entered on the first try. To make the test case explicit, we assume a precondition that the expected PIN is '2468'. The event in parentheses in

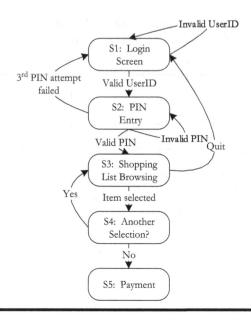

Figure 13.2   Highest Level of Foodie Wish List Shopping Session.

Table 13.9   Port Event Sequence for Correct PIN on First Try

Port Event Sequence for Correct PIN on First Try	
Input Event	*Output Event*
	Login Screen displayed with '- - - -'
2 pressed	
	Login Screen displayed with '- - - *'
4 pressed	
	Login Screen displayed with '- - * *'
6 pressed	
	Login Screen displayed with '- * * *'
8 pressed	
	Login Screen displayed with '* * * *'
(valid PIN)	
	Shopping List displayed

the last row of Table 13.9 is the logical event that "bumps up" to the parent state machine and causes a transition there to the Shopping List Browsing state.

The PIN Entry state S2 is decomposed into the more detailed view in Figure 13.3. The adjacent states are shown because they are sources and destinations of transitions from the PIN Entry state at the upper level. (This approach to decomposition is reminiscent of the old dataflow diagramming idea of balanced decomposition.)

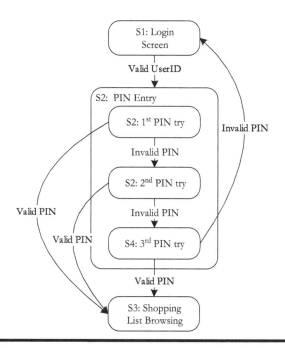

Figure 13.3   Details of the PIN Entry State.

Figure 13.4 decomposes the PIN try states to the penultimate level needed for system testing. (The inputs are still logical rather than actual, but the output events are representative of what the user/system tester would see.) This final state decomposition is applied to see the details of PIN entry tries (see Figure 13.3). Each PIN try is identical, so the lower level states are numbered S2.n, where n signifies the nth PIN attempt. We almost have true input events. If we knew that the expected PIN was "2468" and if we replaced the digit entries, e.g., "1st digit", with "2", then we would finally have true port input events. A few abstract inputs remain—those referring to valid and invalid PINs and conditions on the number of tries. The result of this process is in Table 13.9. Observe that this is exactly the Event Sequence of a use case, and also, the sequence of events and actions in a corresponding system test case.

13.2.3.2 How Many Paths?

The most common products for Model-Based Testing start with a finite state machine description of the system to be tested and then generate all paths through the graph. If there are loops, these are (or should be) replaced by two paths, as we did at the program graph level in Chapter 8. Given such a path, the port inputs that cause transitions are events in a system test case; similarly for port outputs that occur as actions on transitions. There are 21 paths from the Login screen to the Shopping List screen: three PIN attempts, one successful PIN entry attempt, and six ways to fail each attempt. Does this mean we would have to create 21 test cases to test the Login constituent? We will discuss system coverage metrics later.

Here is a hard lesson from industrial experience. A telephone switching system lab tried defining a small telephone system with finite state machines. The system, a Private Automatic Branch Exchange (PABX) was chosen because, as switching systems go, it is quite simple. There was a grizzled veteran system tester, Casimir,

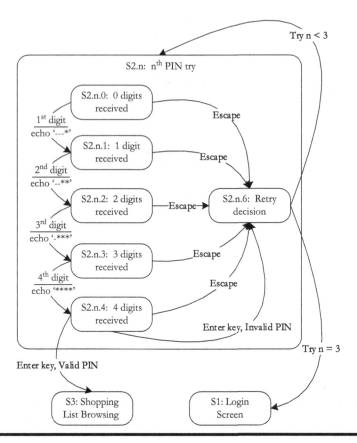

Figure 13.4   Details of the PIN Try States.

assigned to help with the development of the model. He was well named. (According to wikipedia, his name means "someone who destroys opponent's prestige/glory during battle" [http://en.wikipedia.org/wiki/Casimir]). Throughout the process, Casimir was very suspicious, even untrusting. The team reassured him that, once the project was finished, a tool would generate literally several thousand system test cases. Even better, this provided a mechanism to trace system testing directly back to the requirements specification model. The actual finite state machine had over 200 states, and the tool generated more than 3000 test cases. Finally, Casimir was impressed, until one day when he discovered an automatically generated test case that was logically impossible. On further, very detailed analysis, the invalid test case was derived from a pair of states that had a subtle dependency (and finite state machines must have independent states). Out of 200-plus states, recognizing such dependencies is extremely difficult. The team explained to Casimir that the tool could analyze any thread that traversed the pair of dependent states, thereby identifying any other impossible threads. This technical triumph was short-lived, however, when Casimir asked if the tool could identify any other pairs of dependent states. No tool can do this because this would be equivalent to the famous Halting Problem. The lesson: generating threads from finite state machines is attractive and can be quite effective, but care must be taken to avoid both memory and dependence issues.

13.2.4 Atomic System Functions

Atomic System Functions (ASFs) work well in single-processor applications, and less well in our swim lane architecture. We define 19 ASFs that pertain to various shopping scenarios.

ASF-1: Enter Existing (in FoodieDB) UserID
ASF-2: Enter New UserID
ASF-3: Enter Existing (in FoodieDB) User PIN
ASF-4: Enter New (not in FoodieDB) User PIN
ASF-5: Approve UserID
ASF-6: Reject UserID
ASF-7: Approve User PIN Entry
ASF-8: Reject User PIN Entry
ASF-9: Browse Shopping List
ASF-10: Cancel Shopping List Browsing
ASF-11: Move Shopping List item to Shopping Cart
ASF-12: Remove Shopping List item from Shopping Cart
ASF-13: Move Shopping Cart to Checkout
ASF-14: Cancel Checkout
ASF-15: Checkout with valid credit card payment
ASF-16: Checkout with invalid credit card payment
ASF-17: FoodieDB inventory update
ASF-18: FoodieDB ledger update
ASF-19: FoodieDB query response

Here are the five Login scenarios expressed as sequences of ASFs:

Scenario 2.1 < ASF-1, ASF-19, ASF-5, ASF-3, ASF-19, ASF-7>
Scenario 2.2 < ASF-1, ASF-19, ASF-5, ASF-4, ASF-8, ASF-3, ASF-19, ASF-7>
Scenario 2.3 < ASF-1, ASF-19, ASF-5, ASF-4, ASF-8, ASF-4, ASF-8, ASF-3, ASF-19, ASF-7>
Scenario 2.4 < ASF-1, ASF-19, ASF-5, ASF-4, ASF-8, ASF-4, ASF-8, ASF-4, ASF-8, ASF-3, ASF-19, ASF-7>
Scenario 2.5 < ASF-2, ASF-19, ASF-19, ASF-6>

13.3 Identifying Threads in Systems of Systems

By definition, a system of systems (sometimes abbreviated SoS) contains at least two constituents, there are seven in the Foodies Wish List system. The three ways we used to identify threads in a single-processor system also apply to system level SoS threads: as dialogues among constituents, as communicating finite state machines, and as sequences of ASFs.

13.3.1 Dialogues

Use cases are pre-disposed to single processor systems, although the inputs and outputs can be annotated to show processor residence. In this section, we introduce the idea of "dialogues" among constituents. A dialogue has one column for each constituent—it seems that four constituents are a maximum for this book. In practice, it is easier to use columns in a spreadsheet. The dialogue below is our first example; as with use cases, dialogues describe how the user and customer think/assume the eventual system will operate. Dialogues begin in natural language, very much like User Stories. They eventually are formalized as scenarios.

In Scenario 1.1, a new Foodie User proposes a UserID, sends it to Admin. Admin sends the proposed UserID to the FoodieDB. The FoodieDB checks and finds no duplicate, so it approves the new UserID, and confirms this to Admin. In turn, Admin confirms this to Account Creation. The newly approved User then creates a PIN and sends it to Admin. (No check is made on validity of a PIN, since it is local to a User.) Admin sends the PIN to the FoodieDB, so that the FoodieDB can send it as the "Expected PIN" to Login. The numbers show the sequential flow of actions across constituents (and therefore across swim lanes).

Scenario 1.1: Create a valid account		
Pre-Condition: The UserID is not in FoodieDB		
Account Creation	Admin	FoodieDB
1. e11: Enter UserID (original)		
2. Send m7: Propose UserID to Admin	3. Receive m7	
	4. Send m8: Submit UserID to FoodieDB	5. Receive m8
	7. Receive m9	6. Send m9: Approve New Member UserID
9. Receive m11	8. Send m11: Proposed UserID Approved	
10. e12: Create User PIN		
11. Send m13: Defined User PIN to Admin	12. Receive m13	
	13. Send m14: Send User PIN to FoodieDB	14. Receive m14
	16. Receive m15	15. Send m15: Confirm User PIN in FoodieDB
18. Receive m15	17. Send m16: Defined User PIN Accepted	
19. Send m4: Account Creation complete		
Post-Condition: The UserID is in FoodieDB		

We will revisit Scenario 1.1 when we discuss test cases derived from dialogues. Here is a closely related dialogue.

Scenario 1.2: Create an invalid account		
Pre-Condition: The UserID is already in FoodieDB		
Account Creation	Admin	FoodieDB
1. e11: Enter UserID (duplicate)		
2. Send m7: Propose UserID to Admin	3. Receive m7	
	4. Send m8: Submit UserID to FoodieDB	5. Receive m8
	7. Receive m10	6. Send m10: Reject New Member UserID
9. Receive m12	8. Send m12: Proposed UserID Rejected	
10. e13: Click on Exit		
11. Send m4: Account Creation complete		
Post-Condition: Attempt failed.		

13.3.2 Communicating FSMs

Finite state machines for each of the seven Foodie Wish List constituents are given in Appendix B. Figure 13.5 shows the finite state machines needed for Scenario 1.1. For clarity, only the states, and messages needed for Scenario 1.1, are shown in Figure

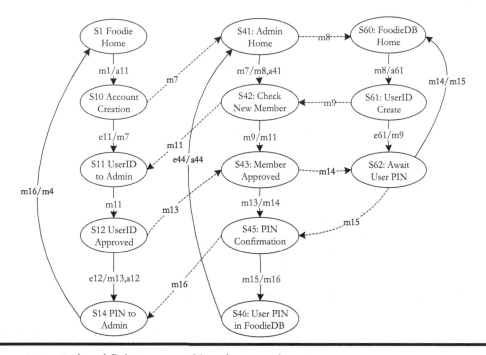

Figure 13.5   Reduced finite state machines for scenario 1.1.

13.5. It is easier to see the flow among constituents in the dialogue for Scenario 1.1. Looking at the message sequence, Scenario 1.1 has the message sequence below:

<m7, m8, m9, m11, m13, m14, m15, m16>

From the message sequence, we can construct the full state sequence of Scenario 1.1.:

<: S1, S10, S41, S1, S61, S62, S42, S11, S12, S43, S62, S45, S14, S1, S41, S1>

We will use state sequences later when we discuss test coverage metrics for dialogues. Scenario 3.1 is a dialogue that involves four constituents:

Scenario 3.1: Normal purchase of One FoodieItem, payment accepted			
Web Swim Lane	**Controlling Swim Lane**		**FoodieDB Swim Lane**
Shopping List	Shopping Cart/ Credit Card	Admin	FoodieDB
e31: Cursor movement			
e32: Select Foodie item			
e33: Move Foodie item to Shopping Cart			
Send m22: Add item to Shopping Cart	Receive m22		
Receive m23	Send m23: Item added to Shopping Cart		
	Send m24: Reduce FoodieItem Count	Receive m24	
		Send m38: Decrease FoodieItem inventory	Receive m38
		Receive m33	Send m33: FoodieItem inventory decreased
	Send m31: Shopping Cart contents	Receive m31 Receive m31	
	e53: Click on Credit Card Interface		
	Send m27: Payment tendered		Receive m27

(Continued)

	Receive m28: Payment accepted		Credit Card sends m28:
			Payment accepted
		Receive m30	Send m30: Payment amount
		Receive m35	Send m35: Payment entered in FoodieDB
		Receive m33	Send m33: FoodieItem inventory decreased
e36: Done shopping	e54: Shopping Cart done	e41: Click on Admin Done	e66: Click on Done

13.3.3 Dialogues as Sequences of ASFs

The 19 atomic system functions identified in Section 13.2.4 can express the more complex dialogues; however, these scenarios can get quite long. Scenario 3.1 can begin only when one of Scenarios 2.1, 2.2, or 2.3 has executed. Here we use the simplest of these, Scenario 2.1 as a prerequisite for the same Scenario 3.1 discussed in Sections 13.3.1 and 13.3.2.

Scenario 2.1 < ASF-1, ASF-19, ASF-5, ASF-3, ASF-19, ASF-7>
Scenario 3.1 < ASF-9, ASF-11, ASF-13, ASF-15, ASF-17, ASF-18>

We can make a slight change to scenario 3.1: this time the shopper moves a second item to the Shopping Cart:

Scenario 3.2 < ASF-9, ASF-11, ASF-9, ASF-11, ASF-13, ASF-15, ASF-17, ASF-18>

Another slight change to scenario 3.1, this time with an invalid credit card payment:

Scenario 3.3 < ASF-9, ASF-11, ASF-13, ASF-16>

13.4 System Level Test Cases

A system level test case contains all the information a system tester (or test automation system) needs to perform a system level test case. In Chapter 12, we saw that some test cases spanned several Foodie Wish List constituents, apparently at the system level. This can be a helpful practice, particularly on projects in which the development machine and the delivery platform are different. In such situations, much of the burden (and difficulty) is shifted from the eventual SoS to the development environment. While this is convenient, it is still necessary to perform system level tests on the actual platform to be delivered.

13.4.1 An Industrial Test Execution System

This section describes a system for automatic test execution that one of the authors was responsible for in the early 1980s. It was intended for executing regression test cases on a telephone switching system (a very boring manual assignment); it was named the Automatic Regression Testing System (ARTS). The system had a human readable system test case language that was interpretively executed on a personal computer. In the ARTS language, there were two verbs: CAUSE would cause a port input event to occur and VERIFY would observe a port output event. In addition, a tester could refer to a limited number of devices and to a limited number of input events associated with those devices. Here is a small paraphrased excerpt of a typical ARTS test case.

CAUSE Go-Offhook On Line 4
VERIFY Dialtone On Line 4
CAUSE TouchDigit '3' On Line 4
VERIFY NoDialtone On Line 4

The physical connection to a telephone prototype required a harness that connected the personal computer with actual system ports. On the input side, the harness accomplished a logical-to-physical transformation, with the symmetric physical-to-logical transformation on output side. The basic architecture is shown in Figure 13.6.

There was an interesting lesson in human factors engineering. The test case language was intentionally free form, and the interpreter eliminated noise words. The freedom to add noise words was intended to give test case designers a place to put additional notes that would not be executed but would be kept in the test execution report. The result was test cases like this (so much for test designer freedom):

As long as it is not raining, see if you can CAUSE a Go-Offhook event right away On Line 4, and then, see if you can VERIFY that some variation of Dialtone happened to occur On Line 4. Then, if you are in a good mood, why not CAUSE a TouchDigit '3' action On Line 4. Finally, (at last!), see if you can VERIFY that NoDialtone is present On Line 4.

In retrospect, the ARTS system predated the advent of use cases. Notice how the event sequence portion of a real use case is dangerously close to an ARTS test case. (The ARTS system evolved into a commercial product that had a 15-year lifetime.)

To extend the ARTS system to our system of systems example, we presume a system testing tool that has the capabilities to send and receive events and messages

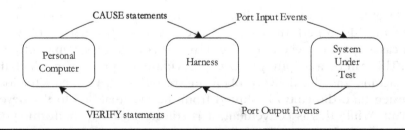

Figure 13.6 Automated Test Execution System Architecture.

between separate swim lane constituents. We use the following test sequence commands (keywords are in all capitals):

VERIFY PRE-CONDITION
VERIFY POST-CONDITION
CAUSE (<eventID>, <value>) IN <SoS constituent>
SEND (<messageID>, <value>) FROM <SoS constituent> TO <SoS constituent>
VERIFY RECEIPT (<messageID>, <value>) FROM <SoS constituent>

Since our intent is to use this extension for progression and regression testing, we will refer to it as the Automatic Test Execution (ATE) system. The automation part can be done either manually, as in the past, or by an engine that executes test scenarios and records the results. The VERIFY portion of such an engine needs, among other things, two additional verbs—EXPECTED and OBSERVED. As other forms of testing, if the expected and observed results are equal (or at least compatible), the test case passes; otherwise it fails. The engine can continue running tests that pass but must stop and report the first point of failure of a failing test scenario. After reporting, the engine can continue running test scenarios.

13.4.2 Use Cases to Test Cases

Recall from Section 13.2.2, there is a hierarchy of ever more detailed use cases: High Level, Essential, Expanded Essential, and Real. Each of these levels is illustrated with an example, Correct PIN on First Try. The conversion process is almost mechanical. An Expanded Essential Use Case converts directly to an abstract system test case— abstract in the sense that there are parameters, not actual values. Because the conversions are so simple, here we show the process for the Real Use Case for Correct PIN on the First Try (see Table 13.4).

Use Case names, Use Case IDs, and Descriptions become system test case names, IDs, and descriptions. Similarly, the pre- and post-conditions of a use case become the pre-and post-conditions of the corresponding system test case. The remainder of a use case is the interleaved sequence of system level inputs and expected system level outputs. Table (Use case) 13.10 is the Real Use Case for Correct PIN on First Try. The system test cases use the CAUSE and VERIFY statements of the Extended ATE system described in Section 13.4.1.

Extended ATE Test Case

Test Case: Correct PIN entry on first try (PIN-1)
Description: A customer enters the PIN number correctly on the first attempt.
Pre-condition: The expected PIN is '2468'

VERIFY	Login Screen display (- - - -)	Pass/Fail?
CAUSE	Keystroke(2)	
VERIFY	Login Screen display (- - - *)	Pass/Fail?
CAUSE	Keystroke(4)	
VERIFY	Login Screen display (- - * *)	Pass/Fail?
CAUSE	Keystroke(6)	
VERIFY	Login Screen display (- * * *)	Pass/Fail?
CAUSE	Keystroke(8)	

Table 13.10 The Real Use Case for Correct PIN on First Try

Use Case Name	Correct PIN entry on first try
Use Case ID	RUC-1
Description	A customer enters the PIN number correctly on the first attempt.
Pre-Conditions	1. The expected PIN is '2468'
Event Sequence	
Input events	Output events
	1. Login Screen shows '- - - -'
2. Customer touches digit 2	3. Login Screen shows '- - - *'
4. Customer touches digit 4	5. Login Screen shows '- - * *'
6. Customer touches digit 6	7. Login Screen shows '- * * *'
8. Customer touches digit 8	9. Login Screen shows '* * * *'
10. Customer touches Enter	11. Login Screen shows 'Correct PIN'
Post conditions	Correct PIN

VERIFY   Login Screen display (* * * *)   Pass/Fail?
VERIFY   Login Screen display (Correct PIN)   Pass/Fail?

We added a test result column to this test case. In practice, it is sometimes possible to organize a sequence of test cases such that the post-conditions of one test case set up the pre-conditions of a successor test case. This can save a lot of test setup time.

The Extended ATE system can recognize when a VERIFY statement fails. Once a test case fails, the system continues with the next test case. Unfortunately, this can lead to a domino effect of failing test cases if successor test cases are dependent on predecessors.

13.4.3 Finite State Machine Paths to Test Cases

The finite state machine in Figure 13.4 is at the level of an abstract expanded essential use case. To convert a finite state machine to a system test case, the abstract inputs must be converted to ones with real values, in our case the Expected PIN is '2468'. Replacing the transition causes (*e.g.*, 1st digit) with the actual digit values, and then replacing the echo actions (*e.g.*, echo '- - - *') with expected screen contents, we derive a system test case identical to that from the use case. It traverses the state sequence <S2.n.0, S2.n.1, S2.n.2, S2.n.3, S2.n.4, S3>.

> Test Case: Correct PIN entry on first try (PIN-1)
> Description: A customer enters the PIN number correctly on the first attempt.
> Pre-condition: The expected PIN is '2468'
> VERIFY   Login Screen display (- - - -)   Pass/Fail?
> CAUSE   Keystroke(2)
> VERIFY   Login Screen display (- - - *)   Pass/Fail?

CAUSE	Keystroke(4)	
VERIFY	Login Screen display (- - * *)	Pass/Fail?
CAUSE	Keystroke(6)	
VERIFY	Login Screen display (- * * *)	Pass/Fail?
CAUSE	Keystroke(8)	
VERIFY	Login Screen display (* * * *)	Pass/Fail?
VERIFY	Login Screen display (Correct PIN)	Pass/Fail?

13.4.4 Dialogue Scenarios to Test Cases

The Extended ATE test case given next is derived from Scenario 1.1; the abstract parameters are replaced with actual values. The first ten test case steps corresponding with the numbering in Scenario 1.1 are as follows:

0. Extended ATE Test Case 1.1
1. VERIFY PRE-CONDITION 'Paul DeVries' is not in FoodieDB
2. CAUSE (e11, 'Paul DeVries') IN Account Creation
3. SEND (m7, Propose UserID to Admin) FROM Account Creation TO Admin
4. VERIFY RECEIPT (m7, Propose UserID to Admin) FROM Account Creation
5. SEND (m8, Submit UserID to FoodieDB) FROM Admin TO FoodieDB
6. VERIFY RECEIPT (m8, Submit UserID to FoodieDB) FROM Admin
7. SEND (m9, Approve New Member UserID) FROM FoodieDB TO Admin
8. VERIFY RECEIPT (m9, Approve New Member UserID FROM FoodieDB
9. SEND (m11, Proposed UserID Approved) FROM Admin TO Account Creation
10. VERIFY RECEIPT (m11, Proposed UserID Approved) FROM Admin

13.4.5 Communicating Finite State Machines to Test Cases

Figure 13.7 contains just the portion of Figure 13.5 that pertains to the ten Extended ATE steps completed in Section 13.4.3.

Here we illustrate the use of noise words (*italic font*) in conjunction with the Extended ATE test case in Section 13.4.3.

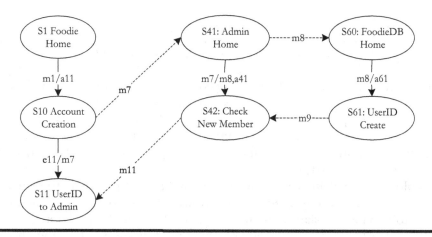

Figure 13.7 A Portion of Figure 13.5.

Extended ATE Test Case 1.1

Please refer to the finite state machine definition for creating a new UserID. Actual user activity begins at the Foodie Home state (S1) and the user input event that causes transition to state S10. Before executing this test case, assure that the UserID 'Paul DeVries' is not present in the FoodieDB.

VERIFY PRE-CONDITION 'Paul DeVries' is not in FoodieDB

In state S10, CAUSE (e11, 'Paul DeVries') IN Account Creation *which sends a message.*

SEND (m7, Propose UserID to Admin) FROM Account Creation TO Admin

and causes a transition to state S11.

Once message m7 is sent, Admin transitions from its initial state, S41, to state S42 where it awaits a response from FoodieDB.

VERIFY RECEIPT (m7, Propose UserID to Admin) FROM Account Creation

While in state S41, Admin forwards the proposed UserID to the FoodieDB and awaits a response in state S42.

SEND (m8, Submit UserID to FoodieDB) FROM Admin TO FoodieDB.

FoodieDB is transitions from its initial state S60 to state S61 where it checks of the string 'Paul DeVries".

On receipt of m8, VERIFY RECEIPT (m8, Submit UserID to FoodieDB) FROM Admin, *FoodieDB transitions from its initial state S60 to state S61 where it checks of the string 'Paul DeVries".*

Since it is not present, FoodieDB, SEND (m9, Approve New Member UserID) FROM FoodieDB TO Admin,

In state S42, Admin VERIFY RECEIPT (m9, Approve New Member UserID FROM FoodieDB

Next, Admin performs a SEND (m11, Proposed UserID Approved) FROM Admin TO Account Creation.

On receipt of message m11, VERIFY RECEIPT (m11, Proposed UserID Approved) FROM Admin, *the Account Creation fsm is in state S11.*

13.5 Coverage Metrics for System Testing

In Part II, we saw the advantage of combining specification-based and code-based testing techniques, because they are complementary. We are in the same position now with system testing: model-based approaches can be combined with use case-based approaches. In this section, we first give an overview of test coverage metrics and associated best practices. The section concludes with two sets of system test coverage metrics: use case-based and model based. But first, we echo some advice from Robert Binder in his blog "Don't Play Developer Testing Roulette: How to Use Test Coverage" [Binder 2019].

In his blog, Binder criticizes organizations that accept less than 100% test coverage of a given metric. Accepting 85% coverage with respect to a chosen metric is very analogous to playing Russian Roulette with a six-shooter. The probabilities of a bad outcome are nearly equal. This is absolutely correct, assuming that the chosen test coverage metric makes sense in a given situation. Test coverage metrics are seldom one-size-fits-all; they need to be mindfully, intentionally chosen based on the nature of the item being tested.

"MBA-Think" refers to management personnel who reduce complex questions to simplified numbers. Test coverage metrics are vulnerable to MBA-Think—they should be mindfully applied. Consider the metric "All program paths for code with no loops": 100% coverage seems like a good idea, but what about infeasible paths? A more mindful metric would be "All feasible program paths for code with no loops." At the other extreme, consider "All program statements": acceptance of anything less than 100% coverage is truly Binder's Russian Roulette.

Best practice? Consider the nature of the item being tested and use that to mandate a test coverage metric. Some examples:

- For code that contains some form of repetition, use Loop Coverage,
- For computational code, use data flow testing, *e.g.*, every definition-clear path for every variable in a calculation,
- For event-driven systems, use test cases that cover: all input events, all output events, and possibly all input events in every context in which they occur.

In other words, the punishment should fit the crime, or more positively, the medicine should fit the disease.

13.5.1 Use Case-Based Test Coverage

In Section 13.2, we saw the process in which customers and developers move from "user stories" to use cases, and then to lists of input events, output actions, and, in the case of systems of systems, messages among constituents. That information serves as a natural basis for our first set of system test coverage metrics.

Consider the space of port input events. Five port input thread coverage metrics are easily defined. Attaining these levels of system test coverage requires a set of threads such that:

Port Input 1: each port input event occurs
Port Input 2: common sequences of port input events occur
Port Input 3: each port input event occurs in every "relevant" data context
Port Input 4: for a given context, all "inappropriate" input events occur
Port Input 5: for a given context, all possible input events occur

The Port Input 1 metric is a bare minimum and is inadequate for most systems. Port Input 2 coverage is the most common, and it corresponds to the intuitive view of system testing because it deals with "normal use." It is difficult to quantify, however. What is a common sequence of input events? Answer: these are probably already present in the use cases. What is an uncommon one? This is more difficult—how do we list things that should not happen? Where does this process end?

The last three metrics are defined in terms of a "context." The best view of a context is that it is a point of event quiescence. In the Foodie Wish List system, screen displays occur at the points of event quiescence. The Port Input 3 metric deals with context-sensitive port input events. These are physical input events that have logical meanings determined by the context within which they occur. In the Foodie Wish List system, for example, the system response to a digit keystroke that occurs in PIN entry is a string on dashes and asterisks (*e.g.*, '- - * *'), but in the Checkout state, the response is the actual digit. The key to this metric is that it is driven by an event in all of its contexts. The Port Input 4 and Port Input 5 metrics are converses: they start with a context and seek a variety of events. The Port Input 4 metric is often used on an informal basis by testers who try to break a system. At a given context, they want to supply unanticipated input events just to see what happens.

This is a specification problem: we are discussing the difference between prescribed behavior (things that should happen) and proscribed behavior (things that should not happen). Most requirements specifications have a hard time even describing prescribed behavior; it is usually testers who find proscribed behavior. The designer who maintains my local ATM system told me that once someone inserted a fish sandwich in the deposit envelope slot. (Apparently someone thought it was a waste receptacle.) At any rate, no one at the bank ever anticipated insertion of a fish sandwich as a port input event. The Port Input 4 and Port Input 5 metrics are usually very effective, but they raise one curious difficulty. How does the tester know what the expected response should be to a proscribed input? Are they simply ignored? Should there be an output warning message? Usually, this is left to the tester's intuition. If time permits, this is a powerful point of feedback to requirements specification. It is also a highly desirable focus for either rapid prototyping or executable specifications.

The situation for output events is simpler—we define two coverage metrics based on port output events:

Port Output 1: each port output event occurs
Port Output 2: each port output event occurs for each cause

Port Output 1 coverage is an acceptable minimum. It is particularly effective when a system has a rich variety of output messages for error conditions. (Our Foodie Wish List system does not.) Port Output 2 coverage is a good goal, but it is hard to quantify. For now, note that Port Output 2 coverage refers to threads that interact with respect to a port output event. Usually, a given output event only has a small number of causes.

In practice, some of the most difficult faults found in field trouble reports are those in which an output occurs for an unsuspected cause. Here is one example: My local ATM system (not the Foodie Wish List) has a screen that informs me that "Your daily withdrawal limit has been reached." This screen should occur when I attempt to withdraw more than the daily withdrawal limit. One Friday afternoon, I tried to withdraw $100 from my local ATM machine. When I saw the daily limit exceeded message, I assumed that my wife had made a large withdrawal. I requested $50 and

Table 13.11 Input Event/Action Coverage

Scenario	e21	e22	e23	e24	a21	a22
2.1	x	—	x	—	x	x
2.2	x	—	x	x	x	x
2.3	x	—	x	x	x	x
2.4	x	—	x	x	x	x
2.5	—	x	—	—	x	—

found out that the ATM also allows a user to request another transaction. With my tester's mindset, I requested and received another $50. I learned later that the system produces the daily limit exceeded message when the amount of cash in the dispenser is low. Instead of providing a lot of cash to the first users, the central bank prefers to provide less cash to more users.

Table 13.11 shows the incidence of our continuing Login scenarios example with input events and output actions.

From Table 13.11, we see that any of scenarios 2.2, 2.3, or 22.4, together with scenario 2.5 provide both Port Input 1 and Port Input 2 coverage. Because failed PIN entry attempts are contexts, we need all five scenarios for Port Input 3 coverage. If we refined our events down to the level of digit keystrokes and the Escape keystroke, as in Figure 13.4, we could postulate the behaviors associated with the point at which an Escape keystroke occurs. We could attain the Port Inputs 4 and 5 coverage. (This raises the number of use cases from 5 to 25.) It might be a better idea to push this down to either the unit or the integration level. Incidentally, this is the intent of the "Shift Left" and "Shift Down" recommendations.

Table 13.12 shows the incidence of our continuing Login scenarios example with messages.

As we saw with event coverage, any of Scenarios 2.2, 2.3, or 22.4, together with scenario 2.5 provide full message coverage.

Table 13.12 Message Coverage

Scenario	m2	m5	m17	m18	m19	m20	m21	m37
2.1	x	x	x	x	—	x	—	x
2.2	x	x	x	x	—	x	x	x
2.3	x	x	x	x	—	x	x	x
2.4	x	x	x	x	—	—	x	x
2.5	x	x	x	—	x	—	—	—

13.5.2 Model-Based Test Coverage

We can use model-based metrics as a cross-check on use case-based threads in much the same way that we used DD-Paths at the unit level to identify gaps and redundancies in specification-based test cases. We really have pseudo-structural testing [Jorgensen, 1994] because the node and edge coverage metrics are defined in terms of a model of a system, not derived directly from the system implementation. In general, behavioral models are only approximations of a system's reality—they might miss important details that should be tested. Computations are a good example of this.

The big weakness of model-based metrics is that the underlying model may be a poor choice. The three most common behavioral models (decision tables, finite state machines, and Petri nets) are appropriate, respectively, to transformational, interactive, and concurrent systems. Decision tables and finite state machines are good choices for testing single processor applications. If a system is described using a decision table, conditions typically include port input events, and actions are port output events. We can then devise test cases that cover every condition, every action, or, most completely, every rule. For finite state machine models, test cases can cover every state, every transition, or every path.

Thread testing based on decision tables is cumbersome. We might describe threads as sequences of rules (even from different decision tables), but this becomes very messy to track in terms of coverage. We need finite state machines as a minimum, and if any form of interaction occurs, Petri nets are a better choice (see Chapter 15).

The finite state machine for the Login constituent is revised to show transition numbers in Figure 13.8. We use it to derive the two most common model-based test coverage metrics: state coverage and transition (edge) coverage. We can identify four test coverage metrics based on finite state machines. Attaining these levels of system test coverage requires a set of threads such that:

FSM1: Every state is traversed
FSM2: Every state transition is traversed
FSM3: Every feasible path (in a finite state machine with no loops) is traversed
FSM4: FSM3 plus every loop is traversed twice, once to enter, and once to exit the loop.
FSM5: Every path (in a finite state machine with no loops) is traversed
FSM6: FSM5 plus every loop is traversed twice, once to enter, and once to exit the loop.

These echo the graph-based coverage metrics we postulated in Chapter 8. They should—finite state machines are an example of directed graphs.

Table 13.13 shows the state coverage of the five Login scenarios. Columns that have only one "x" entry are a quick way to determine FSM1 coverage. Scenarios 2.1, 2.2, 2.3, and 2.4 provide state coverage. Looking at Table 13.14 with the same strategy shows that all five scenarios are necessary for FSM2 coverage. In this example, the five scenarios provide FSM3 coverage (there no loops in the Login FSM.). Because every path beginning with transitions 1, 3, 5 is infeasible, and similarly, the path of transitions 1, 2, 4 is infeasible, the FSM5 and FSM6 test covers cannot be attained. FSM4 coverage is moot for the Login case because there are no loops of states.

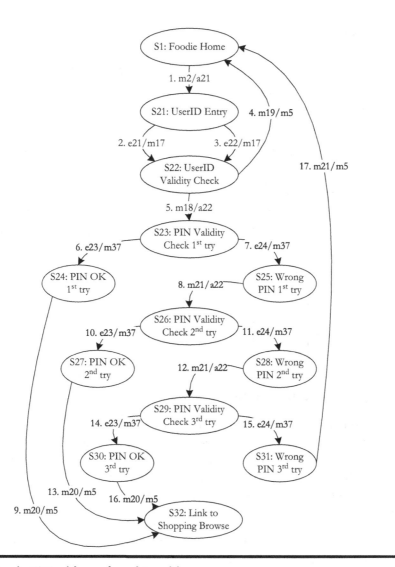

Figure 13.8 Login FSM with numbered transitions.

Table 13.13 State coverage of the five Login scenarios State Coverage

Scenario	S1	S 21	S 22	S 23	S 24	S 25	S 26	S 27	S 28	S 29	S 30	S 31	S 32
2.1	x	x	x	x	x	—	—	—	—	—	—	—	x
2.2	x	x	x	x	—	x	x	x	—	—	—	—	x
2.3	x	x	x	x	—	x	x	—	x	x	x	—	x
2.4	x	x	x	x	—	x	x	—	x	x	—	x	—
2.5	x	x	x	—	—	—	—	—	—	—	—	—	—

Table 13.14 Transition Coverage of the five Login scenarios.

Scenario	e1	e2	e3	e4	e5	e6	e7	e8	e9
2.1	x	x	—	—	x	x	—	—	x
2.2	x	x	—	—	x	—	x	x	—
2.3	x	x	—	—	x	—	x	x	—
2.4	x	x	—	—	x	—	x	x	—
2.5	x	—	x	x	—	—	—	—	—

Scenario	e10	e11	e12	e13	e14	e15	e16	e17
2.1	—	—	—	—	—	—	—	—
2.2	x	—	—	x	—	—	—	—
2.3	—	x	x	—	x	—	x	—
2.4	—	x	x	—	—	x	—	x
2.5	—	—	—	—	—	—	—	—

13.6 Long Versus Short Test Cases

There is an element of foreshadowing in the preceding material. Early on, we spoke of various thread candidates. In that discussion, we saw a range of very short to very long threads. Most writers of use case development consider what we call here "long use cases"—those that are "end-to-end" transactions. We have seen that a system test case can be derived, almost automatically, from a well-formed use case. Since system level test cases traverse some path in the set of communicating finite state machines, these "end-to-end" test cases correspond directly to long use cases. Tables 13.15 and 13.16 show the total number of paths in the two main sets of constituents—some of these are feasible, others are infeasible. The infeasible paths result from dependencies, for example, a rejected Login path cannot be connected to later permissible Shopping List paths.

In this section, we will focus on the main part of the Foodie Wish List application, namely the interactions among Login, Shopping List, Shopping Cart, Admin, and FoodieDB. Of the 5400 total paths in Table 13.16 many are infeasible, leaving 1080

Table 13.15 Paths in Account Creation to Admin to FoodieDB

Constituent	Distinct Paths	Feasible Paths
Account Creation	2	2
Admin	2	2
FoodieDB	2	2
Total paths	8	8

Table 13.16   Login to Shopping List to Shopping Cart to Admin to FoodieDB

Constituent	Distinct Paths	Feasible Paths
Login	8	5
Shopping List	5	5
Shopping Cart	5	6
Admin	6	3
FoodieDB	3	3
Total paths	2700	1080

feasible paths. Clearly, developing and more importantly, testing 1080 feasible test cases is an example of what me might call the test case explosion. To reduce this burden, here we postulate the notion of "short test cases." If we develop short test cases carefully, they can be sequenced by having the pre-conditions of one short test case compatible with the post-conditions of a predecessor short test case.

Seventeen short test cases (abbreviated STC-i) are defined here with short descriptions, pre- and post-conditions, and state sequences.

Login Constituent

STC-1	Rejected UserID
Pre-conditions	UserID not in database, not logged in
State sequence	S1, s21, S22, S1
Post-conditions	UserID not in database, User not logged in

STC-2	Valid UserID, PIN correct on 1st try
Pre-conditions	UserID not in database, not logged in
State sequence	S1, S21, S22, S23, S24, S32
Post-conditions	UserID not in database, User logged in

STC-3	Valid UserID, PIN correct on 2nd try
Pre-conditions	UserID not in database, not logged in
State sequence	S1, s21, S22, S23, S25, S26, S27, S32
Post-conditions	UserID not in database, User logged in

STC-4	Valid UserID, PIN correct on 3rd try
Pre-conditions	UserID not in database, not logged in
State sequence	S1, s21, S22, S23, S25, S26, S28, S29, S30, S32
Post-conditions	UserID not in database, User logged in

STC-5	Valid UserID, PIN failed on 3rd try
Pre-conditions	UserID not in database, not logged in
State sequence	S1, s21, S22, S23, S25, S26, S28, S29, S31, S1
Post-conditions	UserID not in database, User not logged in

Shopping List Constituent

STC-6	User logged in, decides to not shop.
Pre-conditions	User Logged in, ready to shop
State sequence	S1, S32, S1
Post-conditions	User Logged in, ready to shop

STC-7	User logged in, 1 item to Shopping Cart
Pre-conditions	User Logged in, ready to shop
State sequence	S1, S32, S33, S34, S36, S1
Post-conditions	User Logged in, Shopping Cart contents known

STC-8	User logged in, 2nd item to Shopping Cart
Pre-conditions	User Logged in, ready to shop
State sequence	S1, S32, S33, S34, S36, S32, S33, S34, S36, S1
Post-conditions	User Logged in, Shopping Cart contents known

STC-9	User logged in, 1 item selected and then deleted from Shopping cart

Continues shopping.

Pre-conditions	User Logged in, ready to shop
State sequence	S1, S32, S33, S34, S35, S36, S32
Post-conditions	User Logged in, ready to shop

STC-10	User logged in, 1 item selected and then deleted from Shopping cart.

Done shopping.

Pre-conditions	User Logged in, ready to shop
State sequence	S1, S32, S33, S34, S35, S36, S1
Post-conditions	User Logged in, abort shopping.

Shopping Cart Constituent

STC-11	Confirm added item
Pre-conditions	Shopping Cart contents updated
State sequence	S51, S52, S54
Post-conditions	Ready for payment

STC-12	Confirm deleted item
Pre-conditions	Shopping Cart contents updated
State sequence	s51, s53, s54
Post-conditions	Ready for payment

STC-13	Ready for payment, no payment
Pre-conditions	Ready for payment
State sequence	S54, S51
Post-conditions	Shopping cancelled

STC-14	Ready for payment, payment accepted
Pre-conditions	Ready for payment

State sequence	S54, S55, S56, S51
Post-conditions	Payment accepted, inventory reduced

STC-15	Ready for payment, payment rejected
Pre-conditions	Ready for payment
State sequence	S54, S55, S54, S51
Post-conditions	Payment rejected, inventory unchanged

FoodieDB Constituent

STC-16	Payment accepted, inventory reduced
Pre-conditions	Payment accepted, inventory reduced
State sequence	S60, S68, S60, S65, S66, S60
Post-conditions	Payment recorded, inventory changed

STC-17	Payment rejected, inventory unchanged
Pre-conditions	Payment rejected, inventory unchanged
State sequence	S60, S68, S60, S65, S67, S60
Post-conditions	Transaction cancelled

The huge advantage of the short test cases is that they can be chained to express all the long test cases. Figure 13.9 depicts this interconnectivity.

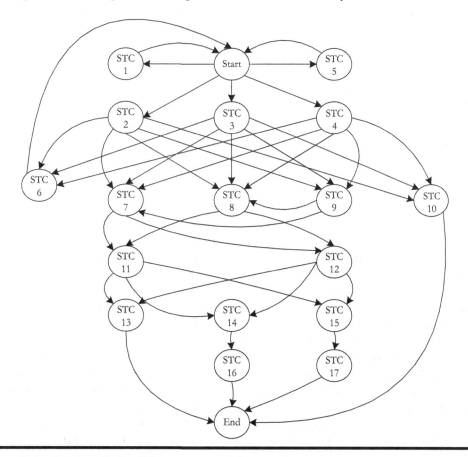

Figure 13.9   108 Locally feasible sequences of short test cases.

As a quick example of a long use case, consider a story with the following sequence:

A Foodie Wish List customer enters a valid UserID, followed by a valid PIN entry on the first try. The customer selects browses the Shopping list, selects an item, and moves it to the Shopping cart. On seeing the price, the customer removes the item and returns to the Shopping List. Once there, the customer selects a less expensive FoodieITem and moves it to the Shopping Cart. The credit card payment is accepted and the Foodie database records both the payment and the reduction in inventory.

As a sequence of short test cases, this becomes the sequence:

<STC-2, STC-9, STC-7, STC-14, STC-16, STC-17>

13.6.1 Supplemental Approaches to System Testing

All model-based testing approaches have been open to the criticism that the testing is only as good as the underlying model. There is no escaping this. In response, some authorities recommend various "random" supplements. One such technique, mutation testing is discussed in Chapter 8. In this section, we consider two fallback strategies, each of which has thread execution probability as a starting point. Both operational profiling and risk-based testing are responses to the "squeeze" on available system testing time.

13.6.2 Operational Profiles

In its most general form, Zipf's Law (also called the Pareto Principle) holds that 80% of the activities occur in 20% of the space. Activities and space can be interpreted in numerous ways: people with messy desks hardly ever use most of their desktop clutter; programmers seldom use more than 20% of the features of their favorite programming language; and Shakespeare (whose writings contain an enormous vocabulary) uses a small fraction of his vocabulary most of the time. Zipf's Law applies to software (and testing) in several ways. The most useful interpretation for testers is that the space consists of all possible threads, and activities are thread executions (or traversals). Thus, for a system with many threads, 80% of the execution traverses only 20% of the threads.

Recall that a failure occurs when a fault is executed. The whole idea of testing is to execute test cases such that, when a failure occurs, the presence of a fault is revealed. We can make an important distinction: the distribution of faults in a system is only indirectly related to the reliability of the system. The simplest view of system reliability is the probability that no failure occurs during a specific time interval. (Notice that no mention is even made of faults, the number of faults, or fault density.) If the only faults are "in the corners" of threads that are seldom traversed, the overall reliability is higher than if the same number of faults were on "high-traffic" threads. The idea of operational profiles is to determine the execution frequencies of various threads and to use this information to select threads for system testing. Particularly when test time is limited (usually the case in many projects), operational profiles maximize the probability of finding faults by inducing failures in the most frequently traversed threads. Here we use our Foodie Wish List system. In Figure 13.13, the short use case labels on the transitions in Figure 13.12 are replaced by estimated transition probabilities.

Finite state machines are the preferred model for identifying thread execution probabilities. The mathematics behind this is that the transition probabilities can be expressed is a "transition matrix" where the element in row i, column j is the probability of the transition from state i to state j. Powers of the transition matrix are analogous to the powers of the adjacency matrix when we discussed reachability in Chapter 4. Once the thread probabilities are known, they sorted according to execution probability, most to least probable. This is done in Tables 13.17 and 13.19. Figure 13.10 shows the connectivity of Login and Shopping List short test cases.

Just as the quality of model-based testing is limited by the correctness of the underlying model, the analysis of operational profiles is limited by the validity of the transition probability estimates. There are strategies to develop these estimates. One is to use historical data from similar systems. Another is to use customer supplied estimates. Still another is to use a Delphi approach in which a group of experts give their guesses, and some average is determined. This might be based on convergence of a series of estimates, or possibly by having seven experts, and eliminating the

Table 13.17 Path Probabilities of Selected Short Test Cases

Test Case ID	Description	State Sequence	Path Probability
STC-1	Rejected UserID	S1, s21, S22, S1	0.01
STC-2	Valid UserID, PIN correct on 1st try	S1, s21, S22, S23, S24, S32	0.9702
STC-3	Valid UserID, PIN correct on 2nd try	S1, s21, S22, S23, S25, S26, S27, S32	0.019404
STC-4	Valid UserID, PIN correct on 3rd try	S1, s21, S22, S23, S25, S26, S28, S29, S30, S32	0.00038808
STC-5	Valid UserID, PIN failed on 3rd try	S1, s21, S22, S23, S25, S26, S28, S29, S31, S1	0.00000792
STC-6	User decides to not shop.	S1, S32, S1	0.2
STC-7	User sends 1 item to Shopping Cart. Done.	S1, S32, S33, S34, S1	0.048
STC-8	User sends 1 item to Shopping Cart. Browse.	S1, S32, S33, S34, S32	0.6
STC-9	User selects and deletes an item from Shopping cart. Browse.	S1, S32, S33, S34, S32	0.006
STC-10	User selects and deletes an item from Shopping cart. Done.	S1, S32, S33, S34, S35, S34, S1	0.00192

Table 13.18   Probabilities of Short Test Case Sequences

Path	STCs	Probability
1	STC-1	0.01
2	STC-5	0.00000792
3	STC-2, STC-6	0.19404
4	STC-3, STC-6	0.0038808
5	STC-4, STC-6	0.000077616
6	STC-2, STC-7	0.0465696
7	STC-3, STC-7	0.000931392
8	STC-4, STC-7	1.86278E-05
9	STC-2, STC-8	0.58212
10	STC-3, STC-8	0.0116424
11	STC-4, STC-8	0.000232848
12	STC-2, STC-9	0.0058212
13	STC-3, STC-9	0.000116424
14	STC-4, STC-9	2.32848E-06
15	STC-2, STC-10	0.001862784
16	STC-3, STC-10	3.72557E-05
17	STC-4, STC-10	7.45114E-07

Table 13.19   Descriptions of the Short Test Cases for the Login and Shopping List constituents

STC ID	Descriptions
STC-1	Rejected UserID
STC-2	Valid UserID, PIN correct on 1st try
STC-3	Valid UserID, PIN correct on 2nd try
STC-4	Valid UserID, PIN correct on 3rd try
STC-5	Valid UserID, PIN failed on 3rd try
STC-6	User decides to not shop.
STC-7	User sends 1 item to Shopping Cart. Done.
STC-8	User sends 1 item to Shopping Cart. Browse.
STC-9	User selects and deletes an item from Shopping cart. Browse.
STC-10	User selects and deletes an item from Shopping cart. Done.

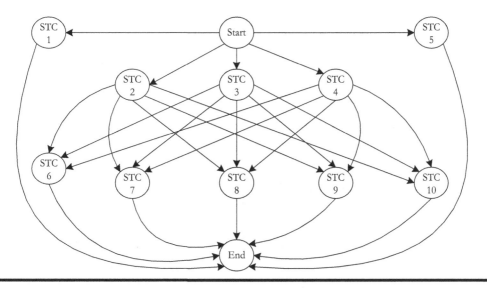

Figure 13.10 Connectivity of Login and Shopping List Short Test Cases.

high and low estimates. Whatever approach is used, the final transition probabilities are still estimates. On the positive side, we could do a sensitivity analysis. In this situation, the overall ordering of probabilities is not particularly sensitive to small variations in the individual transition probabilities. Operational profiles provide a feeling for the traffic mix of a delivered system. This is helpful for reasons other than only optimizing system testing. These profiles can also be used in conjunction with simulators to get an early indication of execution time performance and system transaction capacity.

Figure 13.11 shows the finite state machines for the Login and Shopping List constituents, with the transition probabilities on necessary edges. (By default, the unlabeled edges have probability of 1.00. Notice that the sum of probabilities on outgoing edges is always 1.00.)

Table 13.20 is the list of short test case sequences ordered by probability.

13.6.2.1 Risk-Based Testing

Hans Schaefer, a consultant who specializes in risk-based testing, advises that the first step is to group the system into risk categories. He advises four risk categories: Catastrophic, Damaging, Hindering, and Annoying [Schaefer and Software Test Consulting, 2005]. Next, the cost weighting is assessed. He suggests a logarithmic weighting: 1 for low cost of failure, 3 for medium, and 10 for high. Why logarithmic? Psychologists are moving in this direction because subjects who are asked to rank factors on linear scales, e.g., 1 for low and 5 for high, don't make enough of a distinction in what is usually a subjective assessment. Table 13.21 is the result of this process for our Foodie Wish List use cases in Table 13.20. In this assessment, risk factors include factors such as customer convenience, loss of revenue, and illicit access.

First, we need to consider the risk that failure of a single short test case contributes to the pairs of STCs. Contributions are on a low to high scale 3, 7, 12, 20.

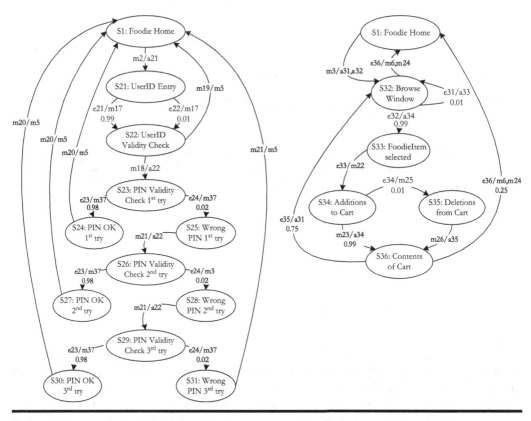

Figure 13.11 Login and Shopping List Constituents with Transition Probabilities.

Failures in short test cases STC-1 and STC-5 are extremely damaging.

STC-1 Rejected UserID: If this test case fails, there is illicit access to the Foodies Wish List system.

STC-5 Valid UserID, PIN failed on 3rd try: This is similar to, and presents a greater risk, than STC-1. Not only does it allow illicit access to the Foodies Wish List system, it could also be that the FoodieDB portion that contains PIN information is corrupt.

Short test cases STC-2, −3, and − 4 all refer to the three PIN entry attempts. The probabilities of STC-3 and STC-4 are greatly reduced due to prior failed attempts. (See Figure 13.11)

STC-2 Valid UserID, PIN correct on 1st try: Failure of STC-2 is inconvenient for the user, but the user still has another chance for PIN entry.

STC-3 Valid UserID, PIN correct on 2nd try: Failure of STC-3 is inconvenient for the user, but the user still has another chance for PIN entry.

STC-4 Valid UserID, PIN correct on 3rd try: Failure of STC-2 is problematic, more than inconvenient, the system would lose a legitimate customer.

Table 13.20 Foodie Wish List Operational Profile

Path	STCs	Probability
9	STC-2, STC-8	0.58212
3	STC-2, STC-6	0.19404
6	STC-2, STC-7	0.0465696
10	STC-3, STC-8	0.0116424
1	STC-1	0.01
12	STC-2, STC-9	0.0058212
4	STC-3, STC-6	0.0038808
15	STC-2, STC-10	0.001862784
7	STC-3, STC-7	0.000931392
11	STC-4, STC-8	0.000232848
13	STC-3, STC-9	0.000116424
5	STC-4, STC-6	0.000077616
16	STC-3, STC-10	0.00003725568
8	STC-4, STC-7	0.00001862784
2	STC-5	0.00000792
14	STC-4, STC-9	0.00000232848
17	STC-4, STC-10	0.0000007451136

Table 13.21 Risk Contribution of Individual STCs

STC ID	Descriptions	Contribution to Risk
STC-1	Rejected UserID	20
STC-2	Valid UserID, PIN correct on 1st try	3
STC-3	Valid UserID, PIN correct on 2nd try	3
STC-4	Valid UserID, PIN correct on 3rd try	7
STC-5	Valid UserID, PIN failed on 3rd try	20
STC-6	User decides to not shop.	3
STC-7	User sends 1 item to Shopping Cart. Done.	3
STC-8	User sends 1 item to Shopping Cart. Browse.	3
STC-9	User selects and deletes an item from Shopping cart. Browse.	7
STC-10	User selects and deletes an item from Shopping cart. Done.	3

Table 13.22 Risk Profile of STC Sequences

Path	STCs	Description	Risk
1	STC-1	Rejected UserID	909494.7018
2	STC-5	Valid UserID, PIN failed on 3rd try	720.3198038
9	STC-2, STC-8	Valid UserID, PIN correct on 1st try; User sends 1 item to Shopping Cart. Browse.	142.1191406
12	STC-2, STC-9	Valid UserID, PIN correct on 1st try; User selects and deletes an item from Shopping cart. Browse.	55.51528931
3	STC-2, STC-6	Valid UserID, PIN correct on 1st try; User decides to not shop.	47.37304688
6	STC-2, STC-7	Valid UserID, PIN correct on 1st try; User sends 1 item to Shopping Cart. Done.	11.36953125
10	STC-3, STC-8	Valid UserID, PIN correct on 2nd try; User sends 1 item to Shopping Cart. Browse.	2.842382813
13	STC-3, STC-9	Valid UserID, PIN correct on 2nd try; User selects and deletes an item from Shopping cart. Browse.	1.110305786
4	STC-3, STC-6	Valid UserID, PIN correct on 2nd try; User decides to not shop.	0.947460938
14	STC-4, STC-9	Valid UserID, PIN correct on 3rd try; User selects and deletes an item from Shopping cart. Browse.	0.867426395
5	STC-4, STC-6	Valid UserID, PIN correct on 3rd try; User decides to not shop.	0.740203857
15	STC-2, STC-10	Valid UserID, PIN correct on 1st try; User selects and deletes an item from Shopping cart. Done.	0.45478125
7	STC-3, STC-7	Valid UserID, PIN correct on 2nd try; User sends 1 item to Shopping Cart. Done.	0.227390625
8	STC-4, STC-7	Valid UserID, PIN correct on 3rd try; User sends 1 item to Shopping Cart. Done.	0.177648926
11	STC-4, STC-8	Valid UserID, PIN correct on 3rd try; User sends 1 item to Shopping Cart. Browse.	0.056847656
16	STC-3, STC-10	Valid UserID, PIN correct on 2nd try; User selects and deletes an item from Shopping cart. Done.	0.009095625
17	STC-4, STC-10	Valid UserID, PIN correct on 3rd try; User selects and deletes an item from Shopping cart. Done.	0.007105957

Figure 13.12   Shopping List Following Correct Pin on the 1st try.

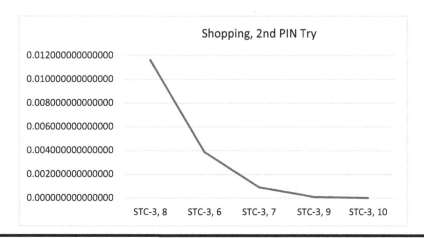

Figure 13.13   Shopping List Following Correct Pin on the 2nd try.

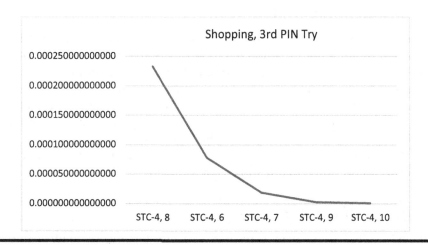

Figure 13.14   Shopping List Following Correct Pin on the 3rd try.

Short test cases 6 through 10 deal with various choices a customer can make on the Shopping List web page.

> STC-6 User decides to not shop: If STC-6 fails, the user could be stuck in the Shopping List constituent. The probable user reaction would be frustration followed by some form of Forced Quit.
>
> STC-10 User selects and deletes an item from Shopping cart. Done: This is similar to STC-6; with a failure, the user could again be stuck in the Shopping List constituent, with the same outcomes as STC-6.
>
> STC-7 User sends 1 item to Shopping Cart. Done: This is normal activity, but if it fails, the user might be stuck in the Shopping List constituent as with STC-6 and STC-10.
>
> STC-8 User sends 1 item to Shopping Cart. Browse: This is desirable activity and can lead to additional purchases. Failure means loss of revenue.
>
> STC-9 User selects and deletes an item from Shopping Cart. Browse: This is a "no harm, no foul" case. However, failure might mean that the Foodie item cannot be deleted from the Shopping Cart. An unintended purchase would certainly aggravate the customer, and ultimately cause item return complexities.

The risk-ordered Foodie Wish List test cases in Table 13.22 differ significantly from their operational profile in Table 13.20.

> Operational Profile Order: 9, 3, 6, 10, 1, 12, 4, 15, 7, 11, 13, 5, 16, 8, 2, 14, 17
> Risk-Based Testing Order: 1, 2, 9, 12, 3, 6, 10, 13, 4, 14, 5, 15, 7, 8, 11, 16, 17

The analysis of operational and risk-based testing orders is very dependent on the transition probabilities that were used to compute the short test case probabilities. Consider three sets of test case sequences. Their probabilities are graphed in Figures 13.12, 13.13, and 13.14.

13.7 Non-functional System Testing

The system testing ideas thus far discussed have been based on specification-based, or behavioral, requirements. Functional requirements are absolutely in the does view, as they describe what a system does (or should do). To generalize, non-functional testing refers to how well a system performs its functional requirements. Many non-functional requirements are categorized onto "-abilities": reliability, maintainability, scalability, usability, compatibility, and so on. While many practitioners have clear ideas on the meaning of the -abilities in their product domains, there is not much standardization of either the terms or the techniques. Here we consider the most common form of non-functional testing—stress testing.

13.7.1 Stress Testing Strategies

Synonymously called performance testing, capacity testing, or load testing, this is the most common, and maybe the most important form of non-functional testing.

Because stress testing is so closely related to the nature of the system being tested, stress testing techniques are also application dependent. Here we describe three common strategies and illustrate them with examples.

13.7.1.1 Compression

Consider the performance of a system in the presence of extreme loads. A web-based application may be very popular, and its server might not have the capacity. Telephone switching systems use the term Busy Hour Call Attempts (BHCAs) to refer to such offered traffic loads. The strategy in those systems is best understood as compression.

A local switching system must recognize when a subscriber originates a call. Other than sensing a change in subscriber line status from idle to active, the main indicator of a call attempt is the entry of digits. Although some dial telephones still exist, most subscribers use digit keys. The technical term is Dual Tone Multi-Frequency tones, as the usual 3 × 4 array of digit keys has three frequencies for the columns and four frequencies for the rows of digit keypads. Each digit is therefore represented by two frequency tones, hence the name. The local switching system must convert the tones to a digital form, and this is done with a DTMF receiver.

Here is a hypothetical example, with numbers, to help understand the compression strategy. Suppose a local switching system must support 50,000 BHCAs. To do so, the system might have 5000 DTMF receivers. To test this traffic load, somehow 50,000 call originations must be generated in 60 minutes. The whole idea of compression strategies it to reduce these numbers to more manageable sizes. If a prototype only has 50 DTMF receivers, the load testing would need to generate 500 call attempts.

This pattern of compressing some form of traffic and associated devices to handle the offered traffic occurs in many application domains, hence the general term, traffic engineering.

13.7.1.2 Replication

Some non-functional requirements may be unusually difficult to actually perform. Many times, actual performance would destroy the system being tested (destructive versus non-destructive testing.) There was a Calvin and Hobbes comic strip that succinctly explained this form of testing. In the first frame, Calvin sees a sign on a bridge: "Maximum weight 5 tons." He asks his father how this is determined. The father answers that successively heavier trucks are driven over the bridge until the bridge collapses. In the last frame, Calvin has his standard shock/horror expression. Rather than destroy a system, some form of replication can be tried. Two examples follow.

One of the non-functional requirements for an army field telephone switching center was that it had to be operational after a parachute drop. Doing this was both very expensive and logistically complex. None of us system testers knew how to replicate this, but in consultation with a former paratrooper, we learned that the impact of a parachute drop is similar to jumping off a ten-foot (three meter) wall. We put a prototype on a fork lift skid, lifted it to a height of 10 feet, and tilted it forward until it fell off the skid. After hitting the ground, the prototype was still operational, and the test passed.

One of the most dangerous incidents for aircraft is a mid-air collision with a bird. Here is an excerpt of a non-functional for the F 35 jet aircraft built by Lockheed Martin [Owens et al., 2009].

The Canopy System Must Withstand Impact of a 4 lb. Bird at 480 Knots on the Reinforced Windscreen and 350 Knots on the Canopy Crown Without:

- Breaking or Deflecting so as to Strike the Pilot When Seated in the Design Eye "High" Position,
- Damage to The Canopy That Would Cause Incapacitating Injury to the Pilot, or.
- Damage That Would Preclude Safe Operation of, or Emergency Egress from the Aircraft.

Clearly it would be impossible to arrange a mid-air bird collision, so the Lockheed Martin testers replicated the problem with an elaborate cannon that would shoot a dead chicken at the windscreen and at the canopy. The tests passed.

There is an urban legend, debunked on Snopes.com, about follow-up a British (or French, or fill-in-your-favorite-country) firm that used the same idea for canopy testing, but their tests all failed. When they asked the US testers why the failures were so consistent, they received a terse answer: "you need to thaw the chicken first." Why mention this? If non-functional testing is done with a replication strategy, it is important to replicate, as closely as possible, the actual test scenario. (But it is funny.)

13.7.2 Mathematical Approaches

In some cases, non-functional testing cannot be done either directly, indirectly, or with commercial tools. There are three forms of analysis that might help—queueing theory, reliability models, and simulation.

13.7.2.1 Queueing Theory

Queueing theory deals with servers and queues of tasks that use the service. The mathematics behind queueing theory deals with task arrival rates, and service times, as well as the number of queues and the number of servers. In everyday life, we see examples of queueing situations: checkout lines in a grocery store, lines to buy tickets at a movie theater, or lift lines at a ski area. Some settings, e.g., a local post office, uses a single queue of patrons waiting for service at one of several clerk positions. This happens to be the most efficient queueing discipline—single queue, multiple server. Service times represent some form of system capacity, and queues represent traffic (transactions) offered to the system.

13.7.2.2 Reliability Models

Reliability models are somewhat related to queueing theory. Reliability deals with failure rates of components and computes characteristics such as likelihood of system failure, mean time to failure (MTTF), mean time between failures (MTBF), and mean time to repair (MTTR). Given actual or assumed failure rates of system components, these quantities can be computed.

A telephone switching system has a reliability requirement of not more than two hours of downtime in 40 years of continuous operation. This is an availability of 0.99999429, or stated negatively, failure rate of 5.7 x 10^{-6}, (0.0000057). How can this be guaranteed? Reliability models are the first choice. They can be expressed as tree diagrams or as directed graphs, very similar to the approach used to compute an operational profile. These models are based on failure rates of individual system components that are linked together physically, and abstractly in the reliability model.

A digital end office intended for the rural U.S. market had to be certified by an agency of the U.S. government, the Rural Electric Administration (REA). That body followed a compression strategy and required an on-site test for six months. If the system functioned with less than 30 minutes of downtime, it was certified. A few months into the test interval, the system had less than two minutes of downtime. Then a tornado hit the town and destroyed the building that contained the system. The REA declared the test to be a failure. Only extreme pleading resulted in a re-test. The second time, there was less than 30 seconds of downtime in the six-month interval.

Reliability models have a solid history of applicability to physical systems, but can they be applied to software? Physical components can age and therefore deteriorate. This is usually shown in the Weibull distribution, in which failures drop to nearly zero rapidly. Some forms show an increase after an interval that represents the useful life of a component. The problem is that software, once well tested, does not deteriorate. The main difference between reliability models applied to software versus to hardware comes down to the arrival rate of failures. Testing based on operational profiles, and the extension to risk-based testing is a good start, but no amount of testing can guarantee the absence of software faults.

13.7.2.3 Monte Carlo Testing

Monte Carlo testing might be considered a last resort in the system tester's arsenal. The basic idea of Monte Carlo testing is to randomly generate a large number of threads (transactions) and then see if anything unexpected happens. The Monte Carlo part comes from the use of pseudo-random numbers, not from the fact that the whole approach is a gamble. Monte Carlo testing has been successful in applications where computation involving physical (as opposed to logical, see Chapter 6) variables are used. The major drawback to Monte Carlo testing is that the large number of random transactions requires a similarly large number of expected outputs in order to determine whether a random test case passes or fails.

Exercises

1. One of the problems of system testing, particularly with interactive systems, is to anticipate all the strange things the user might do. What happens in the Foodie Wish List system if a customer enters three digits of a PIN and then leaves?
2. To remain "in control" of abnormal user behavior (the behavior is abnormal, not the user), the Foodie Wish List system might introduce a timer with a 30-second

time-out. When no port input event occurs for 30 seconds, the Foodie Wish List system could ask if the user needs more time. The user can answer yes or no. Devise a new screen and identify port events that would implement such a time-out event.

3. Suppose you add the time-out feature described in exercise 2 to the Foodie Wish List system. What regression testing would you perform?

4. Make an additional refinement to the PIN Try finite state machine (Figure 13.6) to implement your time-out mechanism from exercise 2, then revise the thread test case in Table 13.3.

5. Complete the Extended ATE test case begun in Section 13.4.4..

6. Does it make sense to use test coverage metrics in conjunction with operational profiles? Same question for risk-based testing. Discuss this.

7. Fill in the input and output events for the last four ASFs in Table 13.16.

References

Binder, Robert V., "Don't Play Developer Testing Roulette: How to Use Test Coverage", *Software Engineering Institute Blog*, https://insights.sei.cmu.edu/sei_blog/2019/10, Oct. 14, 2019.

Jorgensen, Paul C., System testing with pseudo-structures, *Amer. Programmer*, Vol. 7, No. 4, pp. 29–34, April 1994.

Jorgensen, Paul C. *Modeling Software Behavior: A Craftsman's Approach*, CRC Press, New York, 2009.

Larman, C., *Applying UML and Patterns: An Introduction to Object-Oriented Analysis and Design* (2nd Edition), Prentice-Hall, Upper Saddle River, NJ, 2001.

Schaefer, Hans, Software Test Consulting, "*Risk Based Testing, Strategies for Prioritizing Tests against Deadlines*", http://home.c2i.net/schaefer/testing.html, 2005.

Owens, Steve D., Caldwell, Eric O., and Woodward, Mike R., "*Birdstrike Certification Tests of F-35 Canopy and Airframe Structure*" *2009 Aircraft Structural Integrity Program (ASIP) Conference*, December 1–3, 2009, Jacksonville, FL. Also can be found at Trimble, Stephen, July 28, 2010 4:58 PM. [http://www.flightglobal.com/blogs/the-dewline/2010/07/video-f-35-birdstrike-test-via.html] and.[http://www.flightglobal.com/blogs/the-dewline/Birdstrike%20Impact%20Studies.pdf.

Chapter 14

Model-Based Testing

"By my faith! For more than forty years I have been speaking prose without knowing anything about it...."

Monsieur Jourdain in *Le Bourgeois Gentilhomme*

We share the sentiment of Moliere's Monsieur Jourdain; since the first edition, this book has advocated what we now call Model-Based Testing (MBT). In this chapter, we describe the basic mechanism, discuss how to choose appropriate models, consider the pros and cons of MBT, and provide a short discussion of available tools. Actual examples of MBT are (and have been in the earlier editions) scattered throughout this book. The material in Section 14.3 is taken, almost directly, from The Craft of Model-Based Testing (Jorgensen 2017).

There are two important views of a model—as a compromise with reality and as a caricature of reality. Both are important for Model-Based Testing. When we understand a model as a compromise with reality, we accept that the model is essentially incomplete. Taken as a caricature of reality, it is important for the modeler to capture the important aspects of the reality being modeled, much like caricatures of political figures are easily recognized. Further, it is a mistake to force a model to reflect ALL of reality; similarly, it is a mistake to omit important aspects of reality. Modeling, then, is something of an art—it involves talent, understanding, and judgment.

14.1 Testing Based on Models

The main advantage of modeling system behavior is that the process of creating a model usually results in deeper insights and understanding of the system being modeled/tested. This is particularly true of executable models such as finite state machines, Petri Nets, and Statecharts. In Chapter 13, we saw that threads of system behavior, which are easily transformed into system level test cases, are readily derived from many behavioral models. Given this, the adequacy of model-based testing will always depend on the accuracy of the model. The essence of model-based testing is this sequence of steps:

1. Model the system.
2. Identify threads of system behavior in the model.
3. Transform these threads into test cases.
4. Execute the test cases (on the actual system) and record the results.
5. Revise the model(s) as needed and repeat the process.

14.2 Appropriate Models

Avvinare is an interesting Italian word. It refers to a process that many Italian families perform in autumn when they bottle wine. After buying a demijohn of bulk wine, they rinse out the empty bottles that they have saved during the year. There are always small droplets of water clinging to the sides of a bottle, but it is difficult to remove them. Instead, they fill a bottle about half full of the wine to be bottled and shake it up to dissolve the water into the wine. Next, the wine is funneled into the next bottle, shaken, and poured into another bottle. This continues until all the bottles have been rinsed with wine, and they are ready for bottling. Question: would it be the job of a tester to drink the watered-down wine? *Avvinare* is the verb that refers to this entire process. How would you translate this word into English? This activity isn't very common in the English-speaking world. I really don't know, but it won't be easy. Languages evolve to meet the expressive needs of their speakers, and models have evolved to meet the complexity of the systems they describe. This is where Software Engineering meets Epistemology. Since model-based testing begins with modeling, choice of an appropriate model determines the ultimate success of the associated testing. Making an appropriate choice depends on several things: the expressive power of various models, the essential nature of the system being modeled, and the analyst's ability to use various models. We consider the first two of these next.

14.2.1 Peterson's Lattice

James Peterson developed an elegant lattice of models of computation [Peterson 1981] which is summarized in Figure 14.1. The arrows in the lattice signify a "more expressive than" relationship in which the model at the origin of an arrow is more expressive than that at the end of an arrow. In his text, Peterson carefully develops examples for each edge in the lattice. For example, he shows a semaphore system that cannot be expressed as a finite state machine. Four models in his lattice obscure: vector replacement systems, vector addition systems, UCLA graphs, and message systems. There are scores of extensions to Petri Nets; Peterson grouped these together for simplicity. Marked graphs are a formalization of dataflow diagrams, and Peterson shows them to be formal duals of finite state machines.

Peterson's lattice is a good starting point for model-based testing. Given an application, good practice dictates choosing a model that is both necessary and sufficient—neither too weak nor too strong. If a model is too weak, important aspects of the application will not be modeled, and hence not tested. If a model is too strong, the extra effort to develop the model may be unnecessary.

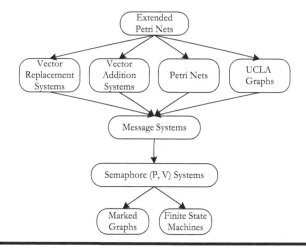

Figure 14.1   Peterson's lattice.

Peterson's lattice predates the invention of Statecharts by David Harel, which raises the question of where they fit in Peterson's lattice. They are at least equivalent, and probably more expressive than most extensions of Petri Nets. Several graduate students at Grand Valley State University have explored this question, with a variety of approaches. Their work is persuasive, but for a long time, I had no formal proof of this potential equivalence. However, given a relatively complex Statechart, it can always be expressed as an Event-Driven Petri Net (as defined in Chapter 4). The rich language associated with Statecharts transitions will probably be difficult to express in most Petri Net extensions. One promising approach offered by DeVries (co-author of this book) [DeVries 2013] is that of "Swim Lane Petri Nets."

Figure 14.2 shows the anticipated placement of Statecharts in Peterson's Lattice. The one-way arrow reflects the fact that a given Statechart can express concurrency (by the concurrent regions), and true concurrency cannot be expressed in a Petri Net, nor in most extensions. Part of the work by DeVries describes "Swim Lane Petri

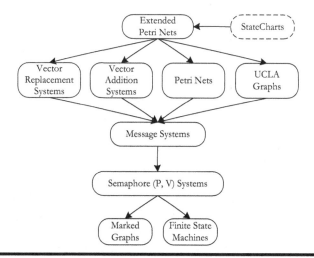

Figure 14.2   Placement of Statecharts in Peterson's lattice.

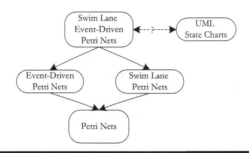

Figure 14.3   Addition to Peterson's Lattice with Swim Lane Models.

Nets." These use the UML notion of "swim lanes" to express parallel activities. We will revisit this concept in Chapter 15 when we use it to describe interactions among constituent systems in systems of systems. There we will use some of the prompts of the Extended Systems Modeling Language to show cross-swim lane communication of Event-Driven Petri Nets. Figure 14.3 shows the anticipated lattice among Event-Driven Petri Nets, Swim Lane Event-Driven Petri Nets, and a sub-class of Statecharts.

14.2.2 Expressive Capabilities of Mainline Models

Peterson looked at four mainline models in terms of the kinds of behavioral issues that they can represent. The Venn diagram in Figure 14.4 shows his summary.

14.2.3 Modeling Issues

Much of the information in this subsection is taken from [Jorgensen 2009]. There are two fundamental types of requirements specification models: those that describe structure, and those that describe behavior. These correspond to two fundamental views of a system: what a system *is*, and what a system *does*. Dataflow diagrams, Entity/Relation models, hierarchy charts, class diagrams, and object diagrams all focus on what a system is—the components, their functionality, and interfaces among them. They emphasize structure. The second type, including decision tables, finite

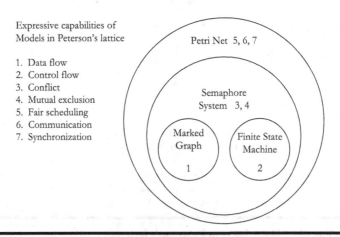

Figure 14.4   Expressive capabilities in Peterson's Lattice.

state machines, Statecharts, and Petri Nets, describes system behavior—what a system does. Models of system behavior have varying degrees of expressive capability, the technical equivalent of being able to express *avvinare* in another language.

The [Jorgensen 2009] reference identifies 19 behavioral modeling issues, subdivided into four groups: the first group contains the code structuring precepts of Structured Programming: sequence, selection, and repetition. The next group is from the Extended Systems Modeling Language group [Bruyn et al., 1988]: enable, disable, trigger, activate, suspend, resume, and pause. These prompts will be used in our modeling of systems of systems using Swim Lane Event Driven Petri Nets in Chapter 17. The task management category consists of the basic Petri Net mechanisms: conflict, priority, mutual exclusion, concurrent execution, and deadlock. The last group deals with issues in event-driven systems: context sensitive input events, Multiple context output events, asynchronous events, and event quiescence.

Table 14.1 maps the 19 behavioral issues to five executable models, each of which is a candidate for model-based testing.

Table 14.1 Expressive Capability of Five Executable Models

Behavioral Issue	Decision Tables	FSMs	Petri Nets	EDPNs	Statecharts
Sequence	No	Yes	Yes	Yes	Yes
Selection	Yes	Yes	Yes	Yes	Yes
Repetition	Yes	Yes	Yes	Yes	Yes
Enable	No	No	Yes	Yes	Yes
Disable	No	No	Yes	Yes	Yes
Trigger	No	No	Yes	Yes	Yes
Activate	No	No	Yes	Yes	Yes
Suspend	No	No	Yes	Yes	Yes
Resume	No	No	Yes	Yes	Yes
Pause	No	No	Yes	Yes	Yes
Conflict	No	No	Yes	Yes	Yes
Priority	No	No	Yes	Yes	Yes
Mutual exclusion	Yes	No	Yes	Yes	Yes
Concurrent execution	No	No	Yes	Yes	Yes
Deadlock	No	No	Yes	Yes	Yes
Context sensitive input events	Yes	Yes	Indirectly	Yes	Yes
Multiple context output events	Yes	Yes	Indirectly	Yes	Yes
Asynchronous events	No	No	Indirectly	Yes	Yes
Event quiescence	No	No	Indirectly	Yes	Yes

14.2.4 Making Appropriate Choices

Choosing an appropriate model begins with understanding the essential nature of the system to be modeled (and tested). Once these aspects are understood, they must be related to the various capabilities just discussed, and then the appropriate choice is simplified. The ultimate choice will always depend on other realities, such as company policy, relevant standards, analyst capability, and available tools. Always choosing the most powerful model is a simple-minded choice; a better choice might be to choose the simplest model that can express all the important aspects of the system being modeled.

14.3 Commercial Tool Support for Model-Based Testing

There are several open source and commercial Model-Based Testing products available. Five open source MBT tools are briefly profiled in (Jorgensen 2017). More importantly, six commercial MBT tool vendors cooperated in providing the results of their products on two specific examples, a variation of the Insurance Premium problem, and a slight simplification of the Garage Door Controller. David Harel identifies two fundamental types of applications—transformational and reactive (Harel 1988). The Insurance Premium problem is an example of a transformational program; it transforms data inputs into computed outputs. The Garage Door Controller is a reactive system, in the sense that it reacts to input events as they occur. Generally speaking, transformational applications are "one shot" programs that execute and finish. Reactive programs may be long running; they maintain a relationship with the environment in which they occur.

Selected portions of the responses from three of the commercial tools are given here. The commercial tools use a variety of models for transformational applications. UML Activity Diagrams, Business Processing Models, Rule-Based (*i.e.,* decision tables) and flowcharts are the most common choices. The consensus among both open-sourced and commercial MBT tools for reactive systems is some form of finite state machines.

Most, if not all, commercial MBT systems are based on finite state machine models of the system being tested. In an ideal MBT world, some graphical form on the system finite state machine would serve as input to the system. The reality is that some form of textual definition is required—usually as code in an object-oriented programming language.

14.3.1 TestOptimal

TestOptimal LLC is located near Rochester, Minnesota, USA. Their product line is extensive and comprehensive, including a very sophisticated set of tools. The company website is [http://testoptimal.com/].

Their solution to the Insurance Premium Problem used the concept of orthogonal arrays to generate a set of nine test cases (Table 14.2) which, taken together, exercise every pair of input parameter values. The tool generates more test cases if three-wise or four-wise orthogonal arrays are used.

The TestOptimal solution to the Garage Door Controller is based on a finite state machine having the input events, input events, and states in Table 14.3. The state diagram is in Figure 14.5.

Table 14.2   Pairwise Abstract Test Cases (Full Set)

Test Case	Age	Claims	Good Student	Non-drinker	Expected Premium
1	16 - 24	0	false	false	$775
2	16 - 24	1 - 3	true	false	$1000
3	16 - 24	4 - 10	false	true	$1150
4	25 - 64	0	true	false	$525
5	25 - 64	1 - 3	false	true	$575
6	25 - 64	4 - 10	true	false	$900
7	65 - 89	0	false	true	$770
8	65 - 89	1 - 3	true	false	$1125
9	65 - 89	4 - 10	false	false	$970

Table 14.3   Garage Door Controller Events and States

Input events	Output events (actions)	States
e1: control signal	a1: start drive motor down	s1: Door Up
e2: end of down track hit	a2: start drive motor up	s2: Door Down
e3: end of up track hit	a3: stop drive motor	s3: Door stopped going down
e4: laser beam crossed	a4: reverse motor down to up	s4: Door stopped going up
		s5: Door closing
		s6: Door opening

The tool generates 13 test cases, once again using the orthogonal array technique. They are shown in Figure 14.5, where they are related to transitions in the finite state machine.

14.3.2 Conformiq

Conformiq Software Oy is located in Espoo, FINLAND. Their product line, Conformiq 360° Test Automation, is very comprehensive and goes far beyond test generation, by integrating with existing software development lifecycle tools in the testing process starting from requirements management and Application Lifecycle Management (ALM) through test management and documentation, and automatic test execution tools. The company website is [https://www.conformiq.com/].

The Conformiq solution to the Insurance Premium Problem begins with a UML Activity Diagram (Figure 14.6).

Based on the Activity Diagram, the Conformiq tool generates 64 test cases that cover all control flows, activity chart nodes, and decisions. Taken together, they constitute Worst Case Normal Equivalence Class testing. Table 14.4 shows the first 16 of the generated test cases.

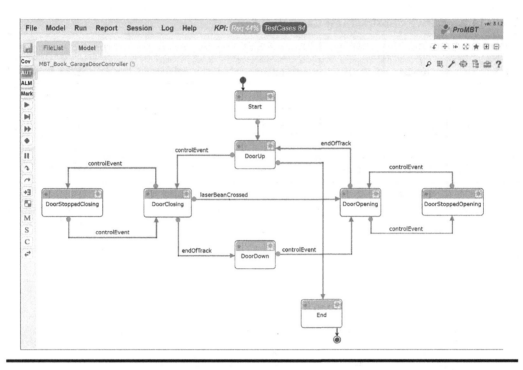

Figure 14.5   TestOptimal FSM Related to Test Cases.

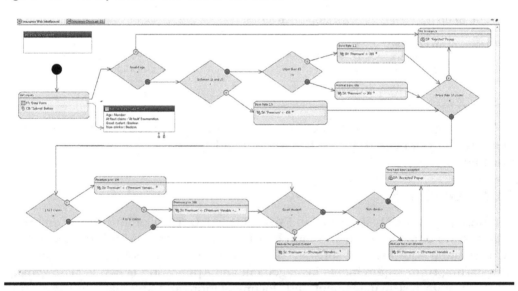

Figure 14.6   Conformiq UML Activity Diagram for the Insurance Premium Problem.

The Conformiq solution to the Garage Door Controller begins with the UML Finite State Machine shown in Figure 14.7.

The 17 test cases in Table 14.5 are derived from the finite state machine in Figure 14.7.

The individual test cases are on state transition sequences. Table 14.6 shows the generated test case 16.

Table 14.4 First 16 of 64 Generated Insurance Problem Test Cases

Test Case	Age	Claims	Good Student	Non-Drinker	Approved?	Premium
1	77	1 to 3	F	T	Yes	$385
2	77	1 to 3	T	F	Yes	$410
3	77	0	T	T	Yes	$235
4	77	4 to 10	T	T	Yes	$535
5	0	0	F	F	No	
6	0	1 to 3	F	F	No	
7	0	4 to 10	F	F	No	
8	0	4 to 10	F	T	No	
9	0	4 to 10	T	F	No	
10	0	> 10	F	F	No	
11	0	> 10	F	T	No	
12	0	> 10	T	F	No	
13	77	> 10	T	T	No	
14	20	0	T	T	Yes	$325
15	77	0	F	T	Yes	$285
16	77	0	T	F	Yes	$310

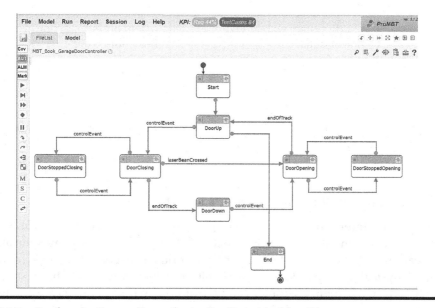

Figure 14.7 Conformiq Garage Door Controller State Machine Diagram.

Table 14.5   Conformiq Test Case Numbers

Test Case	State Sequence	Test Case	State Sequence
1	s1, s5	10	s1, s5, s3, s5, s6
2	s1, s5, s3	11	s1, s5, s2, s6, s1
3	s1, s5, s2	12	s1, s5, s6, s1, s5
4	s1, s5, s3, s5	13	s1, s5, s6, s4
5	s1, s5, s6	14	s1, s5, s2, s6, s4
6	s1, s5, s2, s6	15	s1, s5, s6, s4, s6
7	s1, s5, s6, s1	16	s1, s5, s6, s4, s6, s4
8	s1, s5, s3, s5, s3	17	s1, s5, s6, s4, s6, s1
9	s1, s5, s3, s5, s2		

Table 14.6   Sample Conformiq Generated Test Case

Test case 16:	s1, s5, s6, s4, s6, s4	
Step	Action(s)	Verification Point(s)
1	Provide system with input e1: control signal	System performs action a1: start drive motor "down".
2	Provide system with input e4: laser beam crossed.	System performs action a4: reverse motor down to up.
3	Provide system with input e1: control signal	System performs action a3: stop drive motor.
4	Provide system with input e1: control signal	System performs action a2: start drive motor "up."
5	Provide system with input e1: control signal	

As with the Insurance Premium Problem, the Conformiq tool provides extensive tracking information.

14.3.3 *Verified Systems International GmbH*

Verified Systems International GmbH (https://www.verified.de) was established in 1998 as a spinoff company of the University of Bremen. The company specializes in the verification and validation of safety-critical or business-critical embedded systems and cyber-physical systems. Being a university product, it features the best technology. Verified Systems' main customers come from the avionics, railways, and automotive domains.

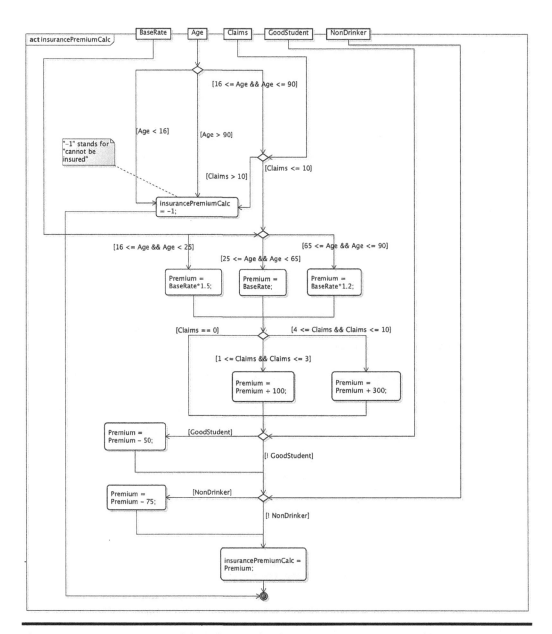

Figure 14.8   UML/SysML Activity Diagram for the Insurance Premium Problem.

Their solution to the Insurance Premium Problem begins with a UML/SysML Activity Diagram (Figure 14.8). The product derives 37 equivalence classes from the inputs. Here are a few sample classes:

(Age == 24) && (1 == Claims) &&!GoodStudent && NonDrinker.
(Age == 16) && (1 == Claims) &&!GoodStudent && NonDrinker.
(Age == 24) && (3 == Claims) &&!GoodStudent && NonDrinker.
(Age == 16) && (1 == Claims) &&!GoodStudent && NonDrinker.

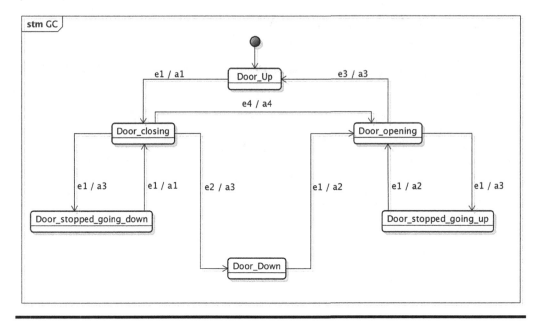

Figure 14.9   Garage Door Controller FSM.

The RT-Tester solution to the Garage Door Controller begins with a UML/SysML finite state machine diagram (Figure 14.9).

The tool derived 252 test cases from the finite state machine diagram. Some of these are listed in Table 14.7. This large number of test cases checks both expected and unexpected sequences of input events.

Table 14.7   Selected Test Case Sequences for the Garage Door Controller

Test Case	Transition Named by Input/Output Event
1	1. (e1/a1).(e2/a3).(e1/a2).(e1/a3).(e1/a2).(e1/a3)
2	2. (e1/a1).(e2/a3).(e1/a2).(e1/a3).(e1/a2).(e2/–)
3	3. (e1/a1).(e2/a3).(e1/a2).(e1/a3).(e2/–).(e1/a2)
4	4. (e1/a1).(e2/a3).(e1/a2).(e1/a3).(e3/–).(e1/a2)
155	155. (e1/a1).(e4/a4).(e4/–).(e3/a3).(e1/a1).(e2/a3)
156	156. (e1/a1).(e4/a4).(e4/–).(e3/a3).(e2/–).(e1/a1)
157	157. (e1/a1).(e4/a4).(e4/–).(e3/a3).(e3/–).(e1/a1)
158	158. (e1/a1).(e4/a4).(e4/–).(e3/a3).(e4/–).(e1/a1)
159	159. (e1/a1).(e4/a4).(e4/–).(e4/–).(e1/a3).(e1/a2)
160	160. (e1/a1).(e4/a4).(e4/–).(e4/–).(e2/–).(e1/a3)
251	251. (e4/–).(e4/–).(e3/–).(e1/a1)
252	252. (e4/–).(e4/–).(e4/–).(e1/a1)

Exercises

An automobile windshield wiper is controlled by a lever with a dial. The lever has four positions: OFF, INT (for intermittent), LOW, and HIGH; and the dial has three positions, numbered simply 1, 2, and 3. The dial positions indicate three intermittent speeds, and the dial position is relevant only when the lever is at the INT position. The decision table below shows the windshield wiper speeds (in wipes per minute) for the lever and dial positions.

c1. Lever	OFF	INT	INT	INT	LOW	HIGH
c2. Dial	n/a	1	2	3	n/a	n/a
a1. Wiper	0	4	6	12	30	60

This may be the most important set of exercises in the 5th edition. Assume you have a test bench for the Windshield Wiper Controller. It includes the following:

- an actual lever, dial and wiper motor (the wiper blades would be too cumbersome)
- the Windshield Wiper Controller
- a 12-V battery connected to the Windshield Wiper Controller with an On/Off switch (replicates the ignition switch)
- a display device showing the number of wiper strokes per minute

In each of the following exercises, use the designated model to describe the system. Use your model to develop test cases of the form:
Test Case ID, Test Case Description (including the underlying model)
Pre-condition(s)

Event Sequence	
Input Event(s)	Output Event(s)

Post-condition(s)
Here is one example:
DT-1 Decision Table Lever moves from INT to OFF
Pre-conditions
    1. Lever at INT
    2. Dial at 1
    3. Wiper motor display shows 6

Event Sequence	
Input Event(s)	Output Event(s)
1. Move lever to OFF position	2. Wiper display shows 0

Post-conditions

1. Lever at OFF
2. Dial at 1
3. Wiper motor display shows 0

Questions to be answered for each model in exercises 1 to 5.

1. How many test cases do you have?
2. Could you derive the event sequence from the model?
3. Did your model contain the basis for identifying pre-conditions? If yes, describe how.
4. Did your model contain the basis for identifying post-conditions? If yes, describe how.
5. Did your model contain the basis for creating the test case description?

1. Describe the Windshield Wiper Controller system with BDD scenarios, then answer the following questions:
   1. How many test cases do you have?
   2. Could you derive the event sequence from the model?
   3. Did your model contain the basis for identifying pre-conditions? If yes, describe how.
   4. Did your model contain the basis for identifying post-conditions? If yes, describe how.
   5. Did your model contain the basis for creating the test case description?
2. Describe the Windshield Wiper Controller system with an extended entry decision table, then answer the following questions:
   1. How many test cases do you have?
   2. Could you derive the event sequence from the model?
   3. Did your model contain the basis for identifying pre-conditions? If yes, describe how.
   4. Did your model contain the basis for identifying post-conditions? If yes, describe how.
   5. Did your model contain the basis for creating the test case description?
3. Describe the Windshield Wiper Controller system as a finite state machine in which states are of the form <lever position, dial position> and transitions are caused either by a single lever event or a single dial event. Answer the following questions:
   1. How many test cases do you have?
   2. Could you derive the event sequence from the model?
   3. Did your model contain the basis for identifying pre-conditions? If yes, describe how.
   4. Did your model contain the basis for identifying post-conditions? If yes, describe how.
   5. Did your model contain the basis for creating the test case description?

4. Describe the Windshield Wiper Controller system as a finite state machine in which states show the wiper speed (0, 6, 12, 20, 30, 60) and transitions are caused either by a single lever event or a single dial event. Answer the following questions:
   1. How many test cases do you have?
   2. Could you derive the event sequence from the model?
   3. Did your model contain the basis for identifying pre-conditions? If yes, describe how.
   4. Did your model contain the basis for identifying post-conditions? If yes, describe how.
   5. Did your model contain the basis for creating the test case description?
5. Describe the Windshield Wiper Controller system as an Event-Driven Petri Net. Use your wiper speed states as places, lever and dial events as port input events, and wiper motor speeds as output events. There is no compelling reason to give names to your transitions, but you may. Answer the following questions:
   1. How many test cases do you have?
   2. Could you derive the event sequence from the model?
   3. Did your model contain the basis for identifying pre-conditions? If yes, describe how.
   4. Did your model contain the basis for identifying post-conditions? If yes, describe how.
   5. Did your model contain the basis for creating the test case description?
6. Write a Retrospective of your answers to questions 1 through 5. Include your conclusions on questions such as the following:
   1. Which models made test case development easy?
   2. Conversely, in which models was test case development awkward or difficult?
   3. There are subtle issues in the Windshield Wiper Controller problem—moving the Lever to the INT position enables the Dial, and conversely, moving the Lever from the INT position disables the Dial. Are these issues "visible" in any of your models? Could your models be extended so they are?
   4. You could extend your finite state machine from question 3 so that each state describes the enabled/disabled status of the Dial. This will double the size of your finite state machine. Would this be helpful?
   5. If you added a condition to your extended entry decision table (question 2) that refers to the enabled/disabled dichotomy, would this be helpful? This change would also double the size of your model.

References

William Bruyn, Randall Jensen, Dinesh Keskar, Paul Ward. "An extended systems modeling language (ESML)", *Association for Computing Machinery, ACM SIGSOFT Software Engineering Notes*, Vol 13 No. 1, Jan. 1988, pp. 58–67.

Byron DeVries, "Mapping of UML Diagrams to Extended Petri Nets for Formal Verification", Master's Thesis, Grand Valley State University, Allendale, Michigan, April, 2013.

D. Harel, "On Visual Formalisms", *Communications of the ACM*, Vol.31, No. 5, May 1988, pp. 514–530.

Paul C. Jorgensen, *Modeling Software Behavior: A Craftsman's Approach*, CRC Press, New York, 2009.

Paul C. Jorgensen, *The Craft of Model-Based Testing*, CRC Press, New York, 2017.

James L. Peterson, *Petri Net Theory and the Modeling of Systems*, Prentice Hall, Englewood Cliffs, NJ, 1981.

Chapter 15

Software Complexity

Most discussions of software complexity focus on two main models—cyclomatic (or decisional) complexity, and textual complexity as measured by the Halstead metrics. Both approaches are commonly used at the unit level—we will use cyclomatic complexity also at the integration and system levels. Although not usually mentioned, program size is another contributor to software complexity. This is most often seen in discussions of program comprehension—sheer size impedes program comprehension.

We take a closer look at software complexity at all three levels—unit, integration, and system. At the unit level, the basic cyclomatic complexity model (also known as McCabe complexity) is extended in two ways. Integration level complexity applies cyclomatic complexity to a Call Graph (a directed graph in which units are nodes and edges represent either object-oriented messages or procedural calls). After discussing the complexities due to object-oriented practice, system level complexity for single-processor applications is expressed in terms of an incidence matrix that relates the *is* and *does* views of a software system. Systems of Systems (SoS) introduce a whole new level of complexity, as we saw in Foodie Wish List examples in Chapters 12 and 13.

Software complexity is usually analyzed as a static (*i.e.*, compile-time) property of source code, not an execution-time property. The approaches discussed here are derived either directly from source code, or in the case of integration and system complexity, from design- and specification-level models. Why worry about software complexity? It has the most direct bearing on the extent of required software testing, but also, it is an indicator of difficulty in software maintenance, particularly program comprehension. As software complexity increases, development effort also increases, although this is a little circular since much of the analysis is based on the development of existing code (too late!). Finally, an awareness of software complexity may lead to improved programming practices, and even better design techniques.

15.1 Unit Level Complexity

We begin our description of unit level complexity with the notion of a program graph from Chapter 8 (Code-Based Testing.) Recall that for a program written in an imperative programming language, its program graph is a directed graph in which nodes are either entire statements or statement fragments, and edges represent flow of control. There is an edge from node i to node j if and only if the statement (fragment) corresponding to node j can be executed immediately after the statement or statement fragment corresponding to node i. Program graphs represent the control flow structure of the source code, and this leads to the usual definition of cyclomatic complexity.

15.1.1 Cyclomatic Complexity

Definition: In a strongly connected directed graph G, its *cyclomatic complexity*, denoted by $V(G)$, is given by V(G) = e − n + p, where

- e is the number of edges in G
- n is the number of nodes in G
- p is the number of connected regions in G

In code that conforms to structured programming (single entry, single exit), we always have p = 1. There is some confusion in the literature about the formula for V(G). There are two formulas commonly seen:

$$V(G) = e - n + p \tag{15.1}$$

and

$$V(G) = e - n + 2p \tag{15.2}$$

Equation (15.1) refers to a directed graph G that is strongly connected, *i.e.*, for any two nodes n_j and n_k of G, there is a path from n_j to n_k, and a path from n_k to n_j. Since the program graph of a structured program has a single entry node and a single exit node, the graph is not quite strongly connected. (There is no path from the sink node to the source node.) The usual way to apply the formula is to add an edge from the sink node to the source node. If an edge is added, Equation (15.1) applies, otherwise Equation (15.2) applies. With this definition, and given a program graph, the cyclomatic complexity is determined by counting the nodes and edges, and then applying Equation (15.2). This is fine for small programs, but what about a program graph such as the one in Figure 15.1? Even for program graphs of this size, counting nodes and edges is tedious. For that matter, drawing the program graph is also tedious. Fortunately, there are more elegant ways, based on an insight from directed graph theory. We next develop two shortcuts.

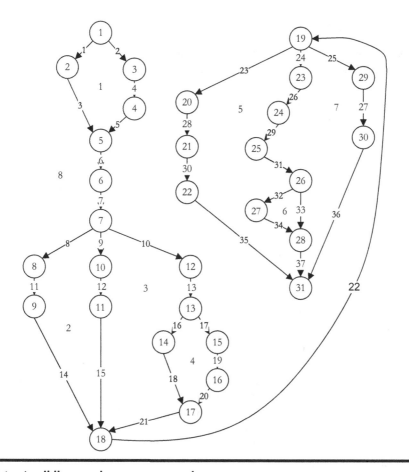

Figure 15.1   A mildly complex program graph.

15.1.1.1 "Cattle Pens" and Cyclomatic Complexity

Cyclomatic complexity refers to the number of independent cycles in a strongly connected directed graph. When drawn in the usual way (as in Figure 15.1), these cycles are easily identified visually, and this can be done for simple programs. Rather than count all the nodes and edges in a larger graph, we can imagine nodes to be fence posts, and edges to be fencing used in a cattle pen. Then the number of "cattle pens" can be counted visually. (The more esoteric term is "enclosed regions," which the topologists prefer.) In the program graph in Figure 15.1, there are 37 edges and 31 nodes. Since the graph is not strongly connected, Equation (15.2) applies, and V(G) = 37−31 + 2 = 8. The eight "cattle pens" are also numbered (notice that one pen is "outside" all the others). Drawing the directed graph to identify cattle pens is still tedious. Again, there is a more elegant way, based on more definitions from graph theory.

15.1.1.2 Node Outdegrees and Cyclomatic Complexity

As we saw in Chapter 4, the indegree of a node in a directed graph is the number of edges that terminate on the node. Similarly, the outdegree of a node in a directed graph is the number of edges that originate at the node. These are commonly denoted for node n as inDeg(n) and outDeg(n). We need another definition to replace the thinking that went into the cattle pen approach:

Definition

The *reduced outdegree of node n in a directed graph* is one less than the outdegree of n.

Denote the reduced outdegree of node n as reducedOut(n); then we can write

$$reducedOut(n) = outDeg(n) - 1.$$

We use the reduced outdegree of nodes in a program graph to compute its cyclomatic complexity. Notice that a cattle pen "begins" with a node with outDeg > = 2. Table 15.1 shows the nodes in Figure 15.1 that satisfy this observation:

The sum of the reduced outdegrees is the number of cattle pens, but this doesn't count the "outside" cattle pen, which makes 8—the cyclomatic complexity of the directed graph. The outdegrees can be determined from the source code, eliminating the need to draw the directed graph, and perform the other tedious steps. As a guideline, a simple loop determines a cattle pen, as do the If, Then and If, Then, Else statements. Switch (Case) statements with k alternatives determine k – 1 cattle pens. So now, finding cyclomatic complexity is reduced to determining the reduced outdegrees of all decision-making statements in the source code. We can state this as a formal theorem (without proof).

Theorem: Given a directed graph G of n nodes, the cyclomatic complexity V(G) of G is given by the sum of the reduced outdegrees of the nodes of G plus 1, *i.e.*

$$V(G) = 1 + \left(\sum i = 1..n \, reducedOut(i) \right)$$

Table 15.1 Reduced Outdegrees in Figure 15.1

Node	outDeg	reducedOut
1	2	1
7	3	2
13	2	1
19	3	2
26	2	1
	Total =	7

15.1.1.3 Decisional Complexity

Cyclomatic complexity is a start, but it is an oversimplification. Why? Because all decision-making statements are not equal—compound conditions add complexity. Consider the following code fragment from the discussion in Chapter 8 Section 8.3.4.3. (Figure 8.9 is repeated here as Figure 15.2.)

The program graph of this fragment is very simple—it has a cyclomatic complexity of 2. From a software testing standpoint, we would apply multiple condition testing, or we could rewrite the fragment as follows (see Figure 15.3), with the resulting cyclomatic complexity of 4:

Notice that the compound condition in Figure 15.2 conceals the decisional complexity that is shown in Figure 15.3. The added complexity of compound conditions cannot be determined from a program graph—it must be derived from the source code.

Doing a full multiple conditional testing analysis for a compound condition entails making a truth table in which the simple conditions are considered as individual propositions, and then finding the truth table of the compound expression. For now,

```
9.    if ((a < b + c) && (b < a + c) && (c < a + b)) {
10.       IsATriangle = true;
11.    } else {
12.       IsATriangle = false;
13.    }
```

Figure 15.2   Fragment of the Triangle Program.

```
1.    if (a < b + c) {
2.        if (b < a + c) {
3.            if (c < a + b) {
4.                IsATriangle = true;
5.            } else {
6.                IsATriangle = false;
7.            }
8.        } else {
9.            IsATriangle =false;
10.       }
11.   } else {
12.       IsATriangle =false;
13.   }
```

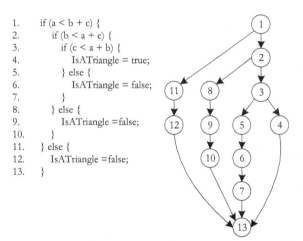

Figure 15.3   Triangle Program Fragment Rewritten with Nested If-Else Statements.

we choose to simplify this and just define the added complexity of compound conditions to be one less than the number of simple conditions in the expression. Why one less? The compound condition creates a unit of cyclomatic complexity, so this avoids "double counting."

15.1.2 Computational Complexity

Thus far, we have focused on what might be called control complexity, or maybe decisional complexity—basically looking at the edges leaving nodes in a program graph. But what about the nodes themselves? Just as with decisions, all nodes are not "created equal." We use the definitions of DD-Path and DD-Path Graph made in Chapter 8.

Recall that DD-Path execution is like a sequence of dominoes, once the first statement executes, every statement in the DD-Path executes, until the next decision point is reached. At this point, we can begin to think about the length of a DD-Path. Since a DD-Path contains no internal decision-making statements for any program P, the cyclomatic complexity of P equals the cyclomatic complexity of the DD-Path graph of P. Our problem is now reduced to considering the computational complexity of a DD-Path, and this is where the Halstead Metrics are useful.

15.1.2.1 Halstead's Metrics

For a given program (DD-Path), consider the operators and operands in the program code. Operators include the usual arithmetic and logical operators, as well as built-in functions such as Square Root. Operands are identifiers. The Halstead metrics [Halstead 1977] are based on the following quantities, derived from the source code of the program (DD-Path):

■ the number of distinct operators, n_1,
■ the number of distinct operands, n_2,
■ the total number of operators, N_1, and
■ the total number of operands, N_2.

Based on these, Halstead defines

■ program length as $N = N_1 + N_2$
■ program vocabulary as $n = n_1 + n_2$
■ program volume as $V = N\log_2(n)$
■ program difficulty as $D = (n_1 N_2)/2n_2$

Of these, the formula for program volume seems to make the most sense, but we could choose to use program difficulty, as this seems to be linguistically related to our goal of describing software complexity.

15.1.2.2 Example: Day of Week with Zeller's Congruence

Here we compare two slightly different implementations of Zeller's Congruence, which determines the day of the week of a given date. The inputs d, m, y respectively are day, month, and year. Tables 15.2 and 15.3 show the values of the inputs to Halstead's metrics.

First implementation

```
if (m < 3) {
    m += 12;
        y -= 1;
}
int k = y % 100;
int j = y / 100;
int dayOfWeek = ((d+(((m+1)*26)/10)+k+(k/4)+(j/4))+(5*j))%7;
```

Second implementation

```
if (month < 3){
    month += 12;
    --year;
}
return dayray[(int)(day + (month + 1) * 26 / 10 + year +
        year / 4 + 6 * (year / 100) + year / 400) % 7];
```

Table 15.2   Halstead's Metrics for the First Implementation

Operator	Number of occurrences	Operand	Number of occurrences
If	1	m	3
<	1	y	3
+=	1	k	3
-=	1	j	3
=	3	dayOfWeek	1
%	2	d	1
/	4	3	1
+	6	12	1
*	2	1	1
n1 = 9	N1 = 21	100	2
		26	1
		10	1
		4	2
		5	1
		7	1
		n2 = 15	N2 = 25

Table 15.3   Halstead's Metrics for the Second Implementation

Operator	Number of occurrences	Operand	Number of occurrences
If	1	month	3
<	1	year	5
+=	1	dayray	1
--	1	day	1
return	1	3	1
+	6	12	1
*	2	1	1
/	2	26	1
%	1	10	1
n1 = 9	N1 = 16	4	1
		6	1
		100	1
		400	1
		7	1
		n2 = 14	N2 = 20

Table 15.4   Halstead Metrics for the two Implementations

Halstead's Metric	Version 1	Version 2
program length, $N = N_1 + N_2$	21 + 25 = 46	16 + 20 = 36
program vocabulary, $n = n_1 + n_2$	9 + 15 = 24	9 + 14 = 23
program volume, $V = N \log_2(n)$	46 ($\log_2(24)$) = 46*4.58 = 210.68	36 ($\log_2(23)$) = 36*4.52 = 162.72
program difficulty, $D = (n_1 N_2)/2n_2$	(9*25)/2*15 = 7.500	(9*20)/2*14 = 6.428

Table 15.4 shows the Halstead metrics for the two implementations. Look at the two versions and decide if you think these metrics are helpful. Remember that these are small fragments.

The calculations in Table 15.4 are rounded to a reasonable precision. Both versions have nearly equal totals of distinct operators and operands. The big difference is in the number of occurrences (21 vs. 16 and 25 vs. 20, yielding program lengths of 46 and 36). However, the Microsoft Word editor provides the text statistics in Table 15.5 which show that the first version is longer in two senses. Does sheer length add complexity? It depends on what is being done with the code. Size, the

Table 15.5   Character Counts in the two Versions

Size Attribute	Version 1	Version 2
Characters (no spaces)	99	107
Characters (with spaces)	147	157
Lines	7	7

number of operators, and the number of operands have clear implications for program comprehension and software maintenance. The testing for the two versions is identical.

15.2 Integration Level Complexity

The entire discussion in Section 15.1 on unit level complexity applies to both procedural code and to object-oriented methods. The differences in these two paradigms are first noticed at the integration level—in fact they are restricted to that level. At the integration testing level, the concern shifts from correctness of individual units to correct function across units. One presumption of integration level testing is that the units have been thoroughly tested "in isolation." That shifts the attention to interfaces among units and what we might call "communication traffic." As with unit level complexity, we use directed graphs to help our discussion and analysis. The starting point is the Call Graph (Figure 15.4) from Chapter 12.

Definition

Given a program written in an imperative programming language, its *Call Graph* is a directed graph in which nodes correspond to methods, and edges correspond to messages.

For object-oriented code, if method A sends a message to method B, there is an edge from node A to node B. For procedural code, if unit A refers to unit B, there is

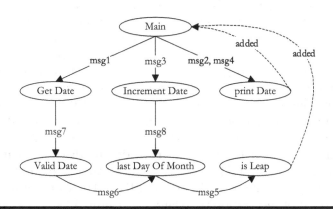

Figure 15.4   Call Graph of Units in procedural integrationNextDate.

an edge from node A to node B. As a general rule, the integration level call graphs of procedural code are less complex than those of functionally equivalent object-oriented code. (We saw this in Chapter 12.) At the same time, the unit level complexity of methods is typically less than that of procedures. This almost suggests a "Law of Conservation of Complexity," in which complexity does not disappear from object-oriented code, it just relocates to the integration level. (This is beyond the scope of this chapter, so it remains a conjecture based on minimal anecdotal evidence.)

15.2.1 Integration Level Cyclomatic Complexity

Cyclomatic complexity at the integration level echoes the approach we took at the unit level, only now we use a call graph instead of a program graph. As before, we need to distinguish between strongly connected call graphs and call graphs that are "almost" strongly connected. Recall we had two equations (15.1 and 15.2) for this distinction:

$$V(G) = e - n + p, \text{ for strongly connected call graphs, and} \tag{15.1}$$

$$V(G) = e - n + 2p \text{ for call graphs that have a single source} \\ \text{node and multiple sink nodes.} \tag{15.2}$$

Notice that the next definitions apply to both object-oriented and procedural code. We repeat two definitions from Chapter 4 next.

Definition

Given the Call Graph of a program (regardless of language paradigm), the *integration level cyclomatic complexity* is the cyclomatic complexity of the call graph.

Definition

Given a directed graph G with n nodes, its *adjacency matrix* is the n x n matrix A = $(a_{i,j})$, where $a_{i,j} = 1$ if there is an edge from node i to node j, 0 otherwise.

As we saw in Chapter 4, all the information in a directed graph can be derived from its (unique!) adjacency matrix, except for the geometric placement of nodes and edges. For example, the sum of elements in row n is the outdegree of node n; similarly, the sum of elements in column n is the indegree of node n. The sum of the indegrees and outdegrees of a node is the degree of the node. Since every edge contributes to the outdegree of some node, this, in turn, together with the number of nodes yields the cyclomatic complexity V(G) = edges – nodes +2p.

Given this, many times it is simpler to provide an adjacency matrix rather than a drawn call graph. Section 15.3 develops a full example of unit and integration level complexity for a rewritten version of NextDate. The call graph of the VBA-like pseudo-code version of integrationNextDate (see Figure 12.17) is in Figure 15.4, followed by its adjacency matrix (Table 15.6).

Table 15.6 Adjacency Matrix of the Call Graph in Figure 15.4

	Main	GetDate	Increment Date	printDate	ValidDate	lastDayOf Month	isleap	row sum (outdegree)
Main		1	1	1				3
GetDate					1			1
IncrementDate						1		1
printDate								0
ValidDate						1		1
lastDayOfMonth							1	1
isleap								0
column sum	0	1	1	1	1	2	1	7

Integration level call graphs are seldom strongly connected, but we can still derive everything we need from the adjacency matrix of a call graph. The sum of the row sums (or column sums) is 7. Nodes with outdegree = 0 must be sink nodes, so for each sink node, we would add an edge to make the call graph strongly connected. There are two such nodes in would add an edge to make the call graph strongly connected. There are two such nodes in Figure 15.4, so the calculation of Integration Level Cyclomatic Complexity is:

$$V(G) = \text{edges} - \text{nodes} + 1 = 9 - 7 + 1 = 3.$$

We can derive a Call Graph for the object-oriented implementation of NextDate (see Figure 12.19). There are 17 methods (nodes) and 25 messages (edges). Repeating the previous calculation for procedural NextDate, we have

$$V(G) = \text{edges} - \text{nodes} + 1 = 25 - 17 + 1 = 9$$

15.2.2 Message Traffic Complexity

As we saw with unit level complexity, only considering cyclomatic complexity is an oversimplification. Just as not all decisions are equal, neither are all interfaces. Suppose, for example, that we find one method repeatedly sending messages to the same destination—clearly this adds to the overall complexity, and we would like to consider this in our integration testing. To do this, we use an extended adjacency matrix of the call graph. In the extended version, rather than just 1's and 0's, an element shows the number of times a method (or a unit) refers to another method (unit). For the Figure 15.4 example, this only happens once, when the Main unit calls printDate twice. We would have this extended adjacency matrix (Table 15.7):

Table 15.7   Extended Adjacency Matrix of the Call Graph in Figure 15.4

	Main	GetDate	Increment Date	printDate	ValidDate	lastDayOf Month	isleap	row sum (outdegree)
Main		1	1	2				4
GetDate					1			1
IncrementDate						1		1
printDate								0
ValidDate						1		1
lastDayOfMonth							1	1
isleap								0
column sum	0	1	1	1	1	2	1	8

15.3 Software Complexity Example

Table 15.8 compares three forms the NextDate program: as a single Java method, as a procedural main program with six procedures, and as a Java implementation with five classes. The Java single method is shown in Figure 15.5, together with its program graph. The procedural and Java implementations of integrationNextDate are taken directly from Chapter 12. When implemented as a single method, this version of NextDate is almost equivalent to a strictly procedural implementation. If you examine the line numbering carefully, you will see that the program graph is

Table 15.8   Complexity of Three Implementations of NextDate

	Java static method nextDate	Pseudo-code integration NextDate	Java integration NextDate
Number of units	1	6	5 classes, 17 methods
Sum of unit complexities	10	14	21
Number of lines of code	55	81	119
Number of messages		7	25
Total unit level complexity	10	14	21
Total integration level complexity		4	45
Total complexity	10	18	66

```
1    public static int nextDate(int day, int month, int year) {
1        int tomorrowDay, tomorrowMonth, tomorrowYear;
2        switch (month) {
         // 31 day months (except Dec.)
3        case 1:
3        case 3:
3        case 5:
3        case 7:
3        case 8:
3        case 10:
4            if (day < 31)
5                tomorrowDay = day + 1;
6            else {
7                tomorrowDay = 1;
8                tomorrowMonth = month + 1;
9            }
10           break;
         // 30 day months
11       case 4:
11       case 6:
11       case 9:
11       case 11:
12           if (day < 30)
13               tomorrowDay = day + 1;
14           else {
15               tomorrowDay = 1;
16               tomorrowMonth = month + 1;
17           }
18           break;
         // December
19       case 12:
20           if (day < 31)
21               tomorrowDay = day + 1;
22           else {
23               tomorrowDay = 1;
24               tomorrowMonth = 1;
25               if (year == 2042)
26                   System.out.println("Date beyond 2042 ");
27               else
28                   tomorrowYear = year + 1;
29           }
30           break;
         // February
31       case 2:
32           if (day < 28)
33               tomorrowDay = day + 1;
34           else {
35               if (day == 28) {
36                   if (isLeap(year))
37                       tomorrowDay = 29;
38                   else {
39                       tomorrowDay = 1;
40                       tomorrowMonth = 3;
41                   }
42               }
43           }
44           break;
45       }
46       return new int[] {tomorrowMonth, tomorrowDay, tomorrowYear};
47   }
```

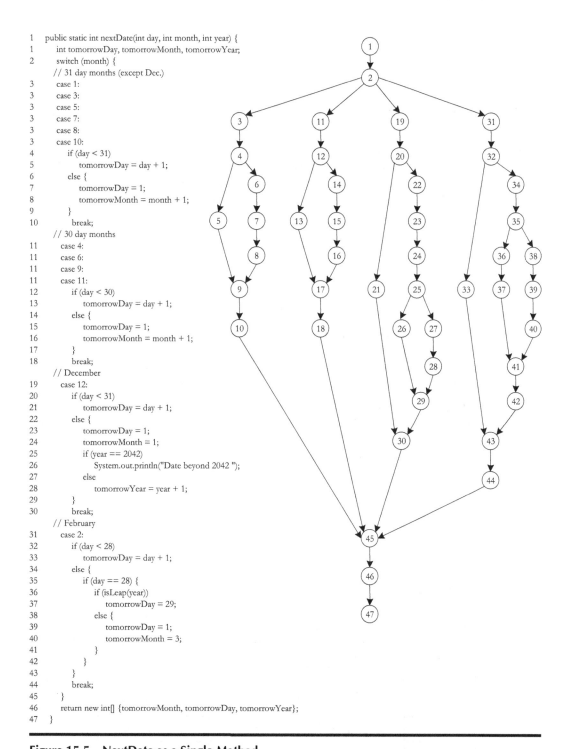

Figure 15.5   NextDate as a Single Method.

technically a DD-Path graph. This has no effect on cyclomatic complexity. There are no complex conditions, so there is no additional decisional complexity.

15.4 Object-Oriented Complexity

The Chidamber/Kemerer (CK) metrics [Chidamber and Kemerer, 1994] are the best-known metrics for object-oriented software. These metrics are discussed in Chapter 9. The names for the six CK metrics are almost self-explanatory; some can be derived from a Call Graph, others use the unit level complexity discussed in Section 15.2. Here we apply the CK metrics to the Java version of NextDate.

15.4.1 WMC—Weighted Methods per Class

Table 15.9 shows the Weighted Methods per Class for the Java version of NextDate (in Chapter 12).

Table 15.9 WMC Metric for the Java Version of NextDate

Class	Methods	Method V(G)	Weight	WMC
DateTest	Main	1	1	1
Date	Date()	1	1	1
	getDate()	1	1	1
	nextDate()	1	1	1
Day	Day()	1	1	1
	getDay()	1	1	1
	getNextDay()	2	2	4
Month	Month()	1	1	1
	getMonth()	1	1	1
	numberOfDays()	4	1	4
	getNextMonth()	2	1	2
	getYear()	1	1	1
Year	Year()	1	1	1
	getYear()	1	1	1
	isLeapYear()	4	4	16
	getNextYear()	1	1	1

15.4.2 DIT—Depth of Inheritance Tree

Current guidelines recommend a limit of DIT = 3. The Depth of the Inheritance Tree for the Java version of NextDate is just 1.

15.4.3 NOC—Number of Child Classes

The Number of Child Classes for The Depth of the Inheritance Tree for the Java version of NextDate is just 1.
just 1.

15.4.4 CBO—Coupling between Classes

The Coupling between Classes in the Java version of NextDate is restricted to data coupling.

15.4.5 RFC—Response for Class

The RFC method refers to the length of the message sequence that results from an initial message. In Chapter 12, we saw that this is also the "length" of the integration-level testing construct, the MM-Path. The longest MM-Path in the Java version of NextDate is 4.

15.4.6 LCOM—Lack of Cohesion on Methods

The methods in the Java version of NextDate all exhibit high cohesion.

15.5 System Level Complexity

Sheer system size is an obvious contributor to system level complexity, as is the underlying system architecture. System vocabulary is another contributor—many systems have a glossary to define jargon and abbreviations. In terms of system maintenance, the documentation of a system is another contributor. Is the document up to date? Is it consistent with the reality of the implementation? Many construction teams keep two definitions of a project, a blueprint (plan) and an "as built" description. We don't have a similar pairing for many systems, and this also contributes to system complexity. In this section, we present a few ideas that can help understanding system level complexity.

15.5.1 Cyclomatic Complexity of Source Code

While it is conceptually possible to consider cyclomatic complexity of the complete program code at the system level, the program size makes this unwieldy. It can be done, and there are commercial tools that support this, but the results are not particularly helpful. In the words of R. J. Hamming: "The purpose of computing is insight, not numbers."

15.5.2 Complexity of Specification Models

Many design models can serve as indicators of complexity, particularly those that can be related to directed graphs (See Table 15.10).

15.5.3 Use Case Complexity

Part of system level complexity stems from how closely intertwined are the software units. This is nicely shown in an incidence matrix that relates use cases to classes (or even to methods) as we noted in Chapter 13. Rows correspond to use cases, and columns to classes (or methods). Then an "x" in row i column j means that class (method) j is used to support the execution of use case i. Note that for procedural code, the incidence is between features and procedures or functions. Now consider whether this matrix is sparse or dense—a sparse incidence indicates that much of the software is only loosely interwoven, making maintenance and testing relatively easy. Conversely, a dense incidence means that the units are tightly coupled and therefore highly interdependent. With dense incidence, we can expect more ripple effect of simple changes, and a greater need for rigorous regression testing after a change is made. As an aside, the incidence matrix serves as a handy way to control the items to be regression tested.

Table 15.10 Complexity Possibilities for Various System Models

Model	Complexity Mechanism
Finite State Machines	Cyclomatic Complexity
Decision Tables	■ Size ■ Density of action entries ■ Connection with other decision tables
Program Design Languages (PDL)	■ Size ■ Number of levels of abstraction ■ Cyclomatic complexity of PDL units ■ Coupling and cohesion of PDL units
Flowcharts	Cyclomatic Complexity

15.5.4 UML Complexity

Many of the UML models have been discussed in the preceding sections. The Chidamber/Kemerer (CK) metrics apply directly to UML class diagrams. We can extend the incidence idea Use Case Complexity (Section 15.5.3) to an incidence matrix in which Use Cases are rows and classes are columns. A cell in this matrix has an "x" if the class is required to implement the use case. As we saw in Section 15.5.3, the density of such a matrix is a good indicator of system complexity.

Exercise

1. Consider a calendar function that finds the zodiac sign for a given date. Compare the total complexities of the Java implementations of zodiac1, zodiac2, and zodiac3.

2. Zodiac1 uses a procedure validEntry to check the valid ranges of month, day, and year.

```
public String zodiac1(int month, int day, int year){
   if (validEntry(month, day, year)){
       if ((month == 3 && day >= 21) || (month == 4 && day <= 19)) {
           return "Aries";
       } else if ((month == 4 || month == 5) && day <= 20) {
           return "Taurus";
       } else if ((month == 5 || month == 6) && day <= 20) {
           return "Gemini";
       } else if ((month == 6 || month == 7) && day <= 22) {
           return "Cancer";
       } else if ((month == 7 || month == 8) && day <= 22) {
           return "Leo";
       } else if ((month == 8 || month == 9) && day <= 22) {
           return "Virgo";
       } else if ((month == 9 || month == 10) && day <= 22) {
           return "Libra";
       } else if ((month == 10 || month == 11) && day <= 21) {
           return "Scorpio";
       } else if ((month == 11 || month == 12) && day <= 21) {
           return "Sagittarius";
       } else if ((month == 12 || month == 1) && day <= 19) {
           return "Capricorn";
       } else if ((month == 1 || month == 2) && day <= 18) {
           return "Aquarius";
       } else {
           return "Pisces";
       }
   } else {
       return "Invalid Date";
   }
}
```

Zodiac2 presumes that the values of month, day, and year are valid. The zodiac signs are assumed to be in an array zodiac(i).

```java
public String zodiac2(int month, int day, int year){
    switch (month){
    case 1: {
        if (day >= 20)
                return zodiac[0];
        else
                return zodiac[3];
    }
    case 2: {
        if (day >= 19)
                return zodiac[7];
        else
                return zodiac[0];
    }
    case 3: {
        if (day >= 21)
                return zodiac[1];
        else
                return zodiac[7];
    }
    case 4: {
        if (day >= 20)
                return zodiac[10];
        else
                return zodiac[1];
    }
    case 5: {
        if (day >= 21)
                return zodiac[4];
        else
                return zodiac[10];
    }
    case 6: {
        if (day >= 21)
                return zodiac[2];
        else
                return zodiac[4];
    }
    case 7: {
        if (day >= 23)
                return zodiac[5];
        else
                return zodiac[2];
    }
    case 8: {
        if (day >= 23)
                return zodiac[11];
        else
                return zodiac[5];
    }
```

```
    case 9: {
        if (day >= 23)
            return zodiac[6];
        else
            return zodiac[11];
    }
    case 10: {
        if (day >= 23)
            return zodiac[9];
        else
            return zodiac[6];
    }
    case 11: {
        if (day >= 22)
            return zodiac[8];
        else
            return zodiac[9];
    }
    case 12: {
        if (day >= 20)
            return zodiac[3];
        else
            return zodiac[8];
    }
    default:
        return zodiac[12];
    }
}
```

The design choice in zodiac3 uses the "ordinal day of the year". Feb. 1 is ordinal day 32. It presumes a function that converts a date to the ordinal day of the year. This version only works for common years. A one day correction would be needed for leap years.

```
String zodiac3(int ordinalDay) {
    if (ordinalDay < 20)
        return "Capricorn";
    if (ordinalDay < 50)
        return "Aquarius";
    if (ordinalDay < 79)
        return "Pisces";
    if (ordinalDay < 109)
        return "Aries";
    if (ordinalDay <= 140)
        return "Taurus";
    if (ordinalDay < 171)
        return "Gemini";
    if (ordinalDay < 203)
        return "Cancer";
    if (ordinalDay < 234)
        return "Leo";
    if (ordinalDay < 265)
        return "Virgo";
```

```
    if (ordinalDay < 295)
        return "Libra";
    if (ordinalDay < 325)
        return "Scorpio";
    if (ordinalDay < 355)
        return "Sagittarius";
    else
        return "Capricorn";
}
```

References

S. R. Chidamber and C. F. Kemerer, (1994). "A metrics suite for object-oriented design," *IEEE Transactions of Software Engineering* Vol. 20, No. 6: pp. 476–493.

Maurice H. Halstead (1977). *Elements of Software Science*. Amsterdam: Elsevier North-Holland, Inc. ISBN 0-444-00205-7.

Chapter 16

Testing Systems of Systems

On March 2, 2012, a Class EF-4 tornado struck the town of Henryville, Indiana (USA). The tornado had winds of 170 mph and left a path of destruction 50 miles long. My wife and I were driving south on Interstate 65; when we were about 50 miles north of Henryville, we saw an Indiana state police car with a sign directing motorists to move to the left lane of the highway. This was the beginning of a direct experience with a "system of systems." Soon, traffic came to a halt, and then impatient drivers started using the right lane anyway, quickly bringing that lane also to a stop. Then we saw emergency vehicles and heavy equipment heading south using the shoulder of the road. We learned from a truck driver that a tornado had hit Henryville about an hour earlier, and that the emergency vehicles and heavy equipment were attempting to reach the devastated area. We noticed that there was very little northbound traffic on Interstate 65, so clearly, northbound traffic south of Henryville was also stopped. The next day, we saw that a highway rest area had been converted to a command center for the Indiana National Guard to coordinate the disaster relief effort. This effort involved:

- The Indiana state police,
- Local and county police departments
- Regional fire departments,
- Regional ambulance services
- Heavy (tree moving) equipment from the public utility companies
- The Indiana National Guard
- Traffic helicopters from Indianapolis television stations.
- The U.S. Weather Bureau
- (and probably many others)

Consider how this all happened. How did these disparate groups come together for an emergency? How did they communicate? Was there any central coordination?

Systems of systems have become an increasingly important topic in several areas of software engineering. In this chapter, we look at some of the early definitions

[Maier 1999], some SysML techniques to specify requirements of these systems, and finally, we develop a new model to describe systems of systems and their model-based testing.

16.1 Characteristics of Systems of Systems

We all experience complex systems every day, but what distinguishes a complex system from a system of systems? Some early attempts to clarify this distinction are:

- A "super system"
- A collection of cooperating systems
- A collection of autonomous systems
- A set of component systems

These early attempts all get at the central idea, but they would also apply to systems such as an automobile, an integrated MIS system in a company, and even the human body. There is a growing clarity of definitions for the underlying nature of systems of systems. Maier begins his distinction by noting two fundamental differences—systems of systems are either directed or collaborative. Initially, he used "collaborative systems" as a synonym for "systems of systems," with the defining characteristic that systems of systems are "built from components which are large scale systems in their own right." He offers air defense networks, the Internet, and emergency response teams as better examples. Maier then provides some more specific attributes:

- They are built from components that are (or can be) independent systems,
- They have managerial/administrative independence,
- They are usually developed in an evolutionary way, and
- They exhibit emergent (as opposed to pre-planned) behaviors.

In addition, he observes that the components may not be co-located, and this imposes a constraint on information sharing. The generally accepted term for the components is "constituent system," and a general architecture is shown in Figure 16.1. Notice that constituent systems may have links other than to the central control point. The control center portion leads to three important distinctions that Maier makes regarding the nature of cooperation among the constituent systems.

Definition

[Maier 1999]

A *directed system of systems* is designed, built, and managed for a specific purpose.
A *collaborative system of systems* has limited centralized management and control.
A *virtual system of systems* has no centralized management and control.

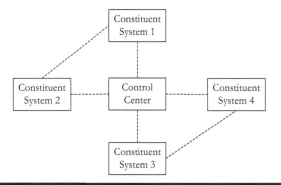

Figure 16.1   Generic view of a system of systems.

The dominant characteristic that distinguishes these categories is the way they communicate and control/cooperate. Maier further asserts that there are two essential requirements that a potential system of systems must satisfy:

1. The constituent systems must be stand-alone systems, and
2. Each constituent has administrative independence from the other constituents.

Maier's three categories were extended [Lane 2012] to include a fourth category: acknowledged. In order from most to least controlling, we have directed, acknowledged, collaborative, and virtual systems of systems.

Systems of Systems (abbreviated as SoS) can evolve. The Henryville tornado incident began as a virtual system of systems—there was no centralized control point. When the Indiana state police arrived, it evolved into a collaborative system of systems. By the next morning, the Indiana National Guard had turned a rest area into a command center, and it was then an acknowledged system of systems. Why is this not a directed system of systems? The constituents are all independent systems that can function, and each has separate administrative control; however, as a system of systems, it was never created with that purpose in mind.

16.2 Sample Systems of Systems

To gain some insight into Maier's categories of systems of systems, we consider one example of each type. The emphasis in this section is how the constituent systems communicate, and how they are, or might be, controlled.

16.2.1 The Garage Door Controller (Directed)

A nearly complete Garage Door Controller system (see Chapter 2) is shown as a system of systems in Figure 16.2. Some elements must be present, namely the drive motor, a wall-mount button, and the extreme limit sensors. The other constituents are

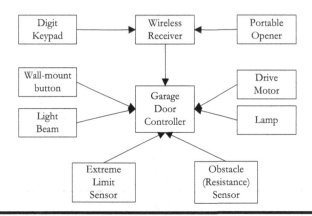

Figure 16.2   Garage Door Controller Constituents.

optional but common. The portable opener is usually kept in a car, and there may be two or more of these. Sometimes a digit keypad is mounted on the outside of a garage, possibly so children can enter after school. The openers and digit keypads send weak radio signals to the wireless receiver, which in turn controls the drive motor. A possible internet-based controller is not shown but could be added. Finally, the light beam and resistance sensors are added as optional safety devices. Many of the constituent systems are made by separate manufacturers and are integrated into a commercial garage door opener system.

The Garage Door Controller satisfies most of Maier's definitional criteria—there is a true central controller, and commercial versions of the full system of systems can evolve with the addition of some constituent systems (*e.g.,* the Digit Keypad).

16.2.2 Air Traffic Management System (Acknowledged)

At a commercial airport (or at any controlled airfield), the Air Traffic Controllers use an Air Traffic Management System (yet another ATM) to manage take-offs and landings. Figure 16.3 shows the major constituent systems for an Air Traffic Control system. The first decision an air traffic controller must make is runway allocation. This depends mostly on the wind direction, but it may also consider local noise restrictions. Arriving aircraft generally has preference over departing aircraft, because an aircraft on the ground can just stay out of the way of landing aircraft. Airborne aircraft is subject to three forms of separation, each of which must be maintained— vertical separation, lateral separation, and time separation. The only exception to these protocols is that, in an emergency, the pilot of an arriving aircraft can request emergency landing priority.

Why is this "acknowledged" and not "directed"? In general, the air traffic controllers, as the name implies, control everything involved with runway use, separation, landing, and departing aircraft. But emergencies can occur, as we shall see later, making this an acknowledged systems of systems.

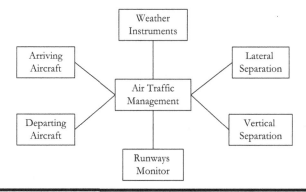

Figure 16.3   Air Traffic Management System Constituents.

16.2.3 The Foodie Wish List System

Our Foodie Wish List System is a good example of a system of systems. (See the full description in Appendix B).

■ three architectural layers of processors
■ web services include account creation, login control, and shopping
■ backend services are general administration and a shopping cart for orders
■ everything is held together by a database.

Figure 16.4 shows the Swim Lane architecture, and Figure 16.5 shows the communication among constituents.

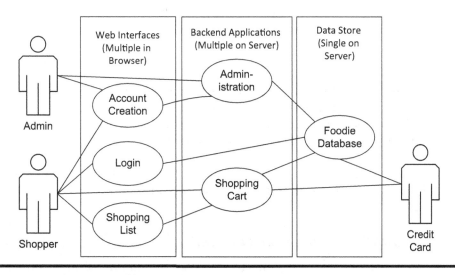

Figure 16.4   Swim Lane Architecture for the Foodies Wish List.

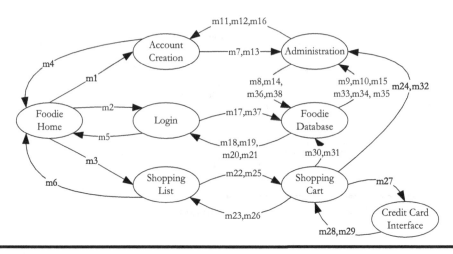

Figure 16.5   Communication among Foodies Wish List Constituents.

16.3 Software Engineering for Systems of Systems

Very little published work exists to apply software engineering principles and techniques to systems of systems. Some of the early work [Maier 1999] and [Lane 2012] is described here, as well as some original material. We will refer to all of this as a UML dialect. After illustrating how this UML dialect can represent systems of systems, we will turn to an approach that supports model-based testing of systems of systems.

16.3.1 Requirements Elicitation

In a webinar, Jo Ann Lane described an emergency response system of systems that dealt with grass fires in Southern California [Lane 2012]. Lane offers a waterfall-like sequence of activities to describe general requirements of a given system of systems. The steps include:

- Identifying resources—potential constituent systems, and modeling them with SysML
- Determining options—responsibilities and dependencies
- Assessing options—expressed as Use Cases
- Identifying a workable combination of constituent systems
- Allocating responsibilities to constituent systems

In the next few sections, we revise and extend the standard UML practices to make them work for systems of systems. These are illustrated with the examples in Section 16.2.

16.3.2 Specification with a Dialect of UML

There are three parts to the UML dialect—class-like definitions of a constituent system in terms of its responsibilities to other constituents and the services it provides. Use Cases show the flow across constituents for overall system of system functions, and traditional UML sequence diagrams to show the incidence of these use cases with constituent systems.

16.3.2.1 Air Traffic Management System Classes

The UML dialect extends and revises some of the traditional UML models. In the UML dialect, constituent systems are modeled as classes in which responsibilities with other classes occupy the position of attributes, and the services take the place of class methods. Two of the constituent systems from Figure 16.3 are described as "classes" in text format here.

Incoming Aircraft

Responsibilities to other constituents

- Communicate with air traffic controller Services
- Fly aircraft
- Land aircraft
- Remain prepared for emergency situations

Air Traffic Controller

Responsibilities to other constituents

Incoming aircraft
Departing aircraft
Runway (status)
Separation instruments
Weather instruments

Services

- Assign runways based on weather conditions
- Monitor separation instruments
- Assign landing clearance
- Assign take-off clearance
- Maintain runway status

16.3.2.2 Air Traffic Management System Use Cases and Sequence Diagrams

In both the standard UML and in the dialect used here, classes constitute the "*is view*" that focuses on the structure and components of a system (and systems of systems).

The *is view* is most useful to developers, but less so for customer/users and testers, who utilize the "*does view*" which focuses on behavior. Use cases are the earliest UML model that relate to the does view, and they are widely recognized as the preferred view of customer/users. The UML sequence diagram is the only place where the *does view* is related to the *is view*. Figure 16.6 is a sequence diagram of the Normal Landing use case. For our dialect, we added Actors (constituent systems) to the use case format. Also, the usual Event Sequence of a standard UML use case is replaced by the sequence of constituent system actions.

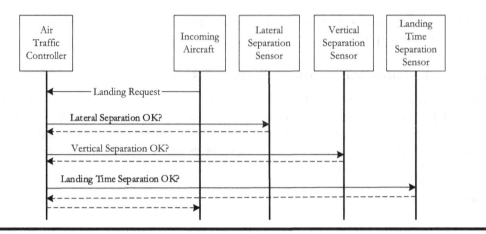

Figure 16.6 Sequence diagram of Normal Landing.

Normal Landing Use Case

10.5	SoS UC1: Normal aircraft landing
Description	The procedure that governs an arriving aircraft under normal conditions.
Actor(s)	1. Air Traffic Controller
	2. Incoming aircraft
	3. Separation sensors (vertical, lateral, and time)
Pre-conditions	1. Designated runway clear
	2. Incoming aircraft ready to land

Action Sequence	
Actor	Action
Incoming aircraft	1. Requests clearance to land
Air Traffic Controller	2. Checks all separation sensors
Lateral Separation	3. OK
Vertical Separation	4. OK
Time Separation	5. OK
Air Traffic Controller	6. Landing clearance given
Incoming aircraft	7. Initiates landing procedures
Incoming aircraft	8. On assigned runway
Incoming aircraft	9. Taxi to assigned gate
Air Traffic Controller	10. Landing complete.

In November, 1993, a commercial aircraft was on its final landing approach to a runway at Chicago's O'Hare International Airport. When the incoming aircraft was at an altitude of about 100 feet, a pilot waiting to take off saw that the landing aircraft had not lowered its landing gear. There is no direct communication between landing and departing aircraft, so the pilot contacted the O'Hare field control tower about the impending disaster. The control tower waved off the landing aircraft, and a disaster was avoided. This is the subject of our second use case and sequence diagram. In this use case, Aircraft L is the landing aircraft, and aircraft G is the one on the ground. We can imagine that the second use case could be a continuation of the first one at action step 7. We can also imagine that everyone involved was very relieved once the post-condition was attained.

November 1993 Incident Use Case

ID, Name	SoS UC2: November 1993 Incident at O'Hare Field
Description	Aircraft on final approach had landing gear up. Pilot on taxi way saw this and notified control tower.
Actor(s)	1. Air Traffic Controller
	2. Incoming aircraft L
	3. Aircraft G waiting to take off.
Pre-conditions	1. Aircraft L cleared to land
	2. Aircraft G waiting to take off
	3. Aircraft L has landing gear up
Action Sequence	
Actor	Action
Air Traffic Controller	1. Authorizes aircraft L to land
Aircraft L	2. Initiates landing preparation
Aircraft L	3. Fails to lower landing gear
Aircraft L	4. 100 feet above end of assigned runway
Aircraft G	5. Aircraft G pilot radios Air Traffic Controller
Air Traffic Controller	6. Terminates landing permission
Aircraft L	7. Aircraft L aborts landing
Aircraft L	8. Aircraft L regains altitude over runway
Air Traffic Controller	9. Instructs aircraft L to circle and land
Air Traffic Controller	10. Thanks pilot of aircraft G
Air Traffic Controller	11. Authorizes aircraft L to land
Aircraft L	12. Landing complete.
Post-conditions	1. Runway available to other aircraft

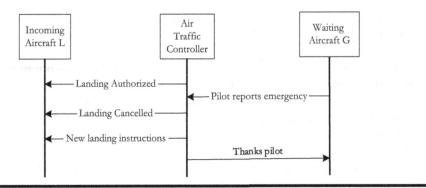

Figure 16.7   Sequence diagram of November 1993 Incident.

This incident happened when one of the authors arrived in Chicago to make a presentation on software technical reviews. Oddly enough, the topic of the day was the importance of review checklists. Obviously, the pilot of the landing aircraft did not pay attention to the landing checklist. In a television news report later, a Federal Aviation Authority official commented that he was far more worried about routine flights than flights during extreme conditions. His reason—people are far more attentive in extreme situations. The sequence diagram for the November 1993 incident is in Figure 16.7. Notice that many of the "internal" actions (2, 3, and 4) are important to the use case, but they do not appear in the sequence diagram.

16.3.3 Testing

Testing for systems of systems must focus on the ways in which constituent systems communicate. Just as integration testing presumes complete unit level testing, the testing of systems of systems must presume that the constituent systems have been thoroughly tested as stand-alone components. The UML dialect models are only general guidelines for system of systems testing. The primary goal of testing for systems of systems is to focus on the communication among constituents. In the next section, we develop a set of primitives that describe the types of communication among constituent systems. They will be presented as Petri nets, and we will use them to describe the control distinctions that are the essence of the four levels of cooperation (directed, acknowledged, voluntary, or virtual).

16.4 Communication Primitives for Systems of Systems

The distinctions among the four types of systems of systems reduce to the way the constituents communicate with each other. In this section, we first map the prompts of the Extended Systems Modeling Language (ESML) into Swim Lane Petri Nets. In Section 16.5, we use the Petri net forms of the ESML prompts in swim lanes to illustrate the communication mechanisms of the four types of systems of systems. We understand swim lanes to be device oriented, like the orthogonal regions of statecharts. More specifically, we will use swim lanes to represent constituent systems, and the ESML prompts to represent the types of communication among constituents.

Finally, in Section 16.5.1, we illustrate the systems of systems communication using Swim Lane Event-Driven Petri Nets on the November 1993 incident.

The first candidate for a set of communication primitives is the set of ESML prompts. Most of these express the power of the central controlling constituent, so they are clearly applicable to directed systems of systems, and probably also to acknowledged systems of systems. We need similar primitives for the collaborative and virtual systems of systems. Here we propose four new primitives: Request, Accept, Reject, and Postpone.

16.4.1 ESML Prompts as Petri Nets

The ESML real-time extension to Structured Analysis [Bruyn et al., 1988] was developed as a way to describe how one activity in a dataflow diagram can control another activity. There are five basic ESML prompts: Enable, Disable, Trigger, Suspend, and Resume, and they are most appropriate to directed and acknowledged systems of systems. Two others are pairs of the original five: Activate is an Enable followed by a Disable, and Pause is a Suspend followed by a Resume. The ESML prompts are represented as traditional Petri nets and briefly described in this section. The marking and firing of Petri nets are described in Chapter 4.

16.4.1.1 Petri Net Conflict

We describe the Petri net conflict first, because it appears in some of the ESML prompts. Figure 16.8 shows the basic Petri net conflict pattern—the place p2 is an input to both the function 1 and function 2 transitions. All three places are marked, so both transitions are enabled, in the Petri net sense. ("Enabling" is an overloaded term here—the ESML sense refers to a prompt, and the Petri net transition sense refers to a property of a transition.) If we choose to fire the function 1 transition, the tokens in places p1 and p2 are consumed, and this disables the function 2 transition, hence the conflict.

In the air traffic management and control example, two constituents, arriving and departing aircraft, both use the same runway, putting them in contention for the limited resource—a good example of Petri net conflict. Since arriving aircraft has preference over departing aircraft, we have an instance of the interlock mechanism described next.

16.4.1.2 Petri Net Interlock

An interlock is used to assure that one action precedes (or has priority over) another. In Petri nets, this is accomplished by an interlock place, labeled "i" in Figure 16.9 that

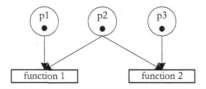

Figure 16.8   Petri net conflict.

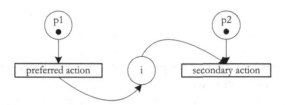

Figure 16.9   Petri net interlock.

is an output of the preferred transition and is an input to the secondary transition. The only way the interlock place can be marked is for the preferred transition to fire.

16.4.1.3 Enable, Disable, and Activate

The Enable prompt expresses the interaction in which one action permits another action to occur. There is no requirement that the second action actually does occur, just that it may occur. In the Petri net in Figure 16.10, the transition labeled "controlled action" has two input places. In order to be an enabled transition, both its input places must be marked. But the place labeled "e/d" can only be marked if the enable transition is fired. The controlled action then has one of its prerequisites, but it still needs to wait for the other input place to be marked. When the controlled action transition fires, it marks the e/d place again, so that is remains enabled.

At a controlled airfield, the air traffic controller selects a runway, and then gives permission to arriving aircraft to land. We can model this with the Enable prompt. Due to the interlock relationship between arriving and departing aircraft, this effectively causes a Disable prompt for the aircraft waiting to take off. Since aircraft landings clearly begin and end, this can also be interpreted as an Activate prompt. The air traffic controller "Activates" the landing process.

The Disable prompt depends on the Petri net conflict pattern. The disable transition and the controlled action transitions in Figure 16.10 are in conflict with respect to the e/d place. If the disable transition fires, the controlled action transition cannot fire. Also, the e/d place acts as an interlock between the enable and disable transitions, so a controlled action can only be disabled after it has been enabled. The original ESML team found that the Enable, Disable sequence occurred so frequently, it acquired a name: Activate.

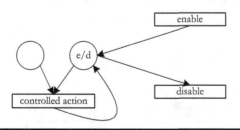

Figure 16.10   ESML Enable, Disable, and Activate.

16.4.1.4 Trigger

The Trigger prompt (Figure 16.11) is a stronger version of the Enable prompt—it causes the controlled action to occur immediately. In ordinary language, we could say that the effect of Enable is "you may" and that of Trigger is "you must, now!" Notice that Trigger has the same renewal pattern that we saw with Enable. We could modify this if necessary so that Trigger is a one-time action. Just removing the output edge from the controlled action back to the trigger place (t) place suffices. The ESML committee never made this distinction.

16.4.1.5 Suspend and Resume

The ESML Suspend and Resume prompts are shown in Figure 16.12. When they occur together, their sequence is known as the ESML Pause prompt. Suspend has the same interrupting power as the Trigger prompt—it can interrupt an ongoing activity, and when the interrupting task is complete, the Resume prompt assures that the interrupted activity does not have to start over—it resumes where it left off. Conversationally, we could say "Stop what you are doing."

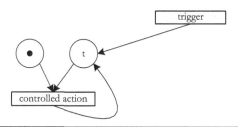

Figure 16.11   ESML Trigger.

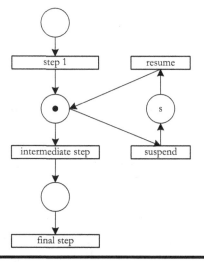

Figure 16.12   ESML Suspend, Resume, and Pause.

As with the Enable/Disable pair, Suspend and Resume have an interlock place, noted in Figure 16.12. An activity can only be resumed after it has been suspended. The labelled s in Figure 16.12 an interlock between the Suspend and Resume actions. Also, the Suspend action and the intermediate step action are in Petri net conflict with respect to the marked input place of the intermediate step. Presumably, a Suspend is followed by a Trigger to another required action which, when complete, leads to a Resume prompt.

The November, 1993 incident described earlier, is a good example where the Suspend and Resume prompts could be used. There is no direct communication between landing and departing aircraft, so the pilot on the ground contacted the O'Hare field control tower about the impending disaster. The control tower waved off the landing aircraft (Suspend), and once the disaster was avoided, issued a Resume.

16.4.2 New Prompts as Swim Lane Petri Nets

The directed and acknowledged systems of systems are characterized by a strong, usually central, controlling constituent. Collaborative and virtual systems of systems do not have this strong position, the constituents are more autonomous. Can a constituent in one of these systems of systems control another? Certainly, but it is more likely that the communication is more collaborative than controlling. Four new primitives are proposed here to capture this more collaborative communication—Request, Accept, Reject, and Postpone. As with the ESML prompts, they can and should interact.

Parallel activities are shown in UML as "Swim Lanes" to connote that a swimmer in one lane is separated from a swimmer in an adjacent lane. In Section 16.4.1, we mapped each of the ESML prompts into Petri Nets. We understand swim lanes to be device oriented, very similar to the orthogonal regions of statecharts.More specifically, we will use Swim Lanes to represent constituent systems, and the communication prompts to represent the types of communication among constituents. Finally, we illustrate the systems of systems communication using Swim Lane Petri Nets on the November 1999 incident. In this subsection, the constituent systems are all members of either collaborative or virtual systems of systems.

16.4.2.1 Request

In Figure 16.13, constituent A requests a service from constituent B, and receives a response to the request. The figure only shows the interaction from the point of view of constituent A because the response choice of constituent B is not known. In general, a response is either Accepted, Rejected, or Postponed.

16.4.2.2 Accept

The Accept and Reject primitives are nearly identical, except for the nature of the response (see Figures 16.14 and 16.15).

16.4.2.3 Reject

The "not done" part of a Reject response could be problematic for testers. How can something that does not happen be tested? The Accept and Reject responses are often subject to a Petri net conflict in the receiving constituent, as in Figure 16.16.

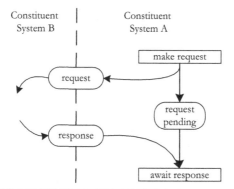

Figure 16.13   The Request Petri net.

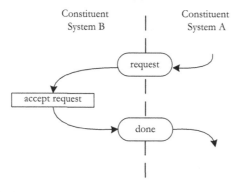

Figure 16.14   The Accept Petri net.

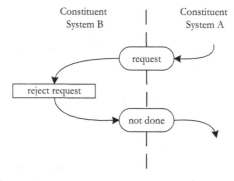

Figure 16.15   The Reject Petri net.

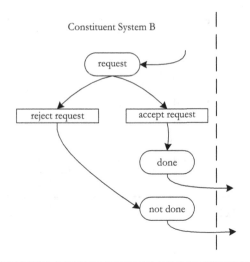

Figure 16.16   Accept and Reject Petri net conflict.

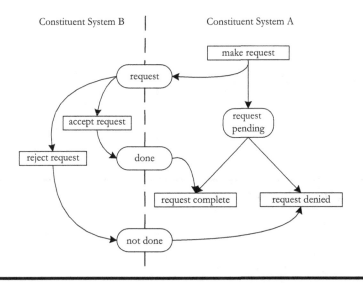

Figure 16.17   The Connections among Request, Accept, and Reject Petri nets.

Figure 16.17 shows a fairly complete picture of the Petri net conflicts in both constituents. Constituent A makes a request of constituent B. In turn, B either accepts or rejects the request, so either the "done" or the "not done" place is marked, and this resolves the Petri net conflict in constituent A.

16.4.2.4 Postpone

What happens if constituent B is busy with an internal priority, and receives a request from constituent A? The interlock pattern is how constituent B completes its preferred task before responding to the request from constituent A (see Figure 16.18).

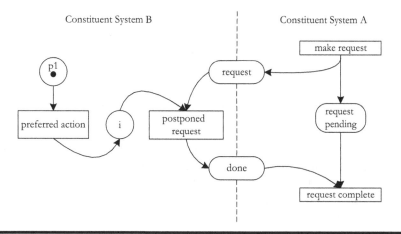

Figure 16.18   The Postpone Petri net.

16.4.2.5 Swim Lane Description of the November 1993 Incident (Figure 16.19)

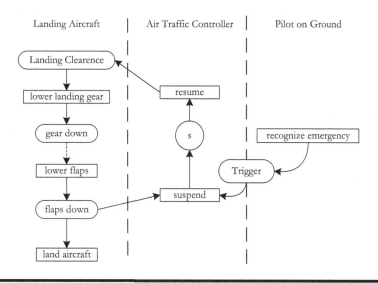

Figure 16.19   Swim Lane Petri net for the November 1993 incident.

16.5 Effect of Systems of Systems Levels on Prompts

When the ESML committee first defined the five prompts, there was some confusion about sequences of prompts. For example, could a Suspend take precedence over a Trigger? Part of the confusion was that the ESML committee was not thinking in terms of systems of systems. To some extent, the definition of the four levels of systems of systems resolves these questions.

One way to begin clarification of this is to postulate two types of communication—commands and requests. The four new prompts are already known as requests, but what about the original ESML prompts. The Trigger, Suspend, Disable, and Resume prompts are all commands, whereas Enable is more of a request.

16.5.1 Directed and Acknowledged Systems of Systems

The central controllers in directed and acknowledged systems of systems are clearly intended to have the "command" power of Trigger, Suspend, Disable, and Resume with respect to their constituents. What about the reverse? Does it make sense for a constituent to "control" the central controller? This seems appropriate when a constituent communicates with what would be an interrupt in software. Consider the safety features in the Garage Door Controller—when an obstacle is encountered, or when the light beam is crossed, the motor immediately stops and reverses to open the garage door.

16.5.2 Collaborative and Virtual Systems of Systems

Because they lack the strong central controlling constituent, both types of systems of systems can use any of the prompts.

Exercises

1. Discuss whether the Disable prompt should have the same interrupting power as the Suspend prompt. Use examples if you wish.

   Questions 2 and 3 revisit the Windshield Wiper Controller in the exercises of Chapter 14.
2. Decide which of the four types of systems of systems best describes the Windshield Wiper Controller.
3. Use Swim Lane Petri Nets to show the interactions in the Windshield Wiper Controller.

References

Bruyn, W., Jensen, D., Keskar Ward, P., "An Extended systems modeling language based on the data flow diagram", *ACM Software Engineering Notes*, vol. 13, no. 1, pp. 58–67, 1988.

Lane, Jo Ann, "System of Systems Capability-to-Requirements Engineering", University of Southern California, Viterbi School of Engineering, webinar given February, 2012.

Maier, Mark, "Architecting principles for systems-of-systems", *System Engineering*, vol. 1 no. 4, pp. 251–315, (1999).

Chapter 17

Feature Interaction Testing

Pamela Zave popularized the feature interaction problem while working at Bell Labs [Zave 1993]. She observed that separately developed software features sometimes interacted in unexpected ways. She offered a few, easily understood examples:

1. the logical conflict between calling party identification service and unlisted directory numbers.
2. call forwarding and call blocking, in which subscriber A forwards calls to subscriber B, and subscriber B rejects calls from subscriber A.
3. the infamous call forwarding loop, in which subscriber A forwards calls to subscriber B, subscriber B forwards calls to subscriber C, and subscriber C forwards calls to subscriber A. What happens when a fourth party calls one of these subscribers? (In fact, most telephone switching systems mark a call as forwarded, and by protocol, a forwarded call cannot be forwarded again. A similar incident once took down the ARPA net is its early days.)

17.1 Feature Interaction Problem Defined

In Chapter 13, we understood threads to be the "atomic element" of system testing. Later, in Chapter 16, we saw system level threads expressed as Event-Dirven Petri Nets (EDPNs). Recall that we described a set of communication primitives, Petri net conflict and Petri net interlock. We also had a list of primitives based on the Extended System Modeling Language (ESML): enable, disable, activate, trigger, suspend, and resume. In addition, we introduced four communication primitives: request, accept, reject, and postpone. All of these primitives are applicable to the feature interaction problem.

Since threads of feature behavior can be modeled as EDPNs, we note here that the EDPNs can exhibit one of three topologically possible forms of connection. EDPN A and EDPN B are:

- 0-connected if there is no edge between any element of EDPN A and any element of EDPN B.
- 1-connected if EDPN A and EDPN B have a common event or place. The connection can be a semi-path to either an ancestor or a descendent event or place.

■ 2-connected if EDPN A creates an output place that is also an input place to EDPN B. Notice that 2-connection occurs only as data places—it is hard to imagine an output event that is also an input event.

■ 3-connected if EDPN A is 2-connected to EDPN B, and EDPN B is 2-connected to EDPN A.

Pamela Zave's second example exhibits 2-connection, and her third example exhibits 3-connection. In the following examples, look for instances of n-connectivity among feature threads, and also, for instances of our 12 communication primitives.

Fundamentally, software must be more than the sum of its parts. That is, the individual component that makes up an integrated piece of software must operate together to add more functionality than each one adds alone – without interacting with the other individual components. This idea is not new. We have already seen the case for integration testing in Chapter 12, which would not be necessary if unit testing of individual components was sufficient. Even Aristotle wrote:

> *In the case of all things which have several parts and in which the totality is not, as it were, a mere heap, but the whole is something beside the parts, there is a cause; for even in bodies contact is the cause of unity in some cases, and in others viscosity or some other such quality.*
> *(http://classics.mit.edu/Aristotle/metaphysics.8.viii.html, n.d.)*

In software, the unity that Aristotle writes of is the beneficial interactions between individual components that enable software to be extended by the beneficial cooperation between some additional functionality, or feature, and the existing functionality. For example, a car's cruise control system interacts with the accelerator functionality to control the speed of the car. Similarly, the brake functionality interacts with the cruise control to turn it off. The accelerator and brake now have *more* functionality than they did when the cruise control system was not included.

However, not all interactions are beneficial. Consider the impact of a cruise control system that did not turn off when the car's brakes were applied, but instead required the driver to manually disable the cruise control through the cruise control interface. There would be a significant impact on the existing accelerator and braking functionality, reducing the safety of the vehicle.

Feature Interactions between features (F) and their expected behavior (ϕ) can be formally described as when a feature, F_i, satisfies a property, ϕ_i, denoted as $F_i \vDash \phi_i$. Features may be combined, or composed, via a composition operator (e.g., $\oplus$). When two features are composed, such as $F_1 \oplus F_2$, we expect that if each feature would satisfy its own expected behavior independently (i.e., $F_1 \vDash \phi_1 \wedge F_2 \vDash \phi_2$) then their composition should satisfy the combination of their respective behaviors (i.e., $F_1 \oplus F_2 \vDash \phi_1 \wedge \phi_2$). However, if the feature's composition does not satisfy the combination of their behaviors, then a feature interaction exists (Calder et al., 2003). In the case of a cruise control system, the existing accelerator and breaking functionality may be a set of base functionality represented by a single feature (i.e., F_1) where the expected behavior is that speed is increased or decreased based on the application of the accelerator or brake, respectively. Cruise control, our second feature (i.e., F_2) attempts to maintain a desired speed. A feature interaction exists if the behavior is altered due to the composition of both features.

Table 17.1   Feature Interaction vs. Correct Behavior

Brakes or Accelerator	Cruise Control	FI Result	Correct Result
Brakes	Off	Slower	Slower
Accelerator	Off	Faster	Faster
Brakes	On	Desired Speed	Slower & Cruise Control Off
Accelerator	On	Desired Speed	Faster (from Desired)
None	On	Desired Speed	Desired Speed

Consider Table 17.1, which includes behavior in terms of several cases. In the case when the cruise control is not applied, we get the expected behavior when either the brakes or the accelerator are applied. Similarly, if the brakes and accelerator are not applied, but the cruise control is, we get the desired result of matching the desired speed. However, when the brakes or accelerator is applied and the cruise control is on, the accelerator still provides faster speed while the brakes still provide slower speed. Additionally, the brakes impact the cruise control feature beyond slowing the car, as the cruise control is also turned off. The difference between the FI Result and the Correct Result is not if there is an interaction, but if the interaction is positive to the system behavior.

While negative feature interactions are problematic for the system they exist in, the *feature interaction problem* is not the individual interactions themselves, but the comparative cost of dealing with feature interactions and the remainder of the development activity. The feature interaction problem occurs when feature development is overwhelmed by detecting, analyzing, and verifying feature interactions (Apel et al., n.d.). For every feature that is added to a system, the possible feature combinations are doubled (i.e., is the feature included or excluded). Since feature interactions could occur between any set of features, the number of system configurations that must be tested is exponential (i.e., $O(2^n)$ where n is the number of features) to the number of features.

Exhaustive testing for feature interactions is infeasible for any sufficiently complex system due to the feature interaction problem. The remainder of this chapter discusses methods of narrowing down where feature interactions might occur and how to reduce the number of tests in order to detect likely interactions.

17.2 Types of Feature Interactions

Detecting feature interactions depends on looking at all the possibilities, which quickly becomes infeasible due to the feature interaction problem, or looking at the *right* possibilities. A subset of likely feature interactions can be identified as interactions on conflicting uses of an input, conflicting attempts at an output, or attempted use of a limited resource. Specific examples are based on the Foodies Wishlist application defined in Appendix B, where Figure 17.1 illustrates the messages passed between the following features where a feature is "an increment of product functionality" (Batory et al., 2006):

- ■ Foodie Home
- ■ Account Creation

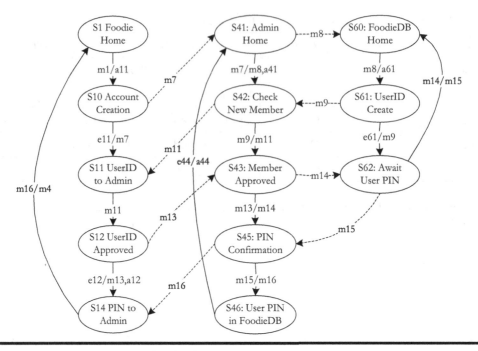

Figure 17.1   Message Communication in Scenario 1.

- Login
- Shopping List
- Administration
- Foodie Database
- Shopping Card

Additionally, each of these increments of functionality may be duplicated, as necessary, to support multiple users. The duplication also indicates an increment of product functionality.

17.2.1 Input Conflict

When represented by a FSM, a conflict between features based on an input can be caused by conflicting transitions based on the same or simultaneous input events or messages.

Consider Scenario 1: Normal Account Creation from Appendix B, B.3.1.1.

1. A Foodie User creates a UserID, sends it to Admin.
2. Admin sends the potential UserID to the FoodieDB.
3. The FoodieDB checks and finds no duplicate, so it approves the new UserID, and confirms this to Admin.
4. In turn, Admin confirms this to Account Creation.
5. The newly approved User then creates a PIN and sends it to Admin. (No check is made on validity of a PIN, since it is local to a User.)
6. Admin sends the PIN to the FoodieDB, so that the FoodieDB can send it as the "Expected PIN" to Login.

The sequence of messages in scenario 1 is m1, m7, m8, m9, m11, m13, m14, m15, m16, m4. The reason for making the state numbers global is so we can describe a

Table 17.2   Conflicting UserIDs

Step	User 1	User 2
1	A Foodie User (1) creates a UserID ("FoodieFan"), sends it to Admin.	
2		A Foodie User (2) creates a UserID ("FoodieFan"), sends it to Admin.
3		The FoodieDB checks and finds no duplicate, so it approves the new UserID ("FoodieFan"), and confirms this to Admin.
4	The FoodieDB checks and finds no duplicate *within the database*, so it approves the new UserID ("FoodieFan"), and confirms this to Admin.	
5	Admin confirms this to Account Creation	
6		Admin confirms this to Account Creation
7	The newly approved User then creates a PIN ("1234") and sends it to Admin.	
8		The newly approved User then creates a PIN ("1111") and sends it to Admin.
9	Admin sends the PIN ("1234") to the FoodieDB, so that the FoodieDB can send it as the "Expected PIN" to Login.	
10		Admin sends the PIN ("1111") to the FoodieDB, so that the FoodieDB can send it as the "Expected PIN" to Login.

scenario as a state sequence across swim lanes. The state sequence for scenario 1 is: S1, S10, S41, S1, S61, S62, S42, S11, S12, S43, S62, S45, S14, S1, S41, S1.

However, consider what could happen when two users creating conflicting UserIDs ("FoodieFan") in Table 17.2.

In this case, the two users are able to create the same account, since the first user's UserID is not stored in the FoodieDB until after the second user's UserID is also checked for duplication. Once *both* user's UserIDs have been approved, both users are able to set their PINs with no additional checks. This results in *both* users having the *last* PIN set, which is the second user's PIN of "1111."

In this case, the additional functionality (i.e., feature) that caused a conflict was the multi-user support. Since only one FoodieDB exists, but multiple instantiations of the Admin functionality are created and operate in parallel, the additional Admin thread caused an input conflict based on multiple messages sent to the FoodieDB when the FoodieDB only expected one set of account creation messages at once.

While, from a design perspective, a single-user Foodie Wish List operates with a single instance of the software in Figure 17.2, the reality includes more than one instantiation.

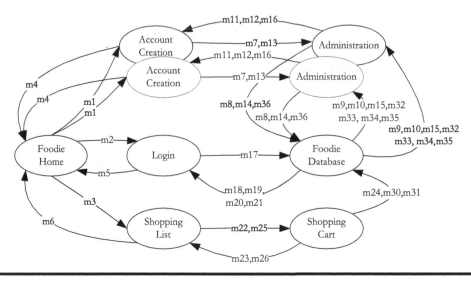

Figure 17.2 Message Communication Among Multiple Instantiations of Finite State Machines.

In Figure 17.2 above, the set of possible interactions is based on the multiple instantiations of Account Creation and Administration. The scenario detailed above is caused by two m8 ("Submit UserID to FoodieDB") and m14 ("Send User PIN to FoodieDB") messages from the Administration FSMs to the Foodie Database. Given the duplication of the instantiations of Account Creation and Administration, the following messages would also be sources of potential duplicate messages Table 17.3:

Table 17.3 Input-Case Test Cases

Test Case	Messages	Source/Destination
1	m4	Account Creation/Foodie Home
2	m1	Foodie Home/Account Creation
3	m8	Administration/Foodie Database
4	m14	Administration/Foodie Database
5	m36	Administration/Foodie Database
6	m9	Foodie Database/Administration
7	m10	Foodie Database/Administration
8	m15	Foodie Database/Administration
9	m32	Foodie Database/Administration
10	m33	Foodie Database/Administration
11	m34	Foodie Database/Administration
12	m35	Foodie Database/Administration

17.2.2 *Output Conflict*

Similar to input conflict, output-based conflict transpires when there are two conflicting transitions. However, in the case of output-based conflict, it is the actions of two different transitions that conflict, often in the form of output or assigning conflicting values, rather than a conflict based on the same or simultaneous input events or messages.

For example, consider the Foodie Database. While the FSMs defined in Appendix B document the behavior of the Foodies Wish List system, the Foodies Database is a single storage point. Consider a family that shares a single Foodies Wish List account where two people are adding and removing things from the card at the same time. In this case, the Shopping List and Shopping Card FSMs have multiple instantiations, one for each shopper, as shown in Figure 17.3.

In Figure 17.3 above, the set of possible interactions is based on the multiple instantiations of Shopping List and Shopping Card. Given the duplication of the instantiations of Shopping List and Shopping Card, the following messages would also be sources of potential duplicate messages Table 17.4:

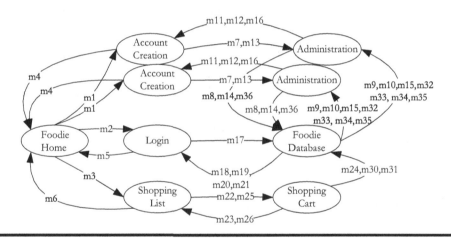

Figure 17.3   Message Communication Among Multiple Instantiations of Finite State Machines.

Table 17.4   Input-Case Test Cases

Test Case	Messages	Source/Destination
1	*m6*	*Shopping List/Foodie Home*
2	*m3*	*Foodie Home/Shopping List*
3	*m24*	*Shopping Card/Foodie Database*
4	*m30*	*Shopping Card/Foodie Database*
5	*m31*	*Shopping Card/Foodie Database*

Table 17.5 Foodie Database Events

Event	Shopping Cart 1	Shopping Cart 2	Foodie Database
1	User 1 adds Vanilla beans		
2		User 2 adds Almas Caviar	
3		m30 to Foodie Database	$11,400.00 Price
4	m30 to Foodie Database		$112.00 Price
5	m31 to Foodie Database		$112.00 Price Vanilla Beans Contents
6		m31 to Foodie Database	$112.00 Price Almas Caviar Contents

Messages m30 ("Payment amount") and m31 ("Shopping Cart Contents") inform the Foodie Database of the cost and the contents of the shopping card. Consider the following events in Table 17.5:

Since the system cannot control the order of events between the parallel instantiations of the shopping cart, it is possible that the price and cost is overwritten for the same user due to a conflict that (in this case) greatly benefits the shopper. Instead of paying $11,400 for a pound of Almas caviar, they are able to purchase it for the price-per-pound of vanilla beans at only $112 a pound.

This output interaction caused by two conflicting actions could be fixed by either:

- Limiting each account to one user logged in at a time, or
- Assigning each order a unique order number rather than storing a single order per customer.

While the FSMs and message view would still identify the possible interaction, testing would indicate that the interaction does not take place and cause a negative impact on the system.

17.2.3 Resource Conflict

Not all interactions are problematic. Often, a change in how the software behaves based on previous or other changes is not only expected but required. Consider the case of a coffee aficionado exploring unique coffee flavors. If the shopper purchased Kopi Luwak coffee, the inventory would be updated to reduce the quantity of coffee due to purchase. Table 17.6 shows the inventory before and after the purchase.

Since the unique Kopi Luwak Coffee made from the undigested coffee beans that remain after the coffee cherry is eaten and digested by civet, replenishing stock is a slow process. However, the shopper (or any other shopper) would be prevented from purchasing the coffee due to a previous interaction that effects how the software will continue to operate.

While not all resource conflicts are desirable, it is important to test for both the negative and positive interactions within a system.

Table 17.6   Foodies Wish List.inventory before and after purchase

Item ID	Name	Before Purchase	After Purchase
1	Vanilla beans	14	14
2	Hop shoots	7	7
3	Italian white truffles:	10	10
4	Kobe beef	8	8
5	Kopi Luwak coffee	1	0
6	Moose House cheese	11	11
7	Saffron	7	7
8	Jamon Iberico de Belotta	3	3
9	Almas caviar	12	12

17.3 A Taxonomy of Interactions

In addition to the types of interactions in the previous section, two aspects of location, time and position, form the starting point of a useful taxonomy of interaction to further classify the types of interactions. Certain interactions are completely independent of time; for example, two data items that interact exhibit their interaction regardless of time. Certain time-dependent interactions also occur, such as when something is a prerequisite for something else. We will refer to time-independent interactions as static and time-dependent interactions as dynamic. We can refine the static/dynamic dichotomy with the distinction between single and multiple processors yielding four categories in which the previous types of interactions (i.e., input-, output-, and resource-interactions) can occur:

Static interactions in a single processor
Static interactions in multiple processors
Dynamic interactions in a single processor
Dynamic interactions in multiple processors

17.3.1 Static Interactions in a Single Processor

Of the five basic constructs, only two have no duration — ports and data. Ports are physical devices; therefore, we can view them as separate processors and thereby simplify our discussion. Port devices interact in physical ways, such as space and power consumption, but this is usually not important to testers. Data items interact in logical ways (as opposed to physical), and these are important to testers. In an informal way, we often speak of corrupt data and of maintaining the integrity of a database. We sometimes get a bit more precise and speak of incompatible or even inconsistent data. We can be very specific if we borrow some terms from Aristotle. (We finally have a chance to use the propositional logic discussed in Chapter 3.)

In the following definitions, let p and q be propositions about data items. As examples, we might take p and q to be:

> p: AccountBalance = $10.00
> q: CartBalance < $1800.00

Definition

Propositions p and q are:

> Contraries if they cannot both be true
> Sub-contraries if they cannot both be false
> Contradictories if exactly one is true
> q is a sub-altern of p if the truth of p guarantees the truth of q

These relationships are known to logicians as the "square of opposition," which is shown in Figure 17.4, where p, q, r, and s are all propositions.

Aristotelian logic seems arcane for software testers, but here are some situations that are exactly characterized by data interactions in the square of opposition:

■ When the precondition for a thread is a conjunction of data propositions, contrary or contradictory data values will prevent thread execution.
■ Context-sensitive port input events usually involve contradictory (or at least, contrary) data.
■ If/else statements are contradictories.
■ Rules in a decision table are contradictories.

Static interactions in a single processor are exactly analogous to combinatorial circuits; they are also well represented by decision tables and unmarked event-driven Petri nets (EDPNs). Features in telephone systems are good examples of interaction (Zave, 1993). One example is the logical conflict between a caller ID service and unlisted directory numbers. With caller ID, the directory number of the source of a telephone call is provided to the called party. A conflict occurs when a party with an unlisted directory number makes a call to a party with caller ID. Which takes precedence—the caller's desire for privacy or the called party's right to know who is placing an incoming call? These two features are contraries: they cannot both be satisfied, but either or both could be waived. Call waiting service and data line

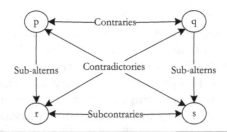

Figure 17.4   Square of Opposition.

conditioning comprise another example of contrary features. In the past, when a business (or home computing enthusiast) pays for a specially conditioned data line, calls on that line are frequently used for the transmission of formatted binary data. If such a line also has call waiting service, if a call is made to the line that is already in use, a call waiting tone is superimposed onto the preexisting connection. If the connection had been transmitting data, the transmission would be corrupted by the call waiting tone. In this case, the resolution is easier. The customer disables the call waiting service before making data transmission calls.

17.3.2 Static Interactions in Multiple Processors

The location of data helps resolve the contraries in the telephone system examples. We would expect that the data for call waiting and data line conditioning are located in the same processor because both refer to the same subscriber line. Thus, the software that controls calls for that line could check for contrary line data. This is an unreasonable expectation for the calling party identification problem, however. Suppose the calling party is a line in an office remote from the office that serves the line with calling party identification. Because these data are in separate locations (processors), neither knows about the other; so their contrary nature can only be detected when they are connected by a thread. To be very precise, we can say that the contrary relationship exists as a static interaction across multiple processors, and it becomes a failure when executing threads in the two telephone offices (processors) interact.

Call forwarding provides a better example of a static, distributed interaction. Suppose we have three telephones in three separate locations for a single person:

Phone A is an office phone in Allendale, Michigan.
Phone B is a home phone in Rockford, Michigan.
Phone C is a cell phone with a mobile location.

We further suppose that each subscriber has call forwarding service, and that calls are forwarded as follows: calls to A are forwarded to B, calls to B are forwarded to C, and calls to C are forwarded to A.

This call forwarding data is contrary—they cannot all be true. Call forwarding data is local to the telephone office that provides the service; it is set by a thread when a subscriber defines a new forwarding destination. This means that none of the offices knows of call forwarding data in the other offices; we have distributed contraries. This is a fault, but it does not become a failure until someone (other than A, B, or C) places a call to any phone in this call forwarding loop. Such a call, say to subscriber B, generates a call forwarding thread in B's local telephone office, which results in a call to C's directory number. This generates another thread in C's telephone office, and so on. For now, please note that the existence of the connecting threads moves us out of the static quadrants and into dynamic interactions. The potential failure still exists; it is just in a different part of our taxonomy.

The bottom line is that static interactions are essentially the same, whether they are centralized into a single processor or distributed among multiple processors. (They are harder to detect when they are distributed, however.) Another common form of static interactions occurs with weak relationships and functional dependencies in a database (centralized or distributed). Both of these interactions are forms of subalternation.

17.3.3 Dynamic Interactions in a Single Processor

While static interactions occur regardless of timing, dynamic interactions require consideration of the implications of time. Among other things, this means we must expand from the data-only interactions to interactions among data, events, and threads. We also must shift from the strictly declarative relationships in the square of opposition to a more imperative view. The notion of n-connectedness in a directed graph (see Chapter 4) serves perfectly. Figure 17.5 shows the four forms of n-connectedness in a directed graph.

Even the data–data interactions exhibit forms of n-connectedness. Data that are logically independent are 0-connected, and subalternates are 2-connected. The other three relationships, contraries, contradictories, and sub-contraries, all pertain to 3-connected data, because each of these is a bidirectional relationship. Six potential pairs of concepts can interact: data–data, data–events, data–threads, events–events, events–threads, and threads–threads. Each of these is further qualified by four degrees of n-connectedness, resulting in 24 elements to our taxonomy for this quadrant. Take some time to think through these interactions. Here are four examples:

1-connected data with data: occurs when two or more data items are inputs to the same action
2-connected data with data: occurs when a data item is used in a computation (as in dataflow testing)
3-connected data with data: occurs when data are deeply related, as in repetition and semaphores
1-connected data with events: context-sensitive port input events

We do not need to analyze all 24 possibilities because faults of interaction only become failures when threads establish some connection. The faults are latent; and when a thread makes a connection, the latent fault becomes a failure. Threads can

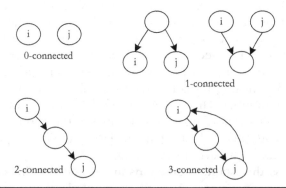

Figure 17.5 Forms of n-connectedness.

only interact in two ways, via events or via data. We will see this more clearly using EDPNs after we make another definition.

Definition

In an EDPN, the *external inputs* (ports or data) are the places with indegree = 0, and the external outputs are the places with outdegree = 0.

In the EDPN in Figure 17.6, p1, p2, and d1 are the only external inputs, and p3, p4, and d3 are the only external outputs. As shown here, data places d1 and d3 are preconditions and postconditions; they are external inputs and outputs, respectively. The best description is that the indegrees of external inputs and the outdegrees of external outputs are always 0.

Now we are at a key point: we can represent the interaction among threads by the composition of their EDPNs. We do this as follows: each thread has its own (unique) EDPN, and within each EDPN, the places and transitions have symbolic names. In one sense, these names are local to the thread; but in a larger sense (when they are composed), local names must be resolved into global synonyms. However, for the input-, output-, and resource-conflicts explored above, we must first describe the threads as EDPNs rather than FSMs. For example, the FSM fragment in Figure 17.7 represents a transition and action between two states (s_1 to s_2) when an event occurs and causes an action.

As a petri-net, Figure 17.7 is represented in Figure 17.8 as two places that pass a single token between them (s1 to s2) and trigger an output action (A) when an event (E) occurs.

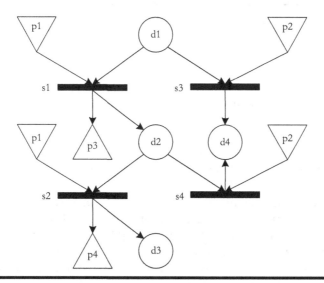

Figure 17.6   External inputs and outputs in an EDPN.

Figure 17.7   FSM Fragment.

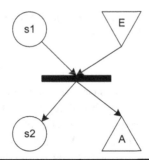

Figure 17.8   Petri-Net Conversion of FSM Fragment.

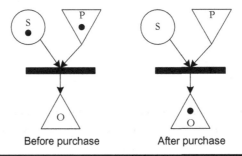

Figure 17.9   Petri-Net Coffee Purchase.

Consider the case of the resource-conflict in Section 17.2.3. We can model the thread for each purchase of coffee in Figure 17.9. S represents the current supply and P, the purchase event, respectively. When a purchase, P, occurs, the petri-net transition fires using the tokens in S and P and causing an output event (O) representing the results of the purchase. As a single thread, no conflict exists in this instantiation. However, the previously discussed resource-conflict chains *two* of these threads together.

The same action: purchasing is attempted twice, in series, resulting in differing results due to the interaction. The left side of Figure 17.10 is a petri-net that represents the initial state of two places (i.e., p1 and p2), each representing the purchase event (P) of coffee. Place S represents a limited supply of coffee. Identical to our resource-conflict, purchasing the single stock of coffee depletes the supply as shown on the right side. Since firing the first purchase transition consumes the token in S (and the coffee!), the second purchase attempt is disabled.

As expected, the second purchase is unable to occur due to the depleted resource. Analyzing the connection between each of the nodes, and we can see that our supply (S) is 1-connected to both purchase action transitions. Place p2 is an interlock that forces the sequence of purchases, but the second purchase is prevented by place S having no tokens.

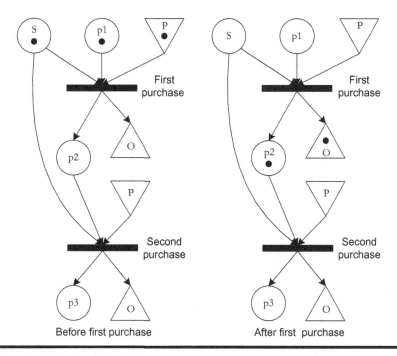

Figure 17.10   Dual Purchase Petri-Net.

17.3.4 Dynamic Interactions in Multiple Processors

While the previous dynamic interaction in a single processor required petri-nets to illustrate the resource-driven conflict over data, input- and output-conflicts can be defined less formally. While still making using of the concept of connectedness, consider the input- and output-conflicts presented above. As previously discussed, the Foodies Wish List operates as multiple instances on potentially multiple processors. However, even on a single processor, the parallel threads of execution operate independently and non-deterministically. For example, in the FSM fragment from Figure 17.2, we can see that both the states *Foodie Home* and *Foodie Database* are 1-connected to multiple instances of *Account Creation* and *Administration*, respectively. (Figure 17.11).

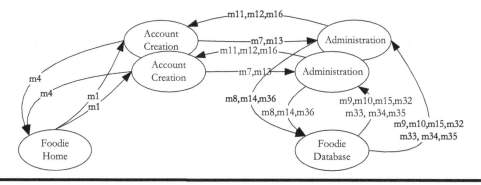

Figure 17.11   FSM Fragment from Figure 17.2.

Due to the parallel execution of the administration and account creation modules, but only one instance of the FoodieDB, the additional threads caused an input-conflict due to conflicting messages sent to the Foodie Database in a nondeterministic order.

17.4 Interaction, Composition, and Determinism

The question of nondeterminism looms as a backdrop to deep questions in science and philosophy. Einstein did not believe in nondeterminism; he once commented that he doubted that God would play dice with the universe. Nondeterminism generally refers to consequences of random events, asking, in effect, if there are truly random events (inputs), can we ever predict their consequences? The logical extreme of this debate ends in the philosophical/theological question of free will versus predestination. Fortunately for testers, the software version of nondeterminism is less severe. You might want to consider this section to be a technical editorial. It is based on our experience and analysis using the EDPN framework. We find it yields reasonable answers to the problem of nondeterminism; you may too.

Let us start with a working definition if determinism; here are two possibilities:

A system is deterministic if, given its inputs, we can always predict its outputs.
A system is deterministic if it always produces the same outputs for a given set of inputs.

The second view (repeatable outputs) is less stringent than the first (predictable outputs), therefore, we will use it as our working definition. Then a nondeterministic system is one in which there is at least one set of inputs that results in two distinct sets of outputs. It is easy to devise a nondeterministic finite state machine; Figure 17.12 is one example (we will see a better example inn Chapter 18).

If it is so easy to create a nondeterministic finite state machine, why all the fuss about determinism in the first place? Recall that in Chapter 12, we took great pains to separate the reality of a system from models of the system's behavior. Finite state machines are models of reality; they only approximate the behavior of a real system. This is why it is so important to choose an appropriate model—we would like to use the best approximation. Roughly speaking, decision tables are the model of choice for static interactions, finite state machines suffice for dynamic interactions in a single processor, and some form of Petri nets is needed for dynamic interactions in multiple processors. Before going on, we should indicate instances of nondeterminism in the

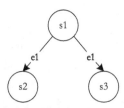

Figure 17.12 A nondeterministic finite state machine.

other two models. A multiple-hit decision table is one in which the inputs (variables in the condition stub) are such that more than one rule is selected. In Petri nets, non-determinism occurs when more than one transition is enabled. The choice of which rule executes or which transition fires is made by an external agent. Notice that the choice is actually another (subtle, often unstated) input.

Exercises

In exercises 1, 2, and 3, assume that feature interaction occurs among sets of feature threads (usually just 2) that are modeled as Event-Driven Petri Nets (EDPNs). For convenience, you may refer to EDPN 1 and EDPN 2 as the EDPNs of threads of interacting features.

1. Describe the n-connectivity of threads in Section 17.2.1, Input Conflict.
2. Describe the n-connectivity of threads in Section 17.2.2, Output Conflict.
3. Describe the n-connectivity of threads in Section 17.2.3, Resource Conflict.
4. Find instances of 2-connected features in the Foodies Wish List example? Any 3-connected examples?
5. Find instances of the Enable prompt among features in the Foodies Wish List.
6. Find instances of the Disable prompt among features in the Foodies Wish List.
7. Find instances of the Trigger prompt among features in the Foodies Wish List.
8. Revisit the Windshield Wiper Controller, this time considering the Lever as one feature and the Dial as a second feature. Find examples of the Enable and Disable prompts between Lever and Dial features.

References

Sven Apel, et al. "Feature interactions: the next generation (dagstuhl seminar 14,281) (n.d.).

D. Batory, D. Benavides, and A. Ruiz-Cortes, "Automated analysis of feature models: challenges ahead," *Communications of the ACM*, vol. 49, no. 12 (2006): 45–47.

Muffy Calder, et al. "Feature interaction: a critical review and considered forecast." *Computer Networks* vol. 41, no. 1 (2003), pp. 115–141. http://classics.mit.edu/Aristotle/metaphysics.8.viii.html.

Pamela Zave. "Feature interactions and formal specifications in telecommunications." *Computer*, vol. 26, no. 8 (1993): 20–28.

Chapter 18

Case Study: Testing Event-Driven Systems

Event-driven systems are exactly what David Harel [Harel 1988] defined as "reactive systems"—they are "long running" and they "maintain a relationship with their environment." Here are some additional characteristics of embedded systems that have implications for system testing:

- input events may be generated asynchronously,
- input events may come from separate devices,
- input events may occur as interrupts,
- input events may have a short duration (*i.e.*, scanning may be necessary),
- processing time for an input event may cause subsequent input events to be ignored (quick example: an impatient hotel guest who presses an elevator call button repeatedly),
- input events may be context sensitive,
- input and output devices may fail,
- independent input and output devices can/should be considered as constituents of a System of Systems.

Due to these characteristics, many of the traditional testing techniques do not directly apply. Instead, the Model-Based Testing approaches are more appropriate. In this chapter, we apply three modeling techniques to a Garage Door Controller: Behavior Driven Development, Finite State Machines, and an extension of Event-Driven Petri Nets that is appropriate for System of Systems. As we progress through the models, we discuss the extent to which they are helpful to testers. As expected, more sophisticated models support more thorough testing. Some of the material is this chapter is taken from *The Craft of Model-Based Testing* [Jorgensen 2017].

18.1 The Garage Door Controller Problem Statement

A system to open a garage door is comprised of several components: a drive motor, the garage door wheel tracks with sensors at the open and closed positions, and a control device. In addition, there are two safety features, a laser beam near the floor, and an obstacle sensor. These latter two devices operate only when the garage door is closing. While the door is closing, if either the light beam is interrupted (possibly by a pet) or if the door encounters an obstacle, the door immediately stops, and then reverses direction. To reduce the size of our models, only the light beam sensor is considered. The corresponding analyses for the obstacle sensor are almost identical. When the door is in motion, either closing or opening, and a signal from the control device occurs, the door stops. A subsequent control signal starts the door in the same direction as when it was stopped. (This is contrary to many garage door systems; it is added here because it lets us illustrate an interesting point.) Finally, there are sensors that detect when the door has moved to one of the extreme positions, either fully open or fully closed. When either of these occurs, the door stops. Figure 18.1 is a SysML context diagram of the garage door controller. In most garage door systems, there are several control devices: a digital keyboard mounted outside the door, a separately powered button inside the garage, and possibly several in-car signaling devices. For simplicity, we collapse these redundant signal sources into one device. Similarly, since the two safety devices generate the same response, we will drop consideration of the obstacle sensor and just consider the light beam device.

18.2 Modeling with Behavior Driven Development (BDD)

In Chapter 11, we have an example of deriving a decision table from a BDD scenario. The BDD process centers on user stories that have a structure that translates easily into a decision table. The Chapter 11 discussion follows an example from Dan North, an early proponent of BDD [Terhorst-North 2006]. If we try to use BDD scenarios for event-driven systems, where order is important, we need to make a more formal definition of a BDD scenario:

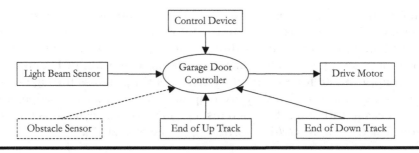

Figure 18.1   SysML diagram of the garage door controller.

Definition

A *well-formed BDD scenario* has the following sections and structure:

> Short ID.
> IF   (<pre-condition(s)>),
> AND   (<data condition(s)>),
> AND   (<input event sequence>),
> THEN (action sequence),
> AND   (<output event sequence>),
> AND   (<post-condition(s>).

We next apply this structure to a few well-formed BDD scenarios for The Garage Door Controller. Our short identifier will be GDCn (for Garage Door Controlle

GDC1		GDC2	
IF	the garage door is Up,	IF	the garage door is closing
AND	a control signal occurs	AND	the End of Down Track signal occurs
THEN	start the motor in the Down direction	THEN	stop the motor
AND	the Door is Closing.	AND	the garage door is Down.
GDC3		GDC4	
IF	the garage door is closing	IF	the garage door is stopped part-way
AND	a control signal occurs	AND	a control signal occurs
THEN	stop the motor	THEN	start the motor in the Down direction
AND	the garage door is stopped part-way	AND	the Door is Closing

Looking at these first four BDD scenarios, we can see three important parts of the Garage Door Controller:

1. Conditions of the door: Up, Closing, Stopped part-way, and Down.
2. Input events: e1: control signal and e2: End of Down Track
3. Actions: a1: Start motor down, a3: Stop motor.

Table 18.1 is a decision table that reflects these four BDD scenarios.

Four test cases are implied by the extended entry decision table in Table 18.1. The first test case is in Table 18.2.

Table 18.1 Decision table derived from GDC1, GDC2, GDC3, and GDC4

c2. Event is	control signal	end of down track	control signal	end of down track	control signal	end of down track
a1. Start motor down	x	—	—	—	x	—
a2. Stop motor	—	—	x	x	—	—
a3. Impossible	—	x	—	—	—	x
BDD Scenario	GDC1		GDC3	GDC2	GDC4	

Table 18.2 BDD Test Case Derived from the Decision Table of Four BDD Scenarios

BDD TC-1	Test case from BDD Scenario 1
Description	When the Garage door is up and a control signal occurs, start the drive motor down.
Pre-condition	Garage door is UP
Input Events	Output Events
1. Control signal	2. Start Motor down
Post-condition	Garage door is closing

18.3 Modeling with Extended Finite State Machines

There are two fundamentally opposed approaches to defining a problem with finite state machines—the bottom-up approach common to agile development and the more traditional top-down approach. Both approaches have advantages and disadvantages, but that discussion diverges from this chapter.

18.3.1 Deriving a Finite State Machine from BDD Scenarios

If we examine the first four BDD scenarios, we can identify input events, output actions, and states of an eventual finite state machine. Doing so, we arrive at the (extended) finite state machine in Figure 18.2. (The black dot shows the initial state.)

Input events	Output events (actions)	States
e1: control signal	a1: start drive motor down	s1: Door Up
e2: end of down track hit	a2: start drive motor up	s2: Door Down
	a3: stop drive motor	s3: Door is closing
		s4: Door stopped part way

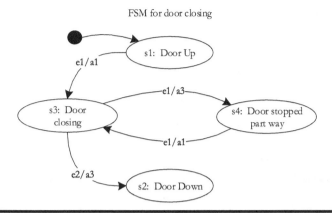

Figure 18.2 **Finite State Machine Derived from BDD scenarios GDC1, GDC2, GDC3, and GDC4.**

The four BDD scenarios are present in Figure 18.2 as follows:

1. GDC1 is the state sequence <s1, s3>
2. GDC2 is the state sequence <s3, s2>
3. GDC3 is the state sequence <s3, s4>
4. GDC4 is the state sequence <s4, s3>

If we executed our BDD scenarios as a sequence <GDC1, GDC3, GDC4, GDC2 >, we have formed a path that traverses every state and every transition in Figure 18.2. The only redundancies are the control signal e1 and the stop motor action a3.

Our first four BDD scenarios have very similar scenarios for a closed door:

GDC5		GDC6	
IF	the garage door is Down	IF	the garage door is opening
AND	a control signal occurs	AND	the End of Up Track signal occurs
THEN	start the motor in the Up direction	THEN	stop the motor
AND	the Door is Opening.	AND	the garage door is Up.
GDC7		GDC8	
IF	the garage door is Opening	IF	the garage door is stopped part-way
AND	a control signal occurs	AND	a control signal occurs
THEN	stop the motor	THEN	start the motor in the Up direction
AND	the garage door is stopped part-way	AND	the Door is Opening

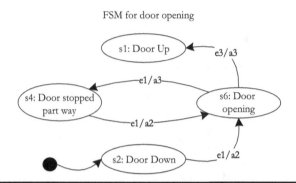

Figure 18.3 Finite State Machine Derived from BDD scenarios GDC5, GDC6, GDC7, and GDC8.

Scenarios GDC5 through GDC8 lead us to the finite state machine in Figure 18.3. They also yielded one new state s6:Door Opening, a new input event e3: end of up track, and one new action a2: start motor Up.

We have reached an interesting example of an inherent problems of bottom-up development. The first four scenarios and the associated finite state machine are correct when taken by themselves, similarly for the second four scenarios. However, when we try to compose the two partial finite state machines, as in Figure 18.4, the result is a non-deterministic finite state machine. When the garage door is in state s4: Door stopped part way, what happens when event e1: Control signal occurs? Does action a1: start drive motor down occur, or does a2: start drive motor up occur? We would hope this inconsistency would be detected by integration testing, but it might not be found until system testing. Part of the reason for this is every bottom-up approach forces a form of "tunnel vision" in which we only gradually see whole picture.

18.3.2 Top-down development of a Finite State Machine

Behavior-Driven Development gave us a good start, but it is time to move to a more sophisticated model—a top-down process. Given the problem statement in Section 18.1, we look for parts of the statement that refer to states, input events, and actions on transition. The components of our system are a starting point to find input events and actions. Signals from the control device(s) are the obvious input event, as is the signal when the light beam is crossed. We also see that there are sensors marking the ends of the track in the up and down directions. The only actions are with respect to the drive motor: start in the up direction, start in the down direction, stop the motor, and reverse the motor direction from down to up. The states of the Garage Door are as they were in the BDD approach: Door is Open, Door is Closed, Door is Opening, Door is Closing, and the problematic Door is Stopped Part-Way.

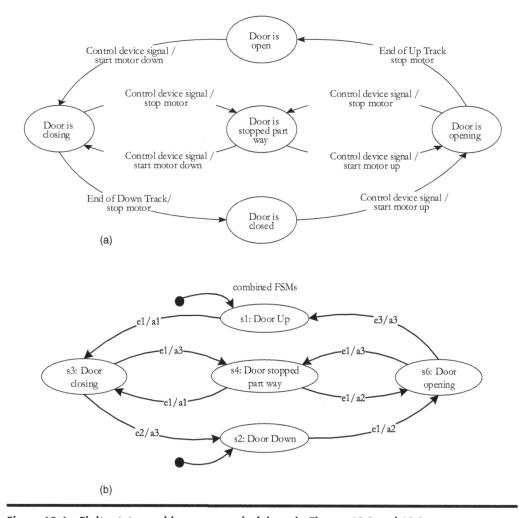

Figure 18.4 Finite state machine composed of those in Figures 18.2 and 18.3.

Input events	Output events (actions)	States
e1: control signal	a1: start drive motor down	s1: Door Up
e2: end of down track hit	a2: start drive motor up	s2: Door Down
e3: end of up track hit	a3: stop drive motor	s3: Door stopped part way
e4: light beam crossed	a4: reverse motor down to up	s4: Door closing
		s5: Door opening

Using just these five states, we would get the non-deterministic finite state machine in Figure 18.4.

It is a fair question to ask when we, as modelers, would recognize the problem in Figure 18.4. If we were lucky, we would recognize the non-determinism immediately. If there were a requirements inspection, the problem would (should!) be found there. If the model was given to the Customer/User as an executable specification, the Customer/User might find the problem. The last resort would be deriving test cases from the model and having unexpected output results. Assuming that, somewhere along the line, the non-determinism was discovered, the most likely correction is a more precise set of states: s1: Door Up, s2: Door Down, s3: Door stopped going down, s4: Door stopped going up, s5: Door closing, and s6: Door opening, as in Figure 18.5.

Given this finite state machine, we follow paths which are early indicators of full system test cases. The simplest way to describe paths is by state traversal sequences, as in Table 18.3. Each such path can then be expressed as a Use Case showing the interleaved sequences of input events and expected output actions. The example in Table 18.4 is for a "soap opera" path (one that is as long and complicated). Notice that the pre- and post-conditions are states in the finite state machine. This corresponds nicely to our earlier definition of a well-formed BDD scenario.

Use case FSM-UC-1 contains five of the six states, three of the four input events, and all four output actions. (Incidentally, this would serve as an excellent regression test cases, because, if it passes, most of the elements of interest are shown to be correct.)

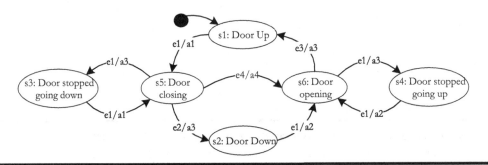

Figure 18.5 Corrected finite state machine for the Garage Door Controller.

Table 18.3 Mapping Paths in the Finite State Machine to State Sequences

Path	Description	State Sequence
p1	Normal door close	s1, s5, s2
p2	Normal door close with one intermediate stop	s1, s5, s3, s5, s2
p3	Normal door open	s2, s6, s1
p4	Normal door open with one intermediate stop	s2, s6, s4, s6, s1
p5	Closing door with light beam interruption	s1, s5, s6, s1
p6	Soap opera test case	s1, s5, s3, s5, s6, s4, s6, s1

Using the automated test execution system described in Chapter 13, the Soap Opera test case would be the following sequence of Cause and Verify statements.

Test Execution Script for test case FSM-UC-1

Pre-conditions: 1. Garage door is Up

1. **Cause** the input event *e1: control signal* **On** the *Control Device*
2. **Verify** that the output event *a1: start drive motor down* occurs **On** the *Motor*
3. **Cause** the input event *e1: control signal* **On** the *Control Device*
4. **Verify** that the output event *a3: stop drive motor* occurs **On** the *Motor*
5. **Cause** the input event *e1: control signal* **On** the *Control Device*
6. **Verify** that the output event *a1: start drive motor down* occurs **On** the *Motor*
7. **Cause** the input event *e4: laser beam crossed*
8. **Verify** that the output event *a4: reverse motor down to up* occurs **On** the *Motor*
9. **Cause** the input event *e1: control signal* **On** the *Control Device*
10. **Verify** that the output event *a2: stop drive motor* occurs **On** the *Motor*
11. **Cause** the input event *e1: control signal* **On** the *Control Device*
12. **Verify** that the output event *a2: start motor up* occurs **On** the *Motor*
13. **Cause** the input event *e3: end of up track hit*
14. **Verify** that the output event *a3: stop drive motor* occurs **On** the *Motor*

Post-conditions: 1. Garage door is up

Table 18.4   Soap Opera Use Case for a Long Path in Figure 18.5

Use Case Name:	Garage Door Controller Soap Opera Use Case	
Use Case ID:	FSM-UC-1	
Description:	Use case for the state sequence <s1, s5, s3, s5, s6, s4, s6, s1>.	
Pre-conditions:	1. Garage Door is Up	
Event Sequence:	**Input Event**	**System Response**
	1. e1: control signal	2. a1: start drive motor down
	3. e1: control signal	4. a3: stop drive motor
	5. e1: control signal	6. a1: start drive motor down
	7. e4: laser beam crossed	8. a4: reverse motor down to up
	9. e1: control signal	10. a2: stop drive motor
	11. e1: control signal	12. a2: start drive motor up
	13. e3: end of up track hit	14. a3: stop drive motor
Post-conditions:	1. Garage Door is Up	

Table 18.5   System-Level, Model-Based Test Coverage Metrics

Test Cover	A Set of Test Cases that	Paths (from Table 18.3)
STC_S	traverses every state	p2, p4
STC_{IE}	uses every input event	p1, p3 p5
STC_{OA}	produces every output action	p1, p3 p5
STC_T	traverses every transition	p2, p4, p5
STC_{PATH}	traverses every path (cycles only once)	p1,p2, p3, p4, p5, p6
STC_∞	traverses every path (repeat cycles <s5, s3> and < s6, s4) > in paths p2 and p4)	Paths containing <s5, s3> and/or < s6, s4)

One of the insights that we gain from finite state machines is that we can recognize context-sensitive input events. Notice that the input event e1: control signal occurs in three different states, with three different system action responses. The finite state machine formulation supports the identification of a set of system level test coverage metrics. Recall that a finite state machine is a directed graph, so we can re-use (and rename) the graph-based test covers developed in Chapter 8. The test coverage metrics defined in Table 18.5 all refer to a given system modeled with a finite state machine. They relate a set of test cases to the test cover metric. Because input events, output actions, states, and transitions are closely coupled, these test coverage metrics overlap with sets of test cases.

18.4 Modeling with Swim Lane Event-Driven Petri Nets

Moving from finite state machines from Event-Driven Petri Nets (EDPNs) (as in Chapter 4) permits a more precise examination of the garage door controller. The system is modeled as a "Swim Lame EDPN" to examine the modes of interaction among the devices in the Garage Door Controller. Finally, we examine failure modes of the light beam mechanism. Some of the material in this subsection appeared in [Jorgensen 2015].

Definition [DeVries 2013]: A *swim lane marked Petri net* is a 7-tuple (P, T, I, O, M, L, N) in which (P, T, I, O, M), is a marked Petri net and L is a set of n sets, where

P is the set of places,
T is the set of transitions,
I is the input mapping of places in P to transitions in T, is the output mapping of transitions in T to places in P,
M is a marking that maps natural numbers to places in P

n ≥ 1 is the number of swim lanes,
L is the union of the places in the n lanes, and
N is the union of the transitions in the n lanes.

Two easy secondary definitions follow almost directly.

Definition

A *swim lane (ordinary) Petri net* is a 6-tuple (P, T, I, O, L, N) in which (P, T, I, O), is an ordinary Petri net (as in Chapter 5). The elements of the 6-tuple are as in the first definition.

Definition

A *swim lane Event-Driven Petri NET (SWEDPN)* is a 7-tuple (P, D, T, In, Out, L, N) in which (P, D, T, In, Out) is an Event-Driven Petri Net (EDPN) (as in Chapter 4). The elements of the 7-tuple are as in the first definition.

In the next three subsections, we develop the Swim Lane Event-Driven Petri Nets for these scenarios: a normal door closing, a door closing with an intermediate stop, and a door closing with a light beam crossing. These correspond to paths p1, p2, p3, and p5 in Table 18.3. Section 18.4.4 contains an extended version of the Door Opening mechanism as a prelude to the failure analysis discussion in Section 18.5.

Since EDPNs refer to port input and output events, we rename the elements of our finite state machine.

Input events	Output events	States
p1: control signal	p5: start drive motor down	s1: Door Up
p2: end of down track	p6: start drive motor up	s2: Door Down
p3: end of up track	p7: stop drive motor	s3 Door Stopped Going Down
p4: laser beam crossed	p8: reverse motor down to up	s4: Door Stopped Going Up
		s5: Door Closing
		s6: Door Opening

We will name the EDPN transitions (drawn as rectangles) and the swim lanes in the accompanying figures.

18.4.1 Normal Garage Door Closing

A normal door closing (path p1 in Table 18.3) begins with the garage door in the s1: Door Up state, a point of event quiescence. If a p1: Control Signal event occurs,

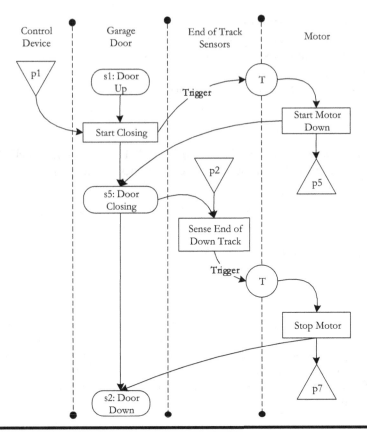

Figure 18.6   Normal Garage Door Closing.

the motor is started in the down direction (p5: start motor down), changing the door state to s5: Door Closing. (The only other event that could occur in the Door Up state would be a laser beam crossing. The mechanism that ignores this possibility is described in Section 18.4.4.) The garage door continues closing until event p2: end of down track occurs. This causes the output event p7: stop drive motor to occur, leaving the garage door in state s2: Door Down. Figure 18.6 uses the ESML Trigger prompt to start and stop the drive motor.

18.4.2 Garage Door Closing with an Intermediate Stop

This scenario (path p2 in Table 18.3) begins as the normal door closing, with the garage door in the s1: Door Up state, a point of event quiescence. If a p1: Control Signal event occurs, the motor is started in the down direction (p5: start motor down), changing the door state to s5: Door Closing. If another p1: Control Signal event occurs, a trigger is sent to the motor, causing the output event p7: stop drive motor to occur, leaving the door in state s3: stopped going down Figure 18.7.

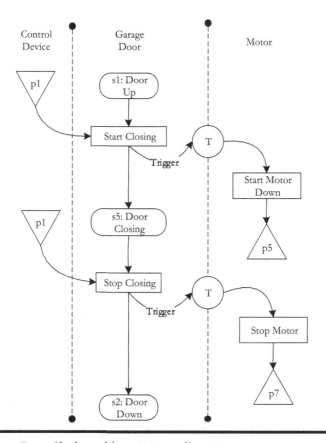

Figure 18.7   Garage Door Closing with an Intermediate Stop.

18.4.3 Garage Door Closing with a Laser Beam Crossing

This scenario (path p5 in Table 18.3) begins as a normal door closing, with the garage door in the s1: Door Up state, a point of event quiescence. If a p1: Control Signal event occurs, the motor is started in the down direction (p5: start motor down), changing the door state to s5: Door Closing. Notice that the Start Closing EDPN transition uses the ESML Enable prompt to enable the Light Beam Sensor. If a p4: laser beam crossed event occurs, this sends an ESML Trigger prompt to the output event p8: reverse motor down to up, leaving the garage door in state s6: Door Opening. We continue this scenario to include the input event p3: end of up track. When that input occurs, a Trigger is sent to the output event p7: stop motor, leaving the garage door in state s1: Door Up Figure 18.8.

18.4.4 The Door Opening Interactions

Figure 18.9 goes through the door opening with one intermediate stop sequence. The initial state is s2: Door Closed. This is a point of event quiescence. If input event p1:control signal occurs, the Start Opening transition is enabled, and when it fires, it marks place s6: Door opening, and sends the trigger prompt to the Start Motor Up transition. That transition fires immediately, marking output event p6: start drive motor up, and the garage door is moving upward. As we saw with the door closing sequence

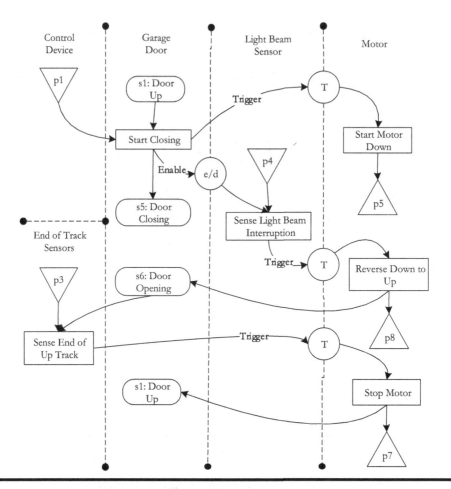

Figure 18.8 Garage Door Closing with a Light Beam Interruption.

(Figure 18.5) two input events can occur when state s6: Door Opening is marked—either p1: control signal, or p3: End of Up Track. Both cases are shown in Figure 18.9.

If event p1:control signal occurs a second time, the Stop Opening transition fires, marking place s4: Door Stopped Going Up and sending a trigger prompt to the Stop Motor transition. When that transition fires, p6 is unmarked, p7 is marked, and place s4: Door Stopped Going Up is marked.

If event p1:control signal occurs a third time, the Resume Opening transition fires, marking place s6: Door opening and sends the trigger prompt to the Start Motor Up transition. As earlier, that transition fires immediately, marking output event p6: start drive motor up and removing the mark from p7: Stop motor. The garage door is moving upward and the system is event quiescent. This is a curious situation: from a Swim Lane Event-Driven Petri Net standpoint: nothing is happening but a system tester would observe that the garage door is in motion. An extremely refined system test case might specify a time interval at this point.

If (when!) event p3: end of up track occurs, the Sense End of Up Track transition fires, sending a trigger prompt to the Stop Motor transition. When that transition fires, p6 is unmarked, p7 is marked, and place s1: Door Open is marked.

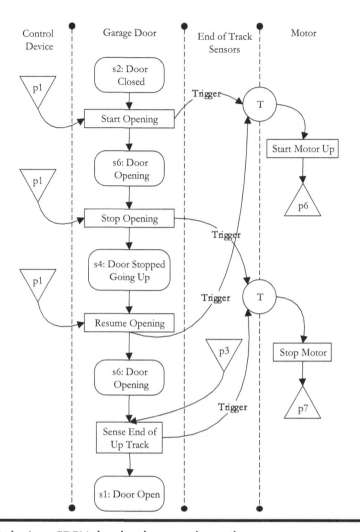

Figure 18.9   Swim Lane EDPN showing door opening options.

Two fine points need to be mentioned here. Theoretically this start/stop loop could continue indefinitely. In practice, pressing the control button is a manual operation that may take 10 milliseconds and the reaction time of the motor stopping is probably about a second. In this time, the door has moved upward a measurable distance. The practical limit on the number of repetitions of the stop/resume cycle as probably about 20. Suffice it to say, this is not an infinite loop. Second, a system test case derived from this scenario will examine the context sensitivity of p1:control signal.

18.5 Deriving Test Cases from Swim Lane Event-Driven Petri Nets

Deriving test cases from a SWEDPN is very similar to the process for deriving test cases from an ordinary EDPN. The difference is that the devices corresponding to the swim lanes need to be added to a test case. Echoing the automatic test execution

Table 18.6 System Level Test Case for Normal Door Closing

Test Case	SysTC-1: Normal door closing			
Pre-conditions	1. Garage door is open			
Cause	**Occurs On**	**Verify**	**Occurs on**	**Observed Action**
1. p1: control signal	Control Device	2. p5: start drive motor down	Motor	Motor starts in down direction. Door begins to close
3. p2: end of down track hit	End of Track Sensors	4. p7: stop drive motor	Motor	Motor stopped. Door is closed
Post-conditions	1. Garage door is closed			

system briefly described in Chapter 13, here is a short test case corresponding the test case in Table 18.6. Reserved words are on bold font, and arguments must be selected from a pre-defined list (italic font). Noise words are permitted for readability (normal font).

Test Execution Script for test case SysTC-1.
Pre-conditions: 1. Garage door is open

Cause the input event *p1: control signal* **On** the *Control Device*
Verify that the output event *p5: start drive motor down* occurs **On** the *Motor*.
Cause the input event *p2: end of down track hit* **On** the *End of Track Sensors*
Verify that the output event *p7: stop drive motor* occurs **On** the drive *Motor*

Post-conditions: 1. Garage door is closed

Depending on the harness used with the automatic test executor, the pre-conditions could be **Caused** and the post-conditions could be **Verified** Table 18.7.

Table 18.7 System level Test Case for Normal Door Closing with Light Beam Interruption

Test Case	SysTC-2: Normal door closing with light beam interruption			
Pre-conditions	1. Garage door is open			
Cause	**Occurs On**	**Verify**	**Occurs on**	**Observed Action**
1. p1: control signal	Control Device	2. p5: start drive motor down	Motor	Motor starts in down direction. Door begins to close
3. p4: laser beam crossed	Light Beam Sensor	4. p8: reverse motor down to up	Motor	Motor reverses direction. Door is opening
5. p3: end of up track hit	End of Track Sensors	6. p7: stop drive motor	Motor	Motor stopped. Door is open.
Post-conditions	1. Garage door is open			

18.6 Failure Mode Event Analysis (FMEA)

Failure Mode Event Analysis deals with physical devices that can fail. Devices can fail for a variety of reasons—physical deterioration, excessive heat, voltage spikes, and so on. Regardless of the underlying cause, there are three failure modes, summarized in Table 18.8.

Here we only consider the two common failure modes: Stuck At One (SA-1) and Stuck At Zero, (SA-0) for the Light Beam Sensor. If the light beam sensor is stuck at zero and the physical event p4: Light beam interruption occurs, no signal is sent. Symmetrically, if the light beam sensor is stuck at one, the signal is always sent, even when the physical event p4 does not occur. We could probably consider the intermittent failure mode by assigning probabilities to the SA-0 and SA-1 faults. It is important to remember (and model!) the fact that the physical input event can occur, but the device may fail. Figure 8.10 shows the normal operation of the light beam sensor.

Now, we consider the failure modes. We begin with the Stuck-At-Zero failure, described as a test case in Table 18.9 and a SWEDPN simulation in Figure 18.11. The Sense Interruption transition in the Light Beam Sensor track has three inputs:

1. event p4: Light beam interruption
2. the SA-0 place
3. the enable/disable input that is/should be set by the Start Closing transition in the Garage Door swim lane

If any of these three inputs is not available to the Sense Interruption transition, it cannot fire. The first case is the normal operation, in which there is no light beam interruption. Figure 18.11 simulates the second case, there is no way to mark the SA-0 place. A third possibility is that the enable/disable prompt does not occur. This is a software fault, not a Stuck-At-Zero fault of the light beam sensor.

If the Sense Interruption cannot fire, the next event will be event 3. p2: end of down track hit. This enables the Sense End of Down Track transition which, when it fires, triggers the Stop Motor transition. The motor stops, and the garage door is closed.

If test case SysTC-3 fails, a tester should try to determine the cause—the physical input event occurred, but the correct response did not occur. The SA-0 fault is a natural first choice. The SWEDPN in Figure 18.11 shows how the SA-0 fault could be simulated. Executing the SWEDPN in Figure 18.11 begins as the normal case in Figure 18.10. The difference is that the SA-0 place is not marked, and there is no transition that could possibly mark it. The Sense Interruption transition can still be enabled, and the p4: light beam interruption can still occur, but the transition can never fire. In Figure 18.11, the door will continue closing until the input event p2: occurs, and the Sense End Of Down Track fires, triggering the Stop Motor transition. The end result is that the door is closed.

Table 18.8   Device Failure Modes

Stuck at zero (SA-0)	*Stuck at one (SA-1)*	*Intermittent*
does not send a signal when it should	always sends a signal, even when it shouldn't	sometimes sends a signal when it shouldn't; sometimes does not send a signal when it should, and usually cannot be repeated

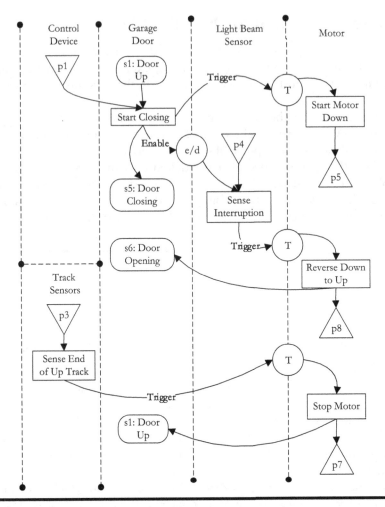

Figure 18.10 Normal operation of an interrupted light beam.

Table 18.9 System level Test Case Resqult for Door Closing with SA-0 Light Beam Sensor Fault

Test Case	SysTC-3: Normal door closing with light beam sensor SA-0 fault			
Pre-conditions	1. Garage door is open			
	2. Light beam sensor has Stuck-At-Zero fault			
Cause	*Occurs On*	*Verify*	*Occurs on*	*Observed Action*
1. p1: control signal	Control Device	2. p5: start drive motor down	Motor	Motor starts in down direction. Door begins to close.
3. p4: laser beam crossed	Light Beam Sensor	4. p8: reverse motor down to up	Motor	Motor continues in down direction
At this point, the test case fails. Test case execution should stop.				

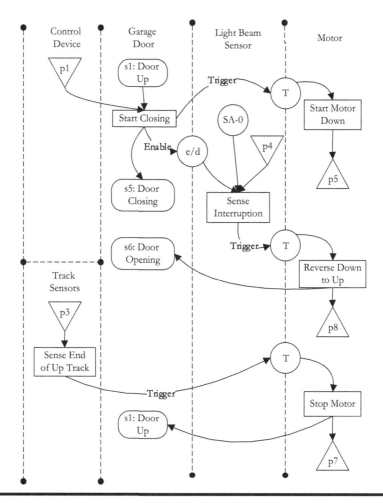

Figure 18.11   Simulating the SA-0 failure mode for the light beam sensor.

Table 18.10 describes the Stuck At 1 fault, and it is simulated in Figure 18.12. As with the SA-0 fault, once the test fails, the tester should determine the cause. Of these two faults, the SA-0 fault could potentially cause harm or injury. The SA-1 fault only makes it impossible to automatically close the garage door.

The Stuck At 1 fault is simulated in Figure 18.12. One way to simulate the SA-1 fault is to just eliminate the input event p4: light beam interruption from the SWEDPN. It is replaced with the SA-1 place. Since that place is both an input to and an output of the Sense Interruption transition, it will always be marked. Once event p1 occurs, the door starts closing, which marks the enable/disable place, thereby allowing the Sense Interruption to fire. The Trigger prompt forces the Reverse Down to Up transition to fire, and immediately the door starts opening, until the end of the up track is reached.

Simply eliminating the p4 event is an undesirable workaround. In fact, the event may or may not occur, but regardless, the trigger should be sent to the Reverse Down to Up transition. A "nicer" way to show just this part is in Figure 18.13. Notice the two connections from output event p4 in Figure 18.13. One (with the arrowhead) is the usual connection. The other, with the small circle termination, is an Inhibitor Arc, defined next.

Table 18.10   System Level Test Case Result for Door Closing with SA-1 Light Beam Sensor Fault

Test Case	SysTC-4: Normal door closing with light beam sensor SA-1 fault			
Pre-conditions	1. Garage door is open			
	2. Light beam sensor has Stuck-At-One fault			
Cause	*Occurs On*	*Verify*	*Occurs on*	*Observed Action*
1. p1: control signal	Control Device	2. p5: start drive motor down	Motor	Motor stops, Door is open. Motor reverses to up direction
At this point, the test case fails. Test case execution should stop.				

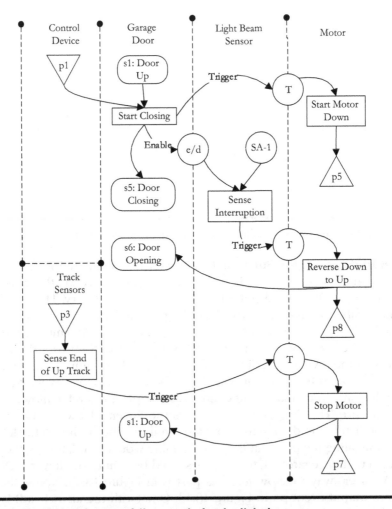

Figure 18.12   Simulating the SA-1 failure mode for the light beam sensor.

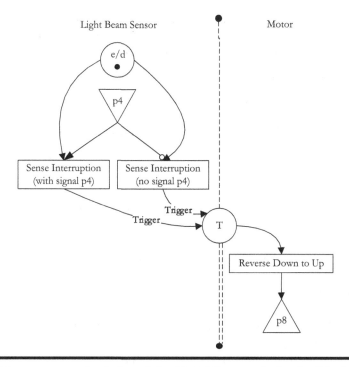

Figure 18.13 **More accurate simulation of the SA-1 failure mode for the light beam sensor.**

Definition

An *inhibitor arc* contributes to the enabling of a transition only when it is not marked.

In Figure 18.13, there are two transitions that can trigger the Reverse Down to Up transition. Assuming that the enable/disable place has already been marked (by the door closing), the port input event p4: light beam interruption either does or does not occur. If it occurs, the Sense Interruption (with signal) is enabled, and when it fires, it triggers the Reverse Down to Up transition. If the p4 event does not occur, the Sense Interruption (no signal) transition is enabled due to the inhibitor arc connection. This representation is more accurate, since the output event p4: light beam interruption is a physical event in the real world. The mechanism that reacts to the inputs and causes the trigger is the item that is Stuck At 1.

We close this chapter with a short comment on where theory meets practice. The Swim Lane EDPNs in Figures 18.11 and 18.12 are clearly very detailed and theoretically correct. Now consider a scenario based on the Automatic Test Executor (ATE) system described in Chapter 13. The first few steps would be as follows:

1. **Cause** the input event *p1: control signal* **On** the *Control Device*
2. **Verify** that the output event *p5: start drive motor down* occurs **On** the *Motor*
3. **Cause** the input event *p4:laser beam crossed* **On** the *Light Beam Sensor*
4. **Verify** that the output event *p8: reverse motor down to up* occurs **On** the *Motor*
5. **Cause** the input event *e1: control signal* **On** the *Control Device*
6. **Verify** that the output event *a1: start drive motor down* occurs **On** the *Motor*

Recall that the ATE engine has two additional verbs, **Expected** and **Observed.** At Step 2, if the light beam sensor has a Stuck-At-One fault, the engine will see **Expected** = *p5: start drive motor down* and **Observed** = *p6: start drive motor up*, and the test case will fail. At Step 4, if the light beam sensor has a Stuck-At-Zero fault, the engine will see **Expected** = *p5: start drive motor down* and **Observed** = *s5: Door Closing*, and the test case will fail.

Observed = *s5: Door Closing*, and the test case will fail

Exercises

These exercises refer to those of Chapter 14 about the Windshield Wiper controller.

1. What modifications (if any) would need to be made to the Automatic Test Execution (ATE) system of Chapter 13? Repeat your version (even if unchanged) here.
2. Use your ATE system to define actual test cases for your BDD scenarios in Chapter 14, Exercise 1.
3. Use your ATE system to define actual test cases for your Extended Entry Decision Table in Chapter 14, Exercise 2.
4. Use your ATE system to define actual test cases for your finite state machine in which states are of the form
   <lever position, dial position> in Chapter 14, Exercise 3.
5. Use your ATE system to define actual test cases for your finite state machine in which states show the wiper
   speed (0, 6, 12, 20, 30, 60in Chapter 14, Exercise 4.
6. Use your ATE system to define actual test cases for your Event-Driven Petri Net in Chapter 14, Exercise 5.
7. Compare your test cases from the two versions of a finite state machine description of the Windshield Wiper Controller (your answers to exercises 4 and 5 here). Are they the same? Should they be the same? If they are different, what implications does this have for choice of states in a finite state machine model of a given system?

References

Byron DeVries, "Mapping of UML Diagrams to Extended Petri Nets for Formal Verification", Master's Thesis, Grand Valley State University, Allendale, Michigan, April, 2013.

David Harel, On visual formalisms, *Communications of the ACM*, vol. 31, no. 5, pp. 514–530, May, 1988.

Paul C. Jorgensen, "*A Visual Formalism for Interacting Systems*" in *Proceedings of the Tenth Workshop on Model-Based Testing*, London. (MBT-2015) [(Eds.) 2015].

Paul C. Jorgensen, The Craft of Model-Based Testing, 2016.

Daniel Terhorst-North, "Introducing Behavior-Driven Development" in Better Software magazine, October, 2006.

Chapter 19

A Closer Look at All Pairs Testing

When it was first introduced, the All Pairs testing possibility was extremely popular. According to James Bach [Bach and Schroeder, 2003], over 40 journal articles and conference papers have been written about the technique. It continues to be discussed in recent books on software testing, it is in the ISTQB Advanced Level syllabi, and the practitioner conferences continue to offer tutorials on All Pairs Testing. It is tempting to say that more has been written about All Pairs Testing than is known. In this chapter, as the title implies, we take a closer look at the All Pairs testing technique, answering these questions:

- What is the All Pairs technique?
- Why is it so popular?
- When does it work well?
- When is it not appropriate?

The chapter ends with recommendations for appropriate use.

19.1 The All Pairs Technique

The All Pairs testing technique has its origins in statistical design of experiments. There, orthogonal arrays are a means of generating all pairs of experimental variables such that each pair occurs with equal probability. Mathematically, the statistical technique derives from Latin Squares [Mandl, 1985]. The NIST papers by Wallace and Kuhn [Wallace and Kuhn, 2000], [Wallace and Richard Kuhn, 2001] captured the attention of the software development community, particularly the agile community. The papers concluded that 98% of the defects in software-controlled medical systems were due to the interaction of pairs of variables.

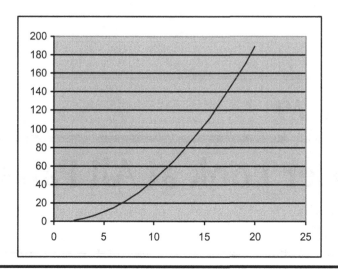

Figure 19.1   The Combinatorial Explosion.

Given a program with n input variables, the All Pairs technique is a way to identify each pair. Mathematically, this is commonly called the number of combinations of n things taken two at a time and is computed by the formula:

$$_nC_2 = (n!) / ((2!)(n-2)!)$$

which is the basis for the well-known "combinatorial explosion." The first 20 values of $_nC_2$ are graphed in Figure 19.1. With the All Pairs technique, for example, the 66 pairs of interactions among twelve variables are exercised in a single test case.

Perhaps the most commonly cited example of All Pairs testing was developed by Bernie Berger and presented at the STAREast conference in 2003 [Berger, 2003]. His paper contains a mortgage application example which has twelve input variables. (In a private email, he said that "twelve" is a simplification). Berger identified equivalence classes for the twelve variables, varying in number between seven classes for two variables to two classes for six variables. The cross-product of the equivalence classes results in 725,760 test cases. Applying the All Pairs technique, this is reduced to 50 test cases—quite a reduction.

The All Pairs technique is supported by several commercial and complimentary tools. The pairwise.org lists 52 currently available pairwise testing tools. Perhaps the most recognized is the Automatic Efficient Test Generator (AETG) system [Cohen et al., 1994]. It is also supported by a free program that is available from James Bach at his website:

(https://www.satisfice.com/download/allpairs).

The technique makes the following assumptions:

- meaningful equivalence classes can be identified for each program input
- program inputs are independent
- there is no order to program inputs
- faults are due only to the interaction of pairs of program inputs

The necessity of each assumption is demonstrated (with counter-examples) next.

19.1.1 Program Inputs

As we have seen in earlier chapters, program inputs can be either events or data. The All Pairs technique refers only to data, that is, inputs are values of variables, not events. It is useful to distinguish between physical and logical variables. As a guideline, physical variables are usually associated with some unit of measure, such as velocity, altitude, temperature, or mass. Logical variables are seldom associated with units of measure; instead, they usually refer to some enumerated type, such as a telephone directory number or an employee identification number. It is usually easier to identify equivalence classes for logical variables.

As a counter-example, consider the Triangle Program. The three sides, a, b, and c, are all integers and are arbitrarily bounded by $1 < = side <= 200$. The sides are physical variables, measured in some unit of length. What equivalence classes apply to a, b, and c? Only the robust equivalence classes that deal with valid and invalid input values of a side:

EqClass1(side) = {x: x is an integer and x < 1} (invalid values)
EqClass2(side) = {x: x is an integer and $1 < = x < = 200$} (valid values)
EqClass3(side) = {x: x is an integer and x > 200} (invalid values)

The actual Notepad input file to Bach's allpairs.exe program (satisfice.com) is:

side a	side b	side c
a < 1	b < 1	c < 1
1 < = a < = 200	1 < = b < = 200	1 < = c < = 200
a > 200	b > 200	c > 200

An interested tester might postulate equivalence classes such as one in which exactly two sides are equal, but such classes are on triples of Triangle Program inputs, not on individual variables. Table 19.1 contains the allpairs.exe output generated for these equivalence classes; the actual test cases are in Table 19.2.

As expected from the allpairs.exe output, there is never an opportunity to choose values for the sides that correspond to an actual triangle. Because six of the nine equivalence classes deal with invalid values, this only exercises data validity, not correct function with valid values.

19.1.2 Independent Variables

The NextDate function violates the independent variables assumption. There are dependencies between the day and month variables (a 30-day month cannot have day = 31) and between month and year (the last day of February depends on whether the year is leap or common). The day, month, and year variables are logical variables, and they are amenable to useful equivalence classes. In Chapter 6, we had the following equivalence classes and we used a decision table to deal with the dependencies. Table 19.3 is an extended entry decision table; it is the result of algebraically reducing the complete decision table in Chapter 6. It is "canonical" in the sense that it exactly represents all the combinations of valid variable values. The dependencies among day, month, and year are all expressed in the canonical decision table for NextDate.

Table 19.1   All Pairs.exe Output

case	side a	side b	side c	pairings
1	a < 1	b < 1	c < 1	3
2	a < 1	1 < = b < = 200	1 < = c < = 200	3
3	a < 1	b > 200	c > 200	3
4	1 < = a < = 200	b < 1	1 < = c < = 200	3
5	1 < = a < = 200	1 < = b < = 200	c < 1	3
6	1 < = a < = 200	b > 200	c < 1	2
7	a > 200	b < 1	c > 200	3
8	a > 200	1 < = b < = 200	c < 1	2
9	a > 200	b > 200	1 < = c < = 200	3
10	1 < = a < = 200	1 < = b < = 200	c > 200	2

Table 19.2   Triangle Program Test Cases Generated by Allpairs.exe

case	side a	side b	side c	Expected Output
1	−3	−2	−4	Not a Triangle
2	−3	5	7	Not a Triangle
3	−3	201	205	Not a Triangle
4	6	−2	9	Not a Triangle
5	6	5	−4	Not a Triangle
6	6	201	−4	Not a Triangle
7	208	−2	205	Not a Triangle
8	208	5	−4	Not a Triangle
9	208	201	7	Not a Triangle
10	6	5	205	Not a Triangle

The base equivalence classes from Chapter 6 are repeated here:

For day: $D1 = \{1 < = day <= 27\}$
            $D2 = \{28\}$
            $D3 = \{29\}$
            $D4 = \{30\}$
            $D5 = \{31\}$
For month: $M1 = \{30\text{-day months}\}$
            $M2 = \{31\text{-day months except December}\}$
            $M3 = \{December\}$
            $M4 = \{February\}$

Table 19.3   Canonical Decision Table of Valid NextDate Variables

Rules	1	2	3	4	5	6	7	8	9	10
day	D6	D4	D7	D5	D7	D5	D1	D2	D2	D3
month	M1	M1	M2	M2	M3	M3	M4	M4	M4	M4
year	—	—	—	—	—	—	—	Y1	Y2	Y2
day =1		x		x		x		x		x
day++	x		x		x		x		x	
month = 1						x				x
month++		x		x				x		
year++						x				

For year: Y1 = {common years}
Y2 = {leap years}

Table 19.3 shows the result of combining rules from a complete extended entry decision table with the day equivalence classes.

$$D6 = D1 \cup D2 \cup D3 = \{1 < = day <= 29\}$$
$$D7 = D1 \cup D2 \cup D3 \cup D4 = \{1 < = day <= 30\}$$

The allpairs.exe test cases for NextDate are given in Table 19.4. Note that the ten canonical test cases are only partly present in the 20 All Pairs test cases. Since the All Pairs algorithm does not merge decision table rules, some of the generated test cases correspond to a single rule in the canonical decision table. For example, All Pairs test cases 1, 3, and 15 all correspond to rule 1; cases 2, 4, 16, and 18 correspond to rule 3; and cases 6, 8, 12, and 14 correspond to rule 5. The redundancy is understandable. The more serious problems are the missing test case (for rule 8) and the invalid test cases (cases 7, 9, and 19). The missing test case consists of the interaction of all three variables, so the All Pairs algorithm cannot be expected to find this one. The invalid test cases are all due to dependencies among pairs of variables; these demonstrate the necessity of the independent variable assumption.

19.1.3 Input Order

Applications that use a Graphical User Interface (GUI) frequently allow inputs to be entered in any order. Figure 19.2 is a GUI for a simplified currency converter. A user can enter a whole US dollar amount up to $10,000, select one of three currencies, and then click on the Compute button to display the equivalent amount in the selected currency. The Clear All button can be clicked at any time; it resets the US dollar amount and resets any selected currency. Once a US dollar amount has been entered, a user may perform a series of currency conversions by first selecting a currency type, then clicking on Compute, then repeating this sequence for other currencies. The Quit button ends the application.

Table 19.4   All Pairs Test Cases for NextDate

case	day	month	year	pairings	valid?	DT Rule
1	1-27	30-day	leap	3	yes	1
2	1-27	31-day	common	3	yes	3
3	28	30-day	common	3	yes	1
4	28	31-day	leap	3	yes	3
5	29	Feb	leap	3	yes	10
6	29	Dec	common	3	yes	5
7	30	Feb	common	3	no	
8	30	Dec	leap	3	yes	5
9	31	30-day	leap	2	no	
10	31	31-day	common	2	yes	4
11	1-27	Feb	~leap	1	yes	7
12	1-27	Dec	~common	1	yes	5
13	28	Feb	~common	1	yes	9
14	28	Dec	~leap	1	yes	5
15	29	30-day	~common	1	yes	1
16	29	31-day	~leap	1	yes	3
17	30	30-day	~leap	1	yes	2
18	30	31-day	~common	1	yes	3
19	31	Feb	~leap	1	no	
20	31	Dec	~common	1	yes	6

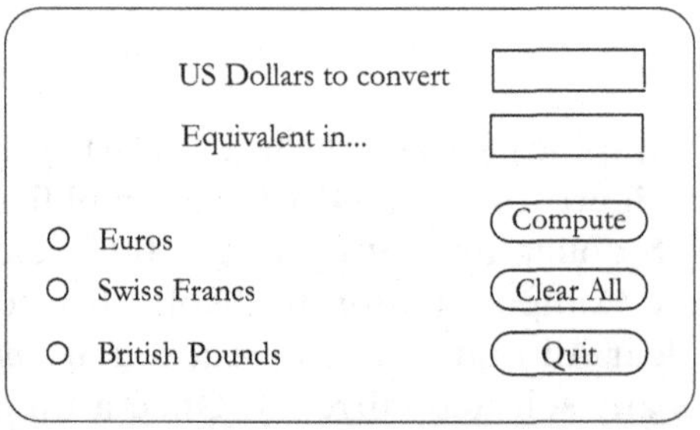

Figure 19.2   Currency Conversion GUI.

Because there is no control on the sequence of user input events, the Compute button must anticipate invalid user input sequences. It produces five error messages:

Error message 1: No US dollar amount entered,
Error message 2: No currency selected,
Error message 3: No US dollar amount entered and no currency selected,
Error message 4: US dollar amount cannot be negative,
Error message 5: US dollar amount cannot be greater than $10,000.

Clicking on the Compute button is therefore a context sensitive input event, with six contexts—the five that result in the error messages, and an input US dollar amount in the valid range. The data contexts of an input event are clearly pairs of interest to a tester, so the All Pairs technique should be appropriate.

At first glance, the Currency Conversion GUI seems to lend itself nicely to the All Pairs technique. The following equivalence classes are derived naturally from the description and are shown in Table 19.5.

USdollar1 = {no entry}
USdollar2 = {< $0}
USdollar3 = {$1 -- $10 K}
USdollar4 = {> $10 K}
Currency1 = {Euros}
Currency2 = {Pounds}
Currency3 = {Swiss Francs}
Currency4 = {nothing selected}
Operation1 = {Compute}
Operation2 = {Clear All}
Operation3 = {Quit}

The first four columns of Table 19.6 are the allpairs.exe program outputs. The (tester provided) expected outputs are in the last column. The "~Compute" in test cases 15 and 16 is an allpairs.exe output that directs the tester to pick an operation other than Compute. (It is an extension of the "Don't Care" entry in decision tables.) Notice that only error messages 1, 4, and either 2 or 5 are generated. Test case 9 generates a fourth context, in which the equivalent currency in Pounds is computed. This is the only actual computation—the All Pairs test cases never check the conversion of dollars to Euros or to Swiss Francs.

Table 19.5   Allpairs.exe Input for the Currency Conversion GUI

US Dollar	Currency	Operation
no entry	Euros	Compute
<$0	Pounds	Clear All
$1 -- $10K	Swiss Francs	Quit
> $10K	nothing selected	

Table 19.6 Allpairs.exe Test Cases for the Currency Conversion GUI

case	US Dollar	Currency	Operation	Expected Output
1	no entry	Euros	Compute	Error message 1
2	no entry	Pounds	Clear All	Pounds reset
3	no entry	Swiss Francs	Quit	Application ends
4	<$0	Euros	Clear All	US dollar amount reset, Euros reset
5	<$0	Pounds	Compute	Error message 4
6	<$0	Swiss Francs	Compute	Error message 4
7	<$0	nothing selected	Quit	Application ends
8	$1—$10K	Euros	Quit	Application ends
9	$1—$10K	Pounds	Compute	Equivalent in Pounds
10	$1—$10K	Swiss Francs	Clear All	US dollar amount and Swiss Francs reset
11	> $10K	Pounds	Quit	Application ends
12	> $10K	nothing selected	Compute	Error message 5 or Error message 2
13	> $10K	Euros	Clear All	US dollar amount reset, Euros reset
14	no entry	nothing selected	Clear All	No change in GUI
15	$1—$10K	nothing selected	~Compute	?
16	> $10K	Swiss Francs	~Compute	?

Table 19.7 Allpairs.exe Input in Different Order

US Dollar	Currency	Operation
<$0	Euros	Compute
$1—$10K	Pounds	Clear All
> $10K	Swiss Francs	Quit
no entry	nothing selected	

There is a more subtle problem with the All Pairs algorithm—the order of inputs can make a surprising difference, even though it should be irrelevant. Table 19.7 just changes the order of USdollar inputs, and the resulting test cases are in Table 19.8. With just this slight change, two currency conversions are performed (to British Pounds and to Swiss Francs), but only error messages 3, 4, and 5 are generated.

The change is caused by the way in which the algorithm picks pairs of variables. The early test cases contain the greatest number of pairs, and the later ones contain

Table 19.8 Allpairs.exe Test Cases (Note Differences with Table 19.6)

case	US Dollar	Currency	Operation	Expected Output
1	<$0	Euros	Compute	Error message 4
2	<$0	Pounds	Clear All	US dollar amount reset, Pounds reset
3	<$0	Swiss Francs	Quit	Application ends
4	$1 − $10K	Euros	Clear All	US dollar amount reset, Euros reset
5	$1 − $10K	Pounds	Compute	Equivalent in Pounds
6	$1 − $10K	Swiss Francs	Compute	Equivalent in Swiss Francs
7	$1 − $10K	nothing selected	Quit	Application ends
8	> $10K	Euros	Quit	Application ends
9	> $10K	Pounds	Compute	Error message 5
10	> $10K	Swiss Francs	Clear All	US dollar amount reset, Swiss francs reset
11	no entry	Pounds	Quit	Application ends
12	no entry	nothing selected	Compute	Error message 3
13	no entry	Euros	Clear All	Euros reset
14	<$0	nothing selected	Clear All	US dollar amount reset
15	> $10K	nothing selected	~Compute	?
16	no entry	Swiss Francs	~Compute	?

the fewest. This means that a potential All Pairs tester needs to be clever about the order in which classes of a variable are presented to the algorithm.

19.1.4 Failures Due only to Pairs of Inputs

By definition, The All Pairs technique only potentially reveals faults due to the interaction of two variables. The NextDate counter-example showed that faults due to interaction of three variables (e.g., February 28 in a common year) will not be detected. This cannot be an indictment of the All Pairs technique—the advocates are quite clear that the intent is to find faults due only to the interaction of pairs of values. Orthogonal arrays and the OATS technique can be used to find interactions among three or more variables. As long as the program being tested uses logical variables, there is not too much risk. If a program involves computations with physical variables, some insight will likely be needed. Suppose, for example a ratio is computed, and the numerator and denominator are from different classes. There may be no problem with nominal values, but a very large numerator divided by a very small denominator might cause an overflow fault. Worst Case Boundary Value testing would be a more likely method to reveal such a fault.

19.2 A Closer Look at the NIST Study

Most introductory logic courses discuss a class of arguments known as informal fallacies. One of these, the Fallacy of Extension, occurs when an argument is extended from a simple to an extreme situation where it is easier to persuade the point to be made. The conclusion is then brought back to the simple case. The Fallacy of Extension most commonly occurs when someone is asking for special consideration, and the response is something like "What if we let EVERYONE have that exception?"

There is an element of the Fallacy of Extension in the myriad of papers that emphasize how the All Pairs algorithm compresses an enormous number of test cases into a smaller, more manageable set. While the popular papers cite the NIST study as the basis for the All Pairs technique, the NIST papers [Wallace and Kuhn, 2000], [Wallace and Richard Kuhn, 2001] never stress this idea of compression; rather, they stress that faults due to more than two variables are relatively rare (2% in the examples they studied). Both papers are concerned with describing faults, identifying root causes, and suggesting standard software engineering techniques to avoid similar faults in future systems.

The closest the NIST papers come to the dominant All Pairs emphasis on test case compression is when they discuss their analysis of 109 failure reports. They note [Wallace and Kuhn, 2000] that "Only three of the 109 failure reports indicated that more than two conditions were required to cause the failure." Further, "The most complex of these [three failures] involved four conditions." The conclusion of that part of the report is that "...of the 109 reports that are detailed, 98% showed that the problem could have been detected by testing the device with all pairs of parameter settings." The report notes that most medical devices only have "a relatively small number of inputs variables, each with either a small discrete set of possible settings or a finite range of values." Then the Fallacy of Extension occurs. Quoting from [Wallace and Kuhn, 2000]:

> *"Medical devices vary among treatment areas, but in general have a relatively small number of input variables, each with either a small discrete set of possible settings, or a finite range of values. For example, consider a device that has 20 inputs, each with 10 settings, for a total of 10^{20} combinations of settings. The few hundred test cases that can be built under most development budgets will of course cover less than a tiny fraction of a percent of the possible combinations. The number of pairs of settings is in fact very small, and since each test case must have a value for each of the ten variables, more than one pair can be included in a single test case. Algorithms based on orthogonal Latin squares are available that can generate test data for all pairs (or higher order combinations) at a reasonable cost. One method makes it possible to cover all pairs of values for this example using only 180 test cases [8]."*

What is really perplexing about this is they preface it with the note that most devices only have a few input settings, so the extension to 10^{20} cases makes little sense.

19.3 Appropriate Applications for All-Pairs Testing

Table 19.9 presents two considerations that help determine whether All Pairs is appropriate for a given application. The first consideration is whether the application

Table 19.9 Applications Appropriate for All Pairs Testing

	Single Processor	*Multiple Processors*
Static	All Pairs potentially OK	All Pairs cannot deal with input orders
Dynamic	All Pairs potentially problematic.	All Pairs cannot deal with input orders

is static or dynamic. Static applications are those in which all inputs are available before calculation begins. David Harel refers to such applications as "transformational" because they transform their inputs into output data [Harel 1988]. Classic COBOL programs with their Input, Processing, and Output divisions are good examples of static applications.

Dynamic applications are those in which not all of the inputs that determine the ultimate path through a program are available at the onset of calculation. Harel uses the term "reactive" to convey the fact that these applications react to inputs that occur in time sequence. The difference between static and dynamic applications is analogous to the difference between combinatorial and sequential circuits of discrete components. Because the order of inputs in important, dynamic applications are not very appropriate to the All Pairs technique. There is no way to guarantee that interesting pairs will occur in the necessary order. Also, dynamic applications frequently contain context sensitive input events in which the logical meaning of a physical input is determined by the context in which it occurs. The Currency conversion example in Section 19.1.3 contains context sensitive input events.

The second consideration is whether the application executes on a single or on multiple processors. The All Pairs technique cannot guarantee appropriate pairs of input data across multiple processors. Race conditions, duration of events in real time, and asynchronous input orders are common in multiprocessing applications, and these needs will likely not be met by All Pairs. Therefore, applications on the dynamic side of the partition, whether in single or in multiple processors, are not appropriate for All Pairs.

The remaining quadrant, static applications in a multiple processing environment, is less clear. These applications are usually computation intensive (hence the need for parallel processing). If they are truly static, within a processor, All Pairs can be an appropriate choice.

19.4 Recommendations for All Pairs Testing

All Pairs testing is just another short cut. When the time allocated for testing shrinks, as it frequently does, short cuts are both attractive and risky. If the following questions can all be answered "yes" then the risk of using All Pairs is reduced.

- Are the inputs exclusively data (rather than a mix of data and events)?
- Are the variables logical (rather than physical)?
- Are the variables independent?
- Do the variables have useful equivalence classes?
- Is the order of inputs irrelevant (i.e., is the application both static and single processor)?

Since the All Pairs algorithm only generates the input portion of a test case, one last question: Can the expected outputs for All Pairs test cases be determined?

Exercises

1. Download the allpairs.exe program form James Bach's website (satisfice.com) and experiment with your favorite example.

References

James Bach and Patrick J. Schroeder, "Pairwise Testing: A Best Practice That Isn't" presented at STARWest, 2003.

Bernie Berger, "Efficient Testing with All-Pairs" presented at STAREast, 2003.

D. M. Cohen, S. R. Dalal, A. Kajla, and G. C. Patton, "*The Automatic Efficient Test Generator (AETG) System*", *Proceedings of the 5th International Symposium on Software Reliability Engineering*, IEEE Computer Society Press, pp. 303–309, 1994.

David Harel, On visual formalisms, *Communications of the ACM*, Vol. 31, No. 5, pp. 514–530, May, 1988.

R. Mandl, "Orthogonal Latin Squares: An Application of Experiment Design to Compiler Testing", *Communications of the ACM*, Vol. 28, No. 10, pp. 1054–1058, 1985.

Dolores R. Wallace and D. Richard Kuhn, "Converting System Failure Histories into Future Win Situations" 2000, available online at http://hissa.nist.gov/effProject/handbook/failure/hase99.pdf.

Dolores R. Wallace and D. Richard Kuhn, "Failure Modes in Medical Device Software: An Analysis of 15 Years of Recall Data", *International Journal of Reliability, Quality, and Safety Engineering*, Vol. 8, No. 4, pp. 351–371, 2001.

Chapter 20

Software Technical Reviews

"Measure twice—Cut once"

(Woodworkers wisdom)

In so many ways, we all depend on forms of reviews—surgical second opinions, movie and restaurant reviews, home safety inspections, Federal Aviation Authority aircraft inspections, and so on (add your favorites).

Are software technical reviews a form of testing? The generally accepted answer is a considered Yes. This is amplified by the chapters on software reviews in the International Software Testing Certification Board (ISTQB) Foundation and Advanced Level Syllabi [ISTQB 2007, ISTQB 2012]. Software testing seeks to identify faults by causing failures, as discussed in Chapter 1. Software reviews try to identify faults (not software failures), but an identified fault typically morphs into faulty code which, when executed, causes a failure.

Much of the material in this chapter is based on experience in the development of telephone switching system software. Those applications could have a 30-year serviceable life; hence, software maintenance could last that long. In self-defense, and for purely economic reasons, that organization refined its review process over an interval of 15 years, resulting in "industrial-strength technical inspections." The industrial strength part refers to a process that was gradually refined, and which contains several subtle checks and balances.

It is helpful to understand software reviews as a critical evaluation of a work product, performed by people who are technically competent. A software review is, or should be, a scheduled, budgeted development activity with formal entry and exit criteria.

20.1 Economics of Software Reviews

Many development organizations are reluctant to institute software reviews, mostly because of a short-sighted view of cost of preparation. As far back is 1981, Barry Boehm [Boehm 1981] dispelled this notion with his graph of fault resolution costs as a function of when they are discovered (see Figure 20.1). This is a remarkable

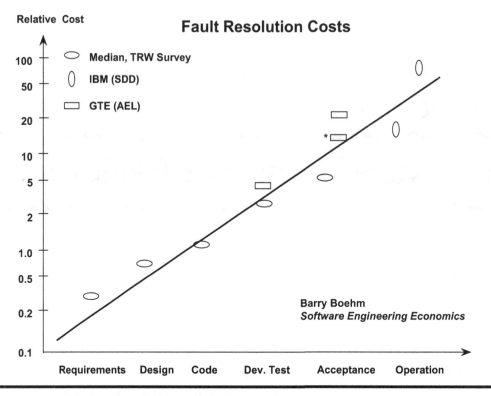

Figure 20.1 Relative costs of defect resolution [Boehm 1981].

comparison as it relates data from three diverse organizations. (As a curious footnote, the GTE Automatic Electric Labs project closest to the line in the Acceptance phase is the project for which one of the authors prepared data at Dr. Boehm's request.) The cost axis is a logarithmic scale, and the straight line of best fit means that correction costs increase exponentially with time.

The IBM corporation [IBM 1981] published a "defect amplification" model that describes how defects from one Waterfall phase might be amplified in a following phase. Some defects might be simply passed through, and others might be amplified by work done in the successor phase. The defects then form their own waterfall, something probably not intended by the waterfall model. The report continues by postulating a defect detection step in which technical inspections detect a percentage of defects before they can be passed on to successor phases. Roger Pressman [Pressman 1992] developed a hypothetical example showing two versions of a waterfall-based software development—one with technical inspections and one without. The result: 12 defects without reviews were reduced to 3 after reviews at three development phases. This is a hypothetical example, but it illustrates a widely agreed-upon fact—reviews reduce faults, and consequently, the overall development cost.

More recently, Karl Wiegers [Wiegers 1995] reports that, in an unnamed German company, correcting defects found by testing was 14.5 times the cost to find the problem in an inspection, and this grew to 68 times the inspection cost if the defect was reported by a customer. Wiegers continues with an updated IBM statistic: correcting defects found in a released product was 45 times the cost if the defect was fixed at design time. He asserts that, while technical inspections may constitute 5 to 15 percent of total project cost, "Jet Propulsion Laboratory estimated a net savings of $7.5 million from 300 inspections performed on software they produced for NASA" and "another company reports annual savings of $2.5 million." One last Wiegers statistic: in another unnamed company, the cost to fix a defect found by inspection was $146 compared to the cost to fix a defect found by customer: $2900, resulting in a Cost/Benefit ratio of 0.0503.

The bottom line? People in development organizations make mistakes, and the earlier these are caught, the cheaper they are to resolve. To be effective, reviews need both process and reviewer credibility, and they must consider human factors. In the next sections, we describe the roles in a review, we then look at and compare three types of reviews, the materials needed to conduct a thorough review, a time-tested review process, and review etiquette. The chapter concludes with a rather surprising study done at Grand Valley State University.

20.2 Types of Reviews

There are three fundamental types of software reviews: walkthroughs, technical inspections, and audits. Each of these is described here, and then compared with the others. Before doing that, we clarify reasons to conduct a review. Here is a list of frequently given reasons:

- communication among developers
- training, especially for new personnel, or for personnel recently added to a project
- management progress reporting
- defect discovery
- performance evaluation (of the work product producer)
- team morale
- customer (re)assurance

All of these can happen with a software review; however, the best (some say only!) reason to have reviews is to discover defects. With this focus, all of the other "reasons" turn out to be diversions, and each diminishes the defect discovery goal.

20.2.1 Walkthroughs

Walkthroughs are the most common form of review, and they are the least formal. They often involve just two people, the producer and a colleague. There is generally no preparation ahead of the walkthrough, and usually little or no documentation is produced. The producer is the review leader; therefore, the utility of a walkthrough depends on the real goal of the producer. It is easy for a producer/review leader to direct the walkthrough to the "safe" parts of the work product and avoid the portions where the producer is unsure. This is clearly a degenerate case, but it happens, particularly when technical people resent the review process. Walkthroughs are most effective at the source code level, and on other small work products.

20.2.2 Technical Inspections

Pioneered by Michael Fagan while he was at IBM in the 1970s, technical inspections are the most effective form of software reviews. They are a highly formal process,

Table 20.1 Comparison of Review Types

Aspect	Walkthrough	Inspection	Audit
Coverage	Broad, sketchy	Deep	Varies with auditor(s)
Driver	Producer	Checklist	Standard
Preparation time	Low	High	Could be very high
Formality	Low	High	Rigid
Effectiveness	Low	High	Low

and more details of technical inspections are given in Sections 20.4 and 20.5. The effectiveness of technical inspections is a result of several success factors, including:

- a documented inspection process
- formal review training
- budgeted review preparation time
- sufficient lead time
- thoughtful identification of the inspection team
- a refined review checklist
- technically competent participants
- "buy in" by both technical and management personnel

20.2.3 Audits

Audits are usually performed by some external group, rather than the development team. Audits may be conducted by an SQA group, a project group, an outside agency, or possibly a government standards agency. Audits are not primarily concerned with finding defects—the main concern is conformance to some expectations, either internal or external. This is not to diminish the importance of audits—they can be very expensive because they require significant preparation time. Whereas a technical inspection meeting may last 60 to 90 minutes, an audit may last a full day or more. Audits may be required by contract, and an unsatisfactory audit usually results in expensive corrective actions.

20.2.4 Comparison of Review Types

The main characteristics of the three review types are summarized in Table 20.1.

Because technical inspections are the most effective at finding defects early, they are the focus of the remainder of this chapter.

20.3 Roles in a Review

In all three types of reviews, there are similar roles. A review team consists of the person who developed the work product, reviewers, a review leader, and a recorder. These roles may involve some duplication, and in some cases, some may be missing. Reviews are an interesting point in a software project because the technical and management roles intersect there. The outcome of each type of review is a technical recommendation to the responsible administrator, and this is a crucial point at which responsibility transfers from developers to management.

20.3.1 Producer

As the name implies, this is the person who created the work product being examined. The producer is present in the review meeting but might not contribute much as one of the reviewers. Why? We all know it is much easier to proofread someone else's work rather than one's own. The same holds true for technical reviews. At the end of all types of technical reviews, the producer will be the person who resolves the action items identified during the review meeting.

20.3.2 Review Leader

Review leaders are responsible for the overall success of the review. They have the following duties:

- schedule the actual review meeting,
- assure that all members of the review team have the appropriate review materials,
- conduct the actual review meeting, and
- write the review report.

To do all of this, a review leader must be technically competent, be well organized, have leadership ability, and must be able to prioritize. Above all, a review leader must be able to conduct an orderly, well-paced business meeting. There are lessons to be learned from a poorly run business meeting. Such meetings are characterized by some or all of the following:

- participants see them as a waste of time
- the wrong people are at the meeting
- there is no agenda, or if there is, it is not followed
- there is no prior preparation
- no issues are identified
- the discussion is easily side-tracked
- time is spent fixing problems rather than just identifying them

Any one of these will doom a review meeting, and it is the responsibility of the review leader to assure that they do not occur.

20.3.3 Recorder

Because of connotations associated with "secretary," the preferred term for this role is review recorder. As the title implies, the recorder takes notes during the review meeting. To do this, recorders must be able to track conversations and write notes in parallel—quite a skill, and not all of us have that ability. It is helpful if recorders can write clearly and succinctly, because the recorded notes will be the basis for the formal review report. Often the recorder helps the review leader write the review report. It is a good practice for the recorder to have a "mini-review" in the last few minutes of the review meeting to go over the notes to see if anything was missed.

20.3.4 Reviewer

The individual reviewers are responsible for objectively reviewing the work product. To do this, they must be technically competent, and should not have any biases or irrelevant personal agendas. The reviewers identify issues and assign a severity level to each item. During the review meeting, these issues are discussed, and the severity level may be changed by consensus. Before the review meeting, each reviewer submits a review ballot that contains the following information:

- reviewer name
- review preparation time
- a list of issues with severity
- an overall review disposition recommendation (OK as is, accept with minor rework, major rework with a new review needed)

20.3.5 Role Duplication

In smaller organizations, it may be necessary for one person to fill two review roles. Here are some common pairings, and a short comment on each possibility:

- review leader is the producer—this happens in a walkthrough. It is usually a poor idea, particularly if the producer is technically insecure.
- review leader is the recorder—this can work, but it is difficult.
- review leader is a reviewer—this works reasonably well, but is very time-consuming.

20.4 Contents of an Inspection Packet

One of the success factors of a technical inspection is the packet of materials that the inspection team uses in its preparation. Each inspection packet item is described in the succeeding subsections. Appendix A contains a sample inspection packet for a Use Case inspection.

20.4.1 Work Product Requirements

As mentioned earlier, technical inspections are valuable because they find faults early in a development process. In the Waterfall lifecycle, and in many of its derivatives, the early phases are characterized by tight what/how cycles, in which one phase describes what must be done in the next phase, and the successor phase describes "how" it responds to the "what" definition. These tight what/how cycles are ideally suited for technical inspections; therefore, one important element in the inspection packet is the work product requirements. Without this, the review team will not be able to determine if the "how" part has actually been accomplished.

20.4.2 Frozen Work Product

Once an inspection team has been identified, each member receives the full inspection packet. This is a point at which three software project disciplines converge: development, management, and configuration management. In the configuration management view, a work product is called a "Design Item." Once a design item has been reviewed and approved, it becomes a "Configuration Item." Design items can be changed by the responsible designers (producers), but configuration items are frozen, meaning that they cannot be changed by anyone unless they are first demoted to design item status. Once a design item enters the inspection process, the producer may no longer make changes to it. This insures that the full inspection team is literally on the same page.

20.4.3 Standards and Checklists

When given a work product to inspect, how does a reviewer know what to do? What to look for? In a mature inspection process, the organization has checklists appropriate to the various work products subject to inspections. A checklist identifies the kinds of problems that a reviewer should look for. Checklists are refined over time, and many companies consider their inspection checklists to be proprietary information. (Who would like to share with the world what their product weak points and concerns are?)

A good checklist is modified as it is used. In fact, one inspection meeting agenda item can be to ask whether any changes in the checklist are needed. Checklists should be public in a development organization. One side benefit is that checklists can improve the development process. This is very similar to the use of grading rubrics in the academic world. If students know the grading criteria, they are much more likely to submit a better assignment. When developers consult a checklist, they know what historical situations have been fault-prone, and therefore, they can proactively deal with these potential problems.

There is a wealth of online material to get started with developing checklists. This paper [http://portal.acm.org/citation.cfm?id=308798] surveys 117 checklists from 24 sources. Different categories of checklist items are discussed and examples are provided of good checklist items as well as those that should be avoided. Karl Weigers' website is another good source for checklists. [http://www.processimpact.com/pr_goodies.shtml]

Applicable standards play a role similar to checklists. Development organizations may have code naming standards, for example, or required templates for test case definition. Conformance to applicable standards is usually required and is therefore an easy item on an inspection checklist. As with checklists, standards may be subject to change, albeit more slowly.

20.4.4 Review Issues Spreadsheet

Individual reviewers identify issues and submit them to the review leader. A spreadsheet with columns as shown in Table 20.2 greatly facilitates the process that the review leader uses to merge the inputs from the full inspection team.

Information in the individual reviewer issues spreadsheets is merged into a master issues spreadsheet by the review leader (Table 20.3). The spreadsheet can then be sorted by location, by checklist item, by fault severity, or some combination of these. This enables the review leader to prioritize the issues, which then becomes the skeleton of the review meeting agenda. This overview of the full set of identified issues can also be used to estimate the length of the review meeting time. In extreme cases, the faults might constitute a "showstopper"—faults so severe that the work product is not yet ready for a review, and is returned to the producer. The producer can then use the combined issues list to guide revision work.

Table 20.2 Individual Reviewer Issues Spreadsheet

<Work Product Information>					
<Reviewer Name>					
<preparation date>					
<Reviewer Preparation Time>					
	Location		Checklist		
Issue #	Page	Line	Item	Severity	Description
1	1	18	typo	1	change "accound" to "account"

Table 20.3 Review Report Spreadsheet

<Work Product Information>						
Review Team Members		Preparation time				
Leader						
Recorder						
Reviewer						
Reviewer						
Reviewer						
Reviewer						
	total prep time					
Meeting Date						
<Review Recommendation>						
		Location		Checklist		
Issue #	Reviewer	Page	Line	Item	Severity	Description
1		1	18	typo	1	change "accound" to "account"

20.4.5 Review Reporting Forms

Once reviewers complete their examination of the work product, they submit an individual review report form to the review leader. This form should contain the following information:

- Reviewer name
- Work product reviewed
- Preparation hours spent

- Summary of the review issues spreadsheet showing the number of issues of each severity level.
- Description of any "showstopper" issue(s)
- The reviewers recommendation (OK as is, minor rework needed, or major rework with new review needed)

This information can be used to analyze the effectiveness of the review process. The Software Quality Assurance group at a telephone switching systems development organization made a study of the severity of found defects as a function of preparation hours. They proved the obvious, but the results are interesting: out of four severity levels, the only reviewers who found the really severe faults were those who spent six to eight hours of preparation time. At the other end of the severity spectrum, those who only found the lowest severity faults only spent one to two preparation hours.

There are other possible analyses, and they relate to the whole idea of openness and accountability. The underlying assumption is that all review documents are open, in the sense that they are available to everyone in the organization. Accountability is the desired consequence of this openness. Consider reviewers who report significant preparation time, yet they do not report the severe faults that other reviewers find. If there is a pattern of this, some supervisory intervention is appropriate. Conversely, reviewers who consistently find the severe faults can be recognized as effective review team members, and this can be a consideration in an annual performance review.

20.4.6 Fault Severity Levels

It is helpful if items in an inspection checklist are given severity levels. Appendix A contains a sample definition of severity levels for use cases. More recently, the IEEE Standard Classification for Software Anomalies Working Group has published (and sells) 1044-2009 IEEE Standard Classification for Software Anomalies [IEEE 2009]. While examples are nice, detailed fault severity levels are awkward in practice. Rather than have a debate about whether a discovered fault is severity level 7 or 8, it is more productive to have a simple 3- or 4-level severity classification (such as the one in Appendix A).

The order of severity levels is less interesting: usually the simplest faults are of severity 1 and the most complex are the high end of the scale (3 or 4). This avoids the confusion that sometimes occurs with priority levels. (Consider priority = 4 and priority = 1: does the 4 mean high priority, or does the 1 mean first priority?)

20.4.7 Review Report Outline

The review report is the point where technical responsibility ends and administrative responsibility begins, so the review report must serve the needs of both groups of people. It also becomes the basis for accountability, because the management relies on the technical judgment of the review team.

Here is a sample outline of a review report:

1. Introduction
    a. Work product identification
    b. Review team members and roles

2. Preliminary Issue List
   a. Potential fault
   b. Severity
3. Prioritized Action Item List
   a. Identified fault
   b. Severity
4. Summary of Individual Reports
5. Review Statistics
   a. Total hours spent
   b. Faults sorted by severity
   c. Faults sorted by location
6. Review recommendation
7. Appendix with the full review packet

20.5 An Industrial-Strength Inspection Process

This section describes a process for technical reviews that gradually evolved over a period of 12 years in a research and development lab that developed telephone switching system hardware and software. Since the commercial lifetime of these systems could reach 30 years, the developing organization had to produce nearly fault-free systems as a matter of economic necessity. As they say, necessity is the mother of invention—certainly true in what is termed here an "industrial-strength inspection process." Some of the checks and balances will be highlighted, as well as some of the resolutions to hard questions.

Figure 20.2 shows the stages in the industrial-strength inspection process. Even these stages were carefully devised. As presented, it happens to resemble common depictions of the Waterfall lifecycle mode, but there are several important differences. The sequence of stages is important, and deviations from the sequence simply do not work. The activities of each stage, and some of the reasons for them, are described in the next subsections.

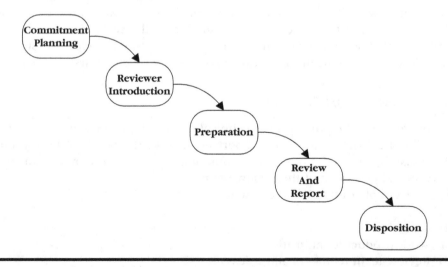

Figure 20.2 Stages in the industrial-strength inspection process.

20.5.1 Commitment Planning

The technical inspection process begins with a meeting between the producer of the work product and his/her supervisor. Working together they identify an appropriate review team and the review leader. In a degenerate case, this can be mildly adversarial—the producer may wish to "stack the deck" with close friends while the supervisor may wish to "send a message" to the producer. Both possibilities are clearly regrettable, but they can happen. On the positive side, if the producer and the supervisor both agree on the value of inspections, they will both see it as a way to promote their own self-interests. After some negotiation, both the producer and the supervisor need to accept and approve the identified review team. In a truly formal process, both parties might even sign off on this agreement.

Once the review team is identified, the supervisor completes any necessary administrative approval. One curious question can arise at this point. What if a review team member is from another supervisory group? Even worse, what if the other supervisor feels that the requested reviewer is on a critical path and cannot be spared? This becomes a question of corporate culture. A good answer is that, if the organization is truly committed to technical inspections, everyone understands that such conflicts can occur. This should be discussed and agreed upon at the project initiation, thereby preventing future conflicts.

The supervisor should have a commitment meeting, with other supervisors if necessary, to obtain commitments for all review team members. Any task approvals are communicated at this meeting. Once all this is done, the results are given to the review leader. This is the point where administrative authority is handed over to the technical people. It is also the point at which management separates from the inspection process.

20.5.2 Reviewer Introduction

Once the review process is turned over to the review team. The review leader assembles the team for a brief meeting. In preparation for this meeting, the producer prepares the full review packet and freezes the work product to be examined. At the preliminary meeting, the review leader delivers the review packet and gives a brief overview of the work product. There may be a discussion of the work product, including any special concerns. Since the review team is accountable for the technical recommendation, the team should decide whether or not the review packet is complete. One item of business is to select the review recorder and to schedule the review meeting time. The meeting ends with all team members either committing to the process or possibly disqualifying themselves. In the latter case, the process may go back to the commitment planning stage (this is, or should be, rare).

20.5.3 Preparation

The review team members have approved preparation time—this is important. It is simply not realistic to rely on a team member's good will to spend personal time (*i.e.*, unpaid) on review preparation. The preparation interval for a review of normal duration (60 to 90 minutes) should be five full working days, in which up to eight hours of preparation time can be used by each review team member. Allowing a five-day interval should be enough for reviewers to meet most of their other commitments.

As part of the preparation, reviewers examine the work product with respect to the review checklist and their own expertise. As issues are recognized, they are recorded into the individual reviewer issues spreadsheet (see Table 20.2). Reviewers should describe the issue, provide a short explanation or description, and then make a severity assessment. At least one full day before the review meeting, the reviewers send their individual spreadsheets to the review leader, along with their ballots showing actual time spent, and their preliminary recommendations.

Once all the individual reports are in, the review leader merges them into a single spreadsheet and prioritizes the issues. This involves some insight, because often two reviewers may provide slightly different descriptions of the same underlying issue. The location information usually is enough to recognize this problem. Given a final issues list, the review leader makes a Go/No Go decision based on the number and severity of the issues. (Review cancellation should be rare, but it is wise to allow for the possibility.) Assuming the review will occur, the review leader prepares the final agenda by prioritizing the merged issues—a form of triage.

20.5.4 Review Meeting

The actual review meeting should be conducted as an effective business meeting. In Section 20.2.2, there is a list of characteristics of a poorly run business meeting. Some steps in the review process have already been taken to assure an effective review meeting:

- The review team was carefully selected, so the right people will be in the meeting.
- The agenda is based on the prioritized list of issues, so there should not be a sense that the meeting is a waste of time.
- The process calls for budgeted preparation time in which issues are identified before the meeting.

Normally, the first order of business is to decide if the meeting should be postponed. The main reasons are most likely absent or unprepared team members. Assuming that the review will proceed, the main job of the review leader is to follow the agenda and make sure that issues are identified, and agreed upon, but not resolved. Once the agenda has been completed, the review leader asks for a consensus of the review recommendation. Recall that the options are Accept as is, Accept with minor rework, but no additional review is needed, or Reject. The review meeting ends with a short wrap-up conducted by the recorder in which the issues list is finalized, the individual ballots are collected, and the team checks that nothing was forgotten.

20.5.5 Report Preparation

The review leader is primarily responsible for writing the review report, but assistance from the recorder is certainly in order. The report is a technical recommendation to management, and it ends the technical responsibility (but not the accountability). If there are any issues, they are noted as action items, that require additional work from the producer. The review report and all other materials should be open to the entire organization, as this enhances accountability.

20.5.6 Disposition

Once the producer's supervisor receives the report, it becomes the basis of a management decision. There may be pressing reasons to ignore the technical findings, but if this happens, it is clearly a management choice. Assuming the recommendation is to accept the work product, it becomes subject to the configuration management function, and the work product is no longer a Design Object, it is a Configuration Item. As such, it can be used in the remainder of the project as a reliable component, not subject to change. If the review recommendation lists action items, the producer's supervisor and the producer make an estimate of the effort required to resolve the action items, and the work is done by the producer. Once all action items are resolved, the supervisor either closes the review or starts a re-review process.

20.6 Effective Review Culture

All forms of reviews are social processes, hence they become corporate culture considerations. In addition, reviews can be quite stressful, and this also requires social considerations. Reviews are a group activity, so group size becomes a question. In general, technical inspection teams should have from four to six members. Fewer members might be necessary in small development organizations. More than six team members is usually counter-productive.

Part of an effective corporate culture is that reviews must be seen as valuable activities by both management and technical people. Reviews must have formally budgeted time for all the activities described in Section 20.5. Human factors are important. Long reviews are seldom effective—psychologists claim that the attention span of most adults is about 12 minutes. Consider what effect this can have on a two-hour meeting. Most review meetings should be in the 60 to 90 minute range, with shorter meetings preferred. Furthermore, review meetings should be viewed as important, and interruptions should not be tolerated. (This includes cell phones!)

The best time to have a review meeting? About an hour after the normal start of the working day. This allows review team members to take care of little things that otherwise might be distractions. The worst time? Just after lunch, or maybe beginning at 3:00 on a Friday afternoon.

20.6.1 Etiquette

To reduce the stress that can accompany a review, the following points of review etiquette should be observed.

1. Be prepared. Otherwise, the review effectiveness will be diminished. In a sense, an unprepared team member is disrespecting the rest of the review team.
2. Be respectful. Review the product, not the producer.
3. Avoid discussions of style.
4. Provide minor comments (*e.g.*, spelling corrections) to the producer at the end of the meeting.
5. Be constructive. Reviews are not the place for personal criticism, nor for praise.
6. Remain focused. Identify issues, do not try to resolve them.

7. Participate, but do not dominate the discussion. Careful thought went into selection of the review team.
8. Be open. All review information should be widely available to the full organization.

20.6.2 Management Participation in Review Meetings

Many organizations struggle with the question of management participation in reviews. Generally, this is a bad idea. Management presence in a review easily creates additional stress on all team members, but in particular, on the producer. If management participation is common, the whole process can easily degenerate into unspoken agreements among the technical staff (I won't make you look bad if you don't make me look bad.) Another possible consequence is that management might not want negative results to be public—clearly a conflict of interest. How credible might a management person be as a reviewer? Willing to do the normal preparation? Capable of doing the normal preparation? Failing either of these questions, a management person becomes a drag on the review meeting. To be fair, there are managers who are technically competent, and they can be disciplined enough to respect the process. The admission ticket would be to do the normal review preparation and set aside any managerial objectives.

20.6.3 A Tale of Two Reviews

The Dilbert comic strip of Scott Adams usually contains poignant insights to software development situations. What follows are two possible reviews that would fit into an extended Dilbert scenario.

20.6.3.1 A Pointy-Haired Supervisor Review

1. The producer picks friendly reviewers.
2. There is little or no lead time.
3. There is no approved preparation time.
4. The work item is not frozen.
5. The review meeting is postponed twice.
6. Some reviewers are absent, others take cell phone calls.
7. Some designers never participate because they cannot be spared.
8. There is no checklist.
9. No action items are identified and reported.
10. The review leader proceeds in a page-by-page order. (No triage)
11. Faults are resolved "while they are fresh in mind."
12. Coffee and lunch breaks are needed.
13. Reviewers float in and out of the meeting.
14. The producer's supervisor is the review leader.
15. Several people are invited as spectators.

Just imagine this as a review!

20.6.3.2 An Ideal Review

Here are some characteristics of a review in a desirable review culture.

1. Producers do not dread reviews.
2. Reviewers have approved preparation time.
3. A complete review packet is delivered with sufficient lead time.
4. All participants have had formal review training.
5. Technical people perceive reviews as productive.
6. Management people perceive reviews as productive.
7. Review meetings have high priority.
8. Checklists are actively maintained.
9. Top developers are frequent reviewers.
10. Reviewer effectiveness is recognized as part of performance evaluation.
11. Review materials are openly available and used.

20.7 Inspection Case Study

One of the few things that can be done in a university setting that cannot be done in industry is repetition. Industrial development groups cannot justify doing the same thing multiple times. This section reports results of a study done in a graduate course on software testing at Grand Valley State University. Five groups of graduate students each performed a Use Case Technical Inspection using the review packet of materials in Appendix A (The use cases have been simplified in Appendix A.). The team members in the class are fairly representative of development groups in industry—a range of experience from new hires through people with two decades of software development. Table 20.4 summarizes the experience profiles of the five review teams.

Table 20.5 clarifies the experience levels in terms of years of industrial experience.

The class had three hours of instruction based on materials that were precursors to this chapter. The review teams were identified in a class meeting, and they used the review packet in Appendix A. The teams had a full week for review preparation, and communicated via email. The following week, each team conducted a 50-minute technical inspection.

Table 20.4   Experience Levels of Review Teams

Group	Experience
1	1 very experienced, 3 with some experience
2	4 with significant experience
3	2 with significant experience, 2 with little experience
4	2 with significant experience, 2 with little experience
5	2 with little experience

Table 20.5 Experience Levels of Review Teams

Experience Level	Years
Little	0 to 2
Some	3 to 6
Significant	7 to 15
Very	Over 15

Table 20.6 Preparation Time and Fault Severity of Each Team

Group	Total Preparation Time (hours)	Low Severity	Medium Severity	High Severity	Total Issues Found	Review Action Items
1	7		33		33	18
2	6	32	27		59	26
3	36	66	27		93	12
4	21	24	20	9	53	46
5	22	13	4	10	27	10

In Table 20.6, the last two columns need explanation. The total number of issues reported to the review leader is typically reduced during the review to a shorter list of action items that require additional work. In the case of Group 3, for example, many of the low severity issues were just simple corrections. Also, there will be duplication among the reported issues—something that the review leader must recognize and collapse into one agenda item.

It would be nice to have a Venn Diagram showing the final action items of each review team. This is topologically impossible with five circles. Instead, Table 20.7

Table 20.7 Demographics of Faults Found by Inspection Teams

Groups	Issues	Groups	Issues
1 only	4	2 and 4 only	6
2 only	9	3 and 4 only	1
3 only	6	1, 2, and 4	3
4 only	27	1, 2, and 5	1
5 only	4	2, 4, and 5	1
1 and 2 only	2	1, 2, 4, and 5	1
1 and 3 only	1	1, 3, 4, and 5	1
1 and 4 only	3	2, 3, 4, and 5	1
2 and 3 only	1	All groups	1

describes the overlap among groups. Of the 32 possible subsets of groups, only those with an overlap are listed. After the review meetings, the five groups found a total of 116 action items.

When all of these are aligned (by eliminating separate appearances of the same underlying fault), Table 20.7 is alarming. Consider the first few rows, in which 50 faults are found only by one group. Even worse, look at the last four entries, where only one fault was found by all five groups, and only four faults were found by four of the five groups.

The implications of this are enormous—companies simply cannot afford to have duplicate inspections of the same work product, so it behooves companies to provide review training, and inspection teams need to use their limited time as effectively as possible.

References

Boehm, B., *Software Engineering Economics*, Englewood Cliffs, NJ; Prentice-Hall, 1981.

IBM System Sciences Institute, "*Implementing Software Inspections*", 1981.

IEEE Standard Classification for Software Anomalies Working Group, 1044-2009 IEEE Standard Classification for Software Anomalies, 2009.

International Software Testing Certification Board, Foundation Level Syllabus, 2007.

International Software Testing Certification Board, Advanced Level Syllabus, 2012.

Pressman, R.S., *Software Engineering: A Practitioner's Approach*, New York: McGraw-Hill, 1992.

Wiegers, Karl, "Improving Quality through Software Inspections," *Software Development*, vol. 3, no. 4 (April 1995). Available at http://www.processimpact.com/articles/inspects.html

Chapter 21

Epilogue: Software Testing Excellence

Finishing a book is almost as hard as beginning one. The ubiquitous temptation is to return to "finished" chapters and add a new idea, change something, or maybe delete a part. This is a pattern that writing shares with software development and both activities endure small anxieties as deadlines near.

This book started as a response to Myers' *The Art of Software Testing*; in fact, the original working title was "The Craft of Software Testing" but Brian Marrick's book with that title appeared first. In the years between 1978 (Myers' book) and 1995 (the first edition of this book), software testing tools and techniques had matured sufficiently to support the *craft* motif.

Imagine a continuum with Art at one end, leading to Craft, then to Science, and ending with Engineering. Where does software testing belong on this continuum? Tool vendors would put it all the way at the engineering end, claiming that their products remove the need for the kinds of thinking needed elsewhere on the continuum. The process community would consider it to be a science, arguing that it is sufficient to follow a well-defined testing process. The context-driven school would probably leave software testing as an art, due to the need for creativity and individual talent. Personally, we still consider software testing to be a craft. Wherever it is placed on the continuum, software testing can also be understood in terms of *excellence*.

21.1 Craftsmanship

First, a disclaimer. The more politically correct *craftspersonship* word is too cumbersome. Here, *craftsman* uses the gender-neutral sense of the *–man* suffix. What makes someone a craftsman? One of our grandfathers was a Danish cabinet maker, and that level of woodworking is clearly a craft. One father was a tool and die maker—another craft with extremely stringent standards. What did they, and others recognized as craftsmen, have in common? Here is a pretty good list:

- Mastery of the subject matter
- Mastery of the associated tools
- Mastery of the associated techniques
- The ability to make appropriate choices about tools and techniques
- Extensive experience with the subject matter
- A significant history of high-quality work with the subject matter

Since the days of Juran and Deming, portions of the software development community have been focused on *quality*. Software Quality is clearly desirable, but it is hard to define, and harder still to measure. Simply listing quality attributes, such as simplicity, extensibility, reliability, testability, maintainability, etc., begs the question. The *–ability* attributes are all similarly hard to define and measure. The process community claims that a good process results in quality software, but this will be hard to prove. Can quality software be developed in an *ad hoc* process? Probably, and the agile community certainly believes this. Do standards guarantee software quality? This, too, seems problematic. Imagine a program that conforms to some set of defined standards, yet is of poor quality. So where does this leave the person who seeks software quality? Craftsmanship is a pretty good answer, and this is where *excellence* comes in. A true craftsman takes pride in his work—he knows when he has done his best work, and this results in a sense of pride. Pride in one's work also defies definition, but everyone, who is honest with himself, knows when he has done a really good job. So we have craftsmanship, pride, and excellence tightly coupled, recognizable, yet difficult to define, and hence to measure, but all are associated with the concept of best practices.

21.2 Best Practices of Software Testing

Any list of claimed best practices is subjective, and always open to criticism. Here is a reasonable list of characteristics of a best practice:

- They are usually defined by practitioners
- They are "tried and true"
- They are very dependent on the subject matter
- They have a significant history of success

The software development community has a long history of proposed "solutions" to the difficulties of software development. In his famous 1986 paper, "No Silver Bullet," Fred Brooks suggested that the software community will never find a single technology that will kill the werewolf of software development difficulties [Brooks, 1986]. Here is a partial list of "best practices," each of which was intended as a silver bullet. The list is in approximate chronological order.

- High-level programming languages (FORTRAN and COBOL)
- Structured programming
- Third-generation programming languages
- Software reviews and inspections
- The Waterfall Model of the software development life cycle

- Fourth-generation programming languages (domain specific)
- The object-oriented paradigm
- Various replacements for the Waterfall Model
- Rapid prototyping
- Software metrics
- CASE (Computer-Aided Software Engineering) tools
- Commercial tools for project, change, and configuration management
- Integrated development environments
- Software process maturity (and assessment)
- Software process improvement
- Executable specifications
- Automatic code generation
- UML (and its variants)
- Model-driven development
- Extreme programming (with its odd acronym, XP)
- Agile programming
- Test-driven development
- Automated testing frameworks

Quite a list, isn't it? There are probably some missing entries, but the point is, software development remains a difficult activity, and dedicated practitioners will always seek new or improved best practices.

21.3 Our Top 10 Best Practices for Software Testing Excellence

The underlying assumption about best testing practices is that software testing is performed by software testing craftsmen. Per the earlier discussion, this implies that the tester is very knowledgeable in the craft and has both the tools and the time to perform the task with *excellence*. There is a perennial debate as to whether a tester should be a talented programmer. To us, the answer is an emphatic yes. As a craftsman, programming is clearly part of the subject matter. Other attributes include creativity, ingenuity, curiosity, discipline, and, somewhat cynically, a can-I-break-it mentality. Our collective "top ten" best practices are only briefly described here; most of them are treated more completely in the indicated chapters.

21.3.1 Carefully Performed Technical Inspections

In addition to finding defects before coding begins, a good technical inspection will/ should make recommendations about the type and extent of appropriate testing (See Chapter 20).

21.3.2 Careful Definition and Identification of Levels of Testing

Any application (unless it is quite small) should have at least two levels of testing— unit and system. Larger applications generally do well to add integration testing. Controlling the testing at these levels is critical. Each level has clearly defined objectives, and these should be observed. System level test cases that exercise unit level considerations are both absurd and a waste of precious test time.

21.3.3 Model-Based Testing at All Levels

If an executable specification is used, a large number of system level test cases can be automatically generated. This offsets the extra effort of creating an executable model. In addition, this enables direct tracing of system testing against a requirements model. Because executable specifications are provocative, the automatically generated system test cases include many possibilities that otherwise might not be created.

Given the three fundamental approaches to integration testing discussed in Chapter 12, MM-Paths are demonstrably superior. They can also be used with incidence matrices in a way that parallels that for system level testing.

At the unit level, using appropriate models guarantees a form of testing that is as complete as the underlying model.

21.3.4 System Testing Extensions

For complex, mission critical applications, simple thread testing is necessary but not sufficient. At a minimum, thread interaction testing is needed. Particularly in complex systems, thread interactions are both serious and difficult to identify. Stress testing is a brute force way of identifying thread interaction. Many times, just the sheer magnitude on interactions forced by stress testing reveals the presence of previously undiscovered faults [Hill 2006]. Hill notes that stress testing is focused on known (or suspected) weak spots in the software and that pass/fail judgments are typically more subjective than those for conventional testing. Risk-based testing is a shortcut that may be necessary. Risk-based testing is an extension of the Operational Profiles approach discussed in Chapter 13. Rather than just test the most frequent (high probability) threads, Risk-Based testing multiplies the probability of a thread by the cost (or penalty) of failure. When test time is severely limited, threads are tested in terms of risk rather than simple probability.

21.3.5 Incidence Matrices to Guide Regression Testing

Both traditional and object-oriented software projects benefit from an incidence matrix. For procedural software, the incidence between mainline functions (sometimes called features) and the implementing procedures is recorded in the matrix. Thus, for a particular function, the set of procedures needed to support that function is readily identified. Similarly for object-oriented software, the incidence between Use Cases and Classes is recorded. In either paradigm, this information can be used to:

- determine the order and contents of builds (or increments)
- facilitate fault isolation when faults are revealed (or reported)
- guide regression testing

21.3.6 Use of xUnit and Object Mocking at the Unit Level

Mock objects replace the stubs and drivers used in unit testing of procedural code. Since they dovetail well with test frameworks such as JUnit, they make it easy to increase the scope of the test framework to include the mock objects.

21.3.7 Intelligent Combination of Specification-Based and Code-Based Unit Level Testing

Neither specification-based nor code-based unit testing is sufficient by itself, but the combination is highly desirable. The best practice is to choose a specification-based technique based on the nature of the unit (see Chapter 10), run the test cases with a tool to show test coverage, and then use the coverage report to reduce redundant test cases and add additional test cases mandated by coverage.

21.3.8 Use of Appropriate Tools at All Testing Levels

Software testing tools greatly augment what a tester can do, from automating tedious processes to expanding the types of questions testers can ask. Artificial Intelligence extensions to testing are increasingly effective.

21.3.9 Exploratory Testing During Maintenance

Exploratory testing is a powerful approach when testing code written by someone other than the tester. This is particularly true for maintenance on legacy code.

21.3.10 Test-Driven Development

The agile programming community has demonstrated success using Test-Driven Development (TDD) in applications where an agile approach is appropriate. The main advantage of TDD is the excellent fault isolation capability.

21.4 Mapping Best Practices to Diverse Projects

Best practices are necessarily project dependent. The software controlling a NASA space mission is clearly distinct from a quick-and-dirty program to develop some information requested by someone's supervisor. Here are three distinct project types. After their description, the top ten best practices are mapped to the projects in Table 21.1.

21.4.1 A Mission Critical Project

Mission critical projects have severe reliability and performance constraints and are often characterized by highly complex software. They are usually large enough so that no single person can comprehend the full system with all its potential interactions.

21.4.2 A Time Critical Project

While mission critical projects may also be time critical, this section refers to those projects which must be completed rapidly. Time-to-market and the associated loss of market share are the usual drivers of this project type.

Table 21.1 Best Testing Practices for Diverse Projects

Best Practice	Mission Critical	Time Critical	Legacy Code
Model-Driven Development	x		
Careful Definition and Identification of Levels of Testing	x	x	x
System-Level Model-Based Testing	x		
System Testing Extensions	x		
Incidence Matrices to Guide Regression Testing	x		x
Use of MM-Paths for Integration Testing	x		
Intelligent Combination of Specification-Based and Code-Based Unit Level Testing	x		x
Code Coverage Metrics Based on the Nature of Individual Units	x		
Exploratory Testing During Maintenance			x
Test-Driven Development		x	

21.4.3 Corrective Maintenance of Legacy code

Corrective maintenance is the most common form of software maintenance. It is in response to a reported fault. Software maintenance typically represents three-fourths of the programming activity in most organizations, and this is exacerbated by the pattern that maintenance changes are usually done by someone who did not create the code being changed.

21.5 An Extreme Example

Take time to look for an article titled "They Write the Right Stuff." It is an example of what can be done with discipline (and a big budget). The "on board shuttle group," as its name implies, writes the software for the space shuttle missions [Fishman 1996]. Here is one quote from the referenced article:

"This software is bug-free. It is perfect, as perfect as human beings have achieved. Consider these stats: the last three versions of the program — each 420,000 lines long-had just one error each. The last 11 versions of this software had a total of 17 errors. Commercial programs of equivalent complexity would have 5,000 errors."

The article also contains some devastating comments on the state of software development:

1. "The way we build software is in the hunter-gatherer stage." -Brad Cox, a professor at George Mason University
2. "Cave art,"… "It's primitive. We supposedly teach computer science. There's no science here at all." -John Munson, a software engineer and professor of computer science at the University of Idaho

The article continues…

"the on-board shuttle group produces grown-up software, and the way they do it is by being grown-ups. It may not be sexy, it may not be a coding ego-trip — but it is the future of software. When you're ready to take the next step — when you have to write perfect software instead of software that's just good enough — then it's time to grow up."

The shuttle group has four guiding principles, again quoting from the article:

1. The product is only as good as the plan for the product.
2. The best teamwork is a healthy rivalry.
3. The database is the software base.
4. Don't just fix the mistakes — fix whatever permitted the mistake in the first place.

One last quote:

"The most important things the shuttle group does — carefully planning the software in advance, writing no code until the design is complete, making no changes without supporting blueprints, keeping a completely accurate record of the code — are not expensive. The process isn't even rocket science. Its standard practice in almost every engineering discipline except software engineering."

What does all this mean for software testing excellence? Much like those "who write the right stuff," software testers need planning not "seat of the pants" *ad hoc* testing. Carefully planned testing echoes several items on our list of top ten best testing practices. To do good planning, the tester needs extensive knowledge of the product to be tested, effective testing techniques, and the judgment to make good choices among alternatives. As we saw in earlier chapters, testing tools enable testers to be more effective. As with and craft, a software tester needs sufficient time to complete carefully planned testing. One example? A GVSU graduate student came to class one evening, slammed his books down on a lecture table, and asked "How much time should be allowed for system testing?" One good rule of thumb is that the time for unit, integration, and system testing should be about what was spent in development. Walt's frustration was that, on a Tuesday, his project manager told him to start testing, because the 800,000 line project would be shipped on Friday. (Thanks Walt.)

We need to move beyond the "cave art" stage. Software testing craftsmanship requires a mindset much like that of those who "write the right stuff."

References

Brooks, Fred P. (1986). "No Silver Bullet — Essence and Accident in Software Engineering". Proceedings of the IFIP Tenth World Computing Conference: 1069–1076. Also found at (April 1987). "No Silver Bullet — Essence and Accidents of Software Engineering". *IEEE Computer* **20** (4): 10–19.

Fishman, Charles, "They Write the Right Stuff", *Fast Company*, 1996. [https://www.fastcompany.com/28121/they-write-right-stuff].

Hill, T. Adrian, "Importance of Performing Stress Testing on Embedded Software Applications", *Proceedings of QA&TEST conference*, Bilbao, Spain, Oct. 2006.

Appendix A: Complete Technical Inspection Packet

This Appendix contains all the items needed for a technical inspection of a set of use cases for an ATM Simulator described here.

A.1 Customer Requirements: ATM Simulator

The ATM system communicates with credit union customers via the Graphical User Interface shown in Figure A.1 and the 15 screens shown in Figure A.2. ATM customers can select any of three transaction types: deposits, withdrawals, and balance inquiries. To simplify the review, and the use cases, these transactions are only done on a checking account.

When a customer arrives at the ATM station, screen 1 is displayed. The customer accesses the SATM system with a virtual plastic card encoded with a personal account number (PAN), which is a key to an internal customer account file, containing, among other things, the customer's name and account information. If the customer's PAN matches the information in the customer account file, the system presents screen 2 to the customer. If the customer's PAN is not found, screen 4 is displayed, and the card is kept.

At screen 2, the customers are prompted to enter their personal identification number (PIN). If the PIN is correct (i.e., matches the information in the customer account file), the system displays screen 5; otherwise, screen 3 is displayed. The customer has three chances to get the PIN correct; after three failures, screen 4 is displayed, and the card is kept. Technically, this would require another screen with a different message. We will just assume this is a user-hostile ATM system.

On entry to screen 5, the customer selects the desired transaction from the options shown on screen 5. If balance is requested, screen 6 is displayed. If a deposit is requested, the status of the deposit envelope slot is determined from a field in the terminal control file. If no problem is known, the system displays screen 7 to get the transaction amount (deposit or withdrawal). If a problem occurs with the deposit envelope slot, the system displays screen 12. Once the deposit amount has been entered, the system displays screen 13, accepts the deposit envelope, and processes the deposit. The system then displays screen 14.

If a withdrawal is requested, the system checks the status (jammed or free) of the withdrawal chute in the terminal control file. If jammed, screen 10 is displayed;

469

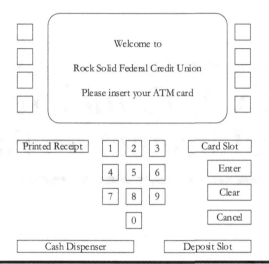

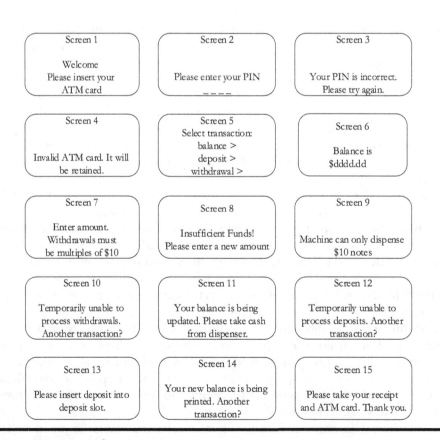

Figure A.1 ATM Customer Interface.

Figure A.2 15 User Interface Screens.

otherwise, screen 7 is displayed so the customer can enter the withdrawal amount. Once the withdrawal amount is entered, the system checks the terminal status file to see if it has enough currency to dispense. If it does not, screen 9 is displayed; otherwise the withdrawal is processed. The system checks the customer balance (as described in the balance request transaction); if the funds in the account are insufficient, screen 8 is displayed. If the account balance is sufficient, screen 11 is displayed and the cash is dispensed. The balance is printed on the transaction receipt as it is for a balance request transaction. After the cash has been removed, the system displays screen 14.

When the "No" button is pressed in screens 10, 12, or 14, the system presents screen 15 and returns the customer's ATM card. The buttons to the right of the screen in Figure 2.2 are associated with different, screen-dependent choices. In screen 5, they correspond to transaction choices. In screens 10, 12, and 14, they correspond to "yes" and "no" answers. Once the card is removed from the card slot, screen 1 is displayed. When the "Yes" button is pressed in screens 10, 12, or 14, the system presents screen 5 so the customer can select another transaction.

The following high-level input events can occur in the SATM system:

e1: Valid ATM card swipe
e2: Invalid ATM card swipe
e3: Correct PIN
e4: Failed PIN
e5: Choose Balance
e6: Choose Deposit
e7: Insert deposit envelope
e8: Choose Withdrawal
e9: Valid withdrawal amount
e10: Withdrawal amount not a multiple of $10
e11: Withdrawal amount greater than account balance
e12: Withdrawal amount greater than daily limit
e13: Remove cash
e14: Yes
e15: No

The output events are simply the 15 screens. (This is a simulator, no actual cash is returned, nor are there any actual ATM cards.)

screen 1:   Welcome screen
screen 2:   PIN Entry
screen 3:   Incorrect PIN
screen 4:   Invalid ATM Card
screen 5:   Select transaction (balance, deposit, withdrawal)
screen 6:   Balance is…
screen 7:   Enter withdrawal amount
screen 8:   Insufficient funds
screen 9:   Only $10 notes
screen 10:   Unable to process withdrawals
screen 11:   Please take your cash

screen 12: Unable to process deposits
screen 13: Insert deposit
screen 14: Another transaction?
screen 15: Take your ATM card and receipt

A.2 Base Use Cases

These base use cases are designed to be the subject of a technical inspection. There are faults deliberately present.

Line	Use Case ID, Name	UC1: Present valid ATM Card	
1	Description	Customer swipes a vaild ATM card	
2	Pre-conditions	1. screen 1 displayed	
3	Event Sequence		
4	Input Events	Output Events	
5	1. e1: Valid ATM card swipe	2. display screen 2	
6	Post-Conditions	1. screen 2 displayed	
7			

Line	Use Case ID, Name	UC2: Present invalid ATM Card	
1	Description	Customer swipes an invaild ATM card	
2	Pre-conditions	1. screen 1 displayed	
3	Event Sequence		
4	Input Events	Output Events	
5	1. e12: Invalid ATM card swipe	2. display screen 4	
6	Post-Conditions	1. screen 4 displayed	

Line	Use Case ID, Name	UC3: Correct PIN entered
1	Description	Costumer enters a correct PIN (this use case applies to all three possible PIN entry attempts)
2	Pre-conditions	1. screen 2 displayed
3	Event Sequence	
4	Input Events	Output Events
5	1. e3: Correct PIN enterede	2. display screen 5
6	Post-Conditions	1. screen 6 displayed

Line	Use Case ID, Name	UC4: Failed PIN entry
1	Description	Customer failed to enter a correct PIN on the third attempt
2	Pre-conditions	1. screen 2 displayed 2. previous two PIN attempts failed
3	Event Sequence	
4	Input Events	Output Events
5	1. e4: Incorrect PIN entered	2. display screen 1
6	Post-Conditions	1. screen 1 displayed

Line	Use Case ID, Name	UC5: Transaction choice: Balance Inquiry
1	Description	Customer selects the Balance Inquiry transaction
2	Pre-conditions	1. screen 5 displayed
3	Event Sequence	
4	Input Events	Output Events
5	1. e5: Choose Balance	2. display screen 6
6	Post-Conditions	1. screen 5 displayed

Line	Use Case ID, Name	UC6: Transaction choice: Deposit
1	Description	Customer selects the Balance Inquiry transaction
2	Pre-conditions	1. screen 5 displayed
3	Event Sequence	
4	Input Events	Output Events
5	1. e6: Choose Deposit	2. display screen 6
6	3. e7: Insert deposit envelope	4. display screen 14
7	5. e15: No	6. display screen 11
8	Post-Conditions	1. screen 1 displayed
		2. account balance is updated

Line	Use Case ID, Name	UC7: Deposit slot jammed
1	Description	Customer selects the Deposit transaction; deposit slot is jammed
2	Pre-conditions	1. e6: Choose Deposit
3	Event Sequence	
4	Input Events	Output Events
5	3. e15: No	2. display screen 12
6	Post-Conditions	1. screen 1 displayed
7		

Line	Use Case ID, Name	UC8: Normal withdrawal
1	Description	Customer selects the withdrawal transaction; valid withdrawal amount
2	Pre-conditions	1. screen 5 displayed
3	Event Sequence	
4	Input Events	Output Events
5	1. e8: Choose withdrawal	2. display screen 7
6	3. e9: Valid withdrawal amount entered	4. display screen 11
7		5. display screen 14
8	6. e15: No	
9	Post-Conditions	1. screen 1 displayed

Line	Use Case ID, Name	UC9: Withdrawal amount not a multiple of $20
1	Description	Customer selects the withdrawal transaction; valid withdrawal amount
2	Pre-conditions	1. screen 5 displayed
3	Event Sequence	
4	Input Events	Output Events
5	1. e8: Choose withdrawal	2. display screen 7
6	3. e10: Withdrawal amount not a multiple of $10	4. display screen 7
7		5. display screen 9
8	Post-Conditions	1. screen 1 displayed

Line	Use Case ID, Name	UC10: Insufficient funds
1	Description	Customer selects the withdrawal transaction; withdrawal amount > account balance
2	Pre-conditions	1. screen 5 displayed
3	Event Sequence	
4	Input Events	Output Events
5	1. e8: Choose withdrawal	2. display screen 7
6	3. e11: Withdrawal amount greater than account balance	4. display screen 8
7		5. display screen 1
8	Post-Conditions	1. screen 1 displayed

Line	Use Case ID, Name	UC11: Daily limit exceeded
1	Description	Customer selects the withdrawal transaction; withdrawal amount > daily limit
2	Pre-conditions	1. screen 5 displayed
3	Event Sequence	
4	Input Events	Output Events
5	1. e8: Choose withdrawal	2. display screen 7
6	3. e12: Withdrawal amount greater than daily limit	4. display screen 10
7		5. display screen 11
8	6. e15: No	
9	Post-Conditions	1. screen 1 displayed

A.3 Base Use Case Standard

Line	Use Case ID, Name	
1	Description	
2	Pre-conditions	
3	Event Sequence	
4	Input Events	Output Events
5		
6	Post-Conditions	
7		

1. **Use Case Name**
   The Use Case name should be short and indicative. Since use cases capture the behavior of a system, it is handy (but not mandatory) if their names begin with a verb.
2. **Use Case ID**
   The Use Case ID should be very short, and possibly linked to the major function, or to an actor in the application.
3. **Description**
   This is a narrative description that should be easily understood by the customer. To improve communication between the customer/user and the developer, system-specific jargon should be described in a supplemental glossary.
4. **Pre-conditions**
   Pre-conditions describe the state of the system before the use case is executed. It is easy for this section to become too general. Pre-conditions should be just those pertinent to the use case.
5. **Event Sequence**
   There are two portions of the event sequence: system inputs and system responses. Whether these are shown in two columns or in one column, they should be numbered to show the interleaved sequence of inputs and responses. Since this standard is for base use cases, there should be no pseudo-code logic expressing alternatives "within" a use case.
6. **Post-conditions**
   Post-conditions describe the state of the system after the use case has executed. As with the Pre-conditions, it is easy for this section to become too general. Post-conditions should be just those pertinent to the use case.

A.4 Base Use Case Checklist

1. Format complete?
   - Use Case Name
   - Use Case ID
   - Narrative description

- Preconditions
- Sequence of inputs
- Sequence of outputs
- post conditions

2. Logic Questions?
   - Any missing pre-condition?
   - Any missing post-condition?
   - Input sequence OK?
   - Output sequence OK?
   - "correctness" (no $5 notes)

3. Consistency
   - Naming conventions acceptable?
   - Are synonyms present?
   - Are synonyms "standardized" into one consistent term?

4. "Completeness"
   - Any missing use cases?
   - Flow across use cases?
   - Matching Pre-conditions with Post-conditions?
   - Extra use cases?
   - Traceable to specifications?

5. Conformance to Base Use Case Standard

A.5 Base Use Case Fault Severity Levels

For the purpose of the review exercise, three fault severity levels are sufficient. These levels are defined with respect to the Use Case Review Checklist.

Fault Severity 1 (least severe)

- use case format correct
  - Use Case Name
  - Use Case ID
  - Narrative description
  - Preconditions
  - Sequence of inputs
  - Sequence of outputs
  - Post conditions
- typographical errors
- grammar errors
- conformance to Use Case Standard

Fault Severity 2

- consistency faults
  - Naming conventions
  - Synonyms
  - Ambiguous/too general

- Logic Questions
  - Any missing pre-condition?
  - Any missing post-condition?
  - Input Sequence OK?
  - Output Sequence OK?
  - "correctness" (e.g., no $5 notes)

Fault Severity 3 (most severe)

- Completeness
  - Any missing pre-condition?
  - Any missing use cases or features because they are not specified in the Customer Requirements?
- Flow across Use Cases
- matching Preconditions with Postconditions
- Extra Use Cases
- Traceable to specifications? "Incorrectness"
- Missing steps/use cases?
- Extra steps/features. They should be removed because they are not included in the Customer Requirements.

A.6 Base Use Case Technical Inspection Forms

The reviewers, including the review leader and recorder, presents the result of their work product examination on a form similar to the one in Table A.1. These individual reports are merged by the review leader into the preliminary issues list.

Table A.1   Individual Inspection Ballot

Work Product Information					
Reviewer Name					
Preparation date					
Reviewer Preparation Time					
	Location		Checklist		
Issue #	Use Case	Line	Item	Severity	Description
1	1	1	typo	1	change "vaild" to "valid"
2					
3					

Table A.2 Inspection Summary

Work Product Information							
Review Team Members							
Leader							
Recorder							
Reviewer							
Reviewer							
Reviewer							
Producer							
Meeting Date							
total preparation time							
Team Recommendation							
		Location		Checklist			
Action Item #	Who?	Use Case	Line	Item	Severity	Description	
1	PCJ	1	1	typo	1	change "vaild" to "valid"	

A.7 Sample Inspection Report Outline

Technical Inspection Report

For

ATM System Simulator Use Case Descriptions

By

<Inspection Team Members>

Table of Contents

I.   **Introduction and Technical Inspection Process**
II.   **Preliminary Issue List**
III. **Prioritized Action Item List**
IV.   **Summary of Individual Ballots and Product Metrics**
V.   **Summary of Process Evaluations**
VI.   **Conclusion**

Reference

Attachments

Attachment A: ATM Simulator Use Cases
Attachment B: ATM Simulator Customer Requirements
Attachment C: Technical Review Forms
    1. Review Report
    2. Individual Ballots
Attachment D: Fault Classification (by Severity)
Attachment E: Use Case Review Checklist
Attachment F: Technical Review Agenda

Appendix B: Foodies Wish List Example

B.1 General Description

Foodies-Wish-List is an online shopping service for rare, expensive gourmet foods. Table B.1 lists the full inventory:

Table B.1   Foodie Wish List Inventory and Prices

Foodie Item	$/pound	$/ounce	$/gram
Vanilla beans	$112.00	$7.00	$0.25
Hop shoots	$128.00	$8.00	$0.28
Italian white truffles:	$200.00	$12.50	$0.44
Kobe beef	$300.00	$18.75	$0.66
Kopi Luwak coffee	$300.00	$18.75	$0.66
Moose House cheese	$450.00	$28.13	$0.99
Saffron	$450.00	$28.13	$0.99
Jamon Iberico de Belotta	$2,200.00	$137.50	$4.85
Almas caviar	$11,400.00	$712.50	$25.11

The high-level architecture of the application consists of three "swim lanes" as shown in Figure B.1. Each of the six components is further described by individual finite state machines (fsms).

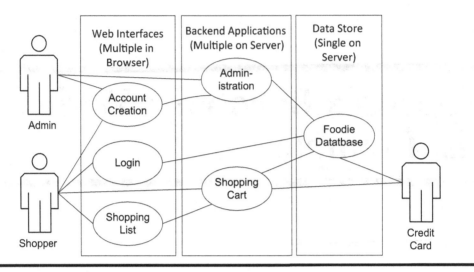

Figure B.1 Foodies Wish List Architecture.

B.2 Messages Among Finite State Machines

The connections among individual fsms in separate swim lanes are meant as communicating fsms. Typically, an output action in one fsm appears as an input event in an adjacent fsm. Finally, the numbering of input events, output actions, states, and messages is global and organized by decades. The Account Creation fsm decade is 10 to 19, Login is the 20's, and so on. After a few iterations, we identified the set of messages shown in Table B.2.

Table B.2 Messages Among Fsms

Message	From	To	Content
m1	Foodie Home	Account Creation	Open Account Creation
m2	Foodie Home	Login	Open Login
m3	Login	Shopping List	Open Shopping List
m4	Account Creation	Foodie Home	Close Account Creation
m5	Login	Foodie Home	Close Login
m6	Shopping List	Foodie Home	Close Shopping List
m7	Account Creation	Admin	Propose UserID to Admin
m8	Admin	FoodieDB	Submit UserID to FoodieDB
m9	FoodieDB	Admin	Approve New Member UserID
m10	FoodieDB	Admin	Reject New Member UserID

(Continued)

Table B.2 (*Continued*)

Message	From	To	Content
m11	Admin	Account Creation	Proposed USerID Approved
m12	Admin	Account Creation	Proposed USerID Rejected
m13	Account Creation	Admin	Defined User PIN to Admin
m14	Admin	FoodieDB	Send User PIN to FoodieDB
m15	FoodieDB	Admin	Confirm User PIN in FoodieDB
m16	Admin	Account Creation	Defined User PIN Accepted
m17	Login	FoodieDB	Entered UserID to FoodieDB
m18	FoodieDB	Login	User ID OK; expected PIN
m19	FoodieDB	Login	UserID not recognized
m20	FoodieDB	Login	User PIN OK
m21	FoodieDB	Login	User PIN failed
m22	Shopping List	Shopping Cart	Add item to Shopping Cart
m23	Shopping Cart	Shopping List	Item added to Shopping Cart
m24	Shopping Cart	Admin	Reduce FoodieItem Count
m25	Shopping List	Shopping Cart	Remove item from Shopping Cart
m26	Shopping Cart	Shopping List	Item removed from Shopping Cart
m27	Shopping Cart	Credit card	Payment tendered
m28	Credit card	Shopping Cart	Payment accepted
m29	Credit card	Shopping Cart	Payment rejected
m30	Shopping Cart	FoodieDB	Payment amount
m31	Shopping Cart	FoodieDB	Shopping Cart Contents
m32	Shopping Cart	Admin	Increase FoodieItem Count
m33	FoodieDB	Admin	FoodieItem inventory decreased
m34	FoodieDB	Admin	FoodieItems inventory increased
m35	FoodieDB	Admin	Payment entered in FoodieDB.
m36	Admin	FoodieDB	Increase FoodieItem inventory
m37	Login	FoodieDB	Entered PIN
m38	Admin	FoodieDB	Decrease FoodieItem inventory

External communication (input) events can originate from the Administrator or from any Shopper. This diagram does not show concurrency, but the interactions among concurrent shoppers are clearly important. Within each fsm, transitions are labeled as e/a, where e is an input event (or possibly a data condition) and a is an output action. The input events (and responses) local to a fsm are derived from elements of the windows corresponding to an fsm. Finally, there is an overall web page fsm. The fsm-based inputs, together with their global names and descriptions, are shown next.

B.2.1 Foodie Wish List Finite State Machines

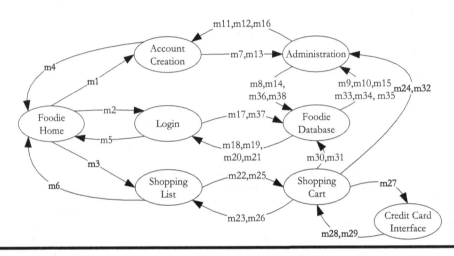

Figure B.2 Message Communication Among Finite State Machines.

B.2.1.1 Foodie Home

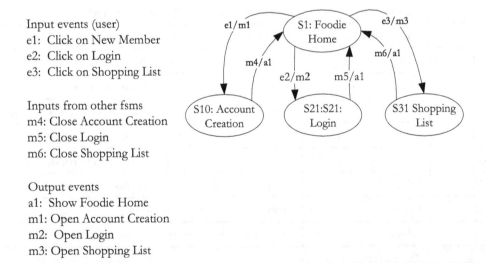

Input events (user)
e1: Click on New Member
e2: Click on Login
e3: Click on Shopping List

Inputs from other fsms
m4: Close Account Creation
m5: Close Login
m6: Close Shopping List

Output events
a1: Show Foodie Home
m1: Open Account Creation
m2: Open Login
m3: Open Shopping List

Figure B.3 Foodie Home fsm.

B.2.1.2 Account Creation

Input events (user)
e11: Enter UserID
e12: Create User PIN
e13: Click on Exit

Inputs from Foodie Home
m1: Open Account Creation

Inputs from Admin
m11: Proposed USerID Approved
m12: Proposed USerID Rejected
m16: Defined User PIN Accepted

Output events
a11: Show account creation window
a12: Show PIN Creation window

Output events to Admin
m7: Propose UserID to Admin
m13: Defined User PIN to Admin

Output events to Foodie Home
m4: Close Account Creation

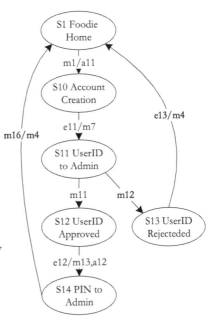

Figure B.4 Account Creation fsm.

B.2.1.3 Login

Input events (user)
e21: Enter valid UserID
e22: Enter invalid UserID
e23: Enter PIN = Expected PIN
e24: Enter PIN ≠ Expected PIN

Input events from FoodieDB
m2: Open Login
m18: UserID OK
m19: UserID not recognized
m20: User PIN OK
m21: User PIN failed

Output events
a21: Show Login window
a22: Show PIN Entry window

Outputs to FoodieDB
m5:   Close Login
m17: Entered UserID to FoodieDB
m37: Entered PIN

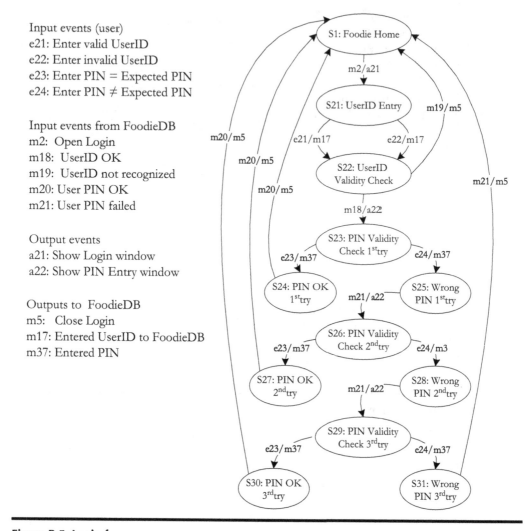

Figure B.5 Login fsm.

B.2.1.4 Shopping List

(Note: State 31 was needed for Login FSM)

Input events
e31: Window: Curser movement
e32: Select Foodie item
e33: Move item to Shopping Cart
e34: Remove item from Shopping Cart
e35: Click on Continue Shopping
e36: Done shopping

Inputs from Shopping Cart
m23: Item added to Shopping Cart
m26: Item removed from Shopping Cart

Inputs from Foodie Home
m3: Open Shopping List

Output events
a31: Show Browse window
a32: Curser at top of list
a33: New cursor position
a34: Increment FoodieItem Count
a35: Decrement FoodieItem Count

Output events to Shopping Cart
m22: Add item to Shopping Cart
m25: Remove item from Shopping Cart

Output events to FoodieDB
m24: FoodieItem count

Output events to Foodie Home
m6: Close Shopping List

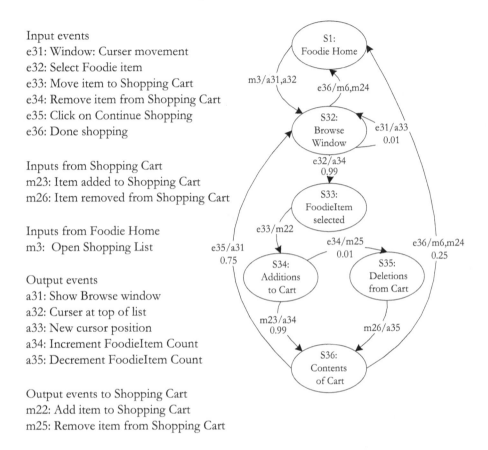

Figure B.6 Shopping List fsm.

B.2.1.5 Admin

Input events
e41: Click on Admin Done

Input events from Account Creation
m7: Propose UserID to Admin
m13: Define User PIN to Admin

Input events from FoodieDB
m9: Approve New Member UserID
m10: Reject New Member UserID
m15: Confirm User PIN in FoodieDB
m33: FoodieItem decreased
m34: FoodieItem added
m35: Payment entered in FoodieDB

Inputs from Shopping Cart
m24: Reduce FoodieItem Count
m32: Increase FoodieItem Count

Output events
a41: Show New Member window
a42: Show Ledger Window
a43: Return to Admin Home

Output events to Account Creation
m11: New Member USerID Approved
m12: New Member USerID Rejected
m16: Defined User PIN Accepted

Output events to FoodieDB
m8: Submit UserID to FoodieDB
m14: Send User PIN to FoodieDB
m36: Increase FoodieItem inventory
m38: Decrease FoodieItem inventory

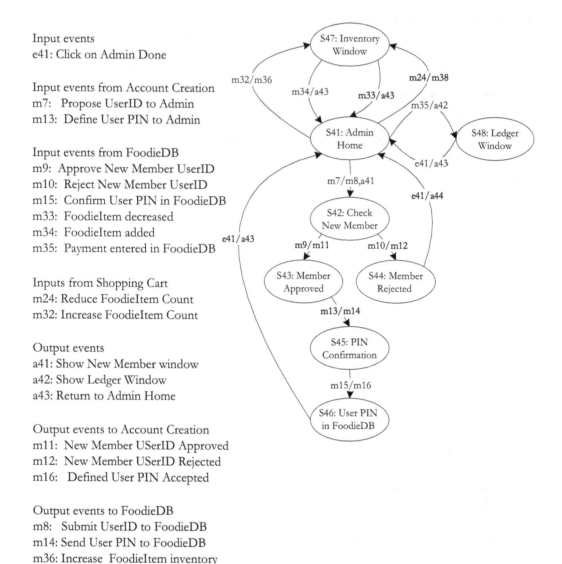

Figure B.7 Admin fsm.

B.2.1.6 Shopping Cart

Input Events
e51: Click on Checkout
e52: Click on Credit Card Interface
e53: Shopping Cart done

Inputs from Shopping List
m22: Add item to Shopping Cart
m25: Remove item from Shopping Cart

Inputs from Credit Card
m28: Payment accepted
m29: Payment rejected

Output Actions
a51: Show Checkout window
a52: Show Shopping Cart Home

Outputs to Shopping List
m23: Item added to Shopping Cart
m26: Item removed from Shopping Cart

Outputs to Credit Card
m27: Payment tendered

Outputs to FoodieDB
m30: Payment amount
m31: Shopping Cart Contents

Outputs to Admin
m24: Reduce FoodieItem count
m32: Increase FoodieItem count

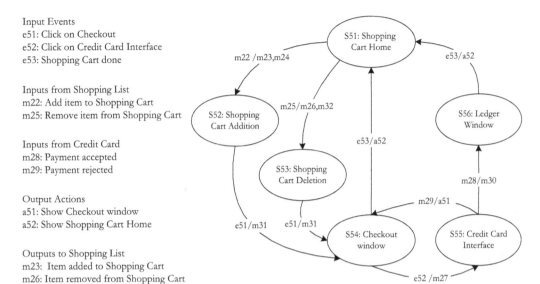

Figure B.8 Shopping List fsm.

B.2.1.7 FoodieDB

Input events
e61: User ID Found
e62: User ID Not Found
e63: Correct User PIN Entered
e64: Wrong User PIN Entered
e65: Item Count adjusted
e66: Click on Done

From Admin
m8: Submit UserID to FoodieDB
m14: Submit User PIN to FoodieDB
m36: Increase FoodieItem inventory
m38: Decrease FoodieItem inventory

From Login
m17: Entered UserID to FoodieDB
m37: Entered PIN

From Shopping Cart
m30: Payment amount
m31: Shopping Cart Contents

Output events
a61: Show UserID window
a62: Show PIN Entry Window
a63: Show Inventory Window
a64: Show Ledger Window
a65: Show Login Window
a66:Show Foodie Home

To Admin
m9: Approve New Member UserID
m10: Reject New Member UserID
m15: Confirm User PIN in FoodieDB
m33: FoodieItem inventory decreased
m34: FoodieItem inventory increased
m35: Payment entered in FoodieDB

To Login
m18: UserID OK
m19: UserID not recognized
m20: User PIN OK
m21: User PIN failed

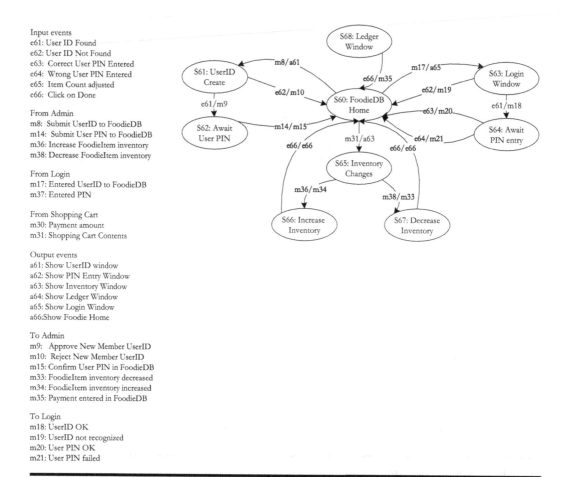

Figure B.9 FoodieDB fsm.

B.3 Dialogs Across Swim Lanes

The Account Creation, Admin, and FoodieDB finite state machines are densely connected (see Figure B.10). Prominent threads among these connections are usefully isolated as simple scenarios, which in turn will evolve into use cases and finally, system test cases. The finite state machines in Figures B.11, B.12, and B.13 are simplified versions of the full fsms, showing only those states and transitions necessary for a scenario.

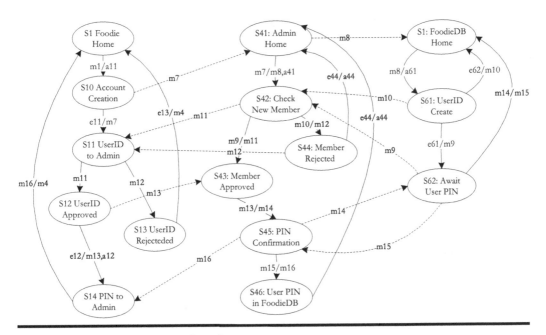

Figure B.10 Messages Among three fsms.

B.3.1 Scenarios

Scenarios are numbered according to their FSM number, (*e.g.*, Account creation scenarios are 1.1, 1.2, …)

Scenarios 1.1 and 1.2 are very detailed and complete. The interactions connected with the Foodie database are more complex (three other fsms), so those scenarios will be expressed both as state sequences and as message sequences.

B.3.1.1 Scenario 1.1: Normal Account Creation

A Foodie User proposes a UserID, sends it to Admin. Admin sends the proposed UserID to the FoodieDB. The FoodieDB checks and finds no duplicate, so it approves the new UserID, and confirms this to Admin. In turn, Admin confirms this to Account Creation. The newly approved User then creates a PIN and sends it to Admin. (No check is made on validity of a PIN, since it is local to a User.) Admin sends the PIN to the FoodieDB, so that the FoodieDB can send it as the "Expected PIN" to Login.

The sequence of messages in scenario 1 is m1, m7, m8, m9, m11, m13, m14, m15, m16, m4. The reason for making the state numbers global is so we can describe a scenario as a state sequence across swim lanes. The state sequence for scenario 1 is: S1, S10, S41, S1, S61, S62, S42, S11, S12, S43, S62, S45, S14, S1, S41, S1.

Scenario 1.1: Create a valid account		
Pre-Condition: The UserID is not in FoodieDB		
Account Creation	Admin	FoodieDB
1. e11: Enter UserID (original)		
2. Send m7: Propose UserID to Admin	3. Receive m7	

(Continued)

Scenario 1.1: Create a valid account		
	4. Send m8: Submit UserID to FoodieDB	5. Receive m8
	7. Receive m9	6. Send m9: Approve New Member UserID
9. Receive m11	8. Send m11: Proposed UserID Approved	
10. e12: Create User PIN		
11. Send m13: Defined User PIN to Admin	12. Receive m13	
	13. Send m14: Send User PIN to FoodieDB	14. Receive m14
	16. Receive m15	15. Send m15: Confirm User PIN in FoodieDB
18. Receive m15	17. Send m16: Defined User PIN Accepted	
19. Send m4: Account Creation complete		
Post-Condition: The UserID is in FoodieDB		

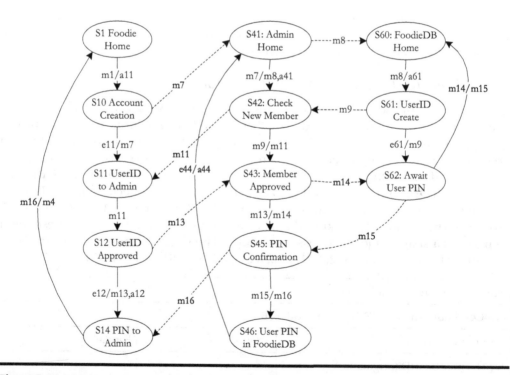

Figure B.11   Message Communication in Scenario 1.

B.3.1.2 Scenario 1.2: Duplicate UserID found

Foodie User creates a UserID, sends it to Admin. Admin sends the potential UserID to the FoodieDB. The FoodoeDB checks and finds a duplicate, so it rejects the new UserID, and confirms this to Admin. In turn, Admin confirms this to Account Creation. This rejection makes user PIN creation impossible.

The sequence of messages in scenario 2 is m1, m7, m8, m10, m12, m4. The reason for making the state numbers global is so we can describe a scenario as a state sequence across swim lanes. The state sequence for scenario 1 is: S1, S10, S41, S1, S61, S42, S44, S11, S13, S1.

Scenario 1.2: Create an invalid account		
Pre-Condition: The UserID is already in FoodieDB		
Account Creation	Admin	FoodieDB
1. e11: Enter UserID (duplicate)		
2. Send m7: Propose UserID to Admin	3. Receive m7	
	4. Send m8: Submit UserID to FoodieDB	5. Receive m8
	7. Receive m10	6. Send m10: Reject New Member UserID
9. Receive m12	8. Send m12: Proposed UserID Rejected	
10. e13: Click on Exit		
11. Send m4: Account Creation complete		
Post-Condition: Attempt failed.		

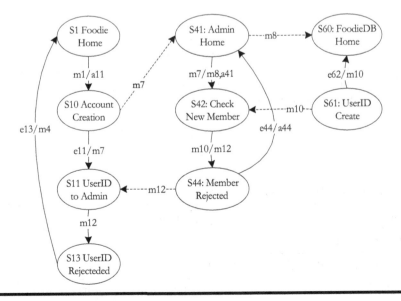

Figure B.12   Message Communication in Scenario 1.2.

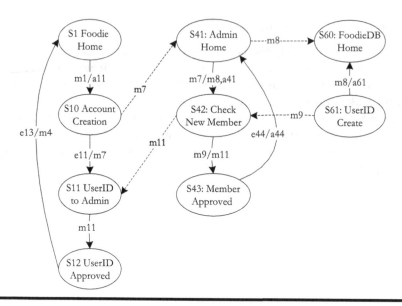

Figure B.13   Message Communication in Scenario 1.3.

B.3.1.3 Scenario 1.3: Partial Account Creation (no PIN definition)

A Foodie User creates a UserID, sends it to Admin. Admin sends the potential UserID to the FoodieDB. The FoodieDB checks and finds no duplicate, so it accepts the new UserID, and confirms this to Admin. In turn, Admin confirms this to Account Creation. The newly approved user chooses to define a PIN at some later session.

The sequence of messages in scenario 1 is m1, m7, m8, m9, m11, m4. The reason for making the state numbers global is so we can describe a scenario as a state sequence across swim lanes. The state sequence for scenario 1 is: S1, S10, S41, S1, S61, S42, S11, S12, S1.

B.3.1.4 Scenarios and Test Coverage for Login

In this subsection, we develop Login constituent Scenarios 2.1 through 2.5. Foe each scenario, we identify the state sequence and the sequence of events and messages embedded in the state sequence. These reappear in chapter 13 in the discussion of test coverage for Systems of Systems.

B.3.1.4.1 Scenario 2.1: Valid Login, PIN correct on 1st try

Scenario 2.1: Valid Login, PIN correct on 1st try	
Pre-Condition: The UserID and PIN are in FoodieDB	
Account Creation	FoodieDB
1. e21: Enter valid UserID	
2. Send m17: Entered UserID to FoodieDB	3. Receive m17
5. Receive m18	4. Send m18: User ID OK; expected PIN
6. e23: Enter User PIN = expected PIN	

Scenario 2.1: Valid Login, PIN correct on 1st try	
7. Send m37: Entered PIN	8. Receive m37
10. Receive m20	9. Send m20: User PIN OK
11. Send m5: Close Login	
Post-Condition: The UserID is logged in	

State Sequence: <S1, S21, S60, S63, S22, S23, S24, S1>
Event/Message/State Sequence: <S1, m2, S21, e21, S22, m17, S60, S61, m18, S23,
                                       e23, S24, m37, S64, e23, m37, m20, m5>

B.3.1.4.2 Scenario 2.2: Valid Login, PIN correct on 2nd try

Scenario 2.2: Valid Login, PIN correct on 2nd try	
Pre-Condition: The UserID and PIN are in FoodieDB	
Account Creation	FoodieDB
1. e21: Enter valid UserID	
2. Send m17: Entered UserID to FoodieDB	3. Receive m17
5. Receive m18	4. Send m18: User ID OK; expected PIN
6. e24: Enter User PIN ≠ expected PIN	
7. Send m37: Entered PIN	8. Receive m37
10. Receive m21	9. Send m21: User PIN failed
11. e23: Enter User PIN = expected PIN	
12. Send m37: Entered PIN	13. Receive m37
15. Receive m20	14. Send m20: User PIN OK
16. Send m5: Close Login	
Post-Condition: The UserID is logged in	

State Sequence: <S1, S21, S22, S23, S25, S26, S27, S1>
Event/Message Sequence: <m2, e21, m17, m18, e24, m37, m21, e23, m37, m20, m5>

B.3.1.4.3 Scenario 2.3: Valid Login, PIN correct on 3rd try

Scenario 2.3: Valid Login, PIN correct on 3rd try	
Pre-Condition: The UserID and PIN are in FoodieDB	
Account Creation	FoodieDB
1. e21: Enter valid UserID	
2. Send m17: Entered UserID to FoodieDB	3. Receive m17

Scenario 2.3: Valid Login, PIN correct on 3rd try	
5. Receive m18	4. Send m18: User ID OK; expected PIN
6. e24: Enter User PIN ≠ expected PIN	
7. Send m37: Entered PIN	8. Receive m37
10. Receive m21	9. Send m21: User PIN failed
11. e24: Enter User PIN ≠ expected PIN	
12. Send m37: Entered PIN	13. Receive m37
15. Receive m21	14. Send m21: User PIN failed
16. e23: Enter User PIN = expected PIN	
17. Send m37: Entered PIN	18. Receive m37
20. Receive m20	19. Send m20: User PIN OK
21. Send m5: Close Login	
Post-Condition: The UserID is logged in	

State Sequence: <S1, S21, S22, S23, S25, S26, S28, S29, S30, S1>
Event/Message Sequence: <m2, e21, m17, m18, e24, m37, m21, e24, m37, m21, e23, m37, m20, m5>

B.3.1.4.4 Scenario 2.4: Invalid Login, PIN failed on 3rd try

Scenario 2.4: Invalid Login, PIN failed on 3rd try	
Pre-Condition: The UserID and PIN are in FoodieDB	
Account Creation	FoodieDB
1. e21: Enter valid UserID	
2. Send m17: Entered UserID to FoodieDB	3. Receive m17
5. Receive m18	4. Send m18: User ID OK; expected PIN
6. e24: Enter User PIN ≠ expected PIN	8. Receive m37
7. Send m37: Entered PIN	9. Send m21: User PIN failed
10. Receive m21	
11. e24: Enter User PIN ≠ expected PIN	
12. Send m37: Entered PIN	13. Receive m37
15. Receive m21	14. Send m21: User PIN failed

Scenario 2.4: Invalid Login, PIN failed on 3rd try	
16. e24: Enter User PIN ≠ expected PIN	
17. Send m37: Entered PIN	18. Receive m37
20. Receive m21	19. Send m21: User PIN failed
21. Send m5: Close Login	
Post-Condition: The UserID is NOT logged in	

State Sequence: \<S1, S21, S22, S23, S25, S26, S28, S29, S31, S1>
Event/Message Sequence: \<m2, e21, m17, m18, e24, m37, m21, e24, m37, m21, e24, m37, m21, m5>

B.3.1.4.5 Scenario 2.5: Invalid Login, no PIN try

Scenario 2.5: Invalid Login, no PIN try	
Pre-Condition: The UserID and PIN are in FoodieDB	
Account Creation	FoodieDB
1. e22: Enter invalid UserID	3. Receive m17
2. Send m17: Entered UserID to FoodieDB	4. Send m19: User ID not recognized
5. Receive m19	
6. Send m5: Close Login	
Post-Condition: The UserID is not logged in	

State Sequence: \<S1, S21, S22, S1>
Event/Message Sequence: \<m2, e22, m17, m19, m5>

B.3.1.5 Summary of Event/Message Sequences for Scenarios 2.1 to 2.5

Scenario 2.1: Valid Login, PIN correct on 1st try
Event/Message \<m2, e21, m17, m18, e23, m37, e23, m37, m20, m5>

Scenario 2.2: Valid Login, PIN correct on 2nd try
Event/Message Sequence: \<m2, e21, m17, m18, e24, m37, m21, e23, m37, m20, m5>
Scenario 2.3: Valid Login, PIN correct on 3rd try
Event/Message Sequence: \<m2, e21, m17, m18, e24, m37, m21, e24, m37, m21, e23, m37, m20, m5>

Scenario 2.4: Invalid Login, PIN failed on 3rd try
Event/Message Sequence: <m2, e21, m17, m18, e24, m37, m21, e24, m37, m21, e24, m37, m21, m5>

Scenario 2.5 Invalid Login, no PIN try
Event/Message Sequence: <m2, e22, m17, m19, m5>

B.3.1.6 Test Coverage of Scenarios 2.1–2.5

To have full state coverage, we can test scenarios 2.2, 2.3, 2.4, and 2.5. To have full event coverage and full message coverage, we can test scenarios 2.1 and either 2.3 or 2.4. To have full state, event, and message coverage, we must test scenarios 2.1, 2.2, 2.3, 2.4, and 2.5.

Scenario 4: End-to-End Login to Purchase Transaction

1. A Foodie User logs in with a valid UserID that is sent to the FoodieDB. (m11). S1, S22, S23, S1
2. It is recognized with a message back to Login (m12). S1, S62, S1
3. The Foodie user then enters a valid PIN on the first try (m14); S1, S24, S27, S1
4. it is sent to the FoodieDB (m14), S1, S64, S1
5. and FoodieDB acknowledges this (m17), and the Foodie user is returned to the main menu at Foodie Home (S1).
6. From the Foodie Home screen, the Foodie user navigates to the Browse Window. After a series of cursor movements, selects a FoodieItem and sends it to the Shopping Cart (m19). S1, S32, S33, S35, S1
7. The Shopping Cart confirms this (m20); S51, S52, S53,
8. and the User goes to the Checkout window S54
9. The User enters a credit card payment (m24) S55 and receives confirmation from the credit card company (m25). S56, S1 and records this with the FoodieDB (m27) and requests the appropriate inventory reduction (m28). S1, S69.
10. The Admin (S41) receives the message (m28), S47 and instructs the FoodieDB to add the needed Foodie items
11. (m 33)
12. The FoodieDB confirms the payment (S69) and notifies the Admin (m32). In response to message m33 (from Admin) the FoodieDB updates the inventory (m33) and confirms this to Admin (m 31). S1, S69, S1,
13. Also, in response to message m28, the Foodie DB S67, S68 and sends message m30 to Admin.

State sequence for Scenario 3: S1, S22, S23, S1, S62, S1, S24, S27, S1, S64, S1, S32, S33, S35, S1, S51, S52, S53,S54, S55, S56, S1, S69, S1, S67, S68, S1.

Scenario: Normal purchase of one FoodieItem, payment accepted			
Web Swim Lane	Controlling Swim Lane		FoodieDB Swim Lane
Shopping List	Shopping Cart/ Credit Card	Admin	FoodieDB
e31: Cursor movement			
e32: Select Foodie item			
e33: Move Foodie item to Shopping Cart			
Send m22: Add item to Shopping Cart	Receive m22		
Receive m23	Send m23: Item added to Shopping Cart		
	Send m24: Reduce FoodieItem Count	Receive m24	
		Send m38: Decrease FoodieItem inventory	Receive m38
		Receive m33	Send m33: FoodieItem inventory decreased
	Send m31: Shopping Cart contents	Receive m31 Receive m31	
	e53: Click on Credit Card Interface		
	Send m27: Payment tendered		Receive m27
	Receive m28: Payment accepted		Credit Card sends m28:Payment accepted
		Receive m30	Send m30: Payment amount
		Receive m35	Send m35: Payment entered in FoodieDB
		Receive m33	Send m33: FoodieItem inventory decreased
e36: Done shopping	e54: Shopping Cart done	e41: Click on Admin Done	e66: Click on Done

B.4 Object-Oriented Design

The FSMs introduced earlier (e.g., Account Creation, Login, Shopping List, Administration, Shopping Cart, Foodie Database) define behavioral specifications that can be used to create analogous implementations. In object-oriented design, each of the FSMs represents the collective behaviors of a thing or an *object* or multiple things or objects. The messages in Table B.3 define the messages, or function calls, between the objects in the implementation represented by classes.

Importantly, the classes created for each of the FSMs fall into three different categories or *tiers* or *layers* in an *n-tier* architecture where tiers are physically separated (e.g., separate servers) and layers are only logically separated. In the case of the Foodies Wish List application, there are three categories, or tiers/layers, composing a three-tier application. The first of these tiers is the *presentation* tier that resides on the user's device to create the interface for the user. One tier removed from the user is the *domain logic* tier that typically resides on the server in a client-server architecture and manages domain logic and rules that support the expected behavior of the application. Finally, the *data storage* tier resides in the database server and stores the application data. The three tiers match the swim lanes presented in Figure B.1. An intermediate object is added (e.g., FoodieDBAccess) to accomplish communication across a tier (e.g., when the Login use-case directly communicates with the Foodie Database).

Organizationally, the classes communicate with each other across tiers as shown in Figure B.14. Classes in the presentation tier communicate with classes in the domain logic tier which then communicate with the FoodieDB in the data storage tier.

Table B.3   Class Categories

FSM	Class Name	Category or Tier/Layer
Account Creation	AccountCreationPage	Presentation
Login	LoginPage	
Shopping List	ShoppingListPage	
Shopping Cart	ShoppingCartPage	
	ShoppingCart	Domain Logic
Administration	AdministrationRules	
Foodie Database	FoodieDBAccess	
	FoodieDB	Data Storage

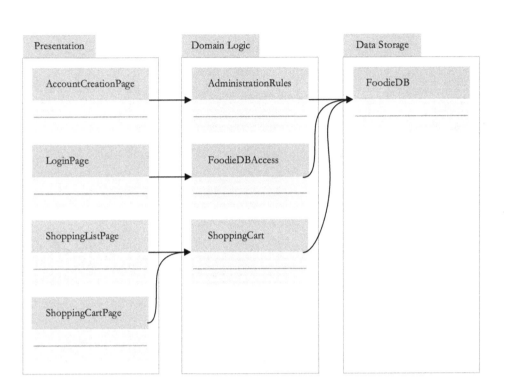

Figure B.14   Foodie Wish List Classes.

Index

Page numbers in *italics* refer to figures and those in **bold** refer to tables.

A

accountability, 451, 453–454
Account Creation (Foodies Wish List), 405,
    405, 482, **482–483**, *484–485*, 488,
    491–497, *501*
Account Creation FSM, 482, *485*, 490, 500, **500**
acknowledged systems of systems (Lane),
    375–376, 383, 386, 390
    Air Traffic Management System, 376, *377*
action coverage, **317**
action entries, 116, 119–120, 123, 235, **237**, **368**
action items, 447, 452, 454–455, **458**, 458–459
actions, 70, 121, 123, **139**, **145**, 235, 237–240, 268,
    303, 306, 318, 384, 403, 411, 413–414
action stub, 116, 122
Activate (ESML prompt), **341**, 383–384, *384*, 391
active state (notion), 66
activities and space (Zipf's Law), 22, 324
Actors, 379, **380–381**
Ada®, 59, 79, 81, 133
Adams, Scott, 456
addition, 156–157, 164
adjacency matrices, *55*, 55–56, **56**, 57, 62, 325
    Calendar call graph, **263**, **264**, 265
    definition, 362
    directed graph, 60–61, **61**
    integrationNextDate, 363
Administration (Foodies Wish List), 405, *405*, 406,
    482, 482, *484–485*, 489–491, 491–493,
    494, 498, 499, *501*
Administration FSM, 283–284, 396, *488*, 490,
    500, **500**
age ranges
    endpoint, 217
    insurance premium case study, **214**, 215, *216*
agile development, 197, 412
agile lifecycles, 232–233
    characteristics, 234
Agile Manifesto (2001), 234
agile methods, 231
    bottom-up, 230

agile model-driven development (AMDD), 245
agile programming, 191, 249, 463, 465
agile testing, 234–246
    agile model-driven development, 245
    behavior driven development, 235–240
    extreme programming, 242
    generic agile lifecycle, *234*
    model driven agile development, 245–246, *246*
    scrum, 242–243, *243*
    test-driven development, 243–244, *244*
    use cases, 241
    user stories, 234–241
    user story granularity, **247**
Agresti, W.W., 229
Air Traffic Management System, 383–384
    acknowledged SoS, 376
    Chicago incident (1993), 381, **381**
    classes, 379–380
    constituents, *377*
    use cases and sequence diagrams, 379–382
aircraft, mid-air collision with bird, 334
all pairs algorithm, 435, 438–440, 442
allpairs.exe program (Bach), 433, **434**, 442
    input for currency conversion GUI, **437**
    input in different order, currency
        conversion GUI, **438**
    test cases for currency conversion GUI,
        437, **438**
    test cases for NextDate, 435, **436**
all pairs technique, 431–439
    failures due only to pairs of inputs, 439
    independent variables, 433–435, **436**
    input order, 435–439
    program inputs, 433
all pairs testing, 81, 231, 431–442
    appropriate applications, 440–441, **441**
    NIST study, 440, 442
    recommendations, 441–442
all possible paths coverage (Miller), 140
alphanumeric characters, **16**
Ambler, Scott, 245

Anna Karenina principle, 143
anomaly, 10, 239
ANSI Standard 187B, 137
Apel, Sven, 393
application lifecycle management (ALM), 343
arcs, same as "edges", 53
Aristotle, 392, 399–400
army field telephone switching center, 333–334
ASF graph, definition, 293
ASF sequences, 305, 309
assert mechanism (JUnit), 258
associative laws, **39**, **48**
ATM Simulator, 469–472
ATM system, 316–317
ATM user interface screens, *470*
atomic propositions, same as simple
    propositions 141
atomic system function (ASF), 291–292–293,
    305, 336
    definition, 293
audits, **446**, 446
automated object mocking, 169–171
automatic regression testing system (ARTS),
    310, *310*
automatic test execution (ATE) system, 311, 343,
    417, 423–424, 430
avvinare, 338, 341

B

Bach, James, 431, 442
backward slices, 191, 199, 203, 209
balanced decomposition, 302
Ball, Thomas, 190
banking system, UML inheritance, 184, *184*
baseline method (McCabe), 157–158
basis (mathematical notion), 156
basis of vector set, definition, 157
basis path algorithm, 158, 160
basis path technique, **212–213**
basis path testing, 156–162, 203, *203*
Batory, D., 393
BDD decision table, 235–240
    action added for customer notification, **239**
    action entries added, **237**
    conditions interchanged, **237–238**
    final version, **241**
    group of rules collapsed into one rule, **238**
    response to invalid card, 237
    rules, **236–240**, 238–240
    rules combined, **239–240**
    rules completed, **240**
BDD scenarios, 350, 410, 430
    definition, 235, 411
    Extended FSM, 412–414
    Garage Door Controller, 411, **412**
Beck, Kent, 165, 242

behavior, 340–341
    "prescribed" *versus* "proscribed", 316
behavioral issues, **341**
behavioral models, 318, 337
behavior-driven development (BDD), 25–28,
    234–240, 409
    bottom-up approach, 239
    completeOrder method, 108
    Garage Door Controller, 410–411, *410*, **411–412**
Beizer, Boris, 138
Berger, Bernie, 432
best practices, 462–465
    careful definition and identification of levels of
        testing, 463, **466**
    carefully performed technical inspections, 463
    exploratory testing during maintenance, 465
    incidence matrices to guide regression
        testing 464
    intelligent combination of specification-based
        and code-based unit level testing, 465
    model-based testing at all levels, 464
    system testing extensions, 464
    test-driven development, 465
    use of appropriate tools at all testing
        levels 465
    use of xUnit and object mocking at unit
        level 464
best practices (mapped to diverse projects),
    465–466, **466**
    legacy code, **466**, 466
    mission critical project, 465, **466**
    time critical project, 465, **466**
beyond unit testing, 225–468
    all pairs testing, 431–442
    feature interaction testing, 391–407
    integration testing, 253–289
    life cycle-based testing, 227–251
    model-based testing, 337–352
    software complexity, 353–372
    software technical reviews, 443–459
    software testing excellence, 461–468
    system testing, 291–336
    testing event-driven systems (case study),
        409–430
    testing systems of systems, 373–390
Bieman, 190
"big bang" approach, 229, 253–254, 258–259,
    261, 289
Big Design Up Front (BDUF), 245
binary arithmetic operators, **16**
Binder, Robert V., 183, 314–315
bipartite graph, 67–68
black box testing, 7, 7, 8
blobs: interpreted as states, 73
Boehm, B., 230, 232, 234, 443–444, *444*
    spiral model, 231
Boolean expressions, 140–141–142

Boolean functions, 249
Boolean operators, **140**, 140–141
Boolean variables, **16**, 82, 140, 143
bottom line, 205
    definitions, 156–157
    Efficient Triangle Program, 204–205,
        206–207, **212**
    effort and efficacy, *203*
    essential complexity, 160–162
    McCabe's method, 157–163
bottom-up approach, 244, 247–248, 295, 412
bottom-up development, 234, 413
bottom-up integration, 229, 258, *258–259*
bottom-up testing order, 227–228
boundary value analysis, 8, 222, **222**
boundary value technique, **212–213**
boundary value test cases, 163
    insurance premium case study, 213, 218–220
boundary value testing (BVT), 79–95, 98–99, 101,
        108, 110, 128, 138–139, 202, *202*, 203
    effort and efficacy, *203*
    guidelines, 93–95
    independent considerations, 79
    input domain of function of two variables, *80*
    normal BVT, 80–82
    path coverage of normal boundary values,
        210, **211**
    path coverage of worst-case values, 210, **211**
    random testing, 92, **92–93**
    rationale, 80
    robust BVT, 82–83
    shortcomings, 97
    special value testing, 85
    traversing test method pendulum, 210, **211**
    worst-case BVT, 83–85
boundary value testing (examples), 85, **86–91**
    NextDate function, 85, **87–91**
    normal test case, **86**
    test cases for Triangle Problem, 85, **86–87**
    worst-case boundary value test cases, **86–87**
bounded function, 111
bounded variables, 92, 98
Bourgeois Gentilhomme (Molière, 1671), 337
Brooks, Fred P., 462
Brown, J.R., 19, 204
Bruyn, W., 383
bugs, xix, 466
    definition, 3
builds, 264, 464
build sequence, 230, *230*, 231
Busy Hour Call Attempts (BHCAs), 333

C

C, 59, 133
C#, 166
C++, 166

calculus, 33–34, 36, 53
Calder, Muffy, 392
Calendar call graph (adjacency matrix), **264**,
    265, 265
Calendar Program
    call graph-based integration, 260–265
    cyclomatic complexities of MM paths, *268*
    functional decomposition tree, *254*
    lexicological inclusion, 256
    neighborhood integration, 262–264
    procedural integrationNextDate, 269–275
    pseudo code, 255–256
    top-down integration, 256–258
call forwarding, 391, 401
call graph-based integration, 260–265, 268
    Calendar Program, *260*
    neighborhood integration, 262–264
    pairwise integration, 261–262
    procedural integrationNextDate, 270–275
    pros and cons, 264–265
call graphs, 181–182, 280, 353
    comparison with other integration testing
        strategies, **275**
    definition, 361
    directed graph, 261
    procedural integrationNextDate, 269, 272
    units in procedural integrationNextDate, *361*
    units replaced by numbers, *263*
calling party identification problem, 400–401
Calvin and Hobbes, 333
capacity testing, same as "stress testing", 332–334
cardinality, 42–43, *44*, 48–49
    "essentially a binary property", 44
Cartesian product, 36, 39–40, 42–43, 84, 100, 102,
        121–124
    definition, 37
case/switch, *65*, 141–142
    program graph, *132*
"cattle pens", and cyclomatic complexity, 355,
        355, 356
CAUSE, 287, **288**, 310–314, 417, **424**, **426**, 429
cause and effect graphing, 115, 127–128, *128*
caviar, **398**, 398, 481
century years, 21–22
chain coverage, definition, 136
chain, definition, 62, *134*, 134
checklists, 10, 382, **446**, 446, 449, 451, 454,
        456–457, 476–478
Checkout, 316, 498
Chellappa, Mallika, 19
Chicago aircraft incident (1993), 381, **381**, *382*,
        383, 386
    swim lane description, *389*
Chidamber, S.R., 181
Chidamber/Kemerer (CK) metrics, 181, 369
Chilenski, John Joseph, 140–143
circuits, 57, 127

Clarke, Lori A., 19, 171
class aggregation, 174
class diagrams, 340
classes, 77, 183, 185, 202, 214, 347, **364**, 364,
        368–369, 378–380, 432, 439, 464, 500
    use cases, 300–301
class/object definition, **19**
clear box testing, same as "code-based testing", 8
COBOL, 59, 97, 133, 171, 462
    static applications, 441
code-based techniques, comparison with
        specification-based techniques, **212–213**
code-based testing, xix, 8–9, 12, 15, 98, 131–164,
        201–204, 244, 246, 249, 291, 314, 354
    basis path testing, 156–162
    code coverage metrics, 135–156
    comparison of test case identification
        methods, *8*
    DD-Paths, 132–135
    detractors, 132, *134*
    distinguishing characteristic, 131
    guidelines and observations, 163
    insurance premium case study, 218–220
    intelligent combination with specification-
        based unit level testing, 465, **466**
    path testing (two most common forms), 131
    program graphs, 131–132
    punishment-fits-crime approach, 222
code-based testing examples
    capabilities of selected code coverage
        tools, **156**
    compound condition from NextDate, 143–147
    compound condition from Triangle Program,
        149–150
    condition with two simple conditions, 143–147
    Java code for NextDate function tests, 151–155
    JUnit test results, 155–156
    model-based (decision table) code coverage
        metrics, 147–148, **148**
    program graph-based coverage metrics,
        147–148
    test coverage analyzers, 150
code coverage metrics, 135–156, 222, **466**
    compound conditions, 140–143
    examples, 143–155
    Miller's coverage metrics, 136–140
    model-based (decision table), 147–148, **148**
    program graph-based coverage metrics,
        135–136
code coverage tools: capabilities, **156**
code structuring precepts (sequence, selection,
        repetition), 341
code with compound conditions, 143–155
coffee, 398, **399**, **481**
    Petri nets, 404, *404–405*
co-functionality testing, **275**
co-functioning, 265

cohesion, 182–183
collaborative systems of systems, 375, 383,
        386, 390
    definition (Maier), 374
combination (functional/structural) testing, 265
combinatorial circuits, 400, 441
combinatorial explosion, *432*
comments, 66, 249
commercial tools (model-based testing), 342–348
    Conformiq, 343–346
    "reactive" versus "transformational"
        (Harel), 342
    TestOptimal, 342–343, *344*
    Verified Systems International GmbH, 346–348
communicating finite state machines, 320
    dialog involving four constituents, **308–309**
    identifying threads in systems of systems, 305,
        307–308, **308–309**
    normal purchase of One FoodieItem, **308–309**
communicating FSMs to test cases (system level),
        313–314
communication primitives for systems of systems,
        382–389, 391
    ESML prompts as Petri nets, 383–386
    new prompts as Swim Lane Petri Nets,
        386–389
communication traffic (interfaces among
        units), 361
commutative law, **39**, **48**
compilers, 112, 171
complementation laws, **39**, **48**
complement, definition, 36
complete decision tables, 116–117, 119–120
completeness (notion), 45, 97, 100
completeOrder method, 112
    coverage of strong normal equivalence
        classes, **110**
    coverage of weak normal equivalence
        classes, **110**
    equivalence class testing, 108–110
    reduced decision table, **109**
    robust forms of equivalence class testing, 110
    strong normal equivalence classes, *109*
    weak normal equivalence classes, *109*
complete statement, "default" statement fragment,
        131
complexity, 248; *see also* software complexity
complexity metrics, 181–182
complex loop coverage, 138–139, *139*
complex system, *versus* "system of systems", 374
components, 228, 392
    early delivery, 234
    failure rates, 334
components of graph, 58
    definition, 57
composition, 183, 264
compound condition coverage, **148**

compound conditions, 138, 143–155, 220, **223**, 250, **250**, 357–358
   Boolean expression, 140–141
   coupled conditions, 141
   masking conditions, 141
   modified condition decision coverage, 142–143
   NextDate, 143–147
   program graph, *143*, 147
   Triangle Program, 149–150
compound If statement, 250
compound proposition, 140–141
compression (stress-testing strategy), 333, 335
computational complexity, 358–361
   Day of Week with Zeller's Congruence, 359–361
   Halstead Metrics, 358
computation faults, **11**
computation use (C-use), 172–173, *174*, 192, 207
computer-aided software engineering (CASE), 36–37, 73, 80
concatenated loops, 138, *139*
concurrency, 318, 339, 484
concurrent statecharts, *74*, 74–75
condensation graphs, 57–58, 136, 138, 140, 160
   DD-Path graph, 134–135, *135*
   strong components, *64*
condensing nodes, 57
conditional statements, **17–18**
condition coverage, 149, 220
condition, definition, 141
   operand of Boolean operator, 141
condition stub, 116
condition test, 136
conditions, **119**, 121, **122**, **145**, **150**, 212, 235, **237–238**, 237–240, 318
   choice, 116
   NextDate, 116–117, **118**
   strong or weak coupling, 141
   triplet (weakly coupled), 141
configuration item, 449, 455
configuration management, 246–248, 257, 448–449, 455
conflicting UserIDs, **395**
Conformiq, 343–346
   Garage Door Controller, 344, *345*, **346**
   insurance premium problem, 343, *344*
congruence, 45, 50
conjunction, **17**, 46–47, **50**, 142, 313, 327, 336, 400
connectedness, 57, 73
connectivity, 55, 58, 61, 202, 325, *327*
constituents, 320, **320–321**, 321–323, **326**, 386, *387–389*, 390
   dialogs among, 305–309
contradiction (proposition always false), 47–49, 149
contradictories, 400, *400*, 402

contraries, 400, *400*, 401, 402
contribution (notion), 191–192
control center (system of systems), 374, *375*
control complexity, 358
control flows, **17–19**, 343
controlled action (transition), 384, *384*, 385
control signals, 422–423
control statements, 142
control transfer, 265–266
cooperation, four levels, 382
corporate culture, 453, 455
cost-benefit ratio, 445
cost weighting, 327
coupling, 141, 183
Coupling between Classes (CBC), 181–182, 367
coverage metrics for system testing, 314–320
   best practice, 314–315
   input event and action coverage, **317**
   model-based test coverage, 314, 318, *319*, **319–320**
   use case-based test coverage, 314–317
coverage report, 150, 465
Cox, Brad, 467
CPPUnit for C++, 166
craft motif, xix–xx, 9, 85, 99, 104, 111, 163, 201, 204, 253, 291, 461–463, 467–468
creativity, 461, 463
Credit Card Interface, 282–283, **308**, *378*, *484*, *489*, 499
cross-check, 250, 268, 318
cross product, 85, 108, 173, 215, 432
   same as "Cartesian product", 37
currency conversion GUI
   allpairs.exe input, **437**
   allpairs.exe input in different order, **438**, 438
   allpairs.exe test cases, 437–439, **439**
currency converter, 435–437, 441
   allpairs.exe program outputs, 437, **438**
   equivalence classes, 437, **437**
   error messages, 437
customer-driven development, 228, 234
customer requirements, *234*, 469–472
customers, 229, 232, 445
cycle, definition, 61
cyclomatic complexity, 58, 128, 143, 160–162, 182, 204, 219, **223**, 251, 269, 353–358
   "cattle pens", 355, *355*, 356
   decisional complexity, 357–358
   definition, 354
   effect of adding edges, *75*
   integration level, 362–363
   MM-Paths, 268, *268*
   node outdegrees, 356
   reduced outdegrees, **356**, 356
   source code, 368
   theorem, 356
cyclomatic number, 58, 157–158, 160

D

data, **12**, 45, 165, 168–169, 171, 182, 213, **213**, 253, 266, 325, 367, 399–403, 405, 433, 437, 441, 444, 484
databases, 41, 169, 295, 321, 377, **395**, 399, 402, 467
  intension and extension, 191
data declaration statements, 66, 191, 197
dataflow analysis, 165, 171, 275
  traversing test method pendulum, 204–205, *205*, **206**
dataflow diagrams, 60, 302, 338, *339*, 340, 383
dataflow technique, 139, **212–213**
dataflow testing, 138, 162–163, 171–181, 202, *202*, 206–207, 221, **223**, 315
  define-use testing definition, 171–172
  define-use testing example, 174–181
  define-use testing metrics, 173, *174*
  Foodies Wish List, 24–29
  insurance premium case study, **220**
  reality check on path testing, 171
  revelation of "deeper faults", 248
data interactions in square of opposition, 400
data items, 400
data modeling, 42–43, 191
data places, 70–71, **71**, 72, 392, 403
data storage tier, 500, **500**, *501*
dateToDayNum (Calendar Program), *262*, **263**
dayNumToDate, 261, *261–262*, **263**
DD-Path coverage, 136–137, **137**, 150, 163, 218
DD-Path graph, 134, 136–137, 266, 358, 366
  Triangle Program, *135*
DD-Path testing, 137
DD-Paths (decision-to-decision paths), 132–135, 139–140, 160, 246, 266–267, 292, 318, 358
  definition (chain of statement fragments), 134
  dependent pairs, 138
  raison d'être, 135
  program graph, 134
DeMorgan's laws, **39**, **48**
DeVries, Byron, xix–xx
  biography, xxi, 418
  master's thesis (2013), 339–340
decisional complexity, 357–358
decision coverage, 143, 145, 150
decision rules, advantages and disadvantages, 34–35
decisions, 66, 343, 358
decision tableau method, 115
decision table-based testing, 8, 115–129
  cause and effect graphing, 127–128, *128*
  guidelines and observations, 128
  test cases for NextDate function, 121–127, **125–127**
  test cases for Triangle Problem, 120, **121**

decision table rules, 435
decision tables, 82, 112, 150, 229, 249, **249**, 340, 342, 400, 407, 410, 437
  basic information, 115–116
  BDD, 235
  BDD scenarios (Garage Door Controller), 411, **412**
  complexity mechanism, **368**
  condition portion and action portion, 116
  example program fragment, **139**
  expressive capability, **341**
  first rule, **26**
  Foodies Wish List, **26–29**
  force top-down view, 239
  impossible rules, 119, **119**
  inconsistent type, **120**
  insurance premium case study, 217, **217**
  iteration, 128
  model of choice for static interactions, 406
  mutually exclusive conditions, **118**
  nondeterministic type, 120
  redundant type, **119**, 120
  rules, 116
  sample, **115**
  scalability issue, 128
  thread testing "cumbersome", 318
  three conditions, seven actions, 108
  Triangle Problem, 116, **117**, **150**
  use cases, 297
decision table techniques, 116–120, 122, **212–213**
decision table terms, **115**
decision table test cases, insurance premium case study, **217**
decision table testing, 202, *202*, 203, 222, **222**
  effort and efficacy, *203*
declarative programming languages, 59
decomposition, 183, 302
decomposition-based integration, 253–260, 268
  bottom-up integration, 258, *258–259*
  procedural integrationNextDate, 269–270, *271–272*
  pros and cons, 259–260
  sandwich integration, 258–259, *259*, 260, 263–264
  top-down, 256–258, *257*; see also functional decomposition
decomposition tree, 253–254, *254*, 258–260, 262
deduction, 47
deductive syllogism, 47
defect, definition, 3
defect discovery, 445
define/reference relationship, 138, 171
define/use notions, 54, 165, 191, 203, 275
define/use testing
  definitions, 171–172
  example, 174–181
  metrics, 173, *174*

defining nodes, 191–192, 206
    definition, 172
definition-clear path with respect to variable
        (dc-path), 172, 181, 203, 207
definition-use path with respect to variable
        (du-path), 172, 181, 197, 206–207,
        209, 221
    all-du-paths criterion, 173
    disadvantage versus slice-based testing, 209
    feasible, 207, **208**
    possible, 206
    testing (effort and efficacy), *203*
degree of node, 54, 362
dependencies, 143, 169, 202–203, 304, 320,
        378, 433
    input domain, 121
Depth of Inheritance Tree (DIT), 181–182, 367
design code test, *234*, 243
design object, 248, 455
design phase, 125, 229, 245, 444
detailed design phase, 12, 230, *230*, 231
determinism, definitions, 406
Deutsch, Michael S., 254
development phase, 4, 10, 227, 444, 446, 449
devices, 70, 440
    failure modes, **425**
dialogs
    across swim lanes (Foodies Wish List),
        490–499
    formalized as scenarios, 306, **306–307**
    as sequences of ASFs, 305, 309
dialogs among constituents, 305–306, **306–307**
    test cases derived from, 306
dialog scenarios to test cases (system level), 313
digraph, same as "directed graph", 58
directed acyclic graph (DAG), 64, 132, 136
directed graphs, 36–37, 53, 58–64, 157–158, 163,
        204, 262, 267, 318, 335, 354–356,
        361–362, 368, 418
    adjacency matrix, 60–61, **61**
    chain of nodes, *134*
    with a cycle, *63*
    definition, 58–59
    EDPNs, 70
    equivalent graphs, 61, *61*
    example, *59*
    finite state machines, 66
    four forms of n-connectedness, 402, *402*
    indegrees and outdegrees, 59–60, *59*
    n-connectedness, 63
    nodes (types), 60
    paths and semipaths, 61–62
    Petri nets, 67–68
    program graphs, 65, 131
    reachability matrix, **62**, 62–63
    recording family relationships, 61
    strong components, 63–64, *64*

strongly connected, 268
structured programming constructs, *65*
directed path, definition, 61
directed semipath, definition, 62
directed systems of systems, 383, 386, 390
    definition (Maier), 374
    Garage Door Controller, 375–376, *376*
discrete mathematics for testers, 33–51
    applicable to specification-based testing, 33
    functions, 39–42
    propositional logic, 45–50
    relations, 42–45
    set theory, 33–39
disjunction, 46–47, **50**
distributive laws, **39**, **48**
documentation, 249, 445–446
"does" view (behavior) *versus* "is" view
        (structure), 241, 294, 332, 340–341,
        353, 379
domain, 7, 40–41–42, 79
domain elements, 41–42
domain logic tier, 500, **500**, *501*
domain testing, 222
domination laws, **39**, **48**, 141
don't care entries, 116–117, 120, 123–124, 238,
        240, 437
driver classes, 286
driver development, 263, 268
drivers, 229, 258, 260–261, 464
dual tone multi-frequency (DTMF), 333
dynamic applications, **441**, 441
dynamic interactions, 402–406
    multiple processors, 405–406
    single processor, 402–405
dynamic program slices, 191

E

eagle and mouse, 249, 251
edge coverage, 138, 142, 318
    definition, 136
edges, 55, 58, 60, 62, 157–158, 171, 191, 202, 270,
        327, 338, 353–356, 391
    directed graphs, 59
    initial and terminal, 61
    interpreted as transitions, 73
    as "messages", 361–363
    messages and returns from one unit to
        another, 267
    program graphs, 131
    as "sequential flow", 293
edge sequences (paths), 56
edge sets, 59
edge testing, 98, 110, 112
Efficient Triangle Program
    basis path testing, 204–205, **206**, *207*, **208**
    decision tables, **212**

Efficient Triangle Program flowchart, *205*, 211–212
  feasible paths, **206**
Efficient Triangle Program program graph, *206–207*
  feasible paths, **208**
  one set of basis paths, **208**
  possible and feasible paths, **206**
Einstein, A., 406
emergency response SoS, 378
empty set, 35–36, 49
enable/disable, 341, 383–384, *384*, 386, 391, 425, 427, 429
enabling, meanings, 383
encapsulation, 183
endpoints of arc, same as "nodes", 53
entity/relationship model, 59, 340
equivalence classes, 45, 97–98, 116–117, 121–122, 432, 441
  currency converter, 437, **437**
  elements (use in identification of test cases), 98
  logical variables, 433
  Triangle Problem, 433
  valid and invalid, 102, 105
equivalence class technique, **212–213**
equivalence class testing, 97–113, 202, *202*, 203, 222, **222**
  completeOrder method, 108–110, **109–110**
  coverage of feasible paths, **206–208**, 211
  "edge testing", 110, 112
  effort and efficacy, *203*
  guidelines and observations, 111–112
  improved, 99–102
  insurance premium case study, 215, *216*
  invalid classes, 111
  NextDate function, 104–108
  robust forms, 111
  strong forms, 111–112
  traditional, 98–99, *99*, 106
  Triangle Problem, 103–104, **206**, *207*, 210–211
  weak forms, 111
  weak robust, 98
equivalence relations, 45, 63–64, 97, 106
  defining properties, 57
  induced by partition, 45
  used to define classes, 104
equivalent graphs, *55*
error, 10
  definition, 3
error messages, 83, 93, 437, **438**, 438, **439**
"error" test cases, 112
errors, 4, 80, 163, 169
Escape keystroke, **317**, 317
ESML (Extended System Modeling Language), 340, 341, 382, 391
  basic prompts, 383

Enable prompt, 421
  Trigger prompt, 420, *421*, 421–422
ESML prompts as Petri nets, 383–386
  enable, disable, activate, 384, *384*, 390
  Petri net conflict, 383, *383*, 384, 386, *388*
  Petri net interlock, 383–384, *384*
  suspend and resume, *385*, 385–386, 390
  trigger, 385, *385*, 386, 389, *389*, 390
essential complexity (McCabe), 160–162
  condensing structured programming constructs, *161*
essential use cases, 294, *294*, **295**
event-driven Petri nets (EDPNs), 15, 70–73, 293, 339–340, 400, 406–407, 409, 419, 430
  definition, 70
  enabled and fired transitions, **72**
  example, *71*
  expressive capability, **341**
  external inputs and outputs (definition), 403
  important difference from traditional Petri nets, 72
  markings, 71, **71–72**
  topologically possible forms of connection, 391–392; *see also* Petri nets
event-driven systems, xix, 233, 293, 315, 341, 409–430
  BDD scenarios, 410–412
  characteristics, 409
  deriving test cases from swim lane EDPNs, 423–424
  exercises, 430
  FMEA, 425–430
  Garage Door Controller problem statement, 410
  modeling with extended finite state machines, 412–418
  modeling with swim lane EDPNs, 418–423
event/message sequences, 495–498
event quiescence, 70–71–72, 293, 316, 341, 419–422
events, 49, **301**, 303, 310–311, 433, 494
event sequences, 303, 349–350, **472–476**, 476
evolutionary development, 230–231
exception handling, 83, 222, **222**
exclusive OR (EOR), **46**, 46–47, 127, *128*
executable specifications, *233*, 233–234
expanded essential use cases, 294, *294*, 311
  correct PIN on first try, **296**, 312–313
"expected" (ATE engine), 311, 430
exploratory testing during maintenance (best practice), 465, **466**
extended ATE test cases, 311–314, **312**, *313*, 336
extended entry decision tables (EEDT), 116, 122, 128, 430
  NextDate, 433, **435**, 435

extended finite state machines
  derived from BDD scenarios, 412–414
  insights, 418
  modeling event-driven systems, 412–418
  non-deterministic, *415*, 416
  top-down development, 414–418
external inputs, 403, *403*
external outputs, 403, *403*
extreme programming lifecycle, *242*
extreme programming (XP), 242

F

Facebook, 75
Fagan, Michael, 445
failure, 324
  definition, 4
Failure Mode Event Analysis (FMEA)
  light beam sensor, 425–430, **425–426**, **428**,
    426–429
failures, 10, 401–402, 440, 443
Fallacy of Extension, 132, 440
fault discovery, 443, 448, 464
fault isolation, 221, 244, 248, 251, 258–261, 264,
    275, 289, 464–465
fault isolation capabilities continuum, 289, *289*
fault resolution costs, 443–444, *444*
fault resolution step, *4*, 4
fault severity, 449, 451, 454, **458**
fault severity levels, 477–478
faults, 4, *4*, *9*, 9, 80, 137–138, 201, 221, 401–402,
    432, 439–440
  definition, 3
faults of commission, 3–4, 6
faults of omission, 3–4, 6
fault taxonomies, 10, **10–12**
feasible paths, 203–204, 266, **320–321**
feature, definition (Batory et al.), 393
feature interaction exercises, 407
feature interaction problem, xix
  definition, 391–393
feature interactions
  nondeterminism, 406–407
  versus correct behavior, **393**
feature interactions (taxonomy), 399–406
  dynamic interactions in multiple processors,
    405–406
  dynamic interactions in single processor,
    402–405
  static interactions in multiple processors,
    401–402
  static interactions in single processor, 399–401
feature interactions (types), 393–399
  input conflict, 394–396
  output conflict, 397–398
  resource conflict, 398, **399**

feature interaction testing, 391–407
feedback, 229–230, 232–233
final node, 134, *134*
final state (notion), 66
finite state machine message path (FSM/M
    path), 285
  continuum of fault isolation capabilities,
    289, *289*
  definition, 286
finite state machine message path integration,
    286–287, **288**
  message and state flow, *287*
  partial test procedure, **288**
finite state machines (FSMs), 15, 64, *67*, 233, 280,
    282, 337–338, *340*, 340–342, 350–351,
    394, *403–404*, 409, 430, 481
  complexity mechanism, **368**
  conventions, 66–67
  definition, 66–67
  dynamic interactions in single processor, 406
  examples of directed graphs, 318
  expressive capability, 341, **341**
  Garage Door Controller, 67
  hierarchy, 301, *302*
  identifying threads in systems of systems, 305,
    307, 307–308, **308–309**
  Login and Shopping List constituents, 327, *328*
  Login constituent, 318, *319*
  message communication, *283*
  message communication among multiple
    instantiations, *396–397*
  nondeterministic, *406*, 414, *415*
  numerators and denominators, 66
  paths to test cases (system level), 312–313
  reduced (Foodies Wish List), *283*
  "special case of Petri nets", 70
  state explosion problem, 73
  states "never actually defined", 66
  tendency to look like "spaghetti code", 74
  thread execution probabilities, 325
  transitions, 343
  Windshield Wiper Controller, 70
finite state machines (identifying threads from
    models), 301–304
  paths, 301–303, *304*
  paths (quantity required), 303–304
Fishman, Charles, 466
flattened classes (Binder), 183–184, *184*
flexibility, 64, 234
flipping, **158**, 158, **159**, 163, 203, 205, **208**
flowcharts, 204, 342
  complexity mechanism, **368**
  Efficient Triangle Program, *205*
flow of control, 54, 65, 354
FoodieItem inventory, *488*, *490*, 499
FoodieItems, **483**, *487–489*, 498, 499

Foodies Wish List, xix, 15, 24–29, 280, 291, 320, 324, 353, 393, 405, 481–501
  Account Creation FSM, *485*
  architecture, *482*
  building an order, 25–28, **26–29**
  candidate threads, 292
  computing final price, 25–28, **26–29**
  conflicting User IDs, 395, **395**
  decision tables, **26–29**
  dialogs across swim lanes, 490–499
  digit entry, 292
  end-to-end login to purchase transaction, 498
  inventory and prices, **481**
  inventory before and after purchase, **399**
  message communication, *279, 281,* **394**
  messages among FSMs, 482, **482–483**, *484, 491*
  model-based integration testing, 280–289
  normal account creation, *394*, 394
  normal purchase of one Foodie item, payment accepted, 499
  object-oriented design, 500, **500**, *501*
  pairwise integration, 282–286
  PIN entry, 292–293
  problem statement, 25
  real use cases, 295
  reduced finite state machine, *283*
  risk-based testing, 327
  scenarios (full FSM/M Paths), 286–287, **288**
  shopping session, 292–293, 301, *302*
  simple transactions, 292–293
  threads in finite state machines, 301–309
Foodies Wish List classes, 500, **500**, *501*
Foodies Wish List Database (FoodieDB), 286, **288**, **297–300**, 305, **306**, **308–309**, *313*, 314, **320–321**, 328, *377–378*, 394, **395–396**, *396–397*, 405, 406, *482*, **482–483**, *484*, *486–492*, 491–500, *493–494*, **493–497**, **500**, *501*
  events, **398**
  FoodieDBStub, 283–284, **284–286**
  FSM, *489–490*, 500, **500**
  long use case, 324
  short test case, 323
Foodies Wish List Home (Foodie Home), *405*, *482, 484–487, 490–492, 494*, 498
  FSM, *484*
Foodies Wish List scenarios, 490–499
  duplicate userID found, *493*, **493**
  normal account creation, 491–492, **491–492**
  partial account creation (no PIN definition), *494, 494*
Foodies Wish List scenarios and test coverage for Login, 494–498
  invalid login, no PIN try, **497**
  invalid login, PIN failed on 3rd try, **496–497**
  summary, 497–498

  valid login, PIN correct on 1st try, **494–495**
  valid login, PIN correct on 2nd try, **495**
  valid login, PIN correct on 3rd try, **495–496**
Foodies Wish List (slice-based testing), 192–196
  program graph of private static double updateShoppingCart, *193*
  program graph of slice on truffleSales, *194*
  reduced Foodie inventory, **192**
  shopping cart user interface, *192*
  subset lattice of "interesting" slices, *196*
Foodies Wish List system, 316, 335–336
  communication among constituents, *378*
  constituents, 305, 307
  illicit access, 328
  operational profiles, 324–327, **329**
  swim lane architecture, *377*
  system of systems, 377, *377–378*
Foodies Wish List Users, 110
  creation of invalid account, **307**
  creation of valid account, **306**
  creation of valid account (reduced FSM), *307*, 307–308
FORTRAN, 59, 97, 133, 462
forward slices, 191, 199
Friday13th (Calendar Program), *254*, 255–257, *258–262*, **263**
frozen work product, 448–449
functional decomposition, 39, 229–230, 232, 259–260, 269
  comparison with other integration testing strategies, **275**
  procedural integrationNextDate, 269, *272*; see also decomposition
functional decomposition tree, 254, 260
functionality, 171, 183–184, 190, 203, 231, 257, 392, 394–395
functional testing, 7, 44, 120, 137, 201, 210, 227–228
  appropriate choices, **222**
  decision tables, 115
  hybrids, 268
  punishment-fits-crime idea, 221
  special value testing, 85
functions, **19**, 39–42, 79, 94, 99, 269
  composition, 41–42
  definition, 40
  domain and range, 40
  one-to-one, 42
  one-to-one *versus* many-to-one, 41
  types, 40

G

Gallagher, K.B., 190–191
gaps, 38, 97–98, 135, 137, 163, 202, 219, 318
gaps of untested software, 7, 9

Garage Door Controller, 15, 29, 342–344, *345*, *348*, 390, 409
    Behavior Driven Development, 410–411, **411–412**
    constituents, *376*
    corrected FSM, *416*
    corrected FSM (soap opera use case for long path), **417**
    directed SoS, 375–376
    extended FSM, 412–418
    finite state machine, 66, *67*, *348*, 348, **348**
    FMEA, 425–430
    light beam sensor, 410
    mapping paths in FSM to state sequences, **416**
    modeling with swim lane EDPNs, 418–423
    problem statement, 410, 414
    SysML context diagram, 410, *410*
    system level test case for normal door closing, **424**
    system level test case for normal door closing with light beam interruption, **424**
    test cases derived from swim lane EDPNs, 423–424
    top-down development, 414–418
Garbage In, Garbage Out (GIGO), 98
getDate, *254*, 255–257, *258–262*, **263**, *268–269*, 270, *271–274*, **363**, **366**
getDigits, 261, *261–262*, **263**
Given, When, Then (BDD keywords), 25–26
Go (oriental game), 245
good programming practices, **223**
grading rubrics (academic world), 449
Grand Valley State University, 457
granularity, 106, **247**, 248, 292, 294
graph-based coverage metrics, 318
graphical user interfaces (GUIs), 98, 469, *470*
    currency converter, 435–437
graphs, 53–58
    adjacency matrices, *55*, 55–56, **56**
    components, 57
    condensation graphs, 57–58
    connectedness, 57
    cyclomatic number, 58
    definition, 53–54
    degree of node, 54
    external boundary (source and sink nodes), 60
    incidence matrices, 54–55, **55**
    paths, **56**, 56–57
    with seven nodes and five edges, *54*
graphs for testing, 64–75
    event-driven Petri nets, 70–73
    Petri nets, 67–70
    program graphs, 64–66
    statecharts, 73–75
graph theory, 8, 147, 157, 160, 261, 292, 355
    pertains to structural testing, 33

graph theory for testers, 53–75
    directed graphs, 58–64
    graphs, 53–58
graphs for testing, 64–75
Gregorian calendar, 21–22
Gruenberger, F., 19
GTE Automatic Electric Labs, *444*, 444
Guest, 24–25, **28–29**, 108, *109*, **109–110**

H

Halstead, Maurice H., 358
Halstead Metrics, 353, 358–361
    Day of Week with Zeller's Congruence, 359–361
Halting Problem, 304
Hamming, R.J., 368
hardware, 127, 335, 452
Harel, D., 73–74, 233, 339, 342, 409, 441
Hetzel, Bill, 19, 254
hierarchy charts, 3, 340
high-level use cases, 294, *294*, **295**
Hill, T. Adrian, 464
Hoffner, T., 198
Huang, J.C., 138
human factors, 310, 445, 455
hybrid functional testing, 217–218, *218*

I

IBM Corporation, 37, 137, *444*, 445
    defect amplification model (1981), 444
    website, 73
idempotent laws, **39**, **48**
identity laws, **39**, **48**
IEEE Standard Classification for Software Anomalies (1993, 2009), 10, 451
if-else construct, 161, *357*, 400
If statements, 142
if-then connective, 46–47, *65*, 137, 141, 235, 356
if-then-else logic, *65*, 128, 132, 136–137, 141, 356
    program graph, *132*
imperative programming languages, 59, 65, 131, 134, 265, 361
implementation of code examples, 15
implementation philosophy, 83
implementation, procedural versus O-O, **278**
impossibilities, **249**, 250–251
"impossible" action, 121
impossible cases, **212**, 212
impossible combinations, 203
impossible interfaces problem, 258
impossible paths, 204
impossible rules, 120–121, **122–126**, 127, 143, 145, 149, **150**
impossible test cases, 121

impossible test pairs, 260
improved equivalence class testing
    incidence matrices, 54–55, **55**, 295–297,
        300–301, 353, 368–369, 464, **466**
    regression testing, 464, **466**
    strong normal ECT, 100–101, *101*
    strong robust ECT, 102, *102*
    weak normal ECT, 100, *100*
    weak robust ECT, 101–102
incident, definition, 4
inconsistency, 119–120
incremental development, 230–231
IncrementDate, *269–270*, 270–272, *272–274*, **363**
indegree of node, 60
    definition, 59
indegrees, 62, 134, 262, 356, 362, 403
independence, 84, 108, 112, 142, 145
independent circuits, 157
independent variables, 82, 93, 105, 149, 222,
    222, 441
    all pairs technique, 433–435, **436**
industrial-strength inspection process, 452–455
industrial test execution system, 310–311
infeasible paths, 138, 202–204, 284, 315, 318, 320
inferior nodes, same as "transfer nodes", 60
informal fallacies, 440
information hiding, 248
inheritance, 174, 182, 185
    testing object-oriented software, 183–185
    UML diagrams of banking system, 184, *184*,
        190, 190
inhibitor arc, 427
    definition, 429
initial (or start) nodes, 59, 66, *134*, 134
initial state (notion), 66
input conflict, 394–396, 403, 405–406
    message communication among multiple
        instantiations of FSMs, *396*
    test cases, **396**
    userIDs, **395**
input data, 98
    defined in terms of intervals and sets of
        discrete values, 111
input devices, 409
input domain, *80*, 93, 104, 111
    true partition, 122
input domain dependencies, 121
input domain testing
    same as "boundary value testing", 79
input (domain) equivalence classes, 8
input events, **317**, 342, 409, **412**, 413–414, *415*,
        416, **417**, **419**, 421–422, 471, **472–476**,
        482, 484
    context-sensitive, 341, 418, 437, 441
input events and messages
    expansion with added use cases, **300**
    use cases, 297–300

input order, 435–439, 441
input-output, 4–5, 7, **16**, 19, 21, 30, 40, 69–70, 72,
        79, 83, 97, 100–101, 127–128, 241, 268,
        292–293, **295**, 297, 301, **302**, 305,
        310–311, 315, 318, 342, **348**, 349,
        406, 441
    cause-and-effect relationships, 128
    conditions and actions (decision tables), 116
    faults, **10**
    Login scenarios, **301**
inputs, 407
    equivalence classes, 116
    invalid combinations, 21
input sequence, 477–478
input variables, 80, 139, 440
    logical relationships, 21–24, 128
    subsets, 128
inspection checklist, 451
inspection packet contents, 448–452
    fault severity levels, 451
    frozen work product, 448–449
    review issues spreadsheet, 449, **450**
    review report outline, 451–452
    review reporting forms, 450–451
    standards and checklists, 449
    work product requirements, 448
inspection process, 452–455
    commitment planning, *452*, 453
    disposition, *452*, 455
    preparation, *452*, 453–454
    report preparation, *452*, 454
    review meeting, *452*, 454
    reviewer introduction, *452*, 453
    stages, *452*
inspection report outline, 479
Institute of Electronics and Electrical Engineers
    (IEEE) Computer Society, 3
insurance premium case study, 213–219, **220**
    age class, *218*
    boundary value test cases, 219
    boundary value testing, 214–218
    code-based testing, 218–219
    data, **214**
    data boundaries, **214**
    dataflow testing, 221
    decision table approach, 217, 220
    decision table test cases, 220
    detailed worst-case boundary value test cases
        for one age class, *215*
    detailed worst-case values, **216**
    equivalence class testing, 215, *216*
    error-prone aspects, 217
    feasible paths, 219, **220**
    hybrid test cases for, 35–45
    Java code, 218, *219*
    path-based testing, 219–220, **220**
    path coverage of functional methods, **220**

problem statement, 217
program graph, 218–219, *219*
redundancy point, 215
slice testing, 221
specification-based testing, 214–218, *218*, **220**
specification-based versus code-based testing
    methods, 214–221
weak and robust normal equivalence class test
    cases, *216*, 218
weak normal equivalence class test cases,
    219–220
worst-case boundary value test cases, *214*, 218
insurance premium problem, 342–343, *344*, **345**
    activity diagram, *347*, 347
Integrated Development Environment, 172
integration-level complexity, 361–363, **364**
    call graphs, *361*, 362, 363
    cyclomatic complexity, 362–363
    message traffic complexity, 363, **364**
integration-level cyclomatic complexity, 363
    definition, 362
integration-level thread, 292
integrationNextDate, 364, **364**
    adjacency matrix, **363**
    call graph, *361*
    classes (program graph), *279*
    messages (object-oriented
        implementation), **280**
    procedural version, 269–275
    pseudo-code version, *361*, 362, **363**
integration-system testing, 245
    scrum lifecycle, *243*
integration testing, 228–229, 231–233, *234*, 245,
    253–289, 292, 382, 392, 464, 467
    call graph-based integration, 260–265
    comparison of strategies, **275**
    decomposition-based integration, 253–260
    example (Foodies Wish List), 24–29
    example (O-O integrationNextDate), 275–280,
        281–282
    example (procedural integrationNextDate),
        269–275
    functional decomposition tree (Calendar
        Program), *254*
    model-based, 280–289
    path-based integration, 265–268
integrity checking, 55
interactions, 292, 432, 439, 484
    time-dependent and time-independent, 399
interaction, versus "interfaces", 265
interesting slices, *196*, 197
"interesting" system transactions, 233
interface faults, **11**
interfaces, 363
    versus "interaction", 265
interface testing, **275**
interior nodes, *134*, 262

International Software Testing Qualification Board
    (ISTQB), 12, 98, 133, 227
    Advanced Level Syllabus, 110, 431, 443
    Foundation Level Syllabus, 443
    Glossary, 3
intersection, definition, 36
intervals, 99–100, 104, 111
"into" versus "onto" distinction, 41, 43–44
invalid dates, **88–91**, **127**, 154, 166, 168, **247**
invalid input dates, **106–108**
invalid values, 101–102
"is" view (structure), see "does" view
IsFriday (Calendar Program), *262*, **263**
isLeap (Boolean function), 166–171, 177–178,
    188–189, 249
    Calendar Program, *254*, 255–262, **263**, 269,
        269, 271, *272–274*, **363**, **366**
    decision table, *249*, 251
    MDD version, 249, *250*
    TDD version, *251*, 251
    truth table, 251
isMonday (Calendar Program), *262*, **263**
isolated node, 60, 64
isomorphism, 50
isValidDate (Calendar Program), 262, *262*, **263**,
    268, 271, **363**
iteration plan, *234*
iterative development, *230*, 242–243, 246
iterative lifecycle testing, 230–234
    executable specification, *233*, 233–234
    rapid prototyping, *232*, 232–234
    specification-based models, 232–234
    waterfall spin-offs, 230–232

J

Java, xix, 59, 133, 138, 151–156
    multi-line blocks of code (indentation and
        curly braces), 132
    structural elements, 15, **15–19**
Java code
    insurance premium case study, *216*, *219*
    O-O integrationNextDate, 275–278
Java implementation
    NextDate function, 21–24
    Triangle Problem, 19–21, 132
Java Object class, 182
Java program graph, 158
Java range check code, *144*, 161
Java single method, 364, **364**, *365*
Jet Propulsion Laboratory, 445
Jorgensen, Paul C., xix–xx, 70, 318, 418
    biography xxi
    Craft of Model-Based Testing (2017), xxi, 337,
        342, 409
    Modeling Software Behavior (2009), xxi,
        340–341

JSlice, 198, **198**
JUnit, xix, 166, 204, 258, 464
 ASSERT mechanism, 151–155, 168–170, 175,
  185–186, 258, 275, 281
 automatic dependency removal from test case
  for leap year, 170
 manual dependency removal from test case for
  leap year, 170
 parameterized test case for leap year, 169
 SimpleDate class, 166–168, 171
 test case for leap year, 168
 test environments, 244
JUnitParams, 168
JUnit test, 175, 178
Juran and Deming, 462

K

Kaner, Cem, 254
Kemerer, C.F., 181
kite, 30
 definition, 30
knotted loops, 138, *139*
Kuhn, D. Richard, 431, 440

L

Lack of Cohesion on Methods (LCOM),
 181–182, 367
Lane, Jo Ann, 375, 378
Laplace, Marquis de, 49
Larman, C., 241
 hierarchy of use cases, 294, *294*
lastDayOfMonth (Calendar Program), *262*, **263**,
 268, 269–272, *273–274*, **363**
Latin squares, 431, 440
lattice (directed acyclic graph), 191
Law of Conservation of Complexity, 362
layers, 500, **500**
leap year problem, 21–22, 82, 106, 108, 122–123,
 125, 177–178
 JUnit testing, 166–171
legacy code, 465, **466**, 466
levels of abstraction, 12, *13*
life cycle-based testing, 227–251
 agile testing, 234–246
 configuration management, 246–248
 granularity, 248
 iterative lifecycles, 230–234
 MDD versus TDD, 249–251
 specification-based *versus* code-based, 246
 TDD (pros, cons, open questions), 248–249
 waterfall testing, 227–230
light beam sensor, 414, 418
 failure modes, 425–430
 normal operation, 425, *426*

Stuck-at-One failure, 425, **425**, 427–430, **428**,
 428, 429
Stuck-at-Zero failure, 425, **425–426**, *427*, 430
Limited Entry Decision Table (LEDT), 116–117,
 122, 126, 235
 mechanical expansion, **26**, 27
Linear Code Sequence And Jump (LCSAJ)
 same as "DD-Path", 133
linear graph
 same as "graph", 53
Lipov, M., 204
load testing, same as "stress testing", 332
Lockheed Martin, 334
logarithmic weighting, 327
logical connectives
 same as "logical operators", 46
logical impossibilities, 284, 304
logically complex function, 15
logical operators, 46–47, 358
logical quantities, 222, **222**
logical variables, 82, 439, 441
 versus "physical variables", 433
logic faults, **11**
Login (Foodies Wish List), *482*, **482–483**, *484*,
 487, *490*, *491*, 494–498, *501*
Login FSM, 318, *319*, *486*, 500, **500**
Login scenarios
 expressed as sequences of ASFs, 305
 input event and action coverage, **317**
 inputs and outputs, **301**
 message coverage, **317**
 state coverage, 318, **319**
 transition coverage, 318, **320**
Login use cases, 297, **297–300**, 500
 no PIN try, **299**
 order in which messages recognized, **300**
 PIN correct on 3rd try, **299**
 PIN failed on 3rd try, **299**
long test cases, 320–321, 323–324
long use cases, 320
loop control, 158–160, 172
loop coverage, **137**, 147, **223**, 315
loop coverage metrics, **223**
loops, 57, 64, 66, 80, 132, 136, 142, **223**, 303,
 318, 423
 pre-test and post-test, *65*
loops of states, 318
loop testing, 138, 140

M

Maier, Mark, 374–376, 378
mainline models (expressive capabilities),
 340, *340*
maintenance, 249, 251
management, 229, 447, 451, 454–455, 457
 participation in review meeting, 456

mandatory participation, 43
Mandl, R., 431
many-to-many function, 42
many-to-many mapping, 42
many-to-one function, 42
many-to-one relation, 44
mapping, 43, 70
marked graphs, 338, *339–340*
marked Petri net, 68, *69*
market share, 465
markings, EDPN, 71
marking set (of Petri net), 68
marking vectors, 72
Mars Climate Orbiter mission (1999), 253
masking conditions, 141
masking MCDC, 142, 145
match variable, 204, 206
mathematical approaches (to stress testing),
    334–335
mathematical context, 1–75
    discrete mathematics for testers, 33–51
    examples, 15–32
    graph theory for testers, 53–75
    perspective on testing, 3–14
McCabe, Thomas J., 66, 157, 163, 203
    baseline method, 158, 220
    basis path method, 157–163
    complexity, 160–162, 353
    flipping, 158, **159**, 163
    violations of structured programming
        constructs, 162, *162*
mean time between failures (MTBF), 334
mean time to failure (MTTF), 334
mean time to repair (MTTR), 335
medical systems, 82, 431
Medicine Wheel, 249
Member, 108, *109*, **109–110**
MemorialDay (Calendar Program), *254*, 255–257,
    258–261, 262, **263**
message communication, *394*
    finite state machines, *283*
    model-based integration testing, *279*, 281
    test coverage metrics, 281
message coverage
    Login scenarios, **317**
message flows
    O-O integrationNextDate, *281*
message inputs, **300**
message outputs, **301**
message quiescence, 267–268, 272
messages, 54, 260, **301**, 307, 310–311, 315, **364**,
    494, 500
    definition, 266
    among FSMs, 482, **482–483**
    O-O implementation of
        integrationNextDate, **280**
message sequences, **284–286**, *287*, 308, 367

message systems, 338, *339*
message traffic complexity, 363
    extended adjacency matrix of call graph,
        363, **364**
methods, **364**, 368
    definition, **18–19**
metrics (most common), 318
    weakness, 318
Michigan pension policy for teachers, 129
Microsoft, 75, 360
miles per gallon example, **95**, 95
Miller, E.F., Jr., 132–133, 136–141, 173
Miller's test coverage metrics, 136–140
    all possible paths coverage, 140
    complex loop coverage, 138–139, *139*
    DD-Path testing, 137
    dependent pairs of DD-Paths, 138
    description, **137**
    multiple condition coverage, 139–140
    predicate outcome testing, 138
    simple loop coverage, 138
    statement testing, 137
    "statistically significant" coverage, 140
mission critical project, 465, **466**
mixed entry decision tables (MEDT), 116
MM-Path complexity, 268, *268*, *274*
MM-Path graph
    definition, 267
MM-Paths, 182, 267–268, 272, 284–285, 292, 367,
    464, **466**
    comparison with other integration testing
        strategies, **275**
    definition, 266
    hybrid of functional and structural testing, 268
    hypothetical across three units, *267*
    intersection with a unit, 267
    Method Message (object-oriented
        software), 266
    Module Message (traditional software), 266
    procedural integrationNextDate, 269, 272, *274*
    test coverage metrics for procedural code, 272
mock objects, 169–171
Mockito framework, 170
model-based integration testing, 280–288
    FSM/M Path integration, 286–288
    message communication, *279*, 281
    normal account creation, 286–287, **288**
    pairwise integration, 282–286
    scenarios, 286–287, *287*, **288**
model-based test coverage, 314, 318, *319*,
    319–320
model-based testing (MBT), xix, 246, 291, 303,
    337–352, 409
    advantage, 337
    appropriate models, 338–342
    basic mechanism, 337–338
    best practice, 465, **466**

choice, 342
commercial tool support, 342–348
issues, 340–341, **341**
mainline models (expressive capabilities), 340,
     340, **341**
Peterson's lattice, 338–340
quality, 325
model-driven agile development (MDAD),
     245–246, *246*
model-driven development (MDD)
     versus TDD, 249–251
modeling, xix
modeling issues, 340–341, **341**
modeling skill, 251
models, views (compromise with reality or
     caricature of reality), 337
modified condition decision coverage (MCDC),
     140, 142–143, 148, 150, **223**; see also
     masking MCDC
module execution paths, 267
     definition, 266
Monsieur Jourdain, 337
Monte Carlo testing, 335
     queueing theory, 334
     reliability models, 334–335
mortgage application example, 432
Mosley, Daniel J., 98, 115, 254
multiple inheritance, 183
multiple-condition coverage, **137**, 139–140,
     144–146, 163, 218, **223**, 251
     same as compound condition coverage, 148
multiple-condition testing, 357
multiple-fault assumption, 97, 100, 102, 129, 222
multi-user support, 395
Munson, John, 467
mutation testing, 324
Myers, Glenford J., 19, 98
     Art of Software Testing (1979), 461

N

narrative text, 3
NASA, 445, 465
natural language, 306
n-connectedness, 63
negation, 47, **50**
neighborhood integration, 262–264, 271
nested-If logic, 150, 250–251
nested loops, 138–139, *139*, **223**
nesting, 65
NextDate, 15, 31, 82, 149, 182, 197
     allpairs.exe test cases, 435, **436**
     base equivalence classes, 434–435
     canonical decision table of valid variables, **435**
     classes and test, 175–178
     classes and test with inheritance, 185–189

compound condition code-testing, 143–147
day equivalence classes, 435
decision table, **145**
decision table-based testing "works well", 128
define-use nodes, **178**
extended to Calendar Program, 254
extended entry decision table, 433, **435**, 435
faults due to interaction of three variables, 439
invalid equivalence classes, 111
as Java single method, *365*
line execution, 178, **179–181**
model-based (decision table) code coverage
     metrics, 147–148, **148**
object-oriented implementation (call graph),
     273, 363
program graph, *144*
program graph-based coverage metrics,
     147–148
random testing, 92, **93**
reduced decision table for range check, **146**,
     147
test cases, **145**
UML class diagram for revised Date classes
     using inheritance, *190*
nextDate (Calendar Program), *254*, 255–256, *257*,
     258–261, 262, **263**, *269*
NextDate function, 21–24, 33, 81, 85, 112, 278
     choice of equivalence relation (craft),
          104–106
     decision table-based testing (test cases),
          121–127
     equivalence class test cases, 104–108
     first try, 121–122
     input date, 106
     Java Code for tests, 151–156
     Java implementation, 22–24
     problem statement, 21
     reduced decision table, **126**
     second try, 122–124
     strong normal equivalence class test cases,
          107–108
     test cases, **127**
     third try, 124–127
     violates independent variables assumption,
          433
     worst-case test cases, 85, **87–91**
NextDate Problem
     conditions, 116–117, **118**
     decision tables, 116–117, **118–119**
     expanded rules, **119**
     impossible rules, **119**
     probability theory, 49–50
     rule counts, **118–119**
NextDate program, 34, 39–42, 246
     basis path method, 157
     example of software complexity, 364–366

NextWeek function, 31–32, 95, 113, 128
Niebuhr, Reinhold, 13
NIST, 431
node coverage, 137, 142
    definition, 135
node coverage metrics, 318
node outdegrees, 356
    definition, 356
node pairs, 59
nodes, 55–56, 58–60, 137, 171, 191, 202,
        353–356, 358
    as ASFs, 293
    connectedness, 57
    dependent pairs, 138
    indegrees and outdegrees, 59–60
    initial, 62
    as methods, 361–363
    module execution paths, 267
    statement fragments, 131
    terminal, 62
    types, 60
node sequences (paths), 56
node set of graph, 57
noise words, 310, 313–314, 424
non-constant condition, 142
non-determinism, 40, 406–407, *415*, 416
non-functional system testing, 332–336
    stress testing strategies, 332–334
Normal Boundary Value Testing (NBVT), 79–82
    generalizing ranges, 81–82
    limitations, 82
    test cases, 85, **94**
    test cases for function of two variables, *81*
normal landing
    sequence diagram, *380*
    use case, **380**
Normal Worst Case BVT, 83–84
Northern Cheyenne people, 249
nuclear reactors, 144
Number of Child Classes (NOC), 181–182, 367
number of combinations formula, 432
numerators and denominators, 439
NUnit for C#, 166

O

OATS technique, 439
object diagrams, 340
object instantiation, **19**
Object Management Group, 37
object mocking, use at unit level, 464
object-oriented (O-O) code, 261
    call graphs, 361–362
    integration level cyclomatic complexity, 362
    integration testing, 278
    unit-level testing, 278

object-oriented complexity, 366–367
    Coupling between Classes, 367
    Depth of Inheritance Tree, 367
    Lack of Cohesion on Methods, 367
    Number of Child Classes, 367
    Response for Class, 367
    Weighted Methods per Class, 366, **366**
object-oriented complexity metrics, 181–182
    Coupling between Classes, 181–182
    Depth of Inheritance Tree, 181–182
    Lack of Cohesion on Methods, 181–182
    Number of Child Classes, 181–182
    Response for Class, 181–182
    Weight Methods per Class, 181
object-oriented design
    class categories, **500**
    Foodies Wish List, 500–501, *501*
object-oriented implementation, messages
        (integrationNextDate), **280**
object-oriented integration, 278, **278**
object-oriented integrationNextDate, 275–280,
        281–282
    comparison of procedural and O-O
        implementation, **278**
    message flows, *281*
    message flows for May 27, 2020, *282*
    messages in O-O implementation, **280**
    program graph, *279*
object-oriented paradigm, foundations, 248
object-oriented programming languages, 77,
        182, 342
object-oriented software, xix, 13, 165–199,
        268, 464
    dataflow testing, 171–181
    issues in testing, 183–190
    mock objects and automated object mocking,
        169–171
    object-oriented complexity metrics, 181–182
    unit testing frameworks, 165–169
object-oriented units (nodes), 260
"observed" (ATE engine), 311, 430
one-to-many function, 42
one-to-one function, 42, 44
operational profiles, 48, 324–328, *328*, **329**, **330**,
        331, 335, 464
operational software development nets, 70
ordered pairs, 37, 40, 42–43, 58, 70
ordering relation, 45, 82
ordinary graphs, 37, 59–60
orthogonal arrays, 342–343, 431, 439
outdegree of node
    definition, 60
outdegrees, 62, 73, 134, 172, 182, 262,
        362–363, 403
    cyclomatic complexity, 356
output actions, 315, 403, 416–418, 482, 484

output conflict, 397–398, 403, 405
  FoodieDB events, **398**
  message communication among multiple
    instantiations of FSMs, *397*
output events, 342, **343**, 404, **412**, *415*, **419**,
    420–422, 427, 429, 471, **472–476**
  multiple context, 341
output expected, **86–91**, 100, **103–108**, **121**, **127**
output sequence, 477–478
Owens, Steve D., 334

P

paired programming, 242
pairwise integration, *261*, 261–262, 269–270
  model-based integration testing, 282–286
  test cases, **284–286**
Pareto Principle (Zipf's Law), 22, 324
partial participation, 43
participation, 43, *44*
  "onto" versus "into", 43
partition elements, 38
partitions, 45, 50, 57, 97
partitions and equivalence relations,
    interchangeability, 45
partition subsets, 38
Pascal, 59, 80–81, 133
path-based integration, 265–268
  concepts (new and extended), 265–268
  hypothetical MM-Path across three units, *267*
  MM-Path complexity, 268
  pros and cons, 268
path coverage, 147
  definition, 136
path probabilities, **325**
path testing, 163, 202, *202*
paths, **56**, 56–57–58, 61–62, 66, 318, **320–321**,
    354, 416, **418**, 419–421, 441
  Account Creation to Admin to FoodieDB, **320**
  definition, 56
  finite state machines, 301–304, *304*
  Login to Shopping Cart to Admin to FoodieDB,
    321
  trillions of, 132, *134*
pause (ESML prompt), 341, 383
perfect foresight, 229, 232
performance constraints, 465
performance evaluation, 445
performance testing, same as "stress testing", 332
periodic table of elements, 27
personal account number (PAN), 469
Peterson, James L., 338, 352
Peterson's lattice, 338–340
  anticipated placement of statecharts, 339, *339*
  with swim lane models, *340*
Petri, Carl Adam, 67

Petri net conflict, 70, 383, *383*, 384, 386, 388, 391
Petri net execution, 68–69–70
Petri net interlock, 383–384, *384*, 391
Petri net markings, 73
Petri net mechanisms, 341
Petri nets, 64, 67–70, 233, 293, 318, 337–338, *339*,
    339, *340*, 341, 382, 403
  coffee purchase, 404, *404–405*
  conservative, 69
  definition, 68
  dynamic interactions in multiple processors,
    405–406
  enabled transition, 69–70
  ESML prompts, 383–386
  example, *68*
  expressive capability, **341**
  marking set, 68
  non-determinism, 407
  transition firing, 69, *69*; see also swim lane
    EDPNs
Phoenix, Sky Harbor International Airport, 82
physical inputs, 425, 441
physical quantities, 82, 222, **222**
physical variables, 439, 441
  versus "logical variables", 433
PIN entry, 292–293, **295–299**, 301, **302**, *303*, 305,
    316–317, *319*, 321, 324, **325–326**, 328,
    329, **330**, *331*, 336, 469, 471, 472–473,
    483, *485–486*, **490**, 494–498
PIN try finite state machine, 301, 303, *304*
Poe, Edgar Allan, 202
polymorphism, 174, 183
  testing object-oriented software, 185–190
port boundary, 241
port events, 70, **71**, 72–73, 292–293, 295
port input events, 301, **302**, 303, 310, 315–316,
    318, 400, 419, 429
  context-sensitive, 316, 400
port inputs, **300**, 303
port output actions and messages, Login
    scenarios, **301**
  use cases, 300
port output events, 301, **302**, 303, 310, 316, 318,
    419
port outputs, **301**, 303
ports, 399, 403
post-conditions, 5, 321–323, 349–351, **381**, 403,
    416, **417**, 417, **424**, **472–476**, 476–478,
    492–497
post-test loop, program graph, *132*
pre-conditions, 301, **306–307**, 313–314, 321–323,
    349, 351, **380–381**, 400, 403, 416, **417**,
    424, **426**, **428**, **472–476**, 476–478, 491,
    493–497
predicate outcome testing, 138
predicates, 141, 197, 220

predicate use (P-use), 172, 192, 197, 206
    all C-uses/some P-uses criterion, 173, *174*
    all P-uses/some C-uses criterion, 173, *174*
preliminary design, 12, 230, *230*, 231, 242–243
preparation time, 457, **458**
presentation tier, 500, **500**, *501*
Pressman, Roger S., 19, 204, 253, 444
pre-test loop, program graph, *132*
pride, 462
PrintDate, *269–270*, 270–272, *272–274*, **363**
Private Automatic Branch Exchange (PABX),
    303–304
probability, **93**
probability theory, 48–50
    definition, 48
procedural code, 174, 182, 261, 361, 368
    call graphs, 361–362
    integration level cyclomatic complexity, 362
procedural integrationNextDate, 269–275
    call graph, 269, *272*
    call graph-based integration, 270–275
    decomposition-based integration, 269–270, *272*
    functional decomposition, 269, *272*
    MM-Paths for input date (May 27, 2020), 269,
        272, *274*
    observations and recommendations, 275, **275**
    program graph of units, 269, *273*
    source code, *269–271*
procedural main program, 364, **364**
procedural programming languages, 77, 229, 289
procedural software, 266, 464
procedural units, 278, **278**
procedure, **18–19**, 42, 269
procedure calls, 172, 174
process, 43, 445
    definition, 10
process community, 461–462
processors (multiple or single), 318, 399–406, 441
    thread identification, 294–305
product, definition, 10
product matrix, 56
    p-tuples, 71–72
program behaviors, 9
    specified, implemented, tested (three-way
        relation), 44
    universe of discourse, 36
Program Design Languages (PDL), complexity
    mechanism, **368**
program graph-based testing, 202–204, *205*, *207*,
    208, 284
    effort and efficacy, **203**
program graphs, 64–66, *132–134*, 137–142
    passim, 157–158, 160–161, 171, 190–192,
        210, 223, 261, 265–266, 278, 282, 303,
        354, 356–358, 364
    compound condition, *143*

coverage metrics, 147–148
DD-Path, 134
definition, 131
definitions ("traditional" and "improved"), 65
directed graphs, 131
Efficient Triangle Program, *207*, **208**
four structured pseudo-code programming
    constructs, *132*
insurance premium case study, 219, *219*
integrationNextDate classes, *279*
mildly complex, *355*
O-O integrationNextDate, *279*
paths, 202–203
private static double updateShoppingCart, *194*
problems, 66
procedural integrationNextDate units, 269, *273*
slice on truffleSales, *194*
Triangle Program, *149*
program graph technique, **212–213**
program inputs, 432–433
    allpairs.exe output, **434**
    Triangle Program test cases generated by
        allpairs.exe, **434**
program paths, 202, 267, 315
program slices, 165
    definition, 190–191
program slicing tools, 198, **198**
progression testing, 112, *230*, 231, 311
project management, 229, 260
Prolog, 59
Prompts, effect of SoS levels, 389–390
proper subsets, 38, 40, 195–196
propositional calculus (logical connectives), 36
propositional logic, 45–50, 100, 116, 399–400
    logical equivalence, 47–48
    logical expressions, 47
    logical operators, 46–47
    operations, expressions, identities, 46
    probability theory, 48–50
    set theory, 45
propositions, truth values, 45–46
pseudo-code, xix, *132*, 218, 269, 275, 476
    integrationNextDate, *361*, 362, **363**
    structural elements, 15, **15–19**
pseudo-structural testing, 318
public static, 20, 22, 31
punishment should fit crime, 221–222, 315
    medicine should fit disease, 315

Q

quadrilateral, *30*, 128
    definition, 30
    types, 113
quadrilateral program, 30–31, 113
queueing theory, 334

R

random events (inputs), 406
random testing, 92, **92–93**, 335
    "academic interest only", 92
    NextDate, 92, **93**
    Triangle Problem, 92, **92**
range elements, 41–42
ranges, 7, 40–41, 43, 79, 81, 83, **103–106**
    valid and invalid, 100
rangesOK (function), 166–170
rapid prototyping, 231, *232*, 232–234
Rapps, S., 171, 191
Rapps-Weyuker Dataflow metrics, 173, *174*
reachability matrix, **62**, 62–63
    definition, 62
reactive applications (Harel), 441
reactive systems (Harel), 233, 409
real use cases, 294, *294*, 295
    conversion into system test case, 311
    correct PIN entry on first try, **296**, 311, **312**
rectangle, *30*
    definition, 30
redundancy, 7, 9, 38, 85, 108, 112, 119–120, 122,
    125, 135, 163, 190, 202, 210, 215, 219,
    318, 435, 465
redundancy avoidance, 97–98
redundant test cases, 94, **94**
refactoring, **223**, *244*, 246, 248, 250
refined decision table, Triangle Problem, 116,
    117–118
reflexive relations, 44–45, 57
regression testing, 4, 100, 112, *230*, 230–231, 244,
    311, 416
    incidence matrices, 464, **466**
relational databases, 41, 43
relational operators, **16–17**
relations, 42–45
    examples related to cardinality and
        participation, *44*
    importance, 42
    relation R on sets A and B, *43*
    single sets, 44–45
    three-way, 44
relations among sets, 42–44
    definition, 42
relative complement, definition, 36
release plan, *243*, 242
reliability, 201, 248, 324, 332, 462, 465
    single-fault assumption, 79–81
reliability models, 334–335
repetition (university setting), 457
replication (stress-testing strategy), 333–334
report preparation, *452*, 454
requirements specification, 12, 227, 232–233, 246,
    291, 304
    consistency, completeness, clarity, 229–230

feedback, 316
    types, 340
resource conflict, 398, **399**, 403–404–405
    Foodies Wish List inventory before and after
        purchase, **399**
Response for Class (RFC), 181–182, 367
responsibilities, 378–379
reusability, 165, 182–183
review cancellation possibility, 454
review checklist, 382, 449, 454, 456–457
review culture, 455–457
    etiquette, 455–456
    ideal review, 457
    management participation in review meetings,
        456
    point-haired supervisor review, 456
reviewers, 445, 448, 454, 456–457, **479**
review issues spreadsheet, 449, 451
    individual reviewer's, **450**, 454
review leader, 445–449, 453–454, 456, 458, 478,
    479
review meetings, 447–449, *452*, 453–457, 459
    management participation, 456
review producer, 445–449, 453–457, **479**
review recorder, 447–448, 453–454, 478, **479**
review report, 447, 451–452
review reporting forms, 450–451
review team, 446, 448, 451, 453–456, **479**
    experience profiles, 457, **457–458**
review training, 457, 459
risk, 231, 327
risk-based testing, 217, 324, 327–332, **330**, *331*,
    335, 464
robust boundary value testing (RBVT), 79, 82–83
    generalizations and limitations, 83
    test cases for a function of two variables, *83*
robust forms, problems, 97
robustness testing, 94, 222, **222**
robust worst case boundary value testing
    (RWCBVT), 79, 83–85
    test cases for function of two variables, *84*
robustness testing, 94, 222, **222**
rule counts, 117, **124**
rules, **119–120**, **122–126**, 127, **139**, **145**,
    149–150, 235, 249, **249**, 318
    BDD decision table, **236–240**, 240–242
    decision tables, 116
    equivalence classes of (identification), 126
run-time errors, 83, 111
@RunWith (annotation), 168–169
Rural Electric Administration (REA), 335

S

sandwich integration, 258–260, 270–271
SATM system, 469, 471
scalability, 248, 332

scalar multiplication, 157, 164
scenarios (FSM/M Paths), 286–287, *287*, **288**
Schach, Stephen R., 132, 253
Schaefer, Hans, 327
scrum, 242–243
semantic-based methods, 201
semantic content, 202, *202*, 203, 282–283
semantic meaning, 202–203, 205
semaphore, 338, *339–340*
semipaths, 61–62
Sense Interruption, 425, 427, 429
sequence-changing statements, **18**
sequence diagrams, 379–382
    Chicago aircraft incident (1993), *382*
normal landing, *380*
set identities, 39, **39**
set of discrete values, 111
set of edges, 53–54
set of equivalence classes, 121–124
set of nodes, 53–54
set of test cases, 135
set of test coverage metrics
    definition, 135
set of transitions, 70, **71**
set operations, 36–37
set partitions, 38–39
    definition, 38
set relations, 37–38
    definition, 38
set theory, 33–39, **50**, 173
    empty set, 35–36
    naive versus axiomatic, 33
    notation, 33–34
    and propositional logic, 45
    set definition, 34–35
    set identities, 39, **39**
    set membership, 34
    Venn diagrams, 35–36, *37*
sets
    elements, 42
    finite versus infinite, 36
Shopping Cart (Foodies Wish List), *482*, **483**, *484*,
    487–490, 498–500, **500**, *501*
shopping cart user interface, *192*
Shopping List (Foodies Wish List), *482*, **483**, *484*,
    487, *489*, 499–500, **500**, *501*
short test case probabilities, 328, *328*
short test case sequences
    ordered by probability, 327, **329**
    probabilities, **326**
    risk profile, **330**
short test cases (STCs), 321
    advantage, 323
    connectivity, 325, *327*
    descriptions of for Login and Shopping List
        constituents, **326**
    failures, 327–328

locally feasible sequences, *323*
path probabilities, **325**
risk contribution, **329**
similar treatment principle, 202–203
SimpleDate class, 166–168, 171, *174*
simple propositions, 140
    same as "atomic propositions", 141
simple transactions, 292–293
single-entry, single-exit, 132, 157, 172, 265, 354
single-fault assumption, 79–81, 83, 97, 100–101, **222**
single sets, 44–45
sink ASF, definition, 293
sink nodes, 60, 65–66, 132, 136, 157, 250, 262,
    266, 293, 354, 363
    definition, 266
slice-based testing, 190–199, 207
    advantage over du-paths, 209
    example, 192–196
    program slicing tools, 198, **198**
    slice splicing, 197
    style and technique, 197
    test case values (triangleType variable), **210**
    triangleType variable, 209
slice splicing (Gallagher), 191
slice technique, **212–213**
slice testing, 202, *202*
    effort and efficacy, *203*
    insurance premium case study, 220
Smalltalk, 165
soap opera tests, 231, **416–417**
software complexity, 353–372
    example (NextDate program), 364–366
    exercise, 369–372
    integration level complexity, 361–363, **364**
    object-oriented complexity, 366–367
    system level complexity, 367–369
    unit level complexity, 354–361
software development, 462–463
software development life cycle, 12; see also life
    cycle-based testing
software engineering for systems of systems,
    378–382
    requirements elicitation, 378
    specification with dialect of UML, 378–382
    testing, 382
Software through Pictures (Aonix/Atego), 80
Software Quality Assurance (SQA), 10, 446, 451
software reviews, 227, 443–459
    checklists, 10, **446**, 446
    contents of inspection packet, 448–452
    documentation, 445–446
    economics, 443–445
    effectiveness, **446**
    inspection case study, 457–459
    inspection process, 452–455
    purpose, 10, 445
    review culture, 455–457

software technical reviews (roles), 446–448
   duplication, 448
   producer, 447
   recorder, 447
   review leader, 447
   reviewer, 448
software technical reviews (types), 445–446
   audits, **446**, 446
   technical inspections, 445–446, **446**
   walkthroughs, 445
software testing
   appropriate tools, 465
   Zipf's Law, 324
software testing examples, 15–32
   decision tables, **26–29**
   Foodies Wish List, 24–29
   Garage Door Controller, 29
   NextDate function, 21–24
   Triangle Problem, 19–21
software testing excellence, 461–468
   best practices, 462–465
   extreme example, 466–468
   mapping best practices to diverse projects,
      465–466, **466**
source ASF, definition, 293
source code, 3–5, 64, 131, 135, 137, 192, 269, 353,
      356–357, 445
   cyclomatic complexity, 368
   loops "highly fault-prone portion", 138
   NextDate function, 125
   procedural integrationNextDate, *269–271*
source nodes, 60, 65, 132, 136, 250, 262, 266, 293,
      354
   definition, 265
space shuttle missions, 466–467
"spaghetti code", 65, 74
special value testing, 8, 85, 93, 137
specification-based models, 353
   complexity, 368, **368**
   iterative lifecycle testing, 232–234
   comparison with code-based techniques,
      212–213
specification-based testing, 7–8–9, 12, 37, 41, 79,
      93, 163, 201–204, 210, 246, 249, 291,
      314, 332
   advantages and problems, 7
   comparison of test case identification
      methods, *8*
   discrete mathematics, 33
   fundamental limitation, 135
   insurance premium case study, 213, **213**
   intelligent combination with code-based unit
      level testing, 465, **466**
specification-implementation pairs, 44
specified behavior, 5–7, 9, 35
spiral model (Boehm), 230–231
spreadsheets, 85, 297, 306, 449, **450**, 451, 454

sprints, *243*, 243
square of opposition, 400, *400*, 402
standards, 449, 462
start nodes, 157
statecharts, 15, 37, 64, 73–75, 233, 337, 339–341,
      382, 386
   blobs, *73*
   concurrent states, *74*
   conventions, 74
   default entry into substates, *74*
   expressive capability, **341**
   initial states, 73, *74*
   notations, 36
state contour (Harel), 74
state coverage, 498
   Login scenarios, 318, **319**
StateMate system, 73
"statement complexity" *versus* "path
      complexity", 140
statement coverage, 137, 218
statement fragments, 65, 133–134, 136–137,
      147, 171, 190–192, 195–196, 202,
      266, 354
   immediate execution ability, 131
   nodes, 131, 135, 265
states, 307, 318, 342, **412**, 414, *415*, 418–419,
      482, 490
state sequences, 286, *287*, 308, 321–324, 413,
      416–417, 494–498
   across swim lanes, 493
state transition sequences, 344, **346**
static applications, **441**
static interactions, 399–402
   multiple processors, 401–402
   single processor, 399–401
static slices, 191–192
"statistically significant" coverage, 140
stimulus/response pairs, 291–293
stress-testing strategies, 332–334
   compression, 333
   mathematical approaches, 334–335
   replication, 333–334
strong components, 63–64, *64*
   condensation graph, *64*
   definition, 64
strong normal edge test cases, 110
strong normal equivalence classes
   completeOrder, *109*
   coverage for completeOrder, **110**
strong normal equivalence class test cases
   NextDate function, **107–108**
   Triangle Problem, 103
strong normal equivalence class testing, 97,
      100–101, *101*
strong robust equivalence class test cases
   NextDate function, **104–106**
   Triangle Problem, **103–104**

strong robust equivalence class testing, 97,
    102, *102*
strong typing, 80, 98
strongly connected call graphs, 362–363
strongly connected graph, 157
strongly typed languages, 83, 97, 111–112
structural elements, pseudo-code and Java,
    15–19
structural testing, 7, 44, 92, 171, 173, 201, 219,
    228, 260, 264–265
    best view, 163
    graph theory, 33
    hybrids, 268
    system level, 234
structured analysis, 60, 383
structured programming, 157, 160, 171, **223**, 341
    architecture, 98
    single-entry, single-exit, 354
structured programming constructs, *160*, 161
    condensing, *161*
    directed graphs, *65*
    violations, 162, *162*
stub development, 263, 268
stubs, 229, 256–261, 270, 464
subalternation, 402
subset lattice of "interesting" slices, *196*
subsets, 38, 45, 97, 100, 191, 196
subsumption (Rapps), 173
SUnit, 165–166
supervisors, 453, 455–456
swim lane architecture, 305
    Foodies Wish List, *377*
Swim Lane Event-Driven Petri Nets (swim lane
    EDPNs), 341, 383, 425, *427–428*, 429
    definition, 419
    deriving tests cases, 423–424
    door opening interactions, 421–423, *423*
    garage door closing with an intermediate stop,
        420, *421*
    garage door closing with laser beam crossing,
        421, *422*
    Garage Door Controller, 418–423
    normal garage door closing, 419–420, *420*; see
        also EDPNs
swim lane marked Petri net, definition, 418–419
Swim Lane Petri Nets, 339–340, 382, 386–389
    Accept prompt, 386, *387*
    Chicago incident (1993), *389*
    definition, 419
    Postpone prompt, 388, *389*
    Reject prompt, 386, *387–388*
    Request prompt, 386, *387*
swim lanes, 286, 306, **308–309**, 311, 482, 500
switch clause, **18**, 22, 31
symmetric difference, definition, 36
symmetric relations, 44–45, 57
synthesis, 229–230, 232

SysML, *347, 348*, 374, 378, 410, *410*
system level complexity, 367–369
    complexity of specification models, 368, **368**
    cyclomatic complexity of source code,
        368, **368**
    UML complexity, 369
    use case complexity, 368
system level test cases, 309–314, 337, 464
    communicating FSMs to test cases, 313–314
    dialog scenarios to test cases, 313
    FSM paths to test cases, 312–313
    industrial test execution system, 310–311
    use cases to test cases, 311–312
system test cases, 227, 233–234, 301, 303–304, 490
system testing, 228–229, 231, 242, 245, 253, 265,
    268, 291–336, 463, 467
    coverage metrics, 314–320
    identifying threads in systems of systems,
        305–309
    long versus short test cases, 320–332
    non-functional, 332–335
    supplemental approaches, 324
    system level test cases, 309–314
    threads, 291–294
    threads, identification in single-processor
        applications, 294–305
system testing extensions, best practice, 464, **466**
system threads, 294
    definition, 293
systems of systems (SoS), 15, 309, 315, 353,
    373–390
    characteristics, 374–375
    communication between constituent systems,
        382
    communication primitives, 382–389
    essential requirements, 375
    generic view, *375*
    identifying threads, 305–309
    interactions among constituent systems, 340
    levels (effect on prompts), 389–390
    sample, 375–378
    software engineering, 378–382
    tornado (Henryville, Indiana, 2012), 373, 375

T

tautology (proposition always true), 47–49
teachers, Michigan pension policy, 129
teamwork, 242–243, 467
Teamwork (Cadre Systems), 80
technical inspection packet, 469–479
    base use case checklist, 476–477
    base use case fault severity levels, 477–478
    base use case standard, 476
    base use case technical inspection forms,
        478–479
    base use cases, 472–475

customer requirements, ATM Simulator, 469–472
   inspection report outline, 478–479
technical inspections, xix, 4, 445–446
   carefully performed, 463; see also software reviews
telephone bills, spring and fall (time changes) problem, 112
telephone switching systems, 310, 333, 335, 391, 400–401, 451
   hardware, 452
   software, xix, 443, 452
Terhorst-North, Daniel (Dan North), 235, 410
terminal nodes, 59, 66
@Test (annotation), 151–154, 168–170, 175, 185, 275
test case compression idea, 440
test case identification, 7–9, 227
   degree of difficulty, 202, *202*
   degree of effectiveness, 202, *202*
   NBVT, 80
test cases, 4–5, 37, 44, 244, 246–248, 251, 432, 465
   completeness, 127
   definition, 4
   derived from swim lane EDPNs (Garage Door Controller), 423–424
   long versus short (system testing), 320–332
   NextDate function, **127**
   operational profiles, 324–327, *328*, **329**, **330**
   output portion, 5
   risk-based testing, 324, 327–330, **330**, *331*
   sources, *9*
   specification-based, 42
   supplemental approaches to system testing, 324–330, **330**, *331*
   syntactic *versus* semantic approach, 94–95, **95**
test coverage, 136, 150, 465
   for Systems of Systems, 494
test coverage metrics, 8, 300
   message communication, 281
   system-level, model-based, **418**
test, definition, 4
test-driven development (TDD), 235, 243–246, 258
   best practice, 465, **466**
   lifecycle, *244*
   versus MDD, 249–251
   pros, cons, open questions, 248–249
testing, 3–14
   basic definitions, 3–4
   destructive versus non-destructive, 333
   insights from Venn diagram, 5–6
   levels, 12–13
   mathematical description and analysis, 33
   point at which becomes craft, 9
   software engineering for systems of systems, 382

testing event-driven systems, 409–430
testing levels, careful definition, 463, **466**
testing life cycle, *4*
testing methods, 6
testing object-oriented software, 165–199
   implications of composition and encapsulation, 183
   implications of inheritance, 183–185
   implications of polymorphism, 185–190
   slice-based testing, 190–198
testing standard DO-178B, 142
testing systems of systems, 373–390
test management, 5, 343
test method pendulum, 94, 160, *202*, 202–204, 262, 264
   traversing, 204–213
TestOptimal, 342–343, *344*
   FSM related to test cases, 342, *344*
   Garage Door Controller event and states, 342, **343**
   Insurance Premium Problem, 342, **343**
   pairwise abstract test cases, 342, **343**
   state diagram, 342, *344*
testSimple function, 174, 175, 178
"They Write the Right Stuff" (Fishman, 1996), 466–467
thread executions, 324–325
thread interaction, 248, 464
threads, 70, 291–294, 301, 318, 324, 335, 337, 400, 402, 404, 406, 464
   "atomic element" of system testing, 391
   case-based, 318
   definition, 70, 293–294
   EDPN composition, 403
   generation from finite state machines (warning), 303–304
   levels, 292
   possibilities, 292–293
   shared vision, 291–292
threads, identification in single-processor applications, 294–305
   finite state machines, 301–304
   use cases (quantity required), 295–301
   user stories, use cases, 294–295
threads, identification in systems of systems, 305–309
   communicating FSMs, 305, 307–308, **308–309**
   dialogs among constituents, 305–306, **307**
   dialogs as sequences of ASFs, 305, 309
tiers, 500, **500**, *501*
time, 72–73, 402, 422, **446**, 448–449, 451, 453–457, 463–464, 467
time allocated for testing, 324, 441
time change problem (spring and fall), 112, 129
time-critical projects, 465, **466**
time-to-market, 231, 465

tokens, 68–69, 71–72
tools of trade, 253
top-down approach, 246, 412
top-down development, 229
    Garage Door Controller (Extended FSM), 414–418
top-down integration, 229, 256–258–259
    Calendar Program, 256–258
    steps, *257*
    theory, 258
topologically possible paths, 202–203–204
topology, 53
traffic engineering (compression), 333
training, 445–446
transfer node, 60
transformational applications, 235, 441
transformational systems, 318
transition coverage, 318
    Login scenarios, 318, **320**
transition firings, 69, *69*
transition probabilities, 325–327, *331*
transitions, 66, 72, 303, 318, 350–351, 383–384, 397, 403, 407, 413–414, 418, 421–422, 425, 427, 429, 490
transitive relations, 44–45, 57
trapezoid, *30*
    definition, 30
traversals (thread executions), 324
traversing test method pendulum, 204–213
    basis path testing, 204–205, *206–207*, **208**
    boundary value testing, **208**, 210, **211**
    comparison of code-based and specification-based techniques, **212–213**
    dataflow analysis, 206–208
    decision table testing, 211–212, **217**
    equivalence class testing, *207*, 210–211
    program graph-based testing, 204, *205–207*, **208**
    slice-based testing, 209, **210**
"treated the same", 98, 100, 106, 110, 126
Triangle Problem, 15, 19–21, 40–41, 81, 128, 136, 201
    decision table, 116, **117**
    decision table-based testing (test cases), 120, **121**
    dependent pairs of DD-Paths, 138
    equivalence class test cases, 103–104
    equivalence class testing, 98, *207*, 210–211
    equivalence classes, 433
    Java implementation, 20–21
    normal boundary value test case, **86**
    physical variables (robust equivalence classes), 433
    problem statement, 19–20, 85
    program graph, 132, *133*
    random testing, 92, **92**

refined decision table, 116, **117–118**
rule counts, **118**
strong normal equivalence class testing, 101
test cases (BVT), 85, **86–87**
traversing test method pendulum, 204–213
Triangle Program, 30–31, 34, 39, 197
    basis path method, 157–158, **159**
    compound condition, 149–150
    decision table, **150**
    decisional complexity, *357*
    program graph, *149*
triangleType variable, 207–208
    path coverage of normal boundary values, 210, **210**
    path coverage of worst-case values, 210, **211**
    slice-based testing, 209
    test case values derived from slices, **210**
trigger prompt, 341, *426–427*, 427, *428–429*, 429
truth set, 49
truth tables, **46–47**, 100, 116, 250, **250**, 357
T (testing tool), 80

U

UCLA graphs, 338, *339*
UML activity diagram, 342–343, *344*
UML class diagrams
    NextDate, 185, *190*
    SimpleDate, *174*
UML class inheritance diagram, 182
UML dialect, 378–382
    classes, 378
    sequence diagrams, 379
    three parts, 378–379
    use cases, 378
UML finite state machine, 344, *345*
unary arithmetic operators, **16**
undirected graphs, 53, 58
Unified Modeling Language (UML), 15, 37, 43, 73, 241, 294
    complexity, 369
    diagrams, 3
    notation, 240
unique cause MCDC, 142–143
unit level complexity, 354–361
    computational complexity, 358–361
    cyclomatic complexity, 354–358
unit testing, 15, 64, 77–223, 227–228, 231, 246, 253, 266, 282, 292, 382, 463–464, 467
    BVT, 77–95
    code-based testing, 131–164
    decision table-based testing, 115–129
    definition issues, 77
    equivalence class testing, 97–113
    method level, 278
    object-oriented software, 165–199

retrospective, 201–223
scrum lifecycle, 243
termination point, 201
unit testing frameworks, 165–169
unit testing retrospective, 201–223
code characteristics, 223, **223**
functional testing, **222**
guidelines, 221–223, **222–223**
insurance premium case study, 213–221, **222**
test method pendulum, *202*, 202–204
traversing the pendulum, 204–213
unit test methods, effort and efficacy, *203*, 204
universe of discourse, 35, *35*, 36
partition, *38*
selection, 49–50
Triangle Program, 39
unordered pairs, 37, 53, 58
usage nodes, 192
definition, 172
use case-based test coverage, 314–315–317
use case complexity, 368–369
use case inspection, 448, 457, 469–479
use case review checklist, 476–477
use case technical inspection forms, 478–479
individual inspection ballot, 478
inspection summary, 479
use cases, 234, 294–295, 305, 310, 378–379–382,
417, 464, 490
Chicago aircraft incident (1993), **381**
expansion of input events and messages, **300**
information content (Venn diagram), *241*
Larman's hierarchy, 241
main advantage, 294
normal landing, **380**
technical inspection packet, 469–479
to test cases (system level), 311–312
use cases (quantity required, identifying threads
in single-processor applications),
295–301
incidence with classes, 300–301
incidence with input events and messages,
297–300
incidence with output actions and messages,
300, **301**
order in which messages recognized in Login
use cases, **300**
UserID (Foodies Wish List), **482–483**, *485–486*,
488, 490–492, *492*, 493–498
user interface, 192, 500
users, 4, 228, 231
user stories, 234–248, 250, 294–295, 306, 315, 410

V

variable values, valid and invalid, 98
variables "treated the same", 98, 100, 106,
110, 126

vector addition systems, 338, *339*
vector replacement systems, 338, *339*
vector spaces, 156, 160, 164
definition, 157
Venn diagrams, 5–6, 9, 73, 95, 135, 458
basic sets, *37*
"do not show Cartesian products", 37
information content in levels of use cases, *241*
Larman's hierarchy of use cases, *294*
overlapping circles, 35–36
set of 30-day months, *35*
set theory, 35–36, *37*
shading, 35–36
specified, implemented (and tested) behaviors,
5, 6
Venn, John, 35
Verified Systems International GmbH, 346–348
Garage Door Controller, *348*, 348, **348**
Insurance Premium Problem, *347*, 347
VERIFY, 287, **288**, 310–314, 417, **424**, **426**, **428**, 429
Vertices, same as "nodes", 53
virtual systems of systems, 375, 383, 386, 390
definition (Maier), 374
V-Model, 12, *13*, *14*, 227
Visual Basic, 92, 133, 250
Visual Basic for Applications, 15, **15–19**, 269, 362
VBA pseudo-code, 278

W

walkthroughs, 445, **446**
Wallace, Dolores R., 431, 440
Warshall's Algorithm, 203
Waterfall model, 12, *13*, 231, 260, 268, 289, 444,
448, 452
as V Model, *228*
Waterfall spin-off types, 230–232
evolutionary development, 230–231
incremental development, 230–231
spiral model, 230–231
Waterfall testing, 227–230
pros and cons, 229–230
weak normal equivalence class test cases
insurance premium case study, 219
NextDate function, **105–106**
Triangle Problem, **103**
weak normal edge test cases, 110
weak normal equivalence class testing, 97, 100,
100, 101
weak normal equivalence classes
completeOrder, *109*
coverage for completeOrder, **110**
weak robust equivalence class test cases, Triangle
Problem, **103**
weak robust equivalence class testing, 97, *101*,
101–102
revised, *102*

weak robust test cases, NextDate function, **105–106**

weekDay (Calendar Program), *254*, 255–258, *258–262*, **263**

Weibull distribution, 335

weighted methods per class (WMC), 181, 366
    metric for Java version of NextDate, **366**

Weiser, M.D., 190, 197

well-behaved attribute, 40, 42
    inverse, 41

Weyuker, E.J., 173, *174*

what/how cycles, 227, 448

white box testing, same as "code-based testing", 8

Wiegers, Karl, 444–445
    website, 10, 449

Windshield Wiper Controller, 31, 129, 349–351, 390, 407, 430

Wittgenstein, L., 165

woodworking, 443, 461

workarounds, 183, 427

Work Breakdown Structure, 77

work product, 448, 453–454–455, 478–479

worst-case analysis, 83–84
    best application, 84
    generalization pattern, 84
    limitations, 84
    test cases for function of two variables, *84*

worst-case boundary test cases, 219

worst case boundary value testing (WCBVT), 79, 83–85, 439
    insurance premium case study, 213–218

worst-case normal equivalence class testing, 343, **345**

worst-case testing, 222, **222**

X

XUnit, 166, 464

Y

YesterDate program, 32, 41–42

Yourdon and Constantine, 182

Z

Zave, Pamela, 391–392, 400

Zeller's Congruence, 256, 359–361

Zipf's law (Pareto Principle), 22, 324

zodiac, *254*, 256–258, *258–262*

zodiac exercise, 369–372

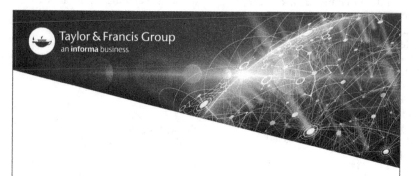

Printed in the United States
by Baker & Taylor Publisher Services